HARVARD SEMITIC MUSEUM

HARVARD SEMITIC STUDIES

Frank Moore Cross, Jr., Editor

Number 25

DICTIONARY OF OLD SOUTH ARABIC
Sabaean Dialect

Joan Copeland Biella

DICTIONARY OF OLD SOUTH ARABIC

DICTIONARY OF OLD SOUTH ARABIC
Sabaean Dialect

JOAN COPELAND BIELLA

Published by
Scholars Press
101 Salem Street
P. O. Box 2268
Chico, CA 95927

DICTIONARY OF OLD SOUTH ARABIC
Sabaean Dialect

Joan Copeland Biella

Library of Congress Cataloging in Publication Data

Biella, Joan Copeland, 1947–
Dictionary of Old South Arabic, Sabaean dialect.

(Harvard Semitic studies ; no. 25) (ISSN 0147-9342)
Arabic (Roman) and English.
Bibliography: p.
1. South Arabic language—Dictionaries. 2. Inscriptions,
Sabaean. I. Title.
II. Series.
PJ6958.B53 492'.9 81-8946
ISBN 0-89130-455-X AACR2

Printed in the United States of America

Table of Contents

I. Introduction

A. Preliminary Remarks vii

B. Sources ix

C. Format ix

II. Abbreviations and Symbols

A. General xi

B. Names of Languages and Dialects xii

C. Symbols xiii

III. A Dictionary of Old South Arabic, Sabaean Dialect

'	1	m	265
b	33	n	289
g	63	s	321
d	79	c	349
ḏ	89	ǵ	391
h	103	f	399
w	119	ṣ	415
z	157	ḍ	433
ḥ	163	q	441
x	195	r	473
ṭ	215	ś	501
ẓ	223	š	509
y	229	t	531
k	237	ṯ	539
l	255		

IV. Selective Bibliography 551

Introduction

A. *Preliminary Remarks*

The dialects of Old South Arabic remain a little-studied branch of the Semitic language family, despite the fact that thousands of texts in Sabaean, Minaean, Qatabanian and Ḥaḍramitic have been published, ranging in type from brief graffiti to substantial historical annals. The lack of attention heretofore paid to these languages has been due largely to the difficulty of access to the texts, and to the absence of even the most basic critical tools, such as dictionaries and concordances, to aid in their study. Since the Second World War a focusing of interest on modern Arabia has led to an expansion of the corpus of Old South Arabian texts available to scholars and, at last, to the preparation of certain essential guides to this material.

Most basic, perhaps, are two concordances, the first prepared by G. Lankester Harding, published in his *Index and concordance of pre-Islamic names and inscriptions* (Toronto, 1971). This publication solves one of the most frustrating problems in the field of Old South Arabic philology: the fact that, typically, any long-known inscription has been edited several times and is citable by several names. The Harding "concordance" provides a cross-reference system to identify these many-named texts for the student and guide him to their various editions. Similar and supplemental to this is the concordance published by A. Avanzini in the first volume (pp.19-185) of her *Glossaire des inscriptions de l'Arabie du Sud, 1950-1973* (Florence: Istituto di Lingue Orientali, 1977), treating much of the more recently-published material.

Next in importance is the concordance to volumes V-VII of the *Répertoire d'épigraphie sémitique*, published in 1968 as volume VIII of the series. These volumes of the *Répertoire* comprise the largest published collection of Old South Arabic texts, including materials of all types and every dialect. Unfortunately, no such work covers the other standard collection, the Pars Quarta (Himyaritic and Sabaean section) of the *Corpus inscriptionum semiticarum*.

Two important grammatical studies have appeared: M. Höfner's *Altsüdarabische Grammatik* (Leipzig, 1943) and A.F.L. Beeston's *Descriptive grammar of epigraphic South Arabian* (London, 1962). Also of special interest are Beeston's *Sabaean inscriptions* (Oxford, 1937)*, which includes a long though incomplete concordance to material of all dialects in the *Répertoire* and the *Corpus inscriptionum*, and A. Jamme's *Sabaean inscriptions from Maḥram Bilqīs* (Baltimore, 1962), which includes a purely Sabaean glossary.

In the field of lexicography proper, we now have the second volume of Avanzini's *Glossaire des inscriptions de l'Arabie du Sud, 1950-1973*, which appeared in 1980. This major work, not yet complete, dealing with a segment of the more recently-published inscriptions, treats all dialects together in a format comparable to that of the present work. It is becoming possible to look forward to the day when various works of this kind, differing in scope, can be combined or used to supplement one another.

Bibliographic coverage of the field of Old South Arabian philology is becoming more comprehensive. In addition to the bibliographies provided in volumes V and VIII of the *Répertoire* (through 1929 and 1968, respectively), an excellent list of recent works compiled by A. Drewes now exists in J.H. Hospers' *Basic bibliography for the study of the Semitic languages*, volume I (Leiden, 1974), pp.336-58. Periodical literature on the subject has increased rapidly in volume since World War II, reaching a peak in the mid-1960's; good current coverage is provided by the index *Elenchus bibliographicus biblicus* (Rome, 1920-   ), especially in its sections "Archaeologia biblica" and "Philologia biblica." Most specialized are the bibliographic reports now published in the journal *Raydan*. This periodical, the first to be devoted to ancient South Arabian studies, has been published since 1978 by the Yemeni Centre for Cultural and Archaeological Research of the People's Democratic Republic of Yemen.

The raw material for philological studies, however, also continues to increase. The vast mass of texts collected by Eduard Glaser at the beginning of this century is now being published by the Austrian Academy of Sciences in the *Sammlung Eduard Glaser* series, of which some thirteen volumes of texts and commentary have appeared. Until his death, each year saw an increase in the collection of texts published by G. Ryckmans in the periodical *Le Muséon*. Another important contributor is A. Jamme, who continues to publish and edit texts collected from museums and his own archeological researches.

In addition to these large collectors of material, several Arab archeologists in recent years have published newly-discovered inscriptions. For Sabaean

---

* I wish to acknowledge a special debt to this work, Beeston's unpublished doctoral thesis, which is one of the best-known and most frequently-quoted contributions to the field of Old South Arabian philology. Its author asked that it not be quoted in the present work because of developments in the forty-four years of scholarship subsequent to it, but readers familiar with it will recognize my indebtedness on almost every page.

studies the most important are A. Fakhry (whose finds were edited by G. Ryckmans), H.Y. Nāmī, M. Iryānī and A. Sharafaddīn.

B. Sources

The material in this work is derived from many published sources. All the Sabaean references have been culled from the glossary of C. Conti Rossini's *Chrestomathia arabica meridionalis epigraphica* (Rome, 1931) and W.W. Müller's *Wurzeln mediae und tertiae Y/W im Altsüdarabischen* (Tübingen, 1962). This material is combined with references from the concordances mentioned in the preceding section (volume VIII of the *Répertoire* and the appendix to Beeston's *Sabaean inscriptions).*

The glossaries of several other collections have been consulted, including the various volumes of the *Sammlung Eduard Glaser,* G. Ryckmans' "Epigraphical texts" volume of Fakhry's *Archaeological journey to Yemen,* Jamme's *Sabaean inscriptions from Mahṛam Bilqis,* and Iryānī's *Fī ta'rīx al-Yaman.* I have attempted to include all words and forms appearing in these works (with the exception of proper names), even when doubtful or much-restored, if they have been the subject of scholarly comment, in the hope that a relatively complete and systematic digest of such comment will be of benefit to students.

The references so far described have been supplemented by many drawn from other published collections, though these have not been examined in such detail. Among them are the *Corpus inscriptionum semiticarum,* Pars Quarta; the Ryckmans collection edited in *Le Muséon*; the inscriptions edited by Jamme and Nāmī; and numerous other editions of texts published in monographs and periodicals. Many philological and lexicographical studies have been consulted, notably those of A.F.L. Beeston, A.K. Irvine, J. Ryckmans, and W.W. Müller.

In the compilation of this widely-dispersed material I have, no doubt, made many errors of detail and judgment, but I have tried to provide enough information to guide other students to clearer and more accurate formulations.

C. Format

Entries in the dictionary are arranged by root, in the order of the Hebrew alphabet (with additions):

' b g d d̲ h w z ḥ x ṭ ẓ y k l m n s ᶜ ǵ f ṣ ḍ q r ś š t t̲

For many words in which the triliteral root is not immediately apparent, cross-references of the "See" and "See also" type have been provided to guide the reader to the appropriate entry.

Under each root derived forms are listed in order, beginning with verbs (if any), in the sequence v, D, L, N, ti, tp, h, st. Nouns follow in order of increasing complexity of form: simple root, root with suffixed -t, root with prefixes m- and t-. The order is sometimes interrupted by entries illustrating the extended use of certain nouns as prepositions and conjunctions, and in cases where one noun is derived directly from another. Adjectives, adverbs, interjections and the like are treated in the vicinity of semantically-related parts of speech. Homonymous roots are distinguished by Roman numerals.

At the beginning of each entry is a listing of the forms in which the word is found in the corpus of material consulted. For nouns these include variant singulars and plurals, with and without suffixes; for verbs, forms in various moods, tenses and persons, with and without suffixes. A citation from the corpus is given for each form so listed, with an indication as to whether the form also appears elsewhere in the corpus. These listings are as complete as possible for that part of the corpus of Sabaean material examined in detail, as defined in the preceding section.

For most entries a brief etymology is given in the form of citation of cognates (certain or proposed) from related languages. When a word has clear cognates in Classical Arabic, only these have been cited, unless forms from other languages seem particularly helpful for an understanding of Sabaean nuances. In the case of words of doubtful sense, etymological conjectures of various scholars are usually summarized.

Each entry includes one quotation or more from the corpus, with English translation, including the word in question and illustrating its use. Notes are provided in many cases to give additonal information or speculation on use and derivation.

A list of abbreviations and symbols follows on pp.xi-xiii. A selective bibliography, including only works cited in the text, appears on pp.551-61.

I wish to express my thanks for their help to T.O. Lambdin, Clarke Berry, and all those who helped in the years of preparation, typing, and retyping of this work--especially to Sandra Levine, who prepared the final typescript, and Richard Brennecke, who drew the chapter-headings. Following a tradition well-established among Sabaean scholars, I dedicate this study to my mother, Anne Biella, who helped me most of all (and probably knows more Sabaean than I think she does--still waters run deep).

Joan Copeland Biella,
W.F. Albright Institute
of Archaeological Research,
Jerusalem

Abbreviations and Symbols

A. General

ab	abbreviation
act	active voice
adj	adjective
adv	adverb
aux	auxiliary verb
av	adverb
caus	causative
coll	collective noun
cf	compare
cj	conjunction
d	dual
D	verb stem with doubled second radical (cf Ar *fa*^{cc}*ala*)
denom	denominative verb
dm	demonstrative
esp	especially
etym	etymology
exp	expression
f	feminine
h	verb stem with h-prefix (cf Ar *'af*^{c}*ala*, Heb *hip*^{c}*īl*)
ib	the same inscription or work
id	the same meaning
ij	interjection
imv	imperative
inf	infinitive
inscr	inscription
ipf	imperfect
L	verb stem with long vowel in first syllable (cf Ar *fā*^{c}*ala*)
lit.	literally
m	masculine
mng	meaning
n	noun; note
N	verb stem with n-prefix (cf Ar *infa*^{c}*ala*, Heb *nip*^{c}*al*)
n.loc	name of a place
n.pr	name of a person, place or building
p	plural; page
pass	passive voice
pf	perfect

phps	perhaps
p.maj	plural of majesty
pn	pronoun
pp	preposition
prob	probably
prt	participle
pt	part; particle
q.v.	which see
rl	relative
s	singular
sim	similar(ly)
s.o.	someone
s.th.	something
s.v.	under the word in question
st	verb stem with st-prefix (cf Ar *istafᶜala*)
syn	synonym
ti	verb stem with t-infix (cf Ar *iftaᶜala*)
tp	verb stem with t-prefix (cf Ar *tafaᶜᶜala, tafāᶜala*)
tr	translates; translation
uned	unedited
unpub	unpublished
v	simple verb stem (Sab fᶜl; includes stems represented in Ar by *faᶜala, faᶜᶜala,* and *fāᶜala*)

B. *Names of Languages and Dialects*

Akk	Akkadian
Amh	Amharic
Ar	Classical Arabic
Aram	Aramaic
Daṯ	Daṯina (MSA dialect)
Ḍof	Ḍofari (MSA dialect)
Eng	English
Eth	Classical Ethiopic (Geᶜez)
Gk	Greek
Ḥaḍ	Ḥaḍramitic (OSA dialect)
Heb	Biblical Hebrew
J.Aram	Jewish Aramaic
Liḥ	Liḥyanite
MSA	Modern South Arabian
Mh	Mehri (MSA dialect)
Min	Minaean (OSA dialect)
ModḤaḍ	Moḍern Hadrami (MSA dialect)
ModYem	
Nab	Nabataean
OSA	Old South Arabic
Om	Omani (MSA dialect)
PBH	Post-Biblical Hebrew
Palm	Palmyrene
Phoen	Phoenician
Qat	Qatabanian (OSA dialect)
Sab	Sabaean (OSA dialect)
Saf	Safaitic
Sem	(general) Semitic
Šx	Šxawri (MSA dialect, also spelled Sḫauri)
Sq	Soqoṭri (MSA dialect)
Syr	Syriac
Te	Tigre
Tña	Tigriña
Ug	Ugaritic
Yem	= ModYem

C. *Symbols*

+ marks forms which occur more than once in the corpus of material included

* marks forms of which all instances recognized in the corpus are cited

▯ represents the Sabaean "number symbol" which sets off symbols representing numerals

/ marks the end of a line in the original text of an inscription, when relevant

[] enclose reconstructed letters, words, and sequences of these

() enclose emendations of actual readings

Note on the transliteration of Classical Arabic: in the transcription of words from III-weak roots, the symbol $\bar{a}$ represents final long 'alif (from original *aw-); the symbol â represents 'alif maqṣura (from original *ay-).

In quoting passages in Sabaean I have frequently abbreviated names of persons, tribes, and places by giving the first consonant only, capitalized. Since single 'alifs and ^{c}ayns look awkward to the Western eye, I have follow d these in my transliterations with supporting vowels (e.g., 'I, ^{c}A), and omitted them in my translations (e.g., I., A.). These letters are not intended to represent serious reconstructions of OSA vowels.

I have not attempted to produce a consistent transliteration system for citations from the various Ethiopic dialects, but have reproduced forms as quoted in my sources.

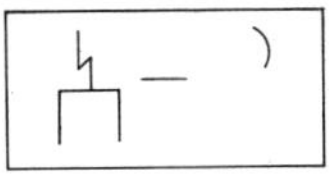

'

ab ' R3943/2+

SYMBOL FOR NUMBER 1000

[Initial of Sab 'lf "thousand."]

R3943/2: 'rb^{c}y wxms[t 'lf]m · □'''''cccc□. "five thousand forty"; R3945/3: tmnyt 'lfm □''''''''□ "eight thousand"

'B

n s 'bhw J550/2+; 'bhmy J585/4+; d 'byhmw C29/3; p 'bhhw Gl533/5+; ''bwhmw C332/7; 'bwthmw C609/2

(1) FATHER, FOREFATHER

[Ar 'ab, ps 'ābā', 'abahāt, id; Heb p 'ābôt.]

C37/6: 'bhhw w'^{c}mmhw "his fathers (paternal ascendants?) and paternal relations"; C332/7: 'šms ''bwhmw "the sun-goddesses (patron deities) of their forefathers"; Gl533/5: s'l b^{c}ly 'bhhw "the obligation (which lay) upon his forefathers"

(2) SPIRITUAL FATHER, ABBOT

[Sense common in Aram.]

C541/67: qssm 'bmstlh "a priest, the abbot of (the church's) monastery"

'BD I

n^{1} s 'bd Gl572/6*

ETERNITY; k-'bd: FOR EVER

[Ar 'abada "endure," 'abad "time without end, eternity."]

Gl572/6: sm^{c} ybln k'bd...'LMQH "a document which prescribes tribute for ever to (the god) I."

n^{2} s t'bdhw R3202/2*

PART OF A SANCTUARY (the living quarters?)

[Ar 'abada "stay, dwell (in a place)."]

R3202/2 (in full): ...]hmw bn h[...] t'bdhw wmdqnth[w] "their...from...its t'bd and its oratory"

'BD II

n p 'bdtm J633/7-8*

"WILD" TRIBESMEN, IRREGULARS attached to a military force

[Ar 'ābid "wild, untamed" (BeNL7/537-8).]

J633/7-8: to fight b^{c}m 'ḤMRN b'bdtm dkwnw byn xmsnhn "against the Himyarites with the irregulars who were among the 2 armies"

'BH

tp pf t'bhhw J555/3*

PUT s.th. IN S.O.'S CARE > ENTRUST WITH (e.g. an office), APPOINT

[Ar 'abaha "observe," wabaha "be careful, take care" (MüRev/105A.]
J555/3: when the god granted him what He had promised wywm t'bhhw qyn M "and when He appointed him administrator of (the city) M."

'BY

n s t'by R4176/10* (D inf?)
DISPUTATION, CONTENTION
[Eth ta'ābaya "contend with one another."]
R4176/10: ḥẓr T'LB R bn klt'by ym T "(the god) T. has prohibited (the people of) R. from all disputation on the day of T."
Note: In C527/2 T'BY prob n.pr (nisba?).

'BL

D? pf 'blw J665/38*
GATHER livestock TOGETHER as booty
[Cf Ar 'bl D "gain possession of camels," denom from 'ibil "camels" (Sab 'bl). Cf also, phps, Sem root WBL "lead, bring," Sq tebil "bring (cattle) together."]
J665/38: 'blw tlty 'frsm "they gathered together thirty horses (as booty)," with parallels hqd and stqd (root NQD) in same inscription

n s 'bl(m,n) R3910/3+; 'blhw J619/7+; s.f 'bltn Ry548/3+; coll 'bl(m,n) R4229/4+; d 'blnhn C535/4; p''bl(m,n) R 3943/2+; ''blhmw R4386+
CAMEL
[Ar 'ibil "camels."]
J643/3: 'liberated' 'frshmw...w''blhmw "their horses and camels (as booty)";
J619/7: dqt wdq ᶜln 'blhw "the fall he took because of (?) his camel";
Ry548/3: 'bltn dt smhw X "the she-camel whose name is X."

'BMSTLH, C541/67--see under 'B, SLY

'BN

n s 'bnm C540/30; p ''bnm C540/74
STONE
[Eth 'ebn, Heb 'eben id.]
C540/30: 'bnm wgyrm "stone and lime": ib/74: msrw ᶜrmn...msrm wšṣnm b''bnm "they packed in the earth for the dam, packing earth and facing with stones"

'BQ, J594/10-11--see under BRQ

'BR

n s t'brm C461/3* (D inf?)
BURNT OFFERING
[Cf Akk abru "firewood," abre nupuḫū "wood is ignited."]

C461/3: dbḥhw d[bḥm w]t'brm "he sacrificed to (the god) a sacrifice and a burnt offering"

'GL

n s m'glm C107/2; d m'glyhmw R4196/2; p m'glthmw C621/7
CISTERN
[Ar m'jl "large cistern" (Dol/11).]
C621/7: gn'thw wxlfhw wm'glthw "its walls, gates and cisterns"; C107/2: they built krfm bY wm'glm bxlf hgrhw "a krf-cistern at Y. and a m'gl-cistern outside their city"

'GR I

n s 'gr R3079/1*
SERVANT of a god (?)
[Ar 'ajīr "hireling," Min 'gr "servant (of a god)."]
R3079/1: 'gr^{c}[..., for 'grW[D?] "servant of (the god) WD" (?)

'GR II

n p/coll 'grn J577/10+
CITIZENS OF NAGRAN
[MüTa^{c}izz/96 suggests phonetic development *'angārān > *'aggārān.]
J577/10: nblw hmw 'GRN b^{c}br 'ḥzb ḤBŠT "they sent those Nagranites against the hordes of Ḥabashat"--and similar military contexts in J577
Note: J tr "mercenaries," after 'GR I n.

'D'

n s (t)'d'm J750/7* (D inf?)
PAYMENT
[J read z'd', emended by BeJSS14/229, who takes root 'D' as a var of 'DY, cf Ar ta'diya^{t} "payment, fulfillment."]
J750/7: šm l'LM[QH] (t)'d'm bhbtn "promised to (the god) l. a payment, consisting of this gift"

'DB I

v pf 'db J540/3; ipf y'dbhmw J576/10
SEPARATE, DELIMIT
[Cf Ar hadaba (= qaṭa^{c}a) "separate, divide" (BonVar/334n'k').]
J576/10: wy'dbhmw hmt 'ḤMRN klyqdmnn "these Ḥimyarites separated them (from the main army?) in order to attack them"; J540/3: ^{c}syh 'xry 'dbn 'db W wR "he made (for) him the excellent boundary stone (which) separates/delimits (the lands) W. and R."

n s 'dbn J540/2+; d 'dbnn J541/8

BOUNDARY STONE (cf 'tb)

J540/2: he constructed and built d(n) 'dbn...w'l t^{c}ly l'wtnh "this boundary stone--let his boundary stones not be removed"

'DB II

n p 'dyb[t] C80/8*

DEPENDENTS (?)

[Cf Ar 'db in sense of "invite," esp to a meal; the 'dybt (and m'db†, below) = "those nourished (by their lord)"?]

C80/8: 'ḥrrhmw w'ḥrrthmw w'dyb[t...] "their freemen, freewomen and dependents (?)"

n^{2} s [m']dbhmw J618/8--read m'xdhmw, with RycHim2/480, root 'XD.

n^{3} p m'dbthmy R4708/1; m'dbthmw R4194/5+

DEPENDENTS (?) (cf 'DB II n^{1})

R4194/5: 'xyhmw wm'dbthm[w] "their brothers/allies and dependents"

'DB III

D? pf 'db C939/2-3*

PUNISH

[Ar 'db D "discipline, chastise."]

C939/2-3: dhrg b^{c}ly msqt hrthw 'db "whoever litigates over the irrigation of his plain will be punished"

'DB IV--obscure in R5067, which consists of the monogram 'DB (n.pr?)

'DW

v pf 'dw R4144/4*

GIVE, PROVIDE (?)

[Ar 'dw D "help, equip."]

R4144/4: he dedicated to the god because 'dw lhw w[fy 'bl]n "He provided (?) for him (the camel's) health"

'DM I

v pf 'dmhmw J643/22*

RESIST (?)

[RycBiOr25/8B cfs the root sense in Ar "be chief, be at the head of."]

J643/22: w'dmhmw 'b^{c}l hmt hgrnhn...wtmn^{c}hmw "the citizens of those 2 cities resisted (?) them and defended themselves against them"

n d t'dmynhn J644/24*

REBELLION (?)

J644/24: all the blood-revenge they took bkly t'dmynhn bn š^{c}bn Š "in the 2 rebellions (?) from tribe Š."

'DM II

n coll 'dm J689/1+; 'dmhw J643/27-8+; 'dmhmy J568/21-2; 'dmhmw R2726/5+; p 'dwmthmw ib/7; 'dymthmw C609/2

(1) SERVANTS, SERFS of a landowner

[Cf esp ModYem 'awādim "domestics."]

C609/2: qnyhmw w'dymthmw w'mhhmw "their livestock/slaves and their servants and maidservants"

(2) CLIENTS, SUBJECT TRIBES of a king

R4188/3: bnw M...'dm mlkn "the clan M., clients of the king"

(3) WORSHIPERS of a god

J561b/6: hwš^{c}...'LMQH 'dmhw bny H "(the god)I. has helped His worshipers, the b.H." AND OFTEN SIM

Note: 'dm occurs in all the senses of ^{c}bd, which it serves as p.

'D̲ I

cj 'd̲ C547/4*

WHEN + pf (Harami subdialect)

[Ar 'id̲, 'id̲ā id.]

C547/4: they did not render to the god His ritual hunt bd̲M 'd̲ ẓ^{c}nw lY bdr ḤḌRMTM "in (the month) d̲M. when they journeyed to Y. in the Hadramite war"

Cf the exp šlt̲t̲'d̲ "three times" under ŠLT̲.

'D̲ II

v ipf y'd̲ C523/6*

PUT ON clothing, DRESS ONE'S SELF (b in) (?)

[Sense from context.]

C523/6: he confessed because y'd̲ b'kswt(h)w ǵr ṭhr "he had dressed himself in his clothes without purification"

'D̲N

v pf 'd̲nw C541/76+; inf 'd̲n J643/16

LET (GO), DISCHARGE (b, l s.o.)

[Ar 'ad̲ana la- "give ear to>permit," denom from 'ud̲un (Sab 'd̲n) "ear"?]

C541/76: b^{c}dn d̲'d̲nw b'š^{c}bn "after they discharged the tribes"; ib/74 'd̲nw lhmw "they discharged them"

Note also 'd̲nt (pf 3fs?) C615/8, fragmentary context.

st pf st'd̲n J643/14-5*

ASK PERMISSION (?)

[Ar 'd̲n st id.]

J643/14-5: tgb'w N...lmlk...ḥgn st'd̲n b^{c}m mr'hmw "N. (and his soldiers) returned to the king as he had asked permission (?) (to do) from their lord"

n[1] s/coll 'dn(m) J557+; 'dnhw J750/5+; p ''dn(m) J651/47+; ''dnhmw J650/29

(1) PERMISSION; AUTHORITY

[Ar 'idn "permission."]

J750/5: he made a journey bltn 'dnhw [dy dh]^{c}yw "without (the god's) permission, so that they lagged behind"; J557: b'dn 'LMQH wmlk "by authority of (the god) I. and the king"

(2) MIND, (MENTAL) FACULTIES

[Ar 'udun "ear"; cf Akk uznu "ear > mind." "The Mesopotamians believed the ear, not the brain, to be the seat of intelligence..." (T. Jacobsen in The Intellectual Adventure of Ancient Man [Chicago, 1950], p.133; a similar belief is probably in question here.]

J612/14: xmr ^{c}bdhw...mhrgm wǵnmm wbry 'dnm wmqmm "to grant His servant slaughters, booty, and strength of mental and physical faculties" AND OFTEN SIM

Note: When dedicants are plural, the expression bry ''dnm is used.

(3) MIND = SELF

s 'dnhw C356/2; p ''dnhmy C355/4-5

C355/4-5: rtdy...'nfshmy w''dnhmy "they dedicated their souls and minds = themselves"

n[2] coll 'dnn Ir13/8; 'dnh R3957/6; p 'dynt NNAG13-4/3

SUBJECTS, CLIENTS

[Cf Sab 'dn "authority," Te 'əzn "tribe."]

Ir13/8: 'dnn w^{c}qbt mlk Ḥ "the clients and governors of the king of Ḥ"; NNAG13-4/3: 'dynt wxmys w'^{c}rb [m]lk Ḥ "the clients, armies and Arabs (irregular troops) of the king of Ḥ"; R3957/6: slḥt d'dnh "she afflicted (one of?) her clients with ritual impurity"

n[3] s? 'dnt C550/10

context doubtful; n.pr?

C550/10: hqnyw...šymhmw wšfthmw 'dnt dhb wbrr ktm wwrq

Note: WinRefs/343-4 tr "they dedicated to their patron and He granted them a talent of gold and a brr of gold dust and gold leaf," but he offers no etym for 'dnt. It is prob preferable to regard these as nn.loc, as in J550/1: kl 'nxlhw b'DNT KTM wWRQ "all his palmgroves in A., K. and W.," though this interpretation renders the syntax doubtful. Tr phps "they dedicated to their patron and their gift (or the like) was, (for) A., gold, and silver (for) K. and W." 'DNT is common elsewhere as n.loc. (Note also 'dnt in C615/8, in fragmentary context.)

n[4] s m'dn C506/2*

DEPENDENTS (= 'dn n[2], q.v.?)

C506/2: ...]th wm'dnh wm'xdt[h... "its...and its dependents (?) and its booty"--list of booty taken from a certain place

'HB

n? 'hbhmw J746/11*

[Isolated in fragmentary context. J cfs Ar 'uhba† "equipment."]

'HL R4085/5--see under HLL

'HL

n s 'hl R2747/1+; 'hlhw R4230B/4; 'hlhmw C392/6; var 'l R3605b+; p/var 'hlt D50/2; 'hlty Ry554/4; 'hlht F127/4

PEOPLE; FAMILY, CLAN

[Ar 'ahl, Lih 'l id.]

R3193: 'hl thmt wṭwdm "people of the coastland and the highland"; R4230B/4: 'hlhw w'rḍhmw "his family and their land"; R2747/1: 'hl ᶜTTR "the clan of A."; D50/2: 'hlt dt Ḥ[MN] "the clan of dt Ḥ."

Note: The form 'l (as in Lih) occurs only in R3605b (3 times), which contains many incorrect nn.pr and is probably not authentic.

'HN

rl 'hnm C407/28; 'hnn C376/14-5; 'hnnm C609/6; 'hnmw R2724/10; b-'hnmw J623/7+

WHENEVER, WHATEVER, WHEREVER (senses not easily distinguishable)

[Cf Ar 'ayna "where," 'aynamā "wherever."]

J623/7: they campaigned b'hnmw yqhnhmw mr'hmw "when/wherever their lord commanded them"; C407/28: 'hnmw ysb'nn "when/wherever they go on campaign"

'HR

n s t'hrn J702/13* (prob inf of tp)

INFLAMMATION

[Cf Ar 'uwār "heat," 'wr D "inflame."]

J702/13: mr(ḍ) '(ḍ)rshw wṯnhw t'hrn 'ḍrshw wṯnyhw "the disease of his molars and incisors--the inflammation of his molars and incisors"

'HT C369-- = 'ḥt, see under 'ḤD

'W

cj 'w C548/2+; f-'w C74/14-5+

OR

[Ar.Eth 'aw id.]

C548/2: wḍ'm 'w bh'm "going out or coming in"; C126/13: h' 'sn 'w [h]yt 'n[t]tn "this man or this woman"; C74/14-5: bn M f'w ḏyqhn "the b. M., or whoever is in command (in his place)"; C571/8-10: wl yṣdn... f'w ^{c}qbhw "let him or his deputy celebrate the hunt"; C599/6: kl sṭrm kbrm f'w ṣǵrm "every document, large or small"

Note: The form f'w is more common in Sab.

'WD

v *pf* 'wdh Ry508/2*

(a) FOLLOW A LINE OF MARCH(?) or (b) ENTRUST (A MISSION TO), *pass* BE ENTRUSTED (WITH A MISSION) (?)

[(a) Denom from *n* 'wd "demarcating line"? (b) Ar 'awida "weigh on s.o. (burden, affair, etc)," Tna 'awwāwada "prepare tools to undertake a task" > "entrust, charge with" (RodConf'66-7/126).]

Ry508/2: ḏn msndn ḏšmw bsb'tm 'wdh khm ^{c}m mr'hmw "this inscription which they set up on a campaign which they marched out on/were entrusted with (?), when they were (acting) with their lord"

Note: BeOr25/296 suggests 2 other trs: "during an expeditionary march which he (?) made when they were (acting) with their lord," or, taking 'wd as a noun, "during an expedition, whereof the (territorial) boundary was KHM, with their lord."

n^1 *s* 'wd(n) J551+; *p* ''wd(n) J550+; 'wdt C465/5

LIMITING LINE; sense^1 COURSE OF STONES IN A WALL marking point of new construction

[Ar 'awida "bend, turn (intr); be bent, curved."]

J551: he dedicated to the god the whole fill of the wall ln 'wdn ḏn sṭrn ^{c}dy šqrm "from the limit (marked by) this inscription up to the summit"

sense^2: BOUNDARY LINE

R2865/2: hrwḥ 'wd hgrn "he enlarged the boundary of the city"; C465/5: 'wdt ḏn wṯnn "the boundary lines (marked by this boundary stone)"

n^2 *s* m'wdn R3945/2*

BOUNDARY LINE (= 'wd^1, sense^2?), or *n.pr*

R3945/2: ḥmy ḥrthw ^{c}A lm'wdn bn kḏ tḍ'n brḥm "he dammed up his canal A. as far as the boundary line (or, as far as M.), so that it might not flow out unchecked"

'WY

tp *pf* t'w R3945/3*

COLLECT, or CAUSE TO COLLECT (waters)

[Cf Ar 'wy *Dt* "collect, or flock, together (of birds)" (Irv/75-6.]

R3945/3: wdy wt'w zm "the waters flowed and collected" or "the channel system caused (waters) to flow and collect"

h ipf yh'yw R2859/2--see under 'YW h

'WK

n s 'k J720/18*

AFFLICTION

[Cf Ar 'awka† "anger, evil, unhappiness, 'akkā "afflict"; phps also Eth 'awkäka, Amh 'awwäka "bewilder, confuse" (HöASASühne/112).]

J720/18: (let him) offer the goat for his servant; b^{c}dn 'k bn nfshw "then the affliction will be (taken) away from his person"

'WL

v pf 'wlhmw J660/17; 'wly C500/1; 'wlw J577/7+; inf 'wln J700/8+

BRING (BACK)

[Ar 'āla (w) "return," D "cause to return."]

J700/8: she asked the god's help l'wln lhw bnhw "to bring her son back to her"; C500/1: 'wly b^{c}mhmy mngt ṣdqm "they brought back with them a satisfactory outcome"; Ir24: 'wln whkrbn whklln mr'tn "to bring and offer and give the woman in marriage"

tp pf t'wl J579/5+; t'l (?) R4176/12; t'wly J581/5; t'wlw J574/8+; ipf yt'wl J635/37-8; yt'wln J577/5+; y't'wln J2112/3-4; yt'wlw J576/8+; yt'wlnn J576/7+; inf t'wln J577/7+

(1) RETURN, esp from battle

J578/31: the god permitted His servants bt'wln...bwfym w(m)hrgtm wsbym "to return (from battle) with health and slaughters and captives" AND OFTEN SIM; J635/37-8: wyt'wl kl gyšhmw bwfym bn hwt brṯn "and all their troops returned in health from that campaign"

(2) RECOVER from a disease

Ir20: t'wlw bn mrḍm wsdmm "they recovered from a disease and an affliction"

Note specially R4176/12: wḥg qnyn ḏbḥhw ṯny 'sn wt'l "and in respect of the slave whom two men killed and (then) returned (to their own tribal center, for sanctuary?)"

h pf h'wl J670/10*

BRING BACK (= 'wl v)

J670/10: the god rescued His servant wh'wl bnhw...b^{c}ntm "and his son was brought back by (His) aid (?)"

st inf st'wln J577/15*

BRING BACK (= 'wl v, h) (?)

J577/15: the god helped His servant st'wln hw' w'qwlhw...bn kl hn[t ḏby'n sb'w "bringing back (?) him and his chiefs from all those [engagements] they undertook"

'WSLKY, R4350--only word in inscription; n.pr?

'ZD, n Ir12--see under ZYD

'ZY

n p 'zyy(m,n) C540/12+

QUOINS or SILLS

[Rh cfs Ar 'azzâ "supply with an 'izâ'" = "the place where the water is poured into the watering-trough or tank; a mass of stone and what is put for protection [of the brink of the trough or tank] upon the place where the water is poured when the bucket is emptied." In C540 (description of the Mārib Dam) the 'zyy are phps sills or spillways placed at the entrances to the two exit channels (Irv/262).]

C540/12: they repaired the sluices with grbm wlbtm w'zyym frznm "rough stone and polished stone and iron quoins/sills"

'ZL

st pf st'zl Ir7 twice*

FAIL, BE LACKING

[Ar 'zl h "(the year) became severe, distressful," 'āzalahum Allāh "God afflicted them with drought (Lane/53).]

Ir7/2: thanksgiving for rain b^{c}d ḏt st'zl...sqym ^{c}sm xryftm "after floods had failed several years"; ib: st'zl ^{c}dw ^{c}dyhw sqym ^{c}sm xryftm "floods had failed to enter (the control dam) for several years"

'ḤD

n m 'ḥd J693/5+; f 'ḥdy BR-Yanbuq 47/9; 'ḥt C609/3; 'ht C369/1; k-'ḥd R3945/1

(1) ONE; k-'ḥd: TOGETHER, UNANIMOUS (cf k-wḥd)

[Ar 'aḥad, f 'iḥdâ; Eth 'aḥadu, f 'aḥatti, id.]

J693/5: they dedicated 2 statues, 'hd ṣrfm w'hd ḏhbm "one silver and one gold"; C541/133: b'ḥd ^{c}šr '(w)[rx]m "in eleven months"; R3945/1: they were led out and were successful in their expedition, k'ḥd b^{c}sy ṣdqm "unanimous in performing what was right/satisfactory"

(2) A CERTAIN...

IrAppl1/3: His servant was saved bn 'ḥd xṭnm "from a certain plague"

'ḤẒ--for 'ḥẓm C522/5, read k-ḥẓm, see under ḤẒM v

'X--see under 'XW

'XḎ

v pf 'xḏ C350/5+; 'xḏhmw J660/15; 'xḏw J560/13+; ipf y'xḏ[C612/3; inf 'xḏ J665/20+; 'xḏhw J576/2

CAPTURE, TAKE IN WAR; EXACT PAYMENT FROM

[Ar 'axada "take, seize"; with acc of person and bi-,"insist on s.o.'s doing s.th." Cf also Rwala/577: ăḥadhom aḥîdten ğayedaten "[he] looted [the camp] completely."]

J665/20: twrdw hmw 'sdn...l'xd lhw 'xdm "those soldiers went down to make captures (lit, to capture captures) for him"; J560/2: w'x[d]w 'sdn 'rḍn "and the soldiers captured the territory"; J576/2: the god helped them b'xd M...bxfrt "to exact the reparation from M."

tp   pf t'xd R4088/4-5+

BE TAKEN PRISONER = GIVE ONE'S SELF UP, SURRENDER

R4088/4-5: hm 'l t'xd fhlt nfshw "if he does not give himself up, (then) his life is forfeit" (same formula R4558/2)

Lt?   pf t'xdw R4137/12*

STRIVE, CONTEND with one another (?)

[Sense suggested by R; cf Eth Lt id.]

R4137/12: r' kt'xdw b^cm hl[... "now, they have striven with..."--context much damaged, but concerns war and booty

h   pf h'xd C84/3; h'xdw ib/4

ATTEMPT, MAKE AN ATTEMPT

[Cf Ar 'xd "take to, set about" (Lane/29A); discussion BeNL10/407.]

C84/3-4: bkn h'xd SB'YN w'sd h'xdw llqthw "when the Sabaean, and those (others) who made the attempt, attempted to capture"

n¹   s 'xdm J649/12+; d 'xdn J649/36; p 'xdtm J578/32+; 'xydt(m) J576/10+

(1) PRISONER or PRIZE TAKEN IN WAR

[Ar 'axīd "prisoner of war," 'axīda⁺ "booty."]

J649/12: he killed on that campaign xmst 'sdm bd^cm [w'ḥ]d 'xdm "five soldiers killed in battle and one, a prisoner"; J658/17: the god granted them mhrgtm w'xydt wsbym wmltm wǵnmm "slaughters and prizes and captives and property and booty" AND OFTEN SIM

Note: Most authors have considered the (apparent) p 'xydt to refer to human prisoners, and have drawn varying distinctions between these and the sby or "captives." Phps the sby were, specifically, "hostages," or, as HöSEG8/58 suggests, the 'xydt may have been soldiers and the sby civilians.

(2) CAPTURING, CAPTURES (maṣdar?)

J665/20 quoted under 'XD v.

n²   s m'xd(m,n) R3943/5+; m'xdhw R3902b#131/2; m'xdhmw J618/16+; p m'xdthw ib/17; m'xdhmy R4626/1+

CONTROL CHANNEL or DYKE

[Cf Ar ma'xad "place from which one takes s.th., source"; in TA 'ixāda⁺ "place where water is collected." Discussion Irv/188-91.]

R3902b#131/2: he built and brought to completion m'xdhw Y dysqyn nxlhw "his control channel Y. which will irrigate his palmgrove"; C623/2: mxd blq m'xdn R mnxy Y "he quarried the masonry of the control channel R., the primary canal of Y.";R4775/2: m'xd yhtmynn š[c]bn [S] "a control dyke which provides irrigation by embankments for the tribe S."

n3 p? m'xdt Ist7626/7*

SENSE, MEANING, PURPORT (?) = TENOR

[Abstract, prob p of pass.prt, "things contained, contents" (BeFSTI/274-5).]

Ist7626/7: wbgl m'xdt 'dynhmw "and by the entire tenor of their obligations"

'XW

v pf 'xw R3945/13+; 'xww R3946/2

ALLY ONE'S SELF WITH

[Denom from 'x "brother, ally," below. Cf Ar 'āxawa "associate with s.o. as a brother."]

R3945/13: bdt 'xw HDRMWT wQTBN 'LMQH "because H. and Q. allied themselves with (the god) I. = the Sabaean state"; ib/8: consigned its property bn 'A d'xw 'LMQH "away from A. (to) those who had allied themselves with (the god) I."

tp ipf yt'xwnn C308/13; inf t'xwn ib/11

MAKE ALLIANCE, ESTABLISH BROTHERGOOD (bcm, with)

[Ar 'xw Lt "associate with s.o. as a brother."]

C308/13: bshm w'mnm yt'xwnn B wZ wcA... "in honesty and security there should make alliance together B. and Z. and A..."; ib/11: the king sent to him lt'xwn bcmhw "that he might make alliance with him"

h pf hxwhw J577/10*

MAKE ALLIANCE (?) (= 'XW tp)

J577/10: hxwhw bmwcdhmw lnsr cnt 'HBŠN "they (?) made alliance (?) with him (?) concerning their promise to aid the Habashite reinforcements"

n1 s 'x J832/1; 'xhw J558/6+; 'xyhw J561b/1+; 'xhmw J669/23; d 'xyhw J620/1+; p 'xhw C73/1; 'xhw C73/1; 'xyhmw R4194/5; 'xhhw R4712/1; 'xwthw R4109/2-3; 'xwthmw F74/6

BROTHER: ALLY (senses difficult to distinguish unless filiation is given)

[Ar 'ax(ū), p. 'ixwa†, id.]

J652/11: lwfy cbdyhw Š w'xyhw M "for the safety of (the god's) 2 servants Š. and his brother M."; R2695/5: 'LŠRH YHDB w'xyhw Y'ZL BYN mlky SB' "I. Y. and his brother Y.B. the 2 kings of S."; Ry512/3: 'xhw wmr'hw qyln Š "his ally and lord, the ruler of Š."; C73/1: 'xhw bnw M "his allies, the b. M."

Note: The pre-suffixal form 'x- is used for both s and p, and 'xy- for s, d and p.

n[2] s 'xth J1046/2-3; 'xthw R4017+; p 'xthn F76/5-6+; 'xthmw Ir33+

SISTER

[Ar 'uxt id.]

F76/5-6: hnt 'ntn w'xthn wbnthn "those women and their sisters and their daughters"; J1046/2-3: qbr Š w'xth B bnt 'A "grave of Š. and her sister B., daughters of A."

n[3] s 'xwnn C308/11; 'xwnhmw ib/15

ALLIANCE

[Eth 'əxwennā id.]

C308/11: he sent lt'xwn b^{c}mhw wstkml h' 'xwnn bynhmw wbyn G "to make an alliance with him, and that alliance was concluded between them and G."

'XR

D? ipf y'xrn R4230C/2; inf 'xr(n) C573/5+; 'xrnh J558/7

KEEP OFF, KEEP AWAY

[Ar 'axīr "last, rearmost," 'xr D "cause to remain behind = hinder."]

C573/5: lwḍ^c wṯbr wmn^c w'xrn kl ḍrhmw "to lay low and crush and repel and keep away their every enemy"; R4230C/2: wly'xrn (qlmm) wmqṣn "and may (the god) keep off noxious insects and damage"

h pf h'xrw C81/5-6*

KEEP BACK, DELAY (cf 'XR D)

C81/5-6: h'xrw hwfyn mwkln "they delayed the payment of that which was promised"

n[1] s l-'xr J633/12+; as adj, m 'xrn C541/95; f 'xrtn ib/96

THE FUTURE; l'xr: FOR THE FUTURE, HENCEFORTH; adj: LATTER

[Ar al'āxir "the hereafter," 'āxir "last."]

J633/12: to ask the god's help once a year ln tkwn ḏt hqnytn wl'xr "from (the date of) this offering and henceforth" (sim ib/15-6 and C95/3); C541/96: bmdt ḏD 'xrtn "in the latter part of (the month) ḏD."

n[2] s? ''xr C547/12*

ANOTHER (TIME), AGAIN

[Cf Ar 'āxar "another."]

C547/12: fl ḥḏrn mn mṯlh ''xr "so let them beware of (committing) the like of this again"

n[3] s m'xrm J703/12*

ONE WHO MOVES S.TH. AWAY (? prob D prt)

J703/12: they placed their offering under the god's protection bn m'xrm wmśwrm wdśśm "against anyone who (might) move, remove or hide (it)."

'ṬR

n s? 'ṭr R4029/1*

A MEDICINAL PLANT (?)

[Cf phps Akk 'atartu (note non-emphatic t) "an herb used as a medicinal plant" (BronSem24/136).]

R4029/1: w'[t]mrm fr^{c}m w'ṭr bhwt mwtḏn "and valuable crops and 'ṭr-plants (?) from this mwtḏ (type of cultivated land)"

'YD, p of yd--see under YD

'YW

h ipf yh'yw R2859/2*

GIVE REFUGE, SHELTER to

[Ar 'wy h id.]

R2859/2: wmn lyh'yw...'ḥd 's[m] "and whoever gives refuge to a certain/such a man..." (phps sim formula in A769/2)

'YS I

n s 's(m,n) C308/17+; 'ys(m,n) C429/6+; 'shw A788/3+; d 'sn C350/5+; 'syn J612/12; 'syhw J651/27

(1) MAN (cf 'NS); pejoratively, FELLOW

[Cf Heb 'îš "man." Root is prob a by-form of 'NS, q.v.]

J612/12: he came in strength whrg ṯny 'syn "and killed two men"; C308/17: nblw 'ysm b^{c}br 'xhw "they sent to one another (lit, a man to his brother)"; J644/10: tškrw...hw' 'ysn L "they defeated that fellow L."

(2) HUSBAND

A788/3: she dedicated a statue lwfy 'shw "for the safety of her husband"

(3) in exp 'ys nbt, FAMILY HEAD (?)

R4195/1: 'A 'ys nbt bn byt N "A., independent head of a family derived from the b. N."

'YS II

v pf 'sw R4193/8*

BE WEAK, BE AT A DISADVANTAGE

[Ar 'ayisa "despair."]

R4193/8: the god saved His servants from the battle they fought, wbhwt ḍ[w^{c}]n f'sw "for in this battle they were at a disadvantage"

'YS III

tp pf t'ysw J643/17+; inf t'ysn J629/35+

GIVE AID

[Cf Ar 'āsa (y or w) "give a present, a retribution."]

J629/35: they praised the god because stwfy wt'ysn mr'yhmw "He succeeded in giving aid to their 2 lords"; Ir9/3: the god allowed him stwfyn wmḍ' wt'ysn "to succeed in arriving and giving aid"

'KL I

n s 'klm GI537/7; 'kylm C548/12

MEAL or GRAIN, CEREAL CROPS

[Eth 'ekl "wheat, meal," Te 'akēlat "polenta (meal gruel)."]

C548/12: he must make an offering of 'kylm w^{c}qb šnnm "meal and the price of the šnn (a food)"; GI537/7: ṯmr sqym w'klm wbql[m] "irrigation crops and cereals and vegetables"

'KL II

n d? m'kly C570/7*

(a) STOREHOUSE, or (b) MIDDLE

[(a) Cf Eth 'akala "be sufficient, large enough for, hold." (b) Eth mā'kal "middle," here with prepositional suffix -y?]

C570/7: the boundaries are to be mnd̤h[t] mwn wm'kly ṯmrm "the outflows (?) of the water and the 2 storehouses for wheat (or, the middle of the wheat-field)"

'L I

n[1] s 'l(m,n) J631/25+; 'lhw Robin az-Zâhir 1/5: 'lhmw C41/2-3: d 'lyhmw J559/18+; p 'l'lt(m,n) C40/4+; 'l'lthmw R4002

GOD, contrasted with šym "patron deity" (cf 'lh)

[Heb 'ēl, Ar 'ilāh id.]

R3945/1: kl gwn d'lm wšymm "every community (owing allegiance to) a god or patron deity"; J643b/10, end formula: b^{c}TTR wHWBS w'LMQHW w'l'lt hgrn M "by A., H., I. and the gods of the city M."; J631/25: ^{c}r 'ln wsṭ hgrn "the citadel of the god (or, of 'Il) in the center of the city"

Note: As in the last example, 'l my sometimes represent the n.pr of the god 'Il.

n[2] s 'lthmw R4046/3*

GODDESS

R4046/3: brd' 'lthmw "by the aid of their goddess"

'L II

dm d? 'ln R4781/1; p.m 'ln C555/1; f 'lt C353/15

demonstrative adjective, d and p: THESE

[Cf Eth 'ellu and the element 'el-, 'al- in Eth and Ar demonstratives and relatives, and the Ar p demonstrative element -'ūl-.]

R4781/1: 'ln nxlnhn "these 2 palmgroves"; C555/1: ymxrw 'ln 'wṯnn "these boundary stones shall face..."; C353/15: bn kl 'lt sb'tn "from all these campaigns"

pn^1 m.p 'l(n) C600/1+; f.p 'lt R3946/1

demonstrative pronoun, p: THESE (p of hwt, hyt, etc)

C600/1: w'l ḏb^{c}br wb^{c}ly bny B "and these (things) are what is obligatory for and incumbent upon the b. B." (cf the expression ^{c}d'l ḏ-); G1447/1: 'ln 'b^{c}l xdrn "these are the owners of the grave"; R3946/1: 'lt 'hgrm wbḍ^{c}m gn'...K "these are the towns and districts K. walled"

pn^2 m.p 'l R3946/7; 'lw C570/10+; f.p 'lwt (?) R3605b/7+ (all doubtful); m.f.p 'ly(m) C375/1++; f.p 'lt C548/4; m.f.p 'lht (late Sab) C541/54-5+; m.p 'lh C568/3

relative pronoun, p: THOSE OF, THOSE WHO (p of ḏ-, ḏt)

[For forms with -h-, cf Te lahā, lahāy "each," and usages of Sab 'hl "people (of), family (of)."]

pre-nominal uses

genitive: R3946/7: w^{c}sy mfrśtn 'l mḥmyn "and acquired the weirs of the embankment system"; C375/1: ln ''wdn 'ly sṭrn "from the lines of this inscription"

Note esp R3911/4: 'nxl...'lym ḏhbn "palmgroves belonging to the irrigated zone"

to indicate material: C544/3: 'rb^{c}t 'ṣlmn 'ly ḏhbm "four statues of gold"

to indicate clan-affiliation: C548/4: l'lt ^{c}TTR "to (the people, the community) of A." (sim usage of 'lh and 'lht)

Note also G1533/2: hmẓ'...l'ly st 'qyn "he ceded... to those of (the vassals of?) the six administrators"

pre-verbal uses

C541/54-5: 'qwln 'lht qsdw "leaders who rebelled"; J558/2: 'mṯln...'ly stwklhw "images which they entrusted to Him"; C435/3: qbltn 'ly ysmynn ḏY "tribes who are called ḏY."

pre-prepositional uses

C570/10: 'lw b^{c}mhw "those who were with him"; R3945/10: lands 'lt ^{c}ly bḥrm "which are by the sea"

'L III

av 'l R4088/4++

negative particle: NOT, NO ONE; 'l 's, 'l ḏ-: NO ONE

[Eth 'al-bo, Heb 'al, id.]

with perfect verb

R4088/4: hm 'l t'xḏ fḥlt nfshw "if he does not give himself up, his life is forfeit"; J578/42: an enemy ḏbnhw d^{c}w wḏbnhw 'l d^{c}w "of whom they have knowledge, or of whom they do not have knowledge"; J665/48: 'l tfqd bn gyšhmw ǵyr 'sm "no one was missing from their army except (one) man"

with imperfect verb

R4815/6: wbnw S...f'l ymn^{c}w "and (as for) the b. S., let them not hinder"

with non-verb

J720/13: a disease d̲'l mn š^{c}r kmhn h' "(about) which there was no one who knew what it was"

compound expressions

R3902b#130/3: w'l 's s'lhmy bḫrthmy "and let no one (lit, no man) lay claim to their aqueduct"; J651/25-6: 'l d̲fqdw bn 'šr^{c}hmw "there was nothing which was missing from their booty (?)"; Ist7626/2: w'l d̲bhw yt̲bnn "let (there be) no one who will settle there"

'L IV

pt 'l...'l C532/8+ (?)

WHETHER...OR WHETHER (?)

[Cf Heb 'im...wə'im, Ar 'immā...wa'immā, id. The usage is dubious in Sab, C532 being the most probable case. Discussion BeDGESA/55:15.]

C532/8: she confessed sins 'l bhn š^{c}rt w'l lm tš(^{c})r "whether she was aware of them or whether she was not aware"

Note: Interpretation of 'l as a relative ('L II) is also possible: "she confessed those (sins) of which she was aware and those of which she was not aware."

'LH I

n s̲ 'lh(n) R3973/2+; 'lhhw R4084/2; 'lhh R3957/3-4; p̲ ''lhn Ry508/10

GOD

[Ar 'ilāh id.]

R3957/3-4: tnxyt wtnd̲rn l'lhh "she confessed and vowed penance to her god"

Note esp the following expressions: QYNN 'lh XS'M "Q., god of (the tribe) X." R3973/2+; 'lhn b^{c}l smyn w'rḍn "the god, the lord of heaven and earth" C541/81-2 (cf 'ln b^{c}l smyn "the god (or, 'Il),lord of heaven" R5085/8).

'LH II

tp i̲p̲f̲ yt'lhnhmy J578/42*

CURSE or SWEAR

[Heb 'ālāh id, n̲ ta'alāh "curse" (BeRev/351).]

J578/42: may the god preserve them bn 'lhtm d̲yt'lhnhmy šn'hmw b^{c}ly ḥṣy mr'yhmw "from curses (with) which their enemy may curse them (or, oaths which he may swear) to the detriment of (?) the esteem of their 2 lords (i.e., the esteem in which their lords hold them)"

    n p̱ 'lhtm J578/42*
        CURSES or OATHS
        J578/42 quoted under 'LH ṯp
            For 'lht elsewhere (f̱ of 'lh) see under 'L II (relative p̱n)

'LY, relative p̱n--see under 'L II

'LM
    v p̱f 'lm Ry585+
        HOLD A RITUAL BANQUET
        [Cf Ar walīma^t "ritual meal," 'lm Ḏ "convene the meeting," wlm ẖ "come
        together, gather." Discussion RycRepas/329 and passim.]
        A710, Lu16, Ry585, Ry586: ywm 'lm ^{c}TTR dDBN whnrhw btrḥ "the day he held
        a ritual banquet for (the god) A. of D̲., and offered him a burnt sacrifice,
        in return (for a favor or the like?)"
        Note ḏ'lm Ry 584 in fragmentary context.
    n^1 s̱ 'lmn R4176/8; 'lmhw A710; p̱? 'lm(n) R4176/8 twice
        (1) RITUAL BANQUET
        R4176/7-8: wlkd̲ lyf^{c}l T'LB b^{c}šr 'lm wbn H 'lmn bxrf wdyH wdM t̲ny bxrf
        wkwn mrt^c 'lmn xmst b'hdxrf ym T "that (the god) T. hold banquets by
        means of the tithes (= paid for with tithe-receipts). (From the tithes)
        of H. the annual banquet; from the 2 qayls of H. and M. (each) 2 banquets
        a year; and the legal number of banquets is five each year, on the day
        of T."
        (2) BANQUETING PLACE
        [Cf phps Eth 'elām, Heb 'ēlammot "vestibule."]
        A710: bny qyf 'lmhw ywm 'lm ^{c}TTR "he built the altar of his banqueting
        place on the day he held a ritual banquet for (the god) A." (sim in Lu16,
        PalSb 15:78 ('66)/47-53)
    n^2 s̱ m'lmhw A710/1; p̱ m'lmt R4635/4-5
        BANQUETING PLACE (cf 'LM n^1, sense^2)
        R4635/4-5: ywm nql lmbny m'lmt S "the day he transported materials for the
        construction of the banqueting place of S."

'LSN v--see under 'LŚN

'LF
    n s̱ 'lf(m,n) R3943/1+; ḏ 'lfn J643b/2; p̱ ''lf(m) C541/119+
        THOUSAND
    [Ar 'alf id.]
    R3943/1: 'rb^{c}t 'lfn "four thousand" (so-called "emphatic" state); C541/119:
    xmsy ''lf "fifty thousand"; R3945/13: t̲ny 'lfm "two thousand"; J643b/2:

ṯny 'lfn "two thousand"; C376/14: hn blṭn 'lfn "these thousand blṭ-coins" ("emphatic" state); ib/3-4: 'lfm blṭm "a thousand blṭ-coins"; R3945/13: sby 'wldhmw 'lf "he captured their children: one thousand"

'LŚN

v pf 'lśnw C99/9; var 'lsnyhn[w] R3232/2 (late Sab)

NOT TO BE ALLOWED TO

[Quadriliteral development from the expression 'l śn "it is not lawful/allowed to," see under ŚNN v.]

C99/9: 'lśnw xdl hy^{c} "they were not allowed to cease offering sacrifices"; R3232/2 (fragmentary context): 'lsnyhm[w] rsty, no tr (C and R take as p of lsn "tongue," q.v.)

'LT--see under 'L I or 'L II

'M

pt 'm F76/8*

INDEED..., NOW...

[Ar 'ammā id.]

F76/8: 'msṭrw bḏn wtfn "now, they have written this deed of transfer"

For 'm in nouns, see under 'MH, 'MM

'MH

n s 'mt(m) J700/8+; 'mthw J706/5; p 'mh J722/3+; 'mhhw J722+

MAIDSERVANT (serves as f of ^{c}bd)

[Eth 'amat, Ar 'ama^{t}, p 'amawāt id.]

R3910/3: ḏyš'mn ^{c}bdm f'w 'mtm "whoever buys a servant or maidservant"; C435/2: lbn 'dm w'mh bny 'A "for the children of the servants and maidservants of the b. A."; J706/5: may the god h^{c}nn 'mthw N bn mrḍ "save His maidservant N. from the disease"

'MM I

n s 'mhw C543/3; 'mhmy J594/8; 'mhmw J719/7; p 'mhthmw F76/3

MOTHER

[Ar 'umm, p 'ummahāt, id.]

J594/8: may the god grant them [wf]y 'mhmy w'ṯthmy wwld[hm]y "the safety of their mother, their wives, and their children"; F76/3:'mhthmw w'xthmw "their mothers and their sisters"

Note: For 'mhw R4151/5 read prob 'm(t)hw. Cf also the epithet 'M^{c}ṮTR "Mother of (the god) A." = the goddess ŠMS.

'MM II

n s 'mt C570/2; p 'mn ib/1; 'mm C540/75+

CUBIT

[Eth 'emmat, Heb 'ammāh, id.]

C540/75: šmw ^{c}rḍ r'shw sṯ 'mm "they prepared the face of its upper area, six cubits"; C570/2: 'rb^{c} 'mn wšlṯ šwḥṭ b'mt mxḍm "four cubits and three spans (?), in standard cubits"

Note also R3890#3: krb...'rb^{c} 'mh "he offered four cubits (or, maid-servants) (?) " (context fragmentary).

'MM III

ti ipf y'tmmw R3945/1*

BE LED OUT

[Ar 'amma, Qat 'mm (R3878/3) "lead the way."]

R3945/1: h^{c}ḏ[b] m^{c}šrt SB' y'tmmw wyḥtẓyw mnš'hmw "(the king) reinaugurated the tribal assembly of the Sabaeans, so that their tribal levies were led forth successfully"

Note also C45/5: H bn [...] T 'mm wb[ny?...] tsn mfg[... C takes as n, cf Ar 'imām "head, chief, leader," but this interpretation is not justifiable from the fragmentary context. If 'mm is a v here, cf phps Ar 'amma in sense "aim at, intend," and tr "H son of...planned (?) and b[uilt the ...?] which is near the..."

'MN

h inf h'mnn J633/13+

GIVE ASSURANCE TO, ASSURE

[Ar 'mn D "assure, guarantee."]

J633/13: as for the god, fšft wh'mnn wṣry wtbšrn "He decreed and gave assurance and decided and announced (oracularly)"; Ir24/2: the god hwfyhw wh'mnn b'ml' "granted him and assured (him with) oracular responses"; R3960/2: hknn wh'mnn wẓrbn lmr'hmw "to arrange and assure and acquire legitimately for their lord"

n^{1} s 'mn(m) C308/13+

SECURITY

[Ar 'aman id; cf Heb.Aram 'āmēn.]

C308/13: bṣḥm w'mnm yt'xwnn B wZ "in honesty and security B. and Z. should make alliance together"; Ry513/3-5: wtrḥm ^{c}ly bny M...RḤMNN w'mn "and may (the god) R. have mercy upon the b. M. And (let there be) security!" (RyMus66/313 calls this a "judaizing" inscription)

n^{2} s 'mnt R3945/13, 18*

SECURITY, PROTECTION in exp ḏ'mnt: THOSE UNDER THE PROTECTION OF, DEPENDENTS OF

[Ar 'amāna† "security." Cf also Min 'hl 'mnhtn "people of the 'amīn class" R3306/1 (BeDGESA/40:4).]

R3945/18: ḥr SB' wḌHR ḏ'mnt K "the freemen of S. and Ḍ., who are under the protection of/dependents of K."; ib/13:hḍb^c ḏ'mnt K "he attacked the dependents of K."

n^3 s 'myntn R4771/1*

DEPOSIT

[Ar 'amāna^t "deposit, deposition in trust."]

R4771/1: w'myntn wš'mtn "the deposit and the contract of sale"

n^4 s t'mn(m,n) C81/9+; p t'mntm J651/34-5

(1) THANK-OFFERING (recompense to the god for favors granted)

[Cf Heb 'amānāh Neh 11:23 "fixed recompense." Discussion BeMus64/311-2.]

J550/2: "he came back safely whṯb lhw...t'mnm "and rendered to (the god) a thank-offering" AND OFTEN SIM

(2) TIME OF THANKSGIVING, when the tribe thanks the god collectively

C126/11: any man or woman with respect to whom a decree is made kt'(m)nn [l']lh[tn] "at a time of (solemn) thanksgiving to the gods"

'MR

v ipf [y]'mrn C464/3*

PROCLAIM

[Cf Heb 'āmar "say," Ar 'amara "command" (BeOracle/220).]

C464/3: f[l y]'mrn hy^{c}m sdy[m] "let him proclaim 'an offering (of blood) poured out'"

n^1 s 'mr(m) R4830/1+; 'mrhw R4998/3+

COMMAND; of a god, ORACLE

[Ar 'amr "command," Heb 'ōmer "utterance."]

C314/8: 'mr wṣḥft "command and rescript (of king)"; R4830/1: 'mr 'LMQH qdm "(by) command of (the god) I. he went forward"; R4998/3: hmt^{c}hw b'mrhw "(the god) assured him of His protection through His oracle"; C575/3: T'LB b^{c}l 'mr R "(the god) T., lord of the oracle of R."; Ry548/3: ḏSMY 'lh 'mrm "ḏS., god of the oracle"

n^2 p 'wmr J576/13*

TOWERS situated on eminences around a fortress, where signal beacons could be lit (?)

[Discussion in BeNL8/444-5. Cf Ar 'amār = ^{c}alam "sign"; 'amara^t "a structure like a manārah [lighthouse]...made in the time of ^{c}Ād and Irem" (Lane s.v.).]

J576/13: kl mḥfdt kwnw 'wmrhw "all the towers (which) were its signal towers" (for a proposed emendation see under NMR II)

n^3 s mh'mrm C363/4 (h prt)*

OFFICER, COMMANDER (?)

[Ar 'amīr "commander."]

C363/4: [w]ḍ^c mh'mrm bḍrn "he laid low an officer in the battle"

'MT--for 'mt "maidservant" see under 'MH. For 'mt "cubit" see under 'MM II.

'N

ij 'n C541/4*

BEHOLD, LO!

[Ar 'inna, Eth 'en, id.]

C541/4: sṭrw dn mśndn 'n 'BRH "he (p.maj) wrote this inscription--lo! Abraha!"

cj b-'n R3910/5*

IF, WHEN

[Ar 'in, id.]

R3910/5: wb'n ymtn bᶜrm bᶜm dyš'mnhw...fbr'm mhš'mn "and if a camel dies on (the hands of) the one who purchased it, the seller is not liable"

'NY I

pn? 'ny P104

personal pronoun, 1st person singular: I (?)

[Cf Ar 'anā, Heb 'ănî, id.]

Note: RyNE4/150 cites appearance of this word in P104, commenting that it is known via Ar transcriptions in Hamdani's Iklīl (no context is quoted).

'NY II

v pf 'nyt R3956/6*

COMPLAIN (?)

[Cf Ug anh id., Heb 'ānāh "mourn" (MüW/26).]

R3956/6: she wore a dirty cloak fxb'ṭ mn 'mr'h d'nyt "and hid (it) from her lords, of which/to whom (?) she complained"

Note: R took as n.pr. Neither solution is completely convincing. Phps the sense is that she was "the subject of complaint."

'NM

n s 'nmhw R3945/11,13*

CIVIL POPULATION

[Cf Ar 'anām "mankind."]

R3945/11: hṯb Y wqsṭhw w'nmhw wbḍᶜhw w'ᶜrrhw...l'LMQH "he gave over Y and its yeomen and civil population and its district and hill-towns to (the god) I."; ib/13: he captured their children wrḍᶜ 'nmhw "and the unweaned children of the civil population"

'NN

? b-'nn R4031/4--context obscure, no tr

'NS

n s 'ns(m,n) C313/3+; p/coll 'ns(n) R3992/8
MAN (cf 'YS 1); pejoratively, FELLOW
[Ar 'ins, 'unās id.]
R3910/3: yš'mnn...bn 'nsm w'b[l]m "(those who) buy any man or camel..."; R4771/1: kl 'l'ltm w['[]mlm w'qwlm w'š^cbm wkl 'nsm bhṯm [wqṭnm] "all gods and kings and chiefs and tribes(men) and all men great and small"; C313/3: the god helped and saved him bn hwt 'nsm "from that fellow"

'NF

n p ''nf C554/1; ''nfhn ib*
FRONTS, NEAR SIDES (?)
[Cf Ar 'anf "nose," Heb 'ap "nose, face."]
C554/1: l''nf 'r^cw sq' ''nfhn "for the near sides (?) of the pastures, (whose) near sides (?) irrigate"--water phps moves through canals from the side of the pasture near the primary canal outward?

'NT--for n 't, Ry508/11, see under 'T

'NṮ

n[1] s 'ṯt(n) J700/7+; 'ṯthw J655/7+; p 'nṯ(m,n) F76/4+; 'nṯhw J576/7; 'ṯthmy J594/8; 'ṯthmw J669/5+; 'nṯt R4176/7+; 'nṯthmw M1/5; ''nṯhmw J575/6
FEMALE; WOMAN; WIFE
[Ar 'unṯâ "female"; Syr 'anttā, Heb 'iššāh "woman," Eth 'anest "women."]
Ry375/6-7: wldm 'sm f'w 'ṯtm "a child, male or female"; F76/5-6: kl hnt 'nṯn w'xthn wbnthn "all these women and their sisters and their daughters"; R4188/5: they dedicated for wfy 'ṯthmw w'wldhmw "the safety of their wives and children"; C523/6: ms 'nṯ ḥyḍ "he touched menstruating women"
Note: MüPoly/129-30 argues that the form 'ṯt is never p, and that texts with such locutions as 'ṯthmy, 'ṯthmw reflect the practice of polyandry in Old South Arabia.

n[2] s 'nṯym C392/9-10*
FEMALE (cf 'ṮY n)
C392/9-10: [ḏb]ḥm ṣḥḥm 'nṯym f'w ḏkrm "a perfect sacrificial victim, female or male"

'S, v 'sw R4193/8--see under 'YS v; n 's--see under 'YS, 'NS, 'SS

'SD

n p/coll 'sd(m,n) C69/3+; 'sdhw J586/22+; 'sdhmy J575/2; 'sdhmw J660/12
SOLDIERS > MEN in general (and see Note)
[Development from Ar 'asad "lion > warrior"? BeJTS2/30-31 sees a possible Heb cognate in 'šdt Deut 33:2 (qere 'ēš dat), probably also a collective.]

J665/15: kl gyšhmw xmsy wsb^c m'tm 'sdm rkbm wsb^{c}y 'frsm "their whole army, seven hundred and fifty mounted soldiers/cameleers and seventy horsemen"; R3960/3+; 'sdn w'n<u>t</u>n "men and women"; R4624/9:'sd mlkn "soldiers/men of the king"

Note: In a few cases 'sd "seems to denote a class of persons settled on land...[perhaps] a technical usage for a person awarded a grant of land in return for military service to the king" (IrvJRAS'64/27). Cf R3951/2: 'sd 'mlkn ['l]w yhwṣtn b^{c}ly 'š^{c}bn "royal soldiers who are being settled on the tribes" (also R3945/9, C82/8, C84/7, C350/2).

pn 'sd Gl573/l+

relative pronoun, <u>m.p</u> = THOSE WHO

[Development from uses of 'sd n^1.]

Gl573/l: R...w'sd t^{c}lmw b^{c}mhw brtm "R. and those who signed with him the document of indebtedness"

Note: In military contexts 'sd n^1 and n^2 are often indistinguishable.

n^2 <u>d</u> 'swdyhmw J665/31*

SOLDIER (of a special class?) (but see also under SWD I <u>n</u>^{2})

[Noun of form f^{c}wl from root of 'sd n^1 "soldier" (RycBiOr25/6A).]

J665/31: 'frsm w'swdyhmw "horsemen and their 2 'swd-soldiers"

'SY I

v <u>pf</u> 'sy C401/7; 'syhw R4356/4; 'syhmw C541/97; 'syw ib/18-9+; <u>ipf</u> y'synn Ir13/10

SEND; specifically SEND/MAKE A RAID

[Sense from context.]

J576/16: as for those Ḥimyarites, f'syw lhmw wkym "they sent aid to them"; C621/8: they returned from the land of Ḥabashat w'syw 'ḤBŠN zrftn b'rḍ ḤMYRM "and the Ḥabashites sent a raid into the land of Ḥimyar"; J578/26: they fought outside the city f'syw bhw K...wxmshw "and K. and his army made a raid there"

Note: DrNote, again from context, suggests the tr "find" in many cases, e.g. C121/8 above: "they found the Ḥabashites pillaging"; J578/26 above: "they found K. and his army there"; Ir28/2: they were grateful k'syw mr'hmw...bwfym "that they found their lord in good health"; Ir13/10: wy'synn bwsṭ hgrn...'rb^{c}t ''lfm 'sdm qrnm "there were (e.g., were found) in the city 400 troops assigned to garrison duty."

h <u>pf</u> h'sy J651/11-2*

SEND (?--cf <u>v</u> above)

J651/11-2: 'sdm <u>dh</u>'sy b^{c}mhw "the soldiers who were sent (?) with him"

'SY II

tp <u>inf</u> t'synhw R4084/4*

BE ASSIDUOUS (?)

[Cf Ar 'usâ "patience."]
R4084/8: she dedicated to the god lqbly dt ['] l t'synhw "because of her not having been assiduous toward Him (?)"

'SS
n s 'shw Ir25/3+
BASE of a statue or stela
[Ar 'uss "base, foundation."]
Ir25/3: they placed it under the god's protection bn 'ys...h'xrnhw wnkthw bn 'shw "against (any) one who would remove it or break it off its base" (sim Ir13/15)

'SR--'srhw C372/3: misreading for 'ŚR v, q.v.

'F--d'fm C540, C541, see under D'F

'FY
n coll? 'fym C562/7*
BAKED GOODS
[Cf Eth 'efuy "baked," Ar mīfâ, mawfâ, Sq mo'fe "oven."]
C562/7: four fig-cakes wbn qrśn 'fym "and part of (?) a qrś-measure of baked goods"

'FKL
n p 'fklt R3945/16*
PRIESTS
[Cf Akk apkallu "wise man, soothsayer"; Nab 'pkl', Palm.Lih 'pkl religious titles.]
R3945/16: bḍ^{c} bẓhr N śl'm 'fklt "he imposed on N a tribute (for?) the priests"

'FL in C380/4--see under FLL

'FS p of nfs, see under NFS

'FQ
v pf 'fq Ir28; ipf y'fqn C541/19+
EXERCISE CONTROL OVER, RESTRAIN
[BeNL7/538-9 cfs Ar 'ufq "horizon," etymologically "frontier, boundary" (cf also RycMus88/202).]
C541/19: they sent him y'fqn bqh mlkn bmšrqn "to exercise control over the east, by order of the king"; J671/16: ky'fqn l[h]mw d^{c}bn ^{c}dy hšqrw nklhmw "since (the god) restrained the flood for them until they had

completed their pebble-pavement"; Ir28: f'fq ndn sb^c^t 'wrxm bbḥrm "so (the god) restrained the wind seven months on the sea (?)"

'ṢF

n p? 'ṣf C87/5*

sense doubtful; phps MAIDSERVANTS (?)

[Cf Ar 'aṣuf = wuṣuf, p of waṣīfa† "maidservant."]

C87/5: dedicated this tablet lqbly 'ṣf y^c^brn fr^c^ lǵlm yldn "for the maid-servants (?) who offer crops, in recompense (?) for the children they will bear"

'ṢR

In R2740/9-10, R has ṣṣyr in the text, 'ṣyr in the commentary: wb hgrn 'ṣyr 'rb^c^ "and in the city ...? four"--n.pr of the city?

'ḌḤ, n in C540/45--see under NḌḤ

'RBY

n coll 'rbym J610/8*

(MIGRATORY) LOCUSTS

[Cf Heb 'arbeh id, Mh harbi "locust."]

J610/8: may the god protect them bn brdm w'rbym w^c^rglm wbn kl qlmtm "from hail and migratory and non-migratory locusts and from all noxious insects"

'RB^c^ and related forms--see under RB^c^

'RY

n p 'rwyn R4176/5-6*

MOUNTAIN GOATS sacred to certain deities

[Cf Heb 'aryeh "lion," Akk arū "eagle," Ar 'arwâ "mountain goat," Eth 'arwē "wild beast." Phps "generic term for the principal wild and strong beast" of the local fauna (UICSH/192-3).]

R4176/5-6: the god has prohibited s'r 'rwyn bn nśg bn mṣrn "the rest of the mountain goats from being prevented from feeding"

'RX

n s 'rxn J669/23; 'rxhw R4624/8; ''rx(n) J567/24+

(1) ROAD

[Cf Heb 'ōraḥ "path; way (of life, etc)."]

R4624/8: [ywm r]tkl 'rxhw "when he took his road on a merchant journey"

(2) AFFAIR, DEVELOPMENT OF AN AFFAIR; PROBLEM, TROUBLE

J567/24: may the god grant them prosperity w''rx wmngt ṣdqm "and satisfying developments and outcomes"; J623/22: may the god preserve them from b'stm ...w''rx sw'm "harm and disastrous developments"; J620/5: tsynt hsyn bn ''rx nhk ^{c}lyhmw šn'n "the injuries he suffered from the troubles the enemy inflicted upon them"

(3) JUDICIAL AFFAIR = JUDGMENT, DECREE

C562/2: ''rx wmḥr "judgments and decree"; J669/23: if the god saves their brother bn hyt 'rxn fyḥqnynn "from this (pending) judgment, they will dedicate..."

'RK

n s 'rkm C570/9; l-'rkn C555/4*

INDEFINITE LENGTH OF TIME = ETERNITY; l-'rkn: FOR EVER

[Ar 'araka "persist, linger," Heb 'ārak "be long."]

C570/9: kl ^{c}frm w'rkm "all space and all time = everywhere and for ever"; C555/4: ymxrw 'ln 'wṯnn nsrn mšrqn l'rkn "these boundary stones shall face the east for ever"

'RF

n s 'rfthw R4922/4*

BOUNDARY STONE (?)

[Cf Ar 'urufa^{+} "boundary," Eth 'araft "partition, wall."]

R4922/4 (fragmentary context): fwkl 'rfthw [..."so he entrusted (?) his/its boundary stone (?)..."

Note: This is the reading of GaAION33/436, after a new photograph. R read fkl for fwkl.

'RḌ

n s 'rḍ(m,n) J555/4+; 'rḍhmw C2/13+; d? 'rḍy C432/4; p 'rḍt(n) J735/14+; 'rḍthw J555/3; 'rḍthmw J563/13+; p? 'rḍhmw J561b/21+

(1) LAND (political entity)

[Ar 'arḍ id, note p 'arāḍi.]

J555/4: 'rḍ QTBN "the land of Q."; J560/10: 'rḍ ^{c}rbn "the land of the Arabs" AND OFTEN, followed by name of the land or its possessors; C81/4: ^{c}ws ḏkwn b'rḍn "the plague which was in the land"

(2) PIECE OF LAND = TERRITORY, FIELD

J561b/21: crops and harvests ^{c}dy kl 'srrhmw w'rḍhmw "in all their valleys and fields" AND OFTEN parallel to 'srr, mfnt, mšymt and the like ('rḍ is probably the least nuanced of the many designations in Sab for types of arable land)

(3) EARTH

MüBilinguis/2-3:mr' smyn w'rḍn "Lord of heaven and earth"--and in several other damaged contexts

'ŚG, n in obscure and fragmentary context C460/2: sfḥ b'ḥt 'śgm "he...? with one ...?"

'ŚS[M]W, in obscure and fragmentary context R3232/3: mn wl'śs[m? or ṣ?]w... 'lsnyhmw rsty

'ŚR

v pf 'śrhmw J665/22; 'śrw Ry506/6; ipf y'śr C603b/28; inf 'śrhw C372/3
BIND; TAKE PRISONER
[Ar 'asara id.]
C603b/28 (fragmentary context): w'l y'śr bs'lhw "he shall not (?) be bound by his obligation (?)"; C372/3: 'śrhw wfqḥ[hw] "binding him and releasing him"; J665/22: hrghmw w'śrhmw klhmw "he slew or took prisoner all of them"

n s? 'śwrhw R4176/13*
PRODUCE (?)
[Sense doubtful. Something "bound" (Ar 'sr "bind) or "gathered" (Heb 'sr "gather") together? Cf Ar 'asīr "collected vegetables."]
R4176/13: ḥrg T'LB 'śwrhw...lqśm 'qwl "(the god) T. commanded His produce (?) (to be) the portion of the tribal leaders"
Note: Cf 'śrm ib/6, phps related to this word (see under ŚRM).

'ŚRM R4176/6--see under ŚRM

'T

pn? 't Ry508/11*
(a) personal pronoun, 2nd singular masculine: THOU; or, (b) ' + t, first and last letters of the alphabet, as a concluding formula (?)
[(a) Cf Ar 'anta, Heb 'attāh id. (b) This is the less convincing conjecture syntactically, but scholars are reluctant to accept an isolated instance of the pronoun.]
Ry508, end: RḤMNN rḥmk mr' 't "O (god) R., thy mercy! Thou art lord! (or, O Lord! 't)"

'TB

n s 'tbn C949/3-4+
BOUNDARY STONE (cf 'db)
[Cf Sab 'db id and Ar hadaba "separate, divide."]
C949/3-4: 'l h^{c}ly dn 'tbn "let not this boundary stone be removed" (same formula NNAG4/6, partly restored in C911/2)

'TW

v pf 'tw J550/2+; 'twy Ir5/3; 'tww J643/3+; ipf y'tw C603/17; y'twn J628/6+; y'tyn J580/5; y'tyw J577/11+; juss (l)y't R4176/11+; inf 'tw J610/5+
COME TO, ARRIVE AT a destination; COME BACK, esp from campaign
[Ar 'atâ, Eth 'atawa id.]

Ir28: the god allowed them 'tw bwfym w'wln bslmm "to arrive safely and return (from campaign) safely"; R4852/1: he dedicated because 'tw bwfym bn kl 'brt bhw sb' "he came back safely from all the expeditions he undertook"; Ir22: the god allowed 'tw wstwfyn hw' brqn "that storm-season to arrive successfully"; R4176/10: lkd ly't ᶜšr "that there shall come in tithes"

D? pf 'twhw C461/4-5; ipf y'tyn C290/5+

BRING, OFFER a sacrifice

[Cf Ar 'atâ bi- "come with = bring."]

C461/4-5: 'twhw tnym t'twm ᶜrbn "he offered (the god) a second (offering) (?), a sacrificial victim"; C290/5: kl ᶜṣmm dy'tyn "every ᶜṣm (tribute? offering?) which he offers"

tp pf t'tww J735/12*

COME (bn away from), RETURN (cf 'TW v)

J735/12: during the rest of that day, t'tww bn mn mḥrmn...dnm "(when) they came away from the mn of the temple, rain fell"

h pf h'tw C338/5+; h'tww C282/9; h'twhn C461/7-8; ipf yh'twn C563/2; yh'tyn C131/4

BRING IN; PRESENT, INTRODUCE (offering, decree)

Ir13/5: h'tw mlkhmw...ᶜdy hgrn "he brought their king into the city"; C131/4: lyh'tyn [']b[ᶜl]hn 'nttm...bhgr "let their husbands bring the women into the city"; C461/7-8: h'twhn ᶜd[y] mxtnhw "he presented them in His shrine"; R3945/6: he destined the Awsanian nation to slaughter and captivity wh'tw xrš bythw "and presented (to the god, as an offering?) the destruction of its palace"; C338/5: h'tw mḥr "he introduced the decree (or pass, the decree was introduced)"

n^1 s 'tw--Instances of a noun 'tw cited in MüW are all more easily taken as verbs.

n^2 s? m't C338/11; p m'tt R4194/3

CHANNEL for water

[Ar 'atiy id, Syr maytəyānā dəmayā "aqueduct," Qat m'tw "channel."]

C338/11: m't mqldtm ᶜdy qdm kwrn "the water channel of the storage basin at the front of the cistern"; R4194/3: qrwt wnqbt wm'tt "canals and cuttings and channels"

n^3 s t'twn C461/4-5* (D inf?)

OFFERING

C461/4-5 quoted under 'TW D?

'TḤ

n s 'tḥn R4410*

THRONE, BALDACHIN (?)

[Cf Eth watḥa motāḥt "erect the canopy" Ex 25:21 (RhSLG2/39).]

R4410 (in full): Y W hqny 'LMQH mbny 'tḥn "Y.W. dedicated to (the god) I. the construction of the throne"

'TY--in verbs, see under 'TW

n[1] s? 'ty[m] R4130/1*

YIELD (?)

[Derived from root sense "come," cf Heb təbû'ah id, from bw' "come."]

R4130/1 (fragmentary): [wr]qm wd^c^tm xrṣm [w]'ty[m... "vegetables and fodder, estimation and (actual) yield (?)"

n[2] s 'tyt J562/4+; 'tythmw Ir9/4

ARRIVAL, ENTRY, including ROYAL ENTRY

J562/4: hwš^c^hmw bstwfyn 'tyt mr'hmw...^c^dy bytn S "(the god) allowed the successful entry of their lord into the (royal) fortress S." (sim Ir7/1); Ir18: mlk wnbtt w'tyt "the kingdom, the (royal) descent, and the (royal) entry"

'TL, n in fragmentary context R4979/3: ...] 'tlt ^c^thyt[..., no tr

'TM

v pf 'tm R3951/4+; 'tmh C37/6; ipf y'tmnn C609/3; inf 'tm(n) J643/29+

(1) MAKE AN AGREEMENT

[Ar 'atama "unite, join."]

C315/10: hslm w'tm Y byn 'mlkn "Y. made peace and concluded an agreement among the kings"; R3951/4: bmsb'n 'tm š^c^bm w'sm lr'shw "in the campaign to which the tribe and the man at its head agreed"

(2) ACQUIRE TITLE TO (land, etc) UNDER AGREEMENT

C37/6: his riverside pasture dt D. w'tm 'tmh bmwhbt whbw 'bhhw "and (it is) an acquisition (to which) he acquired title by the grants given to his forefathers"; R4781/4-5: 'tm w^c^ḍd 'A "he acquired title to and worked (cooperatively) A."

ti ipf y'ttmw J575/5; y'ttmnn J631/26; inf 'ttmn J665/14-5

ASSEMBLE, JOIN FORCES

J665/14-5: tg^c^r w'ttmn kl gyšhmw "their whole troop joined together and assembled"; J575/5: wy'ttmw wtqdmn wrtḏhm b^c^m 'ḤBŠN "they joined forces and attacked and slew the Ḥabashites"

tp pf t'tm J616/21; t'tmw J578/19+

ASSEMBLE (cf 'TM ti)

J578/19: t'tmw wrtḏhn wtqdmn "they assembled and slew and attacked" (sim in R3884/5; cf J575/5, quoted under 'TM ti); J616/13-4: t'tmw wqtḍn kl 'š^c^b "all the tribes(men) assembled and were called up (for military duty)"

n[1] s 'tm C37/6*

LAND ACQUIRED BY AGREEMENT

C37/6 quoted under 'TM v

n^2 s 'tmt C155/4*
PACT, ALLIANCE
C155/4: the god granted ['tmt mlk]hmw w'tmt 'xhw...mlk Ḥ "(an alliance between) their (king) and his ally the king of Ḥ."

n^3 s m'tmn C555/4,6*
ESTATE, LAND possessed by a clan (cf 'TM n^1)
C555/4-6: boundaries ḏbyn m'tmn ḏbn ʿA wm'tmn [ḏ]bn B "which are between the estate of the b.A. and the estate of the b.B."

'TN

h pf? h'tn Ir2I*
TRACK, "RUN DOWN" (the quarry) to a certain place (?)
[RycMus87/505n2 cfs Ar 'atana "remain at a certain place."]
Ir2I: he asked kyhrgn lb'nhn h'tn ʿdy N "to kill the 2 lions (which) had been tracked (?) to N."

'ṮY

n s 'ṯym J752/II*
LARGE, GOOD-SIZED (?)
[Cf phps Ar 'aṯīṯ "large; fleshy"; or, possibly, cf Sab 'nṯy "female" (here with assimilation?).]
J752/II: his filly wldt mhrtm 'ṯym "gave birth to a good-sized (?) filly"

'ṮL

n p/coll 'ṯl(m) R4646/13+; 'ṯlhw C605b/6
(1) TAMARISKS
[Ar coll 'aṯl id.]
C605b/6: the field wkl tlhw wkl 'ṯlhw "and all its tl-palms and tamarisks"
(2) TAMARISK PLANTATIONS (?)
R4646/13: ḥṣm wxṣb 'ṯlm wmhglm "split the wood of or cut down tamarisk plantations and (trees in?) enclosed fields"

'ṮR

n s 'ṯr R3951/5; b-'ṯr J660/11; b-'ṯrhmw J575/4
as pp (b-)'ṯr: AFTER (local and temporal)
[Ar 'aṯar "track, trace," 'iṯra "after"; Syr bātār "in the track of, after."]
J660/11: he ordered him lṭrd whwkbn b'ṯr Ḥ "to pursue and follow after Ḥ.";
R3951/5: bqdmy w'ṯr ḏt mṯbtn "before and after this decree"

Π-B

B I

ab b- R4623A+

ABBREVIATION OF BN, "SON"

[Rare and somewhat dubious; read phps d̲- "he of (+ clan name)"?]

R4623A (in full): sṭr W 'A bGBM bLMDM bMNWR "W.A., son of G., son of L., son of M., wrote (this)"; R5072: B T bRGG "B.T., son of R."

B II

pp b- passim; var b-m C413/4+; var b-mw J653/13+

IN, ON; BY MEANS OF; WITH; BY... (in invocations)

[Cf Ar bi- in these senses; for use with enclitic -m(w), cf Ar bi-mā, Heb bə-mô.]

local: J574/4: bḥrbt ḥrbw...bsrn "in the battle they fought in the valley"; Ir13: bmw wsṭhw "in its midst (= inside it)"; R3104/1: md̲bḥt bh yd̲bḥn mlkn "altar on which the king sacrifices"

temporal: C80/12: bxrf W "in the year of (= named for) W."; J653/13: bmw hwt wrxn "in that month"

instrumental: C40/4: brd' wmqmt 'l'lt "by means of the help and powers of the gods"; J606/5-6: the god commanded them bms'lhw "by means of His oracle"; R3951/5: šrk...bhmw šrkw "partitions whereby they partition"

indicating accompaniment: J574/8-9: t'wlw...bwfym...wsbym wmltm "they returned (from campaign) with health, captives and booty"; N74/3: bmhyt ^{c}qwt "in/during (the commission of) this act of impiety"

indicating exchange (rare): F124/3-5: they dedicated an altar bwfy 'n(f)shmw "in exchange for the well-being of their persons"

invocatory, in closing formula: C493/4-6: b^{c}T̲TR...wbYT̲^{c}'MR wbKTLM "by (the god) A., (the king) Y. and (the town?) K."

with the objects of certain verbs: J574/3: xmr...^{c}bdhw...bnqm "(the god) granted His servant vengeance"; C532/8: xṭ't bllm 'l bhn š^{c}rt "she committed little sins (?), those of which she was conscious..."; R4193/9: š[t]' bhmy t̲lt̲t 'gyšm "three armies fought the two of them"

special use with suffix -hw: e.g. R4842/2: kl 'brt̲ bhw sb' "all the campaigns/battlefields on which he fought," or, as the 3m.s suffix -hw does not correspond to the m.p 'brt̲, tr impersonally "the campaigns where he fought"

compounds of b-: b-'n, see under 'N; b-d̲t, see under D̲T; b-hn, see under HN; b-ḥg, see under ḤG; b-kn, see under K; b-^{c}br, see under ^{c}BR; b-^{c}ly and varr, see under ^{c}LY; b-^{c}m, see under ^{c}M

B'--see under BW'

B'D

n s b'd[m] Gl533/7*

adj: PUBLIC (?)

[Cf Ar badā "appear, be manifest" Sab b'dm "public"? In parallels C609/5, F30/5f = ḥqqm "legally binding" (HöSEG8/32).]

Gl533/7: t^{c}lm...b'd[m] wnfqm wšṣṣm kl ẓhr "signed as public (?), binding and prohibitive every document"

B'L--For b'l J578/39, read b-kl

B'S I

v pf b's J651/43; ipf yb's C522/1

DO HARM, INJURE

[Cf Eth be'sa "be bad, unsafe," Ar ba'isa "be wretched," Sab b's(t) "harm, evil."]

J651/43: may the god save His servant bn kl db's "from anyone who might do harm"; C522/1: yb's wngzn dnfsm "injure or destroy this stela"

h pf hb'sw J577/13; ipf yhb'sn C444/2; act.prt mhb'sm R3972/3+

DO HARM, INJURE (= B'S v)

C444/2: may the god strike down [dyštrn nfshw] wyhb'sn bhw "[anyone who destroys his stela] or injures it" (restoration from sim context C441); R3972/3: they placed their offering under the god's protection bnkl nkym wmhb'sm "from anyone who might harm or injure (it)" AND OFTEN SIM

n^1 s b'sm J615/26+; var b'st(m) R3991/15++

HARM, INJURY; bb'sm: WITH HARMFUL INTENT (?)

J615/26: may the god protect them bn b'sm wnkytm "from harm and injury" AND OFTEN; R3991/15: bn b'stm wnkym "from harm and injury" AND OFTEN; C539/3: šrk lmr'm bb'sm "'associating' (= assigning divine partners?) to the Lord, with harmful intent (?)"--but see B'S II

n^2 p hb's R3232/4*

HARMFUL THING (?)

R3232/4: bn hb's wbšym "from (things that are) harmful or disgusting" (context fragmentary)

B'S II

n p 'b's R4158/3; phps also 'b'[s] C597/4

(COMMON) MEN (?)

[Eth be'si "man." Cf phps Ar ba'usa "be brave, strong in battle" and

Sab b'sn, epithet of the god ᶜTTR, "the Brave in Battle (?)" (HöWdM/498).]
R4158/3: 'q]wlhw 'b's wᶜq[l "its tribal leaders, the (common) men and chiefs"

> Note: Cf phps C539/3, quoted under B'S I n¹: šrk lmr'm bb'sm. Tr "associating the Lord with a man (as a divine partner) (?)"--an anti-Christian, pro-Islamic passage?

B'R

v inf/pf b'r R4194/2+

DIG A WELL; PROVIDE WITH WELLS

[Denom from b'r "well," q.v.]

R4194/2: grb wśwᶜ whrr wb'r "revetted, leveled, built up an embankment and dug wells"; C230/2: hnklw...krfm wb'r wbql "they paved cisterns, dug wells and planted"

n s b'r R4085/3+; b'rhw R4100/3; b'rhmw R3152/2+; p 'b'r(m,n) J735/7+

WELL

[Ar bi'r id.]

R4198/2: hbḥr wḍfr wšrᶜn b'rhmw "excavated, cased with stone and provided with lifting gear their well"; J735/7: wybs ḏbn 'b'rn "some of the wells dried up"

BD'

n s bd'n C548/9*

BEGINNING, FIRST OCCASION

[Ar bad' "beginning."]

C548/9: ᶜlm bd'n lywfyn zlᶜn wḏkr nts "in respect of the first occasion, let (the offender) pay this fine; but whoever repeats (the offense) must leave"

BDD

v inf? bdd C571/10-1*

DISTRIBUTE, SHARE OUT (or read ᶜdd, see Note)

[Ar badda and D id.]

C571/10-1: drm drm b'ḥd xrfm lbdd xrfnhn "once a year distributed among 2 years (?)"

> Note: The original editors (J.H. Mordtmann and D.H. Müller, Sabäische Denkmäler [Vienna, 1883]/55-62) note that b and ᶜ are similar in the script of this text, and read ᶜdd, translating "once a year, to the number of 2 years."

n¹ s bdm G1573/2*

COMPENSATION

[Ar budd id; cf also BeSM2/423, who tr "currency, medium of exchange."]

G1573/2: rtm ḏbdm ḤY'LYm "a claim in regard to a compensation in ḥy'l-coins"

n^2 s mbd P149*

SHARE, PORTION

[Cf Ar mubadda$^+$ "holding of property in common." RyNE4/154 suggests that Sab mbd may designate a piece of property belonging to several owners.]

P149: mbd N "portion of N."

n^3 s tbdd VanLessen 7/3* (maṣdar)

PAYMENT

VanLessen 7/3: 'xd tbdd 'rḍn "payment on the land has been received"

BDL I

pp bdlh C464/4*

EQUIVALENT TO, or IN ADDITION TO

[Cf Ar pp badala "instead of"; n badal "equivalent."]

C464/4: yh^{c}ynn...^{c}ynm wbdlh šlṯ '^{c}ynm "let him turn himself towards...(one) turn, and equivalent/in addition to it, three turns"

n s bdltn R4782/2*

EXPIATION

[Cf Ar badal "substitute, equivalent."]

R4782/2: let him offer to the god parts of the sacrificial animal bdltn wršyn "(which are) the expiation and offering"

BDL II

n s bdln C535/9-10*

INJURY, DISEASE (?)

[Cf Ar badila "be afflicted with pain in the hands and joints"; Te.Amh badala "injure."]

C535/9-10: mt^{c}n...bn bdln b^{c}r yqnyn "to save from injury/disease (any) camels he may acquire"

BD^c--For bd^{c}tn J647/30 read b-d^{c}tn "consisting of d^{c}t-crops" (root D^{cc})

BDR--For bdrn R2864, read as n.pr? Text reads (in full): MRN bdrn "(clan) M., ... (?)"

BDT--For bdthmw C191/2, read bythmw

BḎL I

n s bḏln C609/5*

adj: CONCEDING, LIBERAL

[Ar baḏala "treat s.o. generously" (RyET/22).]

C609/5: let these documents be xd^{c}n wbḏln wḥqqn "restrictive, conceding, and legally binding"

BDL II

n p mhbdlm C540/12-3* (h prt)

INSERTED (?)

[Cf Ar bazala "split," D "broach a jar (of wine)," st "open" (Irv/263).]

C540/12-3: brrm mhbdlm blbt 'zyyn "clamps inserted into the closelaid stonework of the quoins"

BDN--Read b-dn, see under DN

BDT--Read b-dt, see under DT

BH'

v pf bh' J700/9+; bh'w J644/6+; bh't C581/12; ipf ybh' G1642/1; ybh'n R4773/2; act.prt bh'm C548/2; inf bh' J616/17

(1) ENTER, COME (IN); also in sexual sense (cf BW' v "enter")

[Cf Heb bw' id.]

C548/2: wḍ'm wbh'm "going out or coming in"; G1642/1: 'l ybh' Y "let Y. not come"; C523/4-5: bh' ᶜly nfsm...bh' ǵr ṭhr "he had sexual intercourse with a woman unclean after childbirth...in a state of (ritual) impurity"

(2) AGREE TO, CONFORM ONE'S SELF TO

[Ar baha'a "be, become friendly with s.o."]

R2726/2: ᶜd'l dstqr' wxll bh'w dwmm "to that which (the king) publishes and determines have (the Sabaean assembly) conformed forever"; same formula R3951/1

n s bh'thmw J616/ 17, 18, 20*

KIND OF MILITARY UNIT = ADVANCE FORCE (?)

[Derivative of root BH' "come, come in." J unsatisfactorily tr "income."]

J616/17-20: ysrw bh'thmw lbh' lhmw S wthbhmw bh'thmw ᶜdy hgrn R... wbmw ywmn dbhw thbhmw bh'thmw nzᶜw gyšhmw "they sent their advance force (?) to come to them (to) S., and brought back their advance force (?) to the city R.; and on the day on which they (?) brought back their advance force (?), their army revolted..."

BHN--Read b-hn, pp + pn f.p; see also under HN II

BHT I

D? ipf ybht C320/5*

OFFER, DEDICATE (cf BWT h) (?)

[Cf Ar bahata "accept benignly." BeOracle/220 tr "utter a favorable oracular response."]

C320/5 (fragmentary context): let him give produce, honey, a bull... wl ybht[... "and let him offer (?)..."

BHṮ II

n s bhṯm C609/7+

GREAT, IMPORTANT

[Sense from context; for another proposal, see under QṬN n^{1}.]

C609/7: kl 'nsm bhṯm wqṭnm "every man, great or small"

BW'

v ipf yb'hw R4088/3*

ENTER (cf BH' v sense^{1})

[Heb bw' id, Ar bā' "come again."]

R4088/3: mn ^{c}br yb'hw "whoever crosses (the boundary) to enter it"

n s b'th C542/1*

HOUSE (?)

[Ar bī'a^{t} "place of residence."]

C542/1: WHBT...wb'th wfr[... "W., her house (?) and..."

BWN

n p 'bwn R3958/4*

KIND OF TREE (Moringa aptera?)

[Ar bāna^{t}, coll bān id.]

R3958/4: bql w'^{c}lb w'bwn "vegetable gardens, ^{c}ilb-trees and bān-trees (or, plantations of such trees)"

BWR

n s brt C722/2+

TOMB, SEPULCHER

[Cf Heb bôr "cistern; tomb," Ar dār al-bawār "house of perdition = hell."]

C722/2: blw nfs wbrt "he constructed the funerary stela and the sepulcher"; sim C721/1-2

BWṮ

h ipf yhbṯn R4782/1*

OFFER, DEDICATE (cf BHṮ I id)

[Cf Ar bahiṯa "accept benignly" (MüW/30, and see under BHṮ I). For another tr, see under BṮṮ.]

R4782/1: wl yhbṯn l'lhn fxḏm "let him offer to the god the thigh (of the sacrificial animal)"

BHD̤

v pf/inf bhd̤ R3884/12; ipf ybhd̤w J576/5+; ybhd̤n ib/4+

ATTACK, RAID (?)

[Sense from context; phps remotely connected with Eth bas̤h̤a "arrive, invade."]

R3884/12: sb' wbhd̤ b^{c}m 'sd "he campaigned and raided with the soldiers";

J576/: ybḥḍw kl mšrqt Q "they attacked/raided all the eastern parts of Q."

n s bḥḍ(m) J576/6+; p bḥḍt J578/10

ATTACK, RAID

J576/6: yhysrw bḥḍm ḏbn xmshmw "they sent some of their army on a raid"; J578/10: kl b^{c}wt wbḥḍt sb'y wb^{c}w wbḥḍ "all the ambushes and raids they undertook, prepared, and engaged in"

BḤR I

h pf hbḥr R4198/2*

HOLLOW OUT, EXCAVATE a well-shaft

[Ar baḥara "split, make wide," st "become wide, spacious" > "open out, excavate."]

R4198/2: hbḥr wḍfr wšr^{c}n b'rhmw "excavated, cased with stone and provided lifting gear for their well"

n s bḥr(m,n) C30/4+; p 'bḥr R3945/10; var bḥwrm DJE12/3+; d bḥrn ib/4

(1) LAND, REGION; as pp: IN PLACE OF

[Eth beḥēr, Ar baḥra^{+} "land, region."]

R3945/10: kl 'bḥr 'ln 'bḍ^{c}n "all the lands of those districts"; prob also ^{c}d bḥrm, ib; C30/4: mqṭrn bḥr mqṭr srq "an incense burner in place of the incense burner (which) was stolen"

(2) SEA; POOL

[Ar baḥr, Eth bāḥr id.]

R3945/5: 'h[gr]hmw 'lt ^{c}ly bḥrm "their towns which are on the sea"; C308/17: bbḥrn wybsn "on sea and dry land" AND OFTEN; cf also title of the god ^{c}TTR ḏDBN, b^{c}l bḥr ḤTBM "lord of the pool of Ḥ." (HöWdM/552)

(3) FLOOR of a building

[Cf Ar baḥr "bottom (e.g. of the womb, a saddle)," ModYem baḥḥār "man who goes to the bottom of a well to clean it" (MüTa^{c}izz/92).]

DJE12/3-4: sṯt 'sqfm bsṯt bḥwrm wsybhw ṯny bḥrn "six roofs with six floors (= six stories) and its fortification, two floors"; cf also Gl539/5: ...'rb^{c}t bḥwrm... "four floors (?)" or sense^{2}, "four pools"?

n^{2} s mbḥr R3954/2-3+; mbḥrhw C417

(1) TOMB hollowed out in rock

R3954/2-3: he built a quarter of the qbrn...wrb^{c} mbḥr "tomb, and a quarter of the rock tomb"; sim C371/2, C417

(2) ROCK DWELLING

C504/4: he dedicated because ślbt bth...bn mbḥr ^{c}A w'l ẓyt "his daughter had been abducted from the rock dwelling A. but was not held captive"

BḤR II

h ipf yhbḥr C563/3*

CHOOSE

[Cf Heb bāḥar id.]

C563/3: bsr ṯwrm ḏyhbḥr "flesh of a bull which was chosen"

BḤT

n[1] s bḥt R4189/4*

adj: PURE, STANDARD (of gold)

[Ar baḥt "pure, unmixed."]

R4189/4: hqny...ḏhb bḥt "he dedicated pure gold"

n[2] s bḥtm C423/1-2; bḥthw G1194/6; d bḥtnhn J672/1-2+; bḥtnyhn R4203; bḥty R4679

(1) UNIT OF WEIGHT, "STANDARD" UNIT (?) (of gold)

C423/1-2: ṯmny bḥtm ḏhbm "eight 'standard' units (?) of gold"

(2) VOTIVE OBJECT, specifically INSCRIPTIONAL PLAQUE (?)

[No doubt related to sense[1]. Phps these objects were originally of gold (or bronze), and later of blq-stone, the traditional materials of OSA inscriptional plaques. Bḥt is f in J672/1-2.]

J672/1-2: hqny...kl'ty bḥtnhn "he dedicated the 2 votive objects";

R4679: bḥty blqn "2 votive objects of blq-stone"

Note: In C960/2 bḥtn prob n.pr.

BXY--Obscure in R4172/1: ṯwbn bxyn 'db bnxln, no tr. R suggests reading b-xyl, but the passage remains obscure.

BXR

n p 'bxr C582b/2*

FRANKINCENSE (?) or phps n.pr

[Ar baxūr id.]

C582b/2: hqny 'LMQH 'bxr "he dedicated frankincense to (the god) I.";
root also in G1541/1 (TsSEG6/20), prob n.pr, or incomplete for b-xrf

BYD--For pp byd(n), bydy, read b-yd, b-ydy, see under YD

BYN I

v pf byn J619/7-8; ipf ybnn C546/3

(1) BE DISLOCATED

[Ar bāna (y) "be separated."]

J619/7-8: dqt wdq ^cln 'blhw bh' byn kr^c 'blhw "the fall he took because of his camel; in it his camel's knee was dislocated"

(2) CEASE

[Development from sense "be separated" > "be cut off" > "cease."]

C546/3: they made a (public) confession hn ybnn ẓl^cm wtnkrm "when the fine and punishment ceased = at the completion of their penance"; phps also bn C539/3 (see under BN II)

h For yhbn R3910/5, see under WHB v

BYN II

pp byn C140/4+; var bn J700/14+; bynhw J750/14; bynhmw J700/11+

BETWEEN

[Ar bayna id; cf also the Ar exp bayna yadayhi "between his hands" = "in front of him."]

C140/4-5: bḏrm byn ḪMYRM wR wbyn ḤḌRMT "in the war between Ḥimyar and R. (on the one hand) and Ḥaḍramawt (on the other)"; J700/14: tlf R bn ydyhw "R. was struck dead between his hands = on the spot"

n[1] s bynn C609/3*

adv: OPENLY, PUBLICLY (?)

[Ar bayyin "clear, evident."]

C609/3: kl ms[m]ḥ bynn f'w y'tmnn bhyt š'mtn "anyone who accepts (?) publicly (?) or agrees to this purchase..."

n[2] s byn(n) R3954/2+; var bnm C975/6 (?)

(1) INTERIOR CHAMBER

[Cf Ar bayn "that which is between." Discussion BeStI/91).]

R3954/2: bny rb^c qrbn...ḥwln ḏbynn ḏtḥtyn "he built a quarter of the tomb, the tiers of loculi of the interior chamber: namely that which is the lowest one"; sim R3955/2-3

(2) REGION BETWEEN = SURROUNDING DISTRICT, NEIGHBORHOOD

[Ar bīn, p buyūn "horizon, surroundings."]

J577/2: hṣrw ^{c}dy byn hgrnhn "they set out toward the region between the 2 cities"; A452/5: [h]grn Š wbynn "the city Š. and (its) neighborhood"

BY^c

n s b^{c}t(n) C541/66,117*

CHURCH

[Ar bī^{c}a^t, loanword from Syr by^{c}tā "dome > church."]

C541/66: qdsw b^{c}t M "they held a Mass (in) the church of (the town) M."

BYT

n s byt(m,n) C2/6-7+; bythw J552/3+; bythmw J560/6+; bythn J734/5; var bt J702/7+; bthw C368/4-5; bthmw C380/3+; d bytnhn C69/2+; bytnyhn R3958/13; bytnn J706/2; bytyhmw C41/2+; p 'byt(m) R3945/6+; 'bythw J555/3+; 'bythmw J644/13+; var 'bthmw J1028/9

(1) HOUSE = FAMILY, COMMUNITY

[Ar bayt id; discussion BeJESHO15/257.]

R4013/1-2: bythmw wš^{c}bhmw "their family and tribe"; J615/11: kl hgr bythmw "every town of their community"; ib/21: kl 'rḍ...bythmw "all the lands of their community"; cf esp the exp 'b^{c}l bythmw (e.g. J689/5) "patron deities of their family"

(2) SETTLED AREA (contrasted with ^{c}mqt "cultivated area")

N49/1: b^{c}mqt wbytm bhgrn "in the valley (i.e., cultivated land) and the settled area in (the district belonging to) the town"

(2) HOUSE = (FORTIFIED) BUILDING, specifically TEMPLE or FORTRESS

R3624: 'WM byt 'LMQH "A., the temple of (the god) I."; and cf esp the eponym formula (Gl762/3, Gl773b/3+) wfdyhw bn kl 'bythw "(the god) redeemed (the eponym) from (service in) all His temples"; C41/2: they built wt̲wbn bythmw M "and restored their fortress M."; J578/12: mṣn^{c}m w'bytm "strongholds and fortresses"; J576/13: sb^{c}w hyt hgrn...wbyt d̲S "they sacked that city and the fortress of S."

cj bytn J700/14-5*

WHILE, WHEREAS (?)

[BeAdd/292 suggests a comparison with Ar bayda, id. Cf Heb báyit in generalized sense "interior of anything." Ar bayda might be < *bayta, meaning "within."]

J700/14-5: tlf R bn ydyhw bytn sbt yd S "R. was struck dead on the spot, while (?) S.'s hand was slashed (in the struggle)"

BKL (note the common compound b + kl "in all")

v inf bkl R2726/13*

DWELL

[Cf Ar bkl h̲ "conquer and plunder," Sab hbkl "colonize conquered lands." Basic sense of root "dwell," h̲ "cause (others) to dwell"?]

R2726/13: hwṣt whbkln Y...SB' lḥwr wbkl bhgrn "Y. established and settled Sabaeans as colonists to settle and dwell in the city"

h pf hbklh R3945/17; hbklhw ib/7; inf hbkln R2726/13

ESTABLISH persons AS COLONISTS, COLONIZE conquered lands

R2726/13 quoted under BKL v; R3945/17: gn' N whbklh SB' l'LMQH wSB' "he walled (the conquered city) N. and colonized it (with) Sabaeans for (the god) I. and Saba"

n p bklhw J692/6; var bklnhmw G913/1; var 'bkln C334/24

INHABITANTS OF CONQUERED TERRITORY, SUBJECTS

[Discussion of the position and character of the bkl, RycERI/271.]

G913/1: š^{c}bn Ṣ wbklnhmw w'dymthmw "the tribe Ṣ. and their subjects and clients"; R2865/1: SB' wbkln "S. and (its) subjects"

But note also the prominent tribe BKLm (J575/4+), to which many of these passages may refer ('bkl = "members of the tribe BKL").

BKR

n s bkr R3946/8+; d bkryhw C521/4; f.s bkrtn C579/4; bkrthw ib/5-6

(1) FIRSTBORN

[Ar bikr id.]

R3946/8: X bkr d̲M "X., firstborn of (the tribe) M." AND ELSEWHERE SIM

RycRite/386 notes that certain eponyms are described as "firstborn" of the tribe (XLL or SB'N), probably consecrated to the god because of their primogeniture and "redeemed" (fdy) at the end of their service as eponyms (cf Gl678/3, Gl682/1,2,3+).

(2) CAMEL CALF

[Ar bakr id; ModYem f bakrah (RoVoc/301).]

C579/4-6: hqny...bkrtn dt dhbn lw[fy] bkrthw "he dedicated this gold she-camel calf for the safety/health of his she-camel calf"

BL--see under BLW, WBL

BLW

v pf blw C722/2*

CONSTRUCT funerary monuments

[Cf Akk belū "be extinguished, perish," Ar baliya "be old, worn out; decay," D "tie a she-camel to the grave of her dead master (to starve)."]

C722/2: blw nfs wbrt "he constructed the funerary stela and the sepulcher"

Note also the god BLW C924/2+--a death god or death demon?

st inf stbln C343/16*

BURY (?)

C343/16: tny 'sn dhrg wstbln "two men whom he killed and buried (?)"

n s blwt C715/1*

FUNERARY MONUMENT

[Cf Ar balīya† "she-camel tied to her master's grave."]

C715/1: nfs wblwt "funerary stela and monument"

BLḤ

v pf blḥ R4552/1*

FREE from what is unwanted > CLEAN OUT (a canal)

[Cf Eth bāleḥa "free s.o. from danger, save," Te "loosen, free."]

R4552/1 (in full): blḥ kl fnwthw "he has cleaned out his whole canal"

BLṬ I

ti pf btlṭhw R3910/6*

RENDER a contract INVALID (?)

[Cf Ar baṭala "be, become null, void, invalid."]

R3910/6: if a purchased animal dies within a certain period, fbr'm mhš'mn bn mwthw btlṭhw "the seller is not liable for its death; it (the death?) has rendered it (the contract) invalid (?)"

BLṬ II

n s blṭm J624/5+; p blṭ(n) C376/14+; var blṭṭm C73/9+

KIND OF COIN; COINS, MONEY in general

[IrvJRAS'64/22-3 cfs Talmudic bōlēṭ "stamped," PBH bālaṭ "stand forth, project; be cut in relief." He derives these words and Sab blṭ from Gk pallas, p pallades, name of the common Athenian drachma bearing the head of (Pallas) Athena, "extensively used in the eastern trade."]

C376/3-4: 'lfm blṭm mṣ^{c}m ḤY'LYTm blṭ "a thousand standard blṭ-coins, in ḤY'L money"; ib/14: hn blṭn 'lfn "these thousand blṭ-coins"; C73/9: blṭtm rḍym "current coin/money"

BLY

pp bly R5094/3; var bl[t] J745/11; var blty N74/5+; var bltn J750/5+

WITHOUT

[Heb bəlî id; (lə)biltî "in such a way that not" Lev 26:15+.]

R5094/3: bly mrd'm bklm 'wnkrm "without (= let there be no) damage or injury in anything (?)"; J745/11: the two horses were ridden bl[t] š^{c}rhmw "without their knowledge"; N74/5: they invoked the goddess blty kwn bmḥrmn kl b^{c}ltm "without there being present in the temple any priestess"; same context ib/8-9; J750/5: sb'...bltn 'ḏnhw "he journeyed without (the god's) permission"

BLL

n s bllm C547/10-1+

adj: WET, MOIST

[Ar ball id.]

C547/10-1: the god made their watercourses flow mn mwm qllm wbllm "with water in small quantity, but wet (i.e., a trickle of water)"

Note: Other examples of bllm dubious. Cf esp C532/7: she confessed bḏt xṭ't bllm 'l bhn š^{c}rt "because she had sinned...?, of some of which (?) she was conscious..."--usually tr "because she had committed small sins," but no etymology is forthcoming. Tr phps as b-llm, "she had committed sins by night" (see under LLY). For C255/4: n^{c}mtm [w]bllm, tr phps "prosperity and wealth" (cf Ar billa^{t} "wealth"). In C539/6 read ḍllm for bllm; in R3232/2, take as n.pr (?).

BL^{c}

n s mbl^{c}tm F120/12*

sense doubtful; n.pr?

[RyET/72 cfs Ar bl^{c} "pierce, bore," blw^{ct} "underground channel."]

F120/12 (fragmentary context): ...]hw WDYDm bmbl^{c}tm wr' k[..., no tr

BLQ

n s blq(m,n) R2650/2+; blqhw J557

KIND OF STONE

[Cf Ar balaqa "split (stone)," ModYem balag, the white or yellowish sandstone used for most OSA inscriptions (RoVoc/301).]

R2650/2: mxḍ blq m'xḏn "he quarried the blq-stone for the control dyke";

same context R3943/5, C623/2; R4392: kl mbny blq "the whole construction of blq-stone"

BLT (for pp blt and varr, see under BLY)

v pf blt J578/22; blthw J633/6+; blthmw C352/9+; inf bltn C308/10

SEND, DISPATCH a gift, an agent

[Cf Eth bnt D "bring gifts"? Phps a secondary formation from WBL "render," cf Akk biltu "produce, rent"; or from Sab NBL "send."]

C308/10: nbl wbltn "he sent and dispatched"; J578/22: blt K...t^{c}rbm "K. sent pledges"; J633/6: bkn blthw mr'hw lqdmn "when his lord sent him to take charge..."

h pf hblt J2110/7; hbltw J631/15+

PERFORM A (MILITARY) MISSION

J631/15: kl blthmw...dhrḍw mr'hmw bn kl dhbltw "every mission of theirs which pleased their lord, among all that they performed"

n^1 s blt(m,n) C290/4+; blthmw J631/15+; p? bltw J560/8; var bltt F102/10

(1) GIFT, TRIBUTE (cf BLT v, and bnt, "tribute")

C290/4: lydbḥn ^{c}TTR bltn "to offer tribute to (the god) A."; C291/4: stwtqn wstz'dn blt "establishing and increasing the tribute"; phps also R3197/5, context fragmentary

(2) MILITARY MISSION (cf BLT h)

J631/15 quoted under BLT h; J578/39: lbltm wmqrnm wqhtm "for a mission, guard duty or service"; F102/7-11: bkl bltt blthw mr'hw "on all the missions (on which) his lord sent him"

n^2 s tbltn J643/11*

MISSION, MESSENGERS (?)

[Cf, in addition to BLT v "send (agents)," n tnbltm "embassy, messengers" (here with assimilation?).]

J643/11: hysrn b^{c}brhw...tbltn b^{c}m mlk S "to send to him a mission from the king of S."

BM, BMW--see under B II

BN I

pp bn C571/5+; bnhw J572/15+; bnhmw J669/20+; var bn-m C975/7; var bn-mw R3958/5

FROM; FROM AMONG = ONE/SOME OF (cf mn id)

[Usually compared with Ar min id. Alternatively, BeDGESA/47:6 regards bn as an enlargement of the preposition b- with the common enclitic suffix -n found on many prepositions (cf ^{c}br/^{c}brn, ^{c}ly/^{c}lyn, etc); cf Ug b "from." On this hypothesis, bn is not related etymologically to Ar min and its Semitic cognates.]

local: J703/6: 'tmrm w'fqlm...bnkl 'rḍthmw "crops and harvests from all their fields"; C975/7: bnm nxln...^{c}brn QTBN "from the palmgrove toward Q."; R3958/5: bnmw ^{c}lyhw ^{c}d sflhw "from its upper to its lower parts"

temporal: C571/5: bn hwt xrfn "from that year (onward)"

partitive: R4230/7: m'dbthmw bn ḥwr hgrn "their dependents from among the inhabitants of the town"; J669/20: myt byd bnhmw "he died at the hands of one of them"; J561b/11: ḍrm b^{c}ly ḏbn '^{c}rbn "war against some of the beduins"; J574/5: b^{c}mhw ḏbn xmshw "with him (was) part of his army"

explicative: R3910/3: kl š'mt...bn 'nsm w'blm wṯwrm "every purchase, (whether) of a man, a camel, a bull..."; F74/1: br'w (b)n grb wmnhmt "they built (it) of grb- and mnhmt-masonry"

exclusion or prohibition (cf also bn kḏ below): R3945/16: yhḥrm bn mwfṭm "he prevented (it) from being burned"; G1142/8: ḥgr...bn hmlhmw qṭntm "prevent their driving flocks"; J720/15: lḥḏrnn bn hxṭ'n "to beware against sinning"; J561b/22: lxrynhmw bn nḍ^c "may (the god) preserve them against injury"

special use with suffix -hw: J665/27-8: they took booty wbnhw fqflw wḥrbw...wbnhw fghmw bllyn "and then they returned and fought; and then they set out during the night..." (development of temporal usage)

Note: In expressions without f + verb, such as 'tw bnhw bwfym (J656/7, 14; J631/14) the tr should probably be "his son came back in safety."

compounds of bn:

bn ḏ- "some": J635/12: tnš'w...bn ḏymnt wbn ḏš'mt "they undertook a war, some from the south and some from the north"

bn ^{c}lw "from": R4169/2: bn ^{c}lw Ḍ bn S wŠ "from Ḍ., from S., and Š." (as in Qat)

bn ^{c}ly "(incumbent) upon" (= b-^{c}ly): R2726/5: śxlm wnfqm bn^{c}ly 'dmhw "binding and obligatory upon his dependents"; sim R3951/4

bn kḏ "so that not": R3945/2: he dammed his canal bn kḏ tḍ'n brḥm "so that it might not flow out unchecked"; cf also C126/12 for bn ḏ- as negative, quoted under LN

Note: In C343/6 and (phps) J700/14 bn is defectively written for byn pp, q.v.

BN II

pn bn C539/3*

WHOEVER (?) (cf mn id)

[Bn in this sense several times in Min; cf Ar man "who."]

C539/3: let him vow penance; wbn šrk lmr'm bb'sm "and (similarly?) whoever (?) associates (divine partners) with the Lord, maliciously"

BN III

n s bn(m) passim; bnhw J550/1+; bnhmy J818/4; bnhmw J563/6+; var bny R 3990/

7+; bnyh J727/2; bnyhw N19/16+; bnyhmw J560/1+; d̲ bny R2627/2-3+; bnyhw J566/9+; bnyhmw J615/2+; var bnhw R4174b/2; var bnhy R5085/3; p bny Ry509/7+; bnyhw J589/1-2+; bnyhmw C75/1+; var bnw(n) C30/1+; var bnn J736/7+; bnhmw C77/2; var 'bny Ry513/4; f.s bt R4156/1+; bthw R3960/4+; bthmw R4057C/3; var bnt R4489; bnth J764/5; bnthw J731/5+; d̲ bty R4017; var bnty R2753D/2+; p bnt(m) Ist7630/7+; bnthmw J577/13; bnthn F76/5-6+

(1) SON; f, DAUGHTER (cf B I, BNW, BRW)
[Ar (i)bn^u, ps banūn, 'abnā' "son"; bint, p banāt "daughter."]
C37/1: Y D̲ bn Y bn S mlk SM^{c}Y "Y.D., son of Y., son of S., king of S.";
J550/1: bnhw D̲ wS wkl wldhw "his (2) sons D. and S. and all his children";
N19/16: ^{c}A wbnyhw Š mlky S "A. and his son Š., the 2 kings of S."; R3547:
W H...bn bn S "W.H., son of the son of (i.e., grandson of) S. (?)"; F76/
5-6: 'nt̲n w'xthn wbnthn "women and their sisters and daughters"; J577/13:
bnyhmw wbnthmw "their sons and daughters"

(2) MEMBER OF A CLAN; CITIZEN OF A CITY
J720/15: wlmšw bn d̲DBYN "and (let) a member of (the clan) D. go..."; Ry509/
7: SB' wbny MRB "Saba and the citizens of Mārib"; R3902b#130/1-2: L w'A
bny Y bny T̲MD "L. and A., the 2 sons of Y., members of (the clan) T̲.";
R4938/8: 'A bt bny N "A., member of the (clan) b.N."

(3) f only: FEMALE, WOMAN
Ist7630/7: 'dmm 'sdm wbntm "servants, male and female"

Note: In the exp bnt MRB (J735/8) Ryc sees a class without tribal
affiliation (because of servile or foreign origin), serving as sorceresses and the like (Rite/382); but the case may be a simple instance
of sense^2 "(female) citizens of M."

Note: The exps bnhw and bnhmw are easily confused with forms of the
preposition bn "from" with suffixes.

Note: The construct p, normally bny, is often written defectively
as bn (e.g., C5/1). The form bny (with and without suffixes) is used
for s, d and p. For a discussion of use of bny and bnw in nominative
and oblique cases, see BeDGESA/33:4 (the usage is not consistent).

BNW I
n s bnwhw Ry509/1*; cf also [b]nw[n] R4142/9
    SON (cf bn(y) id)
    [Var of bnyhw "his son," e.g. in N19/16.]
    Ry509/1: 'A wbnwhw Ḥ...mlky S "A. and his son Ḥ., the 2 kings of S."

BNW II
n s bnwt R4772/1; bnwthmw C660/2
    BUILDING, CONSTRUCTION (cf bnyt id)
    [Root is a var of more common BNY "build," q.v.]
    C660/2: ṣllw bnwthmw "they paved their construction"

BNKL--Read bn + kl "from all"; see under BN I and KLL

BNY

v pf bny C657/1+; bnyy R4714/+; bnyw R3977/3+; ipf ybny R3945/16

BUILD, CONSTRUCT

[Ar banâ id.]

R3977/3: bnyw bythmw brd' šymh[m]w "they built their house with the aid of their patron deity"; R4714: bnyy wh^{c}s'n dqnn "they built and constructed the oratory"; cf also bny wml' "built and completed" (J557); bnyy wkll, id (3902b#130/2); bnyy whḥdṯ "built and restored (or, built anew)" (J554)

n^{1} s bny R4635/2; p 'bny R3946/6

BUILDING, CONSTRUCTION

R4635/2: qwm bny qyf ^{c}TTR "he established the construction of the qyf-altar of (the god) A."; R3946/6: bny whqm 'bny Y "he built and erected the constructions of Y."

n^{2} s bnyt C608/7; p 'bnytn R4788/4

BUILDING, CONSTRUCTION (cf bny, bnwt id)

C608/7: he erected this inscription lš'm wbnyt wfym "as a dedication and perfect (?) construction"

n^{3} s? bnyy'--in obscure context R4763/1, no tr (n.pr?)

n^{4} s mbny R4392+; var mbn R4127/2; p mbnt R3889/4

BUILDING, CONSTRUCTION (cf bny(t), id)

[Ar mabnī id.]

R4392: kl mbny blq "the whole construction in blq-stone"; R4127/2: kl m^{c}s' wmbn "the whole construction and building"

BNT

n s bnt R4772/2; bnth[ib/1

KIND OF TAX, RENT (?)

[Cf Eth benat, Qat bnt "tribute, taxes," prob from Akk biltu id (cf also Sab blt "tribute").]

R4772/1-2: w'l b^{c}ly bnwt wbnth[...] mn bnt nhmt bn ^{c}lm b[... "that which is necessary for (lit., incumbent upon) the construction and its bnt-rent/tax (?)...tax on pecked masonry, according to the document (?)"

Note: In the context, it is possible that bnt is a derivative of root BNY, related to bnwt "construction" in the same passage.

For n bnt elsewhere, see under BN III.

BSL

v inf? bsl R2859/1*

OFFER A (BURNT?) SACRIFICE

[Cf Heb bāšal "cook" and Sab mbsl below.]

R2859/1: bsl ḏbḥm bn ^{c}bdm "(let him?) offer a sacrifice against (?) the slave"

n s mbsln C434/6*

ALTAR for burnt sacrifice

[Cf Heb məbašlôt Ez 46:23 "cooking-places."]

C434/6: they built ḏn mḥrmn wmbsln "this temple and altar (?)"

BSR--For tbsrn R4194, read t + b + srn (root SRR), "which is in the valley"

B^{c}D

pf b^{c}dw J631/8; inf b^{c}d C380/4

REMOVE, REPEL

[Ar b^{c}d D id.]

C380/4: f̄'l śn qšbn mḥmyn wb^{c}d 'fl ṣrb[n] "so it is not lawful to clear the embanked land nor to remove the dykes of the harvest field";

J631/8: b^{c}dw whb^{c}ln whrg "they repelled, defeated and killed"

pp b^{c}d J631/34+; b^{c}dhw J576/6+; b^{c}dhmw C407/23; var b^{c}dn R3910/4+; b^{c}dnhw Ry506/7

AFTER (+ noun)

[Ar ba^{c}da id.]

J631/34: wb^{c}d ṯnym ywmm "and after the second day..."; R3910/4: wḏyhgb'n b^{c}dn ^{c}šrt ymtm...'blm "and whoever returns a camel (to the seller) after ten days..."; C407/23: w^{c}dww b^{c}dhmw whrghmw "they launched an attack after them and killed them"

Note esp b^{c}d(n)hw in sense AFTER THAT, AFTERWARD: J576/6: ft'wlw ^{c}dy hgrn Ṣ bwfym...wb^{c}dhw f^{c}dw G "so they returned in safety to the city Ṣ.; and after that G. led an invasion..."; Ry506/7: wrhnw wb^{c}dnhw wś^{c}hmw ^{c}A "and they gave pledges; and after that A. gave them a guarantee"

cj b^{c}d ḏ- C314/17; b^{c}dn ḏ- C541/76; b^{c}dn ḏt NNAG13-4/3

AFTER (+ verb)

[Ar ba^{c}du id.]

C541/76: wb^{c}dn ḏ'ḏnw b'š^{c}bn wrdw 'qwln "and after they discharged the tribes(men), the leaders went down..."

n s b^{c}dn C539/2*

adj: FAR

[Ar ba^{c}īd id.]

C539/2: b^{c}lmn b^{c}dn wqrbm "in the world, far and near"

B^{c}W

v pf b^{c}ww J631/29, Gl177/2*

ATTACK, phps specifically LAY AN AMBUSH

[Cf Ar baǵā "leave an ambush and fall on one's prey" (RycMancie/270 n1). Cf also Ar ba^{c}ā "behave unjustly, commit a crime or a betrayal" (JSIMB/85).]

J631/29: wb^{c}ww bllyn ḥyrt 'ḤBŠN wyhrgn bn 'ḤBŠN "and they attacked the camp of the Ḥabashites by night and killed some of the Ḥabashites" h inf hb^{c}yn J708/9*

ATTACK, or INSTIGATE AN ATTACK (?)

J708/9: the god allowed him to return safely bn ḏb't hb^{c}yn "from instigating attacks (against the enemy) (?)"--syntax doubtful; n.pr?

Note: For [hb]^{c}yw J750/6 (J's reading), see under ^{c}YY h.

n s b^{c}whmw J643/19; p b^{c}wt(m) J578/10+

ATTACK, AMBUSH

J578/10: the god preserved their lords bn kl b^{c}wt wbḥḏt sb'y wb^{c}w wbḥḏ "all the ambushes and raids they undertook, prepared and engaged in"

B^{c}Y--see under B^{c}W

B^{c}L--For pps b^{c}l, b^{c}lw, b^{c}ly, see under ^{c}LW, ^{c}LY

B^{c}L I

v inf b^{c}l R3966/8+

ACQUIRE, POSSESS

[Cf Heb bā^{c}al, Akk ba'ālu "rule over"; Ar ba^{c}ala, Aram bə^{c}al "take to wife."]

R3966/8: kl ḏqnyw wb^{c}l "everything which they acquired and possessed"

h pf hb^{c}l J639/4+; hb^{c}lw J576/13+; inf hb^{c}ln J576/4+

TAKE POSSESSION OF, CONQUER

[Development from sense of B^{c}L I v "acquire" > "acquire forcibly."]

Ir13: ^{c}dw whb^{c}ln wxtršn wdhr hgrn "he invaded, conquered, plundered and burned the city"; IrApp2#1/8: whb^{c}lw 'wṯqhmw "and they took possession of their hostages"

n^1 s b^{c}lm F3/6*

POSSESSION, PROPERTY

F3/6: byt wẓrb...ḏḤ ẓrbm brgm b^{c}l()m "house and property of (the clan) ḏḤ., a legal acquisition and possession"

n^2 s b^{c}l J561b/4-5++; d b^{c}ly J643b/10+; p 'b^{c}l R3910/2+; 'b^{c}lhw J576/7+; 'b^{c}lhn C131/4; f.s b^{c}lt(m) N74/6+; d b^{c}lty C457/18+

(1) LORD, OWNER (esp of gods)

[Ar ba^{c}l "lord, husband," Heb bá^{c}al "owner, lord."]

frequent in epithets of deities, e.g. 'LMQH b^{c}l 'WM "I., lord of (the temple) A." (J558/2++); šmsyhmw b^{c}lty 'wṯnn "their sun-goddesses, the 2 ladies of the boundaries" (J664/20-1); cf esp the 'b^{c}l byt "lords of the house/family," a species of tutelary deity, e.g. C568/2-3: b^{c}l byt 'lh S "the household deity, the god S."

(2) CITIZEN

R3910/2: š^{c}bn SB' 'b^{c}l hgrn MRB "the tribe S., citizens of the city M."

(3) m only: HUSBAND

C131/4: 'nṯtm...wwśqt w[mkb]bt 'b^{c}lhn...lyh'tyn [']b^c[l]hn 'nṯtm bhgr "women and the property (?) and clients (?) of their husbands...let their husbands bring the women into the city"

(4) f only: PRIESTESS

N74/6: they invoked the goddess blty kwn bmḥrmn kl b^c^ltm wḥlmtm "without there being present in the temple any priestess or dream-seeress"

n³ s b^c^lm J722+

LAND BELONGING TO (the god) B^c^L, i.e. NATURALLY IRRIGATED LAND (only in epithet of the god 'LMQH/TWR)

[Cf Ar ba^c^l "land or plants thriving on natural water supply," ba^c^lī "unirrigated (land, plants)." Discussion HöWdM/493.]

J722: 'LMQH...wṯwr b^c^lm wḏt ḤMYM "(the gods) I. and the Bull of B^c^L's land (or, of the naturally irrigated land), and (the goddess) ḏt Ḥ."

n s mb^c^l R4176/5+

PROPERTY, specifically DOMAIN or ESTATE ATTACHED TO A TEMPLE

R4176/5: wqwlnhn...lykwnw b^c^ly mb^c^l T'LB "and as for the 2 tribal leaders, let them be in charge of the property of (the god) T."; J554: bn mb^c^l 'LMQH "part of the property of (the god) I." (end of inscr dedicating part of the temple wall)

B^c^L II

v pf b^c^lw C541/69*

EXCAVATE

[Cf Ar ^c^abala "amputate"; mi^c^wal, mi^c^bala† "pointed iron tool used to break up stone"; Eth mab^c^al, mā^c^bal "pointed iron tool" (lrv/271).]

C541/69: b^c^lw ^c^rn lhwṯrn "they excavated the bedrock to lay the foundation"

n s tb^c^l C541/102-3; tb^c^lhmw Ry446/4; p tb^c^lt C540/21 (Inf D?)

EXCAVATION

C541/102-3: bn tb^c^l ^c^rn ^c^d šqrm "from the excavation (foundation?) of the hill-fortress to the top"

B^c^M--Read b-^c^m, see under ^c^M

B^c^R

n s b^c^r(m) R3910/3+; b^c^rhmw R3945/19+

HEAD OF CATTLE; in p, HERDS, LIVESTOCK, esp CAMEL HERDS, CAMELS

[Ar ba^c^īr "camel," Heb bə^c^ir "herd."]

R3910/3: every purchase they make bn 'nsm w'b[l]m wṯwrm wb^c^rm "of man, camel, bull or head of cattle"; R3945/19: ẓll b^c^rhmw ''blm wbqrm whmrm wqnym "plundered their herds: camels, cattle, asses and sheep"; C563/3: kl ṯwr wb^c^r "all cattle and camels"

B^c^T--For n b^c^t, see under BY^c^

BǴL

n *s* bǵlm R4146/5; bǵlh[mw] id

MULE

[Ar baǵl id.]

R4146/5: hqnyw...bǵlm lbǵlh[mw] "they dedicated (the image of?) a mule for their mule"

BṢL

n *p* bṣln J720/9-10*

ONIONS

[Ar baṣal *coll* id.]

J720/9-10: wystṣyn bn ḏfr'n wbn bṣln "and he stank of strong-smelling vegetables and onions"

Note: bṣlyn in J618/11 may be related to this root; tr "vegetable garden" or the like (J takes as *n.pr*): hfsḥ bṣlyn "he enlarged the vegetable garden (?)"

BḌ^c

v *pf* bḍ^c C563/1+; bḍ^{c}w Ir13/9+

(1) ENACT LEGISLATION concerning tribute, IMPOSE TRIBUTE

[Cf phps Bāḍi^c, ancient name of the island and custom house Maṣṣawa^c (CoRoC/117); Eth baṣ^{c}a, baḍ^{c}a "assess, estimate the price of s.th."]

C563/1: bḍ^c whḥr "he enacted and decreed"; R3945/16: bḍ^c bẓhr N ś1'm "he imposed a tribute upon N."

(2) SLAY (AND STRIP) an enemy in battle

[Ar baḍa^{c}a "cut, slash; take away part of s.th." (RycMus87/255). Another proposed tr from the same etymology is "kill in hand-to-hand combat."

Ir13/9: bḍ^{c}w (85) 'sdm ǵyr ḏnflw xlf bytn "they slew eighty-five men besides those who made the attack (or, fell) outside the fortress"

h *pf* hbḍ^c R3945/13*

ATTACK

R3945/13: hbḍ^c ḏ'mnt K "attacked those who are under the protection of K."

n^1 *p* bḍ^{c}m C407/25+; *var* bḍw^{c}m J631/31

adj: (KILLED AND) STRIPPED on the battlefield

C407/25: the god allowed him hrg ṯlṯ 'sdm bḍ^{c}m wṯny 'xḏn "to kill three soldiers, stripped (of weapons and valuables), and (take) two prisoners"

AND ELSEWHERE SIM

n^2 *s* bḍ^c(m) J555/3+; bḍ^{c}hw R4176/2; *p* 'bḍ^c(m) R3946/1+

TERRITORY, COUNTRYSIDE surrounding a town or temple and administratively dependent on it

[Cf Ar baḍa^{c}a "cut," and cf qaṭī^{c}a^t "fief" from qaṭa^{c}a "cut,"]

R3946/1: 'lt 'hgrm w'bḍ^{c}m gn'...K "these are the towns and territories (which) K. walled"; J555/3: bbḍ^{c} š^{c}bnhn M wY "in the territory of the 2 tribes M. and Y."; R4176/2 : ḥẓr T'LB qsdm bn ḍbḥ bbḍ^{c}hw "(the god) T. has prohibited qsd-citizens from collecting taxes in His territory"

BQY

v ipf ybqyn R4351/3*

a) POUR FORTH, DEBOUCH; or, b) CONTINUE SUPPLYING; or error for SQY q.v.?
[a) Cf Daṯ *bqq: baqqaitu al-mâ' min tummi "I sent out the water from my mouth, spat," also in Q. b) Ar bqy D "preserve" (Irv/58-9).]
R4351/3: the canal which irrigates these valleys, dybqyn 'wṯr ^{c}A "which debouches (on) the plains of A. (or, continues supplying them with irrigation water)"

BQL

D pf bql C378/4+; bqlw R4636/6; inf bqln C11/3+

PLANT

[Ar baqala "sprout (a plant)"; ModYem baggal "plant seedlings at a distance from each other for better development" (RoVoc/301).]
R4636/6: bqlw tbqlt 'rḍhmw "they planted the plantations of their territory"

n^{1} s bql(n) R3958/4+; p bqlt C308/6

VEGETABLES, PLANTS

[Ar baql "herbaceous plants; specifically, legumes"; ModYem bagl id (RoVoc/301).]
R3958/4: wbql kl bql w'^{c}lb w'bwn kwn wsṭhw "and he planted all the vegetables, ^{c}ilb-trees and bān-trees (which) were in it"; F123/9-10: kl tb(q)lt yt'nn bqln wrd 'l "all the cultivated land for which the watering place l. guarantees (water) for the plants"

Note: For '[b]qlm F102/11-2 read prob '[f]qlm "harvests" (RyET/63 tr "vegetables").

n^{2} s t(b)qlhmw R4995/1; p tbqlt(m) R4085/2+; tbqlthmw J650/14b+ (D inf?)

PLANTATION, CULTIVATED LAND

R4085/2: kl ṣyḥ wtbqlt '^{c}md w'^{c}lb "all leveled and cultivated lands, naturally and artificially irrigated"; and cf R4636/6, quoted under BQL D, and F123/9-10, quoted under BQL n^{1}

BQR I

n p/coll bqrm R3945/19+; bqrhmw R4040/4

CATTLE

[Ar baqar coll id.]
R3945/19: wẓll b^{c}rhmw ''blm wbqrm wḥmrm wqnym "and took as booty their livestock: camels, cattle, asses and sheep" AND ELSEWHERE in lists of booty

BQR II

v <u>pf</u> bqr C658/3*

BORE, EXCAVATE in rock

[Ar baqara "open, split," MSA baqara "break up (the surface of the earth)." Lane gives baqqara al-qawm mā ḥawlahum "the people dug the tract around them, and made wells" (Irv/115-6).]

C658/3: bqr whnbṭ wbr' whšqr "he excavated, dug, built and completed"

BR' I

v <u>pf</u> br' R4107/2+; br'w R4775/1+; <u>inf</u> br' R4194/2+; <u>masdar</u> br'm C541/58

(1) CREATE (said of a god)

[Ar bara'a id. Prob loanword from Heb bārā' id in this usage.]

MüBilinguis/2: mr'hw <u>d</u>br' nfshw "his Lord who created his soul"; sim ib/3

(2) CONSTRUCT, BUILD, phps specifically in stone

[For the original sense of the root, cf Punic br' "engraver (?)."]

R4194/2: grbw ws̀w^{c} wḥrr wb'r wbr' "they revetted, leveled, built up embankments, dug a well and constructed..."; R4994/2: qnyw wbr' bythmw "they acquired and built their house"; C541/58-9: msrm wgrbtm wbr'm "packing in earth (to repair the dam) and building up with grb- and mbr'-masonry"

n <u>s</u> mbr'(m,n) C540/11+; mbr'hw R4069/7

MASONRY, STONEWORK (in general, and as contrasted with grb "rough masonry")

C540/11: they repaired the sluices mbr'm grbm wlbtm "(with) stonework: rough and close-laid masonry"; C540/63: mw<u>t</u>rhw mbr'n wgrbn "its foundation (of) masonry and rough stonework"

BR' II

n <u>s</u> br'm R3910/6*

<u>adj</u>: EXEMPT, NOT LIABLE/RESPONSIBLE

[Ar barī' "free, exempt." Cf also Sab bry (BRY I n^{2}) "healthy."]

R3910/6: if a purchased animal dies within a certain period, fbr'm mhš'mn bn mwthw "the seller is not liable for its death"

Note: BeStI/90 connects lbrwhw in J2856/4 with BR' II (q.v.) and tr "for his freedom from responsibility," in a context of sales and contracts.

BRG I

v <u>inf</u> brg(n) F3/1+

ACQUIRE

[RhWZ37/156n1 tr "acquire on good terms." Cf ModYem brig/yibrag "pay, pay back a debt" (RoVoc/301).]

F3/1: qnyn wbrgn wb^{c}ln wẓrbn "possess, acquire, own and have a right to (= own legitimately)"

n s brgm F3/6*

ACQUISITION, PROPERTY

F3/6: byt wẓrb...ḏḤ ẓrbm brgm b^{c}lm "house and property of (the clan) ḏḤ., a legal acquisition and possession"

Note: Cf also phps R4194/2: ḏbrgm bbythmy (R takes as n.pr). Irv/159-60 suggests tr "owning their house by purchase."

BRG II

n p brw[g]hmw Gl537/7*

OPEN LANDS (?)

[Cf Ar barija "be apparent, conspicuous, ample." Discussion RhSLG2/27, 111, and n5, where he tr after root BRG I "land bought on good terms."]

Gl537/7: ls^{c}dhmw bbrw[g]hmw wḥṣwrhmw ṯmr sqym "may (the god) grant them, in their open and enclosed lands, sqy-crops"

BRD I

n s brdm C74/20+

COLD, or HAIL (as injurious to crops)

[Ar bard "coldness," barad "hail."]

C74/20: as for the god, fṣry hmt 'srrn...bn brdm wbnkl ql(m)tm "may He protect these valleys from cold/hail and any noxious insect" AND ELSEWHERE in sim contexts, with qlm(t)

Note: In another sense and in very doubtful context, R2860=C603a/7. Combining the emendations of C and R, we might read wl yh^{c}/ḏb mś(w)dn w(k)[l]/ brd w[... "and repair the fire-altar and ev[ery]...? and...?

BRD II

n d? brdnn C541/48*

COURIER

[Ar barada "send a messenger," Iranian barīd "courier."]

C541/48: this communication reached them, (and) hqdmw brdnn brṯ ydnn ^{c}rbn "they sent forward 2 couriers (to) the place the Arabs were approaching"

BRW I

h inf hbrwn J631/4*

CUT OFF > SLAUGHTER

[Cf Ar barâ "cut, cut off."]

J631/4: the god helped His servant bhrg whbrwn wṯbr "in killing, slaughtering, and crushing (the enemy)"

st pf stbrw J649/16-7+

CONTEND WITH, ATTACK (?) (^{c}l, ^{c}ly against)

[Cf Ar bry L "vie, compete, contend for superiority with s.o.," Lt id, reciprocally (Lane/197BC); or cf Ar barā "do evil" (DozyI/80).]
J649/16-7: sb'...wstbrw bmsgthw ᶜly šᶜbn Ḥ "he campaigned and contended with his bodyguard (?) against the tribe Ḥ."; cf also Ry507/7: wkd' whbt rhnn wst[b]rw ᶜlhmw mgrmtm "and when the hostages had already been given, he contended/attacked against them criminally (?)"--reading of RodConf'65-6/135; but cf other conjectures under WQR st, GWR st

BRW II

n s brw(m) Ir16/2+; brwhw J576/2+; brwhmw N20/8; d brwyhw J716/7-8; p 'brw J591/9

CHILD; SON (cf bn(y) id under BN III; and bnw id)

[Cf Mh beréu "born," birwôt "she gave birth" (Mü/Taᶜizz/98), and Aram bar "son" (prob ultimately connected with root BN III); phps also Akk būru "calf" (often figurative: "offspring").
J2114/6: brwm ḏkrm "a male child"; J576/2: brwhw wbny mr's...K "his son and the sons of the chiefs of K."; Ir16/2: brw lbnyhw "one of his grandsons"

BRḤ

ti For btrḥ R4906/2+, see under TRḤ

n s brḥm R3945/2*

as adv: a) UNCONTROLLED; or, b) FOR PUBLIC USE

[a) Cf Heb bāraḥ "go/pass through (of a bolt)," Ar bariḥa "escape."
b) Cf Ar bariḥa "(the case) became manifest," bi-l-burīḥ "publicly," burīḥ "proclamation, public announcement" (Irv/73-4).]
R3945/2: he dammed up his canal bn kḏ tḏ'n brḥm ḏhbnhn "so that it might not flow out uncontrolled (or, for public use) (over) the 2 fields"

BRY I

D? inf bryn C315/20*

MAKE HEALTHY

[Ar bari'a "be healthy," Sab bry "health."]
C315/20: wz' T'LB bryn ''ḏnhmw wmqymthmw "may (the god) T. continue to make healthy their mental and physical faculties"--cf the common formula bry ''ḏnm w mqymtm under BRY n[I]

Note: For ybryn NNAG6/23-4, J read more plausibly yxryn (J627/23-4), root XRY.

h pf hbryw J616/20-1*

TAKE BOOTY, "LIBERATE" BOOTY from the enemy (?) (but see Note)

[Cf Ar br' D and h "make free, exempt."]
J616/20-1: nzᶜw gyšhmw whbryw ᶜwfhmw "their troops went on a raid and 'liberated' their booty"

Note: Alternatively, hbry might be regarded as a var of hbrw (BRW I h); the tr then would be "they went on a raid and slaughtered their prey."

st inf stbryn C352/8*

KEEP s.o. IN HEALTH (said of a god) (?)

[Cf Ar br' st "restore to health." MüW/29 tr "obtain help," after Tña tabāraya "help one another."]

C352/8: may the god grant stwfyn wstbryn b'hnmw ḏqdmhmw wblthmw 'mr'hmw "that He successfully keep (him) in health wherever their lords lead them or send them"

n^1 s bry J643b/9+; var brytm J635/8+

HEALTH/STRENGTH

[Ar bari'a "recover from an illness; be free, blameless," barī "healthy."]

J643b/9: ys^c dnhw 'LMQHW...bry ''ḏnm wmqymtm "may (the god) I. grant him health/strength of mental and physical faculties" AND OFTEN SIM; J635/8: t'wln bwfym wbrytm "to return (from campaign) with health and strength"

n^2 s bryn J745/10*

adj: HEALTHY

[J took as n.pr; BeRev/353A conjectures adj tr after Ar barī'.]

J745/10: the horses were ridden bn srn bryn...^c dy xbtn "out of the healthy valley to unhealthy pasturage"

BRY II

n s F16+

(CARVED) CULT-STONE (only in exp bry ŠMS)

[J.Aram br' "cut"; Ar bara "make an arrow, cut a feather" (MüW/29).]

F16 (in full): bry ŠMS "cult-stone of/for (the goddess) ŠMS" AND ELSEWHERE SIM

Note: Taking bry as a v, the tr would be "it was carved (for) (the goddess) Š." For a description of a bry, see RyET/15-6 (comments on F16).

BRK I

v pf [b]rk C543/1; ipf ybrkn J1028/1

BLESS

[Ar brk D, L id.]

J1028/1: lybrkn 'LN ḏlhw smyn w'rḍn mlkn Y. "may (the god) I., who owns heaven and earth, bless the king Y."; C543/1: [b]rk wtbrk sm RḤMNN "may the name of (the god) R. be blessed and praised"

h For mh(b)rk F119/8, read mhrk; see under HRK

tp pf tbrk C543/1*

BE PRAISED, or BLESSED

[Ar brk Lt in both senses.]
C543/1 quoted under BRK I v

BRK II

n s brkt(n) C338/12+; p? brkn C302/2
CISTERN
[Ar birka† id.]
C338/12: ʿsn wḍrk brktn dt ʿrn "he dug out and faced with stone/strengthened the cistern of the hill-town"; C380/3: lbt[h]mw wlbrkthmw "for their house and cistern"

BRM--For n brm, see under BRR II, III, IV; for btrm C581/8, see under BTRM

BRḌ

n p 'brḍ R4767/2*
SMALL QUANTITIES (?)
[Ar barḍ id.]
R4767/2: ...sḥ w'brḍ ydbhnn "...and small quantities (?) (which) he sacrificed..."

BRQ

D? pf brq J735/6*
SEND LIGHTNING (of a god; i.e., inaugurate the stormy season)
[Ar baraqa "shine (the sky, with lightning)."]
J735/6: hxb sqy wdnm...bqdmy dt brq "irrigation water and rain had failed before (the god) sent lightning"

n s brq(m,n) J610/9+; d brqn J618/7; p 'brq(m) J610/14+
LIGHTNING STORM > STORMY SEASON (period of rain essential for agriculture)
[Ar barq "flash of lightning"; f in Sab (cf J610/9, below).]
Ir19: 'brq w'dnm "storms and rains"; J610/9: may the god protect them bn kl qlmtm bhyt **brqn**"from any insect pest in this stormy season"; ib/14: the responses they ask of the god l'brq dt' wxrf "regarding the stormy seasons of spring and autumn"; J628/12: may the god fill their control-dam bkl 'brq dt' wxrf "in all the stormy seasons of spring and autumn"

BRR I

v ipf ybrrn J613/28,31*
RUSH OUT, MAKE A SORTIE
[Cf Eth barara "pierce, penetrate." Discussion RycMus87/248 and n5.]
J631/28: wltltm ywmm ybrrn dbn D...wbʿww bllyn ḥyrt 'ḤBŠN "and on the third day some of (the tribe) D. made a sortie and a night attack on the camp of the Ḥabashites"

h pf hbrr J576/16+; hbrrw J575/3+; ipf yhbrr R4787/2; yhbrrw J576/8+
RUSH OUT, MAKE A SORTIE (= BRR I v); pass BE DISLODGED, DRIVEN OUT
J575/3: hbrrw lḍb' bn hgrn "they rushed out to fight from the city"; J644/8: hbrrw wtḏlln L wš^{c}bhmw bn bytn "L. and their tribe were driven out ignominiously from the fortress"

n^1 p brrm C540/12*
CLAMPS (?)
[Irv/263 suggests this tr as clamps "penetrate" the stones they bind together; or, alternatively, the stone might be "pierced" to receive them.]
C540/12: they repaired the sluices mbr'm grbm wlbtm w'zyyn frznm wbrrm mhbḏlm blbt 'zyyn "(with) rough and close-laid stonework, iron quoins, and clamps inserted into the close-laid stonework of the quoins"

n^2 s? mtbrm (?) R2861/[2] in obscure and fragmentary context; no tr

BRR II

h pf hbrrw C581/10; inf hbrrn Gl364/6
(1) MAKE UPRIGHT (?)
[Cf Ar barr "pious, upright."]
Gl364/6: fl yhmt^{c}n whbrrn whṣḥḥn whṣdqn whwfyn l'dmhw "may (the god) save, make upright, make sound, make honest, and grant to His servants...(?)"
(2) PAY a debt
C581/10: fhbrrw lgtzḥn b^{c}m 'sn wnfq bnhw "they paid in order to settle accounts with the man, being indebted to him"

n^1 s brhmw C541/97*
PLEDGE, OATH
[Ar birr "an oath of allegiance" (Irv/312-3).]
C541/97: k'syhmw 'š^{c}bn brhmw ^{c}ḏbw "when the tribes(men) had sent their pledge/oath, they repaired..." (apparently the oath of allegiance was a preliminary formality after the tribes had assembled)

n^2 s brtm Gl574/8*
RESTITUTION, REPARATION (?)
[Eth bert "equivalent."]
Gl574/8: k(n)fq bnhw ^{c}A bṣnqm bbrtm "when A. was indebted regarding him for a debt in reparation (?)"; for brt elsewhere see under BWR

BRR III

n s brm J670/26+
WHEAT
[Ar burr id.]
J670/26: 'ṯmrm sqym wbrm wš^{c}rm "crops of sqy-crops, wheat and barley"; sim C540/40
Note: For brm C73/8, see under BRR V n^1

BRR IV

n s brn J115/5; brhmw J541/8-9; var brr(m,n) F3/8+

OPEN COUNTRY

[Ar barr id, as opposed to towns and settled areas; may refer in Sab to grazing land as opposed to cultivated land.]

F3/8: bhgrm wbrrm bkl brtm "in settled country and open country; everywhere"; G1143/2: rb T'LB...kl brrn "(the god) T. owns all the open country"; J541/8-9: 'dbnn d'db brhmw "the boundary stones which divide their land"

BRR V

n^1 s? brm C73/8*

A UNIT OF WEIGHT (esp for precious metals) (?)

[Development from sense of brr below, "silver"?]

C73/8: kwn myrn tmn brm bdhbn bblṭtm rḍym "(the price of) grain was one-eighth of a br-unit (or, eight br-units) in gold, in current coin"

n^2 s brr C550/10*

SILVER (?)

[Eth berur id, prob connected with root BRR II "be pure."]

C550/10: šfthmw 'DNT dhb wbrr KTM "their offering: (for) A., gold; and silver, (for) K."

BRT--For n brt, see under BWR, BRR II

BRT

v pf brt R4624/4; brtw J651/27-8; inf brtn GaAntYemp540/2

(1) LEVEL land; RAZE an abandoned building

[Cf Ar bart "level ground."]

R 4624/4: wbrt msb' ᶜrn...bn rydhw "and he leveled the road (to) the hill fortress from its foot (upward)"; J651/27-8: brtw mḥqr bytnhn "they razed the rubble of the 2 houses"

(2) DISCHARGE a debt

[Development from sense "make level, even"?]

GaAntYemp540/2: fdyw wqṣṣ wbrtn kl ml' "they acquitted themselves of, repaid, and discharged the whole sum"

n s brt(n) J635/38-9+; brthw J562/21; p brthmw R4986/3; p 'brt J559/9+

(1) PLACE, FIELD

J562/21: they placed their offering under the god's protection bn hnkrnhw bn brthw "against (anyone's) moving it from its place"; C323/3: 'brt bhmw gz w'tw h' tyln "the places/fields through which that flood passed and came"

(2) BATTLEFIELD CAMPAIGN, UNDERTAKING

[Development from basic sense "field."]

R4842/2: 'tw bwfym bn kl 'brt bhw sb' "he came back in safety from all the battlefields/campaigns he had participated in"; J635/38-9: yt'wl kl gyšhmw bwfym bn hwt brṯn "all their troops returned in safety from that battlefield /campaign"; J559/9: kl 'brṯ bhmw hwṣl lbytn S b'ḍrrm wbslmm "all the undertakings in which he joined with the house S., in wars and in peace"

Note: In J516/8, J tr the exp ḏn brṯn as "this proclamation" (sense attested in Qat but not elsewhere in Sab); the fragmentary context does not support this tr.

(3) as cj, WHERE > IN ORDER THAT

[Cf uses of Ar hayṯu (BeNL10/408-9).]

Ir28/1: the god brought him back in safety bn bḥrm brṯ ḥškhw mr'hmw "from overseas, where their lord had despatched him"; C541/48: hqdmw brdnn brṯ ydnn ᶜrbn "(the king) sent 2 couriers, in order that the Arabs should obey" (for other trs of this passage, see under DNY)

BŠM

n p? bšym R3232/4*

DISGUSTING THINGS (?)

[Cf Ar bašama "be disgusted, nauseated."]

R3232/4: bn hb's wbšym "from (things that are) harmful or disgusting" (context fragmentary)

BŠR I

tp pf tbšr J643/16+; tbšrhw J627/4+; tbšrhmw J647/17-8; tbšrw J618/6+; inf tbšrn J614/8-9+

(1) "ANNOUNCE" = GIVE AN ORACULAR RESPONSE (said of a god)

[Ar bšr D "announce (good news)."]

J735/17: xmr...h(y)t brqn ḥgn tbšr 'dmhw "(the god) granted that lightning storm as He had announced (to) His servants"; J647/17-8: lxmrhmw 'wldm... ḥgn [t]bšrhmw bms'lhw "to grant them children as He had announced to them in His oracle"

(2) SEEK/ASK FOR such an oracle response (bᶜm from the god)

[Phps sense² is the passive, sense¹ the active voice of this verb.]

J614/9: the god granted him kl 'ml' wtbšr stml' wtbšrn bᶜmhw "all the ml'- and tbšr-responses he sought and asked for from Him" AND OFTEN SIM

n s tbšrt(m,n) J627/4+; p tbšr J614/8-9+

"ANNOUNCEMENT" = A KIND OF ORACULAR RESPONSE

[Cf Ar tabšīr "announcement (of good news)."]

J647/10: xmrhw tb[š]rtm bms'lhw "(the god) granted him an 'announcement' response in His oracle"; and cf J614/8-9, quoted under BŠR I tp

BŠR II

n s bšr(n) C563/3+

(1) FLESH

[Heb bāśār id; cf Ar bašara† "skin."]

C563/3: an offering of bšr twrm dybḥr "the flesh of a chosen bull"

(2) FLESH-OFFERING

C539/3: šym ᶜl[y]n wbšrn "he arranged for a burnt-offering and a flesh-offering"

BT--For n bt, see under BYT, BN III

BTRM--In doubtful context C581/8. Passage reads: 'sm dmẓ' wwgr bythmw bly sdtm śqt btrm[n? or ᶜ?] C tr: "a man who came and built their house in six nights. It fell (śqt?) in an earthquake [b-trm[ᶜ], allegedly Ar meaning 'agitatus est,' but not in Lane or Dozy]." GressAOT/468 tr "a man who had come and caused (wgr?) much (śqt) disturbance [presumably btrm[], but Gressmann reads btrm[n] and gives no etymology] on the sixth night." Root and tr very doubtful.

BT--For yhbtn R4782, see under BWT h

BTT

v pf (b)ttthw J584/10-1*

COMMUNICATE, MAKE KNOWN phps PROMISE

[Cf Ar batta "spread out, lay out; divulge (a secret), communicate (an idea)" JSIMB/91).]

J584/10-11: hqnythw wqhhw bd (b)ttthw "she dedicated it (to the god) as He commanded, in accordance with that which she promised him"

Note: yhbt in R4782/1, quoted under BWT h, may derive from a sense as in Ar batta, abatta "spread out, lay out": yhbt l'lhn "let him lay out (portions of the sacrifice) for the god" (cf BeNL10/411).

⅂-G

G'M

v inf g'mn J658/13*

sense doubtful: BRING TOGETHER, ASSEMBLE (?)

[Read phps l'm and cf Ar l'm L "reconcile, bring together," ti "become coalesced, consolidated; agree together."]

J658/13: he ordered him to organize a squadron wlg'mn ^{c}šr X b^{c}d ḥrb and to ...? the clans of X after the battle"

GB' I

v pf gb' J643/16+; gb'w J576/10+; ipf ygb'w ib/8; inf gb' Ist1726/2

(1) RETURN, COME BACK

[Eth gab'a "return."]

C541/80: gb' mlkn ^{c}dy hgrn "the king returned to the city"; R2633/8: gb'w bn 'rḍ Ḥ "they returned from the land of Ḥ."

(2) LEASE (?)

[Cf GB' I h sense[4] and n gb'n (BeFSTI/273).]

Ist7626/2: w'l ḏbhw yṯbnn wgb' "and let no one settle in [a certain territory] or lease (?)..."

D? pf gb'hw R3908/5*

CAUSE TO RETURN, BRING BACK

R3908/5: he dedicated to the god bḏt hwfyhw bḏt gb'hw "because He protected him, because He brought him back (from a campaign?)"

ti pf tgb'w J643/13-4*

RETURN, COME BACK (= GB' I v)

J643/13-4: the king of Ḥ. went up wtgb'w N...lmlk Ḥ "and N. [and his soldiers] returned to the king of Ḥ."

h pf hgb' J651/34; hgb'y C376/10; hgb'w J576/2+; hgb'hw C67/13+; ipf yhgb'n R3910/4; inf hgb'n J649/34+

(1) RETURN, GIVE BACK, RESTORE

R3910/4: wḏyhgb'n b^{c}dn ^{c}šrt ymtm "and whoever returns [an animal to its seller] after ten days..."; Gl574/10: xmrhw 'LMQ<H> hgb'n l'A ṣdq "(the god) I. agreed to restore (his) right to A."

(2) REPEL, DRIVE BACK

J649/34: hsḥthmw whgb'n whrg "he destroyed and drove back and killed them"

(3) RESTORE a building; phps more specifically RENDER, i.e. COVER A SURFACE (with plaster, etc.)

[Discussion BeNL10/422.]

R4775/2: hwṯrn whṯbn whgb'n...m'xḏhmw "laid the foundations of, rebuilt and restored / surfaced their control dyke"

(4) LEASE OUT

[Cf Eth gabā'i "mercenary, workman hired for pay."]

C376/10: hgb'y l'LMQH hyt 'rḍn "they leased out that field in behalf of (the god) l." (or tr as sense I, "gave back to l.")

(5) COMMAND

[Cf Amh gabā id (RyET/73), but esp syn hṯb, root sense "return."]

F121: hgb' whṯbn...'dmhw "he commanded and decreed (for) his servants"

st inf stgb'n Ir13/6*

REPEL, DRIVE BACK (= GB' I h)

Ir13/6: stgb'n wtḍʿn "drove back and laid low (the enemy)"

n s? gb'n(m,n) C613/4+

REFUND, REMISSION of taxes or payment due

C613/4: 'ṯwbt wgb'n "repayment and refund"; R2695/6: xmrnm wnḥltm wḏgb'nm "a grant, a gift, and a remission (of taxes)"

GB' II

v pf gb' J656/17-8*

IMPOSE tithes

[Ar jabâ "levy a tax" (BeRev/352).]

J656/17-8: kl ʿšr gb' bʿlyhmw "all the tithes which he imposed on them"

GBḎ

v pf gbḏ R3943/3+; gbḏw C308/23; ipf ygbḏ[w] J577/14

PLUNDER, LAY WASTE cultivated land (cf GBZ v)

[C cfs Eth gabaz "plunder." The word seems not to occur in Geʿez, but is phps Tña.]

R3943/3: gbḏ ḏhby Y "he laid waste the 2 alluvial fields of Y"; J577/14: wygbḏ[w...s]ṯy ''lfm 'ʿmdn "they plundered/laid waste sixty thousand vine-props (a measure of conquered territory)'

GBZ

v pf gbzw J629/28*

PLUNDER, LAY WASTE cultivated land (= GBḎ v)

J629/28: gbzw kl 'srrhmw "they laid waste all their valley-fields"

GBH

n s gbht C504b*

KIND OF HORSE

[Ar jabhat id.]

C504b (on a bronze horse): gbht ḏt B hqnyt L "the horse of (the goddess) ḏt B., offering of L."

GBL

n s gblt(n) C435/3+; gblthw R4923/4+

(HILL) COUNTRY, contrasted with byt "town"; TERRITORY, DISTRICT

[Ar jabal "mountain"; Heb gəbūl "boundary; territory (within boundaries)".]

C435/3: bbytn wgbltn "in town and country"; R4923/4: f]qḥ gblthw "he opened his territory (to irrigation)"

GD, see under GDY

GDD

h pf hgdd R2865/1; hgddw R4176/14

DECIDE, DETERMINE

[Cf Ar jadd "fate, (good) fortune."]

R2865/1: hgdd wᶜzz hrwḥt hrwḥ "he determined and established the enlargement (of boundaries) he brought about"; R4176/14: hgddw whᶜzz mḥr hḥr "he (p.maj?) determined and established the law he passed"

n p gddm Gl537/6

(THE) GREAT, GREAT ONES

[Ar jidd "majesty, exaltedness."]

Gl537/6: gddm wqṭnm "the great and the small"; and often as epithet of the tribe XWLN gddm "X. the great," e.g. J577/8; in this usage also gddn and gddtn.

GDY

h pf hgd C37/7*

ALLOT, CONCEDE

[Heb gdd/gdy "cut off" > "allot"; Ar jadâ "give," Eth gādā "gift, tribute."]

C37/7: gdyt hgd lhw "the concession he made to him"

n s gdyt C37/7+

ALLOTMENT, CONCESSION (kind of tax? MüW/38)

C37/7 quoted under GDY h; ib/8: gdyt wmṯbt "concession and compensation"; C609/4: š'mt wgdyt "purchase and concession"

Note: Cf also n gdym or ldym N17/3 (fragmentary context). In R3439/2 read phps nḥlt wgdy(t) "gift and concession"--R read rdy(t).

GDM, v--in R2859/3 read ᶜBDM n.pr for (w)gdm (TsSEGI1/27).

G<u>DD</u>

n s g<u>dd</u>tm C540/87* (restored in ib/39)

KIND OF GRAIN (SPELT?)

[Daṯ jidû "stubble (which remains after the harvest," Ar jazaz "harvest." CoRoC/122 cfs Amh.Te gažā "andropogon Gayamus," gaža, gāšā "oats," and tr "spelt."]

C540/87: [ś]ᶜrm wgddtm w[t]mrm "barley and spelt (?) and dates"

GDW I
n s̲ gdwyn R4483*
   (THE) SURVIVING, SURVIVER (last living member of tribe)
   [Ar jd̲wy id.]
   R4483: md̲bḥt 'I...gd̲wyn "altar of I., the surviver"

GDW II
n d̲ gdwty R3946/5*
   (a) STONE; or (b) HILL
   [(a) Ar majdâ, Heb gāzît "hewn stone." (b) Ar ja/utwa† id.]
   R3946/5: In gd̲wty Ḥ ᶜd hgrn "from the 2 stones/hills of H. to the city"

GDM
v inf gd̲m[n] G1574/14*
   PRESERVE, RESCUE
   [Ar jad̲ama "cut off" > "set apart" > "preserve" (sim Eth gazama).]
   G1574/14: kh' hsṭw gd̲m[n] bnhw "that (the god) has consented to preserve his son"

GDF
v pf gd̲f C546/6*
   BE STUBBORN, INTRACTABLE
   [Eth gazafa id.]
   C546/6: wd̲gd̲f mnhm lyḥd̲rn wlynd̲rn "and whoever among (those criminals) is intractable, let him beware and vow penance"

GHM
v pf ghmw J665/28*
   DO during the night; SET OUT during the night
   [Ar jahma† "darkest part of the night," Dat̲ jaham "do early in the morning, set out in the morning, attack in the morning."]
   J665/28: fghmw bllyn "and they set out during the night"
      Note: So RycBiOr25/7. J read lhmw.
n d̲ ghmy NNAG12/11*
   prob DARK PART OF THE NIGHT, NIGHT-WATCH
   NNAG12/11: ḥrb bhw ᶜdy ghmy ywm 'rbᶜm "he performed the (ritual) combat there until the 2 dark watches of the fourth day" (discussion RycMancie/269)
cj ghm d̲- Ry510/4*
   AT THE TIME WHEN; WHEN
   Ry510/4: ᶜly mhnsb'tm...ghm d̲ndynhmw ᶜrbn "in the course of the campaign, when the Arabs harrassed them"
      Note: Ry read lhm.

GW, see under GWY, NGW

GWB

n s̲ gwbn C373/3; p̲ 'gwbt R3619/1
   (1) KIND OF STONEWORK
   [Ar jāba (w) "break stone"; ModYem giwāb "basin excavated in rock," tigwab "wall surrounding a terrace" (RoVoc/302).]
   (2) STONEMASONS (? or n̲.pr)
   R3619/1: lḥwt 'gwbt B "for the life of the stonemasons (?) of B."

GWD

n s̲ gwdm J665/44*
   SWIFT RIDING ANIMAL (esp horse?)
   [Ar jawād "runner"; Eth gayd "swift, racehorse"; Te gēda "hurry."]
   J665/44: he took from the enemy kl gwdm frsm wnqt "every swift riding animal, horse or she-camel"

GWZ

v p̲f̲ gz C373/3; gwzt J525/1; i̲p̲f̲ ygzn J711/1+
   PASS, GO; PASS THROUGH
   [Heb gwz "pass by," Ar jāza (w) "pass through, cross."]
   J711/1: may the god grant him prosperity 'hnmw ygzn "wherever he may go";
   C323/3: all the places bhmw gz w'tw h' ṯyln "through which that flood passed and came"; R3910/6: wygzn sb^{c}m ywmm "and seven days have passed";
   J525/1: gwzt mḥrmhw ġyr ṯhrm "she passed through (the god's) temple (in a state of) impurity"

n^1 s̲ gwz F55/8*
   TERM, DATE OF PAYMENT
   [Cf use of GWZ v̲ in R3910/6 quoted above.]
   F55/8: hmhr...bnhmw gwz "he has fixed the term of payment for them"

n^2 s̲ mgzt J635/37*
   CROSSING, FORD
   J635/37: bknf 'rḍ 'l mgzt mwnhn d̲T̲ "at the border of the land of I., at the ford of the 2 watercourses of T." (J took as n̲.pr)

GWY

v ygwnhmw J567/8--see under NGW
n s̲ gw R4638/2; gwy C570/9; gwm C366/3+; gw[h]mw C131/6
   ASSOCIATION of tribes, COMMUNITY bound together on a religious basis
   [Phoen gw "community"; Heb gôy "troop, crowd; people," gēw "midst."]
   R3945/1+: gwm d'lm wšymm "a community (owing allegiance to) a god or patron deity"; ib/6: wld 'LMQH wgwm "the children of (the god) I. (= the Sabaeans) and the association of tribes"; C570/9: SB' gwy qhlm "Saba in full assembly"; C131/6: mḥmyt gw[h]mw "irrigated lands of their community";

Gl772/5+: sqy ^{c}<u>T</u>TR SB' wgwm "(the god) A. provided irrigation for S. and the community"

GWL

n^{1} <u>s</u> gl Ist7626/7*

ENTIRETY

[Ar jāla (w) "go around, enclose."]

Ist7626/7: bgl m'x<u>d</u>t 'dynhmw "by the entirety of the contents of their obligations"

n^{2} <u>s</u> gwlm R3945/12+

as adv: AS ONE'S OWN PROPERTY, AS PRIVATE PROPERTY

[Ar jawl "coherent, enclosed property"; Eth g^{w}elt "estate or other object transferred for use and enjoyment; feudal benefice." Alternatively, RycERI/273 cfs Heb g'l "redeem, free from obligation," tr Sab gwl as "property so redeemed and held." Some authors tr "entirely," cf GWL n^{1}.]

R3945/12: he acquired the yeomen of K. w'wldhmw wqnyhmw gwl[m] l'LMQH wlSB' "and their children and possessions as property for I. and for S."; ib/8: '^{c}rrhmw w'srrhmw wmr^{c}yhmw gwlm "its towns, valleys and pastures as property" (reference is to state property acquired by conquest) R4231/3: ^{c}sy wbny xdrhw...gwlm "he constructed and built his tomb as his own property"; R3902b#130/4: 'l 's s'lhmy bḥrthmy...gwlm "let no one challenge their possession of their aqueduct as (their) own property" (reference is to private property in which the owner has invested labor)

GW'

n <u>adj</u>: <u>p</u> gw^{c}m J631/35*

HUNGRY

[Ar jā^{c}a (w) "be hungry."]

J631/35: after the second day t'wlw 'ḤBŠN...gw^{c}m "the Ḥabashite (troops) withdrew, hungry"

GWR

v <u>pf</u> gr C548/1; grhmw Ry507/10

(1) DWELL in a place for a certain length of time > SOJOURN/BECOME A PROTEGÉ, or VISIT

[Phoen.Heb gwr "dwell as a protege/resident alien" (cf Ug gr "foreigner"), Ar jāra (w) "turn aside, tarry," <u>L</u> "be the neighbor of."]

C548/1: mngr ḥm[y]m "whoever visits/becomes a protegé of the sanctuary"

(2) ASSIST

[Cf esp Ar jwr <u>h</u> "stand by s.o., aid s.o."]

Ry507/10: wgrhmw 'Z'N qrnm b^{c}m mlkn "and certain Yaz'anite tribesmen assisted them in battle along with the king"

Note: MüW/39 and others read Ry507 as n (p/coll?): 'xwthw wgrhmw "his allies and their clients"

n s gwrhw J2856/3*

PARTNER, CO-OWNER

[Ar jār id (BeStI/90).]

J2856/3: no objection having been raised ḥbln lmš'mhw gwrhw "to the contract effected on the part of the vendor, by a partner (of the vendor)"

GZ, see under GWZ, GZZ, NGZ

GZZ

v ipf y(g)zzn R4767/4* (R emends from ylzzn)

CUT, HARVEST (?) (cf GDD n "kind of grain")

[Ar.Eth.PBH gzz "cut off, shear," ModḤaḍ gzz "cut (corn, mustache)."]

R4767/4: ...]y(g)zzn ḏhwfrhw[... "he will harvest what it has produced (i.e. its crops)"

h hgzz R2865/1--read h^{c}zz, see under ^{c}ZZ h

n s gzztm R3956/4*

RAGGEDNESS, STATE OF BEING TORN

R3956/4: ^{c}ṭf ṭm'm wgzztm "a dirty, torn mantle (lit, of impurity and raggedness)"

Note: For gzzt C540/87 read gddt, see under GDD

GZḤ

ti inf gtzḥn C581/10*

sense doubtful: CONCLUDE, SETTLE ACCOUNTS (?)

[Cf phps Ar.Sab gz^c "cut off, cut down."]

C581/10: hbrrw lgtzḥn b^{c}m 'sn wnfq bnhw "they paid in order to settle accounts (?) with the man, being indebted to him"

GZY

v pf gzy J629/39; gzyw J564/9; inf gzy J629/38

PERFORM THE DUTIES OF A COMMISSION OR OFFICE

[Cf Ar jazâ "share," Daṯ gazā "pass (the time)" (RycMus87/245-6 and n4.]

J629/37-9: stwfy gzyt M...bhgrn Ṣ w'qwl wqhy mr'yhmw...lgzy bR...wstwfy gzyt M w'qwl gzy b^{c}mhw "(the god) prospered the commission of M. in the city Ṣ., and (that of) the chiefs whom their 2 lords ordered to perform a commission in R.; and He prospered the commission of M. and of the chiefs who performed their commissions with him"; J564/9: bgzyt gzyw bhgrn M "during (the performance of) the commission which they performed in the city M."; Ir12: gzy ltnṣf wqrn "he performed his commission to provide protection and guard"

n s gzyt(n) J629/37+

(1) OFFICE, COMMISSION

J629, J564 quoted under GZY v

(2) DECREE, DEFINITION

[Cf here also root GZZ "cut, define, decide" (BeFSTI/274).]

Ist7626/5: sm^{c}n wgzytn "(document of) attestation and definition"

GZM

v pf gzm R3957/6; gzmw J576/3+; inf gzmn J575/2

(1) CUT to pieces, DESTROY (an enemy in battle)

[Ar.Heb.Eth gzm "cut."]

J575/2: their lord sent them lgzmn hmt 'ḤBŠN "to destroy those Ḥabashites"

(2) SWEAR, PLEDGE ONE'S SELF; of a god, DECIDE, DECREE

[By extension from sense "cut" > "decree" > "make obligatory" > "pledge one's self to do."]

J576/3: b^{c}d slm wgzm gzmw "after the peace and the oath they swore"; C435/1: gzmw gzm ^{c}ṮTR "they swore/pledged themselves by the oath of (the god) A."; C449/3: gzmw wrṯdw[... "they pledged themselves and placed under (the god's) protection..."; R3957/1: gzm sw' ḏS ^{c}ly ršdh "(the god) dS. decided adversely against her conduct"

tp pf tgzmw C308/12*

SWEAR TO ONE ANOTHER, AGREE BY OATH

C308/12: tgzmw kwḥd ḍrhmw wslmhmw "they agreed/swore to one another that their war and peace should be in unison (or, they agreed as one, i.e. together, concerning their war and peace)"

n s gzm(n) J576/3+

OATH, OBLIGATION CONFIRMED BY OATH

J576/3: gzm gzmw "the oath they swore"; C541/10: hxlf bgzmn "he made (him) lieutenant by an oath (of fealty)"

GZ^c

v pf gz^c C292/4*

CUT DOWN, HEW wood

[Ar jaza^{c}a, Eth gaz^{c}a "cut wood."]

C292/4: h̤sm wgz^c bn kl h̤sm "he cut down and hewed some of the wood"

n[1] gz^{c}m R3945/13--reading uncertain. BeSI/69 takes as n.pr G/LZWM.

n[2] s mgz^{c}m C612/1*

WORK OF HEWN WOOD (?)

C612/1: mgz^{c}m h̤smm mbr'm "mgz^c-woodwork, h̤sm-woodwork, stonework"

n[3] p? mgz^{c}t C291/1*

KIND OF PAYMENT or TAX (?)

C291/1: ṣrf w'kry wmgz^{c}t "expenses, rents (?) and payments (?)"

GZF

v pf gzft R4469/1; pf/inf gzf R3951/5

SELL, or REQUIRE S.O. TO BUY, WHOLESALE

[Ar jzf "buying or selling a thing in the lump, without weighing or measuring"; also "wholesale purchase."]

R3951/5: 'rzm w'gzf bhmw šrkw...wh^{c}db wgzf b^{c}ly mśwd "commandeerings and wholesale purchases wherein they share out...and renew and make wholesale demands on the council"; also R4469/1 in fragmentary context

n p/coll gzfm R3951/3; p 'gzf ib/5

WHOLESALE PURCHASES

R3951/5 quoted under GZF v; ib/3: mnṣḥtm wgzfm wmnqlm "demands and wholesale purchases and transfers (of goods)"

GZR

v pf gzr DJE7*

SLAUGHTER AN OFFERING, SACRIFICE

[Ar jazara "slaughter."]

DJE7: gzr N "N. has sacrificed"

GY'--for n mg't J647/26 read ml't, see under ML'

GYB

v ipf ygbnhmw Gl441/5; inf gybhmw C86/8-9+

SAVE, PROTECT (bn from) (cf KYB v id)

[Ar jwb D "protect," jawb "shield"; Mh gob, Šx gieb "(small) shield."]

C86/8-9: wlgybhmw bn ḥry "and to protect them from injury"; Gl441/5: kygbnhmw bn xybtm "that (the god) may protect them against drought"

GYL

n s gyl R4646/19-20*

COURSE, PERIOD

[Ar jāla (w) "go around, circle"; jawlān "circuit."]

R4646/19-20: the month of dN gyl xrf M "(in) the course of the year (named for) M."

GYR

v inf gyrn Ist7630/4*

PLASTER

[Ar jayr "gypsum, lime"; J.Aram gyr D, Eth gayara "whitewash."]

Ist7630/4: yqṭ wgyrn whqšbn krfm "they dug, plastered, and prepared for use a cistern"

n^{1} s gyr(m,n) C540/25+

PLASTER, LIME

R5085/7: they prepared it bgyrm wqṣm "with plaster and gypsum"; C540/25:

mbr'n wgyrn "stonework and plaster"

n² mtgyr? R4469/2: ...ḥrmmmmtgyr, no tr

GYŠ

n s gyš(m,n) J665/41+; gšhw Ir32; gyšhmw J635/38+; p 'gyš(m) C26/4+; 'gyšhw Ry508/8; 'gyšhmw C541/25

TROOP of riders, ARMY

[Ar jayš "army," J.Aram gaysā "robber-troop"; Mh giyṓś "call (people) together." DoughtyI/478 and Rwala/506 cite jaysh/gejš as ModAr p of "camel," "camel-rider."]

J635/38: wyt'wl kl gyšhmw bwfym bn hwt brṯn "and all their army came back safely from that campaign"; J665/42: 'frsm bn gyšhmw "horsemen from their troop"; ib/49: 'l tfqd bn gyšhmw ǵyr 'sm "only one man was missing from their army"; J577/14: 'gyš wǵzwy "troops and 2 raiding parties"; C541/25: gm^c w 'gyšhmw "they assembled their troops"

GMD, v in C540/78--see under LMD v

GML

n p/coll gmlm J576/3+

CAMELS, phps specifically TRANSPORT CAMELS

[Ar jamal, p jimāl "camel."]

J576/3: rkbm wgmlm "riding camels and transport camels"; J649/40: gmlm wbqrm wḍ'nm "camels, cattle and sheep"; Ry507/9: gmlm wbqrm w^cnzm "camels, cattle and goats"

GMS?

n p? g[ms]t R2861/[1]* (reading doubtful)

UNRIPE DATES (?)

[Ar jumsa† id. Another proposed reading is l[s]s(n), cf Ar lsās "first shoots of grass."]

R2861/[1]: lyhb g[ms]t "that he devastate the unripe dates..." (context obscure)

GM^c

v pf gm^c C541/21+; gm^c w ib/25

ASSEMBLE, BRING TOGETHER

[Ar jama^c a and D id.]

C541/21: gm^c ḏhṯ^c hw bn K "he assembled those of K. who owed obedience to him"; ib/25: gm^c w 'gyšhmw "they assembled their troops"

tp pf tgm^c Ry508/4*

BE BROUGHT TOGETHER

Ry508/4: wtgm^c kl ḏhrgw wǵnmw...ṯlṯt ^c šr ''lfm mhrgtm... "and all that they slew and took as booty was brought together, (there being) thirty thousand slain, etc"

Note: For 'gm^c R4964/8, read 'LMQH with HöSEG8. For [g]m^c Ry533/12, read [q]m^c, q.v.

GN'

v pf gn' R2850A+; ipf ygn' R3945/14

WALL, ENCLOSE WITH A SIEGE WALL

[Phps related to Sem root GNN "protect."]

R2850A: gn' hgrhw "he walled his town"; R4006: ḫ]ṣr wgn' mwṭn(h)mw "he built a wall and a siege-wall around their residence"; R3945/14: wygn' gn'm "he built a siege-wall"

n s gn'(m,n) J557+; p gn't R2633/7; 'gn' J651/31

(LARGE) WALL, esp DEFENSIVE, SIEGE-WALL

J557: gn' 'WM "the wall of (the sanctuary) A."; J550/1: kl tml' gn'n "all the fill of the wall"; R2633/7: kṯwbhw gn'thw "when he restored (for) it its walls"; J651/31: 'gn' wmḥfdt hgrn "the siege-walls and towers of the city"; C40/4: gn'n bhyt nṭ^{c}tn "the wall(ing) in that fortification"; ib/3: mwrt wgn' "wall and siege-wall"

GNB

v pf/inf gnb J597/1*

BE/FIGHT ON THE SIDE OF, FOR s.o.

[Ar jānaba "stand by the side of."]

J597/1: sb]'t sb' wgnb 'A "campaigns A. undertook and fought for..."

GNW

n p 'gnw J574/6*

GARDENS (?)

[Ar janna† "garden," janā "gather fruits; harvest." Cf GNY, GNN.]

J574/6: he fought ^{c}dy 'gnw srn Ś "in the gardens (?) of the valley Ś."

GNZ I

n p gnwzhw DJE12/4*

STOREROOMS

[Loanword from Iranian "treasure, treasure room, storeroom." Sq ginz "arsenal," Bib.Aram+ ginzā "treasure house" (MüTa^{c}izz/94).]

DJE12/4: ṯny bḥrn wkl gnwzhw "two floors (of a building) and all its storerooms"

GNZ II

n p? gnztn J702/10*

CORPSES, THE DEAD; mḥrm gnztn: CEMETERY

[Ar ji/ānaza† "corpse; bier"; Eth genzat "funeral."]

J702/10: 'l ś́nyw ś́yq bwst mḥrm gnztn "they are forbidden to drive (cattle) through the cemetery"

GNY

n *s/coll* gnyn J650/6*

GARDEN CROPS, GARDEN HARVEST

[Cf GNW, GNN.]

J650/6: they dedicated a statue from the tithes bn qyẓn wgnyn "from the summer harvest and the garden crops/harvest"

GNN

ti *inf* gtnn(n) J570/8+

GATHER GARDEN CROPS; HARVEST

[Cf GNW, GNY.]

C74/13: gtnnn lhmt 'srrn "let (them) gather the garden crops of those valleys"; J570/9: bn gtnnn l'LMQH "from harvesting for (the god) I."

Note: In C74 quoted above, gtnnn may be *n* with *l-* possessive.

tp *pf* tgn J570/3*

GATHER GARDEN CROPS (= GNN ti?)

J570/3: lqbl]y ḏ'l tgn bywm ṯmny[m] "because he did not gather garden crops on the eighth day..."

h hgn Ry512/1--prob *n*, see under HGN

G^{c}R

tp *pf* tg^{c}r J511/13+

BE CALLED TOGETHER; JOIN TOGETHER

[Eth ge^{c}ra "cry out."]

J577/13: tg^{c}r kl d̲h̲ḍr^{c} "all whom he had defeated were called together"; J665/14: tg^{c}r w'ttmn kl gyšhmw "their whole army was called together and assembled"; Ir32/5: tg^{c}r b^{c}mhmw xmsy 'frsm "fifty horsemen joined together with them"

GFY, *v* in J576/9 = Ry535/4+--read LFY, q.v.

GFN

n *p* gfnt C522/4*

VINES

[Ar jafn "vine" cited in TA as from Yemenite dialect; Heb gepen id (RabAncWar/20).]

C522/4: wḏ yḍwn wynm [...] gfnt... "and whoever injures a vineyard... vines..."

GR, see under GWR

GRB I

n s grb R4842/7+; grbhw J571/4+; p grbthmy J594/7; grbthmw J654/10+; grybt(m) J567/14+; grybthmw ib/10+

BODY; (BODILY) LIFE, HEALTH; PERSON

[Te garob "body"; Ar jirāb "(sheepskin) bag for provisions." Cf also Ar jirm "body," Aram garmā "bone, body, self," Sab grm "body."]

R4842/7: may the god hwfyn grb ^{c}bdhw "protect the body/person of His servant" AND OFTEN SIM; R4938/8: may the god allow lḥyw grb 'ṯthw "to live/recover (from illness) the body of his wife"; J586/10: šrḥ wrtṯdn grybt mr'yhmw "to prosper and guard the lives of their 2 lords"

Note: In the common expression lwfy gr(y)bthmw "to protect their gr(y)bt," ns from GRB I and GRB II (presumed) cannot be distinguished.

GRB II

v pf grbw R4194/2+; inf grb R5085/5

MAKE A GRB-FIELD = REVET, TERRACE; WALL UP

[Ar jirba^{t} "field prepared for sowing, or land cleared for sowing and planting"; ModḤaḏ garb "any field, cultivated or not, surrounded by a wall against torrents"; MSA usage generally, "a walled field." Discussion Irv/161-2. For sense of root, cf Heb.Aram GRP "sweep clean; clear." Sab v is denom from n grb, see below.]

R4194/2: grbw wśw^{c} wḥrr "they revetted, leveled, and built up an embankment"; R5085/5: hqšbw wgrb ǵlhmw "they cleared and terraced their lowland"; R5094/2: grbw mqbrtm "they walled up tombs"

n? p grbthmw C87/9; grybthmw C535/5+

CULTIVATED FIELD; WALLED or TERRACED FIELD (?)

Note: The existence of this n in Sab is questionable, since all cited instances occur in the phrase wfy gr(y)bthmw "protect their fields (?)" and may be instances of the n from GRB I "body, health." A n grb "field" is attested unambiguously in Qat (e.g., R3856/1: 'srrs wgrwbs "his valleys and fields"), and the Sab v grb is no doubt ultimately derived from a similar noun.

n^{2} s grbm C540/11+

ROUGH STONE

[MSA gurūb id. Phps originally the kind of stone employed in building terracing and revetting walls of fields: roughly squared but not smoothed (Irv/260-61).]

C540/11: grbm wlbtm "rough stone and close-laid stonework"; C325/1: [g]rbm wrb^{c}tm "rough stone and squared stone"; ib/9: mnhmtm wgrbm "pecked masonry and rough stone"

n^{3} s grbtm C541/58*

BUILDING UP WITH STONE (maṣdar?)

C541/58: msrm wgrbtm "packing in earth and building up with stone"
Note: The term grbym C485+, hitherto interpreted as a "tribal" name, may in some cases be a professional designation or derived from such a designation ("the stonemason") (BeNL10/413).

GRB III

n s grbhw R3992/7*
LEGAL ADVERSARY, OPPONENT IN A LAWSUIT
[Ar jrb D "tempt, test" (BeNL6/316).]
R3992/7: grbhw M "his adversary M." (after lacuna)--context thanks god for securing dedicant's legal rights.

GRW

n p grtn Gl143/3*
YOUNG, OFFSPRING OF ANIMALS
[Ḥaḍ ǧarû "young animals"; cf also Heb gûr "young of any animal, cub."]
Gl143/3: wḥg 'xd grtn bn kl qṭntm "(the god) has the right to take young animals from all (these) flocks"

GRḤ

n p/coll grḥ J643b/3*
a) DOMESTICATED ANIMALS; or, b) FEMALE BEASTS kept for breeding
[a) Eth garḥ "well-trained horse," cf Te garḥa "become tame," Tña garḥa "break (a horse)" (MüRev/107). b) Ar jāriḥa† id (BeRev/351).]
J643b/3: ''blhmw wḥmrthmw wkl grḥ "their camels and asses and all the domesticated (or, breeding) animals"
Note: For grḥ mnm C548/1 read gr ḥmnm (or ḥm(y)m), see under GWR.

GRM I

n s grm J752/9; d grmy J750/7
(1) BODY; (BODILY) LIFE, HEALTH (cf GRB I n id)
[Ar jirm "body."]
J752/9: they dedicated frsm...lgrm mhrthmw "a horse for the health of their filly" (grm here may be for more common grb, with dittography of following m)
(2) WATERSKIN, WATERBAG
[Daṯ garm "sheepskin coat," ModYem garm "roughly tanned cowhide used for coats" (RoVoc/302). Cf also Ar jirāb "(sheepskin) bag."]
J750/7: grmy mwn d[ys]tqynn "2 waterskins from which they quenched their thirst"

GRM II

h ipf yh(g)rm R2860/4*
COMMIT A CRIME, BE GUILTY OF

[Ar jarama id.]

R2860/4: wmn lyh(g)rm nkr qntm "and whoever is guilty of damaging a storage pit..."

n s̲ mgrmtm Ry507/7*
    MONETARY PENALTY (?)

[Ar jarīma[+] id (BeOr25/298). RyMus66/292 tr "crime, criminally," Rod Conf'65-6/135 tr "terror"--depending on restoration of preceding v̲; cf WQR st, BRW st.]

Ry507/7: st[q]rw ᶜlhmw mgrmtm "imposed on them a monetary penalty"

GRN

n s̲ grnh J514*
    THRESHING FLOOR

[Ar jurn, Heb gōren id.]

J514: ng' kl ᶜbrhmw...wgrnh "he walled all their field and its threshing floor"

GRT, n̲ in Gl143/3--see under GRW

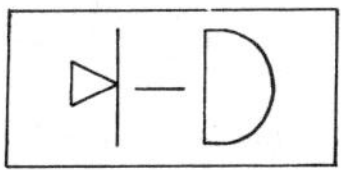

D

pn d- C539/4*

relative pronoun, *m.s.*: HE OF (= *d*)

[See etym under *D*.]

C539/4: ʾlsm RḤMNN dKL^{c}N "in the name of (the god) R., He of K." (cf KL^{c}N as *n.loc* in, e.g., C541/85); for C540/67 see under D'

D'

pt d' Ry507/7+; *var* d- C540/67

ALREADY

[Cf phps Eth wd' *D* used before pf *v* to convey sense "already"; particle dā'mu in several modal senses.]

Ry507/7: wkd' whbt rhnn wst[q]rw ^{c}lhmw mgrmtm "and when the hostages had already been given, they imposed on them a monetary penalty"; C540/66-7: 'š^{c}bm *dd*' ḥr ^{c}lyhmw tqh bM w^{c}rmn drᶜẓm hr^{c}ẓhmw "the tribes on whom it was already incumbent to bring (the building works) to completion in M. and (on) the dam, (the king) having already (?) sent a summons to them"

Note: In C540/67, the d in dr^{c}ẓm may phps more plausibly be interpreted as substituting for *d*-, the spelling being influenced by the sequence *dd* in the line above. The form d- phps also occurs in Ry507/2, and d' phps also in C541/12-3.

D'B--For 'dyb, C80/8 (assigned here by CoRoC/124B), see under 'DB

DBB

v *pf* db R4546/2*

FURNISH WITH BATTLEMENTS, FORTIFY (?)

[Cf Eth tadbāb "battlements" (RhSLGI/70n2).]

R4546/2: ^{c}A wM db b^c*T*TR... "A. and M. have fortified (?), by (the god) A..." (syntax doubtful; could db be *n.pr*, cf Ar dubb "bear"?)

h *pf* hdbwhw C448/3*

FORTIFY (?) (cf DBB *v*)

C448/3: hdbwhw wh^{c}qbn "they fortified and restored it"

DBW--For hdbwhw, C448/3, see under DBB *h*

DBL

v ipf ydblnhw J2856/4*

sense doubtful; PERFORM DULY, COMPLY WITH (?)

[Cf Ar dabala "put in order, in good condition (a field or the like)" (Lane /849C) (HöSEG8/23, and cf BeStl/90).]

J2856/4: b^{c}d yhḥmnhw wydblnhw "after (the vendor) shall have safeguarded and duly performed it (the contract)"

n s/coll dblm C562/6*

LUMP OF PRESSED FIGS, FIG-CAKE (?)

[Heb dəbēlāh id.]

C562/6: ^{c}gdm xbṭn wdblm "pressed grapes and pressed figs (?)"

DBS

n s dbsm C548/12-3+

HONEY or the like

[Heb dəbaš "honey," Ar dibs "syrup, molasses."]

C548/12-3: šnnm wdbsm wlbbm "šnn (a milk food), honey and cake"; C540/96: dbsm wxm'tm "honey and butter"

DBR

st For [st]dbrn, C291/7 in fragmentary context, see under TWB st

n s dbr Ry551/3; p 'dbr R3439/2

PAYMENT in the form of work (?)

[Cf phps Ar dbr D "make arrangements, plan, organize."]

R3439/2: nḥlt wrdy(t) w'dbr "payments, profits, and payments in work (?)"; Ry551/3: bdbr in fragmentary context

DHR

v pf dhrw Ry507/4; inf dhr Irl3+

a) BURN; or b) DESTROY (?)

[a) Te dähära "be very hot" (RycMus87/249 and n9). b) Ar dahr "end, limit, destiny"--v here would be D, "bring to an end"? (RodConf'65-6/133).]

Irl3: ^{c}dw whb^{c}ln wxtršn wdhr hgrn "invaded, conquered, destroyed and burned the town"; Ry508/3-4: hrg kl ḥwrhw wdhr qlsn "killed all the colonists and burned (?) the church"; ib: dhr ^{c}sm sfnm bḥyqn "burned (?) a number of boats in the creek"

DWL

n s [m]dwln N28/6-7*

ALTERATION, REPAIR of a building (?)

[RyNE4/164-5 cfs Ar dāla (w) "change periodically, alternate."]

N28/6-7: kl nkl m[bny m]dwln "all the pebbled paving of the con[struction of the re]pair (?)"

DWM

n as adj: f.s dmtn C548/17* (act.prt?)

LASTING, PERMANENT

[Ar dāma (w) "be lasting, permanent."]

C548/17: after committing certain sacrilegious acts, a man shall pay fines, but ^{c}rthw dmtn "his defectiveness/fault is permanent" (context is damaged and first word may be incomplete)

n s dwmm R2726/3+

as adv: FOREVER

[Ar dawm^{an} "constantly, forever."]

R2726/3: thus ordained the king of Saba, w^{c}d'l dstqr' wxll bh'w dwmm "and to that which he publishes and decrees have (the Sabaean freemen) conformed forever"; sim context R3951/1

DWN--For v dn see under DNY

DWS--The phrase 'ḥgkm dt dwsm, J647/14, is prob n.pr.f; J tr "the laws which were abused" (discussion BeNL9/195)

DWR

n^1 s drm J633/9+; exp drm drm C571/10+

TIME,OCCASION; as adv, drm and drm drm: ONCE, ON ONE OCCASION

[Ar dawr "(one's) turn," dawra^{+} "turn, revolution, circuit."]

J633/9: yḥḷẓn hwt ḥḷẓn drm bxrfm "he suffered from that sickness once a year," and the god commanded him lst^{c}nnhw drm bxrfm "to ask His help once a year"; J576/11: the king made a sortie from the city drm tntm "a second time"; C571/10: ^{c}qbhw drm drm b'ḥd xrfm "he acted as his deputy once a year"

n^2 s dwrm R2861/12*

GENERATION > PEOPLE

[Ar dawr "age, era," Heb dôr "generation."]

R2861/12: appointed to rule qwm[m w]dwrm "the community and the people"

n^3 p 'dwr(m) J574/7+; 'dyrm J577/4

BEDUIN CAMP, CLAN

[Ar dār, p 'adwār "settlement with a few houses or tents; tribe of Beduins."]

J574/7: ḥrbw...xmst w^{c}šry 'dwrm bn 'dwr 'A "twenty-five beduin clans fought" AND ELSEWHERE SIM

n^4 For mhdrn C359/8 and GI443, see under HDR

DYN--For dn see under DNY

D ipf ydynn R4626/2; inf dyn Ry554/3

(1) IMPOSE A FINE (?)

[Ar dāna (y) "be indebted," Min dyn (R2833/1) "impose an obligation."]
Ry554/3: ...]wl dyn kbrn M "and let the kabir M. impose a fine (?)"
(2) BE SUBJECT TO TAX, BE INDEBTED TO; BE THE RESPONSIBILITY OF
R4626/2: 'srr ydynn '^{c}rrn T wH "the valleys which are tributary to/the responsibility of (the fortresses) T. and H."
Note: Cf also ydnn C541/48: hqdmw brdnn brṯ ydnn ^{c}rbn, which BeNL10/409 tr "(the king) sent out 2 couriers, in order that the Arabs should obey (his summons)," but for this see also under DNY

n^1 p 'dynhmw Ist7626/7*
MONETARY PENALTIES, or OBLIGATIONS in general
[Ar dayn in both senses. Cf BeMus65/275.]
Ist7626/7: wbgl m'xḏt 'dynhmw "and by the entirety of the contents/tenor of their obligations"

n^2 s tdyn J1028/10-11* (tp inf?)
PIETY
[Ar tadayyana "profess a religion with sincerity, be zealous in belief" (RodBiOr26/32A), tadayyun (inf) "piety."]
J1028/10-11: bxfrt smyn wtdyn w''ḏn 'sdn ḏn msndn "this inscription [was erected] by the protection (?) of Heaven and the piety and power/strength of the soldiers"

DYT--For dytm R4779/4 see under WDY

DKṮ

v ipf ydkṯn R4176/8*
VIOLATE (?)
[Sense conjectured from context.]
R4176/8: t^{c}lmn ^{c}ṮTR...ḏydkṯn ṯḥrm kḥrm "let (the god) A. take cognizance of him who violates the taboo (on the tithe), for it is sacred"

DL, see under DLW

DLW

n s mdlt R4191/6; mdlthw J572/4+; mdlthmy J669/6-7
WEIGHT, or VALUE
[Eth mädlot in both senses (IrvJRAS'64/25). Cf mdlwṯ id in Ḥaḍ.]
J608/5-6: he dedicated ṣlmn ḏṣrfn ḏmdlthw 'l(f)n rḏym "a statue of silver, of which the weight/value was a thousand rdy" AND ELSEWHERE SIM

DLL

v pf dllw J575/4; inf dll ib/3
GUIDE, POINT OUT
[Ar dalla "show, indicate."]
J575/3: ysrw bqdmyhmw dlwlm **ldll** '^{c}ṣd "they sent guides before them to

point out for them/guide them to the (enemy) warbands"; ib/4: '^{c}ṣd dllw lhmw "the warbands they had pointed out to them"

n p dlwlm J575/3*

GUIDES

[Ar dalīl "guide."]

J575/3 quoted under DLL v

DM, see under DWM, DMW, DMN

DMW

v ipf ydmw C548/6*

BLEED, or DRAW/SHED BLOOD

[Ar damiya, Tña damawa "bleed"; D causative.]

C548/6: if there is blood on his garments in the temple whm lm ydmw lyẓl^{c}n "and if he is not bleeding (i.e., if the stain is old), let him pay a fine," or "and if he has not shed blood (i.e., used his weapon aggressively in the sanctuary, but has carried it only for show?), let him pay a fine"

n s dm C464/9; p or var dmwm C548/3

BLOOD

[Ar dam, Heb dām, dāmîm id.]

C548/3: hn lyngsn slḥhw wdmwm bšy^{c}hw lyẓl^{c}n "if he should defile his weapons, or if there is blood on his garment, let him pay a fine" (cf continuation quoted under DMW v); C464/9: dm ṭlyn [...] wdyn bqḥfm "blood of a (sacrificed) lamb flowing in streams"

DMN (?), v in R4158/8: ...] wydmnh bqbr m[... "and he ...ed her/it in the grave (?)"

DN, see under DNY

DNY

v pf dn C541/74; dyn ib/74; dnw Ry506/6-7; ipf ydnn C541/49

DRAW NEAR, APPROACH; in p, ASSEMBLE

[Ar danâ "come nigh upon," but cf other suggestions below.]

C541/74: kdny ḍlln ^{c}ly š^{c}bn "when the sickness drew near the tribe" (Irv/374n175 cfs Daṯ dannâ ^{c}alâ "overlook" overhang, tr "demoralize"-- see also under XNY); ib/64: the king sent a summons wdn ^{c}rbn ^{c}dyw hgrn "and the Arabs drew near (and) entered the city" (Irv/302-3 cfs Ar dāna in sense "comply"); ib/49: he sent a courier brṯ ydnn ^{c}rbn "(to) the place the Arabs were approaching/assembling (in)"; Ry506/6-7: dnw kẓl "(the king, p.maj) approached as a protector" (RodConf'65-6/126 cfs Ar dāna "judge")

DNN, see under DNY

D^c

v pf d^{c}w C429/7+

KNOW, HAVE KNOWLEDGE (sometimes with bn of)

[Cf Heb yādā^c id; phps also Ar da^{c}ā "call."]

C429/7: 'nsn wḏbnhw 'l d^{c}w wš^{c}rw "men, including those of thom they have no knowledge or cognizance"; C411/9: šn'm ḏbnhw d^{c}w wḏbnhw 'l d^{c}w "any enemy, those whom they know and those whom they don't know" AND OFTEN IN THIS FORMULA; for n d^{c}t see under D^{cc}

D^{c}B, R4785/4: ...] (w)ḍ^{c}m wr d^{c}b mrn xmrhmw [..., no tr

D^{c}Ṭ

v pf d^{c}ṭ P135a*

ATTACK (?)

[Cf phps Ar da^{c}aṣa "crowd, press," da^{c}aḍa "crush almost to death" (JDN/170).]

P135a (edited in RyNE4): kn d^{c}ṭ hgrn N wysḥtw NBṬ "when the city N. attacked (?) and destroyed the Nabataeans"

D^{c}M

n s d^{c}mt C505/1*

BUTTRESS or some supportive construction for an (embanked?) field (?)

[Ar di^{c}āma$^+$ "buttress; pillar."]

C505/1: mlkw d^{c}mt mšrqh[w] "they owned the buttress (?) of his east-lying field"

D^{cc}

n s? d^{c}tm J691/9+

PRODUCTS OF THE SOIL, CROPS (prob those grown on land naturally irrigated, contrasted with sqy "artificially irrigated crops")

[Cf Ar du^{c}ā^c "a kind of plant growing close to the ground, with berries which...can be roasted and eaten"; also "palms planted separately" (JSIMB/113). Nuance of natural irrigation deduced from contrast with sqy.]

J691/9: 'ṯmrm šfqm d^{c}tm [ws]qym "abundant crops, (both) d^{c}t and sqy (i.e., naturally and artificially irrigated)"; Ir22: 'tw wstwfyn d^{c}t kwnt bmqy(ẓ)hmw w'rḍhmw "(the god) successfully sent the d^{c}t-crops which were in their summer-crop lands and fields"; R3951/3: xrṣ...b^{c}mhmw wrqm wd^{c}tm wṭḥnm "he estimated for them (the value of their) vegetables, d^{c}t-crops and meal" AND SEVERAL TIMES WITH wrq

For wd^{c}t R4176/12, see under WD^c n

DFL

n s dflm C541/59*

a) PITCH, or b) CLAMPS (?)

[a) Ar difal "tar extracted from the juniper or savin tree"--used to render parts of the sluices watertight? b) Akk dapālu, syn of riksu "bond" (Irv's reading and suggested etymologies).]

C541/59: grbtm wbr'[m] wdflm wnh[m]t "building up with grb- and br'-stonework, pitch/clamps (?) and pecked masonry"

Note: C and SoSoDGI read xfgm, see under XFG

DFN

n p mdfn C553/3*

UNDERGROUND CHAMBERS

[Eth dafana "dig; conceal," madfen "(underground) storehouse."]

C553/3: bmdfn ᶜsnn "in the underground chambers of the cistern"

DFQ

v pf dfq R4964/6*

sense doubtful

R4964/6: d̲mrw wtṣl'n...kdfq bnhw "they ordained and proclaimed...when his son (?) ...ed (?) (or, he ...ed from him)"

DQQ

n s dqqm C541/120*

FLOUR

[Ar daqīq id.]

C541/120: t̲mn m'tm wst̲m dqqm wᶜˇsry ''lfm tmrm "eight hundred and six (measures of) flour and twenty thousand dates"

DR, see under DWR

DR'

h pf hdr' Ry508/4*

CAPTURE BY A SURPRISE ASSAULT (?) (b- + obj)

[Ar dara'a "fall on the enemy unexpectedly," h "deceive, take treacherously, trap (a wild beast, etc)" (RodConf'66-7/127).]

Ry508/4: whdr' mlkn b'A "the king captured A. by a surprise assault (?)"

DRK

v ipf ydrkhmw Ir12/3*

OVERTAKE by pursuit

[Ar daraka "reach, overtake s.o. by pursuit" (RodConf'65-6/129).]

Ir12/3: ydrkhmw bllyn t̲ntn "they overtook them on the night of the next day" h pf hdrkhmw (m.s) J574/10; hdrkthmw J576/12; hdrkhmw (m.p) J574/4+; ipf yhdrkhmw J577/5; inf hdrkn J629/33

(1) PURSUE (b'tr, b^{c}d "after")

J575/4: hdrkhmw b'trhmw "they pursued (after) them"; J629/33: hdrkn b^{c}d 'HDR "to pursue (after) the Hadramis"

(2) OVERTAKE (cf DRK v)

J574/10: hdrkhmw tnbltm...tdr^{c}m "an embassy overtook them, (offering) surrender"; C353/12: hdrkhmw bK whqdhmw "they overtook them in K. and captured them"

DRF

n p? drft C197/6*

SIDES, FLANKS (?)

[Ar darf id.]

C197/6: the god granted him m^{c}ls sdqm kl drft $[m]^{c}$ls "a satisfying battle, on every flank (?) of the battle"

DRR

n^{1} s drrhmw C615/8*

PLENTY > HARVEST (?)

[Ar darra "be abundant, plentiful."]

C615/8: 'DNT wdrrhmw "A. (place-name) and (its) harvest (?)"; note also R4760/5 (damaged context): wdrrh[...]

n^{2} as adj: m.p mdrrm R4907/8*

FLOURISHING, LUXURIANT (of trees)

[Ar darra "said of herbage, it became tnagled or luxuriant by reason of its abundance" (BeAIP/448).]

R4907/8: ...] swd ^{c}rrm mdrrm [... "a hillside (plantation) of flourishing cypresses"

DŚŚ

n s dśśm J703/12* (act.prt?)

ONE WHO HIDES an inscription (by re-using the stone for building?)

[Ar dassahu fī -lturāb "he hid, buried it in the ground" (BeNL7/539).]

J703/12: they dedicated it to the god for protection bn m'xrm wmśwrm wdśśm "against (any)one who might move (it) away or injure or hide (it)"

DT'

n s dt' J610/14+

(1) SPRING (season)

[Cf Heb deše' "fresh herbage"; ModYem dite' "spring harvest" (RoVoc/302); and esp dathiathum, Pliny's word for the spring incense harvest (Hist. nat.xii.60).]

J610/14: 'brq dṯ' wxrf "rainstorms of spring and autumn" AND OFTEN SIM; C967/4: sqy xrf wdṯ' SB' "(the god) irrigated S. in autumn and spring" AND OFTEN SIM IN EPONYM FORMULAE

(2) SPRING HARVEST

J617/8: xrf wdṯ' ws^{c}s^{c}m wmlyn ^{c}dy kl 'rḍthmw "autumn, spring, summer and winter harvests in all their fields" AND OFTEN SIM; J661/7: fr^{c} 'myrt dṯ' wxrf "cereal crops of the spring and autumn harvests" AND OFTEN SIM

Ḥ-D

D

rl d- passim

relative pn, m.s. (use sometimes extended to d and p, and to f)

(1) before verbs: (HE) WHO, (THAT) WHICH

[ModYem di id (m and f).]

C407/26: ǵnmm dhrḍhw "booty which satisfied him"; C334/15: ṯty zxntn dzxn "two wounds which he received"; R4663/4-5: s[c]dhmw n[c]mtm wdqnyw "grant prosperity to them and (to) that which they possess"; R4090/3: may the god strike down dynhkn wšṭrhw "(anyone) who injures or destroys it (a gravestone)"

(2) before non-verbs: (THAT) WHICH (IS), (HE) WHO (IS)

[Ar dū id.]

R4938/20: bn dbsrn "from that which is in the valley"; R4174b/9: mqṭrnhn db 'A "the 2 incense burners which are in A."; J564/3: ṣlmn dbhw ḥmd "this statue, by (the dedication of) which he praised (the god)"

periphrasis for genitive: C555/4: m'tmn dbn 'A "landed property of the b.A."; C571/7: hmt ymtn dtnd[c]tn "those days of the song-ritual (?)"; C374: ''wdn dsṭrn "the lines of the inscription"; without antecedent: R3945/13: hbḍ[c] d'mnt K "attacked (those) of the 'security' of K. (i.e., his dependents)"

to indicate clan affiliation: C512/1-2: 'A...d'hl R "A. of the clan R."; C528/1-2: 'A dG "A. of (the clan) G." AND VERY OFTEN

Note also the common locution d + n.pr of tribe X, "those of (the tribe) X" = "(the tribe) X." Such a form may phps in some cases designate specifically the "chief" of the tribe ("he/the one of X"); cf e.g. R4176/8: dMDNḤN "the chief of (the tribe) M. (shall prepare a banquet)"; the tr "(the tribe) M." is equally plausible.

in epithets of gods: J559/9+: [c]TTR dDBN "(the god) A. of (the sanctuary) D." AND OFTEN SIM

to indicate material: J615/9+: ṣlmn ddhbn "this statue of gold" AND OFTEN SIM

with enclitic -mw (really a subclassification of sense[1], usage before verbs): F55/6: wdmw yhr'bnn b[c]ly (ẓ)hrm "and (anyone) who accepts this document..."

Note: For d + m (phps the shortened form of the enclitic?), see under DM. This form seems to function as a demonstrative, and may be more closely related to the demonstrative dn than to the relative d. (See DM also for the compound dmdn.)

compounded with prepositions: for such compounds as d-b, d-l, d-bn, see under the second member of the compound. Prepositional phrases including d are usually written in one word with what follows, e.g., bdtxmr J2116/4, wldyz'n R3902b#149/1, etc.

For the compound d'l, see under D'L.

Note the corresponding f.s dt (see under DT) and p 'l(y) (see under 'L II), and the variant spelling z (see under Z). A unique use of d as dm phps occurs in MüAf024/153: wd bytn msgdn "and this house is the place of prayer."

D'B--In C540/10, MD'B is the n.pr of the northern sluices of the Mārib dam (cf phps Ar di'b "wolf," a common element in nn.pr): ᶜdbw MD'Bn bn sflhw "they repaired M. from its foundation" (tr Irv/258-9)

D'L

rl d + 'l (negative) F30/7+

relative pn + negative: THAT NOT, SO THAT NOT

[Discussion RycMus67/339-48.]

F30/7: let this written acknowledgment of debt be a prohibition wd'l yhknn ᶜln bny dY "so that no (more) will be imposed on the b.Y."; R4964/13: hsṭw gdm[n] bnhw lqbly d'l yẓbnn ᶜtlhw "(the god) agreed to save his son because (the dedicant) had not refrained from besieging Him (with prayers)"; J702/4-5 (doubtful context): wl(ḥd)rn kl ršym d'l yšrḥn ṣythw "let every priest beware who does not (?) protect his reputation"

D'F

n p? d'fn C540/29-30+

CANALS; or n.pr

[Irv/275,37ln141 cfs PBH zûf "drip, be viscid," Om dzûf "flow over." Ar roots z'f, d'f refer to (sudden) death, phps including sense of flowing/passing away.]

C540/29-30: fqḥ mḍrft d[']fn 'bnm wgyrm "he opened the revetments of the canals (recently made) of stone and plaster"; C541/45: tbr ᶜrmn wᶜwdn... wmḍrft d'fn "the dam, settling basin and revetments of the canals broke"

D'T--in broken contexts R3605b/11, R4763/1--doubtful.

DBḤ

v pf dbḥ C957; dbḥhw R4176/12; ipf ydbḥn R3104/1-2+; ydbḥw C74/11-2; ydbḥnn R4767/2

(1) SACRIFICE an animal ritually

[Ar ḏabaḥa "kill (by slitting the throat)," in ritual and profane senses.]
R3104/1-2 (on an altar): mḏbḥt bh yḏbḥn mlkn ṯwrm "altar on which the king sacrifices a bull"; C957: ywm ḏbḥ ^{c}ṮTR "when he sacrificed (to the god) A."

(2) KILL, MURDER

R4176/12: qnyn ḏbḥhw ṯny 'sn "the slave whom two men killed"

n^{1} s ḏbḥ(m) R2740/8+; p ḏbyḥm C541/124+; var 'ḏbḥm R3945/1+

(1) BLOOD SACRIFICE

[Ar ḏibḥ id.]
R2740/8: ^{c}sy ḏbḥm "he made a sacrifice"

(2) ANIMAL FOR BUTCHERING or SACRIFICE (phps specifically camel)

[Ar ḏibḥ, Daṯ ḏabīḥa id.]
R3945/1: ḏbḥ ^{c}ṮTR šlṯt 'ḏbḥm "he sacrificed three animals to (the god) A."; C541/124: ṭbxm...ḏbyḥm wbqrm "animals for butchering--camels (?) for butchering and cattle" (part of provisions for workmen on the Mārib dam); also with cattle and sheep in C540/42-3

n^{2} s mḏbḥt R3104/1+

ALTAR for blood sacrifice

[Heb mizbē^{a}ḥ id; Ar maḏbaḥ "slaughterhouse; altar (in Christian usage)."]
R3104/1 quoted under ḎBḤ v sense^{1}; R2643 (in full): mḏbḥt ḏB bH "altar of (the clan) B. at (the sanctuary) H." AND OFTEN with owners' names

ḎHB I

n^{1} s ḏhb(m,n) J559/3-4++

GOLD (term also sometimes describes objects made of bronze)

[Ar ḏahab "gold."]
J559/3-4: hqnyw...ṣlmnhn ḏy ḏhbn "he dedicated 2 statues of gold" AND VERY OFTEN SIM, with varying syntactic form: C352/4: ṣlmn ḏḏhbm; C534/4-5: ṣlmn ḏḏhbn (more common); in other contexts: Ir13/13: ḏhbm wǵnmm "gold and booty"; C73/8-9: a price bḏhbn bblṭm rḍym "in gold, in current coin"; R4184/4: ḏhb bḥt "pure gold"

n^{2} s ḏhb C338/12+

KIND OF AROMATIC GUM used as incense, phps called "GOLDEN" from its color

[Most probably cf Ar ḏahab "gold" (contrast other types of incense, e.g. ṣrf "silver" and lbn "white"). Or phps cf Ar ḏāhib "resin of a tree" which flows out (ḏahaba, Sab ḎHB III) (RyRB58/373). Cf Is 60:6, where the Sabaeans offer zāhāb ûlbonāh as tribute.]
C683 (on an incense altar): rnd ḏhb n^{c}m qsṭ "nard, 'golden' incense, 'sweet' incense, costus"; C338/12: mslmn ḏḏhb "altar for 'golden' incense (or, altar of gold, n^{1}?)"

DHB II

n¹ s̱ dhb(n) R4815/3+; dhbh R3946/4+; d̲ d̲hbnhn R3945/2; d̲hby R3943/3+; p 'd̲hbn J735/2; 'd̲hbh R3950

IRRIGATED LAND in a wadi bed; CULTIVATED LAND, FIELD

[RhSLG2/113-4, quoting Hamdānī 199.20, calls d̲hb "the rain-water stream, similarly the land watered by it" (BeSI/66). The 'd̲hb are part of the syr or common land belonging to the city. RoVoc/303 cites West Yem zähäb or zahb "field."]

R3943/3: gbd̲ d̲hby [Y] "he plundered the 2 cultivated territories of Y. (one on each side of the wadi bed?)"; R3945/2: he banked up the aqueduct lest water td̲'n brḥm ld̲hbnhn "flow out unchecked to the 2 irrigated territories"; R4815/3: fnwtm...dt tnš'n mwn bn d̲hbn "a canal which carries water from the irrigated field A."

n² p? d̲hb C540/55,58*

(MONSOON) RAINS, FLOOD; SAYL FLOOD

[Phps a separate root. Cf Ar d̲ahba⁺, p dihab "light rain."]
C540/55-8: tbr [b]n d̲hb xrfn wsqyw...'rd̲n bn d̲hb dt'n "(the dam) had broken because of the autumn monsoon rains, and the land was watered by the spring flood"

DHB III

n¹ s? d̲hb C541/112*

EXIT, OUTFLOW CHANNEL(S) (?)

[Ar d̲ahaba "go; leave," d̲ahab "passage; departure."]
C541/112: whqšbw d̲hb XBŠ "they prepared for use the outflow channel(s) of X. (the northern sluices of the Mārib dam)"

n² p? md̲hbthw J618/16*

PASSAGE, OUTFLOW (?) (cf d̲hb n¹ sim)

[Ar mad̲hab "passage, way out."]
J618/16: m'xd̲hmw...wmd̲hbthw "their control dyke and its passages/outflows (?)"

DHW (?)

n s? md̲ht N19/2*

sense doubtful

[MüW/52 tr "might" after Ar d̲ahā "be proud, boast," but context seems unsuitable.]
N19/2: [lw]fy md̲ht T'LB bwfym "to protect (?) the ...? of (the god) T. in safety"

DWD

n p d̲wwdtn R2861/3*

PASTURE LANDS (?) (reading very doubtful)

[Cf Ar madād id (Lane/998A).]

R2861/3 (obscure and fragmentary): mtbmdgblw/ dwwdtn wm/ n lyš'm bn ᶜbd'sm... (context unhelpful for tr)

Note: R prints śwᶜltn, and quotes other readings: swwdtn, swᶜdtn. RhGr/9 read dwwdt from Glaser's squeeze. For dwwdt C376/8, read (?) śwwdt; see under ŚWD.

DXR

n s d[x]r J591/1*

TREASURER (?) (reading doubtful)

[Cf Ar daxara "hoard, treasure (s.th.)" (Lane/956C).]

J591/1: R...d[x]r blt 'l "R., treasurer (?) of the taxes/tributes of (the king) l."

n[2] In fragmentary context R4787/1, n mdxr. Cf Min id "funerary monument" (R2918/2) and Eth zexr id.

DY

rl dy C655/1+

relative pn, m.d: THE TWO OF (examples all express clan affiliation)

[Cf d-, m.s id; dyn, m.d demonstrative adj (see under DYN).]

C655/1: H wN dy ḤBB "H. and N., the two (members of the clan) Ḥ." AND OFTEN

DYB

n p mdbn Gl442/3*

WATERCOURSE, CANAL

[Ar dāba (w) "melt, flow away" (SchSEG7/35).]

Gl442/3: xmst 'ᶜnbm mdbn dS "five vineyards of the canal dS."

DYN

dm dyn F71/3-4*

demonstrative adj, m.d: THESE TWO (cf dn dm[2] id)

[Cf dn, m.s id; dy, m.d relative pn.]

F71/3-4: hqny...dyn ṣlmnhn "he dedicated these 2 statues"

DYR

n s dyrm R3945/2*

a) SILT FIELD; or, b) RAISED PLOT

[a) Cf Ar dūr = turāb "(silt) field" (Q, cited by Irv/72-3). b) Analyze as d-yrm (root RW/YM "be high") and tr "that which is raised" = "raised plot."]

R3945/2: he repaired the irrigation system of his land wykn fnwtm fnwtm wdyrm dyrm "(so that) it was (arranged) channel by channel and silt field by silt field"

ḎKW I

D *pf* ḏkww J665/17; *inf* ḏkwn J631/27

KILL, SLAUGHTER (in battle)

[Cf Ar ḏakkā "slaughter (an animal)" and ḏakāh "slaughter" (BeNL7/539).]

J631/27: hrgw wḏkwn whsḥtn 'ḤBŠn bn wsṭ hgrn "they killed, slaughtered and destroyed the Ḥabashites from the center of the city (outward)"

Note: For ḏkw J665/19, see Note to ḎKY *v*.

ḎKW II

n *s* hḏkwt J541/6*

INDICATION, DELINEATION

[Cf Ar ḏakuwa, ḏakiya, ḏakâ "be sharp-witted, intelligent." Sab h "know clearly" or "cause (others) to know, recognize"? (cf BonVar/333n).]

J541/6: wkwn lhḏkwt 'ln 'wṯnn qf msqy "and let the boundary stone of the irrigation system (serve as) the indication of these boundaries"

ḎKY

v *pf* ḏky C541/56+; ḏkyhw Ry508/3+; ḏkyw C541/33+; *var*? ḏkw J665/19 (see Note)

SEND

[Cf Ar 'aḏkaytu -l-^{c}uyūna "I sent against him the scouts," root ḎKW (Lane/971C).]

Ry508/3: wwrd mlkn 'A wḏkyhw bgyšm "and the king went down (to) A. and sent him to (supervise?) the troop"; ib/6: ḏkyhw...lqrn ^{c}ly N "he sent him to fight against N."; C541/56: wmlkn ḏky ^{c}ẓtm ^{c}ly 'š^{c}bn "as for the king, he sent a summons to the tribes"

Note also J665/19: mqdmtn...bn Ḥ ḏḏkw mlk Ḥ l'x̱ḏ lhw 'x̱ḏm. Normal sense of *v* ḏkw "slaughter" is not suitable here. Tr as ḏky, misspelled by attraction to ḏkww in ib/17?--"the advance troop from Ḥ. which the king of Ḥ. sent (?) to make captures for him."

Note: For ḏkyn Ry502/4, J601/10, NNAG7/10, read ḏ-kyn and see under KYN *v*.

h *pf* hḏky Ir28; hḏkyw C541/79+

SEND (= ḎKY *v*)

Ir28: hḏky...tnbltm "he sent an embassy"; C541/79: srwtn 'lht hḏkyw lqrnhmw "the troops which they sent to fight/guard them"; sim ib/53-4

n *s* ḏky Ry507/6*

MISSION (?)

Ry507/6: ...bḏky ṯny b^{c}()ly N "on the second (?) mission (?) to N." (context damaged)

Note: BeOr25/298 reads kḏky ṯny, tr "when he sent two (persons)." In R4369/2, read ḏky as ḏ-ky, *rl* + *pp*, and see under KY *pp*.

D̲KN--For n md̲knt C224/2,3-4, read md̲qnt; see under D̲QN

D̲KR I
  v pf d̲kr F30/1+; for d̲kr C548/10, see under KRR
      (1) MENTION, MAKE KNOWN, ANNOUNCE
      [Ar d̲akara id.]
      F30/1: d̲kr (Z̲) F kr' kwhbyhw "Z̲. F. announces as follows: now they have given to him..."; G1573a/1: d̲kr bnw d̲H...k'l śnhmw [... "the b.H̲. have announced that it is not lawful for them..."
          Note: Obscure in R5094/5: whmw d̲kr sm^c... Tr "they have made known the testimony (?)," or the like?
      (2) NEGOTIATE (?)
      [Ar d̲ākara id.]
      J643/14: mt̲bt mngyt d̲kr b^{c}mhw "the successful diplomatic mission he negotiated (?) with him"
  n s d̲krn GaMosna^c/10-1+
      MEMORIAL
      [Nab d̲krwn, Heb zikkārôn id.]
      GaMosna^c/10-1: mnqlt d̲krn "the roads of the memorial (consisting of this inscription)" (cf BeSM/399); stela in Mārib Museum, photographed by Condé and reported in RyNE5/127: d̲krn T̲M "memorial of T̲."

D̲KR II
  n s d̲kr(m) J588/4+; p d̲kwr[m] J594/9; var 'd̲krm J564/19+; var 'd̲krwm J561b/20+
      adj: MALE
      [Ar d̲akar id.]
      J729/10: [km^c?]nmy yldn lhw d̲krm "if a male (child) should be born to him..."; J588/4: xmrhw...wldm d̲krm "(the god) granted him a male child"; J564/19: may the god grant him 'wld[m] 'd̲krm hn'm "male, pleasing children" AND OFTEN

DLL
  tp inf tdlln J644/7-8*
      BE HUMBLED, ABASED; as aux, (DO) IN IGNOMINIOUS FASHION
      [Ar dll D̲t "humble one's self."]
      J644/7-8: hbrrw wtdlln...bn byt "they were dislodged ignominiously from the fortress"
  h pf hdll J669/21-2; ipf yhdlln C81/7
      (1) MAKE VILE > FIND AGAINST in a legal proceeding, REJECT
      [Ar dll h "debase, humiliate."]
      J669/21-2: dmr...mr'hmw...whdll m^{c}brn "their lord pronounced sentence and found against/rejected the (previous) m^{c}br procedure"

(2) RAVAGE

C81/7: yfthn bythmw wyhdlln qnyhmw "their house was laid waste and their property ravaged"

st inf stdlln Robin UmmLayla 1/4*

OBEY

Robin UmmLayla 1/4: stwddw wstdlln ltṣn^c^n bn ḤBŠN "they agreed to obey the reinforcement against the Ḥs."

DM

dm dm C435/1+

demonstrative pn (?) + enclitic (?): THIS

[Cf rl d- "that which, that of" and dm dn "this."]

C435/1: gzm ^c^TTR...kdm yt^c^lmnn "the decision of (the god) A. (is) as follows (lit., like this): they shall take cognizance..."; F55/4: gzmw...kdm ylqḥnn kl 'nsm "they pledged themselves as follows: they will arrest any man..." (Ry restored as dm(w), prob mistakenly)

Note also the exp dmdn, prob d (rl) + m (enclitic) + dn (dm): OF THE SAME, OF THIS; e.g. in J653/10: wrx dM dmdn xrfn "the month dM. of the same year"; sim Sh18/2, NNAG12/10 (J emended unnecessarily to d(mnd) in J653).

DMDN--see Note to DM

DMW--rl + enclitic, see under D

DMR I

v pf dmr J669/20-1+; dmrhw C963/3; dmrw R4964/4-5+; ipf ydmrn C392/10; inf? dmrn C293/4

ORDAIN, PRONOUNCE judicial SENTENCE

[Cf Eth zmr h "declare solemnly, religiously."]

C293/4: wl [xryn w]dmrn 'mr'hmw...bn nḍ^c^wšṣy "may their lords [protect and] ordain (?) against injury and evil eye"; J669/20-1: wdmr b^c^mhmw mr'hmw whdll "and their lord pronounced sentence in their presence and found against (them)"; R4964/4-5: dmr wtṣl' dmrw wtṣl'n "the edict and proclamation (which) they ordained and proclaimed"; same formula Ry365/11

n s dmr R4964/4; p 'dmrn Gl193/2

EDICT, JUDGMENT

R4964/4 quoted under DMR I v; Gl193/2: b]qdmy 'dmrn w'[fth]n "before the edicts and [ordinance]s"

DMR II

n d mdmrn C542/6*

PLANTATIONS (?)

[Cf Heb zāmar, Ar zabara "prune (vines)"; Amh azmärä "cultivator; harvest" (Irv/134).]
C542/6: t̲ny md̲mrn wt̲nty mwqntn "two plantations (?) and 2 cisterns (?)"

D̲N

dm[1] d̲n passim

demonstrative adj, m.s.: THIS

[Cf Ar deictic element du-, da- and Sab d- (relative pn, m.s); here extended by the "nominalizing" suffiz -n.]

R4187/4: hqnyw...d̲n ṣlmn "they dedicated this statue" AND VERY OFTEN; R4176/1: bḥg d̲n mḥrn "according to this ordinance"; R4416/2: 'lw sṭrw bd̲n wtfn "those who wrote (in) this wtf-document"

Note also the obscure passage F64/6: wmn d̲nmn bš'mtn '[... "and whoever, by a purchase (?) .." Cf the f dt, p 'ln ('L II).

dm[2] d̲n J614/5-6*

demonstrative adj, m.d: THESE TWO (cf d̲yn id)

[Prob defective spelling of d̲yn, q.v. under D̲YN.]

J614/5-6: hqnyy...d̲n ṣlmnhn "they dedicated these 2 statues"

Note: This form is conceivably an error, after the common phrase d̲n ṣlmn "this statue."

D̲NB

n p d̲nb(n) C334/24+

CLIENTS

[Ar d̲ānib "follower, adherent."]

C334/24: sᶜdhw...bkln wd̲nbn "(the god) granted him subjects and clients"; in fragmentary context C140/13

D̲NM

v pf d̲nm J735/12+

RAIN

[Eth zanma id.]

J735/12: ws'r bn hwt ywmn...d̲nm wmẓ' d̲ᶜbn bl[l]yn "during the rest of that day it rained, and flash floods came in the night"; J651/17: d̲nm d̲nmn "rain fell"

n s d̲nm(m,n) J735/5+; p 'd̲nm Ir19+

RAIN

[Eth zenām id.]

Ir19: 'brq w'd̲nm "storms and rains"; J735/5: hxb sqy wd̲nm 'rḍn "irrigation water and rain failed (in) the land"

D̲ᶜB

n p d̲ᶜb J651/33+; p 'd̲ᶜb(m,n) Ir22/1,2

FLASH FLOOD, SAYL; FLOOD WATERS

[Ar d̲^{c}b N̲ "it [water]...flowed in a continuous stream" (Lane/965C).]
J735/12: mẓ' d̲^{c}bn bl[l]yn wml'w 'mṭrn wsqyw kl 'srrn "flash floods came in the night, filled the rain-watered fields and provided irrigation for all the valleys"; Ir22/1: 'd̲nm w'd̲^{c}bn mhšfqn wmh^{c}mmn "abundant and ample rains and flash floods"

D̲FR'

s p̲ d̲fr'n J720/9*

ILL-SMELLING PLANTS

[Ar d̲afira "emit a strong odor," d̲afrā' "an herb of foul odor" (Lane/967AB).]
J720/9: he sat in the temple wystṣyn bn d̲fr'n wbn bṣlm "stinking of ill-smelling plants and of onions"

D̲QṬ

v i̲p̲f̲ yd̲qṭ C462/3+; yd̲qṭn C970/3+

a) SACRIFICE (?); or, b) CLAIM OWNERSHIP RIGHTS (?)

[a) BeOr/216 suggests relationship with Ar saqaṭa "fall" (here in a causative sense). b) LuSemAS5/65 cites this root in Akk and Ar in sense "sting, pierce"; in Sab it may be connected with the Near Eastern practice of driving a peg when land is acquired.]
C970/3: bn tḥty d̲n wṯnn yd̲qṭn N "N. sacrifices beneath this boundary stone," or, "according to this boundary stone, N. claims ownership rights"; same formula C466/3 and prob elsewhere in fragmentary contexts

D̲QN

n^{1} s̲ d̲qn(n) R4050/2+; b-d̲qnhw C618/4

FORE PART, VESTIBULE; in p̲p̲ b-d̲qn: IN FRONT OF

[Ar d̲aqan "chin." For prepositional use, cf Heb lipnê, le'appê "before, in front of" (lit., "at the face," "at the nose").]
R4050/2: hḥd̲]ṯw kl nkl qdm d̲qn m[qbrthmw] "they repaired all the pavement in front of the vestibule (?) of their burial place"; C619/4: 'l bn 'dm... qtbrn bqbrhmw...wb qbr bd̲qnhw "let no servant be buried in their tomb nor in the tomb in front of it"

n^{2} s̲? md̲qnt J552/3+; md̲qnthmw R3564/2; md̲qnthw F95+94/2; p̲? md̲qn C660/4

PLACE FOR RITUAL PROSTRATIONS = ORATORY

[Cf Ar d̲aqan "chin"--which the worshiper holds between his hands (or touches to the floor) during the prostration.]
R4198b/3-4: br'w whšqrn mknt wmd̲qnt "they built and completed a chapel and an oratory"; C660/4: kl md̲qn 'bythmw "all the oratories of their temples"; F77: md̲qnt mśwdhmw "the oratory of their shrine"

Note: R4905/[3] has been restored as d̲n md̲[qn]n, establishing this form unquestionably as the singular; but other restorations are possible.

DR--For n mdrn R2876/6, see under DR'; for dr elsewhere, see under DRR

DR'

v pf dr'w P123/2*

SOW

[Cf Ar zar^c, Eth zar' "seed"; Yem dirē' or direh "durra" (RoVoc/303).]

P123/2: dr'w mhql rh "they sowed the fields of the plateau"

n p mdr' R2876/2; var mdrn ib/6

SOWN FIELDS

[Cf the v dr' "sow" and the month name dMDR'n.]

R2876/2: [']nxl w'^{c}nb wmdr' "palmgroves, vineyards and sown fields"; ib/6: 'nxln w'^{c}nbn wmdrn, same tr

DRW--For v hdrw J575=Ry539/4, see under DRR h

DR^c--In fragmentary context, n? dr^c F120/7: ...] ^{c}dy dr^c 'blm wbn dr[... no tr. RyET/72 cfs Ar name of a measure dr^c "arm's reach." In fragmentary context, n mdr^{c}m R4158/9: ...] wtryd mdr^{c}m w[..., no tr.

DRR

h pf hdrw J575/4; pass.prt m.s mhdrm F71/6+

SCATTER, DISPERSE an enemy; prt mhdrm: WIDESPREAD, EXTENSIVE

[Ar darra "strew, scatter"; cf also Ar roots drw, dry same senses.]

J575/4: wrdw...b^{c}ly '^{c}sd...hdrw hmt '^{c}sdn "they came down upon the enemy warbands and scattered those warbands"; F71/6: sqym mhšfqm bMRB wsryhw mhdrm "abundant irrigation water in M. and its 2 valleys, widespread"; note also J851/7: sqym mhdrm "widespread irrigation water"

n^1 s drm J735/13*

adv: WIDELY, EXTENSIVELY (cf mhdrm "widespread, extensive")

J735/13: flash floods sqyw kl 'srrn drm "provided irrigation water for all the valleys, extensively"

n^2 s? hdrn Sh8/3; d hdry Sh18/2

FLOOD BASIN (contexts somewhat obscure)

Sh18/2: wsqy(n) whšfqn MRB whdry srrnhn "irrigated abundantly M.and the 2 flood basins of the 2 valleys"; Sh8/3: sqym whdrn (read hdrm?) 'srr MRB "irrigation and flood basin (?) of (?) the valleys of M."

n^3 For n tdrm J720/5, see under NDR I

DT

dm^1 dtn J652/22-3*

demonstrative pn, f.s: THIS (ONE)

[Cf Ar f.s relative ḏāt.]

J652/22-3: hqny ḏtn bywm wqhhw mr'hw "he dedicated this (hqnyt 'offering' understood?) when his lord commanded him"

Note: For ḏt in J584/7, see under ḎT rl.

dm[2] ḏt passim; ḏtn Gl537/3 (but see Note)

demonstrative adj, f.s: THIS

Gl537/3: hqnyw...ḏtn mwqntn "they dedicated this reservoir"; J567/13: hqnyw ḏt hqnytn "they dedicated this offering"; J735/6: bqdmy ḏt brq "before this stormy season"

Note: Conceivably the form ḏtn in Gl537 is a demonstrative adj, f dual (no other examples extant).

rl[1] ḏt passim

relative pn, f.s: (THAT) WHICH; (SHE/IT) WHO, (SHE/IT) OF (cf senses of ḏ, rl m.s)

before verbs: C657/3: fnwthw ḏt tsqynhw "its canal which irrigates it"; C375/1: ywm hwfy dt tnb'hw "when (the god) brought about that which He had promised him"

before non-verbs: C579/4-5: bkrtn ḏt ḏhbn "a she-camel calf of gold"; C40/2: nṭ^{c}thmw...ḏt bfnw hwr mḥfdn "their nṭ^{c}t building which is in front of the cistern of the tower"

to indicate clan affiliation, after f.nn.pr: R4057/1: D ḏt S hqnyt "D. of (the clan) S. dedicated" AND ELSEWHERE; after m.n.pr (once): J741/2-3: [H] bn K...SBY'n ^{c}bd ḏt N^{c}MBRL "H., son of K., the Sabaean, servant of (the clan?) N." (or read, the lady--human or divine--of N.?)

in epithets of goddesses, e.g., ḏt B^{c}Dn, ḏt ḤMYm, etc (passim)

Note: The expression šwf ḏt lnh' J584/7, which J tr "he applied himself to it until this...," is prob a f.n.pr "Š. of (the clan) L." Note also an apparent use of ḏt as a p relative in J738/9: 'ṯthmw bnt ḏt G "their wives, daughters of (the clan) G."

cj b-ḏt C76/4 and passim; l-ḏt R3991/13 and commonly; b-ḏtm R4169/3

(1) BECAUSE (usually b-ḏt in this sense)

[Compounds of pps b-, l- + rl ḏt; the form bḏtm shows Qat influence.]

C308/3: they dedicated three statues ḥmdm bḏt hwš^{c}hmw T'LB "in praise because (the god) T. had bestowed on them..." AND OFTEN; R4169/3: ...] wbḏtm hwfyw Y [... "and because they had protected Y."; and cf other examples in the citations under sense[2]

(2) IN ORDER THAT, SO THAT

C76/4: they dedicated this inscription bḏt hwfyhw bms'lhw wbḏt yz'n hwfynhw bms'l because (the god) had granted him (a response) in His oracle and so that He would continue to grant him (responses) through the oracle"; R3991/13: they made a thank-offering bḏt šf [w]mt^{c}n ^{c}bdhw...wl ḏt yz'n T'L[B] šwf wmt^{c}n "because (the god) had saved and delivered His servant, and so that (the god) T. would continue to save and deliver"; J626/17: wkwnt dt hqnytn ldt n^{c}mt wtn^{c}mn lY "and this offer was (made) in order that it might have gone well and will go well for Y."

rl[2] dty J686/2+

relative pn, f.d: THEY TWO OF

J686/2: Ḥ wN dty G hqn[y]tw "Ḥ. and N., the 2 (women) of (the clan) G., dedicated..."; R3913/2: bny...ḥrtnhn dty šltn klwtn "he built the 2 aqueducts of the three water drops"

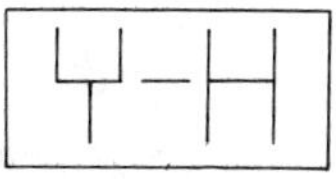

H

ij h- R4589C*

O... (?) (but read prob as part of n.pr)

[Ar hā, Heb ha- id.]

R4589C (in full): hlh HWD^{c}TT mqs[rn] "O God (? elision for h-'lh)! H. (is?) a bondman"--but tr prob "HLH HWD^{c}TT, the bondman"

H II

pn -h passim

suffix pn (f, m and common gender) after verbs and non-verbs

[Cf Ar -hā, -hu id.]

feminine (most common usage): N14/7: hqnyt...lwfy mqmh wls^{c}dh n^{c}mtm "she dedicated (so that the god) would protect her health and grant her prosperity" AND VERY OFTEN

masculine (occasional examples): A682/2: mdbḥt 'BKRB...wrtd mdbḥth "altar of A.; and he placed his altar under the god's protection"

common gender (unique example?): C126/11: 's] 'w 'ntt lh yryśn "[any man] or woman with respect to whom a decree is made" (f pn used by attraction to 'ntt?--common gender represented by -hw elsewhere in the inscription)

H'--defective spelling for HW', HY', q.v.

HB--See under HBB, WHB

HBB

v ipf yhb R2861/1+

INJURE (but see Note)

[Cf Ar hbb D "tear, rend," Akk abbu "devastation."]

R2860/5: ...]wmn lyh(g)rm nkr qntm...wl yh(b) db mś(w)dn [... "and whoever is guilty of damaging a storage pit, or whoever injures what is in the field (?)..."; also in damaged context R2861/1

Note: An alternate tr of R2860/5 would read, "whoever gives (root WHB) what is on the altar/in the shrine..." The n mśwd does not have the sense "field" elsewhere in Sab.

HBṬ

v ipf yh[b]ṭn N74/12-3*

BEAT

[Ar habaṭa id (BeNL4/146).]

N74/12-3: wl yqtrn bmḥrmn [w]l yh[b]ṭn wl y^{c}ḏbn ^{c}šry bl[ṭm] "let him be punished in the temple, let him be beaten and let him be fined twenty blṭ-coins"

HGM--For hgm J578/11, see under HYG

HGN

n s hgn Ry512/1+

(BASTARD) SON, phps specifically SON OF A SLAVE WOMAN

[Ar hagīn "half-breed, the father being nobler than the mother" (RodConf -'69-70/180).]

Ry512/1: Ḥ...hgn qyln Š "Ḥ., (bastard) son of the tribal leader Š." (Ry took as v); R3904/15: hgn 'bhmw "their father's (bastard) son"

HGR

n^{1} s hgr (m,n) J615/11++; hgrhmw C107/2; d hgrnhn J576/4+; hgrynhn N76/2 (RyNE4/168 takes as nisba, unconvincingly); hgry R3946/2; p hgr(n) J576/4+; var 'hgr(m,n) C126/9+

(1) TOWN, CITY--administrative center of a s^{c}b (group of clans)

[Eth hagar id; cf Hamdānī Gaz. 86:3: al-hajar = al-qarya†. ModYem hajar "ruins of an ancient city" (CoRoC/131A). Discussion, BeSemAS4/26-8.]

C126/9: Š w'hgrm "Š. and the (neighboring) towns"; J615/11: kl hgr bythmw "all the towns (or, every town) of their house (= clan-group)"; J629/30: kl hgr wmṣn^{c} "all the towns and fortresses"; AND VERY OFTEN followed by the name of the town, e.g. hgrn MRB "the city Mārib" (J572/7 and often sim)

(2) SETTLED TERRITORY

C37/3: ḥqlm whgrm "cultivated and settled territories"; Ir31: hgrn wsrrn "settled and cultivated territories"

n^{2} p? hgrhmw Ry508/7*

TOWN-DWELLERS

[Metonymically from sense "town"? Cf Eth hagar "town; town-dweller" (DiLLA/20).]

Ry508/7: 'š^{c}b ḏH whgrhmw w'^{c}rbhmw "the tribes(men) of H. and their town-dwellers and their beduins"

HD--For rbHD J1028/12, see under RBB n^{1}, HWD

HDB--For v hdbwhw C448/3, see under DBB h

HDY

v pf hdy RyGrafp561; act.prt m.s hdym J750/11-2

LEAD, GUIDE

[Ar hadâ id.]

RyGrafp561: hdy ^{c}rn ymnytn wš'mytn "he guided the caravan (to) southern and northern parts"; J750/11-2: ftḥm ḏkyn bnhmw b[^{c}m] hdym ḏkd 'fshmw "a lawsuit which was originated by them against the guide who had treacherously endangered their lives (by losing them in the desert)"

HDR

n^{1} p 'hdr C308/7; 'hdrhw ib/9

CISTERNS, or some other part of the irrigation apparatus

[Akk adāru "container (for water)" (cited from Bezold by Irv/331n178); cf also Ar hadīr "noise of running water."]

C308/7: 'hdr msqytn wmštr^{c}n "cisterns (?) of the canal-irrigated and well-irrigated lands"; ib/9: qšmtn w'hdrhw w'kfrhw wṣwrthw "the orchard, its cisterns (?), sluices and embankments"

n^{2} s mhdrn C359/8+

GRAVE, TOMB (?)

[Cf Sab xdr, Phoen hdr id. But as the consonant does not correspond, cf also Akk adāru "Metalgefass" (rare) -- phps a hollowed rock container (for water, or for use as a grave).]

C359/8: trṯḏ T'LB ḏn mhdrn "this tomb is placed under (the god) T.'s protection"; G1443: he acquired xdrn wmhdrn "the grave and the tomb"

Note: C emended to mxdrn in C359, prob unnecessarily. Note also a possible cognate in Talmudic hădar "return, go back, repeat."

HW

pn^{1} hw C518/3*

independent personal pn, 3m.s: HE/IT

[Ar huwa id.]

C518/3: ḏhw bydn ḏqlḥn "which is near the cultivated land"

pn^{2} -hw passim

suffix pn (3s, m, f and common gender), after verbs and non-verbs

[Ar -hu, hā id. For discussion of f use in Sab, see BeDGESA/37:3.]

masculine usage passim: J664/8-9: hqnythw ḏšfthw "his offering which he had promised Him (i.e. the god)"; R4935/4: kl ḏlhw "all that belonged to him" AND VERY OFTEN

feminine usage, after verbs: C581/13-4: stml't b^{c}m 'LMQH wh' [y]ṯbhw "she asked (a response) of (the god) I. and He answered her" AND ELSEWHERE; after non-verbs: J770/9: bnhw ^{c}mn 'shw "her son by her husband"; A788/2: hqnyt mr'hw "she dedicated to her lord" AND ELSEWHERE

and normally to indicate common gender

HW'

pn h' J702/15+; var hw' J631/14+ (and cf under HY' pn)

demonstrative pn, m.s, used pre-verbally and, with compound subjects, post-verbally: HE, HIM

[Cf Ar huwa, Eth we'etu "he (independent pn)."]

pre-verbal: J702/15: wh' fl śyf "and as for Him, may He grant..." AND ELSEWHERE

post-verbal: J631/14: t'wlw...hw' wkl šw^chw "they returned, he and all his followers"; J564/12: wqhhmw lnẓr...h' w'xhw "he ordered them to guard, him and his brother" AND ELSEWHERE

dm h' J720/13+; var hw' C99/6+

demonstrative adj, m.s.: THAT (sometimes used pejoratively; cf hwt id) J720/13: h' ḥlzhw "that disease of his"; R4767/3: h' dbḥ "that sacrifice"; C99/6: hw' srn "that valley"; AND OFTEN, usually followed by a nunated noun; note esp pejorative use, e.g., J585/15: stškr h' 'sn "that fellow (= the enemy) was defeated"

HWD

n p HD J1028/12; var HWD Ry515/5

JEWRY, THE JEWS, in exp rbH(W)D "Lord of the Jews," epithet of the god RḤMN (cf YHD sim)

[Ar al-hūd id, secondary form from YHD, q.v.]

Ry515/5 (end of inscription): rbHWD bRḤMNn "Lord of the Jews. By (the god) R."

HWN

D inf hwn J722/c*

SOOTHE, APPEASE

[Ar hwn D "render light, easy," hawn "comfort."]

J722/c: wlyxmrn...'mhhw hwn lhn lbhw "may (the god) grant to His maid-servants to appease His heart toward them"

n s hwnt Gl773b/3*

COMFORT, CONVENIENCE (?)

[Ar hīna[†] id.]

Gl773b/3: wsqy ^{c}TTR hwnt [hmythw w]hḍybhw "(the god) A. has provided irrigation waters (with) the comfort (?) of [His rains and] showers"

HW^c--For hw^c R4585B, see under W^cY h

HWF

n s hwfm C545/3*

SLAVE, SERVANT (?)

[CoRoC/131B cfs Ar hūf "idle, stupid man"; MüW/110 considers the comparison too uncertain.]

C545/3: hqny...^{c}bdm whwfm "he dedicated a slave and a servant (?)"

Note: In C372/1, hwfhmw is phps a n.pr.

HWR I

n s hwr C40/2+; hwrhmw C540/17; var? hwrtn C421/5; d hwry R3943/5

(1) BASIN for ritual ablution

[Ar hūr "pond, natural basin."]

R3943/5: bny...hwry xlf mḥdrn "he built the 2 basins outside the (temple) forecourt"; C434/4: bnyw...mḥrmn...bn dt hwrtn ^{c}dy ṣlwt "they built the temple from this basin to the side (of the building)"

(2) CHANNEL or WATERCOURSE

C540/17: ǵyln hwrhmw...whwr MFLLm "the bed of the exit channel and the bed of M. (the righthand channel)"; C40/2: they built their bastion dt bfnw hwr mḥfdhmw "which is in front of the watercourse of their tower"

Note: In some instances (e.g., C40/2), the tr "behind" has been proposed, after Ar warā'a id. In C434/4, CoRoC/132A and MüW/110 tr "back part of a building." For hwry C318/4, see under WRY h.

HWR II

v ipf yhwr Gl767*

DESTROY (?) (cf n hyrt under HYR II)

[Ar hāra (w) "be destroyed, collapse."]

Gl767: ...]n yhwr ^{c}d[... "...he shall destroy (?)..."

HWT

pn hwt J584/3+

demonstrative pn, 3m.s: THAT ONE, HIM (used post-verbally with compound subject, like hw'; both examples accusative)

[Cf Eth we'etu "he."]

J584/3: mt^{c}hw...hwt wbnhw "(the god) saved him, him and his son"; J649/27: wqhhmw...hwt wsb^{c}y wm't 'sdm "he commanded them, him and 170 soldiers"

dm hwt J577/7+

demonstrative adj, m.s: THAT (cf hw' id; all clear examples accusative, post-prepositional, or adverbial); sometimes pejorative

accusative: J577/7: škr hwt 'χsn "he defeated that fellow (= the enemy)"

post-prepositional: J590/2: t'wln bn hwt tqdmn "to return from that battle"; J653/13: bmw hwt wrxn "in that month"

adverbial: tqdmw b^{c}mhmw hwt ywmn "they attacked them (on) that day"; J633/9: yḥlẓn hwt ḥlẓn "he suffered (from) that disease"

Note unique usage with plural n: R4193/11: kl hwt 'gyš[n] "all those troops"

HḤR--For v ḥhr, see under ḤWR h

HY

pn -hy Sh18/2+

suffix pn, 3f.s, post-nominal: HER/ITS (rare; but see Note)

[Cf Ar -hā id, hiya "she."]

Sh18/2: 'DNT w'^{c}ḍdhy "(the area) A. and its diversion moles" (cf the parallel text F71/8: 'DNT [w]'^{c}ḍdhw); J629/29: mḥrmt whyklt w'b'r wmsqy bxlfhy "temples and palaces, and the wells and irrigation works in their (lit., her--f.s for inanimate p as in Ar?) vicinity"

Note: LuMus86/185 considers these rare examples errors for more common -hw.

HY'

pn h' J619/7-8* (and cf under HW' pn)

demonstrative pn, 3f.s: THAT ONE, IT (cf hyt id)

[Cf Ar hiya, Eth ye'eti "she (independent pn)."]

J619/7-8: dqt wdq ^{c}ln 'blhw bh' byn kr^{c} 'blhw "the fall he took because of his camel, in which his camel's knee was dislocated"

dm h' R4815/5+; var hy' C40/4

demonstrative adj, f.s: THAT

R4815/5,7: h' fnwtn "that canal"; C40/4: rfdt hy' mwrtn "the revetments of that retaining wall"

HYG

n p? hgm J578/11*

DISTURBANCE > WAR

[Cf Ar hayjā "tumult, disturbance, war" (BeNL7/540-1).]

J578/11: ^{c}sm sb'tm wb^{c}wtm whgm "numerous campaigns, attacks and wars"

HYHR

n s hyhr(n) C82/5+

HARVEST (?); or specific KIND OF CROP

[Sense from contexts.]

C82/5: s^{c}dhw...hyhrn bṯwrhw "(the god) granted him a harvest (?) in exchange for (?) his bull"; C408/11: xmr ^{c}bdhw...hyhr wfr^{c} "(the god) granted His servant hyhr-crops (?) and fr^{c}-crops (or, a harvest and first-fruits)"

Note: For hyhr elsewhere, see under YHR h.

HYKL

n p hyklt J629/28-9*

PALACES or TEMPLES

[Cf Ar haykal "temple," Heb hêkāl "palace; temple."]

J629/28-9: wṯr wqm^c mḥrmt whyklt "he leveled and destroyed temples and palaces"

HYL

n *s* hyl R4818/6*

ASSAULT; or, FEAR (?)

[Cf Ar hāla (y) "pour," *L* "shower (upon), assail, fall (upon)"; or, cf Ar hawl "terror."]

R4818/6: may the god keep away hyl [w']ṭly wmnḍ^c šn'm "assault/fear, insults and injury (caused by any) enemy"

HY^c

v *pf* h^c R4963/2+; *var* hy^c R3946/7+; *ipf* yh^{c}n Gl532; *inf* hy^c C99/9+

CAUSE TO FLOW > (1) OFFER, SACRIFICE (libations, blood sacrifices?)

[Cf Ar hā^{c}a (y) "flow, spread out (of dense liquids, esp molten metals)" (BiKa/1467-8). Sab *v* is transitive and may include *D* forms, though the stem h^c in *pf* and *ipf* suggests that not all are *D*.]

C99/9: f'lśnw xdl hy^c "and they are not allowed to cease sacrificing"; R4963/2: ym h^c śl' "when he offered an offering"; C306: ywm h^c ḥrmtm "when he sacrificed (in) the sanctuary"; R3946/7: ywm hy^c mhy^c L ^{c}ṮTR "when he sacrificed (in) the shrine of L. (to the god) A."

(2) PROVIDE WATER FOR

Gl532: lyh^{c}n...hy^{c}m "to provide water (by means of) a flow"; C617/1-2: w'l śn hy^c msb'n 'nsm sb^{c}rm "this conduit must not provide water for man or beast"; R4815/7: 'l ymn^{c}w bny R...bn hy^c lhmw h' fnwtn "the b.R. shall not prevent this canal from providing water for their benefit (i.e., for the benefit of the b.S.)" sim exp C611/7-8

(3) SPREAD (?) (transitive or intransitive?--context obscure)

F3/8: wlhy^c whwṣln lkl ḥšk "and let (knowledge of this edict) spread/be spread and be propagated (?) (down) to every prohibition"

(4) PERFORM (?)

J831/2: kl 'ḍb' wmwṣtt hy^c "all the engagements and affrays he has performed (?)"

Note: Cf also *v* hw^c, under W^{c}Y *h*.

n^1 *s* hy^{c}m C464/3+

(1) FLOW OF WATER

Gl532 quoted under HY^c *v* sense^2

(2) LIBATION

C464/3: f[l y]'mrn hy^{c}m sdy[m] "and let him proclaim 'a libation (of blood) poured out'"

n^2 *s* mh^c Ry507/7*

LIBATION (?) (cf hy^c sense^2)

Ry507/7: mh^c wxmrtm 'xny "a libation (?) and numerous gifts (?)"

(context obscure)

n[3] s mhy^c(n) R3946/7+; p mhy^{c}tn C338/10

PLACE OF LIBATIONS = SHRINE, SANCTUARY

J550/1: he dedicated kl mǵbb wmḥfdt dn mhy^{c}n "all the ramparts and towers of this sanctuary (= the Mārib temple)"; R3946/7: ywm hy^c mhy^c ...^{c}TTR "the day he sacrificed (in) the shrine (to the god) A."; ib/15: mhy^c 'wtnn "shrine of the boundary stones"; C338/10: tqdm...'ln mhy^{c}tn "he undertook (the building of) these sanctuaries"

HYR I

n s hrthw C939/3-4; hrthmw C378/4-5+

PLAIN; LEVEL, CULTIVATED LAND

[Yem hayra† "plain," Mh hôyer "abyss, precipice" (MüW/111); Ar hūr "swampy terrain"--moist ground in a depression (Irv/213).]

F124/7: 'bythmw whrthmw "their settled and cultivated territories"; C378/4-5: bql bhrthmw "he planted in their level land"; C392/4-6: 'tmr w'f[ql] yknn bhrthmw "the crops and harvests which are in their level land"

Note: In R4085/4-5 read prob br' w^{c}s' bh(m)t [not hrt] ['n]xln "constructed and built in those palmgroves"

HYR II

n s hyrtn C334/9*

DESTRUCTION, CRUSHING DEFEAT (?) (cf HWR II v)

[Cf Ar hāra (y) "be destroyed, collapse."]

C334/9: [^{c}syw] hyrtn š^{c}bn R bhwt ywmn dtq[dmw] "the tribe R. [inflicted] a crushing defeat (?) in that battle which they fo[ought]"

HYT

dm hyt J576/5+

demonstrative adj, f.s: THAT (only in oblique cases?)

[Cf Ar hiya, Eth ye'eti "she."]

accusative: J576/5: hb^{c}ln hyt hgrn "to take possession of that city"; J686/5: xmrhw wldm hyt mr'tn "(the god) granted her a child, (namely) that girl" AND ELSEWHERE

genitive: J576/5: sby wqny hyt hgrn "prisoners and livestock of that city" AND ELSEWHERE

post-prepositional: J610/9: hwfyhmw bn brdm...bhyt brqn "(the god) protected them from cold in that stormy season" AND ELSEWHERE

Note unique usage with plural n: C334/21: bn kl hyt sb'tn "from all those campaigns" (normally kl hnt sb't, J650/22 and elsewhere sim). (But phps this instance should be tr as s "that campaign.")

HLL

n p 'hlm R4085/5*

CISTERNS (?)

[Cf Ar halla^{t} "vessel containing a lampwick and oil = a lamp" (Freytag 4/401, quoting Q.]

R4085/5: br' w^{c}s' bh(m)t ['n]xln 'rb^{c}t 'hlm w'ḥrrhmw "he built and constructed in those palmgroves four cisterns and their (outlet) canals"

HLK

v pf hlky N27/4-5*

CONFORM, COMPLY (?)

[Sense suggested by RyNE4/164, who cfs Qat yhlkwn R3691/9 id, and Heb hālak "go, direct one's self."]

N27/4-5: whlky ywm fdyt mwklh "and they complied (?) on the day she acquitted herself of her payment"

HLM--For v hlm, see under LMM h

HM I

cj hm C548/6+

IF (cf hn id, under HN I)

[Cf Ar 'in, Heb 'im, Mh hem id.]

C548/6: whm lm ydmw "and if blood is not flowing (the penalty is less severe)"; R4088#55/4: whm 'l t'xd fhlt nfshw "and if he does not give himself up, his life is forfeit" AND ELSEWHERE SIM

HM II

pn^{1} hm Ry508/2*

independent pn, 3m.p: THEY (cf more common hmw id)

[Ar hum id.]

Ry508/2: khm ^{c}m mr'hmw "when they were with their lord"

pn^{2} -hm C20/2+

suffix pn, 3m.p: THEM, THEIR (cf more common -hmw id)

[Ar -hum id.]

C20/2: ^{c}s'w...mqbrhm "they built their tomb"; C341/8: wl s^{c}dhm "and may (the god) grant them..." AND ELSEWHERE

HMW

pn^{1} hmw J574/8+

independent pn, 3m.p: THEY (pre-verbal, or post-verbally with compound subjects)

[Ar hum(^{u}) id.]

2/7-8: whmw fḥmdw "and as for them, they praised..."; J574/8: t'wlw hmw w'qwlhmw "they returned, they and their tribal leaders" AND OFTEN pn^2 -hmw J588/7++

suffix pn, 3m.p: THEM, THEIR

[Ar -hum(^{u}) id.]

after verbs: J588/7: wlxmrhmw ḥẓy wrḍw "may the god grant them favor and good will" AND VERY OFTEN

after non-verbs: J588/11: ls^{c}dhmw...wfy grybthmw "may He grant them the safety/well-being of their bodies"; J586/18: hrgw bnhmw sb^{c}t w^{c}šry "they killed some of them--twenty-seven" AND VERY OFTEN

Note: Sometimes written independently, as in J644/30: hqnyt hmw "their offering"; Fl19/8: 'tw hmw "(He) brought them back."

dm hmw C609/5+

demonstrative adj, m.p: THOSE (sometimes pejorative) (cf hmt id)

[Cf Ar hum(^{u}) "they."]

C609/5: hmw 'sṭrn wš'mtn "those documents and deeds of sale" AND ELSEWHERE; pejorative sense, e.g. J576/16: whmw 'ḤMRn f'syw lhmw wkym "and as for those Ḥimyarites (= the enemy), they sent them aid"

HMY I

D pf hmy Gl772/4+

CAUSE RAIN TO FALL (said of a god)

[Cf Ar hamâ "flow, pour forth (said of tears)." Also of clouds shedding rain (Dozy2/765A); hamya^t "light rain."]

Gl772/4: wfdyhw whmy ^{c}TTR SB'n wgwm "when (the god) A. freed him (the eponym) and caused rain to fall (over) S. and the community" (v is sqy in parallel texts); Gl687 end: whmy[...] whmy xrf wdt' SB' "He caused rain to fall (over) S. (in) autumn and spring"

HMY II

pn^1 hmy J578/31+

independent pn, 3d: THEY TWO, THOSE TWO

[Ar humā id.]

J578/31: ^{c}bdyhw...hmy wš^{c}bhmy "(the god's) 2 servants, they two and their tribe"; J576/10-1: stml'w b^{c}m 'LMQH khmy bṣdqm "they asked of (the god) I. that those two (bulls seen in a vision) should (exist) in reality" AND ELSEWHERE

Note: J tr the compound k-hmy in J567 and elsewhere as "if," treating it as a var of k-mhnmw, k-m^{c}nmw (see under MHN II, M^{c}N). But in the relevant texts J567 and C581/9 dual referents are present, and in J729/9 the damaged context throws doubt on the reading; phps [km^c]nmy (or the like) should be restored.

pn^2 -hmy J594/6+

suffix pn, 3d: THEM BOTH, THEIR

[Ar -humā id.]

J594/6: wl s^cdhmy 'LMQH...wfy grybthmy "may (the god) I. grant them both the safety/well-being of their bodies"; J629/9: S wM wb^{c}mhmy 'dmhmy "S. and M. and their servants with them" AND ELSEWHERE

Note: In 4985/2 the fragment [...]ṯhmn has been interpreted as a noun or verb with a variant dual suffix.

dm^1 hmy J651/20*

demonstrative adj, d: THOSE TWO (m only? cf hmyt, dm^2 id)

[Cf Ar humā "they two (independent pn)."]

J651/20: wdqy hmy btnhn "those 2 houses collapsed"

dm^2 [h]myt C326/1(+?); var hmt J629/39+

demonstrative adj, d (m and f): THOSE TWO (cf hmy dm^1 id)

[For the final -t, cf the dm hmw and its var hmt.]

J629/39: bhmt sb'tnhn "in those 2 campaigns"; J643/22: 'b^{c}l hmt hgrnhn "the citizens of those 2 cities"; also with hgr ib/23; C326/1: [h]myt š^{c}bynhn "those 2 tribes"

Note also J574/7: bhmyt 'kdnn "in those 2 plowed fields (?)"--root of the n is presumably KDN, and the form, if dual, may be aberrant. The normal d kdnn occurs in ib/4.

HMS

v inf hms(n) J574/13+

BREAK DOWN an enemy

[Ar hamasa id.]

J574/13: hwš^{c}nhmw bwḍ^c wṯbr whms whkms kl ḍrhmw "to help them in humbling, crushing, breaking down and subduing their every foe" AND ELSEWHERE in similar contexts

HMR

n s hmr C523/8*

EJACULATION of semen (?)

[Cf Ar hamara "flow out (water, etc)."]

C523/8: he vowed penance because nḍx 'kswt(h)w hmr "he had spattered his clothes (with) semen (?)"--in an enumeration of various sexual offences

HMT

dm hmt J564/14+

demonstrative adj, 3m.p: THOSE (only in oblique cases? and often in pejorative sense; cf hmw id)

[Cf Eth 'emuntu, Phoen hmt "they."]

J564/14: bkl hmt 'wrxn "during all those months"; C74/14: lgtnnn lhmt 'srrn "to gather the produce (?) of (?) those valleys"; in pejorative sense, e.g. J601/9: yṯbrw...hmt 'ḤBŠn "they crushed those Ḥabashites"

Note: For a possible var hmyt, see Note to HMY II dm^2.

HN I

cj hn C542/7+; b-hn C523/2+

(1) WHEN; IF

[Ar 'in, Mh hen "when; if." Cf also Sab hm "if" (HM I).]

C542/7: [bR]ḤMNn...hn ᶜnn "[by the god] R., when He manifests Himself"; C548/2: hn lyngsn slḥhw...lyzlᶜn "if he defiles his weapons, let him pay a fine"

(2) BECAUSE

[Extension from conditional use.]

C523/2: he confessed bhn qrb mr'tm...whn bh' ᶜly nfsm whn bh' ǵrṭhr "because he had approached a woman (sexually), and because he had had intercourse with a woman unclean after childbirth, and because he had had intercourse (in a state of ritual) impurity..."; sim in other confessions, R3956/3, R3957/5, C533/2; C547/3: they confessed hn 'l hwfyhw mṭrdhw "because they had not duly rendered to (the god) his mṭrd-ritual"

HN II

pn -hn J804/2-3+

suffix pn, 3f.p: THEM, THEIR (used only of animate beings)

[Ar -hunna id.]

post-verbal: J804/2-3: [wlx]mrhn rḍw "[may the god gr]ant them good will" AND ELSEWHERE

post-nominal: J649/40: rkbm brḥlhn "(female) riding camels with their saddles"; F3/5: 'nṯn wkl 'wldhn "the women and all their children" AND ELSEWHERE

post-prepositional: J722/c: may the god grant hwn lhn lbhw "(that he may) appease His heart toward them"; C532/8: she confessed certain sins, 'l bhn šᶜrt w'l lm tš(ᶜ)r "those of which ('l bhn) she was conscious and those which ('l) she was not (lm) conscious of" (syntax somewhat doubtful)

Note: For hnm Ry443/4, see under HNM.

dm hn C376/14(+?)

demonstrative adj, f.p: THOSE (cf hnt id)

[Cf Ar hunna "they (independent pn, 3f.p)."]

C376/14: hn blṭn 'lfn "those thousand blṭ-coins"; phps also C562/6: 'l s'l...hn ḥrḍm wᶜgdm xbṭm "let no one lay claim to those (?) ...s and pressed grapes"

Note: C562/6 may represent a usage in which collective nouns are treated as feminines (here f.p, as several ns which may be collective appear). C suggests, however, than hn in this instance is a unique example in Sab of a pp also found in Ḥaḍ (R2640/2), where it is clearly synonymous with bn; C would tr "no claim arising from (?) ...s," or the like.

HN'

n adj: m.s hn'(m,n) C86/5-6+; f.p? hn't R3966/9

adj: PLEASING

[Cf J.Aram hn' "be pleasant, be of use," Ar hani'a "take pleasure in, enjoy."]

C86/5-6: 'wldm 'd̲krwm hn'm "male, pleasing children" AND OFTEN SIM; J704/4: 'wldm 'd̲krm hn'n "male, pleasing children"; R4193/16: 't̲mrm 'ly kwkbt ṣdqm hn'm "fortunate, satisfying, pleasing crops"; R3966/9: hn't bn 'ẓrbhmw "pleasing (crops?) from their landed property"

HNW--In C325/6, hnwm (isolated after lacuna). C takes as n.pr; MüW/109 takes as n, tr "success" (cf root HN').

HNM

? hnm Ry443/4*

sense doubtful; see Note

Ry443/4: w'l db^{c}lyhmw d̲'A hnm w'l d̲[... "and these things (??) are what is incumbent upon d̲A., and what is..."

Note: Such a tr would associate the word with hn (independent pn, 3f.p), phps with enclitic -m, but this analysis is doubtful (cf Be DGESA/40:12).

HNT

dm hnt J577/16+

demonstrative adj, f.p: THOSE

[Cf -hn, 3f.p suffix pn (HN II); for final -t, cf hmw and hmt, m.p demonstrative adjs.]

J577/16: hmt ḍby'n wsby'n "those battles and campaigns"; J578/13: hnt sb'tn "those campaigns"; F76/4: hnt 'nt̲n "those women"

H^{c}--See under HY^{c}

HF^{c}

n s hf^{c} J651/53*

sense doubtful; an injury inflicted by an enemy

J651/53: may the god protect him bn b'stm wnkytm...wšf^{c} whf^{c}...kl šn'm "from harm, injury, invasion or...? of any enemy"

Note: JSIMB/159 cfs implausibly Ar nafa^{c}a "be useful," tr advantage."

HḌB

n p hḍybhw GI773b/4*

SHOWERS of rain

[Ar haḍba† "a rain consisting of many drops, a lasting rain" (Lane/2896C).]

Gl773b/4: sqy ^{c}T̠TR hwnt [hmythw w]hḍybhw "(the god) A. provided irrigation waters (with) the comfort (?) of [His rains and] His showers"

HḌG--In obscure and fragmentary context C405/12: ...] hḍgm b(ǵ)zwtm b'^{c}rr[n... "...? in raids (?) in the mountains..."--C cfs Ar ḍagama "be oblique," Eth ḍagām "left (hand)," tr "adversus est."

HQB--For hqb C149/1, C462/6, see under QBB h̠ and n̠

HQF--For hqwf J541/8, see under QWF h̠

HQR

n s hqrn BeGlean51-2/2*
TOWN (var of hgr id)
[BeGlean/52 cites the frequent confusion of q and g in many Arabic dialects, including those of present-day South Arabia.]
BeGlean51-2/2: bbḍ^c hqrn H "in the territory of the town H."

HRB

v pf hrbw Ry507/5*
FLEE (?)
[Ar haraba id.]
Ry507/5: whrgw...whrbw k[... "they killed...and fled (?)"
Note: Ry wrongly cfs C365/6, where this root is not found.

HRG I

v pf hrg J575/7+; hrghmw J665/22+; hrgw J586/18+; ipf yhrgn J631/30+; yhrgnhw R4088#55/6+; yhrgw J575/7+; yhrgwhmw J644/19 (doubtful form; read prob yhrg(n)hmw); inf hrg J575/7+
KILL
[Heb hārag id; cf Ar hrj D̠ "drive a camel roughly and without rest," harj "bloodshed."]
C78/4: s^{c}dhw hrg mhrg ṣdqm "(the god) allowed him to make satisfactory killings (in battle); R3945/18: hrghmw šlṯt 'lfm "he killed them (to the number of) three thousand"

ti inf htrgn Ir32/25*
BEAT ONE ANOTHER TO DEATH
Ir32/25: wtqdmw whtrgn "they fought together and beat one another to death"

tp pf thrgw J649/32*
EFFECT A SLAUGHTER
J649/32: twś^{c}w wtqdmn...wthrgw b^{c}mhmw "they attacked in force and effected a slaughter among them"

n p mhrg(m) J576/9+; var mhrgtm J629/18+
SLAUGHTERS, KILLINGS (one of the desirable things obtained in battle);

phps also BATTLE

J576/9: yhrgw bnhmw mhrgm $\underline{d}^c$sm "they made a number of killings among them (= the enemy)"; J644/24: wkwn kl mhrg lfyw $\check{s}^c$bn "and (these) were all the killings (by which) the tribe obtained blood revenge"; J629/18: they returned from campaign bmhrgt wǵnmt ṣdqm "with satisfying killings and booty" AND OFTEN SIM; R3945/13: wrww bmhrg G "they rebelled in the slaughter (battle?) of G."

HRG II

v   pf hrg C939/2-3*

LITIGATE

[Cf MSA haraja "speak, discuss," Te täharädä "haggle, jest" (Irv/328n126).]

C939/2-3: $\underline{d}$hrg b^{c}ly msqt hrthw 'db "he who litigates over the irrigation of his level ground will be punished"

HRY

v   pf hryt J751/6*

BE COLD (temperature, weather)

[Cf Ar huri'a "be very cold (wind, atmospheric temperature)."]

J751/6: mt^{c}n grbhw bn hry hryt bxrf S "saved his life from the bitter cold which befell in the year (named for) S."

n   s hry J751/6* (takes f verb)

BITTER COLD, LOW TEMPERATURE

J751/6 quoted under HRY v

HRK

n   s mhrkm F119/8*

BOOTY

[Eth mehrekā id (BeNL7/542).]

F119/8: w'tw hmw bwfym wmhrkm "(the god) brought them back (from campaign) with health and booty"

Note: Ry emended to mh(b)rkm; MuW/58 assigns to root RWK, tr "together" after Ar mal al-rōk "common property."

HRM

n   s hrm C86/10; p 'hrm C429/5

WEAKNESS

[Ar harima "become decrepit" (HaAED/817).]

C86/10: wl gybhmw bn hry wlsn wm^{c}ḍw whrm "may (the god) protect them from harm, calumny, despite and weakness"; C429/5: $\check{s}$ṣyt w'ṭly w'hrm "evil eye, insults and weaknesses"

HRS--For v hrs, see under RSY h

HRT-- For n hrt, see under HYR I; for n mhrt R4069/5, read mḥrg (?) and see under ḤRG

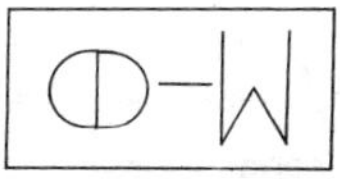

W

cj w- passim

coordinating conjunction: (1) simple, AND

[Ar wa- and many Sem cognates. Discussion BeDGESA/52:1-9, HöASG/166.]

J617/8: xrf wdṯ' ws^{c}s^{c}m wmlym "autumn and spring and summer and winter harvests"; R4196/2: br'w whwṯr whšqr m'glyhmw "they built and laid the foundations of and completed their 2 cisterns"

(1a) TOGETHER WITH

R4627/6: S...wkl qnyhw w'dmhw "S., together with all his slaves/livestock (?) and clients"

(2) adversative, BUT

R3945/15-6: he destroyed the wall of his town N., whgrn N yhḥrm bn mwftm "but the town N. he forbade to be burnt"

(3) OR

C126/8: mn 's w'nṯt "whoever, man or woman..."

(4) introducing second part of sentence

apodosis: F30/7: 'hnmw ^{c}kr wl yyf^{c}n "whenever it is contested, yet let it be upheld"

description of attendant circumstances (cf Ar ḥāl-clauses): C548/2-4: hn lyngsn slḥhw wdmwm bšy^{c}hw "if he has defiled his weapons, there being blood on his garment..."

introducing predicate when subject or verbal complement precedes the verb (cf usage of f-): C334/12-3: wḥrt mr'hmw...wwfyt "and as for the camp of their lord, it was saved"; R4193/10: wbxlf bythmy wxmrhmy "and outside their house, there (the god) granted to them both..."

(5) as first word in inscription

C570/1: wkwn lnxln "Now, let the palmgrove have..."; C376/1: wśxly "Now, they two bound themselves..."

Note: When w- links vs in sequence, the first is typically finite, the rest infinitives, e.g. F72/2-3: hwṯrw wbr' whšqrn "they laid the foundations and built and completed."

When w- precedes the ipf, a modal or consequential translation is often required: R3945/16: ^{c}tb... 'l wḍ^{c}t šfthmw...wyhrgw "he designated those whose dedication was ordained, so that they would be slain"; ib/2: hṯb mwy dhbhw...wykn fnwtm fnwtm "repaired the water (-supply) of his alluvial land so that it should be arranged canal by canal"

W'Y

ti ipf yt'nn F123/9-10*

ASSURE OF, PROMISE

[Ar wa'â id, ti (itta'â) "exact a promise from" (MüW/111).]

F123/9-10: tb(q)lt yt'nn bqln wrd 'l "plantations (for which) the watering-place l. assures the plants (of water)"

WBL

v ipf ybln G1572/6; [y]blnn R2695/3

PAY TRIBUTE

[Cf Heb hôbîl "bring offerings," Sab blt "send a gift," Akk biltu "tribute."]

G1572/6: sm^{c} ybln k'bd bn Ẓ "a document which prescribes tribute (lit, which pays tribute) forever from Ẓ."; R2695/3: [y]blnn 'kbrw'QYNM...l'mr'-hmw "(let) the leaders of 'A. pay tribute to their lords"

n^{1} s wblm C518/4*

TAX

C518/4: 'rḍ ytlwn lmlk SB' bfnwn wblm "land which shall pay to the king of S. for (its) canals a tax" (C took as n.pr)

n^{2} s? hwbltm C289/15+

TRIBUTE

J576/10: yt'wlw...bhwbltm wmhrgtm w'xydtm "they returned (from campaign) with tribute, slaughters and prisoners/booty"; C289/15: t'wlw...bwfym wḥmdm whwbltm "they returned with safety, praise and tribute" (C emends unnecessarily to hwkltm)

WGH

v inf wgh Ry509/10*

SURPASS IN DIGNITY

[Ar wajaha id (cf wajh "face") (RyclHS/328).]

Ry509/10: wswd wwgh wh[... "and be the chief and surpass in dignity and..." (context doubtful)

Note: Ry read wlh, took as n.pr.

WGL--For n mwgln, see under WLG

WGR

v inf C581/7-8*

CONSTRUCT THE SUPERSTRUCTURE of a building (?)

[Eth wagr "tumulus," Aram yəgar "heap of stones." In Ḥasa and Baḥrayn the superstructure of a tomb is such a heap of stones or earth (RyNE5/

139).]

C581/7-8: 'sn dmz' wwgr bythmw "the man who came and constructed the superstructure of their house (?)"

n s wgr C984/1+

TUMULUS, SUPERSTRUCTURE OF A TOMB

C984/1: wgr wqbr "tumulus and grave"; same formula C985/1

WDD

v ipf ydd D69/1*

LOVE

[Ar wadda id.]

D69/1: lydd ᶜSTR Y bn R "may (the god?) A. love Y. son of R."

st pf stwddw Robin UmmLayla 1/4; inf stwddn Robin al-Mašamayn 1

AGREE

[Geᶜez astawādada "arrange harmoniously" (RobAtt/48).]

Robin UmmLayla 1/4: stwddw wstdlln "agreed to obey"; Robin al-Mašamayn 1: tqhw wstwddn "imposed on themselves and agreed"

n¹ s wdhw R4993/1*

OFFERING (to win favor?)

[Cf Ar wdd Dt "try to gain favor, ingratiate one's self." Also in Min and Qat.]

R4993/1: [hq]ny S wdhw w[b](n)hw...wwldhw "he dedicated to (the god) S. his offering, his son and his children"

n² s? wdd R5059--only word in inscription. A salutation (cf Ar wadd "friendship") or n.pr?

n³ s mwd C967/2+

FRIEND, ADHERENT

[Ug mwdd id, Ar mi/awadd "very loving or affectionate (man)" (Lane/2931B).]

C967/2: ᶜA bn ᶜA bn ḤZFRM dXLL mwd Y wY wK ywm ršw ᶜTTR "A. son of A. of (the clan) Ḥ. of (the tribe) X., friend of Y. and K., when he acted as priest of (the god) A." (typical introduction to an eponym-list inscription; for parallels cf RyclMAM/90-92, 35-7)

WDW

n p 'wdwn C563/2*

WADIS = RIVER VALLEYS (cf WDY n)

[Ar wādī, p 'awdā', 'awdiya† id.]

C563/2: 'wdwn wmsqyn "river valleys and canal-irrigated land"

Note: MüW/78 read 'ᶜdwn, tr "fords" (cf root ᶜDW).

WDY

v pf wdy R3945/3; act.prt m.s wdyn C464/10

FLOW, or CAUSE TO FLOW

[Eth wadaya "pour," Ar 'awdâ "remove, take away"; Ar wādī "watercourse."]
G929/2: 'srr ydynn '^{c}rrn T "wadis which flow (by) the hills (or, citadels) of T."; R3945/3: wdy wt'w zm W "the water of W. flowed and collected (or, the water-system of W. caused (water) to flow and collect)"; C464/10: blood of a sacrificial lamb wdyn bqḥfm "flowing in streams"

n s wd Ry506/5; wdy(n) C540/9+; p 'wdytn J616/26, phps also R4779/4 [...]dytm
WADI = RIVER VALLEY (cf WDW n)
C407/18: ḍb' wdy S "he fought (in) the wadi S." (C emends to ^{c}dy); J616/26: ḥrbhmw bsfl 'wdytn dB "fought them in the lowland of the wadis of B."; Ry506/5: bwd bmnhg T "in the wadi (?) on the road to T."; Ry509/4-5: wdyn M'SL "wadi Māsil" (still so named)

WDN

v inf wdn R3958/2*
PREPARE FOR FLOODING or IRRIGATION
[Cf Ar wudn (Hamdānī, Jazīra^{+} 199.20) "field on a riverbank flooded after sowing"; wadana "moisten" (Irv/153).]
R3958/2: ḥyf wnš' wwdn...kl ḥrt "revetted, banked up and prepared for flooding the whole aqueduct"

st pf stwdn R3945/2*
BE IRRIGATED, RECEIVE IRRIGATION WATER
R3945/2: zm ḥmy M dstwdn bn Ḥ "the channel-system (which) irrigates M., which receives irrigation water from Ḥ."

WD^{c}

st pf std^{c}t F87/7*
ASK FOR (?)
[Cf Ar wada^{c}a "put down"; st may mean "seek/ask for s.th. to be provided"? RyET/57 tr "be desirable (of goods)" from a (dubious) tr of n d^{c}t as "goods."]
F87/7: they dedicated lqbly dxmr dstd^{c}t N "because of what (the god) granted of that which N. asked for (?)"

n s d^{c}t R4176/12*
DEPOSIT (PRICE)
[Cf Ar wadī^{c}a^{+} "deposited amount."]
R4176/12: wḥg qnyn dbḥhw ṯny 'sn...wm'tn d^{c}t "and in respect of the slave whom two men killed, two hundred was the deposit price" (Be2SAIn/71 suggests that this was a public slave, leased to a master who forfeited his deposit when the slave was killed)
For d^{c}t elsewhere see under D^{cc}

WDQ

v pf wdq J619/7; wdqy J651/20

FALL, COLLAPSE

[Eth wadqa id.]

J619/7: dqt wdq ᶜln 'blhw "the fall he took because of his camel"; J651/20: rain fell wwdqy hmy btnhn "and those 2 houses collapsed"

n¹ s dqt J619/7*

FALL

[Eth deqat id.]

J619/7 quoted under WDQ v

n² s wdqt(n) J651/12+

FALL (= WDQ n¹)

J651/12: wdqt wmḥqr bytnhn "the fall and ruin of the 2 houses (after the rainstorm)"; C396/9: ...] bn wdqtn [... "from the fall (?)" (fragmentary context)

WD'

v pf [w]d' R4011/9; ipf yd C335/4 (but see Note)

aux: CONTINUE to do (= WZ' v)

[See under WZ' v.]

R4011/9: [w]d' 'LMQHW m[tᶜ w]hᶜnn "may (the god) I. continue to save and help"; C335/4: wldt yd T'LB sᶜdhw "because (the god) T. continued to bestow on him..."

Note: In R4011/9, this is the reading of HöWZ42/106; R read [w]r'. In C335/4, this is the reading of CoRoC; C read yz.

WDY--For hw[d]yw Ist7630/3, see under WKY h

WHB

v pf R3945/1+; whbhw ib/15+; whbhmw R4049; whbt Ry507/7; whbyhw F30/1; whbw R4134/1+; ipf yhb R2860/5+; yhbn R3910/5

GIVE

[Ar wahaba id.]

J574/11: whbw 'wldhmw 'wtqm "they gave their children as hostages" AND OFTEN with the giving of hostages, 'wtqm or rhnn); R3910/5: flyhbn ᶜśbhw śᶜtn dysb'n bᶜlyhw "let (the person who hires an animal) give (i.e., pay) its hire-price (for) the period he worked it"; R2860/5: wlyh(b) db mś(w)dn "let him give that which is on the altar"

ti ipf ythbnn Gl573/2*

RECEIVE

[Reflexive of WHB v "give" (HöSEG8/40).]

Gl573/2: a claim to money dythbnn l'wrxn kbrhn "which they will receive in several (?) months"

h pf hw[hb]y R4545/[2]*

GIVE (?) (= WHB v)

R4545/[2]: X and Y hw[hb]y 'LMQH "gave to (the god) I...."

n[1] s hbtn J750/7*

GIFT

[Ar hiba† id.]

J750/7: šm l'LMQH (t)'d'm bhbtn "he promised to (the god) I. a payment, consisting of this gift"

n[2] p mwhbt C37/6+

GIFTS, DONATIONS (?) (cf WHB n[1])

C37/6: mwhbt whbw 'bhhw "gifts made (to) his ancestors": ib/7 mwhbt wgd[yt] "donations and gifts"; C131/4: wśqt w[mwh]bt "property (?) and gifts (?)" (RhSLGI/65 read [wh]bt; C read [mkb]bt)

WHN--For n mhn Ry510/4, see under MHN

WHR

tp ipf? [y?]twhr R4920/3 = J527*

SET IN ORDER (?)

[Cf Ḥaḍ mawhar "stick with which beasts are driven" (LaH/738). Other possible cognates are Heb yhr "be stiff, arrogant"; Himyaritic wahar "blaze of the sun," Mandaic yĕhar "shine" (phps related to the Heb) (RabAncWAr/27).]

R4920/3: he worked the land he had leveled w[y?]twhr ᶜMNBṬ "and set ᶜA. (n.loc?) in order" (building context, fragmentary; J read [ys]twhr)

WHT

n p mwhtn R2876/2,4,6*

(WINE?) PRESSES

[Ar wahata "press."]

R2876/2: 'nxl w'ᶜnb wmdr' wmwhtn wmqblt "palmgroves, vineyards, seeded fields, wine presses and leased lands"; other contexts similar

WZ'

v pf wz' J627/9+; wz'y ib/15-6+; wz'w J644/17+; ipf yz R4142/6+; yz' J643b/7+; yz'n C3/9++; tz'n R4149/4; yz'nn J567/18-9+; inf wz' C82/8++; z'n J664/9+

(1) aux: CONTINUE to do (cf WD' v)

[Cf Ar wazaᶜa "distribute among many" (CoRoC/135-6)?]

C82/8: wl wz' 'LMQH šwf wmtᶜn ᶜbdhw "and may (the god) I. continue to assist and save His servant" AND VERY OFTEN in wishes for the god's favor); C3/9: wl yz'n hwfynhmw "and may (the god) continue to protect them" AND VERY OFTEN SIM

(2) aux: DO IN ADDITION or GO ON TO DO

F74/2: wz'w šrᶜw bythmw "in addition, they provided a water supply for their house"; Ir13: dwz'w hrg "those whom they went on to kill"

(3) EXTEND, ADD TO (?) (one example of transitive use)

C541/103-4: wz'w bqdm ^{c}wdn "they extended (?) the settling basin at the front (or, on the east)"

WZ^c

n^1 s z^c Ist7608b/9*

DEFENSE (maṣdar?)

[Ar wizā^c id, waza^{c}a^t "bodyguards."]

Ist7608b/9: s]txlhmw lz^c bḥrn wlṣlḥ Ḥ[MYR] "he appointed them for the defense of the sea and the maintenance of order in Ḥ."

n^2 s wz^c J655/2+; d wz^{c}y J662/3

OFFICER with lawkeeping functions

[Ar wazī^c "chief, officer" (cf BeNL4/139).]

J662/3: wz^{c}y š^{c}bn [S]B' "the 2 officers of the tribe S." (and elsewhere with names of tribes)

WḤB

v pf hwḥbw C291/8; ipf yhwḥbn R3910/7+

sense doubtful

[C and R tr "make a deposit" after the root WHB "give," but the proposed exchange of h and ḥ is unlikely. Cf rather (?) Ar ḥbw "present, give," and phps also Old Aram myḥb (D prt?), last word before signatures in a list of bequests (Papyrus 9/22 in Kraeling, E.G., Brooklyn Museum Aramaic Papyri, Yale Univ. Press, New Haven, 1953, p. 243).]

R3910/7: wmnmw dyhr'bn wyhwḥbn wrqm wd^{c}tm "and whoever enters an agreement and ...s vegetables and d^{c}t-crops..."; also with hr'b C291/9; C291/8: fl ygb'n lb^{c}lh 'nsm dhwḥbw "let the man whom they ...ed return to take possession of it"

WḤD

n cardinal number: k-wḥd C308/12*

ONE, SINGLE; k-wḥd: AS ONE, IN UNISON, TOGETHER (cf k-'ḥd id)

[Ar wāḥid "one," Heb kə'eḥād "together."]

C308/12: tgzmw kwḥd ḍrhmw wslmhmw "they agreed that their war and peace should be in unison (i.e., that they would make war only together)"

WḤL

v inf wḥ[l] R2695/[l]*

WAIT, ALLOW TIME (for a debtor to pay)

[Cf Heb yḥl D "wait."]

R2695/[l]: xmry whnqṣn w'xrn wwḥ[l] "they acted graciously and reduced (the sum owed?) and delayed the time (allowed to pay)"

WXR

v <u>inf</u> wxr R2876/6*

DELAY

[Cf Ar 'xr D̲, Sab 'XR h̲ id.]

R2876/6: qblw wwrd wwxr wtrdn sntn 'rḍtn "they have leased out (lands), and (if? they?) neglect (?) or delay, the law will take effect (?) on the lands"

WṬN

n <u>s</u> mwṭnn C82/7+; mwṭnhmw C408/12+

(1) FORECOURT of temple (?)

[Eth waṭana "begin."]

C532/6: she committed a sin and wḍ't ^{c}dy mwṭnn ǵyr ṭhrm "went out to the temple forecourt (?) (in a state of) impurity"

(2) PLACE OF RESIDENCE

[Ar mawṭin id, prob related to sense ^{1}.]

C408/12: the god granted fr^{c} bm^{c}ls̲tn bmwṭnhmw "crops from the wheatfields in their place of residence"; R4006: gn' mwṭn(h)mw "he walled his place of residence"

(3) BATTLEFIELD

[Ar mawṭin id Qur 9:25+]

C82/7: zxnt zxn bmwṭnn "the wounds he received on the battlefield"; C343/17: hfyhw bn mwṭnn "(the god) protected him from the battlefield"

WẒB--For yẓbnn R4964/13, see under ẒBN

WẒM

h <u>inf</u> hẓmn J700/6+

FREE FROM REPROACH

[Cf Ar waṣama id (IrvBSOAS30/287-8). BeAddenda ib/292 refers to a conjectured NẒM, related to Heb NṢL (in hiṣṣîl); he tr "save, deliver."]

J700/6: the god agreed xlyn whẓmn nfs ^{c}bdhw "to protect and free from reproach the person of His servant"; Ir9/4-5: xmr ṣḥḥ whẓmn bn ǵlyt "agreed to restore and free (them) from hatred"

WYL

ij wylyw R4775/4*

WOE (<u>l-</u> to) (? see Note)

[Cf Ar wayl "distress, woe," Eth waylē "woe!"]

R4775/4 (invocation at end of inscription): b^{c}T̲TR [w]'LMQH wwylyw SMYD^{c} wb'šms wmndḥt 'mlk SB' "by (the gods) A. and I.--and woe to S.! (?)--and by the sun-goddesses and irrigation-gods of the kings of S."

Note: The position is syntactically unlikely for an interjection.

Inscription concerns the breaking of a dam; was S. the perpetrator, here being cursed? RycMus87/257 cites another invocation of SMYD^{c} (without wylyw) in Ir14.

WYN

n s wyn(m) C276/3+; wynhmw C228/2+; wynyhmw GaAntYem/p.540; p 'wyn NNAG13-4/3; 'ywnm R4230C/1; 'ywnhw Robin az-Zâhir 1/3; 'ywnhmw R4194/3

GRAPES > VINEYARD

[Ar.Eth wayn "grapes."]

R4194/3: kl ^{c}šq 'ywnhmw w'rḍhmw "all the strip-cultivated land of their vineyards and field(s)"; also with ^{c}šqt R4230C/1; also with 'rḍ NNAG13-4/3; R4196/2: m'glyhmw...b^{c}ly wynhmw "their 2 cisterns (which are) above their vineyard"; cf also C522/2-3: ...]mḍwn wynm bn ḏysrqn mḥrmhw [...] bn mḥrmhw bqrm wḏ yḍwn wynm [... "the laying waste of a vineyard on the part of (?) one who steals from (the god's?) temple... cattle in His temple; and whoever lays waste a vineyard..." Is this a reference to misuse of temple land (by letting cattle graze on it, or the like)?

Note: In C522 some authors have interpreted w-ynm as a v, see under NWM.

WKB

v pf wkb J575/8+; wkbw J567/11+; ipf ykbnn J576/8 (only this inscription)

(1) ACQUIRE, OBTAIN

[Cf Eth tawakfa, tawakkafa "receive; receive s.o. kindly, for supporting and helping him."]

J567/11: stml'w...wwkbw b^{c}m 'LMQH "they asked and received from (the god) I."; C314/11: wkbw...'ml' ṣdqm "they received satisfying favors" AND OFTEN SIM

(2) HELP, ALLY SELF WITH

[Development from sense^{1} as in Eth.]

J575/8: he dedicated bḏt wkb 'xhw "because (the god) helped his brother"; J576/8: ykbnn bhw ḏM wš^{c}bn M wyhbrrw š^{c}bn M "ḏM and the tribe M. allied themselves there and the tribe M. made a sortie"; sim in ib/9,15, and cf C398/11 under WKB n^{1}

(3) PERFORM a mission, or the duties of an office

Ir13/11: wkb blt(h)mw "he performed their mission" (cf RycMus87/249-50); IrAppII#13/15: wkb ^{c}bdhw...^{c}qbm bhgrn "his servant performed as governor in the city"

h pf hwkbhmw C407/21; ipf yhwkbn R2861/19+; yhwkbnn J576/14; yhwk[..] R2724/[10]; inf hwkbn J660/11

(1) COMPEL, BIND s.o.'s actions

[Cf Eth 'awkafa "accept (a command)."]

C609/4: bhmw yhwkbn kt^{c}lm "whereby he is bound, since he signed"; obscure in R2861/19: hm yhwkbn kḏ yhšfqhw ṯmrn "if he (the god?) be compelled to enrich him with crops..."

(2) COMPEL TO MOVE > MUSTER; PURSUE

J660/11: he commanded him lṭrd whwkbn b'ṯr Ḥ "to hunt and pursue Ḥ."
C407/21: ḥrbhmw...whwkbhmw...^{c}dy ḥmlhmw bḥrn "he fought them and pursued them until he drove them into (?) the sea"; J576/14: yhwkbnn bhw...lšrḥhw "they mustered there to protect/reinforce (?) him"

st pf [st]wkbw J560/12; inf stwkbn ib/10

GIVE AN EXCORT, ACCOMPANY

[Cf Ar wākaba id.]

J560/10-12: blt[hw] mr'hw...^{c}dy 'rḍ ^{c}rbn lstwkbn [whn]qḏn 'ṣ̈ḥb "his lord sent him on a mission to the land of the beduins to escort and rescue the allied troops" [wst]wkbw whnqḏn w'xḏ hmt 'sdn 'ṣ[ḥb]h(mw) "and they escorted and rescued and took possession of those soldiers their allies"

n^{1} s wkbhw C398/11* (or inf, see WKB v sense^{2})

HELP (?)

C398/11: xmrhw...wkbhw b'rḍ X "(the god) granted him His help (?) (or, agreed to help him) in the land of X."

n^{2} D prt?: f.p mykbt J702/16*

THINGS (TO BE) OBTAINED (cf WKB v sense^{1})

J702/16: ^{c}ln dśf dwkb wh' fl śyf ḥwlm mykbt bhw "because he has given that which he obtained, may (the god) give a dream in which (there will be) things to obtain" (discussion RycMancie/265)

n^{3} as adj: f.s. R4781/[2]*

WELL WORKED, WELL CULTIVATED

[Cf Ar wakaba "apply one's self constantly, assiduously to a thing" and Sab mhwkb "well cared-for estate" (Irv/50).]

R4781/[2]: wl t(k)nn 'ln n[xl]nhn fdfdtm m[w]k[b]tm "and let these 2 palmgroves be a source of increase, well cultivated"

n^{4} p mhwkbhmw C308/5,9*

CULTIVATED PLOTS, ESTATES

[Cf WKB n^{3} and Ḍof ukbīt "plantation," ModYem wakab "boundary stone" (RoVoc/303).]

C308/5: kl mhwkbhmw wmsqyhmw "all their estates and canalized land"; ib/9: kl mhwkbhmw krrm wšr^{c} qšmtn "all their estates, all together, and the water channels of the orchard"

WKY

h pf hw[k]yw Ist7630/3*

CAUSE TO BE SUPPORTED = RE-ERECT a building (?)

[Ar wakâ = waka'a "support one's self" (HöSEG8/33).]

Ist 7630/3: hw[k]yw wṯwbn bythmw...wyśfhw sqfm "they re-erected (?) and restored their house and added to it a roof"

Note: BeFSTI/280 read hw[d]yw but did not translate.

tp pf twkyw GI533/12*

SUPPORT ONE ANOTHER, COME TO AN AGREEMENT TOGETHER (?)

GI533/12: kwn dn mṣdqn bkn twkyw bdN "this contract was executed when they came to agreement together (?) in (the month of) dN."

n s wkym J576/16*

SUPPORT

[Cf WKY v and Ar wikāya^t "stick, support."]

J576/16: 'syw lhmw wkym ^cdy dt mẓ'w xlf [hg]r[n] "they sent them support until they arrived outside the city"

Note: For wky Ry507/7, read w-ky and see under KY.

WKL

v pf wkl R4922/4*

ENTRUST TO S.O.'S PROTECTION

[Ar wakala and D id.]

R4922/4: ...]hm ^cx fwkl 'rfthw [... "...15. And he entrusted its boundary stone to (the god's?) protection"

Note: R read fkl; reading fwkl from new photo, GaAION33/436.

tp pf twklhw C528/5*

a) PLACE CONFIDENCE IN; or b) ENTRUST TO a god's PROTECTION (= WKL v)

[a) Ar wkl Dt id. b) Cf WKL v.]

C528/5: ...hgn twklhw...wśf n^cmtm "as he trusted in Him (or, entrusted [an offering] to His protection), He granted him abundant prosperity" (context fragmentary)

st pf stwkl J611/7+; stwklhw J704/3+; stwklw J605/4+; inf stwkln J611/15+

(1) TRUST TO S.O. to do

[Cf Ar ti, Dt id.]

J655/5: stwkl b^cmhw lxmrhw "he trusted to (the god) to grant him..."; J605/4: he dedicated to the god ṣlmn ḥgn stwklhw lwfy bnhw "this statue, as he trusted to Him to protect his son"

(2) ENTRUST TO S.O.'S PROTECTION (cf WKL v and tp)

J611/15: the god bestowed on His servant bkl 'ml' whwkl[t] yz'n stml'n wstwkln lxyl 'LMQH "all the favors he continues to seek and the gifts he entrusts to the power of (the god) I."; sim J653/17, J611/7; J568/6-7: they dedicated as the god commanded the king lqbly hwkl stw[kl] mlk... l^cbdyhw "when the king entrusted gifts to his 2 servants" (RycHim2/476 sees this as an "adoption" of the 2 servants by the king, granting them the right of succession); J558/2: images 'ly stwklhw...lwfyhmw "which he entrusted to (the god) (in exchange) for their safety"

n^I p hwkl J568/6+; hwklt J611/7+

GIFT, THING ENTRUSTED to s.o.

J611/15, J568/7 quoted under WKL st; J568/13: the god protected His servant according to (= in measure equivalent to?) these gifts"

Note: For hwkltm C289/15, see n hwblt under WBL.

n^2 s mwkl(m,n) C81/9+; mwklh N27/4-5

PAYMENT, S.TH. HANDED OVER IN PAYMENT

[Cf Ar muwakkal "handed over" (D pass.prt).]

C81/9: h'xrw hwfyn mwkln "they delayed the paying of the (promised) payment"; N27/4-5: ywm fdyt mwklh "the day she acquitted herself of her payment"; C80/9: he dedicated twrm [mw]klm bkn yfqln "a bull as payment when he gathered the harvest"

WKN

h inf hwknn C19/9+

ESTABLISH FOR, BESTOW UPON (b- + obj)

[Ar wakana "set up," Dt "be stable."]

C19/9: šft whwknn ^{c}bdhw...bwfy hwt ǵlmn "(the god) granted and bestowed (on) His servant the safety of this boy"; R4233/7: xmr whwknn 'LMQ[H] ^{c}bdhw...hwfynhw "(the god) I. granted and bestowed (on) His servant to protect him"

WLG I

n s mwlg(m) C325/1+; var mwgln R4170

MATERIAL USED IN BUILDING (type of stone?)

[Sense from context.]

C325/1: [g]rbm wrb^{c}tm mwl[g]m "rough stone and squared masonry in mwlg-stone"; R3966/3-4: they restored m^{c}mr mwlgm "the tomb (using?) mwlg-stone"; R4170 (in full): [tq]dm mṣrb mwgln ^{c}d^c "he directed (the construction of) this incense-altar of mwgl-stone..."

WLG II

n s mwlg F77*

ENTRANCE (?)

[Ar mawlij id (cf RyET/54).]

F77: ^{c}s'w...mdqnt...wmwlg ^{c}r mśwdhmw "they built the oratory and entrance (?) of the citadel of their assembly"--or could this be a "construction in mwlg-stone," from WLG I?

WLD

v pf wld J669/8; wldt J752/10+; wldthw C19/7; ipf yldn (3m.s) J669/10; tldn C978/4+; yldn (3f.p) C87/6

BEAR a child; pass BE BORN

[Ar walada, pass wulida, id.]

J669/8-10: he dedicated lqbly dwld lhmw bnm...wšftw 'LMQHW kmhnmw yldn lhmw bnm...fyhqnynn "because a son was born to them, and they had promised (the god) I. that if a son were born to them, they would dedicate"; C19/7: he asked the god lwfy ǵlm wldthw M "to protect the boy whom M. bore him"; C87/6: they dedicated lqbly 'ṣf y^{c}brn fr^{c} lǵlm yldn "for the women who offer crops in recompense for the children they will bear"

tp inf tldn R4151/6; var 'tldn F3/7

BE BORN

[Ar wld Dt id.]

R4151/6: ṣdǵhw btldn bnm wwldt "(the god) manifested to him the birth/being-born of a son, and she gave birth..." (cf n tld "birth"); F3/7: let these men be mt̲l wmknt 'dm d̲D 'tldn 'sd bytn "interchangeable with the men of (the clan) d̲D, having been born (?) men of (its) family"

h ipf yhwldn C131/4-5; inf hwld[n] C350/14

BEGET

[Ar wld h id.]

C131/4-5: 'nt̲tm [w']wld yhwldn bnhn "(their) wives and the children they begot upon them"; C350/14: xmrhw T'LB hwld[n] ^{c}sm ǵlmm "(the god) T. allowed him to beget numerous boys"

n^{1} s wld(m,n) J717/7+; wldhw J550/1+; p wld R3946/2+; wldhw C375/1; wldhmw J703/7+; 'wld(m) R4938/15+; 'wldhw J755/6; 'wldhmw R4188/6+; 'wldhn Ir34+; var 'lwdhw R3966/1+; 'lwdhmy R5094/1+; 'lwdhmw R4195/2

CHILD; SON

[Ar walad, p wuld, 'awlād, id.]

R4938/15: 'wldm 'd̲krm 'ly kwkbt "numerous male children" AND OFTEN; J558/4: yśfnhmw 'LMQHW wldm wqnym hn'm "may (the god) I. grant them abundance of pleasing children and slaves/livestock"; R2726/6: 'dmhw... w'wldhmw wd̲'^{c}d̲rhmw "his servants and their children and dependents"

Note esp wld ngšyn J577/3+ "son of the Negus (king of Ethiopia)"; wld 'LMQH "children of (the god) I. = the Sabaeans" R3945/6; wld ^{c}M "children of (the god) A. = the Qatabanians" J576/16+. For a discussion of wld as a technical term, "clan-members subject to the patria potestas of the head of the clan" (with reference to the exps wld 'LMQH, wld ^{c}M), see BeFSTI/279.

n^{2} s mwld J2109/7-10*

CHILDBIRTH, DELIVERY

[Ar mīlād "time of birth."]

J2109/7-10: šw[^{c}] wwfyn wmt^{c}n 'LMQH...grb 'mthw...bn mwld wldt ǵlmm "(the god) I. protected and saved the life of his maidservant from the delivery (in which) she bore a boy-child"

n^{3} s tldm J721/8*

BIRTH

[Cf Ar tawlīd "delivery" and Sab tldn, inf of WLD tp.]
J721/8 in fragmentary context; lines 5-6 read "she asked the god for a child and He granted her a child"

WLW--For v tlw, ns tlw, 'tlwt, see under TLW. For n mstl, see under SLY

WLY--For proposed h 'wly see under 'WL v. For ns tly, 'tly, see under TLW

WM'

n s wm' F120/17*

SIGN OF ASSENT (?); l-wm': AS ASSENT > INCLUDING (?)

[Ar wm' h "make a gesture," 'īmā' "gestures, nods" (RyET/72).]
F120/17 (context fragmentary): ...]wlwm' HRN xlw [... "and including (?) H., with the exception of (?)..."

WSṬ

h For hsṭw, R4964/12, see under SṬW

n[1] as adv: wsṭ C140/12; wsṭhw R3958/4+; b-wsṭ R3945/16+; var b-ysṭ N74/2+

MIDST, MIDDLE; adv: IN THE MIDDLE OF

[Ar wasṭ "middle," wasṭa "in the middle of."]
C407/9-10: bwsṭ hgrn "in the middle of the city"; C140/12: wsṭ ḍr Ḥ[MY]RM "in the middle of/during the war (with) Ḥ."; Ir13/8: yhrgw bwsṭhw wbxlfhw "they slew (the enemy) inside (the fortress) and outside it"; R3958/4-5: kl bql...kwn wsṭhw "all the vegetable gardens (which) were within it"

n[2] s mwsṭ C308/10*

INTERIOR; as pp: IN THE INTERIOR OF (?)

C308/10: kl mwsṭ hyt mkntn "everything in the interior of this cella"

WSY

h pf hwsyhmw J647/26; hwsyw ib/25

CAUSE or REQUIRE TO BE DONE, ASSIGN A TASK

[Ar wassâ "do a kindness"; Daṯ wssy "do"; cf Ar 'sy L "aid...do, undertake."]
J647/25-6: the god allowed them stwfyn kl syt hwsyw 'mr'hmw...bkl syt hwsyhmw bml't sb^c^t xryftm "to bring to a successful conclusion all the tasks their lords assigned...in all the tasks they assigned them in the course of seven years"

n p? syt J647/25,26; sythmw ib/27-8

ASSIGNMENTS, TASKS

J647/27-8: mqwlthmw wsythmw "their duties and assignments"; ib/25-6 quoted under WSY h

WSM

n[1] s smt C553/2*

MARK, INSCRIBED SYMBOL

[Cf Ar sima† "mark impressed by hot iron on the skin = brand" (BronSem24/135-6).]

C553/2: let the boundary be established b^{c}br smt sṭr bṣlwt Ǵ "according to the mark inscribed on the face of Ǵ."

Note: Another tr "delimitation," after Ar samata "direct one's course," samt "way, road."

n^2 s̲ wsm Sha^{c}ib ^{c}Arjan*

BRAND on an animal

[Ar wasm id.]

inscr of Sha^{c}ib ^{c}Arjan, above a drawing of a camel: wsm (one-word inscription quoted in BeAIP/44 n1)

WSN

n s̲ snthw J567/6+

SLEEP

[Ar sina† "slumber, doze," wasina "sleep."]

J567/6: he dedicated ḥgn d̲t hr'y 'LMQH ^{c}bdhw...bwsṭ snthw "as (the god) I. showed His servant in his sleep (i.e., in an oracular dream)"; R3929/5: ḥgn khr'yhw bsnthw "as (the god) showed him in his sleep"

Note: For snt elsewhere see under SNN

WS^c

v p̲f̲ ws^{c}w Ry507/7; i̲p̲f̲ yws^{c}n R4351/1

GIVE, SUPPLY GENEROUSLY WITH (specifically, water) (cf WŚ^c v̲)

[Cf Ar wasa^{c}a "be sufficiently capacious for, be ample."]

Ry507/7: st[q]rw ^{c}lhmw mgrmtm wky ws^{c}w [...] "they imposed on them a monetary penalty, and when (?) they gave generously..."; R4351/1: ^{c}brn...d̲yws^{c}n 'srrn "the canal which abundantly supplies (with water) these valleys"

n 'ws^{c}m C174/1--read s^{c}s^{c}m, see under S^{c}S^c

WSF

v i̲n̲f̲ wsfhmw Ir23*

GRANT IN ABUNDANCE (cf WŚF v̲?)

[RycMus87/512 considers this spelling an unusual variant of root WŚF in a relatively ancient text.]

Ir23: lwsfhmw 'LMQH bry ''d̲nm "may (the god) I. grant them abundant health of mental faculties"

W^{c}B

v i̲n̲f̲ w^{c}b R4069/10*

FINISH, COMPLETE (?)

[Cf Ar w^{c}b h̲ "he went to, or attained...the utmost limit in anything."]

R4069/10: they built its canal ww^{c}b kl w^{c}b qhhw "and achieved the full completion of its construction"

h pf hw^{c}bw C325/3+; inf hw^{c}bn R5085/6-7

FINISH, COMPLETE (cf W^{c}B v)

R5085/6-7: hqšbhw whw^{c}bn bn ^{c}lyhw ^{c}dy sflhw "they furbished and completed it from top to bottom"; C325/3: hw^{c}bw kl qh Y "they completed the whole construction of Y." (cf R4069/10, quoted under W^{c}B v); C540/30: tqhhw wfqḥ mḍrft ḏ[']fn...whw^{c}bw klhmw "he constructed it and opened the channels of the sluices and they all were completed (?)"

n s w^{c}b(m) R4069/10+

COMPLETION (maṣdar)

R4069/10 quoted under W^{c}B v; F74/2: in that year tnbth(m)w w^{c}bm "the completion (of the building project) was brought about for them"

W^{c}D

v pf w^{c}dhmw J577/9 twice*

PROMISE

[Ar wa^{c}ada id.]

J577/9: w^{c}dhmw kyṣrynhmw mlk Ḥ b^{c}br 'mr'hmw...ww^{c}dhmw š^{c}bn N ṯny wrxyn ltṣryn b^{c}br 'mr'hmw "the king of Ḥ. promised them that he would protect them against their lords, and the tribe N. promised them (for?) two months to protect them against their lords"

h pf hw^{c}dhmw C541/61-2*

MAKE AN APPOINTMENT, SUMMON AT AN APPOINTED TIME

[Cf Heb hô^{c}îd Jb 9:10 "summon at an appointed time"; also Ar wā^{c}ada "make an appointment."]

C541/61-2: he summoned the tribes to repair the dam whw^{c}dhmw bwrxn ḏS "and he summoned them (to meet) in the month ḏS."

n^{l} s m^{c}d(m) C548/1+; m^{c}dhw R3910/4

(1) (TIME) LIMIT, DEADLINE; APPOINTED TIME > FEAST-DAY (?)

[Ar mī^{c}ād "time agreed on, deadline."]

R3910/4: ḏyš'mn ^{c}bdm...flyknn m^{c}dhw 'ḥd wrxm "whoever buys a slave, let his time limit (of guarantee) be one month"; C548/1: mngr ḥm(y)m...m^{c}d Ḥ "whoever visits a sanctuary on the feast-day (?) of (the god) Ḥ..." (cf BeSl/53)

(2) ORACULAR PROMISE or RESPONSE

[Cf Ar mī^{c}ād "promise."]

R4370: bšft wm^{c}d ^{c}Ṯ[TR] "by the oracular promise and response of (the god) A."; N74/7: ḥgn yqht ḏt B bm^{c}dm "as (the goddess) ḏt B. commanded, by an oracular response"; C315/11: bml' wm^{c}d wwš^{c}n šymhmw "by the ml' ('fulfillment') response and the m^{c}d ('promise') response and the aid of their patron deity"

Note: For m^{c}d J647/29, see under M^{c}D

n^{2} s m^{c}dtn C262/3*

PLEDGE, COMMITMENT

[Cf Ar maw^{c}ida^{+} id.]

C262/3: bn h' m^{c}dtn bnyy [mk]nt "on account of this commitment (made between them), they two built the cella"

n^{3} s mw^{c}d J577/10; mw^{c}dhmw ib/10+

PROMISE (cf m^{c}d sense^{2})

[Ar maw^{c}īd id.]

J577/10: nẓrw mw^{c}d 'GRN ltṣryn b^{c}br 'mr'hmw...whxwhw bmw^{c}dhmw lnṣr "they bethought themselves of the promise of the Nagranites to protect (them) against their lords, and allied with him (?) through/because of their promise to help"; C541/95: the tribes came down ^{c}ly mw^{c}dhmw "in accordance with their promise"

W^{c}Ẓ--For w^{c}ẓm C318/6, read w-^{c}ẓm, see under ^{c}ẒM

W^{c}Y

h pf hw^{c} R4585B*

CAUSE TO BE REMEMBERED > COMMEMORATE (?)

[Cf Ar wa^{c}â "remember."]

R4585B (in full): ^{c}LQ^{c}TT mqsrn hw^{c} "A., the subjected (a religious title), has commemorated (?)"

Note: Grimme considered hw^{c} a variant of hy^{c}, q.v.; tr "he has sacrificed."

W^{c}L I

v inf w^{c}l R2861/11*

RULE OVER (?)

[Cf Ar wu^{c}ūl "noble (persons)" (Lane/3056C).]

R2861/11: wd[š']m lw^{c}l qwm[m w]dwrm "and whoever is appointed to rule over the community and the people..."

Note: For w^{c}lt J560/3-4 read w-^{c}lt "and the highlands," see under ^{c}LY n^{2}. For w^{c}ln R2695/2 read w-^{c}ln "and (incumbent) upon," see under ^{c}LY pp^{1}.

W^{c}L II

n p 'w^{c}l(n) C397/4+

IBEX, MOUNTAIN GOAT (in epithet of the god 'LMQH)

[Ar wa^{c}l, p 'aw^{c}āl, id.]

R3649b: 'LMQH b^{c}l 'w^{c}ln "(the god) I., lord of the ibexes"; C397/4: 'LMQH-b^{c}l'w^{c}lṢRWḤ "I., lord of the ibexes of (the city) Ṣ." AND ELSEWHERE SIM

WF'

h pf hwf' J555/4*

PROVIDE (?)

[Cf Ar wfy D "he paid, or rendered, to him fully...his right, or due" (Lane/3057B), h "fulfill, accomplish."]

J555/4: he fought with S. whwf' kl nṭʿ wkśwy wkl mwf' ḍb' S "and provided (?) all the tents (?) and garments and all the provisions (?) for S.'s campaign"

n s mwf' J555/4*

PROVISIONS for a campaign (?)

J555/4 quoted under WF' h

WFD

v pf wfd C516/19; wfdt C978/5; ipf yfdnhw C612/2

(1) PRODUCE (e.g., crops) ABUNDANTLY (?)

[Cf Ar wafada "travel; arrive; come, or go, as an ambassador" (cf Lane/2955A).]

C516/19: wwfd F mmd "and (the cultivated area) F. produced (crops) abundantly (?)"; C978/5: he asked the god ktldn 'ṯ[thw...] wfdt ǵlmm "that his wife might give birth [and] she produced a son" (but read prob wldt, as in parallel context R4151/6)

(2) aux: CONTINUE to do, DO AGAIN (?)

C612/2: ḏyfdnhw wyḍʿn ʿynm "whoever continues to neglect the spring (?)" (reading and translation uncertain)

h ipf yhwfd (?) R2865/3* (reading doubtful; see also WFR h)

CAUSE TO PRODUCE crops > CULTIVATE (?)

R2865/3: w'l yhwfd bh ʿmd wʿlbm w'l hṯmr kl ṯmrm 'l sqy "let no one cultivate (?) there naturally or artificially irrigated lands, nor those (which) yield any crop without irrigation"

n[1] s fdfdtm R4781/2*

(SOURCE OF) INCREASE or PRODUCE

[Cf Eth fadfada "increase."]

R4781/2: wl tknn 'ln n[xln]hn fdfdtm m[w]k[b]tm "and let these 2 palmgroves be a source of increase, well cultivated"

n[2] s tfd(m) C516/18+

HARVEST (?)

R2740/8: ʿsy ḏbḥn tfd mmd "he offered a sacrifice (for?) the prolonged harvest (?)"; C516/18: tfdm m'tm mmd "harvest, a hundred (measures?), prolonged (?)"

WFṬ

v pf/inf wfṭ R3943/3+

SET AFIRE, BURN

[Eth wafaṭa "burn; cook."]

R3943/3: _t_br wxrš wwfṭ R "crushed, destroyed and burned R."; R3945/3: mxd S wwfṭ N wkl 'hgr M "he defeated S. and burned N. and all the towns of M." AND SEVERAL TIMES in this inscr in sim contexts

n _s_ mwfṭm R3945/16*

BURNING, BEING BURNT (maṣdar)

R3945/16: hgrn N yhḥrm bn mwfṭm w^c tbhw xrš bythw "the town N. he reserved from burning (= forbade to be burnt), but ordered (concerning) it (?) the destruction of its palace"

WFY

v _pf_ wfyt C334/13; _ipf_ yfyn R3910/6; yfyhmw R3909/5

(1) BE SAFE, SAVED

[Ar wafâ "be perfect, complete; pay a debt."]

C334/13: as for the camp of their lord, wwfyt wst[r]ḥ[t] "it was safe/saved and delivered" (cf WFY _D_; this may be _D_ _pass_)

(2) PAY A DEBT

R3910/6: the seller is not liable, wl yfyn lmhš'mn šr^c hw "and let (the buyer) pay to the seller his due" (cf C548/9 quoted under WFY _D_)

Note also lyfyhmw R3909/5 in fragmentary context (phps _n_ ^1 ?)

ti _inf_ wtf Ry510/3*

PUBLISH (?), or COMMISSION (?)

[Cf senses of Ar wfy D. Form is dubious if it represents the _ti_ of a I-w root--cf Sab t', _ti_ of root W'Y (?). JPDSM/173-6 suggests reading wtq from Ar waqâ "guard, keep," but this tr is not significantly better. Cf also the _n_ wtf (WFY _n_ ^2).]

Ry510/3: hwrw wwtf _d_n msndn "he displayed and commissioned (?) this inscription"

D _pf_ wfyw J729/11-2; _ipf_ ywfyn C380/4+; twfyn R3959/3; _inf_ wfyn R4134/5+; wfyhmw R3908/7

(1) MAKE SAFE > PRESERVE, PROTECT

[Factitive of WFY _v_ sense ^1.]

J582/6-7: lwfyhw wlxmrhw ḥzy "to protect him and grant him favor"; C380/3-4: lywfyn 'šrmn lbrktn...lywfyn fnwhw "to make safe/protect the foundation of the cistern; to make safe his/its canals"; J606/7: ls^c dhmw ..n^c mtm...wlwfy mr'hmw "to grant them prosperity and to protect their lord" AND OFTEN IN SIM CONTEXTS; J616/12: lsb' wwfyn 'š^c b "to campaign and protect the tribes"; F3/9: ^c lmw _d_Ḥ lywfyn "(the clan) _d_Ḥ. signed (the agreement) that it might be preserved"

Note: In some contexts infinitives of this _v_ are indistinguishable from instances of the _n_ wfy "well-being, safety."

(2) PAY a debt (cf WFY _v_ sense ^2)

J729/11-2: wfyw mr'hmw...dšfthw "they paid to their lord what they had promised Him"; C548/9: lywfyn ẓl^{c}n "let him pay this fine"; R2726/16: kl ywfyn š'mtm w'ṯwbtm ḥg '[s]ṭrhmy "that the purchases and payments may be paid according to their documents (= contracts)"; R4134/5: wlmw bny Ḥ lwfyn 'rḍhmw b^{c}lm ẓrbm "they pledged themselves (for) the b.Ḥ. to pay for their land by a document of guarantee" (sim context R3959/3)

tp pf twfyw G1573/3; [t]wfyt G1655/19?; inf twfyn A452/5

(1) BE SAFE, SAVED

G1655/19: [wt]wfyt hgrhmw...bn h['... "and their city was saved from that..." (only instance of this sense; read [w]wfyt, WFY v or D?)

(2) BE UNDER AN OBLIGATION, PLEDGE ONE'S SELF

[Hö SEG8/41 suggests development from WFY v "be valid, guaranteed, pledged" to Dt "pledge one's self (to fulfill, to pay)."]

G1573/3: twfyw bhyt rtn "they pledged themselves (to pay) by that (document of) indebtedness"; A452/5: the clients of S. and F. tsb'w wtwfyn [r]z' wḥly "are compelled and under obligation regarding expenses and gifts"

h pf hwfy J561b/6+; hfy J752/11; hwfyhw J551+; hfyhw C343/16; hwfyhmw C398/4+; hfyhmw ib/14; hwfyhmy J624/6; hwfyw J656/16; [hw]fythmw F106; ipf yhwfyn J551+; inf hwfyn R4012/4+; hwfynhw J580/13+; hwfynhmy C314/8; hwfynhmw J561b/15+; hfynhmw J752/14-5

(1) MAKE SAFE, PROTECT (cf D sense^{1})

J561b/6: hwfy 'LMQH ^{c}bdhw...bsb't...sb'w "(the god) I. protected His servant in the campaigns they undertook"; R4842/7: may the god continue hwfyn grb ^{c}b[d]hw "to protect the life of His servant" AND OFTEN in these two contexts

(1a) aux: DO SAFELY

Ir28: 'wlhw whwfyn bn bḥrm "(the god) brought him back safely from (over)-seas"

(2) PAY, GRANT; FULFILL OBLIGATIONS, RENDER s.o. HIS DUE

[Ar 'awfâ "give to the full."]

J656/16: hwfyw mr'hmw 'LMQH...kl ^{c}šr "they paid to their lord I. all the tithes"; R4962/6: xmr whwfyn ^{c}bdhw...bkl 'ml' stml' b^{c}mhw "(the god) bestowed and granted to His servant all the oracles he sought" AND OFTEN; J551: hwfyhw 'LMQH wyhwfyn dṯ tnb'hw "(the god) I. granted to him and will grant what He promised him"; C547/3: hn 'l hwfyhw mṭrdhw "because they did not render duly to (the god) His ritual hunt"; C99: 'lsnw xdl hy^{c} whwfyn ['L]MQH "they were not to cease offering sacrifices and rendering His due to I."

st pf stwfy J560/7+; stwfyw R4636; stwfyt F71/7; ipf ystwfynn R2695/4; inf stwfyn J562/4+; stwfn N74/10

(1) MAKE SAFE, PROTECT (cf WFY h sense^{1})

Ir12/2: stwfy kl 'wṯn hgr "to protect all the borders of the town"; F71/7: he dedicated because stwfyt 'A [w]'^{c}ḍdhw "A. and its plantations had been protected"

(2) aux: DO SUCCESSFULLY, BRING TO A SUCCESSFUL CONCLUSION (cf WFY ḫ sense^{1a})

J647/24: xmrhmw 'LMQH...stwfyn kl syt "(the god) I. allowed them to bring all the tasks to a successful conclusion"; Ir24: ystkmln wstwfyn "accomplished successfully"

(3) GRANT; specifically, TRANSFER PROPERTY by means of a wtf-deed (cf WFY ḫ sense^{2})

J560/7: stwfy ṣry "(the god) granted a ṣry-oracle"; R2695/4: lystwfynn bḏn wtfn bqlw "to transfer the vegetable gardens by means of this wtf-deed"

n^1 s wfy(m) R4842/1+; wfyhw J604/2+; wfyhmw R3990/7-8+; wfyhn Ir34

SAFETY, WELL-BEING (cf var yfy id)

[Ar wafâ "be complete, perfect," wafā' "completeness."]

R4842/1: the god allowed him 'tw bwfym bn kl 'brṯ bhw sb' "to return in safety from all the battlefields on which he fought" AND OFTEN SIM; R4671/3: a dedication for [w]fy wṣḥ mqymthmw "the well-being and health of their faculties"; C2/5: they dedicated lwfyhmw wwfy 'wld xmrhmw T "for their (own) well-being and the well-being of the children (the god) T. granted them" AND OFTEN SIM

Note: Obscure in J616/17: wbmw hwt wfyn "and in that...?"

n^2 s wtf(m,n) R4646/19+

(1) DEED OF TRANSFER of property (esp to a god)

[Eth 'awfaya "deliver, entrust," Amh watafa "leave s.o. one's place, put s.o. in one's place." For the institution, cf the Ar waqf and RhBod/174.]

R4133/3: wtfn whqnytn "deed of transfer and dedication"; R4646/19: xmrnn wwtfn "this grant and deed of transfer"; C99/11: sṭr wṣ[ḥfṭ ḏn] wtfn "text and document of this wtf"

(2) PROPERTY TRANSFERRED by wtf-deed

Ist7626/1: wtfn H lḏS "this wtf-territory (named) H. belongs to (the god) ḏS."; R4727/3: [st]wfyw ḏn wtfn lhwfy W 'dmhw "they transferred this property so that (the god) W. would protect His servants"

Note: This n and the v wtf cited herein as WFY ti may be derived from a separate but secondary root WTF (cf Amh watafa cited in the etymology of wtf n).

n^3 s mwfyhmw C152/2*

PROTECTOR

C152/2: mkrbn mwfyhmw "the mkrb (= chief Sabaean official), their protector"

WFR I

tp inf tfr R4176/7*

JOURNEY, MAKE A PILGRMAGE

[Cf Eth wafara "go into the country"; and cf prob also Ar farâ "cross country."]
R4176/7: ltfr qsd T'LB ᶜdy T̲ wᶜdy 'A "so that the yeomen of (the god) T. might journey to (the shrines) T̲. and A."

h pf hwfr MüAfO24/p151; inf hwfrnn J669/14-5
MAKE A PILGRIMAGE (cf WFR I tp)
J669/14-5: if they receive the favor they ask, lhwfrnn 't̲thmw wbnhmw ᶜdy mḥrmn wlḥmdnn mqm 'LMQHW "let their wives and sons make a pilgrimage to the temple and praise the power of (the god) I." uned inscr MüAfO24/p151 (photo): ywm hwfr mhwfrt 'LMQH b'BHY "when he undertook the pilgrimage of (the god) I. in (the month of) A."
Note: RycRite/380n3 cites the suggestion of Ghul to cf Ar wafra† "lock of hair" and the propitiatory sacrifice of hair in cases of "extreme need." Tr would be "make an offering (of hair)."

n¹ s mfr C546/2+; var mwfr C506/3
COUNTRY, DISTRICT AROUND A CITY
[Eth mufār "fields, farm or village with fields."]
C506/3: sr wmwfr hgrn "common land of and country surrounding the city"; C546/2: syr wmfr hgrn, same tr

n² s mhwfrt MuAfO24/p151*
PILGRIMAGE
uned inscr MüAfO24/p151 quoted under WFR I h

WFR II

h pf hwfrhw R4767/4; ipf yhwfr R2865/3
PRODUCE crops (?)--both contexts questionable
[Cf Dat̲ wafara "be saturated with water" > "be fertile, produce crops"? Cf also phps Heb pārāh, Eth farya "bear fruit."]
R2865/3: 'l yhwfr bh ᶜmd wᶜlbm "let no one produce in it naturally or artificially irrigated crops" (or read yhwfd, WFD h, q.v.); R4767/4: y(g)zzn d̲hwfrhw "let him harvest what it has produced (?)" (context fragmentary)

WṢḤ

v pf wṣḥhmw C541/24; wṣḥw C540/7
REACH, COME TO
[Cf Eth baṣḥa "arrive."]
C540/7: wṣḥw qdm ᶜA "they came to (the area) before A."; C541/24: wwṣḥhmw ṣrxn "the summons reached them"

WṢL

h pf hwṣl J559/1+; hwṣlw J651b/11+; ipf yhwṣlnn Ry502/6; inf hwṣln F3/8
(1) ASSEMBLE (of troops)

[Ar wṣl h̲ "join, combine with."]

J576/4: wbnhw fhwṣlw ^{c}dy byn hgrnhn wbnhw fybḥḏn mlkn "and then they assembled in (the area) between the 2 cities, and then the king attacked"; J665/24: hwṣlw gyšhmw "their troops assembled"

(2) JOIN IN, TAKE PART IN a campaign or war

J559/9: bkl 'brṯ bhmw hwṣl lbytn S b'ḍrrm wslmm "in all the undertakings in which they joined for the house S. in wars and peace"; J561b/11: kl 'brṯ ^{c}dyhmw hwṣlw lḍrm "undertakings in which they joined for war"

(3) INCLUDE

F3/8: wlhy^c whwṣln lkl hšk "let (knowledge of this decree) spread and include every prohibition"

n s̲ ṣlthmw R3232/2*

KIN, RELATIVES (?)

[Ar ṣila^t id.]

R3232/2 (fragmentary): ṣlthmw...ḥywhmw "their kin (?)...their clan (?)"

For ṣlt elsewhere see under ṢLW and ṢLL

WṢ^c

tp pf twṣ^{c}t C365/5*

BE RUINED (?), CAPTURED (?)

[Cf Te waṣṣa^{c}é "harm, injure," tawaṣṣa^{c}é "be injured, ruined" (CoRoSab/31), and Sab wḍ^c v̲ "lay low, defeat."]

C365/5: bkn twṣ^{c}t ḏt mṭrn "when this rain-watered field was ruined/captured (?)"

WṢR--For ipf (?) yṣr R2648/1, see passage quoted under YṢR

WṢT I

h pf hwṣt R3945/1+; hwṣthw J550/2+; ipf yhwṣtn R3951/2; yhwṣthw Ir13/14; yhwṣthmw Ry533/28; inf hwṣtn Ir13/11

(1) COMMAND, ORDAIN

[Etymology doubtful. HöWar?/80-81 cfs Ar waṣâ "join, unite," D̲ "recommend, empower, entrust to," h̲ id. WṢT may be a development of this root. Cf also Eth ṣōtā "order, species, class," Amh ṭayyata "bind together."]

Ir13/11: wqh whwṣtn "he ordered and commanded"; Ry533/27-8: 'brṯ bhw yhwṣthmw mr'hmw "campaigns on which their lord commanded them"

(2) GIVE LEGAL STATUS TO various entities

a political group: R3945/1: ['l]t hfṭn K...mkrb SB' bmlkh[w] l'LMQH wlSB' ywm hwṣt kl gwm "these (lands) did K., mkrb of S., in his function as king, assign to (the god) I. and to S. on the day he gave legal status to the whole community"; sim formula R3946/1, 3948/3, 3949 and elsewhere

Note: For discussions of this formula see RycER2/155; HöWar? passim.

colonies: C601/11: _d_bhw hwṣt whbkln...mlk SB' "in which the king of S. gave legal status to (colonies) and settled colonists"; R3951/2: 'sd mlkn ['l]w yhwṣtn b^{c}ly 'š^{c}bn "the king's soldiers whom he established (as colonists) upon the tribes"

an individual's personal authority: J550/2: hwṣthw Y...wy^{c}qb bkbtn "Y. established him in authority and he acted as (Y's) deputy in the campaign"

n _s_ mṣt R4176/9; _var_ mwṣt C338/10+

ORDINANCE, DECREE

R4176/3: whwṣt T'LB...wyǵrdw...bḥg mwṣt T "(the god) T. ordained, and they ...ed? according to the ordinance of T."; ib/9: lṭbb mṣt 'LMQH w T'LB "to proclaim the decree of (the gods) I. and T."; sim in C338/5,10

WṢT II

n _p_ mwṣtt J831/2*

BURNT SACRIFICES (?) (in military context; conquered property burned in honor of the god?)

[Cf Heb yāṣat "set on fire," in military contexts.]

J831/2: the god protected him bkl 'ḍb' wmwṣtt hy^c b^{c}m mr'hw "in all the battles and burnt sacrifices (?) he offered together with his lord"

WḌ' I

v _pf_ wḍ't R3945/16+; wḍ'y Ir13; _ipf_ yḍ'n C570/6+; tḍ'n R3945/2; _prt_ wḍ'm C548/2

(1) GO OUT, FLOW OUT

[Eth waḍ'a, waṣ'a, Heb yāṣā' "go out"; for use with the casting of lots (R3945/16?), cf Josh 19:1 wayyēṣē' haggôrāl.]

C548/2: wḍ'm 'w bh'm "going out or coming in"; R3945/2: he dammed up his canal bn _kd_ tḍ'n brḥm "so that it might not flow out unchecked"; ib/16: ^{c}tb bn N 'l wḍ't šfthmw nsrn 'l'ltn "he gave command (concerning) those of (the conquered territory) N., those, the offering of whom to the gods had come out (by lot?)"

(2) DIE

Ir13: fbmw wsṭhw wḍ'y bn ẓm'n "and there they died of thirst"

(3) RESULT, FOLLOW > BE ESTABLISHED

C570/6: so that along the length of the palmgrove yḍ'n tḥrw byn nxlnhn "the delimitation between the 2 palmgroves may be established"

D _pf_ wḍ' J557; _ipf_ ywḍ'n C603/29

(1) SEND OUT (= EXPORT) (?), or PULL UP, GATHER (?) fodder

[Eth wḍ' _D_ "cause to go out."]

C603/29 (obscure context): wmn lywḍ'n s^{c}m s[']l "and whoever exports/gathers (?) fodder (which is not his own property?) shall be held responsible (?)"

(2) ANNOUNCE (?)

[Eth wḍ' D "announce."]

J557: wwḍ' 'A b'ḏn 'LMQH "and A. has announced, by permission of (the god) I..." (J's tr; or read as WḌ' v, "A. has gone out"?)

h ipf yhwḍ'n C615/5; inf hwḍ'n R4176/6

(1) DRIVE OUT

R4176/6: the god has prohibited the doorkeepers bn hwḍ'n 'śrm...kḥrmw "from driving out the herds, for they are sacred"

(2) EXTEND (?)

C615/5 (fragmentary context): yhwḍ'n fnwtn "he will extend (?) the canal"

st inf st(w)ḍ'n C126/4+

DRIVE OUT > EXILE, PROCLAIM AN OUTLAW (?) (cf WḌ' h sense[1])

[Discussion BeSabPL/307.]

C126/4: mn ḏlhw yr[y]śn [S]B' wstwḍ' "anyone with respect to whom S. makes a decree so that (thereby) he is proclaimed an outlaw..."; prob also C546/8, a confessional inscr, after lacuna: ...] ystḍ'n kḥwr bqdmy ḏt tnxytn "let him/them be outlawed as it was ordered before this confession"

n s mwḍ'hw R2861/24*

TRIBUTE (?)

[Cf Eth wādā "gift."]

R2861/24: (y)nq(d)n mwḍ'hw wmnš'hw "he paid his tribute (?) and tax (?)"

WḌ' II

ti inf tḍ'(n) C321/2+

PURIFY ONE'S SELF (?)

[Ar waḍu'a "be clean," Dt "perform a ritual ablution."]

C321/2: w]l tḍ'n nfshw b[... "to purify (?) himself" (context fragmentary; also in fragmentary context R3917/2)

WḌN--For n mwḍnhmw C408/12 (reading of MoMiSI/163), read mwṭnhmw with C; see under WṬN

WḌ^{c}

v pf wḍ^{c}w C541/70-71; inf wḍ^{c} J616/16+

(1) LAY LOW, DEFEAT

[Ar waḍa^{c}a "lay down; humble, humiliate."]

J616/16: lṯbr wwḍ^{c} wdr^{c}...kl ḍrhmw "may he crush, lay low and humble their every foe" AND OFTEN SIM

(2) LEVEL GROUND (?)

C541/70-71: kwḍ^{c}w lhwṯrn ^{c}wdn "when they leveled the ground (?) to lay the foundation for the settling basin"

Note: For ipf yḍ^{c}n see under ḌW^{c}, ND^{c}

ti inf tḍ^{c}n J581/8*

LAY LOW (cf WḌ^{c} v)

J581/8: they dedicated bḏtbry wtḍ^{c}n ḍrhmy "because they had crushed and laid low their foe"

Note: For tḍ^{c} elsewhere see under NḌ^{c} tp, to which this instance also might be assigned.

h inf hwḍ^{c} J652/24-5*

BE IN CHARGE OF, CONTROL (?)

[Cf senses of Ar waḍa^{c}a "appoint for; impose or remit a tax or the like" (Lane/3053BC).]

J652/24-5: wqhhw mr'hw...lhwḍ^{c} wšrḥ bbytn S "his lord ordered him to be in charge of and protect the house S."

n^{1} as adj: f.s wḍ^{c}t DJE10/3*

(WHAT IS) LOW, BELOW (?)

[Ar waḍī^{c} "low, inferior."]

DJE10/3: ['r]ḍn wwḍ^{c}t smyn "[the ear]th and (what is) below the heaven"

Note: BeSt1/95 suggests reading as plural n and trs "[creators of] earth and founders of heaven."

n^{2} s wḍ^{c}n J647/13-4*

UNVEILED WOMAN (?)

[BeNL9/195 cfs Ar wāḍi^{c} id. He suggests the term refers to a normal accompaniment of cultic acts.]

J647/13-4 (fragmentary context): 'ḤLKM ḏt DWSM wḍ^{c}n "A. of (the tribe) D., the unveiled woman (?)"

Note: J read here 'ḥgkm ḏt dwsm wḍ^{c}n and tr "the laws which (were) abused and lost" (root ḌW^{c}).

WQH

v pf wqh R4938/4+; wqhhw J583/6+; wqhw (for wqhhw) C378/5+; wqhhmy J616/10; wqhmy (for wqhhmy) C389/6; wqhhmw J563/4+; wqhy J586/14+; wqhw R3960/5+; note esp yqht N74/6; ipf yqhn J662/17; yqhnhmw J578/39+; yqhnn R4137/5+; yqhnnhmy J578/37-8; yqhnnhmw J668/13

(1) OBEY (l- s.o.)

[Ar waqiha "hear, obey."]

C140/12: kbr ḍr Ḫ wkl ḏyqhn lhw "the leader of the war of Ḥ. and all who obeyed him"; sim in R3958/12, phps also C74/15

(2) ORDER, COMMAND

R4938/4: they dedicated the statue ḏwqh 'LMQH 'dmhw bms'lhw "which (the god) I. commanded His servants (to dedicate) through His oracle" AND OFTEN SIM; R3884/12: X and Y b^{c}m 'sd wqhw "with the soldiers they commanded"; J578/39: bkl 'brṯ yqhnhmw mr'yhmw "in all the campaigns (on which) their lords commanded them"

Note esp pf 3f.s yqht in N74/6--the dialect of this inscr typically replaces initial w with y.

ti pf tqh C541/98+; tqhhw C540/29; tqhw Robin al-Mašamayn 1

(1) ORDER FOR, IMPOSE UPON ONE'S SELF

[Reflexive of WQH "command."]

Robin al-Mašamayn 1: ḥgn ktqhw wstwddn bnw G "According to what the b.G. imposed on themselves and accepted"

(2) CONSTRUCT, COMPLETE

[Ar ittaqah (root WQH) "complete."]

C540/29: wzlw msrn wšṣnm bsbᶜt wᶜšry ymtm wtqhhw "and they finished the packing in of earth and facing with stone in twenty-seven days, and completed it"

n[1] s qh C541/19-20; var qht(m) J565/6+; qhthw J564/12

OBEDIENCE; AUTHORITY, COMMAND (senses often indistinguishable)

[Cf Ar waqha† "obedience."]

J565/6: sb'w bqht 'mr'hmw "(campaigns) they undertook by command of (or, in obedience to) their lords"; C541/19-20: bqh mlkn "by command of the king"; C308b/25: slmw wsmᶜn qhtm "they made peace and declared their obedience (or, submitted to the [royal] authority)"; J564/12: qhthw bhgrn "his authority in the city"; F3/8: mwṣt wqht 'mr'hmw "decree and command of their lords"

n[2] s qh C325/3; qhhw R4069/10

COMPLETED CONSTRUCTION (cf WQH ti, sense[2])

C325/3: hwᶜbw kl qh Y "they completed the whole construction of Y."; R4069/10: wᶜb kl wᶜb qhhw "he achieved the full completion of its construction"

WQL

h pf hwqlw C540/68+

BE IN CONFUSION, ACT IN A CONFUSED MANNER (?)

[C alleges an Ar 'ūqila (h pass) "be senseless, rage" > "be confused."]

C540/68: hwqlw 'šᶜb rḥbtn ḏllm wmwtm "the lowland tribes were in confusion (?) (with) disease and death"; R4157/2: [h]wqlw lhw ''b[lm] "camels behaved in a confused manner around him (?)"

WQM

v inf wqm J652/20*

TREAT HARSHLY (?)

[Ar waqama "treat with violence and harshness" (JSIMB/27).]

J652/20: wlnqm wwqm 'LMQH kl ḏyxrgnhmy ᶜbr mr'hmy "and may (the god) I. take vengeance on and treat harshly anyone who brings a legal action (?) against their lord"

n s qmtm J558/5*

HARSH TREATMENT (?)
J558/5: may the god save them bn ʿdqm wqmtm "from persecution (?) and harsh treatment (?)"

WQN

n *s* mwqntn G1537/3; *d* mwqntn C542/6
CISTERN, RESERVOIR (?)
[Cf Ar wuqna† "hollow in the earth," and cf Sab qnt (= Ar qana†?) "storage pit" under QNY.]
G1537/3: they dedicated to the god ḏtn mwqntn "this cistern (?)" C542/6: ṯny mḏmrn wṯty mwqntn "two plantations and two cisterns (?)"
Note: Irv/134 suggests tr "sunken fields."

WQF

v *pf* wqf C81/2*
MAKE OVER property to the god, for pious purposes
[Ar wqf *D* "institute a religious endowment (waqf)."]
C81/2: he dedicated a tablet to the god wwqf lhw ṯwrm "and made over to Him a bull"

WQR I

v *pf* wqr R2861/9*
INSCRIBE, CARVE a law, in stone
[Ar waqara "split stone," and cf Ḥaḍ mwqrt "carved object" Ry4c and Sab derived *ns* below.]
R2861/9: lkḏkbr ḏwqr ḥḏrn "now, whoever behaves arrogantly (regarding) that which is legally inscribed, the warning..."

st *pf* st(q)rw R507/7*
ORDAIN, IMPOSE a penalty (?)
[Development from sense of WQR v "inscribe a law" > "make legal."]
Ry507/7: w(k)d' whbt rhnn wst(q)rw ʿlhmw mgrmtm "when the hostages had already been given, they imposed on them a monetary penalty"
For other readings of this passage see under BRW st and GWR st.

n¹ *s* wqr(n) R2726/14+
EDICT carved in stone (?)
R2726/14: bḥg wqr wmḥr hḥr "according to the edict (?) and decree (which) he decreed"; and read hwt wqrn "that decree" in R2724/(5), fragmentary context

n² *s* mqrm C438/4+
ORACULAR DECREE (?)
C438/4: mqrm [w]nʿmt "oracular decree (?) and (divine) favor"; C460/1: bmqrm "by an oracular decree (?)" (context damaged)

n^{3} s mwqrn R3943/5,6*

ROCK BASIN, CISTERN (?)

[Cf Ar waqīr "large trench in rock, containing water." Also in unintelligible context in Ḥaḍ R3512/3--the depression cut in the top of the altar? (Irv/204).]

R3943/5-6: bny mzff mwq[rn w]ml...y mwqrn wklwt mzff "he built the sluices of the rock basin (?), and...the rock cistern and the water drops of the sluices"

n^{4} s tqr R3918/2--see under QYR

WQR II

n wqr J1026a (graffito)

A TERM OF SALUTATION (?)

[RycBiOr26/249 interprets this usage as a term of salutation well-known in Thamudic; cf also RycBiOr17/204, commenting on A. van den Branden, *Les textes thamoudéens de Philby*, v.I, Louvain, 1956.]

J1026a (in full): MDKM wqr "M. (gives) greetings!" (J read fqr and took as a n.pr)

WR

?--R4785/4: ...](w)ḍ^{c}m wr d^{c}b mrn xmrhmw [... (context obscure)

n s mwrt, see under MWR

WRD

v pf wrd Ry508/3+; wrdw J575/4+; ipf yrd R3916/1; yrdnn R3946/3; inf wrd R2876/6

(1) COME DOWN; FALL (rain)

[Ar warada id.]

R3946/3: 'srr yrdnn bn M "the valleys (which) come down from M."; C540/59: kḥgn wrd dṯ'n "when the spring (rain) fell"

(1a) BE SET DOWN in writing (?)

R2726/10: ...] ^{c}kr lyr[dn] wyf^{c}n h' (^{c})lm[n] "(For anyone who) raises objections, let this document be set down (?) and recorded"

(3) NEGLECT (?)

[Cf Heb yārad id Dt 28/43 (so R).]

R2876/6: qblw wwrd wwxr wtrdn sntn 'rḍtn "they have leased out (lands), and (if?) (they?) neglect (?) or delay, this law will take effect (?) on the lands..."

D pf wrd C540/64-5; wrdhmw C405/13

SEND FORTH or DOWN

[Ar wrd D "make (s.th.) reach" (Irv/282-3).]

C405/13: [ywm wr]dhmw bshln "[when he se]nt them down into the plain";

C540/64-5: kwrd mlkn...r^{c}ẓm "when the king sent forth a summons"

tp pf twrdw J665/18; inf? trdn R2876/6

(1) GO DOWN

J665/18: rqyw bn M wdkww tlty rkbm...wtwrdw hmw 'sdn mqdmtn "they went up from M. and killed thirty cameleers and those soldiers, the vanguard, went down..."

(2) TAKE EFFECT ON (?)

[Cf usage of Ar nazala "do down" > "happen, occur."]

R2876/6: if they neglect the lands (?) wtrdn sntn 'rḍtn "this law will take effect (?) on the lands"

h pf hwrd J550/2; hwrdhmw R4158/4

LEAD, CONDUCT

[Ar wrd h "bring; convey."]

J550/2: kl 'rgl hwrd ^{c}d hgrn "all the footsoldiers he led to the city";

R4158/4: whwrdhmw mš[rqn] "and he led them toward the east (?)"

n s wrd C204/4+; d wrdnhn C549/2-3

(1) FALL or ARRIVAL (of rain) (maṣdar of WRD v sense[1])

C204/4: kqṣr bn wrd dnmn "when he brought in the harvest, away from/against the fall/arrival of rain" (reading of BeSI/108)

(2) WATERING PLACE (?)

[Ar wird id.]

F123/10: tb(q)lt yt'nn bqln wrd 'l "plantations (for which) the watering place (?) l. makes the plants secure (i.e., it supplies them with water)";

C549/2-3: hqny wrdnhn "he dedicated the 2 watering placed (?)"

WRW I

v pf wrww R3945/13; ? wrw[R4689/3

FIGHT, phps specifically REBEL

[Cf Eth warawa "throw," Te warā "fight," Syr eštawri "advance, come to meet; fight" (MüW/112). The nuance "rebel" is suggested by the context in R3945.]

R3945/13: he overthrew K. bdt wrww bmhrg G "because they fought/rebelled in the battle of G."

For yrn in Ry507/9 read qrn.

n p? wrwtn C320/2*

sense doubtful

C320/2 (fragmentary context): ^{c}śbn šwbn wtwrn wwrwtn "fodder of various kinds (?), a bull, and...?

Read phps ^{c}rwtn and tr with C "precious things," after Ar ^{c}urwa^t.

WRW II

h pf hwrw Ry510/3*

DISPLAY (?) (cf WRY h)

[Cf Ar wry h "show, display." RyMus66/308 tr "cause to be carved."]
Ry510/3: hwrw wwtf dn msndn "he displayed (?) and commissioned (?) this inscription"
Note: BeOr25/294 reads (tḥ)wrw with Ryc, from root ḤWR "decree, ordain."

WRX

n s wrx(m,n) J653/13-4; wrxhw C540/98+; d wrxn J577/8; wrxyn ib/9; p 'wrx(m,n) J720/12+
MONTH
[Eth warx "moon; month."]
C343/12: kwn[t] dt hqnytn bwrx [d]DT' dxrf S bn Ḥ "this act of dedication was made in the month dD. of the year (named for) S. son of Ḥ." AND OFTEN in dating documents; J720/12: stt 'wrxm mrḍm "a six-months' illness"; C540/98: wrxhw dD dlxmst wsty wxmsm "its month (i.e., the date of this document) is dD. of (the year) 565" AND ELSEWHERE in closing formulas

WRY

h pf hwry C318/4*
MAKE KNOWN, ANNOUNCE (cf WRW h)
[Ar wry h "show," Heb tôrāh "instruction," Te.Amh wārē "information, news" (MüW/112).]
C318/4: wkn hwry ^{c}A w'l kd 'l s'l xdrn "thus have A. and I. announced (by means of this inscription) that no one may lay claim to this tomb"
Note: hwry cited by MüW/112 in R4176/4 does not exist. For hwr elsewhere, see under HWR

WRK

v inf wrk R4142/6*
SUPPORT, AID (?)
[Cf Ar wark "hip," Heb yārēk "thigh."]
R4142/6: a dedication made lqbly dlyz wrk bn[hmw] "so that (the god) would continue to support (?) (their) son"

WR^{c}

h pf hwr^{c} Ir13/6; hwr^{c}w C353/16
FRIGHTEN (?)
[Cf Ar wari^{c}a "be timid," Heb yāra^{c} "tremble."]
C353/16: he dedicated bdt hwr^{c}w ws[... "because they had frightened (?) and ... (an enemy?)"; Ir13/6: hwr^{c} wstgb'n wtḍ^{c}n kl wld ^{c}M "he frightened (?) and defeated and laid low all the children of (the god) A. (= the Qatabanians)"

WRQ

n s wrq(m,n) R3946/7+; wrqhmw R55/7

(1) GOLD

[Ar.Eth warq id.]

R3946/7: bny ᶜṮTR wrqm "he constructed an (image of?) (the god) A. in gold"

(2) GREENSTUFF, VEGETABLES

[Ar wariq "leafy, green," Heb yereq "vegetables." Original sense of root prob "greenish-gold."]

R3951/3: wrqm wdᶜtm wṭḥnm "vegetables, (cattle-)fodder and meal" AND OFTEN with dᶜtm; GI361/3: yḥmln wrqn mfrᶜn "they will pay (as tribute) first-fruit vegetables"

For wrq C550/10-11 see under 'ḎN n^3 where passage is quoted.

WRṮ

tp pf twrṯy C37/3*

INHERIT FROM

[Ar wrṯ Lt "possess an inheritance."]

C37/3: 'rḍt twrṯy 'bhmy "the lands they 2 inherited from their father"

h pf hwrṯhw C516/27; inf hwrṯ R3951/5

ACQUIRE, TAKE POSSESSION OF

[Cf Ar wariṯa "be heir, inherit," Heb hôrîš "dispossess, take possession of."]

C516/27: ...]whᶜšr ḏhwrṯhw "he offered as a tithe what he had acquired" (context fragmentary); R3951/5: hṯb whwrṯ whᶜḏb "he set in order, took possession of and repaired"

n s wrṯthw C95/2 (f.s); p 'wrṯhw ib/5

HEIR > OWNER, MASTER/MISTRESS

[Ar warīṯ "heir"; cf usage of Latin heres for "heir" and "master."]

C95/2: the god agreed to protect them when he returned to the city Išwᶜn wrṯthw Q "to help his mistress Q." ib/5: the god granted His servant ḥẓy wrḍw 'wrṯhw bny M "the favor and good will of his masters the b.M." (formula normally ḥẓy wrḍw 'mr'hw)

WŚY

v inf wśy J737/2; wśyhmw ib/3

ASSIST

[Ar wsy L id, var of root 'sy.]

J737/2-3: may the god grant them children wl wśy bny G wl wśyhmw wl hᶜnnhmw "and assist the b.G.; and let Him assist them and help them"

WŚL

h ipf yhślnn J669/24*

MAKE A PROPITIATORY OFFERING

[Cf Ar wsl D, Dt "he sought...to approach him, to gain access to him, or to advance himself in his favour" (Lane/3053C).]

J669/24: yhqnynn wyhślnn t̲wrn "they would dedicate and make a propitiatory offering of 2 bulls"

For hśl elsewhere see under ŚLL

n   d̲ mwśltnhn G1743/1*

    PROPITIATORY OFFERING (?)

[Cf Ar wisāla^t "means of access to a thing," Ḍof ūsal "recourse, support in time of need" (MüOriens20/268).]

G1743/1: hqny ^{c}T̲TR mwśltnhn "he offered (the god) A. 2 propitiatory offerings"

WŚ^c

v   inf wś^c R4646/1*

    GRANT, GIVE (cf WŚ^c v)

[Ar wś^c D "give generously, grant s.o. the use of s.th." (RyMus66/283).]

R4646/1: hḥ]r wryśn wwś^c mr['hmw]...dn wtfn "their lord ordained, enacted, and granted this edict"

tp   pf twś^{c}w J649/30; inf twś^c(n) J646/7+

    aux: DO AMPLY, IN FORCE

J646/7: the god allowed His servant nqm wtwś^c "to take ample vengeance";
J649/29-30: the king ordered them ltqdm wtwś^{c}n...wtwś^{c}w wtqdmn "to attack in force, and they attacked in force"

WŚF

v   pf wśf R3946/7; wśfhw J757/4+; wśfhmy R4123/2; wśfhmw J567/21-3+; wśfw C448/2; ipf yśf R3946/8; yśfmw ib/4,6; yśfnhw F88/3; yśfnhmw J558/4+

    (1) ENLARGE

[Cf Heb yāsap "add, increase," Sq sef "come after, increase."]

C448/2: wśfw wrymw kl gn'hw "they enlarged and raised all its wall"

    (2) INCREASE with, GRANT ABUNDANCE OF

R3946/6: w'ln nxlm ^{c}sy bY wyśfmw qnyhw... "and these are the palmgroves he acquired in Y. and (so) increased his property: (list follows)";
J558/4: bd̲t yśfnhmw 'LMQHW wldm wqnym "because (the god) I. granted them abundance of children and property"

For śf J570/5 see under ŚYF

WŚQ

v   ipf yśq R4689/4*

    BRING TOGETHER, GATHER (?)

[Cf Ar wasaqa id.]

R4689/4 (context fragmentary): ...w]yśq dh[... "he gathered (?)...";
cf also wśq R4635/6--n.pr?--quoted under RYD v

h inf hwśqn J557*

HEAP UP the fill of a wall

[Ar wsq D "bring (grain) together in a heap."]

J557: hml'n whwśqn gn' 'A "he filled in and heaped up the wall of (the temple) A."

n p? wśqt C131/3-4*

RICHES, PROPERTY (?)

[Cf Ar wasq "ass-load (of grain)."]

C131/3-4: 'nṯtm wwśqt w[wh]bt [']b^{c}lhn "women and the property (?) and gifts (?) of their husbands"

WŠ', n mwš'hw, R2861/24--misprint in R for mnš'hw, see under NŠ'

WŠḤ

v ipf ywšḥ R3103/1*

SACRIFICE

[Ar wšḥ D "put a belt (or the like) around the waist; strike on the waist," wišāḥa$^+$ "sword."]

R3103/1: mḏbḥt b(h) ywšḥ...bḏ'A "altar on which (the king?) sacrifices (on a certain day in the month) ḏA." (parallel context R3104/1-2 has yḏbḥn)

WŠ^c

h pf hwš^c J561b/6+; hwš^{c}hmw J562/4+; hwš^{c}t C427/1; inf hwš^{c}n J574/3+; hwš^{c}nhmw ib/12+

BESTOW, GRANT; GIVE AID (2nd obj with b-; said of a god)

[Ar ws^c D "be generous," h "give generously"; cf also, phps, Eth 'awše'a "answer; give an oracular response" (HöSEG8/58f). May be related, with metathesis, to root ŠW^c, q.v. (so BePESA/16; Hö ib rejects this suggestion).]

Ry533/27: hwš^{c}hmw bbry ''ḏnm "(the god) bestowed on them health/strength of mental faculties"; C343/15-6: hwš(^{c}) ^{c}bdhw...bṯny 'sn ḏhrg "(the god) granted to His servant two men, whom he killed (i.e., He allowed him to kill two men)"; C314/6: xmr whwš^{c}n [mr'yh]mw...bhwfynhmy "(the god) granted and bestowed on their 2 lords His protection of them"; J629/25: hwš^c whwfyn ^{c}bdhw...bkn sb'w "(the god) aided and protected His servant when they campaigned"

st pf stwš^c J700/10; stwš^{c}thw ib/7

ASK THE ASSISTANCE OF

J700/7-10: stwš^{c}thw 'ṯtn B...l'wln lhw bnhw...wbh' l^{c}br R...ḫgn stwš^c "the woman B. asked his assistance to bring to her her son, and he went to R. as he had been asked"

n s wš^{c}n C315/11-2+

STRENGTH/AID

[Cf Ar wus^{c} "ability, capacity" and Sab WŠ^{c} h "give aid."]
C315/11-2: bml' wm^{c}d wwš^{c}n šymhmw "by the oracular response, promise and aid of their patron deity"; C339/4: brd' wtḥrg 'mr'hmw...wbwš^{c}n 'xhmw š^{c}b[n ḏ]M "by the help and command of their lords, and by the strength/aid of their ally, the tribe ḏM."
For n tš^{c}t C308/17, see under ŠW^{c}

WTW

h pf hwtwhmw J560/14*
CAUSE TO RETURN = BRING BACK
[Prob causative of a var of root 'TW "come (back)." Cf also Min pp wtw "in the direction of," Ḍof wtty "cause to reach" (MüW/III on wtw pp).]
J560/14: the soldiers captured the territory and riding animals whwtwhmw ^{c}dy hgrn "and brought them back to the city"

WTN

n s mhwtnm J627/12+
PERPETUALLY FLOWING WATER
[Ar watana "be perpetual, never-failing (esp of water)."]
J627/12: let the god fill their dam with water bkl brq dṯ' xrf mhwtnm "in every stormy season of spring and autumn, perpetually flowing water"; sim J628/13

WTF, v and n--phps a triliteral var of root WFY, but see under WFY ti and n^{2}.

WṮ'

v pf wṯ' Ry507/3*
WOUND (?)
[Cf Ar waṯa'a "bruise, wound" (RodConf'65-6/133).]
Ry507/3: mlkn...wṯ' kdhrw qlsn whrgw 'ḤB(ŠN) "the king was wounded (?) when they burned the church and killed the Ḥabashites"

WṮB

v ipf yṯbn R4782/3; yṯbnn Ist7626/1+; prt? wṯb J720/7-8
(1) SIT, STAY
[Himyarite waṯaba "sit" (Nashwan, Extr/133 etc., cited in RabAncWar/27); Heb yāšab "sit, dwell."]
J720/8: 'l ṣbnw wṯb bmḥrmn "they did not reject the (person who) was sitting in the temple" (tr HöASASühne/107)
(2) SETTLE, DWELL
Ist7626/1: w'l ḏbhw yṯbnn wgb' "and let no one settle therein or lease (?) ..."; sim context A452/4; R4782/3: lyṯbn b^{c}m š^{c}bn "in order that he may dwell with the tribe" (but cf also ṮWB v "return")

tp p̱f twṯbhw J725/8*
    ASSAULT, INFLICT wounds UPON (?)
    [Cf Ar wtb h "cause to leap, jump," Dt "take possession illegally of s.o.'s property" (Lane/2930A).]
    J725/8: zxn w'ṯ['r] twṯbhw wṯ'rhw "the wounds and acts of vengeance he inflicted (?) and wreaked on him"

h p̱f hwṯb R2657+; hwṯbt R2659
    SET UP, ESTABLISH (?) (all contexts fragmentary)
    [Cf Heb hôŝîb "settle, cause to dwell."]
    R2657: ...] ṢRWH whwṯb ᶜ[... "(the city) Ṣ., and established (?)...";
    R4499 phps sim; R2659 (in full): ...] hwṯbt mḥwlm wdstqr' ṯṯ(y) [... "the encircling wall was set up (?), and that which he announced (?), two..."

n¹ ṣ ṯbt R4531/1*
    SEAT, SHRINE of a god (?) (cf WTB n²)
    R4531/1: mbny ṯbt 'l'ltn "the construction of the shrine (?) of the gods"; for ṯbt elsewhere see under TWB n²

n² ṣ mwṯb(n) J600/8; mwṯbhw C396/4; mwṯbhmw C308/4+; p? mwṯbtm J575/5
    SEAT, SHRINE of a god (?) (cf WTB n¹)
    C308/4: all the incense they planted lmwṯbhmw YHGL "for their shrine Y."; mwṯbn Y also in J600/8; G1644: hḥdṯw mwṯbhmw "they repaired their shrine (?)"
    Obscure in J575/5: dkwn kwnhmw dSHRTM mwṯbtm "those who were allied with them from (the place) S., the shrines (?)"--epithet of SHRTM?

WTD
n ṣ mwṯdn R4029/1*
    KIND OF CULTIVATED FIELD or LAND (?)
    [Reading and interpretation doubtful; context suggests kind of land.]
    R4029/1: '[ṯ]mrm frᶜm w'tr bhwt mwṯdn "valuable crops and 'tr-plants (?) from this mwṯd-land"

WTM--For twṯm R4779/1, see under TWTM
n ṣ wṯmt G1142/7-8*
    OPEN COUNTRY
    [Cf Heb yĕšîmōn "wilderness," Ar wuṯima "produce little grass and fodder."]
    G1142/7-8: wṯmt wmrᶜt ᶜrn "the open country and the grazing land of the hill-town"

WTN
v p̱f wtn R3945/1+
    DELIMIT, ESTABLISH BOUNDARIES
    [Eth wsn D "delimit, determine."]
    R3945/17: bn X ln 'wṯn wṯn K "from X. to the boundaries K. established";
    C610/2: sṯr wtwṯn sṯr wwṯn "the document he drew up and the delimitation

he established"

n¹ s wtn(n) C949/4+; p 'wtn(m,n) R3945/15+; 'wtnh ib/5

(1) BORDER, BOUNDARY

R3945/15: 'wtn wtn K "the boundaries K. established"; ib/5: he acquired N. bn Š wbn X l'wtnh "between Š. and X., to its borders"

(2) BOUNDARY IDOL or BOUNDARY STONE (often difficult to distinguish from sense¹)

C949/4: w'l hᶜly dn 'tbn wtn "let no one remove this 'tb, (that is) this boundary stone"; R3945/15: he conquered its territory lmhyᶜ 'wtnn ᶜd wtn M "up to the temple of the boundary idols, as far as the boundary of M."

Note also the title of the two sun-goddesses, bᶜlty 'wtnm "mistresses of the boundaries" C457, J664.

n² s twtn R2865/2* (D inf?)

SETTING OF BOUNDARIES, DELIMITATION

R2865/2 quoted under WTN v

WTQ

v imv? m.s tq P135c*

HAVE FAITH, CONFIDENCE IN (?)

[Ar watiqa id. Discussion RyNE4/152.]

P135c: tq 'SD "have confidence, A.! (?)"

h ipf yhwtqnhw F55/5; inf hwtqn R2724/4

CERTIFY, GUARANTEE (?)

[Cf Ar wtq D id.]

F55/5: whr'š]nn kl z'dm ldyhwtqnhw "they will lay down every deposit for the person who will guarantee it (?)"; R2724/4: ...dhr'šhmy lhwtqn hwt (wq)rn "which he laid down to certify (?) this edict"

st inf stwtqn C291/5*

MAKE CERTAIN, ESTABLISH

[Ar wtq h id.]

C291/5: stwtqn wstz'dn blt H "to establish and increase the tribute of H."

n¹ s tqthw R2876/3*

GUARANTEE

[Cf Ar tiqaᵗ "trust, confidence," watīqaᵗ "document, voucher."]

R2876/3: its claim, purchase deed, payments, wᶜlmhw wtq[t]hw "and its document and guarantee"

n² p 'wtqm J574/11+; 'tqhmw IrApp11/1

HOSTAGES (cf WTQ n¹)

J574/11: whbw 'wldhmw 'wtqm "they gave their children (as) hostages"; IrApp11/1: ḥmlw hgrn qrnm whbᶜlw 'wtqhmw "they took (into?) the city a guard and took possession of their hostages"

WTR

v pf wtrw J576/12; ipf ytrw J577/15; inf wtr J629/28

FLATTEN, LEVEL; of a well, FILL IN to ground level

[Cf Ar watara "flatten, trample upon."]

J629/28: wtr wqm^{c} mḥrmt whyklt "leveled and destroyed temples and palaces"; J576/12: wtrw kl 'b'rhmy wqm^{c}w... "they leveled all their wells and destroyed..."; J577/15 also refers to wells

h pf hwtry C655/1; hwtrw R4663/2; inf hwtr(n) R4196/2+

LAY THE FOUNDATION OF (usually with hšqr "roof" or "complete")

[ModYem wattar id (RoVoc/304).]

R4196/2: br'w whwtr whšqr m'glyhmw "they built and laid the foundation for and completed their 2 cisterns" AND OFTEN SIM

n^{1} s trt C608/1; trthw C448/3

FOUNDATION, SUBSTRUCTURE (= WTR n^{3})

C448/3: he walled it bn mrymhw ^{c}dy trthw "from its superstructure to its substructure = from top to bottom"; cf also C608/1: ...]trt mtwl "the foundation of the highway (?)"--C proposes the reading ^{c}M^{c}]TRT 'TWL (two nn.pr)

n^{2} p 'wtr R4351/3*

PLAINS, LOWLANDS

[Cf Sab trt, mwtr "foundation of a building."]

R4351/3: the canal which irrigates these valleys, dybqyn 'wtr ^{c}A "which debouches on the plains of A."

n^{3} s mwtrm R4626/1+; mwtrhw R4107/3

FOUNDATION, SUBSTRUCTURE (= WTR n^{1})

R4626/1: ^{c}s'y m'xdhmy...bn mwtrm ^{c}dy šqrn "they constructed their control dam from foundation to top" AND ELSEWHERE SIM

X-Z

Z

pn z- D71/2+; zn D71/2

HE OF, THE ONE OF (= d-); THIS (ONE) (cf dn)

[See under d-, and cf Eth ze, zeni.]

D71/2: zn wz "this one and that one"; R5085/10: wrxhw zṢRBn "its month (was) zṢ" (elsewhere dṢRBn); R5073 (in full): zNBLT "he of/member of the clan of N." AND SEVERAL TIMES with nn.pr

Z'D

st inf stz'dn C291/5*

INCREASE s.th.

[Cf Ar zyd st "demand more."]

C291/5: stwṭqn wstz'dn blt Ḥ "to establish and increase the tribute of Ḥ."

n s z'dm R3910/7+

EXTRA sum of money put down as a deposit

[Ar zāda (y) "become great, increase," ziyāda^{t} "increase; surplus; extra pay."]

R3910/7: whoever enters an agreement f'w yhr'šn z'dm f'w s'rt ṭmrm "or lays down an extra (sum) as a deposit, or any other security..."; sim F55/5?; C291/10: ...z]'dm f'w ǵ[yr] z'dm "with or without an extra (sum as a deposit)"

Z'D'--For n z'd'm J750/7, read (t)'d'm; see under 'D'

Z'K

v pf/inf z'k J720/16*

PAY, COMPENSATE > OFFER, SACRIFICE as a penance

[HöASASühne/III-2 cfs Ar zaka'a "pay in ready money, quickly or promptly."]

J720/16: wlmšw m^{c}rbtm bn dD wz'k šhn "and let a member of (the clan) D. go to a place of sacrifice and offer a goat (as the penance of a fellow clan-member)"

Z'N--For wz'n Ry507/10, read 'Z'N "Yaz'anite tribesmen" (BeOr25/300)

ZBD

n p? zbd C308/17+

GIFT(S)

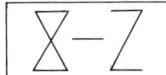

[Ar zabada "bestow," Heb zebed "gift."]
C308/17: kl tš^c t wzbd ysrw 'ysm "all aid/presentation(s) and gift(s) (which) (each) man sent"; also in R2753B/1 in obscure context (n.pr?)

ZBY--For dzby R2861/14, read dxṭ' with R? No etymology or translation has been proposed for zby.

ZBR

v inf zbrn C287/1+
CONSTRUCT, BUILD
[Cf ModYem zābūr "mud wall," zawbar "to construct a mud wall" (RoVoc/304).]
C287/1: hẓlw wzbrn dM "they roofed over and built dM."; sim ib/3, also with hẓly

ZDM--For zdm R3067, read 'dm "servants of," or take as n.pr? Inscr reads (in full): ^c MYT^c zdm S^c D mt

ZHD

n p 'zhd R2726/8*
KIND OF LEGAL DOCUMENT, phps (STATEMENT OF) LACK
[Cf Ar zahīd "little, insignificant; a small amount."]
R2726/8: kl s'wlt w'sm^c w'zhd w'try "all claims (to the harvest), attestations, and (statements of?) lack and surplus (?)"

ZWY--For n 'zyy C540, see under 'ZY

ZWYR--For n zwyr C308b/6, see under ZWR

ZWL

v pf zlw C540/28*
FINISH, COMPLETE
[Ar zāla (w) "go away, cease," Mh zôl "cease" (MüW/61).]
C540/28: wzlw msrn wšṣnn bsb^c t w^c šry ymtm "they finished packing in earth and facing (the construction) with stone in twenty-seven days"

ZWR

n p? zwyrn C308b/6*
WATER DIVERTERS or DISTRIBUTORS
[Cf Ar zīr, zūrā' "vase" > "cistern"; or cf Ar zāra (w) "turn aside"--here sense would be "deflect (and distribute) water" (Irv/137-8).]
C308b/6: kl šr^c qšmtn wzwyrn "all the water channels of the orchard and the water distributor(s)"

ZḪḪ

h ipf yhzḥ R4197b/2*

OVERFLOW

[Eth zaḥzeḥa id, zeḥzuḥ "excess."]

R4197b/2: mqldhw...yhzḥ lhw "his storage cistern which overflows for his benefit"

ZXN

v pf zxn J649/19+; zxnhw J687/7

INFLICT A WOUND; pass, BE WOUNDED, RECEIVE A WOUND

[Cf Ar zaxama "beat violently, thrust away," maxana "wound."]

J687/7 (context fragmentary): ...] zxnt zxnhw [... "the wound he inflicted on him"; J649/19-21: wzxn bhw xms zxnm mḍytm fxḏyhw...wfrshw N. wzxn "he received there five wounds (which) penetrated his thighs, and (as for) his horse N., it was (also) wounded"

n^{1} s zxnt C82/7+; d zxntn C334/15; p zxn(m) J649/19+

WOUND

C82/7: may the god save him bn zxnt zxn bmwtnn "from the wound he received on the battlefield"; J725/7: zxn w'ṯ['r] twṯbhw "the wounds and acts of vengeance he inflicted on him"

n^{2} p zxyntm Ir13+

WOUNDED (men)

Ir13/9: they slew eighty-five men besides those who fell (?) outside the fortress, ḏhbrrw bnhw zxyntm "those who made a sortie from it, wounded"; Ir32/8: (1300) bḍ^{c}m w(700) zxyntm w(3000) sbym "thirteen hundred slain, seven hundred wounded, and three thousand captives"

ZYD

n p 'zd Ir12/4; 'zdhmw ib/5

AUXILIARY TROOPS

[Ar zāda (y) "augment, increase" (RycMus87/246 and n9). (Ryc suggests an alternative tr "provisions" after Ar zād, zawād id, less plausibly.)]

Ir12/4: lḥrb 'zd G "to fight the auxiliary troops of G."; ib/5 sim

ZYY--For n 'zyy C540, see under 'ZY

ZKW

n s zkt MüBilinguis/2*

ALMS, ZAKĀ^{t}-TAX

[Like Ar zakā^{t}, a loanword from Aram zākūtā id.]

MüBilinguis/2: br'...bythw...brd' wbzkt mr'hw "he built his house with the help and alms (paid to) his Lord (the god)"

ZKT--For n zkt MüBilinguis/2, see under ZKW

ZL--See under ZWL, ZLL

ZLL

n *s* zlt C373/3+

FORTIFICATION(S)

[Ar zilla^{t} "stones; smooth stones" (Lane/1242B).]

C373/3: zlt nkl gwbn "fortification(s) of pebbled stonework"; C40/4:mslfhw ZLT FRZNM "its glacis, the Iron Fortification"; C62: ẓllm zlt hgrhmw "roofed chambers of the fortification(s) of the town"

ZM--For *n* zm, see under ZMM

ZMX--In R3945/8, for zmx read s]tmx[ḍ? (signs doubtful)

ZMM

n *s* zm R3945/2+

SYSTEM OF WATER CHANNELS

[Ar zamma "fasten, tighten, bridle"--some kind of controlled canal or canal system? Cf phps Amh zäma "running water, (small) river" (Irv/74-5); and phps Ar zamzam "copious, abundant (esp water)."]

R3945/2: hṯb zm ḥmy M "he restored the channel-system (which) irrigates M."; ib: kl msqy zm W "all the canals of the channel-system of W."; ib/3: wdy wt'w zm "the channel-system caused (water) to flow and collect"

ZN--For *pn* zn D71/2, see under Z

ZNM--In C541/23, read mznm as a *n.pr*

Z^{c}M

v *inf* z^{c}mh N74/3*

INVOKE, CALL UPON a deity

[Cf Heb z^{c}m "threaten"--force the deity to respond? Cf also Ar za^{c}ama "state an opinion," za^{c}m "assertion" (BeNL4/144).]

N74/3-5: nṣfw khyf^{c}t ḏt B wz^{c}mh bysṭ mḥrmn ṯlṯ 'z^{c}mm "they had performed the ceremonies at the time when (the goddess) ḏt B. was 'exalted' and had invoked Her in the sanctuary on three occasions"

n *s* z^{c}mhw C396/7; *p* 'z^{c}mm N74/5

INVOCATION of a deity

N74/5 quoted under Z^{c}M *v*; C396/7: ln sm^{c} z^{c}mhw "when He heard his invocation..."

ZFF I

n *p* zfn C540/84*

UNSKILLED LABORERS

[Cf Ar izdaffa al-ḥimla^{t} "he carried..., or raised upon his back, the load" (Irv/289).]

C540/84: expenditure lf^{c}ln wlzfn "for the craftsmen and unskilled laborers (in the dam-repair project)"

ZFF II

n s mzf R3943/5; mzfh R3946/6; mzfhw ib; p mzff R3943/5+

EXIT CHANNEL, DISTRIBUTOR SLUICE

[Cf Eth zafzafa, Ar zaffa "spread the wings" > equipment designed to spread water? Cf also Ar istazaffahu al-sayl "the torrent found it light to carry, and took it away"; ModYem mazaff "wooden conduit to carry water" (Irv/202-3).]

R3943/5: mxḍ blq mzf m'x<u>d</u>n "he quarried stone for the exit channel of the control dyke"; R3946/6: m^{c}sn Y wmzfhw "the cistern Y. and its exit channel"; R3943/6: mzff nmrn "the exit channels of the control wall"

ZR, ZRM--For mzr GI539/4 (fragmentary context), see passage quoted under KS' v; for n mzrm C540/50, see under MZR

ZRF

n s zrftn R2633/8*

INCURSION, INVASION

[Cf Ar zarāfa† "troop, band of men," Tña zäräfa "abduction, sack, pillage" (sim in other Eth languages); Syr zərīfūtā "aggression, assault," zarīftā "violent rain; attack, assault" (RodConf'68-9/107-8).]

R2633/8: 'syw 'ḤBŠn zrftn b'rḍ ḤMYRm "the Ḥabashites sent an incursion/invasion into the land of Ḥ."

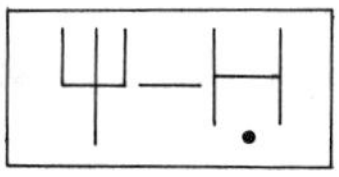

ḤBB

v *pf* ḥb Serjeant-Hûd2+

LOVE

[Ar ḥabba id.]

Serjeant-Hûd2: ^{c}M'D^c ḥb "A. He loved"; sim Ry429d; Serjeant-Hûd10: ḥb LBKH "L. loved"

n *p* mḥbbt Ir16/1*

CLIENTS, DEPENDENTS

[Cf Daṯ ḥabāb "master, patron (of servants or slaves);" Sab mwd "friend" of the king (RycMus87/500).]

Ir16/1: mḥbbt ḏt Y "clients of Y."

ḤBL I

v *pf* ḥbl J577/6; ḥblw J576/3+

(1) LIE, DECEIVE

[Eth ḥabala "deceive," Tña ḥabälä "lie"; Ar ḥabala "catch with a net."]

J577/6: tnblt ḥbl 'sd nbl b^{c}brhw 'mlk S "messengers who deceived those whom the king of S. sent to him"

(2) ENGAGE IN HOSTILITIES AFTER SWEARING PEACE

J576/3: the god helped his servant bḥbl ḥblw b^{c}d slm wgzm gzmw "in the hostilities/revolt they engaged in after the peace and oath they swore"

n *s* ḥbl(m) J589/11+

DECEIT > TREACHEROUS REVOLT

J589/11: ḥbl wḍr hšt'w...b^{c}br mr'yhmw "the revolt and war they began against their 2 lords"; J667/8: ḥbl wqsdt "revolt and rebellion"; J576/3 quoted under ḤBL I *v*

ḤBL II

n *s* ḥbl(m,n) R3945/1+

(1) BOND, ALLIANCE

[Ar ḥabala "make an alliance, a treaty," ḥabl "alliance, protection"; Heb ḥébel "troop, band" I Sam 10:5,10 (HöWar?/82).]

R3945/1: kl gwm ḏ'lm wšymm wḏḥblm wḥmrm "every community (owing allegiance to) a god or patron deity, or (bound by) an alliance or treaty"; same formula R3624, R3948/4+

(2) SALE CONTRACT

J2856/3: w'l kbḥ bydy š'mn ḥbln "no objection having been raised, in the presence of the purchaser, to the contract"

ḤBL III

n s ḥbln F2*

GATE, DOOR (?)

[Akk 'abullu "gate, large gate (of town or building)," ModHaḍ ḥabl "course of stones in a wall or dam" (RyET/3).]

F2 (on the wall of the Mārib temple): ...]dn ḥbln šlṯ ᶜšr ḏbr's m[... "this gate (?); thirteen which are at the top of..."

ḤBL IV

n p ḥb(l)tn Ir24; ḥblthmw Gl441/3+

VINES, VINEYARDS

[Ar ḥabalat "grapevine, vinestock."]

Ir24: qlmt ḥb(l)tn wṯmrn wsqym "vermin of the vines, of crops and sqy-crops"; Gl441/3: xybt nkrw b'ᶜnbhmw wḥblthmw "the drought (with which) they were afflicted regarding their vineyards and vines"; C308/23: qmᶜw ḏbn Ḥ wgbḏw kl ḥblthw "they subdued the people of Ḥ. and plundered all its vineyards"

ḤBN

tp inf tḥbn J578/11*

CARRY OUT A VIOLENT ACT

[Ar ḥabina "become angry against s.o."]

J578/11: the god preserved them bn kl bᶜwt wbḥḍt sb'y wbᶜw wbḥḍ wtḥbn "from all the ambushes and raids they undertook and prepared and engaged in and carried out"

ḤBS

v ipf yḥbs Ry507/6*

WITHHOLD (?) or CAPTURE

[RodConf'65-6/135 cfs Ar ḥabasa "withhold"; also "hold in custody; arrest."]

Ry507/6: yḥrbh[mw] yḥbs wkd' whbt rhnn "he fought them and withheld/captured (?) and refused to give hostages" (Rod's tr)

Note: Ry read yḥks, but did not tr.

ḤBR

v ipf yḥbr J635/35*

ALLY WITH, JOIN WITH (?)--but prob n.pr

[Heb ḥābar, Eth xabara "be joined."]

J635/35: lḥrb ᶜš[r]t yḥbr 'sd kwnw kwn bny Y "to fight the clans with whom those who were (allied) with the b.Y. had joined (?) (or, to fight the clans of YḤBR who were (allied) with the b.Y.)"

N inf? nḥ(b)rn J702/3--Passage reads l/ nḥ(b)rn/ wl (/d)rn; RycHim2/484 n27 considered the two phrases "almost certainly a graphic corruption" of lḥḏrn "beware," root ḤḎR.

n s ḥbrm R4230C/3*

SPELL, ENCHANTMENT (or metathesis for ḥrb "battle"?)

[Heb ḥéber id.]

R4230C/3: wly'xrn (qlmm) wmqṣm wbrdm wḥbrm wšn'm "may (the god) keep away noxious insects, loss (of crops), cold and any spell or enemy"

ḤBT--For ḥbtn lr24 read ḥb(l)tn, see under ḤBL IV

ḤG

cj ḥg R3946/1+; ḥgḏt J551; b-ḥg C37/7+; ḥgm k- R3951/5; ḥgn ḏt J567/5+; ḥgn k- J568/4+; k-ḥgn C540/59

AS, BECAUSE; ACCORDING TO, BECAUSE OF (cf ḥng); k-ḥgn: WHEN

[See etymology under ḤNG.]

J568/4: they dedicated ḥgn kwqh 'LMQH "as (the god) I. had commanded" AND OFTEN SIM; J551: he dedicated ḥgḏt wqh 'LMQH "according to that which (the god) I. had commanded"; C74/16: ḥg ᶜlm bhw tᶜlm "according to the oracular sign whereby he had been instructed"; C37/7: bḥg gdyt hgd lhw "because of the concession he granted him"; R3946/1: wḥg qnyn ḏbḥhw ṯny 'sn "and because of (?) the slave whom two men killed (or read as n: the law/judgment (in the case of) the slave (?))"; C540/59: kḥgn wrd ḏt'n "when the spring (rain) fell"

Note: For ḥg elsewhere see under ḤGG.

ḤGG I

v pf ḥgw C547/6*

MAKE A PILGRIMAGE

[Ar ḥajja id.]

C547/6: ḥgw ḏS bY "they made a pilgrimage to (the god) ḏS. at Y."

n s ḥgtn C533/4*

PILGRIMAGE

[Ar ḥijja† id.]

C533/4: a man approached her sexually ywm ṯlṯ ḥgtn "on the third day of the pilgrimage"

Note: The month-names formerly read as ḏḥgtn (e.g. R2633) and ḏmḥgtn (C46/6) are now read by Be (NewL/2) as ḏḥltn and ḏmḥltn.

ḤGG II

v pf ḥg GI143/3*

CLAIM, HAVE A RIGHT TO (?)

[Cf Ar ḥaqqa "have a right," ḥaqq "right, title" (HöTPK/36); or Eth ḥeg, Sab ḥg "statute."]

GI143/3: wḥg 'xd̲ grtn bn kl qṭntm "and (the god) has the right to take young ones from all flocks (or read as n: and (this is) the law: He may take...)"

n s ḥgn C548/14; ḥghmy R3945/2

(1) STATUTE, LAW

C548/14: ywfyn d̲n ḥgn ^{c}šrt 'xrftm "let this law be preserved ten years"

(2) OBLIGATION

R3945/2: ywm ṣdq ^{c}TTR w'LMQH ḥghmy wyhṯb mwy d̲hbhw "the day when (the gods) A. and I. fulfilled their obligation and sent water (for) his land"

ḤGK--For 'ḥgkm J647/13-4 read 'ḤLKM, n.pr.f (BeNL9/194)

ḤGL

n s mḥgl(m,n) R4646/13-4+; p mḥglt ib/9

ENCLOSED FIELD

[Ar ḥajl "anklet, fetter," Aram ḥgl "make a circle" (RycHimI/97-8).]

R4646/13-4: d̲y^{c}dwn lxd^{c}n wḥṣm wxṣb 'ṯlm wmḥglm bhwt srn "whoever trespasses to injure, split the wood of, or cut down tamarisk-plantations or enclosed fields in that valley..."

Note: Obscure in J2109/7-10: the god saved His maidservant's life bn mwld wldt ǵlmm d̲krm myt ǵyr qllt mwnn bmḥgln "from childbirth: she bore a male child (who?) died without (even?) a small quantity of food in the field (i.e. without shelter?)."

ḤGR I

v pf ḥgr R4176/3+; ipf yḥgrnn Robin al-Mašamayn/3; inf ḥgr GI142/7

ENCLOSE, SET APART (esp land): MAKE S.TH. TABOO or FORBIDDEN

[Ar ḥjr D "he made a bound or an enclosure around his land" (Lane/516C).]

GI142/7: kyqfnn wḥgr mrbd̲n kl r^{c}y "they shall delimit and forbid this sheep-fold to any herdsman"; C646/6: ...wḥgr 'b'r wy[... "and he set apart the well and..."; R4176/3: ywm ḥgr srn lǵrḍ bḥw "when (the god) set apart the valley as taboo, to ... with the serfs"

Robin al-Mašamayn/3-4: yḥgrnn w^{c}rbn d̲t brkt "set apart and dedicate this basin (to a god)"

Note: For ḥgr R4176/13, see under ḤRG v.

n s ḥgr(m) C559+

(1) CONSECRATION, DEDICATION

C559: ḥgr ^{c}ZYN ^{c}ly N "the consecration of (the goddess) U. (is) over N. =

N. is consecrated to U." (on an amulet)

(2) adj: CONSECRATED

N19/9: wl]dt...ǵlm[m] ṯnym ḥgrm "she bore a second, consecrated boy-child"

Note: Include here, phps, ḥgrm C325/9 (fragmentary context).

n² s mḥgr R4920/2+; p mḥgrtn C204/3+; mḥgrthmw C546/11

ENCLOSED (PASTURE) LAND

[Ar maḥjar "tract surrounding a town or village" (Lane/518), Daṯ maḥjar "territory reserved for pasturage."]

C546/11: srhmw wmḥgrthmw wmrᶜyhmw "their valley, enclosed pastures and pasture lands"; R4920/2: wbny bmḥgr ṣyḥ [... "and he built in the enclosed land (which) he had leveled..."

ḤGR II

n s ḥgrm R3478*

STONE > WEIGHT

[Ar ḥajar in both senses.]

R3478 (on a bronze weight with a handle): ḥgrm "weight"

ḤDṮ

v pf ḥdṯt C80/4; ḥdṯw J643/9

OCCUR, TAKE PLACE

[Ar ḥadaṯa id. For use of root in divine epithets, see HöRelig/267, WdM/543.]

C80/4: he sought an oracle bᶜd ḥdṯt ḥdṯt bbyt bn Q "after the event/disaster which occurred in the fortress of the b.Q."; J643/9: mngt ḥdṯw bhgrn M "the events which took place in the city M." (or read as D, "events which they brought about"?)

h pf hḥdṯ R4388; hḥdṯy R3902b#152/3-4; hḥdṯw C11/1+; inf hḥdṯ(n) C191/1+

RENEW, REPAIR; or MAKE NEWLY (senses not always distinct)

[Ar ḥdṯ h "produce, create"; cf also ḥadīṯ "new." Discussion RycInsAnc/84-5.]

C11/1: hḥdṯw qyf šmshmw "they renewed the cult stone of their sun goddess"; R3966/1-2: hḥdṯw whqšb...mᶜmr "they repaired and refurbished the tomb"; C191/1: br' whḥdṯn whšq[rn "constructed, made newly and completed"

n s ḥdṯt(n) C80/4,6*

EVENT, phps specifically DISASTER

[Ar ḥadaṯ in both senses.]

C80/4 quoted under ḤDṮ v; ib/6: mtᶜ ᶜbdhw...bn hyt ḥdṯtn "(the god) saved His servant from that disaster"

ḤḎK

n s ḥḏk C684+ (all on incense burners)

KIND OF INCENSE = "PUNGENT" INCENSE (cf n^{c}m "sweet incense")

[Cf Ar ḥḏq "sting, bite, burn the mouth."]

C684: ḥḏk ḍrw rnd qsṭ "pungent incense, ḍrw-incense, nard, costus"

ḤḎR

v pf ḥḏr J649/21; ipf yḥḏrn C546/6; inf ḥḏr(n,nn) J720/14+

FEAR; BEWARE

[Ar ḥaḏira id.]

J649/21: zxn wḥḏr ktxd^{c}nn rglhw "he was wounded and feared that his legs were injured"; J720/14: wbnw ḏḎ lḥḏrnn bn hxṭ'n "let the b.Ḏ. beware of sinning"; C546/6: lyḥḏrn wl ynḏrn "let him beware and vow penance"

Read prob lḥḏrn in J702/2-4 (passage quoted under ḤBR N̲).

ḤW--see under ḤWY

ḤWB

v pf ḥbt R4938/9*

SIN

[Heb ḥiyyēb, Aram ḥwb "be guilty," Ar ḥawba^{t} "sin."]

R4938/9: they asked the god lḥyw grb 'ṯthw...wḥbt kxmrhmw bms'lhw "to cure the body of his wife, she having sinned,as He granted them through His oracle"

n s ḥbhmw C539/1*

SIN

C539/1: ykfrn ḥbhmw wyqbln qrbnhm[w] "he expiated their sin and (the god) accepted their offering"

ḤWD

n s ḥwdn J542/2*

CISTERN (?) or other construction; phps a WATER DEFLECTOR (?)

[Ar ḥawd id (Bon2T/138n3)? Cf also Ar ḥāda (w) "turn aside, turn away."]

J542/2: h^{c}ḏb wkll kl ḥwdn "he repaired and walled round the whole cistern"

ḤWZ

h inf hḥznhw Ir25/3*

SEIZE

[Ar ḥāza (w) "gain possession of, seize."]

Ir25/3: they put their offering under the god's protection bn 'ys hḥznhw wh'xrnhw "against (any) man who would seize it or remove it"

ḤWY

v ipf yḥw D58+; tḥw D65+; tḥwm (enclitic m̲) D65; inf ḥwyhmw Ir32/7

(1) LIVE (cf ḤYW, ḤYY id)

[Cf Sab ḥyy, id; Heb Ḥawwāh (n.pr).]

D58: 'A bn W lyḥw ᶜA "A., son of W.--may A. live!"; D65: ᶜWBymt...lṭḥw ḏt Ḥ "may A. die; may ḏt Ḥ. live!"

(2) ALLOW TO LIVE, SPARE (?) (phps D)

Ir32/7: ᶜdww hgrhmw sḥtm wḥwyhmw wẓwrn "they entered their town with destruction and spared them (?) and laid siege"

n¹ s ḥw R4176/3; ḥwhw R3946/4,8

CLAN, phps specifically SERF CLAN

[Ar ḥawâ "collect, gather," ḥiwā' "circle of tents"; Heb ḥawwāh "tent village, tent camp." For nuance "serf," cf Min R2771/7: ḥrsm wḥwsm "their freemen and serfs"]

R4176/3: ḥgr srn lǵrḍ bhw "(the god) set apart the valley, that they should ... with the serfs"; R3946/8: yśf ḥwhw F 'dm hš'mhw Ḥ "he increased his clan F. with the clients Ḥ. sold him"

Note: Also referred to this word is the form ḥywhmw R3232/2 where it occurs near ṣlthmw in fragmentary context. Tr "their kin (slt) ...their clan"?

n² s ḥwy NNAGI/5*

LIFE (= ḥyw id)

NNAGI/2: he dedicated bḏt hw[šᶜ]hw 'LMQH bḥwy "because (the god) I. had granted him life"

ḤWL

pp ḥwl R3945/10*

AROUND, NEIGHBORING

[Ar ḥawla id.]

R3945/10: 'bḍᶜ ḥwl bḍᶜ T "districts around the district T."

n¹ s ḥwl R3955/2; p ḥwln R3954/2+

PART OF A TOMB = TIER(S) OF LOCULI (?)

[From sense of "encircling" inner wall of tomb? Discussion BeStI/91.]

R3954/2: bny rbᶜ qbrn...ḥwln ḏbynn ḏtḥtyn "he built a quarter of the tomb, the tiers of loculi of the interior chamber: namely, the lowest one"; R3955/2: one quarter of the tiers of the interior chamber, ḥwl tḥtyn "the tier of the lowest part"

For ḥwlm J702/16, see under ḤLM

n² s mḥwl(m) R2659+; p mḥwlt C325/6

(1) ENCLOSING, ENCIRCLING WALL

[Ar ḥāla "turn," ḥawla "around."]

R2659: hwṯbt mḥwlm "the encircling wall was set up"; R4773/2: mᶜrby wmṣrᶜy wfnwt mḥwl "the 2 entrances, the 2 doors, and the road (leading to?) the enclosing wall"

(2) PILLAR (?)

[Cf Eth ḥawelt id.]
C325/6: 'rbʿt flśtm ʿlwm w'rbʿt mḥwlt "four tops of columns above, and four pillars (?)"

ḤWR

v *pf* ḥwr C546/8; ḥwrw C102/4+; *ipf* yḥwr R3945/16; *inf* ḥwr R2726/13

(1) GO to a place > SETTLE in a place

[Cf Eth ḥora "go," Daṯ ḥāra^{+} "village," Ar ḥāra^{+} "quarter of a city".]
R2726/13: lḥwr wbkl bhgrn Ṣ "to settle and dwell in the city Ṣ."; R3945/16: he instructed them kḏ yḥwr SB' bhgrn N "that Sabaeans should settle in the city N."

(2) PUBLISH an edict, COMMAND by means of an edict (phps D?)

[Development from sense "go": the edict "goes out," "is published."]
C546/8: ...] sṭd'n ḥwr bqdmy ḏt tnxytn "let him (?) be outlawed (as) it was commanded before this confession"; Ry510/3: (ḥ)wrw wwtf ḏn mśndn "(they) commanded and commissioned this inscription" (for another reading, see under WRW *h*)

h *pf* hḥr R2726/14+; hḥrw R3951/5+; *inf* hḥr(n) R3910/1+

CAUSE an edict TO GO OUT > PUBLISH an edict (cf ḤWR *v* sense^{2})

R3910/1: wqh wryśn whknn whḥrn mlkn "the king commanded, ordered, established and published (by edict)"; R2726/14: bḥg wqr wmḥr hḥr lhmw "according to the edict and statute he decreed for them"

n^{1} *p/coll* ḥwr(n) C405/3+; ḥwrhw Ry508/4; *p* ḥwrw C102/4+

SETTLERS, INHABITANTS (cf ḤWR *v* sense^{1})

C609/3: ḥwr w'dym[t] bny ḏM "settlers and clients of the b.M."; Ry508/4: ḥrb M whrg kl ḥwrhw "he fought (the city) M. and killed all its inhabitants"; C102/4: bnw M...ḥwrw hgrn ʿA "the b.M., inhabitants of the city A."; sim F3/5

n^{2} *s* mḥr(n) C563/5+

(1) STATUTE, DECREE (cf ḤWR *v* sense^{2}, *h*)

C563/5: ḏyʿdwn bʿly ḏn mḥrn wlystʿḏbhw "whoever violates this statute, let him fine him"; and cf R2726/14 quoted under ḤWR *h*

(2) THING DECREED = SACRIFICE (?)

G1209/5: h'tw mḥr hnṭf bḏn ẓrn "he offered a sacrifice (?) (whose blood) he caused to flow on this mountain"; C460/3: hʿ mḥr "offered a sacrifice (?)"

ḤZ--For hḥznhmw Ir25/3, see under ḤWZ *h*

ḤZB

n *p* 'ḥzb J577/3+

WARBAND, GANG of enemy soldiers (always in phrase 'ḥzb ḤBŠT "the warbands of Ḥabashat")

[Ar ḥizb, p 'aḥzāb "group, troop, gang," esp in pejorative uses; prob loanword from Eth.]
J577/3: ^{c}dw G wld ngšyn w'ḥzb ḤBŠT "G., child of the Negus, invaded (with) warbands of Ḥabashat"; C314/19: xmr mr'yhmw 'L[M]QH tdr^{c}n Š...w'ḥzb ḤBŠ[T] tḥt m[r']yhmw "and (the god) I. granted to their 2 lords to subjugate Š. and the warbands of Ḥabashat to their 2 lords"

ḤZN--For hḥznhmw Ir25/3, see under ḤWZ h

ḤẒW

v pf ḥẓww C660/2; inf ḥẓwn J603/5+

"INAUGURATE" = determine the fate of a newly completed building (= ḤẒY v) (?)

[Discussion RycExpAst/529; cf Ar ḥaẓẓ "fate," ḥuẓwa† "favor, good will," ḥaẓiya "obtain s.o.'s favor."]
J603/5: they dedicated because br'w whšqrn wḥẓwn sqh wmśwd "they had constructed and completed and 'inaugurated' (?) the cistern and the sanctuary"; C660/2: bnyw...mhẓllm lbythmw...wḥẓww ḥẓyhmw wṣllw bnwthmw "they built roofed passages for their house and 'inaugurated' them (lit., determined their fate) and paved their buildings"

Note: Traditionally the vs ḥẓw and ḥẓy have been translated as terms concerned with the building of ramps or slopes, from the (presumed) basic sense "inclination" of the Ar root ḥẓw/y "favor, good will."

ḤẒY

v inf ḥẓyn C648/4+

"INAUGURATE" a new building (= ḤẒW v) (?)

[See etymology under ḤẒW v.]
C648/4: ^{c}dbw whẓl whṣr[h] wḥẓyn tḥẓyt wnkl kl ṣdqm "they repaired, roofed, built upper chambers, 'inaugurated,' and paved everything (?) satisfactorily"; R4671/2: [h]qšb wḥẓyn l^{c}TTR "they renovated and 'inaugurated' (it) for (the god) A."

ti ipf yḥtẓyw R3945/1*

BE FAVORED by the gods > SUCCEED

[Ar ḥaẓiya "enjoy s.o.'s favor."]
R3945/1: he reinaugurated the tribal assembly of the Sabaeans wy'tmmw wyḥtẓyw mnš'hmw k'ḥd "so that their tribal levies were led forth and succeeded communally"

n^{I} s ḥẓy(m) J561b/18++; ḥẓyhmw C660/2

FAVOR, (GOOD) FORTUNE or FATE bestowed by a lord or god

[Cf Ar ḥuẓwa† "favor."]
J561b/18: may the god grant them ḥẓy wrḍw mr'hmw "the favor and good will of their lord" AND VERY OFTEN SIM; Ir24: ḥẓy wrḍw lb mr'hmw wḥẓy wrḍw

š^c byhmw "the favor and good will of their lord's heart and the favor and good will of their 2 tribes"; J567/22: may the god grant them n^c mtm wwfym wḥẓym "prosperity, health and good fortune"; and cf C660/2 quoted under ḤẒW v

n² s tḥ(ẓ)t F55/3 (copy: tḥyt); tḥẓthw GaAlON31p590; var tḥẓyt C648/4
FATE, FORTUNE (?)
C648/4 quoted under ḤẒY v; GaAlON31p590, F55/3 fragmentary
Note: In C40/3, read tḥyt with C (?).

ḤẒM

v pf ḥẓm C522/5; inf ḥẓmn Gl369/2
sense doubtful; DEPART (?)
[Proposed sense from context.]
Gl369/2: kxdg wḥẓmn wṣwr "when he left, departed (?) and separated"; C522/5: wdS fr' kḥẓm mḥrmn "and as for (the god) dS., He has departed from (?) the temple (as a punishment for sacrilege committed there?)"

ḤẒR

v pf ḥẓr R4176/2+; ipf yḥẓr GaAlON33/2; yḥẓrn ib/5
PROHIBIT, EXEMPT (bn from); "BAN" in a ritual sense
[Ar ḥaẓara "forbid, prohibit."]
R4176/2: ḥẓr T'LB qsdm bn ḏbḥ "(the god) T. has prohibited the qsd-class from collecting taxes"; GaAlON33/2-5: kmnm 'ns dyḥẓr wl ydbḥn dbḥm f'w y'xrn ršwn ḥẓrhw 'ns yḥẓrn wlydbḥn "whenever (there is) a man who has been 'banned,' let him offer a sacrifice, or let the priest remove his ban; (as for) the 'banned' man, let him sacrifice"

n s ḥẓrm R4646/10; ḥẓrhw GaAlON33/4; var ḥẓrnh R4176/10
(1) BAN, INTERDICTION
[Ar ḥaẓr id.]
GaAlON33/4 quoted under ḤẒR v; R4176/10: ḥẓr...R bn kl t'by ym T wḥẓrnh nfsm "(the god) prohibited R. from all disputation on the day of T., and its (R.'s) ban is (inscribed on?) a stela"
(2) ENCLOSED/FENCED TERRITORY (cf ḤṢR n² sim)
[Cf Ar ḥaẓīra⁺ "fence, hedge; field."]
R4646/10: mḥglm wḥẓrm "enclosed field and fenced land"

ḤY'L

n s ḤY'LYTm C376/4; p ḤY'LYm C548/5,7
KIND OF COIN
[Nisba from the n.pr ḤY'L.]
C376/4: 'lfm blṭm mṣ^c m ḤY'LYTm "a thousand coins of standard weight, ḤY'L-coins"; C548/5,7: lyẓl^c n l'lt ^c TTR...^c šr ḤY'LYm...xms ḤY'LYm "let

him pay to the community of A. ten ḤY'L-coins...five ḤY'L-coins"

ḤYW

v pf ḥyw Ry375/2+; ipf yḥywn J669/11+; inf ḥyw J655/9+

LIVE; SURVIVE (cf ḤWY, ḤYY id)

[Eth ḥaywa, Ar ḥayya id.]

J669/11: šftw 'LMQH kmhnmw yldn lhmw bnm wyḥywn fyhqnynn ṣlmn "they promised (the god) I. that if a son were born to them and lived/survived, they would dedicate a statue"; J648/4: xmrhw ḥyw lhw brwhw "(the god) allowed his son to live for him"; Ry375/2: 'l ḥyw lhw wldm "no child has lived/survived for him"

h ipf yhḥywn C336/7*

CAUSE TO LIVE > CURE

C336/7: he promised to dedicate k[m^c?]nmy yhḥywn K...bn mrḍ mrḍ "if (the god) would cure K. of the sickness he was suffering"

n^1 adj m.p? ḥym J635/32*

ALIVE

[Ar ḥayy id.]

J635/32: sbym...dhrgw wd'xdw ḥym "captives whom they killed or captured alive"; cf also ḥyy N11/2 in fragmentary context

n^2 s ḥyn MüBilinguis/2; var ḥyw(m) Sh18+

(1) LIFE

[Ar ḥayya†, Sab ḥ(y)wt id.]

Sh18: may the god grant them n^{c}mtm wwfym wḥywm wsqym "prosperity, health, life and irrigation water"; J736/13: yxmrhmw ḥyw grbthmw wḥẓy 'mr'hmw "(the god) granted them the life of their persons and the favor of their lords"; MüBilinguis/2: mr' ḥyn wmwtn "Lord of life and death (a divine epithet)"

Note: Cf also C6/4, isolated at end of inscr, after date: ḥyw, tr "Life!"? Sim ḥh (read ḥy?) P139e.

(2) HEALTH (?) (cf ḤYW h "cure")

J633/14: rbx wḥyw bn hwt ḥlẓn "relief and cure from this disease"

n^3 s ḥywt J764/3+; var ḥwt R3619

LIFE (= ḥyw)

[Eth ḥeywat id, and cf Sab ḥyw "life."]

J764/3: [šf?]th ḥywt wldm "(the god granted) her the life of a child"; R3547: W^{c}RN ḥywt mlkn "W., the life (?) of the king" (phps a bodyguard?); R3619 (in full): lḥwt 'gwbt B R "for the life of the stonemasons (?) of B.R."

ḤYY

v inf ḥyy Ry520/6*

LIVE (cf ḤWY, ḤYW id)

Ry520/6: may the god allow his wives and children ḥyy ḥyw ṣdqm wmwt mwt ṣdqm "to live a proper life and die a proper death"

ḤYN

pp ḥyn C547/14*

AT THE TIME OF

[Ar ḥīna id.]

C547/14: lyṯwbnhmw ṯwb yn^{c}m ^{c}rt tnxytm ḥyn ḏM "may (the god) bestow on them a pleasing reward in exchange for this confession, at the time of (the month) ḏM."

ḤYF I

v pf ḥyfhmw J577/2*

COMMIT AN INJUSTICE against s.o.

[Ar ḥāfa (y) id.]

J577/2: they returned from campaign b^{c}m ḥyf ḥyfhmw Š...w'š^{c}b ḤMYRM "with (= because of?) the wrong which Š. and the tribes of Ḥ. committed against them"

n s ḥyf J577/2*

ACT OF INJUSTICE, WRONG

J577/2 quoted under ḤYF v

ḤYF II

v inf ḥyf R3958/2*

REVET, SHORE UP

[Ar ḥifa† "side, edge, slope of a mountain," ḥāfa† "side of a wadi" (lrv/151-2).]

R3958/2: bql wḥyf (w)nš' wwdn...kl ḥrt "he planted (?), revetted, banked up and prepared for flooding all the aqueduct"

ḤYḌ

n s ḥyḍ C523/3+; p ḥyḍ ib/7

MENSTRUATING WOMAN

[Ar ḥā'iḍ (f) id, ḥayḍ "menstruation."]

C523/3: qrb mr'tm bḥrmw wmlṯ ḥyḍ "he approached a woman (sexually) at a forbidden (time), and had intercourse (?) with a menstruating woman"; ib/7: ms 'nṯ ḥyḍ wlm yǵtsl "he touched menstruating women and did not wash himself"

ḤYQ

n s ḥyqn Ir13*

COVE or other body of water

[Cf Ar ḥāqa (y or w) "enclose, surround;" Eth ḥayq "shore."]
Ir13: they occupied and burned a number of boats bḥyqn Q mkdḥ mlk Ḥ "in the cove (?) Q., depot of the king of Ḥ."

ḤYR

v pf ḥyr J1013c; ḥyrw J631/22+
MAKE CAMP, CAMP in a place
[Central Ar ḥyr "remaiǹ," Syr ḥīrtā "camp."]
J631/22: B. and the Ḥabashite force traveled to the city wḥyrw bxlf hgrn "and camped outside the city"; J1013c (graffito): ^{c}A G ḥyr "A.G. camped (here)"

n^1 s ḥrt(n) C334/12+; var ḥyrt J631/30+; ḥyrthmw J576/12+; p? ḥyrn Ir12
MOBILE CAMP
[Syr ḥīrtā id, Ar ḥayr "enclosure." Cf also Ar al-Ḥīra†, capital city of the Lakhmids.]
J576/12-3: hdrkthmw ḥyrthmw ^{c}dy Q...qdmthmw ḥyrthmw ^{c}dy xlf [... "their mobile camp overtook them at Q...their camp preceded them to the vicinity of...";C334/12:wḥrt mr'hmw...wwfyt "and as for their lord's camp, it was saved"; ib/11: they expelled the tribe bn ḥrtn "from the camp"
For ḥrt elsewhere, see under ḤRR I n^1

n^2 s? mḥ(y)rhmw C542/6*
ENCLOSURE, ENCLOSURE WALLS
[Ar ḥayr "[an enclosure] like a ḥaẓīra†: or a place of pasturage in which it is prohibited to the public to pasture their beasts" (cf Irv/327n113).]
C542/6: ṯny mḏmrm wṯṯy mwqntn bmḥ(y)rhmw "two plantations and two cisterns within their enclosure"
Note: Text reads mḥ()rhmw; C emends to mḥ(my)hmw "their embanked land."

ḤKS--For yḥks Ry507/6, read yḥbs (?) and see under ḤBS

ḤL--For yḥln C523/9, see under ḤL' v

ḤL'

v ipf yḥl' R2888; var yḥln C523/9
PAY A REPARATION
[Ar ḥala'a "give money to s.o." (RycConf/2).]
C523/9: hḍr^c w^{c}nw wyḥln "he submitted and abased himself and paid a reparation (for his sin)"; R2888: LB' yḥl' "L. paid a reparation"

tp inf tḥl'n R3956/9+
PAY A REPARATION (cf ḤL' v)
R3956/9: hḍr^{c}t w^{c}nw wxṭ't wtḥl'n "she submitted and abased herself, made a sin-offering and paid a reparation"
Note: ḤL' v may be a D form, with tḥl'n as its inf.

ḤLB

n s ḥlb C541/130*

DATE WINE

[Ar ḥlb usually "milk," but refers to various liquids including wine (Irv/319-20); Eth ḥalib "juice of figs, dates."]

C541/130: 'hd ᶜšr ''lfm 'l ḥlb sqym ḏtmrm "11,000 (measures?) which are (of) wine, the beverage of dates"

ḤLẒ

v pf ḥlẓ J583/7+; ipf yḥlẓn J663/8

BE SICK; SUFFER FROM A DISEASE (esp of legs or hips?) (cf ḤLṢ)

[No convincing etymology. Cf Ar lḥṣ D "drive into a corner," Heb lāḥaṣ "press, oppress," and Mandaean ḥlaṣa "torture, torment"?]

J633/8: yḥlẓn hwt ḥlẓn drm bxrfm "he suffered from that disease once a year"; J583/7: bkn ḥlẓ rglyhw "when his feet/legs suffered from a disease"

n s ḥlẓ(m,n) C411/7+; ḥlẓhw J720/14; p? ḥlẓtm Ir20/2

DISEASE (esp of legs or hips?)

J720/14: mrḍm...ḏ'l mn šᶜr kmhn h' ḥlẓhw "a sickness about which no one knew what that disease of his (was)"; C411/7: kl ḥlẓm wmrḍ[m] "every disease and sickness"; J711/4-6: ḥlẓ ḥqwnhn wḥlẓ ymrnhw drm bxrfm "the disease of hips and the disease which attacks him once a year"

ḤLY I

n s ḥlynn R3895/6; p ḥly A452/5

GIFT

[Cf Ug ḥlym, parallel to mlk "kind of offering"; Ar ḥalā "he obtained, got from him good; he gave him a thing as property" (Lane/633-4).]

A452/5: tsb'w wtwfyn [r]z' wḥly "they are compelled and under obligation regarding all expenses and gifts"; R3895/6: ...]t ḥlynn wgb'nn [... "..., gifts and remission of taxes"

ḤLY II--For mḥly Gl142, 1143, read mxly and see under XLY

ḤLL I

v pf ḥlt R4088#55/5+; ḥllw Ry509/5; ipf yḥlln R3247

HARM, DESTROY; pass BE DESTROYABLE = BE FORFEIT (a life)

[Ar ḥalla "untie, dissolve, break up."]

R3247: SMW lyḥlln ḏ ysrq mqd(ḥ)n "may (the god) S. destroy anyone who steals this bowl"; R4088#55/5: whm 'l t'xḏ fḥlt nfshw lḏyhrgnhw "if he does not give himself up, his life is forfeit to anyone who may kill him" (same exp R4088#56/5-6, R4558/2); Ry509/5: ksb'w wḥllw 'rḍ M "when they campaigned and harmed/destroyed the land of M."

Note: RyMus66/306 tr ḥllw in Ry509/5 "dwell," after Saf, Qat ḥl, ḥll "camp, dwell."

n <u>d</u>? mḥlnn C542/5; <u>p</u>? mḥl[lt] R4197/1-2

OUTFLOW

C542/5: ...] mḥlnn 'rḍtm [... "the 2 outflows, the lands..."; R4197/1-2: hš]qr whqḥ mrw wmḥl[lt] "completed and prepared for use the irrigated field and (its) outflows"

Note: In C542/5, C emends to RḤMNN without improving sense.

ḤLL II

n <u>p</u> 'ḥll(m) C79/6+

BOOTY, phps specifically GARMENTS or WEAPONS stripped from a fallen foe = SPOILS

[Ar ḥulla† "garment." Cf also ModAr ḥalāl "movable property" (LaH/555, Rwala/268)--sense includes slaves, flocks, herds. HöSEG8/57 cfs Ar ḥalāl "permitted," tr "legitimate booty" (property which may be lawfully taken from the vanquished foe).]

C79/6: the god granted him mhrgt w'ḥll w'sby ṣdqm "satisfactory slaughters, booty and captives"; C334/17: the god helped him bt'wln bwfym w'ḥllm w[sby]m wǵnmm ḏhrḍwhmw "to return (from campaign) with safety, 'ḥll-booty, captives and ǵnm-booty which satisfied them" AND OFTEN SIM

ḤLL III

n <u>s</u> ḥllt R3945/8+

VILLAGE

[Ar ḥilla† "tents, collection of tents."]

R3945/8: hṯb ḥllt Y...[w]kl bd^{c}hw w'A w'hgrhw "made over the village of Y. and its district, and A. and its villages (etc., to the Sabaean state)"; same exp R3916/2

ḤLM

n^1 <u>s</u> ḥlm(m,n) Ir15/1+; <u>var</u> ḥwlm J702/16

DREAM

[Ar ḥulm id.]

Ir15/1: the god granted him ḥlmm whr'yt "a dream and an oracular vision"; J567/11-2: stml'w b^{c}m 'LMQH khmy bṣdqm whkn hwt ḥlmn wwkbw b^{c}m 'LMQH kbṣdqm whkn hkn hwt ḥlmn "they asked of (the god) I. that the 2 (bulls which he saw in a vision) might be real and that dream might come to pass, and they received from I. as (if it were) real and that dream had come to pass"; J702/16: fl śyf ḥwlm mykbt "may He give a dream (promising) things to obtain"

n^2 <u>s</u> ḥlmtm N74/6*

DREAM-SEERESS

[Ar ḥalama "dream."]

N75/6: z^{c}mh...blty kwn bmḥrmn kl b^{c}ltm wḥlmtm "they invoked (the goddess) without there being (present) in the temple any priestess or dream-seeress"

ḤLF

n s ḥlf R2625*
ALLIANCE (?)
[Ar ḥilf id.]
R2625 (fragmentary): ...]bḥlf šqr[... "in a firm (?) alliance (?)"

ḤLṢ

n s ḥlṣm J650/32*
OPPRESSION (cf ḤLẒ)
[Cf Heb lāḥaṣ "oppress," Mandaean ḥlaṣa "torture, torment," and Sab ḥlẓ "suffer from a disease"; ḥlṣ may be var of ḥlẓ "disease."]
J650/32: the god protected him bn b'stm wnkytm wnḥtm wḥlṣm...šn'm "from harm, injury, beating and oppression (by any) enemy"

ḤMD

v pf ḥmd R3992/10+; ḥmdhw C357/10; ḥmdt J751/4+; ḥmdy J568/9+; ḥmdw Mül/3; ipf yḥmdnn ib; inf ḥmd(nn) J629/16+
PRAISE
[Ar ḥamida id.]
R3993/10: ḥmd...xyl wmqm T...bḏt mt^{c}...^{c}bdhw "he praised the might and power of (the god) T. because He saved His servant" AND VERY OFTEN SIM; J564/3: he dedicated a statue ḏbhw ḥmd...mqm [']LMQH bḏt stwfy... "by which he praised the power of (the god) I. because He had granted ..." AND OFTEN SIM; Mül/3: yḥmdnn mqmhw bkn yqnynn 'wldm...wḥmdw mqm 'LMQH "they praised (the god's) power when they acquired children, and they praised the power of I."

h inf hḥmdn J668/12-3*
BEHAVE IN A PRAISEWORTHY WAY, EARN PRAISE
[Ar ḥmd h id.]
J668/12-3: the god allowed His servants hḥmdn whyhrn 'hnmw yqhnnhmw 'mr'hmw "to earn praise and conquer where/whenever their lords commanded them"

n[1] s ḥmd(m) C308/3++; ḥmdhw C357/10+
PRAISE
[Ar ḥamd id.]
C308/3: hqnyw šymhmw T...'ṣlmn...ḥmdm bḏt hwš^{c}hmw "they dedicated to their patron deity T. these statues in praise because He had helped them" AND VERY OFTEN SIM; J575/8: yt'wlw bwfym wḥmdm wmhrgm "they returned (from campaign) with health, praise and slaughter" AND OFTEN SIM; C541/93: tryd ḍlln bḥmd RḤMNN "the illness abated, with praise to (the god) R."; J649/14:

ḥmdm bsb't wz'w sb' "in praise for the campaigns they continued to undertake" (unique example of ḥmdm + b + n)

Note: In J657/4: šfthw ḥmd bdxmrhw read ḥmdm "he promised him (the offering) in praise because He had granted him"? (Cf C308/3 quoted above.) In R3884/2: ṣlmn dbhw ḥmdm read ḥmdw "this statue by which they praised"? (Cf J564/3 quoted under ḤMD v.)

n[2] s mḥmd J1028/12*

(THE) PRAISED ONE, divine epithet

[Ar maḥmūd, muḥammad id.]

J1028/12: rbHD bmḥmd "Lord of the Jews. By the Praised One" (closing formula)

ḤMẒ

n? s? ḥmẓ J726/1*

sense doubtful; phps n.pr

[JSIMB/207 implausibly tr "skinner," after Ar ḥamaṭa "peel, skin."]

J726/1: TWBM ḥmẓ YSR 'dm bn ᶜA hqny... "T., ...? of (the clan?) Y., clients of the b.A., dedicated..."

ḤMY

v pf ḥmy R3945/2 twice; ipf yḥmynhw J651/33

(1) EMBANK a canal

[Ar ḥamâ "defend, shield," Heb ḥômāh "wall."]

R3945/2: ḥmy ḥrthw "he embanked his aqueduct"; J651/33: mḍrfn...dyḥmynhw bn dᶜbn "the channel which he embanked against floods"

(2) IRRIGATE by means of embankments

R3945/2: zm ḥmy M "the channel-system (which) irrigates M. (by embankments)"

h ipf yhḥmnhw J2856/4*

SAFEGUARD, PROTECT

J2856/4: bᶜd yhḥmnhw wydblnhw "after (the vendor) shall have safeguarded and duly performed it (the contract)"

ti ipf yḥtmynn R4775/2; inf ḥtmyn N74/9-10

(1) PROTECT

N74/9-10: wl ḥtmyn wstwfn bn hᶜfšn "may (the goddess) protect and deliver from (the consequences of) the sacrilege"

(2) PROVIDE IRRIGATION by embankments

R4775/2: m'xd yḥtmynn š[ᶜ]bn [S bn mt]br[n] "the control dyke (which) provided irrigation for the tribe [S. before (?) the br]each (in the dam?)"

n[1] s ḥmym F90/1+

(1) SANCTUARY

[Ar ḥimâ id.]

C548/1: mn gr ḥm[y]m yḥrṭ slḥm "whoever visits the sanctuary bearing weapons..."

(2) EMBANKMENT, DAM

R90/1: ...]ym bnhw ḥmym wqẓ't [... "from it a dam, and the distance (?)..."

n^2 *p* ḥmyt F127/4*

PROTEGES, CLIENTS

[Ar ḥamiya "protect," ḥimya$^+$ "that which is defended."]

F127/4: wldhmw ḥmyt w'hlht H "their children, the clients and clans of H."

n^3 *s* mḥmy(m,n) C660/3+; *p* mḥmyt(n) R4176/4

(1) TABOO AREA, part of a sanctuary (cf ḥmy)

C660/3: ^{c}smym wmḥmym wmḥḍrtn lmknt mwṯbn "an ^{c}smy, a taboo area and a shrine for the cella of the mwṯb-sanctuary"

(2) EMBANKED LAND, EMBANKED FIELD

C380/3: lywfyn fnwhw wkl mḥmym "to make safe his canals and all the embanked land"; C37/3: mḥmyt w^{c}brt w'byt w'rḍt "embanked lands, meadows, settled areas and fields"; R4176/4: ^{c}šr mḥmytn "the tithes of the embanked fields"

n^4 *s* mḥmt(m) R3686/1+

SYSTEM OF IRRIGATION by means of embankments

R3686/1-2: mḥmt wmsqt 'nxlhmw...w'l 's s'l mḥmtm wṣ^{c}tm [w]mflqm "the embankment system and canal system of their palmgroves...let no one lay claim to the embankment system, the diversion system or the dispersion system"

ḤML

v *ipf* yḥmln G1361/3; *inf* ḥmlhmw G1142/9+

(1) DRIVE

[Ar ḥamala "transport, carry, convey."]

G1142/9: ḥgr...kl r^{c}y...bn ḥmlhmw qṭntm "prohibited any herdsman from (their) driving (of) flocks"; J576/16: hsḥthmw ^{c}dy ḥmlhmw mṣr^{c}t hgrn "they slaughtered them until (they) drove them to the gates of the city"; C407/22: hwkbhmw...^{c}dy ḥmlhmw bḥrn "he pursued them until he drove them to the sea"

(2) PAY as tribute

[Ar ḥamala "pay as tribute" (SoSoSEG4/37-8).]

G1361/3: yḥmln wrqn mfr^{c}n "he will pay as tribute vegetables, first-fruits"

ḤMN--For ḥmnm C548/1 read ḥm(y)m, see under ḤMY *n*^{1}; for yhḥmnhw J2856/4, see under ḤMY *h*

ḤMR

n^1 *p* ḥmr(m) R3943/2+; *var* ḥmrthmw J643b/3; *var* 'ḥmrm Ir12/6

ASS

[Ar ḥimār id.]

R3943/2: t̲ll qnyhmw ''blm wbqrm wḥmrm wqnym "took their livestock as booty: camels, cattle, asses and sheep and goats" AND ELSEWHERE SIM

n² s̲ ḥmrm R3945/1+

KIND OF TREATY (?) (phps solemnized by the sacrifice of an ass)

[HöWar?/82-3, cfing M. Noth, "Das alt-testamentliche Bundschliessen im Lichte eines Mari-Textes" (in Gesammelte Studien zum Alten Testament, v.6 [Munich, 1957], pp. 142-54), suggests this tr--cf Ar ḥimār, Sab ḥmr "ass."]

R3945/1: kl gwm d̲'lm wšymm wd̲ḥblm wḥmrm "every community (owing allegiance to) a god or patron deity, or (bound by) an alliance or ḥmr-treaty" same formula R3624, R3948/4+

Note: Read ḥmrt R3945/15 as n.pr.

ḤMT

n? s̲? ḥmtm R4763/1*

context obscure; sense doubtful

R4763/1: ...]' mrb bnyy' ḥmtm [..., no tr

ḤNG

cj ḥngn J753/2*

AS (= ḥg, see under ḤG)

[This is the non-assimilated form of the common cj ḥg(n). Cf Himyaritic ḥinj = Ar mit̲l "like, as" cited by Nashwān (Extr, p.29) (BeRev/353B); Ar ḥinj "root, origin" (JSIMB/225).]

J753/2: [hq]n(y)[w]...ṣlmnhn ḥngn wqhhmw [b]ms'lhw "they dedicated these 2 statues as (the god) commanded them in His oracle"

ḤNN--In R4142/10, read ḥ(g)n? Passage reads: ...] ḥnn bšft[... Cf the phrase ḥgn šfthw "as he promised Him" R3399B+

ḤNT--For ḥnt R3605b/1 read snt with Ry547/1? See under SN.

ḤSM

v inf ḥsm J643b/5+

CUT/HACK TO PIECES in battle

[Ar ḥasama "sever."]

J643b/5: the god helped him bškr wsḥt wḥsm mlk Ḥ wmṣrhw bhwt tqdmn "in defeating, slaughtering, and cutting to pieces the king of Ḥ. and his force in that battle"; J575/7: ḥsm whrg whsḥtn...hmt 'ḤBŠN "cutting to pieces, killing and slaughtering those Ḥabashites"

ḤFD

n s̲ mḥfdn J554+; mḥfdhmw R2720/3+; mḥfdhmy R4194/3; d̲ mḥfdnhn J557; p̲ mḥfdt R3943/4+

TOWER (in agricultural and cultic contexts); FORTIFICATION

[Eth māxfad id; Sab usage seems to include other fortified building works.]

R4194/3: qrwt wnqbt wm'tt wmḥfdhmy "canals, cuttings and channels and their tower"; R4648/2: mḥfdhmw Ṣ mḥrm Q "their tower Ṣ. of their temple Q."; J551: mḥfdt b^{c}ly dn mhy^{c}n "towers above this sanctuary"; R3943/4: gn' M mḥfdt blqm "he walled (the city) M. (with) fortifications of blq-stone"

ḤFN

n d ḥfnnhn R4930*

CONTAINER, or UNIT OF MEASURE

[Ar ḥafana "scoop up with both hands," ḥafna^{t} "handful"; cf phps Akk ḫupunnu "bowl."]

R4930: he dedicated ḥfnnhn bn fr^{c}t fr^{c}hw "these 2 containers (or, ḥfn-measures) of the first-fruits he had rendered to (the god)"

ḤFF

n^{1} s ḥf J558/5*

ENCIRCLEMENT (but see Note)

[Ar ḥaffa "surround."]

J558/5: may the god protect them bn ml' wḥf šn'm "from the abundance or encirclement of any enemy"

Note: Or read phps as var of ḥyf "act of injustice, wrong"--see under ḤYF n.

n^{2} s mḥfn Gl209/14*

ENCLOSING WALL

[Cf Ar ḥaffā^{t} "border, enclosure."]

Gl209/14: bny wgn' hgrn...wmḥfn db D "he built and walled the city and the enclosing wall which is at D"

Note: The parallel text C338 reads mḥfdn here.

ḤFR

v pf ḥfrw C541/68; inf? ḥfr C399/2

DIG, DIG OUT

[Ar ḥafara id; ḥafar "a newly dug well" (Irv/98-9).]

C399/2: hn[b]ṭ wḥfr [b]'rhw "he dug down to water and dug out his well"; C541/68: ḥfrw ṯw wṣḥw ^{c}rn "they dug until they reached bedrock"

ḤFŠ

v inf? ḥfš C462/4*

INQUIRE, SEEK an omen or oracle

[Cf Heb ḥāpaš "search, search out."]

C462/4: ...]tm wḥfš b[...] ṯny šmlm "... and inquire...a second bad omen..."

ḤṢY

n s ḥṣy J578/42-3+

FAVOR (= ḥẓy)

[See etymology under ḤẒY n¹.]

J578/42-3: may the god protect them against curses with which their enemies may curse them b^{c}ly ḥṣy mr'yhmw "to the detriment of the favor (shown to them by) their lords"; J657/12: ḥṣy wrḍw mr'hmw "favor and good will of their lord" AND ELSEWHERE SIM, paralleling ḥẓy

ḤṢM

v pf ḥṣm C292/4; inf ḥṣm R4646/13

CUT, SPLIT WOOD (?)

[Etymology doubtful. Cf phps Ar ḥaṣab "firewood" and Sab ḥsm "cut to pieces." Ar xṣm h "break apart (intransitive, said of wood)" is sometimes cited, but does not appear in Lane.]

C292/4: ḥṣm wgz^c bn kl ḥṣm "he split and hewed some of the split wood"; R4646/13: xd^{c}n wḥṣm wxṣb 'ṯlm "injure, split the wood of, or cut down tamarisks"

Note: Obscure in C290/5: ḥṣm kl ^{c}smm ḏy'tyn lM "...? every offering which they offer to M." Phps refer to root ḤṢṢ?

n s ḥṣm(m) C292/4+; ḥṣmhw C325/8

(1) SPLIT WOOD, LUMBER (?)

C325/8: qṣ^{c}w ḥṣmhw "they cut down its wood (?)"; C292/4 quoted under ḤṢM v

(2) KIND OF WOODWORK, made of split wood (?)

C612/1: mgz^{c}m ḥṣmm mbr'm "mgz^c-woodwork, ḥṣm-woodwork, stonework..."

ḤṢN

n¹ s ḥṣn C287/3*

FORTRESS

[Ar ḥiṣn id.]

C287/3: hẓly wzbrn G wḥṣn R "they roofed over and built G. and the fortress of R."

n² p ḥṣn(h)w G913/3; var 'ḥṣnhw J619/11-2; 'ḥṣnhmw R3/9

PROTÉGÉS, CLIENTS

[Ar ḥaṣuna "be fortified" > "be protected."]

F3/9: 'ḥṣnhmw 'dm ḏḤ "their (fellow-)clients, the clients of ḏḤ.";
J619/11-2: mt^{c}hw wkl 'ḥṣnhw...b'bythw bn sdm wmrḍ mrḍw "(the god) saved him and all his clients in his fortresses (or, dependent clans) from the sickness they suffered"; C913/3: ^{c}mn ḥṣn(h)w bhṯm wqṭnm "with his clients, great and small"

ḤṢṢ

n p ḥṣṣm R3945/2+; var? ḥṣ(t?) R4646/9

SECTIONS of land, parcels of LAND SECTIONED by walls

[Ar ḥiṣṣa†, p ḥiṣaṣ "part, portion," PBH ḥāṣaṣ "cut off, divide."]

R3945/2: ᶜsy ḥṣṣm wṯᶜrtm ḏhb M "he made sections and sluices (in) the irrigated land M."; sim J541/2; R4646/9: mḥglt w'ṯl wḥṣ(t?) "enclosed fields, tamarisk plantations and sectioned land"; J542/4: let no one deceive K bḏhbhw ḥṣṣm wb fnwthw "concerning his irrigated land, the sectioned land, nor concerning his canal"

Note: In R4646/9, RycMus69/98 reads ḥṣ[d], tr "harvest" after Ar ḥaṣīd id.

ḤṢQ

n s? ḥṣq Ry502/3; ḥṣqhmw J644/20-1+

BAGGAGE TRAIN (?)

[Sq ḥáṣaq "bind, tie," Heb.Aram ḥṣq "tie, bandage, saddle"--reference is to baggage tied onto transport animals (BeNL7/541).]

Ry502/3: ḥṣq sb' bᶜm hwt gyšn "the baggage train which set out with this army"; J644/20-1: 'frshmw wrkbhmw wbᶜrhmw wḥṣqhmw "their horses, riding camels, (transport) camels, and baggage train"

ḤṢR

v inf? [ḥ]ṣr R4006/1*

SURROUND WITH AN ENCLOSURE

[Eth ḥaṣara "provide with a wall," Heb ḥāṣēr "court, enclosure (around a building)," Ar ḥaẓara "fence in."]

R4006/1: [ḥ]ṣr wgn' mwṭn(h)mw "(they) surrounded with an enclosure and walled their residence"

n¹ s ḥṣrhw C542/3*

ENCLOSING WALL

C542/3: mqby[hmw] wḥṣrhw wb'ryhw "their drinking cistern and its enclosing wall and its 2 wells"

n² p ḥṣwrhmw Gl537/7*

ENCLOSED LANDS (cf ḤẒR n²)

Gl537/7: may the god grant them bbrw[g]hmw wḥṣwrhmw ṯmr sqym "in their open and their enclosed lands, sqy-crops"

ḤḌR I

tp pf tḥḍr J1526/3*

PERFORM A PILGRIMAGE (?)

[Be2SAIn/63 on ḤḌR h derives it from ḥḍr "court of a temple" (n², sense² below); v will mean "do something in the temple" > "present one's self in the temple, make a pilgrimage to it."]

J1526/3 (graffito): tḥḍr "he performed a pilgrimage (?)"

h inf hḥḍrn R4176/1*

PERFORM A PILGRIMAGE (= ḤḌR tp)

R4176/1: the god commanded lkd 'l y^{c}tnn S bd'A bn hḥḍrn 'LMQH ^{c}dy M "that (the tribe) S. in (the month) dA. not neglect to make a pilgrimage to (the god) l. at M."

n[1] s ḥḍr J651/17+; ḥḍrhw C79/4+

(1) DWELLING PLACE

[Ar ḥaḍar "settled region," ḥaḍīra$^+$ "place of assembly, vestibule," Heb ḥāṣēr "court."]

C79/4: he dedicated lqbl dhwfyhw bḥḍrhw dM "because (the god) protected him in his dwelling-place dM"; same exp C82/4

(2) COURT of the temple (= mḥḍr)

[Dwelling-place of the god? Min ḥḍr part of the temple associated with sacrifices.]

R4228/7: bny byt S wym nql lḥḍr [... "he built the temple of (the god) S.; and when he provided stone for the court..."

(3) PILGRIMAGE (cf ḤḌR tp, h)

J651/17: lnẓr wtnṣfn (b)hgrn M lḥḍr 'A "to guard and maintain order in the town M. for the pilgrimage of (the month) A."; IrApp2#3/12: ḥḍr SYN "pilgrimage of (the god) S."

n[2] s mḥḍrn R3943/5; p mḥḍrtn C660/3

COURT of the temple (?) (cf ḥḍr sense[2])

R3943/5: bny ^{c}A whwry xlf mḥḍrn "he built A. and the 2 cisterns outside the temple court"; C660/3: ṣllw mwtbhmw...wqdmhw...mḥḍrtn...lmknt "they paved their shrine and, in front of it, the courts for the cella"

ḤḌR II

n p 'ḥḍr J629/33+

nisba: ḤAḌRAMIS (?)

[From n.loc ḤḌRM(W)T; for loss of final radicals, cf Ar ḥaḍārim "Ḥaḍramis." (RycBiOr25/6B). JaSIMB/130 tr "dwellings," identifying the word in these passages with n[1] sense[1] from ḤḌR I.]

J629/33: hdrkn b^{c}d 'ḤḌR w^{c}rb "to pursue the Ḥaḍramis (?) and beduins"

Note: Cf also ḤḌRM C140 "Ḥaḍramis."

ḤQW

n d ḥqwnhn J711/5; ḥqwyhw J700/13

HIPS

[Ar ḥaqw "waist, flank."]

J700/13: xrṭ R šzb S bn ḥqwyhw "R. drew the dagger of S. from his hips"; J711/5: ḥlẓ ḥqwnhn "the disease of his hips"

ḤQL

n[1] s ḥql(m) J578/8+

CULTIVATED LAND, COUNTRY (contrasted with hgr "town")

[Ar ḥaql "field; domain."]

J578/8: tqdmw...bḥql Ḥ "they fought in the cultivated land of Ḥ."; also with a n.loc ib/34, J590/10; bḥqlm whgrm "in country and town"

n[2] p? mḥql P123/2*

CULTIVATED LAND, FIELDS (cf ḥql)

[Ar maḥqala[†], p maḥāqil "fields" (RyNE4/150-1).]

P123/2: dr'w mḥql rḥ "they sowed the fields of the plateau"

adv nḥql(m) R2726/15*; nḥql-mw Ir12/2; nḥql bn Hö43+

IN PARTICULAR, PARTICULARLY

[Development from basic sense "part," cf Heb ḥéleq id, Ar ḥalq "field" (BeNL10/415).]

R2726/15: all those claims, nḥql bn š'mtm w'ṯwbtm ṯmrtm "particularly as regards purchases and payments (for) crops"; Ir12/2: slmw...nḥqlmw dwrm "made peace, in particular on one occasion"

ḤQQ

n s ḥqq(m,n) C609/5+

CONTRACT; as adj: LEGALLY OBLIGATORY/BINDING

[Ar ḥaqq "right, title, legal claim; sound, valid."]

C609/5: xd[c]n wbdln wḥqqn "restrictive, conceding (?) and legally binding"; R2724/11: lyknn ḥqqm wnfqm "let (this edict) be legally obligatory and binding"; same exp ib/6

ḤQR

n s mḥqr J651/12,28*

RUIN, RUBBLE

[Ar ḥaqura "be low, contemptible."]

J651/12: wdqt wmḥqr bytnhn "the fall and ruin of the 2 houses"; ib/28: ln brṯw mḥqr bytnhn "after they razed the rubble of the 2 houses"

ḤR--See under ḤWR, ḤRY, ḤRR

ḤRB

v pf ḥrbhmw C407/20; ḥrbw J577/4+; ipf yḥrbhmw ib/11+; yḥrbw J574/6; inf ḥrb J616/23+; ḥrbhmw ib/26; act.prt? ḥrb(m,n) NNAG12/17+

(1) FIGHT, RAVAGE

[Ar ḥāraba id.]

J616/23: hgrw wṣbḥn wḥrb "they made a raid and a morning attack and fought"; C407/20: they campaigned and fought bkn ḥrbhmw mr'hmw "when their lord fought them"; J577/4: lnqm bḥrbt ḥrbw "to take vengeance for the battle they fought"; C713/2: nṣb Q...ḥrbm šhrm "grave stela of Q., a famous fighter (?)"

(2) "FIGHT," i.e., PERFORM THE RITUAL OF PASSING THE NIGHT IN THE AREA OF THE TEMPLE CALLED "MIḤRĀB"

[Denom from mḥrb (ḤRB n^2). Discussion RycMancie/264 and passim.]

NNAG12/6: wkbw ml'm IN...lḥrb byn t^cmtn "they received an oracle regarding N. that (he should) 'fight'/perform the ḥrb-ritual between 2 night watches"; ib/17: sb' ḥrbn lḥrb "to compel the 'fighter' to 'fight'"; and several other examples of this sense in this inscr

n^1 s ḥrbn NNAG12/4-5*

(RITUAL) COMBAT

NNAG12/4-5: the god commanded him lšym ḥrbn bmḥrmn "to prepare (or, consult) the ritual combat in the temple"

n^2 s ḥrbt(n) J685/2+; ḥrbthmw J665/40; p ḥryb J650/20+

BATTLE, WAR

[Ar ḥarb (f) id.]

J650/20: sb't wḥryb sb'w wšw^{c}n mr'hmw "the campaigns and battles they undertook, aiding their lord"; J685/2: mt^{c}hw bn ywm ḥrbt "(the god) saved him from (harm on) the day of battle"

n^3 mḥrbn C106/3; [m]ḥrbhw R4108/3

PART OF THE TEMPLE where tḥrb-visions are obtained

[Cf Ar miḥrāb "recess" or "niche" in the mosque; for discussion of ancient forms of the miḥrāb, see SerjMiḥr/443n3,446,448; BafIns/33.]

C106/3: br'w whšqrn mḥrbn K "they constructed and completed the mḥrb K."

n^4 s tḥrbn C357/12+; p tḥrbt(n) R4632/2+

VISION obtained by incubation in the miḥrāb

[Inf of ḤRB v sense^2--prob D?]

C357/12: hr'yt hr'y lhm[w] btḥrbn "visions he showed them through the tḥrb-vision"; R4632/2: šmw tḥrbt(n) lwfyhw "they consulted (?) tḥrb-visions for (the sake of) their well-being" C289/20: tḥrbt w'ml' "tḥrb-visions and oracle responses"

ḤRG

v pf ḥrg R4176/13; inf ḥrgn R4137/5

COMMAND

[Frequent in this sense in Qat; cf Ar ḥarraja "forbid."]

R4137/5: sb]'t yqhnn wḥrgn ['mr'hmw] "[the cam]paigns [their lords] ordered and commanded"; R4176/13: ḥrg T'LB 'śwrhw wmrḍ ṯlṯ lqśm 'qwl "T. commanded His produce and a grant (?) of one third (to be) the portion of the tribal leaders"

st pf stḥr(g)w G913/1*

ALLOT FOR ONE'S SELF (?)

[Sense derived from ḥrg "command"?]

G913/1: sthr(g)w "they alloted for themselves (?)" (inscr much restored, HöSEG8/22)

n[1] s mḥrg C648/2; p mḥrg R2633/6

(TRIBAL) LEADER (lit., "COMMANDER")

R2633/6: kbwr wmḥrg S "chiefs and leaders of (the tribe) S." (at end of a list of witnesses); C648/2: qwl wmḥrg R "chief and leader of (the tribe) R."

In R4069/5: mhrt wkbwr š^cbn, read prob mḥrg (cf R2633/6 quoted above).

n[2] s tḥrg C41/4+

COMMAND

C41/4: brd' wtḥrg mr'hmw "by the aid and command of their lord"; sim C339/3

ḤRD

n s ḥrdn R3616*

ALTAR FOR BLOOD (?) SACRIFICE

[Cf Eth ḥarda "slaughter."]

R3616 (fragment of an incense altar): ḥrdn ISN [... "sacrificial altar for (the god) S."

ḤRW

n s tḥrw C570/6*

DELIMITATION, REGULATION OF BOUNDARIES

[Cf Ar ḥry Dt "examine, investigate."]

C570/6: lkd...yd'n tḥrw byn nxlnhn "in order that the delimitation between the 2 palmgroves may be established"

ḤRṬ

v ipf yḥrṭ C548/1*

BEAR arms (?)

[No convincing etymology; sense from context. Cf phps Ar xrṭ h "draw (a weapon)."]

C548/1: mn gr ḥm(y)m yḥrṭ slḥm "whoever visits a sanctuary bearing (?) arms..."

ḤRY I

v pf ḥr C540/66*

BE INCUMBENT (^cly upon)

[Ar ḥry Dt "need to" (Dozy), ḥarī "proper, right" (Irv/284).]

C540/66: 'š^cbm dd' ḥr ^clyhmw tqh bM w^crmn "the tribes upon whom it was already incumbent to bring to completion (the repairs) in M. and (on) the dam"

ḤRY II

n s ḥry C86/9*

LOSS, HARM

[Ar ḥry "decrease, be diminished."]

C86/9: may the god protect them bn ḥry wlsn wmʿḍw "from loss, calumny, and despite"

ḤRM

v *pf* ḥrm J723/4+; ḥrmw R4176/6

(1) BE SACRED, TABOO

[Ar ḥarama "be forbidden," ḥaram "sacred, taboo."]

R4176/6: the god prohibited the doorkeepers bn hwḍ'n 'ś́rm ḏystʿḏbn kḥrmw "from driving away the flocks which betake themselves (there), for they are sacred"; ib/8: let the god take cognizance of ḏydkṯn tḥrm kḥrm "him who violates the taboo (on the tithe), for it is sacred"

(2) INCUR INTERDICT, BE "BANNED"

J723/4: the god saved His servant bn ḥrmn ḥrm "from the interdict he had incurred"

h *pf* hḥrm R4233/5+; *ipf* yhḥrm R3945/16

PREVENT, INTERDICT; *pass* INCUR INTERDICT (cf ḤRM *v* sense^2)

[Eth 'aḥrama "prevent."]

R3945/16: hgrn N yhḥrm bn mwfṭm "he prevented the town N. from being burnt"; sim ib/7, [h]ḥrm; R4233/5: ...]hw bn ḥrmn hḥrm "(to free?) him from the interdict he had incurred"

n^1 *s* ḥrmw C539/3*

"FORBIDDEN" or CONSECRATED PERIOD

[Ar ḥaram "forbidden, taboo, sacred."]

C539/3: qrb mr'tm bḥrmw wmlṯ ḥyḍ "he approached a woman (sexually) at a time forbidden, and had intercourse (?) with a menstruating woman"

n^2 *s* ḥrmn R4233/5+

INTERDICT

R4233/5 quoted under ḤRM *h*; J723/4 quoted under ḤRM *v*

n^3 *s* ḥrmt(m,n) R4176/7+

SANCTUARY (but see Note)

R4176/7: tfr qsd...ʿdy...'A whṣr bḥrmt 'A "the qsd-citizens journeying to (the shrine) A. and enacting the hṣr-procession (?) in the sanctuary A." (in ib/10, cf ḤRMT *n.loc*); C282/2: hqny...S ʿdy ḥrmtn "he dedicated to (the god) S. in the sanctuary," or tr as epithet, "S. of the sanctuary" or "of Ḥ."; C366: hʿ ḥrmtm šlṯṯ'ḏ "he sacrificed (in) the sanctuary three times"

Note: In C366 and parallel texts, some consider ḥrmt a type of incense (named for the district ḤRMT?) (TsSEG6/7). In C414/2-3, read ḥrt for ḥr[m]t (ḤRR I *n*^{1}).

n^4 *s* mḥrm(m,n) R4648/2+; *d* mḥrmnhn J577/17; mḥrmynh[C40/5; *p* mḥrmt J629/28;

mḥrmthmw C323/5

(1) TEMPLE, SANCTUARY

[Eth meḥrām id.]

R4648/2: br'w...mḥfdhmw Ṣ mḥrm Q "they constructed their tower Ṣ. of the temple/sanctuary of (the god) Q."; C323/5: mt^{c} mḥrmthmw whgrhmw bn hwt ṯyln "(the god) saved their temples and villages from that flood"; J629/28: mḥrmt whyklt "temples and palaces (?)"

(2) FORTIFIED CAMP

[Sense from context and basic sense of root: "protected area, immune from violation."]

Ir32: nfṣw ^{c}dy mḥrmn ḏǵrw "they went to the fortified camp which they had provisioned"; sim J643/32,34

Note also the exp mḥrm gnztn "sanctuary of the dead = cemetery," J702/10 (passage quoted under GNZ II).

n^{5} s tḥrm R4176/8*

TABOO (cf ḥrm, ḥrmn "interdict")

R4176/8 quoted under ḤRM v sense^{2}

ḤRF

h ipf yhḥrfn R4133/7*

DISTORT, FALSIFY (?)

[Ar ḥrf Dt id.]

R4133/7: ...] yhḥrfn 's[ṭrn? "(whoever) falsifies doc[uments... (?)"

ḤRṢ

n s ḥrṣm C540/75*

ZEAL, CARE; adv ḥrṣm: CAREFULLY

[Ar ḥara/iṣa "be intent on, strive" (Irv/287-8).]

C540/75: br'w ^{c}glmn wnmryn ḥrṣm bgrbm "they built the diversion mole and the control wall carefully with rough stone"

ḤRḌ

n s? ḥrḍm C562/6*

sense doubtful; prob a KIND OF FOOD

[C tr "cuts of cheese" after Heb ḥărîṣê heḥālāb id 1Sam 17:18 (derivation of ḥāraṣ "cut"), but cf prob Eth ḥariḍ "flour, dough."]

C562/6: ḥrḍm w^{c}gdm wdblm "...?, pressed grapes and pressed figs"

ḤRR I

v pf ḥrrw C541/110-1; inf ḥrr R3958/2+

RAKE UP EARTH for an embankment, CONSTRUCT AN EMBANKED CANAL (= ḥrt)

[MSA ḥarra "rake up earth to build earth dams" (Irv/31).]

R4194/2: grbw wśw^{c} wḥrr "they revetted, leveled and raked up an embankment";

R3958/2: ḥyf (w)nš' wwdn wḥrr wbr' kl ḥrt "revetted, embanked, prepared for flooding, raked up earth for and constructed every ḥrt-canal"; C541/110-1: ḥrrw ^{c}rmn "they raked up earth for the dam"

n^{1} *s* ḥrt(n) C657/3+; ḥrthw ib/2+; *d* ḥrtn C460/5; ḥrty R3911/2; *p* ḥrm Ist 7630/4; *var* ḥrrtn R3945/17; *var* 'ḥrrhmw R4085/5

(1) PRIMARY CANAL, AQUEDUCT with embanked sides

[Cf ḥrr *v* and ModYem ḥarra "stone wall or embankment" (RoVoc/305), "intended to support fields on hillsides against the impetus of the pluvial run-off" (Irv/31). Cf also ModḤaḍ ḥrr^{t} "opening in the levee of earth... of the wadi to regulate the flow of the sêl water if the field is low" (LaH/122).]

C657/2: bḥrthw w[b]fnwthw d̲t tsqynhw bn ḥrtn "in his primary canal and his secondary canal which waters it (a palmgrove) from the primary canal"; C654/2: 'l kmtt ḥrtn wt̲n "let this aqueduct not extend beyond the boundary"; C518/7: rt̲d 'sṭrhw wḥrt "he placed his inscriptions and aqueduct (?) under the god's protection"; R4085/5: br'...'rb^{c}t 'hlm w'ḥrrhmw "constructed four cisterns and their aqueducts"; Ist7630/4: hqšb ḥrm "prepared the aqueducts for use"; R3945/17: stmxḍ mwy d̲Q...wstmxḍ...ḥrrtn d̲t M...bn ḥrrtn...ln 'wt̲n "he confiscated the waters of Q. and the canals of M., from the canals to the boundary stones"

(2) DRAINAGE CHANNEL on an altar, to carry away blood (?)

[Derived from sense "canal."]

C460/5: wt̲nty ḥrtn "and 2 drainage channels" (sacrificial context, fragmentary)

For ḥrt in another sense, see under ḤYR *n*^{1}

n^{2} *s* ḥrrtm C541/57*

BANKING UP of earth (*maṣdar*?)

C541/57: a command to the tribes lḥrrtm wmsrm wgrbtm wbr'[m] "for banking up of earth, packing in of earth, and building up with stone (to repair the dam)"

For ḥrrtn R3945/17, see ḤRR *n*^{1} sense^{1}.

n^{3} *p* ḥrwrhmw R3911/3*

EMBANKED LANDS, or LANDS IRRIGATED BY EMBANKED CANALS (?)

R3911/3: ^{c}s'w ḥrty brfdyhw...bḥrwrhmw d̲ysmynn ^{c}A wS "they constructed 2 embanked canals...in their embanked lands which are called A. and S."

ḤRR II

n *p* ḥr R3945/18; ḥrhw ib/6+; *var* 'ḥrr(m) R4818/5+; 'ḥrrhmw J616/15+; *f* 'ḥrrthmw C80/8

FREEMEN, FREE-BORN MEN (phps also a military class)

[Ar ḥurr id.]

R3945/6: wld 'LMQH wgwm ḥrhw w^{c}bdhw "the children of (the god) I. and the community (= the Sabaean state), its freemen and its slaves";C80/8: 'ḥrrhmw w'ḥrrthmw w'dyb[thmw] "their free-born men, free-born women, and dependents"; R4818/5: 'wldm '(ḥ)rrm 'd̲krwm "free-born, male children"

ḤRR III

n s mḥr J666/6*

DROUGHT (or phps FEVER)

[Ar muḥirr "thirsting" (IrvRev/129-30). RycHim2/495 and n53 cfs Ar ḥūr "injury, loss, ruin," synonym maḥāra† (root ḤWR).]

J666/6: the god saved them bn mḥr kwn b'rḍn "from the drought (or, fever) which was in the land"

For mḥr elsewhere, see under ḤWR.

ḤRT--For n ḥrt, see under ḤYR, ḤRR I

ḤRT̲

n p mḥrt̲thmw R3945/11*

PLOWED (i.e., CULTIVATED) LANDS

[Ar ḥarat̲a "plow, cultivate."]

R3945/11: kl 'hgrhmw wmḥrt̲thmw wmrᶜythmw "all their towns, plowed lands and grazing lands"

ḤŚŚ

n s? ḥśśm C448/2*

MATERIAL USED IN MASONRY

[Sense from context]

C448/2: mbr'm ḥśśm w'bnm "stonework: ...? and stones"

ḤŚR

n p ḥśrw R3951/1; var ḥśrn R2678+

SOCIAL CLASS OF INDIGENTS (?) (cf ḥšr id)

[BeNL9/192 cfs Heb ḥāšar "lack, be indigent" and the ModḤaḍ social class called ḍuᶜafā'; cf phps Ar xasira "suffer from the cold."]

R2678: kbr ḥśrn F "chief of the Indigents of F."; same exp R4798; R3951/1: nzḥt wᶜhrw F w'rbᶜn wḥśrw "the Outlanders, the nobles of (the clan) F., the clansmen and the Indigents"

Note: RhKat1/75n4 cfs Ar ḥuššār "tax collectors" and so translates. For ḥśrm C448/2 read ḥśśm, see under ḤŚŚ.

ḤŠD

n? s? ḥšd F120/14*

sense doubtful; context fragmentary

[RyET/72 cfs Ar ḥšd "join together, assemble," ḥšd "troop of men."]

F120/14: ...]rd ᶜlhmw qsb R ḥšd[... "...upon them, R. ...ed ...(?)"

ḤŠY

n s ḥšym Ry507/6*

BRONCHIAL TROUBLE

[Ar ḥašiya "to breathe short, or unintermittedly; pant for breath" (Lane/578B) (cf DrNote/103).]

Ry507/6: d̠'syw...bn ḥšym̀ wsᶜlm "What they encountered of bronchial trouble and coughing"

ḤŠK

v pf ḥškhw Ir28/1; ḥškhmw ib; inf ḥšk R4962/19+

COMMAND

[Cf Heb ḥāśak "withhold, prevent." BeNL5/109-10 proposes original sense of root to have been "set a limit"; OSA "define" > "ordain."]

Ir28/1: ḥškhmw tnbltm b'rḍ Ḥ "he commanded them (to go) as an embassy into the land of Ḥ."; R4962/19: may the god protect him bkl b[rt̠]m...d̠bhw yqhn wḥšk mr'yhw "in every campaign in which his 2 lords may order and command him"

Note: In R4137/16 read prob ḥšk for ḥšr: [...]m wḥšk 'mr'hmw "...? and commanded (inf, or n "command of"?) their lords."

n[1] s ḥšk(m) R4194/2+

(1) PERSON IN AUTHORITY, STEWARD

R4194/2: 'nsm ḥškm kś' bbythmw "a man, a steward who commanded in their house"

(2) COMMAND

F3/8: kl ḥšk wmwṣt wqht 'mr'hmw "every command, ordinance and order of their lords"

n[2] s ḥškthw R5094/1+;ḥškthmy unpub inscr cited MüPoly/133; p 'ḥškthw Ry520/5-6; 'ḥškthmy Ẓafar1/2-3

WIFE

[Cf Heb ḥāśak "withhold, prevent" and Ar parallel ḥurma[†] "wife" (ḥarama "be sacred, set apart"); or phps sense is "person (f) in authority over a household," cf Sab ḥšk "steward" (BeNL5/110). Discussion of usages MüPoly/133.]

R5094/1: S wḥškthw w'lwdhmy "S., his wife and their children"; C543/3: Š w'mhw...wḥškthw "Š, his mother and his wife"; Ry520/5-6: 'ḥškthw wwldhw "his wives (!) and his children"

n[3] p mḥškt C541/88,89*

PERSONS IN AUTHORITY > EMISSARIES

C541/88-9: wṣḥ[h]mw mḥškt ngšyn w...mḥškt mlk R wtnblt mlk F wrsl M "there reached them the emissaries of the Negus, the emissaries of the king of

R., the embassy of the king of F. and the messengers of M."

ḤŠR

n p 'ḥšrn R2726/4*

SOCIAL CLASS OF INDIGENTS (?) (cf ḥśr id)

[See etymology under ḤŚR.]

R2726/4: ᶜhrw F wnzḥt w'rbᶜn w'ḥšrn wmśwdn "the nobles of (the clan) F., the Outlanders, the clansmen, the Indigents and the council"

For ḥšr R4137/16, read prob ḥšk v.

ḤṮW

v? inf? ḥṯwn R4378/2*

sense doubtful; context fragmentary

[R cfs Ar ḥṯw "spread dust; tread the earth."]

R4378/2: ...] wḥṯwn kl ṯḏ [..., no tr

ḤṮQ

v pf ḥṯq R4176/13*

TAKE CARE (?)

[Cf phps Heb ḥāšaq "give one's self up to a wish, desire."]

R4176/13: ḥṯq bhwfyn bḥg ḏnmḥrn "he is to take care (?) that payment is made in accordance with this decree"

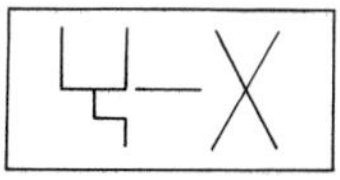

X

ab x R4922+

SYMBOL FOR NUMBER 5

[Initial of Sab xms "five."]

R4922/4: ...] ^{c}x "10-5 (i.e., fifteen)" (note absence of strokes setting off a number); R4199/2: ▯ x ▯ [... "5 ..."; ib/3: ...] ▯ xll ▯ "5-1-1 (i.e., seven)" (context fragmentary)

XB, see under XYB

XB'

v <u>pf</u> xb't R3956/5*

HIDE, CONCEAL

[Ar xaba'a id.]

R3956/5: she wore a dirty mantle (in the temple) fxb't mn 'mr'h "and concealed (it) from her lords"

XBB

n <u>p</u> 'xbb R4231/5+; 'xbbhmw C516/11

PITS or NICHES

[Ar xabba "sink (in sand); be hollow, cavernous (earth, in speaking of a cave," 'axbāb "niches."]

R4231/5: let the tomb belong to the clan B. wkl b'xbb wmdr xdrn gwlm "and everything in the niches and soil of the tomb, as private property"; R4356/4: ^{c}syhw 'xbb[... "he constructed niches for himself (?)"

XBṬ

v <u>pf</u> xbṭ C575/7*

STRIKE, MAKE A SURPRISE RAID (?)

[Ar xabaṭa "strike; travel not by the main road, on a road not open to view" (cf Lane/698A).]

C575/7: to protect the tribe bn xbṭn xbṭ D b'rḍn "from the raid(s?) which D. made in the land"

n^{I} <u>s</u> xbṭn C575/6+

(1) RAID(S?)

C575/6 quoted under XBṬ v

(2) ATTACK of disease

[Ar xabṭa† "blow; attack of disease."]

J751/8: the god cured her bn xbṭn kwn bhwt xrfn "from the attack of disease which befell in that year"

n² p xbṭhmw J616/15*

RAIDERS (?)

J616/15: 'wlw kl 'ḥrrhmw 'wt̲qm wxbṭhmw "they brought back all their freemen as hostages, and their raiders (?)"

Note: Read phps as v, "and struck/punished them," or the like?

n³ as adj: p? xbṭn C562/6*

PRESSED and dried, of fruit (?)

[Ar xabaṭa "trample."]

C562/6: ᶜgdm xbṭn wdblm "pressed (?) grapes and lumps of pressed figs"

XBŠ, C541/44,113--n.pr of the northern sluices of the Mārib Dam (Irv/293-5,318).

XDG

v pf xdg J643/29+; xdgw J644/9

(1) ALLOW

[Eth xadaga "allow; leave (a place)."]

J628/8: the god agreed by oracle that kwn xdg 'tw sqym ᶜdy hwt m'xd̲n "He would allow irrigation water to come to that control dyke"

(2) LEAVE a place

J643/29: xdg hgrn Y w'tw ᶜdy xlf hgrn H "he left the city Y. and came to the neighborhood of the city H."

XDL

v ipf yx[dl] C380/6; inf xdl C99/9

ABSTAIN FROM, BE NEGLECTFUL OF

[Cf Heb ḥādal "cease."]

C99/9: 'lśnw xdl hyᶜ "they are not allowed to abstain from sacrificing"; cf also C380/6: wd̲yd[sl wnm]l nmln fl ynkrn "and whoever is neg[lectful or utters] calumnies (?), let him be fined"

XDM

ti inf xtdmn Ir24*

BE CULTIVATED, BE GROWN (of crops)

[Ar xadama "cultivate (land; plants)," ti id (DozyI/354); sim Dat̲ LaGDI/569-70).]

Ir24: cereal crops 'hnmw ytfrᶜnn wxtdmn "wherever they are cultivated or grown"

n s xdmtn N56/1*

MAIDSERVANT
[Ar xaddāma^{+} id.]
N56/1: Ṣ xdmtn bnt Š "Ṣ., the maidservant, daughter of Š."

XD^{c}

v pf xd^{c}w C448/4; ipf txd^{c}nn J649/21; inf xd^{c}n R4775/3
BE DAMAGED, BE MADE USELESS
[Cf Ar xada^{c}a "it became little (rain)," xada^{c}at al-sūq "the market became dull in respect of traffic" (Irv/221); see also under XD^{c} L.]
R4775/3: t̲br wxd^{c}n hwt m'xd̲n "that control dyke was broken and made useless"; J649/21: zxn wḥd̲r ktxd^{c}nn rglhw "he was wounded and feared that his feet would be damaged/made useless"

L? pf xd^{c}w C448/4; inf xd^{c}n R4646/13
DAMAGE
[Cf Syr Zr xāda^{c} "push, shake brutally" (RodConf'66-7/130).]
R4646/13: wmnmw d̲y^{c}dwn (l)xd^{c}n wḥṣm wxṣb 't̲lm "and whoever enters (the fields) to damage, hew or cut down tamarisks..."; restored ib/7-8; C448/4: xd^{c}w wh^{c}qbw lxlfhw mṣr^{c}tm "they damaged and (then?) repaired, outside it, the double doors" (or read as XD^{c} v, "the double doors were damaged and repaired"?)

n^{1} s xd^{c}n C609/5*
as adj: CONSTRAINING, RESTRICTIVE
[Cf Ar xada^{c}a "refuse, be reluctant" (RyET/22).]
C609/5: let these documents be xd^{c}n wbd̲ln wḥqqn "restrictive, conceding (?), and legally binding"

n^{2} s mxd^{c}m Ry508/11+ (L prt?)
ONE WHO DAMAGES
Ry508/11: bxfr RḤMNN (d̲)n msndn bn kl xssm wmxd^{c}m "this inscription (is) under (the god) R.'s protection against (any)one who would injure or damage (it)"; sim J511/4
Note: Ry tr "alteration, falsification," after Ar xada^{c}a "deceive."

XDQ--R2880 (in full): ǵrf wxdqn wnṭ^{c}, no tr

XDR

n s xdrn R4231/4+; xdrhw ib/3
TOMB, GRAVE
[Ar xadira "stay, abide"; cf Phoen ḥdr "(burial) chamber."]
R4231/4-5: wkwn xdrn lB wkl b'xbb wmdr xdrn gwlm "let the tomb belong to (the clan) B. and everything in the niches and soil of the tomb, as private property"; C318/4: 'l 's s'l w^{c}ẓm xdrn "let no one raise a claim to or enlarge this tomb"

XWB--For xb see under XYB

XWD

v pf xwdhmw NNAG12/26; inf xwdn C429/1+

(1) SEEK TO OBTAIN a favor or response (from a god)

[RycMus87/258n2 deduces sense from context, but cfs Heb ḥīdāh "riddle, puzzling question," in the semantic sphere of "oracular response."]

R4151/5: sflt wxwdn 'm(t)hw...ktldn bnm wwldt "(the god's) maidservant asked and sought an oracular response that she might bear a son, and she did"

(2) GRANT a favor or oracular response

NNAG12/26-8: wxwdhmw 'LMQH bṣdǵ hwt 'sn...l'rx nḍ^{c}w b^{c}br 'LMQH "(the god) I. granted them a response by the manifestation (shown to) that man concerning the litigation they had argued before I."; C429/1: ...]w wxwdn ḏbn mqtt hwt 'ysn "some of the officials ...ed and granted (favors?) to that man"

n s txwd NNAG15/20* (D inf?)

FAVOR or RESPONSE obtained from a god

NNAG15/18-20: the god granted them bkl ṣry wtbšr wšft wtxwd ṣry wšft wxwdn wtbšr "every response, promise, favor and announcement which He gave, promised, granted and announced"

XWX

n d xxnhn J552/3*

DOOR, PASSAGE

[Ar xawxa† "aperture...in a wall,...admitting the light...; passage... between any two houses" (Lane/820B).]

J552/3: kl mbny xxnhn wmḏqntn "all the construction of the 2 passages and the oratory"

XWM

n s xwm(m) R4138/6+

SICKNESS, PLAGUE

[Cf Ar xawma† "country with an unhealthy climate."]

R4138/6: the god protected His servant bn xwm[m ḏ]kyn bkl 'rḍn "from the plague which was in the whole land"; J645/13: xwm w^{c}ws wmwtt "the plague, pestilence and death"

XWS--For xs see under XSS

XX, see under XWX

XṬ'

v pf xṭ' R2861/14; xṭ't R3956/8-9+; ipf yxṭ'n DJE10/5

(1) ERR, SIN (b- against)

[Ar xaṭi'a id.]

J561b/13: 'ᶜrb xṭ'w b'mr'hmw "beduins who had sinned against their lords"; DJE10/5: kl 'ns yxṭ'n bḏt mqb[rtn] "any man who sins with regard to this burial place..."

(2) MAKE A SIN-OFFERING

[Cf Heb ḥăṭā'āh, ḥaṭṭā't "sin-offering."]

R3956/8-9: she had sinned, fhḍrᶜt wᶜnw wxṭ't wtḥl'n "so she humbled and abased herself, made a sin-offering and repented"; sim in C568/6, R3957/9

h pf hxṭ' J702/8; hxṭ't C532/3-4; hxṭ'w J577/9+; inf hxṭ'n J720/15

SIN (b- against) (= XṬ' v sense[1])

[Ar xṭ' h id.]

C532/3-4: she confessed because hxṭ't bbythmw wbmḥrmn "she had sinned in (her family's) house and in the temple"; J601/8: xṭy' hxṭ'w b'mr'hmw "the sins they had committed against their lords"; sim C612/5; J720/15: lhḏrnn bn hxṭ'n b'LMQH "let (them) beware of sinning against (the god) I."

n s xṭ'm R2861/6-7; p xṭy'(n) C612/5+

SIN, CRIME

[Ar xiṭ' id.]

J601/8 quoted under XṬ' h; J720/10: ws'r xṭy'n xmrhmw "and (the god) granted (= forgave) them the rest of their sins"; R2861/6-7: whoever buys and hires out the son of a free man's slave, wkwnt xṭ'm š'mt(n) "the purchase shall be (accounted) a crime"

XṬṬ

v inf xṭṭ A452/4*

FIX THE BOUNDARIES OF a piece of land

[Cf Ar xaṭṭa "draw lines on the sand," xiṭṭa† "a piece of land on which a sign has been put, so that a house may be built there" (Lane/760B, SchSEG7/55).]

A452/4: w'l ḏbhw yṯbnn wxṭṭ šᶜbn S "and the tribe S. shall not dwell there nor fix boundaries (therein)"

n s xṭṭ F119/12*

KIND OF MAGIC performed by drawing lines in the sand

[Ar xāṭṭ "one who draws lines in the sand for magical purposes, magician" (RyET/69).]

F119/12: may the god protect them bn nṭᶜ wšṣy wxṭṭ [š](n)'m "from injury, evil eye or sand-magic of (any) enemy"

XṬL

n s xṭl R4176/7*

IDLE TALK

[Ar xaṭal "loquacity; corrupt speech with loquacity" (Lane/767A).]

R4176/7: wḥẓr ᶜA bn xṭl 'n_t_t bywm sbᶜ _d_Ṣ "(the god) prohibited (the place) A. from the idle talk of women on the seventh day of (the month) _d_Ṣ."

XṬR

n _p_ mxṭr C183*

DANGERS (?)

[Ar maxāṭir id.]

C183: may (the god?) protect them from (?) mxṭr [']bythmw [w]'šᶜbhmw "dangers (to) their communities and tribes"

XẒF

n? _p/coll?_ xẓf C596/8*

THINGS SEIZED = BOOTY (?)

[Cf Ar xaṭifa "seize, make off with."]

C596/8: ...] trymw xẓf wtᶜlyh[... "they took away the booty (?) and carried it off"

XYB

v _ipf_ yxbn C291/5,8; yxbw R3945/3

BE LACKING, NOT PRESENT

[Ar xāba (y) "fail."]

R3945/3: he imposed on them, as an addition to their tribute, bqrm wsfrtm _d_yxbw bᶜm śl'hmw "a cow and a goat which were lacking from their tribute (already paid)"; C291/5: they refused anyone who would stz'dn blt H fl yxbn bn šrᶜhw "increase the tribute of H.; so let it (any increase) be lacking from (H.'s) just payment"; sim ib/8

h _pf_ hxb J735/5; hxbt J635/5; _inf_ hxbn R4176/6-7

(1) CAUSE TO FAIL or BE LACKING

[Ar xyb _h_ id.]

J735/5: they asked the god to grant rain lqbly _d_hxb sqy wdnm..._t_l_t_t 'brqm "because He had caused the irrigation waters and rain to fail for three rainy seasons"; J635/5: hxbt brq "the rainy season was caused to fail = was lacking"

(2) CAUSE TO STARVE

[Cf also Ar xawba† "hunger, famine."]

R4176/6-7: the game-animals of the god T. are sacred, w'l śn hxbn... ṣd T "it is not lawful to cause/allow the game of T. to starve"

n' _s_ xbtn J745/11*

BAD PASTURAGE

[Ar xawba† "land which has had no rain although neighboring land has been watered" (RycHim2/475).]

J745/11: rkby bn̥ srn bryn yrt^{c}nn ^{c}dy xbtn "(the 2 horses) had been ridden out of the healthy valley to graze in bad pasturage"

Note: BeRev/353A tr "unhealthy pasturage" but cfs Ar waxīm id.

n^{2} s xybt G1441/3+

DEARTH or DROUGHT

[Ar xawba^{+} "hunger."]

G1441/3: xybt nkrw b'^{c}nbhmw "the drought they suffered in their vineyards"; J567/27: may the god save them from tlftm wxybtm wqlmtm "loss (of life), dearth and insect pests"; Ir24: xybt 'brqn "dearth of rainstorms"

XYḎ

n s x(y)ḏm F30/6* (F read xlḏm)

as adj: RESTRICTIVE, PROHIBITIVE

[Ar xawada "be in disagreement with, oppose s.o." (RyET/22).]

F30/6: let this document be x(y)ḏm wbḏlm wḥqqm "restrictive and conceding, and legally binding"

XYL

n s xl C2/8+; var xyl C84/8+; xylhmw R5094/3; p 'xyl C448/5+; var xlthmw F74/4-5

POWER, MIGHT (often divine); FORCE, STRENGTH

[Eth xayl id.]

C2/8: ḥmdw xl wmqm T'LB "they praised the might and power of (the god) T." AND OFTEN SIM; R5094/3: bxyl RḤMNN wbxylhmw "by the might of (the god) R. and by their (own) strength"; C448/5: b'xyl wmqymt xmys "by the strength and powers of the troops"; Ist7608b/5: bxylm wbgyšhmw "with force and with their army"

XYS

v inf? xys IrApp2#1/1*

ACT TREACHEROUSLY

[Ar xāsa "break, violate (a pact, an alliance)" (RycMus88/216n4).]

IrApp2#1/1: bkn n()mw 'b^{c}l hgrn...xys b^{c}br ḤḌRMWT "when the citizens of the town plotted to act treacherously for the sake of Ḥ."

XYR

n s xyrhmw R4126/1; p 'xyr C405/11

BEST (?); in p, SUPERIORS, NOBLES (?)

[Ar xayr "good, superior."]

R4126/1 (in full): xyrhmw '...[b]n šrshmw "their best (?)...from their beginning (?)"; C405/11: ...] wb^{c}mhw 'xyr š^{c}bhmw Ṣ "and with him (were) the nobles (?) of their tribe Ṣ."

Note: XYRHMW C937/1,5 prob n.pr.

XL, see under XYL, XLL

XLW

v <u>inf</u> xlwn J572/5+; <u>var</u> xlyn J700/6

GUARD, TAKE CARE OF

[Eth xallawa id.]

J572/5: he dedicated because h^{c}n wmt^{c}n wxlwn grb mr'hmw "(the god) helped and saved and guarded the person of their lord"; sim exp J651/24; J700/6: the god granted to His servant xlyn whẓmn nfs ^{c}bdhw "to guard and deliver (?) the person of His servant"

Note: For J700/6, Irv BSOAS30/289 suggests an etymology from Ar xalā "be free from" and tr "free from reproach" (see under WẒM <u>h</u>)

pp xlw F120/10+

EXCEPT, WITH THE EXCEPTION OF (?) (contexts fragmentary)

[Ar xalā id.]

F120/10: ...]n xlw 'sn Š bn[... "except for (?) the man Š."; ib/17: ...]wlwm' HRN xlw [... "and including (?) H., with the exception of (?)..."

XLY

v <u>inf</u> xlyn J700/6, see under XLW <u>v</u>

n <u>p</u> mxlym GI142/2+

GREEN PASTURES, in epithet of the god T'LB

[Ar xalâ "cut fodder for cattle," xalâ^{n} "fresh fodder." This is a <u>n.loc</u> from the root (discussion HöTPK/29).]

GI142/2: T'LB b^{c}l mxlym "(the god) T., lord of the green pastures"; same exp GI143=R3900

XLL I

v <u>inf</u> xll R2726/2+

SETTLE, DETERMINE

[Cf phps Heb ḥālal "begin"? or Ar xāla (w) "supervise, manage, administer," Qat sxl (<u>h</u>) "determine" (R3566/15).]

R2726/2: kn h<u>t</u>b Y...mlk SB'...w^{c}d'l <u>d</u>stqr' wxll bh'w dwmm "thus ordained Y., the king of S.--and to that which he has published and determined (the Sabaean council) have conformed forever"; same formula R3951/1

st <u>pf</u> [s]txlhmw Ist7608/9*

APPOINT

[Cf XLL <u>v</u> "determine," or phps root XYL "power" (BeNL4/138).]

Ist7608/9: [ks]txlhmw...lz^{c} bḥrn wlṣlḥ Ḥ "when he had appointed them for the defense of the sea and the maintenance of order in Ḥ."

XLL II

n <u>s</u> xlt R3921+

SARCOPHAGUS

[Ar xilla† "box, case," Phoen ḥlt "sarcophagus" Ešm/3,5.]

R3921 (in full): xlt RḤBT "sarcophagus of R." (R notes that nn.pr associated with xlt are all f)

XL^{c}

n? s? xl^{c}n R4172/3*

n.pr? (but see Note)

R4172/3: 'db bnxln dt xl^{c}n nxl mr'hw "the boundary stone in the palmgrove which is ... (or, the palmgrove called dt X.), his lord's palmgrove"

Note: Read phps dt xlfn "which is near, in the vicinity of."

XLF I

h pf hxlf C541/10*

ASSUME THE FUNCTION OF A KHALĪFA, ACT AS A DEPUTY

[Ar xlf h id (CoRoSab/30-31).]

C541/1-13: hxlf bgzmn Y...xlfthmw dstxlfw ^{c}ly K wd' kn lhw xlftn "Y., their xalīfa/deputy whom they had appointed as such over K., assumed the function of xalīfa by (swearing) an oath; but it (K.?) already had a xalīfa..."

st pf stxlfhw Ry506/8; stxlfw C541/10

APPOINT s.o. AS KHALIFA or DEPUTY

[Ar xlf st id.]

C541/10-13 quoted under XLF h; Ry506/8: he made an agreement with the enemy wrhnhmw bnhw wstxlfhw ^{c}ly M "and gave them his son as a hostage (?); and he (the enemy?) appointed him (the son?) his deputy over M."

n^{1} s? xlfm R3945/1*

GARMENT with which a divine statue is dressed

[Cf Heb ḥălîpāh "change of raiment" and Akk naḫlaptu.]

R3945/1: the ruler of Saba ynr btr[ḥ] wwhb ^{c}TTR wHWBS xlfm "made a burnt sacrifice in recompense (for divine favor?) and gave (the gods) A. and H. a garment"

n^{2} s xlftn C541/13; xlfthmw ib/11; p xlyfhmw ib/36

KHALIFA = DEPUTY, LIEUTENANT

[Ar xalīfa† id.]

C541/10-13 quoted under XLF h; ib/36: dkyw srwthmw K...wL wH wxlyfhmw "K., L. and H. sent their troops and khalifas"

XLF II

n s xlf J643/20+; xlfhw R2633/7+; d xlfy R3943/4; p 'xlf C338/11; var? xlfn R4176/6+

(1) GATE

[MSA xalfa "window, opening in a wall."]

R3943/4: ywm bny xlfy M "when he built the gates of (the city) M.";
R2633/7: gn'hw wxlfhw wm'glthw "its walls, gate, and cisterns"

(2) WHAT IS OUTSIDE THE GATE = VICINITY, DISTRICT

[Cf also MSA mixlāf "district; ethnic or administrative subdivision" (RoVoc/305-6), which may be related to XLF I ("area administered by a khalifa"?).]

J643/20: mẓ'w ᶜdy xlf hgrn Y "they (a military force) reached the vicinity of the city Y." AND OFTEN SIM; J631/22: ḥyrw bxlf hgrn Z "they camped in the vicinity of the city Z."; Ir13/9: hsḥthmw bn xlf fnwt hwt bytn "they exterminated them from the vicinity of the front of that fortress"; R4176/6: ḥẓr T'LB xlfn dM wR wM bn hwḍ'n 'ś́rm "(the god) T. prohibited the districts (?) dM, R. and M. from driving out the herds"; Ir13/8: yhrgw bwsṭhw wbxlfhw "they slew (the enemy) inside (the fortress) and outside it (lit., in its interior and in its vicinity)"

Note: Doubtful in BeGlean p42/4: br' mṣnᶜthmw...bxlfn bsrn "(they) constructed their fortress at the ...? in the valley". Be suggests tr "frontier post," cfing MSA xalfa "window, opening in a wall" with Ar ṯaǵr "opening in a coastline, mountain range; frontier." More plausibly, take BSRN as n.pr or tr "in the districts in the valley"

pp xlf C276/3+; xlfhy J629/29; xlfy R4177/3; xlfn J643/31-2+

IN/TO THE VICINITY OF, NEAR; OUTSIDE

[Cf usages of XLF II n sense[2] "vicinity."]

J643/31-2: gb' mlk...xlfn Ḥ "the king returned (to) the vicinity of Ḥ."; C276/3: wyn dxlf bythmw "a vineyard near their house"; R4177/3: qf qyf xlfy N "he erected an altar stone near (?) N"

XLQ

n s xlqn C338/7*

PART OF IRRIGATION APPARATUS (?)

[Cf Ar xalaqa "measure"; Heb ḥālaq "divide, share." Irv/120-21 tr "water-distributor" or the like, a "measurer" or "sharer-out" of water.]

C338/7: tqdm b'rn dt Ẓ wxlqn Y "he undertook (the construction of) the well dt Ẓ. and the xlq-apparatus Y."

XM'

n s xm'tm C540/96-7*

BUTTER or CURDS

[Heb ḥem'ah "sweet, new butter" (Irv/290) or "curdled milk" (BDB s.v.)]

C540/96-7: dbsm wxm'tm "honey and butter/curds"

XMṬ

n s xmṭnm IrApp2#3/14,23*

SICKNESS

[Cf phps Ar xamaṭa "smell, have a certain odor (said of milk, when it has a pleasant or unpleasant smell)" (RycMus88/217n2).]
IrApp2#3/14: the god saved His servant bn 'ḥd xmṭnm dkwn "from a certain sickness that occurred"

XMS

n[1] cardinal number: f xms(n) R3945/13+; m xmst(n) J703/3+

FIVE

[Ar xams, xamsa[+] id.]
R3945/13: xms m'm ▯ mmmmm ▯ "five hundred: 500"; R3960/4: hqnyw... xmstn 'ṣlmn "they dedicated these five statues"; J703/3: hqnyw...xmst 'ṣlmm dhbm "they dedicated five gold statues"

n[2] s xms G438*

FIFTH (fraction) (cf also XMS n[5])

[Ar xums id.]
G438: xms dn qbrn "one fifth of this grave"

n[3] as adj: s.m xmsn NNAGI2/7*

FIFTH (ordinal)

[Ar xāmis id.]
NNAGI2/7: xrf W...xmsn "the year (named for) W., the fifth (year of his eponymate)"

n[4] cardinal number: xmsy R3945/18+

FIFTY

[Ar xamsūn id.]
R3945/18: xmsy wm't 'lfm ▯ m 1/2m ▯ "one hundred and fifty thousand: 150"; J665/34: hrgw bnhmw xmsy wṯmn m'tm bḏ[c]m "they killed of them eight hundred fifty, stripped (on the battlefield)"; J586/22: 'ḥd wxmsy bḏ[c]n "fifty-one stripped"

n[5] s xms(m,n) J643/24+; xmshw J576/4+; xmshmy J629/23+; xmshmw J574/8+; d xmsnhn J633/8; xmsyhw C334/3; p xmys N72+73/3+; var 'xms(m) J576/1+; [']xmshmw Ist7608b/4

ARMY, TROOPS; specifically, INFANTRY

[Cf Ar xamīs id and the expression 'ahl al-xums "long-established Arabs or descendants of slaves" (GReise/24), phps taking their name from the fractional tax levied on them. In Sab these are distinguished from the '[c]rb and 'š[c]b, the beduin and (settled) tribal contingents of the military forces.]
J643/24: mṣrm w'frsm bn xms mlk S "troops and cavalry of the army of the king of S."; J578/7: 'š[c]b wxms ḤMYRM "tribal and xms-troops of Ḥ."; N72+73/3: xmys w'[c]rb mlk S "(regular) troops and beduin irregulars of the king of S."; J576/4: xmshw w'frshw "his infantry and cavalry"; J647/29-30: 'rḍ xmsn "army land"--set aside to provide crops for the

use of the army? (discussion RycHim2/486 and n35)

XMṢ

v ipf yxmṣhw J1028/12*

OBLITERATE writing on a stela (?)

[Cf Ar xmṣ h "make empty; make thinner" (Dozy1/406); the sense here may be that the inscribed surface of the stela is rubbed flat or that the letters are hollowed or hacked away.]

J1028/12: they placed the inscription under the god's protection bn kl mxd^{c}m dyxmṣhw "against any damager who would obliterate (?) it"

XMR

v pf xmr J574/3+; xmrhw J580/9+; xmrhmy J632/6-7; xmrthmy C544/3-4; xmry R2695/1; xmrw F3/6; ipf yxmrn J735/3+; yxmrnhw J736/12+; yxmrnhmw J650/9+; yxmrhmw J736/13; inf xmr J580/12+; xmrhw J570/10+; xmrhmy J614/13+; xmrhmw J563/11+; [x]mrhn J804/2; xmrnhmw J669/26+

GRANT, ALLOW (FOR)GIVE, CONCEDE

[Ar xmr h id (Lane/808B, citing Q and TA, says "the form is common in El-Yemen").]

C581/6: whb wxmr 'LMQH "(the god) I. gave and granted"; J588/3: xmrhw... wldm dkrm "(the god) granted him a male child" AND OFTEN SIM; J587/3: xmrhw hwfynhw bn kl sb't sb' "(the god) granted him to protect him from all the campaigns they fought" AND OFTEN SIM; R4962/6: xmr...^{c}bdhw bkl 'ml' stml' b^{c}mhw "(the god) granted His servant all the favors he sought from Him" AND OFTEN SIM; J610/5: xmrhmw...'tw "(the god) allowed them to come back"; F3/6: xmrw bny dḤ 'mr'hmw 'mlkn "their lords the kings conceded to the b.Ḥ..."; J720/10: ws'r xṭy'n xmrhmw "and (the god) forgave them the rest of the sins"

ti pf (x)tmrw C358/2; inf xtmrn Ga3/4; xtmrnhw Ham9/9

BE GRANTED = RECEIVE

Ham9/9: lxtmrnhw wldm [ḥ]g krt^{c}hw b[m]s'lhw "on account of his being granted a child according to (the god's) truthful declaration in His oracle"; C358/2: ...] (x)tmrw bny bythw "they received (?) the construction of his house" (Halevy read htmrw); Ga3/4: tnhlw wxtmrn "were given and granted"

n^{1} s xmrn(m) R4646/18+; p? xmrtm Ry507/7

(1) CONCESSION, GRANT, GIFT

R4646/18: dn xmrn wwtfn "this concession and transfer (of property)"; R2695/6: wtfm wmṣdqm wxmrnm "a deed of transfer, an affidavit and a concession"; Ry507/7: mh^{c} wxmrtm 'xny "libations and numerous gifts"

(2) GRACIOUSNESS (?)

J646/11: may the god grant him rḍw wxmrn mr'hw "the good will and graciousness of his lord" (parallel contexts have ḥẓy "favor")

n[2] d mxmry R4708/1*

CONCESSION, GRANT (= xmrn)

R4708/1: X and Y šmy mxmry m'dbthmy "established the 2 concessions of (concerning?) their clients"

XNH

n as adj: p 'xnh R4157/3+; var 'xny Ry507/7

MANY

[Cf Ar xaniya "lay many eggs (locust); be abundant in plants (field)" MüW/48).]

R4157/3: ...] wsbym 'xnh w[... "and many captives..."; also in lists of booty in fragmentary contexts C596/7 (mhrgtm 'xnh "many slaughters") and C597/7 (''blm 'xnh "many camels"); Ry507/7: mh^c wxmrtm 'xny "libations and many gifts"

XNY

D? pf xny C541/74*

DESTROY; of a disease, BE SEVERE (^c ly against)

[Ar xny h ^c alâ "corrupt, destroy."]

C541/74: xny ḍlln ^c ly 'š^c bn "the sickness was severe against the tribes-(men)"

Note: Read phps dny, see under DNY v.

For 'xny Ry507/7, see under XNH.

XS, see under XSS

XSS

v pf xsw R3943/1; act.prt xssm Ry508/11

INJURE (cf XSS)

[Mod Ar xassa "be vile, diminish, harm" (StSESA/526).]

R3943/1: mxḍ D 'l xsw 'LMQH wSB' "he overthrew (the people of) D., who had injured (the god) I. and Saba"; Ry508/11: may this inscription be under protection bn kl xss()m wmxd^c m "from anyone who would injure or damage (it)"

Note: BePESA/19 cfs Ar xāsa (w) "act treacherously" for R3943/1; cf Sab XYS v id.

XSŚ

n s xsśm Ry507/11* (act.prt?)

ONE WHO INJURES (cf XSS v)

[See under XSS v.]

Ry507/11: may this inscription be under protection bn kl xśśm "from anyone who would injure (it)"

XFG

n <u>s</u> xfgm C541/59*

ROUGHCAST, PLASTER (?)

[Cf Ar xaffaqa "roughcast a wall, plaster it from top to bottom" (Dozy).]

C541/59: grbtm wbr'[m] wxfgm wnh[m]t "building up with grb and br' stonework, roughcast (?) and pecked masonry"

Note: Some editors read dflm, see under DFL.

XFD, <u>n</u> J598/5 after lacuna: no tr (something granted by the god to His servants)

XFḌ

h <u>inf</u> hxfḍn Ir5/14*

PLEASE, SATISFY (= XDF <u>h</u>)

[Ar xafḍ "tranquillity; quietness" (Lane/773C).]

Ir5/14: victories and numerous slaughters <u>d</u>hrḍw whxfḍn 'lbb mr'yhmw "which satisfied and pleased the hearts of their lords"

XFR

h <u>pf</u> hxfr J576/2*

GIVE PROTECTION, AID

[Ar xafara and <u>D</u> "guard, protect."]

J576/2: the god 'LMQH helped M. in battle bxfrt hxfr M 'LMQH "with the aid I. gave to M."

n[1] <u>s</u> xfr Ry508/11; <u>var</u> xfrt J576/3+

(DIVINE) PROTECTION, AID

[Ar xufra[+] id.]

J1028/11: bxfrt smyn...<u>dn</u> msndn bn kl xssm "this inscription (has been placed) under the protection of Heaven against anyone who would injure (it)"; same exp Ry507/11; with bxfr Ry508/11; J576/3: whbw xfrt 'LMQH... 'frsm wrkbm wgmlm "(the god) I. (and others) gave aid (in the form of) horsemen, cameleers and camels"; ib/2 quoted under XFR <u>h</u>

n[2] <u>s</u> xfrt R4646/16; xfrthw ib/17-8

ENCLOSED FIELD (?)

[Sense of "protection" from XFR <u>h</u>.]

R4646/[8-9]: kl mšym[t xf]rt "all enclosed fields (?)"; ib/16: fl ytqdmn whqmn xfrt mr'hmw "let him take charge of and put in order the enclosed fields of their lord"

XṢB

v <u>pf</u> xṣbw GaMosna[c]/6; <u>inf</u> xṣb R4646/13

CUT, HEW wood or stone

[Cf Heb ḥāṣab id.]
R4646/13: xd^c n wḥsm wxṣb 't̲lm "injure, hew or cut down tamarisks"; GaMosna^c /6: mnqltn ṣrbt xṣbw "these roads were collective enterprises (which) they cut (in rock)"--this inscr marks such a road

XṢR

v pf xṣrw J1028/3*

ACCOMPANY

[Ar xāṣara "walk hand in hand, walk by someone's side" (Lane/748C).]
J1028/3: 'lht Y wG xṣrw mr'hmw...kdhr qlsn "those of (the tribes) Y. and G. who accompanied their lord when he burned the church"

XḌ, XḌM--For mxḍm C570/2, see under MXḌ

XḌF

h pf hxḍf J650/23; inf hxḍfn Ir5/3+

PLEASE, SATISRY (= XFḌ h)

[Apparently a by-form of root XFḌ (q.v.), with metathesis.]
J650/23: they returned from campaign with booty d̲hxḍf whrḍwn 'lbbhmw "which pleased and satisfied their hearts"

XR'

v inf xr'n J576/3*

sense doubtful; prob denotes some military activity

[RyMus69/154 identifies root XR' with XRY, but the sense of the latter ("protect") does not fit the context. Cf phps Ar ḥry D̲t̲ "pursue"?]
J576/3: the god aided His servant bxr'n wškr wnqm 'ḥzb ḤBŠT "in ...?ing and defeating and taking vengeance on the warbands of Ḥ."

XRG

v pf xrghw J646/7+; ipf yxrgnhw J646/9; yxrgnhmy J652/21

BRING A LEGAL ACTION/SUIT AGAINST

[Cf Ar xaraja ^c alâ "reprimand, censure," or phps xaraja 'ilâ "present one's self to s.o." (Dozyl/358); if the latter, the Sab v is prob D. (Discussion RycHim2/497).]
J646/7: the god allowed him nqm wtwś^c d̲xrghw b^c br mr'hw "to take ample vengeance on the person who brought suit against him before his lord"; J712/7: the god saved His servant bn ''rx wxrgt xrghw d̲bn š́^c bhw ...b^c br mr'hmw "from the lawsuits and legal actions some of his tribe brought against him before their lord"; and read xrghw in C398/7 (C emends to hrghw)

n s xrgt J712/7+

(1) LEGAL ACTION

J712/7 quoted under XRG v

(2) RAID

[Cf Ar xurūj id, xarja^{+} "sortie," xaraja "go to war, attack,"]

J665/49: 'l tfqd bn gyšhmw 'sm bn xrgt "not a man was missing from their army from (because of) the raid"

XRW

v pf xrwt N74/8*

CHOOSE to do s.th > DO, COMMIT willfully (?)

[Cf Eth xaraya "choose" (BeNL4/145).]

N74/8: the goddess commanded him to write this inscription ḥgn xrwt hyt ^{c}qwtn "because this act of impiety had been willfully committed (?)"

XRṬ

v pf xrṭ J700/12; inf xrṭ N74/11

(1) DRAW OUT

[Cf Ar xaraṭa "strip off the bark."]

J700/12: xrt R šzb S bn hqwyhw wt^{c}ṣrw bynhmy bšzbn "R. drew the dagger of S. from his hips and they struggled together for the dagger"

(2) COMMIT A CERTAIN SACRILEGIOUS ACT

[Cf sense^{1} "draw out (a daggar)"; or phps Ar xaraṭa "break wind" (Ryc Conf/4).]

N74/11: wmnḏ y^{c}tqwn wxrṭ byṣṭ mḥrmn wl yqtrn "and whoever commits acts of impiety or sacrilege (or, who defecates or breaks wind?) in the temple, let him be punished"

XRY

v ipf yxryn J627/23-4; inf xryn R3992/12+; xrynhw J571/6-7+; xrynhmy J572/14+; xrynhmw J561b/22+

PRESERVE, SAVE

[Cf Eth xaraya "choose" > "keep safe."]

R3992/12: he praised the god bḏt mt^{c} wxryn ^{c}bdhw...bn hyt 'rxn "because He saved and preserved His servant from that affair" AND OFTEN SIM;

R4962/27: wlxryn 'dmhw...bn nḍ^{c} "and may (the god) preserve His servants from injury" AND OFTEN SIM

n adj: s 'xry J540/3*

MOST EXCELLENT (?)

[Cf Ar 'aḥrâ "more/most proper, worthy" (Bon3T/31-2n8); and cf Eth xaraya "choose."]

J540/3: ^{c}syh 'xry 'dbn "he made (for) him the most excellent (?) boundary stone"

XRF

n^{1} s xrf(n) C2/13+; d xrfnhn C83/4; p xrf(n,m) R3945/14+; var xryf R3958/14+;

var xryft Ir19/3+; var xrft(m) C621/10+; var 'xrftm C548/15

(1) AUTUMN, AUTUMN HARVEST

[Ar xarafa "pick fruit," xarīf "autumn"; cf also carfiathum, Pliny's word for the autumn incense harvest (Nat.hist.xii.60).]

R4176/13: ym TRʿT xrf wdṯ' "the day of T. in autumn and spring"; C2/13: frʿ dṯ' wxrf "crops of the spring and autumn harvests" AND OFTEN; Ir19/3: 'brq w'ḏnm wxryft w'ṯmr "storms, rains, harvests and crops" (in list of gifts of the god)

(2) metaphorically, YEAR

[Named as the representative season, cf usage of Eng "winter = year."]

C548/14-5: ywfyn ḏn ḥgn ʿšrt 'xrftm "let this law be preserved (= observed) for ten years"; C83/4: he dedicated this byn xrfnhn "(in the epagomenal period) between the 2 years" (cf BeESACD/18-9)

in dating documents: R2633/10: wrxhw ḏḤ ḏl'rbʿy wsṯm'tm xrftm "its month (of enactment) was ḏḤ. of the year(s) 640" AND OFTEN SIM

in citing eras: R4196/4: xryftm bn xryf NBṬ "years of the years (i.e., reckoning) of N."; C448/6: xrfm MBḤḌ bn 'BḤḌ "years (reckoning) of M. son of A."; also C46/6

in citing eponymates: R2726/18: xrf NŠ'KRB "the year (named for) N." AND OFTEN SIM

n^{2} s xrfy(n) C46/6+

YEAR (= xrf)

C46/6: the month ḏM. ḏbxrfyn xmst wṯmny wṯlṯ m'tm "in the year 385"; R4966/3: bxrfy Ḥ "in the year (named for) Ḥ."; J550/2: bkl xrfy hrs "in the whole year (in which) he commanded"

XRṢ

v inf xrṣ R3951/3,5*

ASSESS the value or probable yield of crops

[ModYem xarraṣ id (RoVoc/306), Daṯ xaraṣa "guess, suppose."]

R3951/3: xrṣ wšrk wrzm bʿmhmw wrqm wdʿtm "assessing, partitioning and commandeering from them greenstuff and fodder"; ib/4-5: kl xrṣ wšrk... bhmw šrkw wxrṣ "every assessment and partition by which they partitioned and assessed"

n s xrṣ(m) C540/83+; p xrṣ(m) R3951/3+

ESTIMATION, ASSESSMENT

C540/83: ḏrz'w...xrṣm l'šʿbn...wnśkm lfʿln "what they spent (in foodstuffs), by estimation for the tribal laborers and in actual expenditure for the (non-tribal) workers"; R4130/1: wr]qm wdʿtm xrṣm [w]'ty[m] "greenstuff and fodder, estimation and (actual) yield"; R3951/4 quoted under XRS v

XRQ

n p xr[q]hw Ry548/5*

ATTACKS, INVASIONS (?)

[Cf Ar xarq "piercing; breakthrough, breach."]

Ry548/5: the god let him conquer bxr[q]hw [']qdmn "in his preceding attacks (?)"

XRŠ

v pf xršh R3945/19+; ipf yxršnhw C445/2+; inf xrš R3943/3

(1) OBLITERATE an inscription

[Ar xaraša "scratch, scrape."]

C445/2: this is the funerary stela of X, wlqm^c^n ^c^TTR...dyxršnhw "and may (the god) A. strike down (any)one who obliterates it"; AND SAME and sim formulae elsewhere

(2) RAZE a city or building

R3943/3: ṯbr wxrš wwfṭ R hgr L "crushed, razed and burned R., the village of L."

ti inf xtršn Ir13/10,13*

RAZE FOR ONE'S OWN BENEFIT > PLUNDER (?)

Ir13/13: xtršn ḏhbm wǵnmm bn hgrn "to plunder gold and booty from the town"; ib/10: ^c^dw whb^c^ln wxtršn wdhr hgrn "invaded, conquered, plundered and burned the town"

n s xrš R3945/6*

DESTRUCTION (maṣdar?)

R3945/6: h'tw xrš bythw "he presented (to the god, as an offering?) the destruction of (the enemy's) palace"

XŚF--n xśftm Ry500/3 in fragmentary context: ...bkl xśftm...

Note: Context refers to "houses." RyMus66/269 cfs xśf, name of a measure in Min R2918/3; JOrAnt9/122 cfs Ar xasf "deep places in the ground," tr "caves."

XTM

n p xtymtn J655/17-8*

SOWN FIELDS (?)

[Ar xitām "first watering of seed-produce, or, of a sown field" (Lane/703A).]

J655/17-8: n'd qyẓ wṣrb mlk m'yltn wxtymtn "produce of the summer and autumn harvests (on the) property (consisting) of gardens and sown fields (?)"

XTN

v pf xtnw J651/14*

HOLD A RITUAL CELEBRATION (?)

[Etymology doubtful. Usually compared with Ar xitān "celebration at the

time of a marriage, circumcision, etc." (cf Lane/704A).]
J651/14: ḏnm ḏnmn...wwdqy hmy btnhn...bkn xtnw bhmy bytnhn "rain fell and those 2 houses fell down when they were holding a celebration in those 2 houses"

n s̲ mxtnhw C462/8+; p̲ mxtntn F3/8

PART OF THE TEMPLE used for ritual celebrations (?)

C462/8: h'twhw ^{c}[rbn] ^{c}dy mxtnhw "offer to (the god) a sacrificial victim in His mxtn"; sim C461/8; F3/8: let the adopted clan members be equal to 'sd 'bytn wmxtntn bhgrn Ṣ "men of the clans and mxtn-sanctuaries of the city Ṣ."

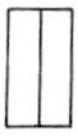 — Ṭ

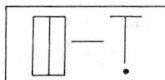

ṬBB

v inf ṭbb R4176/9*

PROCLAIM

[Cf Eth ṭababa "understand." Sense here is causative.]

R4176/9: šm T'LB...'ḥd lṭbb mṣt 'LMQH "(the god) T. appointed one (person) to proclaim the decree of (the god) I."; note also ṭbhw C516/13 in obscure context

ṬBX

n p ṭbxm C541/122-3*

ANIMALS FOR BUTCHERING

[Cf Heb ṭābaḥ "slaughter, butcher," Ar ṭabaxa "cook (meat)."]

C541/122-3: ṭbxm...ḏbyḥm wbqrm "animals for butchering, (camels) for slaughter and cattle" (part of provisions for workmen on the Mārib dam)

ṬBY

v? pf? ṭby Gl733/2*

REQUEST, DEMAND (?)

[Cf Ar ṭabā "call, invite."]

Gl733/2 (syntax somewhat doubtful): bn ṭby w^{c}lmy bhmy "when?/after? he requested (?) and they signed with them"

h pf hṭbw J616/19*

SUMMON (?) (l- s.o.)

J616/19: ṯhbhmw bh'thmw ^{c}dy hgrn R...kr' khṭbw lhmw 'š^{c}b D "they had brought back their advance troops (?) to the city R. when the tribes(men) of D. summoned (?) them"

n s ṭbytm Ir32*

SUMMONS, CALL

Ir32: mẓ't ^{c}brhmw ^{c}ztm wṭbytm ^{c}(m)n mr'hmw "a summons and call reached them from their lord"

ṬBN

v pf ṭbn J541/3*

DECEIVE (?)

[Cf Ar ṭabina "examine s.th. maliciously; deceive" (BonVar/333n.f).]

J541/3: w'l 's ṭbn K bdhbhw...wb fnwthw "let no one deceive (?) K. concerning (the use of?) his irrigated land and his canal"

h pf hṭbn R3946/4,5*

SEE TO, BE IN CHARGE OF (?)

[Cf Ar ṭabina "be intelligent"; Min 'hl ṭbn bmsqy R2791/6 "those in charge of irrigation."]

R3946/4: ᶜsy bn R...kl dhṭbn bW "he acquired from R. all that he had been in charge of (?) in W."; sim ib/5

n s ṭbntm C399/5*

CARE, SURVEILLANCE (?), in exp ['h]l ṭbntm "those keeping watch (over the irrigation system)"

[Cf the Min exp quoted under ṬBN h. In Qat, the ṭbn are part of the citizenry, opposed to (or synonymous with) the mśwd "landowners" (R3566/19+).]

C399/5 (fragmentary context): ...'h]l ṭbntm "group keeping watch (over the irrigation system) (?)"

ṬHR

n s ṭhr(m) C523/5+

(RITUAL) PURITY, CLEANNESS

[Ar ṭuhr id.]

C523/5-6: he confessed because bh' ǵr ṭhr wy'd b'kswthw ǵrṭhr "he had had sexual intercourse (in a state of) impurity (lit., without purity), and had put on his clothes (in a state of) impurity"; C532/6-7: wḍ't ᶜdy mwṭnn ǵyr ṭhrm "she went out to the temple forecourt (in a state of) impurity"

ṬWD

n s ṭwd(m) C540/5+; var ṭdm J546/3

HIGHLAND

[Ar ṭawd "mountain"; here reference is to the highland of Arabia between the Tihāma (coastal plain) and the central plateau (cf Müln566/141-2).]

C540/5: 'ᶜrbhmw ṭwdm wthmt "their beduins of the highland and the coastal plain" AND SEVERAL TIMES in this exp

ṬWY

n s ṭytn C308/7*

WELL LINED WITH STONE

[Ar ṭawīya†, ṭīya† id; ṭawâ "line a well with stone" (RoVoc/306).]

C308/7: kl 'hdr mstqyn...ᶜdy ṭytn "all the cisterns of the canal-irrigated land as far as the well lined with stone"

ṬWL

v For v ṭlwhw R4922/2, see under ṬLW v

h ipf yhṭl R4994/4*

EXTEND, LENGTHEN s.o.'s lifespan

[Ar ṭāla (w) "be long," h "lengthen, prolong."]

R4994=N21/4: šymhmw...lyhṭl bny H "their patron deity...may He lengthen (the lives) of the b.H."

n^1 s ṭlm C541/107*

LENGTH

[Ar ṭūl id.]

C541/107: (45) 'mm ṭlm w(35) 'mm rymm "forty-five cubits in length and thirty-five cubits in height"

n^2 s mṭwl R659/1*

HIGHWAY (?)

[Cf Ar ṭūl "length; geographical longitude"; ModḤaḍ maṭwāl "corridor" (MüW/76).]

R659 (fragmentary context): ...]ṯrt mṭwl "the substructure of the highway (?)"

Note: C read ^{c}M']ṮRT 'ṬWL, nn.pr.

ṬW^c

tp For tṭ^{c}n C308/19, see under NṬ^c I tp

h pf hṭ^{c}hw C541/21*

OWE/YIELD OBEDIENCE

[Ar ṭā^{c}a (w) and h "obey," Te ṭa^{c}a "submit" (MüW/76).]

C541/21: gm^c dhṭ^{c}hw bn K "he assembled those of K. who owed obedience to him"

st pf stṭ^{c}w C401/8*

sense doubtful; fragmentary context

[Cf phps Ar ṭw^c st "be able, capable of," or Sab NṬ^c I tp "begin hostilities."]

C401/8: ...]t stṭ^{c}w ^{c}brnhw wḥmdm b[dt... "(gave thanks to the god because?) they ...? against (?) him; and in praise because..."

n s ṭw^c R4962/29+

SUBJECTION, CONSTRAINT

[Cf Ar ṭw^c D "subject, subjugate."]

R4962/29: may the god protect them bn nḍ^c wššy wṭw^c šn'm "from injury, evil eye, and subjection (by any) enemy" AND OFTEN SIM

Note: Cf phps ḍw^c Ry538/44, sim context--phonetic variant?

ṬWR

n s mṭwr C3/6*

ENCLOSURE for livestock

[Cf Syr ṭiyārā "sheepfold," Heb ṭîrāh "encampment (protected by a stone wall)."]

C3/6: hqny...ʿdy mṭwr 'A lwfy qnyhmw "he made an offering at the enclosure A. for the well-being of their livestock"

ṬWŠ--For v nṭš C548/10, see under NṬŠ v

ṬḤN

n s ṭḥnm R3951/3+

FLOUR, MEAL of various grains

[Ar ṭiḥn "flour, ground wheat."]

C540/86-7: sdlm wṭḥnm dbrm [wš]ʿrm wgddtm w[t]mrm "flour and meal of wheat, barley, spelt (?); and dates"; sim ib/39; R3951/3: wrqm wdʿtm wṭḥnm "greenstuff, fodder and meal"

ṬY--For n ṭyt, see under ṬWY

ṬYB

h For v hṭbw J616/19, see under ṬBY h

n^{1} s ṭyb(n) J762/2+

KIND OF INCENSE = "SWEET" INCENSE; sometimes metonymically PLANT PRODUCING ṬYB-INCENSE

[Cf Ar ṭayyib "sweet-scented," ṭīb "scent, perfume," Heb ṭôb "perfume."]

C686 (on an incense burner): rnd ḏrw ṭyb ldn "nard, ḏrw-incense, 'sweet' incense, ldn-incense"; J762/2: ...]ṭybn dmdl[thw... "(an offering of?) ṭyb-incense, the weight of which was..."; C308/4: kl ṭyb wṣrf tnṭʿw "all the ṭyb and ṣrf-incense (plants) they planted"

Note also ṭbhw C516/13 in obscure context.

n^{2} s ṭybm J635/4-5*

adj: SWEET-SMELLING

[Ar ṭayyib id.]

J635/4-5: qrytm wṭnfm ṭybm "sweet-smelling qryt- and tnf-incense"

n^{3} s ṭyb'l C681*

KIND OF INCENSE = "SWEET-SMELLING INCENSE OF THE GOD" (?)

[Compound of ṭyb n^{1} and 'l "god."]

C681 (on an incense burner): ṭyb'l rnd ḏrw "ṭyb'l-incense, nard, ḏrw-incense"

ṬYT--For n ṭyt C308/7, see under ṬWY

ṬL--See under ṬWL, ṬLW

ṬL'--For v hṭl't R3956/4-5, read hṭm't; see under ṬM' h

ṬLW--In fragmentary context R4922/2: ...]hw dt ṭlwhw ʿMŠBM bnw[..., no tr.

R cfs Ar ṭalā "tie up a young animal to prevent it from suckling; defer, wait" and ṭāla (w) "be long."

ṬLY I

n s ṭlyn C464/9*

LAMB or KID

[Ar ṭalāⁿ id.]

C464/9: [ysd s]'rt dm ṭlyn "[he shall pour out] all of the blood of the lamb/kid"

Note: BeOracle/223 interprets the form as dual.

ṬLY II

n p 'ṭly R4818/6+

ABUSE, INSULTS

[Ar ṭly D "abuse, insult" (MüW/76).]

R4818/6: may the god keep away hyl [w']ṭly wmnḍᶜ šn'm "assault, insults and injury (by any) enemy"; C429/5: šṣyt w'ṭly w'hrm "evil eye, insults and weaknesses"

ṬLF

n s ṭlf R3902b#130/2*

EMBANKMENT, REVETMENT

[Cf Ar ṣalīf "bank, slope of a hill," Sq ṣalfíye "back" (Irv/28-9).]

R3902b#130/2: bnyy wkll ṭlf ḥrt "they built and completed the embankment of the aqueduct"

ṬM'

h pf hṭm't R3956/4-5*

SOIL, RENDER (RITUALLY) IMPURE

[Cf Heb ṭm' D id.]

R3956/4-5: she confessed that lbst ᶜṭf ṭm'm...hṭm't fxb't "she had worn a dirty mantle (which) she had soiled and (then) hidden"

Note: R's reading hṭl't is corrected in RycConf/5n21.

n s ṭm'm R3956/4*

IMPURITY, DIRT

[Cf Heb ṭum'āh "uncleanness."]

R3956/4: ᶜṭf ṭm'm wgzztm "a dirty, torn mantle (lit., a mantle of dirt and tatters)" (cf continuation of passage under ṬM' h)

ṬMR

n s ṭmrm R3910/7*

SECURITY, PROPERTY offered as security (?)

[Sense chiefly from context. Cf Ar ṭūmār, ṭāmūr "roll, scroll on which something is written," muṭammar "accumulated; applied to household goods and property" (Lane/1880BC). JSIMB/368 cfs Ar ḍimār "debt of which the payment is deferred"; cf also another sense of this word, "a sale upon credit, in which the payment is deferred to a definite period" (Lane/1803C).]

R3910/7: yhr'šn z'dm f'w s'rt ṭmrm ᶜbdm f'w 'm[tm... "(whoever) lays down an extra (sum) as a deposit, or any other security (?), (e.g.) a slave or maidservant..."

ṬNY

v pf ṭny R2705/2*

ERECT a statue

[Phoen.Punic ṭn' "set up, erect."]

R2705/2: ṭny mṯln "he erected an image"

ṬNF

n s ṭnfm J635/4*

KIND OF INCENSE, prob RESIN OF ṭnf-TREE

[Cf Ar ṭanaf "kind of red tree" (Lane/1886A).]

J635/4: qrytm wṭnfm ṭybm "sweet-smelling qryt- and ṭnf-incense"

Ṭᶜ--See under ṬWᶜ, NṬᶜ I

ṬᶜM

v inf ṭᶜmn J730/7-8*

CAUSE TO TASTE, FEED (l̲- to)

[Ar ṭaᶜima "eat, taste," h̲ "feed."]

J730/7-8: may the god ṭᶜmn lhmw 'fql yfqlnn "cause them to taste/feed to them the harvests they shall reap"

ṬFF

n s ṭfn J755/4+

PLAQUE, VOTIVE TABLET (cf dfw id)

[Akk ṭuppu/duppu "tablet," Ar ḍaffa† "side of s.th."]

J755/4: hqny...ṭfn ḏṣrfm "he dedicated this silver plaque"; sim C529/4

ṬRD

v inf ṭrd J660/11*

HUNT, CHASE

[Cf Ar ṭarada "drive away"; development in Sab, "pursue game."]

J660/11: wqhhw...lṭrd whwkbn b'ṯr Ḥ "he commanded him to hunt and pursue (after) Ḥ."

n s mṭrdhw C547/3-4*

(RITUAL) HUNT, or HUNTED ANIMALS offered to the god

[Cf here Ar ṭarīda† "stolen animals," as well as Sab ṭrd "hunt." For

discussion of the ritual hunt, cf BeRitH/193 and passim.]
C547/3-4: 'l hwfyhw mṭrdhw bd̲M "they did not render to (the god) His (ritual) hunt/hunted animals in (the month) d̲M."

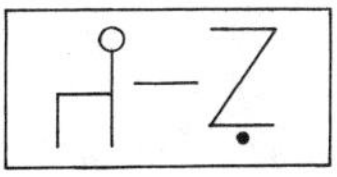

ẒBY

n s ẓbytn R4142/4*

KIND OF SHE-CAMEL = "GAZELLE-AGED," i.e. YOUNG (?)

[Cf Ar snn al-ẓabī "gazelle-aged," i.e. "two-year-old (camel)"; cf ẓabī "gazelle."]

R4142/4: they dedicated ṣ[l]mn w['b]ltn ẓbytn "a statue and a young (?) she-camel"

ẒBN

v ipf yẓbnn R4964/13*

REFRAIN (cf ṢBN v sim)

[Cf Ar ṣabana "avert, divert, refuse; withhold, keep back" (HöSEG8/50).]

R4964/13: hsṭw ǵḏm[n] bnhw lqbly ḏ'l yẓbnn ^{c}tlhw "(the god) agreed to rescue his son because he did not refrain from besieging Him (with prayers)"

ẒBR--In C608=R659/7, read kbrhw for ẓbrhw? Passage quoted under FG

ẒHR I

h pf hẓhr C376/12; hẓhry ib/14

CERTIFY, ATTEST (specifically, indebtedness)

[Cf Ar ẓahara "appear, be clear," h "disclose, announce."]

C376/12: ẓhrn ḏhẓhr ^{c}ly H "the document which attests (the indebtedness which lies) upon H."; ib/14: ḏbhw hẓhry hn blṭn 'lfn "by which they attest (their indebtedness regarding) those thousand blṭ-coins"

n s ẓhr(n) C376/12+

DOCUMENT, ATTESTATION

[Cf Ar ẓahīr "decree."]

C376/12 quoted under ẒHR I h; ib/15: wl yf^{c}n k^{c}d h' ẓhrn "let this document be valid forever"; sim F30b/5; Gl533/7: t^{c}lm...kl ẓhr "he signed every document"; F30b/2: ẓhrn ḏ^{c}md "document of indebtedness"

ẒHR II

n s ẓhr R3945/16*

BACK

[Ar ẓahr id.]
R3945/16: bḍ^c bẓhr N ś́l'm "he imposed a tribute on the back of N."

ẒWR I

v pf ẓwryhmw J578/26; ẓwrw C353/13+; ipf yẓwrw J577/8; pf/inf ẓwrhmw C353/8
BESIEGE
[Though the correspondence of sibilants is incorrect, cf prob Ar ṣīra† "enclosure for sheep or goats," Heb ṣwr "enclose, surround, besiege," Aram ṣəyar "siege, straitness" (cf Irv/27, 324n69).]
C353/6: tṣn^cw bhgrn D wmwrhmw bhw mlk...wẓwrhmw bhw "they fortified themselves in the city D. and the king shut them in there and besieged them"; J577/8: yẓwrw hgrn Ẓ ṯny wrxn "they besieged the city Ẓ. two months"; J578/26: ẓwryhmw...^cdy sb^c wtḍr^cn K "they besieged them until K. was defeated and surrendered"

ẒWR II

n s ẓrn C338/5+
MOUNTAIN
[Cf Aram ṭūrā id.]
C338/5: h'tw mḥr hnṭf bḏn ẓrn "he offered a sacrifice (whose blood) he caused to flow on this mountain"; R4176/15: mḥr hḥr...T'LB...^cdy ḏn ẓrn "the decree (the god) T. enacted on this mountain"
Note: For ẓr elsewhere, see under ẒRR.

ẒWR III

n p? ẓwrm R3946/5*
PILLAR(S)
[Cf Ar ẓi'r id.]
R3946/5: bny tfr^c bythw...ln ẓwrm wrymm "he built the superstructure of his house from the pillar(s) upward"

ẒYW

v pf ẓyt C504/5-6; ẓyw F120/16
a) PUTREFY; or, b) BE HELD CAPTIVE (?)
[a) Cf Ar ẓayya† "corpse"; also Mh ṯôye "to smell," Šx ẓey "smell," Eth ṣe̅'a "to stink." b) Cf Eth ḏ̣ewawa "take captive."]
C504/5-6: ślbt bth...bn mbḥr...w'l ẓyt "his daughter was removed from the tomb, not (yet) having putrefied," or "was taken prisoner from the dwelling, but not held captive"; also in F120/16 in fragmentary context: ...] bkn ẓyw b^cm mrn[... "when they ...ed with ..."
Note: Cf also the n ẓym R4054 (fragmentary context): ...]wn ẓym bkn ykwnn b[... "...? when they were..."

ẒYM--For n ẓym R4054/2, see Note to ẒYW v

ẒYT

n s? 'ẓytm J2109/12(+?)

STRANGULATION (?) (injury caused by an enemy)

[Cf Ar ẓa'ata "choke, strangle."]

J2109/12: mrḏm wnḥtm w'ẓytm wb'stm "sickness, beating, strangulation (?), harm"; phps also in J650/33: '[ẓy]tm wmyqẓ "strangulation and sleeplessness" (cf RycMus88/199n2)

Note: For ẓyt C504/5-6, see under ẒYW v.

ẒKK

n p mẓkkt R4085/2+

SLUICES, WATER CONTROLS

[Cf Ar ṣakka "shut, close (a door)"--here, structures to check the flow of water (Irv/212).]

R4085/2: tqdm...kl ḥrt wmẓkkt wb'rn "he undertook (the construction of) every aqueduct, the sluices and the well"; F61/2: br'...(')rb^c n kl(w)tn mẓkkt [lnxl]h(w) "he built four water drops, the sluices (for) his [palm-grove]"

ẒLL

v inf ẓll R4378/3*

ROOF OVER

[Ar ẓill "shade," ẓll h "shade, screen, protect."]

R4378/3: ...]hy wẓll by(t) "...ed and roofed over the house"

h pf hẓly C287/2-3; hẓlw ib/1; inf hẓl C648/4+

ROOF OVER (= ẒLL v), BUILD A COVERED PASSAGE

C648/4: ^c dbw whẓl whṣr[ḥ] "repaired, roofed over and built upper chambers (for the building)"; C287/1: hẓlw wzbrn dM "they roofed over and built (?) dM."; sim ib/2-3, 11-2

n[1] s ẓl Ry506/6-7*

PROTECTOR (?)

[Cf Ar ẓill "shade > shelter, protection, patronage," Heb ṣēl "protection (of God)."]

Ry506/6-7: mxḏ mlkn bH wdnw kẓl M "the king defeated (them) in H. and approached (the tribe) M. as a protector (?)"

Note: Syntax somewhat doubtful; Ry tr "M. vanished like a shadow."

n[2] s ẓlt C717/1; p ẓllm C62/1+; var? ẓlly C663/1 (fragmentary)

ROOFED TOMB or CHAMBER

C717/1: ẓlt W "roofed tomb of W."; C371/4: ẓllm ḏqny 'A "the roofed tombs/chambers which A. acquired"; C62/1: ẓllm zlt hgrhm[w] "the roofed chambers of the fortification(s) of their town"

Note: In C62, C read ṣllm and emended to ylIm.

n^3 s? mẓllt C648/3; p? mẓll GaAlON33/9 (D prt?)

ROOF, ROOFED PASSAGE

[Cf Ar muẓallil "that which gives shade."]

C648/3: br'w...ṣrḥt wmẓllt bythmw "they constructed the upper rooms and roof/roofed passage of their house"

n^4 s? mhẓll C660/2* (h prt?)

ROOF, ROOFED PASSAGE (cf mẓllt id)

C660/2: bnyw...mhẓllm lbythmw "they built a roof/roofed passage for their house"

ẒLM I

n s ẓlm R4815/8*

WEST (?)--or n.pr

[Cf Ar ẓalām "darkness," associated with twilight, sunset (cf BeJRAS'48/179).]

R4815/8: nxln...d^{c}brn ẓlm "the palmgrove which (lies) toward the west"

Note: In R3945/15, read ^{c}DB ẒLM w^{c}DB ḤMRT as nn.pr. In R4194/3, read tbsrn ẒLMTm sim: "which are in the valley Ẓ."

ẒLM II

n s ẓlm(n) J688/3*

STATUE (var of ṣlm id)

[See under ṢLM.]

J688/3: hqny...ẓlmn ddhbn "he dedicated a statue of gold"

ẒL^{c}

v ipf yẓl^{c}n C548/4+

BE FINED, PAY A FINE

[Cf phps Ar ẓal^{c} "crime" > "penalty for a crime"? (Lane/1918A).]

C548/4: if he defiles his weapons, lyẓl^{c}n l'lt ^{c}TTR...^{c}šr ḤY'LYm "let him pay to the community of (the god) A. a fine (of) ten ḥy'l-coins"; ib/6: lyẓl^{c}n xms ḤY'LYm "let him be fined five ḥy'l-coins"; sim ib/8

n s ẓl^{c}(m,n) C548/9+

FINE, MONETARY PENALTY

C548/9: the first time he sins (?), lywfyn ẓl^{c}n "let him (merely) pay a fine"; C546/4: ẓl^{c}m wtnkrm "fine and reparation"

ẒLF I

ti ipf yẓtlfn C546/7; yẓtlfnn ib/4-5

REFRAIN FROM an action

[Ar ẓalafa id.]

C546/4-7: fyẓtlfnn dmnhw ltrz' 'hlhtn wdgdf mnhm lyḥdrn wlyndrn [wl] yẓtlfn mtlhw "so let them refrain from whatever (tends) to the injury of the clans, and whoever among them is intractable, let him beware, vow penance and refrain from (doing) the like (again)"

ẒLF II

n s? ẓlf R4176/2*

a) BEATING; or, b) HOOVES (?)

[a) Cf Syr ṣlf "beat." b) Ar ẓilf "cloven hoof."]

R4176/2: ḥẓr T'LB R bn ẓlf qnwym ywmy T wẒ "(the god) T. prohibited R. (name of a place) from beating slaves/the cloven hooves of cattle (?) on the 2 days of T. and Ẓ."

ẒM--For v hẓmn, see under WẒM h

ẒM'

v pf ẓm'w J750/6*

BECOME THIRSTY

[Ar ẓami'a id.]

J750/6: ẓm'w wšm l'LM[QH] (t)'d'm...lgrmy mwm ḏ[ys]tqynn "they became thirsty and promised to (the god) I. a payment for 2 skins of water (with) which they might quench their thirst"

n s ẓm'n Ir13/11*

THIRST (cf ṣm' "drought")

[Ar ẓim' id.]

Ir13: wḍ'y bn ẓm'n "they died of thirst"

ẒMM, ẒMN--For v hẓmn, see under WẒM h

Ẓ^{c}N

v pf ẓ^{c}nw J575/4+

JOURNEY

[Ar ẓa^{c}ana "move away, depart."]

J575/4: ẓ^{c}nw lbḥrn whdrkhmw b'ṯrhmw "they journeyed to the sea, pursuing them"; C547/4-5: ẓ^{c}nw lY "they journeyed to Y."

ẒR--For n ẓr, see under ẒWR II, ẒRR

ẒRB

v inf ẓrb(n) R3960/2+

HAVE A RIGHT TO, POSSESS/ACQUIRE LEGITIMATELY

[Cf Ar ẓaraba "adhere"--allusion to the "firmness" of the legal bond? Discussion RhSLG3/12-3.]

R3960/2: hknn wh'mnn wẓrbn lmr'hmw "to arrange, assure and acquire legitimately for their lord"; F3/1: qnyn wbrgn wb^{c}ln wẓrbn "possess, acquire, own and have a right to"; C518/2: ẓrb wnqb(n) Y "acquired and cut channels (for) Y." (signs uncertain)

Note: For ẓbr in F76/1, read ẓrb.

n s ẓrb(m) R3958/13+; p 'ẓrbhmw R3966/6,9

RIGHTFUL PROPERTY/POSSESSION consisting of land; ^{c}lm ẓrbm: DOCUMENT attesting possession, TITLE DEED

R3958/13: wkwn ḏn srn ẓrb wmqny bny M "this valley is the rightful possession and property of the b.M."; R3959/3: ltwfyn 'rḍhmw b^{c}lm ẓrbm "pledged to pay (for) their land by (means of) a title deed"; F3/6: byt wẓrb wrb^c byt ḏḤ ẓrbm brgm b^{c}lm "the house, property and people of the clan ḏḤ., a legal acquisition and possession"; R3966/6: lwfy 'dmhmw w'ẓrbhmw w'qnyhmw "for the well-being of their servants, landed property and livestock"; ib/9: hn't bn 'ẓrbhmw "pleasing (crops) from their landed property"

Note: For ẓbr in F76/5, read ẓrb.

ẒRF

h pf hẓrfw R4194/4*

IMPROVE land

[Cf Ar ẓrf D "adorn."]

R4194/4: hẓrfw whqh kl ḏn ^{c}šqn "they improved and prepared for use all this cultivated land"

ẒRR

n s ẓrhw C540/11*

STONE CASING (?) (but see Note)

[Cf Heb ṣārar "wrap, shut up (a person); be cramped," ṣəror "pebbles (?)" II Sam 17:13, Amos 9:9; Ar ẓirr "a stone" (Irv/259-60).]

C540/11: ^{c}ḏbw M bn sflhw wẓrhw mbr'm grbm wlbtm "they repaired M. (the northern sluices of the Mārib dam) from its foundation, and its stone casing (?) with grb- and lbt-masonry"

Note: If from root ẒWR II "rock, mountain," etc, tr phps "bastion"--part of the northern sluices? For n ẓr elsewhere, see under ẒWR II.

𐩺-Y

YBS

v _pf_ ybs J735/7; ybsw ib/6

DRY UP

[Ar yabisa id.]

J735/7: ybs ḏbn 'b'rn "some of the wells dried up (in the drought)"; ib/6: ybsw 'mṭrn "the rain-watered fields dried up"

n _s_ ybsm J577/18+

(DRY) LAND (always opposed to bḥrm "sea")

[Ar yabs id.]

J577/18: š'mt wymnt wbḥrm wybsm "north and south and sea and land"; same exp J576/2; J585/14: ^{c}ltm wsfylt bḥrm wybsm "highlands and lowlands, sea and land"

YD

n _s_ yd J669/20+; ydhw J570/13+; _d_ ydy C571/6; ydyhw J700/14-5; _p_ 'ydhmw C541/51+; b-yd C576; b-ydn R3894B; b-ydhw R4085/5; b-ydy J2856/3

(1) HAND

[Ar yad id; for _p_, cf Eth 'ed, Syr 'Īdā, Akk idu.]

C369/2: 'ḥt 'ṣb^{c}m bn ṯty yd ^{c}šr "one finger from two hands(s), (i.e.) one-tenth"; J700/14-5: tlf R bn ydyhw "R. perished between his hands (i.e., on the spot)"; ib/15: sbt yd S "S.'s hand was slashed (in the struggle for the dagger)"; note esp use with _vs_ h^{c}d and nz^{c}: C541/51: klhmw h^{c}dw 'ydhmw wrhnhmw "all of them who had withdrawn their hands (from obedience) = rebelled and (then) given them pledges (of submission)"; sim with _v_ nz^{c} J577/8 (see also under ^{c}WD _h_, NZ^{c})

(2) figuratively, ACTION, POWER

J570/13: ydhw wlsnhw "(the god's) hand and tongue, i.e., His action and His oracle"

(3) in exps b-yd(n), b-ydy: AT THE HAND OF = BESIDE, NEAR, IN THE PRESENCE OF

[Cf Heb ^{c}al-yad id.]

R4085/5: ^{c}mnhw [w]bydhw "with it and near it" (Irv/214 tr "on his (own) authority and at his (own) expense"); C518/3: bqlḥ syr hgrn...[w]ḏhw bydn ḏqlḥn "in the cultivated land of the territory of the city...which is near the cultivated land"; J2856/3: w'l kbḥ bydy š'mn ḥbln "no objection having been raised, in the presence of the purchaser, to the contract"

Note: In C191/2: bdthmw w'rḍhmw, read prob b(y)thmw.

YD^c

v pf yd^c C613/2*

sense doubtful; context damaged

C613/2: ...] ḏyd^c wfqḥ ḏ^{c}d'l nxly "who ...?ed and irrigated (?) as far as (?) the 2 palmgroves"

h pf hyd^{c}hw J584/9*

CAUSE TO KNOW > GIVE AN ORACULAR RESPONSE (said of a god)

[Cf Heb hôda^c "cause to know," Eth 'ayde'a (ẖ) "inform."]

J584/9: he dedicated to the god because hyd^{c}hw...b^{c}br 'xyhw "He had given him an oracular response regarding his brother"

st pf styd^{c}thw J721/5; var std^{c}t F87/7; ipf ystyd^{c}nhw C409/7-8; inf styd^{c}n J564/4-5+

ASK TO KNOW, CONSULT (the response of) the oracle

J740/5: the god granted him children ḥgn kstyd^{c}hw "as he had asked Him"; J564/4-5: tqn^{c}w wstyd^{c}n 'SB'n "the Sabaeans were contented with and had sought to know (a certain oracular response)"

n p myd^c J567/18+

INFORMATION, REPLIES delivered by the oracle

J567/18: 'ml' wmyd^c yz'nn stml'n wstyd^{c}n "the (oracular) responses and replies they will continue to seek and ask"; sim Ir9/4

YHD

n s? YHD C543/2*

JEWRY, THE JEWS (cf hwd id)

[Aram yəhûd id.]

C543/2: RḤMNn rbYHD "(the god) R., Lord of the Jews"

YHR

h pf hyhr J564/7; inf hyhrn J668/13

CONQUER (?)

[Sense from context. Cf phps Heb yāhîr "exalted"; sense of "raising one's self over" the defeated enemy?]

J564/7: stwfy mngwm...hyhr mr'hmw K bythmw S "(the god) granted the outcome ...(that) their lord K. conquered (?) their house S."; J668/13: may the god continue to allow His servants hḥmdn whyhrn 'hnmw yqhnnhmw 'mr'hmw "to behave in a praiseworthy way and conquer whenever their lords commanded them"

Note: Sense in J564 may be technical, referring to a ritual (?) of "exalting" the lord at his accession. Cf the better-known ritual of "exalting" a deity (passages quoted under YF^c h, st). For hyhr elsewhere, see under HYHR.

n s yhrm J616/29*

CONQUEST, VICTORY (?)

J616/29: they returned from campaign bwfym wḥmdm wyhrm w'ḥllm "with safety, praise, victory (?) and spoils"

YWM

n^1 s ywm J651/19+; var ym R4176/8+; d ywmy R4176/2; p ywmn (?) C126/12; var ymt(m,n) C540/28-9+; var 'ywm(m) Ir13+

(1) DAY

[Ar yawm id.]

C540/28-9: bsb^{c}t w^{c}šry ymtm "in twenty-seven days"; J651/19: bywm šhrm "on the day of the new moon"; F4176/7: bywm sb^c "on the seventh day (lit., on day seven)" AND OFTEN with cardinal numbers

(2) used adverbially: (ON THE DAY) WHEN

[Ar yawma id.]

R4845b: hqny...ywm šymhw Y "he dedicated (on the day) when Y. appointed him"; C957: gn' 'A...ywm ḏbḥ ^{c}ṮTR "he walled A. (on the day) when he sacrificed to (the god) A."; G1691/3: ywm sqy ^{c}ṮTR "when (the god) A. provided irrigation waters" AND OFTEN; R4230A/2: bym kwn ^{c}qbm bbt "when he was (acting as) steward in the house"

n^2 s ywm(n) Ir6/1+

BATTLE; MILITARY EXPEDITION

[Cf the Ar exp 'ayyām al-^{c}arab "battles of the Arabs."]

Ir6/1: ywm ḏkyn byn 'SB'n wL "the battle which took place between the Sabaeans and L."; Ry538/22-3: bmw sdṯ hwt ywmn "on the sixth (day) of that expedition"; J649/41: wlḏmxr hwt ywmn fšw^{c}w "and (in praise) because he had fought that battle, thus furnishing military service..."

YWN--For n 'ywn, see under WYN

YYN

n s yynhmw Ist/7630/5*

VINEYARD (var of wyn id)

[See under WYN.]

Ist7630/5: fdy yynhmw...wbql wynhmw "they acquired their vineyard... and planted their vineyard"

YKB--For n mykbt J702/16, see under WKB n^2

YMN

h ipf yhymnn C432/6*

GO/TURN TO THE RIGHT

[Cf Ar yaman "right side."]

C432/6: mn^{c} [bnmw ḏ]yhš'mln wbnmw ḏyhymnn bn ḏn š'mn "he forbade [anyone who] might go to the left or to the right of this statute."

n^{1} s ymn Ry507/7; ymnhw C535/8

(1) RIGHT HAND

[Ar yamīn id.]

C535/8: rḍw lbhw ws^{c}d ymnhw "the good will of His heart and the support of His right hand"

(2) SOUTH (?) (cf ymnt id)

[Ar yaman id.]

Ry507/7: kkl fyḥ ymn whbw...rhnm "when all the tribesmen of the south (?) gave hostages" (for an alternate tr, see under FYḤ)

n^{2} s ymnt J577/18+

SOUTH

[Ar yamna^{t} id.]

J577/18: bn š'mt wymnt wbḥrm wybsm "from north and south and sea and land"; same exp J576/1, J635/12

Note: Cf also the name of a kingdom, YMNT "Yemen," e.g. C541/7.

n^{3} p ymnytn RyGrafp561*

SOUTHERN PARTS, PLACES LYING TO THE SOUTH

[Nisba-type adj from ymn "south," f.p.]

RyGrafp561: hdy ^{c}rn ymnytn wš'mytn "he guided the caravan to southern and northern parts"

YMT--For v ymtn, see under MWT; for n ymt, see under YWM n^{1}

YSṬ--For n ysṭ N74/2,4,11-2, see under WSṬ

YS^{c}

h pf hys^{c} R5094/5 (?); hys^{c}w R3431=R5094/2

ENLARGE (?)

[Cf Ar wasi^{c}a "be wide, ample."]

R3431: S wḥškthw w'lwdhmy hys^{c}w wgrbw mqbrtm "S., his wife and their children enlarged (?) and walled (their) tombs"; obscure in R5094/5: whmw ḏkr sm^{c} wsfh hys^{c} bmqbrt, no tr

Note: In his edition of R3431 (namely, R5094), Winnett read hys^{c}m for v hys^{c}w in the first passage quoted, taking it as a n.pr, less plausibly.

YSR

D pf ysr J570/7+; ysrhw J635/32; ysrw J575/3+

CAUSE TO GO STRAIGHT > SEND (context usually military)

[Cf Heb yāšar "be straight," D "direct"; cf Ar ysr Dt "be possible" (BePESA/13).]

J575/3: ysrw bqdmyhmw dlwlm ldll "they sent before them guides to guide (them)"; J635/32: ysrhw mr'hw lsb' "his lord sent him to campaign"

h <u>pf</u> hysr J576/5+; <u>var</u> hsr C396/5; <u>ipf</u> yhysrw J576/6+; yhysrnhmw Ir12/8; <u>inf</u> hysrn J643/10

(1) SEND (= YSR <u>D</u>) (context usually military)

J576/5: 'sd hysr Š...lh^{c}nn ^{c}dy wṯnn "the soldiers whom Š. sent to give aid at the border"; J577/14: 'gyš...hysr ldb' b^{c}lyhmw "the troops he sent to fight against them"

(2) ERECT walls (cf more prob under SWR <u>h</u>)

[Variation on basic sense "make straight, upright"?]

C396/5: hsr gn' hgrn "he erected the walls of the city"

n <u>s</u> mysrm C414/3*

PLAIN; LEVEL LAND

[Heb mîšôr id.]

C414/3: msqy mysrm "irrigation of the plain"

YFY

n <u>s</u> yfym N75/9*

SAFETY, WELL-BEING (<u>var</u> of wfy id)

[See under WFY <u>n</u>^{I}.]

N75/9: may the god grant them yfym wmngt ṣ[dqm] "well-being and good fortune"

YF^{c}

v <u>pf</u> yf^{c}w C541/68+; <u>inf</u> yf^{c}hmw J577/18+

(1) GO UP, RISE; also apparently RISE AGAINST, REBEL

[Cf Ar yafa^{c}a "grow up, grow tall."]

C541/68: yf^{c}w ^{c}rmn "they went up the mound (or, the dam)"; ib/116: yf^{c}w lǵzwhmw "they went up for their task"; J618/18: kl 'ǵyl yf^{c}w "all stream-beds (which) have risen"; J577/18: in laying low kl ḍrm dyz'n yf^{c}hmw "any enemy who continues to rise against them"; sim J585/13

(2) BE MANIFEST/MANIFESTED (a deity)

J619/10: yf^{c} lhw 'LMQH "(the god) I. was manifested to him"; J750/8: yf^{c} xyl 'LMQH "the power of (the god) I. was manifested"

D? <u>pf</u> yf^{c}hw J643/16; <u>ipf</u> yyf^{c}n C949/4+; <u>inf</u> yf^{c}n C376/15

(1) RAISE UP, SET UP

C949/4: w'l h^{c}ly <u>dn</u> 'tbn wṯn yyf^{c}n lmšr^{c}n "and let no one remove this monument, (i.e.,) the boundary stone (which) is set up for the plantation"; cf also NNAG4/6-7: 'l h^{c}ly 'tbn wṯn yf^{c}n bmšr^{c}--yf^{c}n phps is error for yyf^{c}n, or is a <u>D</u> <u>inf</u>

(2) RECORD, PRESERVE (a document)

C376/15: 'hnn ^{c}kr wl yf^{c}n k^{c}d h' ẓhrn "whatever objections may be raised, let (the agreement) be preserved as (recorded) in this document"; R2726/10: ...] ^{c}kr lyr(dn) wyf^c h' (^{c})lm[n] "[whatever] objections may be raised, let this document be set down (?) and recorded (?)"; sim usage with yyf^{c}n F30/7; sim in R4768/3

Note: Forms apparently used in this sense sometimes seem to be D (cf the ipf yyf^{c}n), sometimes simple verbs (cf the inf yf^{c}n).

(3) SUCCOR (said of a deity)

C88/5: the god commanded them, (declaring) kyf^{c}n 'ns "that He would succor the man (whose house was destroyed)"--phps an ipf 3m.s of the simple verb

tp inf tyf^{c}n C314/12*

RAISE UP, EXALT; or, SUPPORT (?)

[Cf senses^1 and ^{3} of YF^c D?]

C314/12: 'ml' ṣd[q]m...lśmk wtyf^{c}n mr'yhmw "fortunate oracle responses... to raise/sustain and exalt/support their 2 lords"

h pf hyf^c R3079/2 (no context); hyf^{c}t N74/4

ELEVATE, EXALT a deity as one's patron (but see Note)

N74/4: nṣfw khyf^{c}t d̲t B wz^{c}mh bysṭ mḥrmn "they had performed the ceremony at the time when (the goddess) d̲t B. was 'exalted' and had invoked Her in the temple"

Note: RycMus67/347 tr "make known, proclaim" and tr N74/4 "in accordance with what d̲t B. proclaimed and (with) Her declaration in the temple." But in view of the proposed sense "be manifest/manifested (a deity)" of the simple v, phps the ceremony called hyf^c was only in fact an invocation of the deity, "causing (Her) to become manifest." Cf also YF^c st for another aspect of this ceremony.

st pf styf^c R4176/1+

BE EXALTED (or manifested?) as a patron deity

[Cf Note to YF^c h.]

R4176/1: hḥr T'LB...bkn styf^c bxrf 'A "(the god) T. ordained, when He was 'exalted'/manifested in the year (named for) A."; R4964/10: ṣdqhmw ḥgn kstyf^c lhmw bms'lhw "(the god) bestowed (favors) on them when He was 'exalted' over/manifested to them, according to His oracle (?)"

n s mtyf^c R5094/4* (tp prt?)

ADULT (?) (context somewhat obscure)

[Cf Ar yf^c Dt "grow up, become adult."]

R5094/4: bly mrd'm bklm 'wnkrm bn mtyf^c "let there be no damaging in anything, nor (any) harm on the part of (any) adult (?)"

YṢR--In obscure context R2648/1: lfnwt dyṣr ylbn 'hl'l (reading of Fresnel), or fnwt dyṣrt bn 'hl'l (reading of Halevy). No tr

YQH--For v yqht, var of wqht N74/6, see under WQH v

YQṬ

v _inf_ yqṭ Ist7630/4*

DIG

[Cf Min wqṭ R2869/6 "hollow out, excavate, dig," Ar waqīṭ "excavation filled with water" (BeFSTI/280; R).]

Ist7630/4: wyqṭ wgyrn whqšbn krfm "dug, plastered and set in order a cistern"

YQẒ

n _s_ myqẓ(m) J650/33+

SLEEPLESSNESS, INSOMNIA

[Cf Ar yaqiẓa "be awake," yaqaẓa[†] "wakefulness."]

J650/33: may the god protect His servant bn b'stm...wmyqẓ wnḍ[c] wšṣy šn'm "from harm, insomnia, injury or evil eye of (any) enemy" AND SEVERAL TIMES in lists of injuries

YŚF

v _inf_ yśfhw Ist7630/3*

ADD TO (cf WŚF _v_ id)

[See under WŚF _v_. BeFSTI/280 considers this form a consecutive infinitive like those that follow, and notes yqṭ (for *wqṭ) in the same inscription.]

Ist7630/3: they restored their house wyśfhw sqfm wyqṭ wgyrn whqšbn "and added to it a roof and dug, plastered and set in order"

YŚQ--For _v_ yśq R4689/4, see under WŚQ

YṮW--For yṯw (_v_?), see under ṮWY

𐩫—K

K

pp k- C126/10+

(1) LIKE, (SUCH) AS

[Ar ka- "like, as."]

C126/10 (fragmentary): bnyhmw wbnthmw k'lw [...] "their sons and daughters, such as those who..."; R3945/1: ḥtẓyw mnš'hmw k'ḥd b^{c}sy ṣdqm "their tribal levies suceeded communally (lit., like one man) in doing good work"

(2) AT THE TIME OF

[Cf Sab k-, ky cj "when."]

Ry446/4: ktb^{c}lhmw "at the time of their foundation"

(3) k + l: FOR

R4905/2: bny kl b^{c}l Š d̲n md̲[q]n "he built for the lord of Š. this oratory"

cj k- C541/67+

(1) causative sense, FOR, BECAUSE

[Cf Ar kay, li-kay "so that, in order that," and senses of Eth kama "(so) that, in order that."]

C541/67: qdsw b^{c}t M kbhw qssm "they held Mass in the church of M., for in it there is a priest"; R4176/6: they shall not prevent the mountain goats from feeding, kḥrmw "for they are sacred"

(2) substantival, THAT (cf 'deictic' k-, sense[5])

C541/73: r'yw kdny ḍlln "they saw that the pestilence was approaching"; J716/7: šfthmw 'LMQH...ky^{c}thdn "(the god) I. promised them that He would take care of..."; sim C88/5+; C333/13: wqh 'dmhw...kl yd̲bḥnnhw "(the god) commanded His servants that they should sacrifice to Him"

(3) final, SO THAT

R4176/6: let the mountain goats feed kstnḥs̤n bnslm "so that they may grow fat with offspring"

(4) temporal, WHEN, AFTER

C88/4: ḥgn wqhhmw...kyf^{c}n "as (the god) commanded them when he was 'exalted'"; C621/8: 'syw 'ḤBŠn zrftn...khrgw mlk ḤMYRm "the Ḥabashites sent an invasion after the king of Ḥ. had been killed"

(5) 'deictic' in certain expressions and contexts

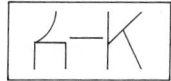

C86/3: he dedicated to the god ḥgn kwqhhw bms'lhw "just as He had commanded him through His oracle" AND OFTEN IN EXP ḥgn k-; J736/8: they promised to dedicate a bull km'nmw kyxmrnhw bnn...wr' kxmrhw...bnyhw "if (the god) would grant him a son; and now He has granted him his 2 sons" AND OFTEN IN EXP r' k- (note also deictic k- introducing the clause "He would grant him a son"); J752/10: hqnyw...frsm d̲t d̲hbm d̲t šfthw lgrm mhrthmw kwldt mhrtm "they dedicated a gold mare which he had promised (the god) for the life of this filly, (saying) 'let a filly be born'" AND OFTEN TO INTRODUCE DIRECT SPEECH

compounds:

k + l WHEN: C541/73: kl r'yw kdny ḏlln ᶜly 'šᶜbn 'd̲nw lhmw "when they saw that the sickness was approaching the tribes, they dismissed them"

Note: For bkl in J550=481=C376/2, see passage quoted under n̲ xrfy (XRF n̲²).

k + d̲, k + d̲ + m, l + k + d̲, l + k + d̲y, k + l + k + d̲y: THAT, SO THAT: R3945/2: he repaired the water system, bn kd̲ tḍ'n brḥm "so that it might not flow out unchecked"; C318/4: kd̲ 'l s'l xdrn "so that no one may claim the tomb"; F55/4: gzmw...kd̲m ylqḥnn "they resolved that they should take ..."; C570/5: wlkd̲ bn sfrt nxln...yḍ'n tḥrw...lkwn...'wt̲nn "and so that along the length of the palmgrove the delimitation may be established, let the boundaries be..."; R3951/2: kn ht̲bw...mlk SB'...lkd̲ 'l s'lw "thus ordained the king of S., that they should not be called to account"; R4176/2: hḥr T'LB...lkd̲ 'l yᶜṭnn...wlkd̲ ḥzr T'LB "T. ordained that they shall not neglect...and that T. has prohibited..."; R4773/1: wqh ᶜT̲TR... lkd̲y 'l yᶜrbn [... "(the god) A. commanded that he not sacrifice..."; R2876/3: bn d̲n] wtfn klkd̲y lyknn s'[wlth]w wš'mthw "[concerning this] property transfer, so that its claims and purchases may be [honored...]"

k + mhn, see under MHN II; k + mhnmw, see under MHN II; k + mᶜnmw/y, see under MᶜN; (b) + k + n, see under KN

K'B

n s̲ k'bt(n) C540/16+; d̲ k'bty ib/80

BUTTRESS (part of the Mārib dam)

[Dat̲ kābah "stone column at Mārib"; C tr "a ridge or bank checking and controlling the flow of water." Irv/266-7 identifies the five k'bt of C540 with the five large buttresses at Mārib.]

C540/16: k'bt ǴYLN "the buttress of Ǵ."; ib/17-8: k'btn tbn ǴYLN wMFLLn wk'bt MFLLm "the buttress between Ǵ. and M. and the buttress of M."; ib/80: k'bty RHBm "the 2 buttresses of R."

KBB

n s̲ kbtn J550/2 twice*

MILITARY CAMPAIGN, HOSTILITIES

[Cf Ar kabba "overthrow"; cf also kabata "crush, repress."]
J550/2: y^{c}qb bkbtn b^{c}ly SB'...bkl xrfy hrs bkbtn b^{c}ly SB' "he acted as governor during the campaign against S...the whole year he commanded during the campaign against S."

Note: For n kbt elsewhere, see under KWB. For [mkb]bt C131/4, read [wh]bt (?); passage quoted under wsqt n.

KBḤ

v pf kbḥ J2856/3*

OBJECT, RAISE AN OBJECTION, CHALLENGE (?)

[Cf Ar kbḥ "restrain, hold in" (BeStI/89).]
J2856/3: w'l kbḥ bydy š'mn ḥbln "no objection having been raised, in the presence of the purchaser, to the contract"

KBY

n^{1} s kbyt G1388/3*

BURNING OF INCENSE (maṣdar?) (but see Note)

[TsSEG6/15 cfs Ar kby D "burn incense."]
G1388/3: ...ḥḏrn ršwm kbyt bytm... "let a priest beware of burning incense (?) (in?) a temple..."

Note: Alternatively, cf Ar kabā "become dim (light)," Heb kābāh "be quenched, extinguished (fire or lamp)." Tr "beware of letting (a fire) go out"?

n^{2} s mkbyhw R2671*

INCENSE BURNER (?)

R2671: M bn M wmkbyhw "M., son of M., and his incense burner (?)" (inscription on the Mārib dam)

Note: HöWZ43/86 tr "sarcophagus," from root KBB.

n^{3} s tkbym C612/3*

BURNING OF INCENSE (?) (maṣdar, cf n kbyt)

C612/3: ḏyn[s]mn tkbym "whoever blows (?) burning incense (?)" (context fragmentary)

KBR

v pf kbr C343/11+; inf kbrn J627/5

(1) ENLARGE

[Ar kbr D "enlarge, increase."]
C343/11: kbr 'mwrtn [l]mšmthmw "he enlarged the walls for their cultivated fields"; C140/12: kbr ḍr Ḥ[MY]Rm "he escalated the war (against) Ḥ." (reading doubtful)

(2) as aux, DO GREATLY, GENEROUSLY

J627/5: the god granted His servant kysqyn wkbrn 'rḍhmw bn 'mrn ḏmlyn "that He would irrigate their land generously with regard to the winter cereal crop"

(3) BEHAVE HAUGHTILY > OPPOSE, RESIST

[Ar kbr L id.]

R2861/8-9: lkḏkbr ḏwqr ḫḏrn "let anyone who opposes what is inscribed (i.e., a law) beware"

n^1 s kbr(n) R4963/1+; p kbwr R2633/6+; var 'kbrw C618/1+; var 'kbrt J576/2+; s kbrhmw Gl679/1+; p 'kbrwhmw R3951/5

TRIBAL LEADER, HEAD OF A CLAN (often serving as eponym)

[Ar kabīr "chief, important (person)."]

R3951/5: mśwd Ṣ wš^{c}bn Ṣ w'kbrwhmw w'dwmthmw "the assembly of Ṣ., the tribe of Ṣ., their clan-heads and their clients"; R2633/6: kbwr wmḥrg S "the clan-heads and tribal leaders of S." (at end of list of witnesses); R2695/2: 'kbrw 'QYNM 'qwl š^{c}bn B "the heads of (the clan) A., tribal leaders of the tribe B."; Gl679/1: X bkr XLL wkbrhmw "X., first-born of (the clan) XLL and their clan-head" AND OFTEN IN EPONYM FORMULAS; C541/86-7: kbr ḤḌRMWT "leader of Ḥaḍramawt"; J576/2: 'kbrt KDT "clan-heads of Kinda"; J665/1: kbr '^{c}rb "leader of the beduins"

Note: BeESACD/45n75 rejects tr "kabirate" in R4768/5: ...] bkbr XLL end of inscription). Be would read [bxrf...bn...b]n kbr XLL "[in the year? of ...? son of ...? of] the kabīr of X." Be equates the exp bn kbr XLL with kbr XLL (ESACD/30), also in C567/5+. For kbrhw C608=R659/7 in obscure context, see quotation of passage under FG.

n^2 s kbr J651/26+

SIZE, BIGNESS (?); ABUNDANCE

[Ar kibr id.]

J651/26: 'l ḏfqdw bn 'šr^{c}hmw kbr rḥlm "nothing was missing from their articles of booty of the bigness (?) of a camel saddle (i.e., not so much as a camel saddle was missing)"; Ir6/2: may the god grant crops wkbr ḏṯ' wxrf "and abundance of spring and autumn harvests"

Note: J takes kbr rḥlm in J651 as the name of a tribe, cf kbr XLL (which others tr "the leader of (clan) X").

n^3 p? kbrm R2695/6; ? kbrhn Gl573/2; (kb)rhmw C575/12

(1) adj: GREAT

[Ar kabīr "great, extensive,"]

R2695/6: kl 'sṭrm kbrm f'w ṣǵrm "all documents, great or small"; C575/12: the tribe, (kb)rhmw wṣ[ǵr]hmw "their great and small"

(2) MANY, SEVERAL (?)

Gl573/2: ḤY'LYm ḏyṯhbwn l'wrxn kbrhn "ḥy'l-money which they will receive in several (?) months" (tr of HöSEG8/41)

KBT--For n kbt, see under KBB, KWB

KD'

v pf/inf kd' Ry507/7*

REFUSE (but read prob k-d', see under D('))

[RodConf'65-6/135 cfs Ar kadâ "give little, be miserly," h "refuse, reject" (and cf Ar kd' "be rare, small (of plants sprouting poorly)").]

Ry507/7: yḥbs wkd' whbt rhnn "he withheld and refused to give hostages"

Note: Ry read sd', Be k-d'.

KDD--For kd J750/12, see under KYD v

KDḤ

n s mkdḥ Ir13*

DEPOT, DOCKYARD

[Cf Ar kadaḥa "toil, labor, slave (with a view to s.th.)." Cf also place-name al-Magdaḥa (RycMus87/253-4 and n23).]

Ir13: ^{c}dww wdhr ^{c}sm sfnm bḥyqn Q mkdḥ mlk Ḥ "they occupied and burned a number of boats in the cove Q., the depot of the king of Ḥ."

KDN

n s kdnn J577/5; d? kdnn J574/6; p 'kdnn ib/7

(PLOWED) FIELD

[Cf Ar kadana "plow with oxen," kadna† "one day's plowing" (JSIMB/62).]

J574/6-7: they fought those Habashites bkdnn ḏW wW wfršt L wḥrbw bhmyt 'kdnn "in the 2 plowed fields of W. and W. and the field of L., and they fought in those fields"

KHY--For khy R4964/12 cited in PirenneGloss, read k + h' (independent pn)

KHL

v pf khlw J651/36*

BE ABLE TO, SUCCEED IN

[Eth kahala, Sq.Daṯ khl id.]

J651/36: he made a thank-offering kkhlw whkmln bkl ḏwqhhmw mr'hmw "when they had succeeded in completing all that their lord had commanded"

n^1 s kh[lm] R4011/12-3*

POWERFUL PERSON (?)

R4011/12-3: may the god protect bn nḍ^{c} wšṣ[y š]n'm [w]ǵlyt kh[lm] "against injury and the evil eye of (any) enemy, and the oppression of (any) powerful person (?)"

Note: khlm in R4964/10 is prob epithet of the god 'LMQHW.

n^2 s khltm J559/12+

ABILITY, POWER

J559/12: may the god grant wfym w^{c}ztm wkhltm wbry 'ḏnm wmqm "health, strength, and ability, and strength of mental and physical faculties"; sim J561/12, C326/3

KHMY--see under HMY

KWB

n[1] s? [k]wbm C571/6, so restored in BeSI/120. C read [š]ᶜbm. Context fragmentary: ...k]wbm (2) ydy ŠRḤ['L..., no tr

n[2] s kbtm Ir10/1*

CUP

[Ar kūba† "drinking glass."]

Ir10/1: dedicant offers a statue wbᶜlyhw kbtm "and in addition, a cup"

Note: For kbt elsewhere, see under KBB.

KWKB

n s kwkbn J649/33; p? kwkbt J567/23+

(1) STAR

[Ar kawkab id.]

J649/33: thrgw...bn šf šrqm ᶜdy mqṭt šmsn wlyl lylm ᶜdy šrq kwkbn dsbḥn "they fought from the appearance of sunrise until sunset and all night long until the rising of the morning star"

(2) STAR(S) (astrological) > (GOOD) FORTUNE

[Ar kawkaba† "star, constellation" (RycExpAst/522n9).]

J655/12: may the god grant 'wldm 'dkrm hn'm dkwkbt wmngt ṣdqm "male, pleasing children of satisfying stars and fate" AND SEVERAL TIMES SIM

KWN

v pf kwn C315/7+; var kyn J601/10+; kwnt C547/15+; kwnw J561b/9+; var knw C541/81-2; ipf ykn R3945/2; yknn R2876/3+; tkwn J633/12; var tknn R4781/1+; yknnn C609/5; var ykwnw R4176/5; ykwnn C380/3+; inf kwn C570/6; kwnhmw J601/10+

(1) BE, OCCUR

[Ar kāna (w) id.]

R4815/5: h' fnwtn w'ᶜmd w'ᶜlb ykwnn bh "this canal and the ᶜmd- and ᶜlb-lands which are on it"; C315/7: dr št' wkwn bkl 'rḍn "the war which broke out and occurred throughout all the land"; MüBilinguis/5: wkd'l yknn lmᶜnhw "let nothing happen to his dwelling"; J601/10: ytbrw...hmt 'šᶜbn wdkyn kwnhmw "they crushed those tribes and those who were (allied with) them"-but see sense[3] for a more plausible analysis

(2) BE MADE, PROMULGATED (dedications and documents)

[Cf Ar kwn D "make, produce"; Heb kwn h "establish."]

J633/12: to ask the god's help once a year ln tkwn dt hqnytn wl'xr "since the making of this dedication and henceforward"; C547/15-6: wkwnt dt tnxtn b'mr Ḥ "and this confession was made by order of (the god) Ḥ."; R3959/3: wkwn dn wtfn bwrx... "and this deed was enacted in the month..." AND OFTEN SIM

Note also kwn in jussive uses:

C553/1 (introduction): wkwn wtn... "Now let the boundary be..."; C570/6: lkwn ᶜbrn N 'wtnn "let the boundaries toward N. be..."; R3910/4: flyknn mᶜdhw 'ḥd wrxm "So let its term be one month"

(3) BE ALLIED WITH, SUPPORT (L?) in exp dkw/yn kwnhmw

[Cf Yem Ar kāwana "join forces with, be on the side of, support" (BeStl/91).]

J601/10: ytbrw...hmt 'šᶜbn...wdkyn kwnhmw "they crushed those tribes and those who were allied with them" AND ELSEWHERE SIM (the exp is frequent, the syntax doubtful)

tp In J633/12,15, read tkwn as ipf 3f.s of KWN v

h pf hkn J567/11,12; ipf yhknnn C609/5+; inf hkn(n) R3910/1+; act.prt? mhkn C310/1; pf hknw Gl142/1

CAUSE TO BE > (1) BRING TO PASS

J567/11-2: stml'w bᶜm 'LMQH khmy bṣdqm whkn hwt ḥlmn wwkbw bᶜm 'LMQH kbṣdqm whkn hkn hwt ḥlmn "they asked of (the god) I. that these 2 (bulls seen in a vision) might be real and that He would bring to pass that dream; and they obtained of I. that it was real and He brought to pass the realization of that dream"

(2) BUILD, ERECT (?)

[Cf Ar kwn D "create."]

C310/1: ...] mhkn mkn[tn... "the builder (?) of this cella (?)"; C321/4: fl y'tyn [mknt]n dyhknnn lhw "let him dedicate the [cella] which they built for (the god)"

(3) DETERMINE, ARRANGE, FIX

[Cf esp Heb kwn h "establish, prepare."]

R3910/1: wqh wryśn whknn whḥrn mlkn "the king commanded, ordered, determined and decreed"; C609/5: everything which (?) yhknnn bn wᶜln bny dM "they determined (to be) obligatory for and incumbent upon the b.M."

st pf stk[n] J721/6-7*

ABASE, HUMBLE ONE'S SELF (?)

[Cf Ar kwn st id.]

J721/6-7: xmrhw wldm bᶜd dstk[n ']LMQH bn R "(the god) granted him a child after the son of (?) R. abased himself (?) to (the god) I."

n¹ s knhmw C204/3

STATE OF BEING (?)

[Cf Ar kawn "being," kiyān "nature."]

C204/3: ...]w mhgrtn ḥgn knhmw bqdmy dn w[tfn] "...these enclosed fields in accordance with their state of being (?) before this trans[fer of property]"

n[2] s mknt(n) R4198b/3+

CHAPEL, "CELLA"--part of the temple

[Ar makān "place," Ḥaḍ makān "small chamber"; cf Heb usage of māqôm "place" for "shrine" or "temple" Dt 12:2,3+. Some authors cf the Sab word with Ar kanna "cover, conceal."]

R4198b/3: br'w...mknt wmdqntn 'l'h "they constructed a chapel and an oratory for the god"; C660/3: mḥḍrtn lmknt mwṯbn "courts for the chapel of the sanctuary"; C240/6: hqnyw [']LMQH...ḏn mkntn ᶜMDn "they dedicated to (the god) I. this chapel (called) 'the Pillars'"

Note: For mknthmw Ir22/1, read mfnthmw; see under FNW n[2].

n[3] s mknt F3/7+

as pp: INSTEAD OF, IN PLACE OF

[Ar makāna id.]

F3/7: wlyknn 'ln 'sdn...mṯl wmknt 'dm ḏD 'tldn 'sd 'bytn "let these men be like and instead of (= interchangeable with) the clients of (the clan) ḏD. born (?) men of (its) families"

Note: SoSoSEG4/34 distinguishes another sense in Gl321/4, tr "intention" after Ar makāna† id): ...]b kwnw mknthmw "their intentions were ..."; but context is too fragmentary to support the suggestion.

KWR

n s kwr(n) C338/3+; d kwrnhn C353/12+

(1) FIRE ALTAR

[Ar kūr "forge, furnace."]

C338/3: ym tqdm hš̌qr kwrn wmhyᶜ ṣrḥn "when he took charge of the completion of the fire altar and the shrine of the upper chamber"

(2) VILLAGE (?)

[Cf Ar kūra† "rural district, village."]

C353/12: hdrkhmw bkwrnhn "they pursued them into the 2 villages (?)"; sim Ir17 (n.pr?)

KY

cj ky Ry507/7*

WHEN (?) (cf cj k-)

[Phps scriptio plena for k-, usually meaning "when"; cf senses of Heb kî (BeOr25/298).]

Ry507/7: st[q]rw ᶜlhmw mgrmtm wky wsᶜw [... "they imposed on them a monetary penalty; and when (?) they had given generously..."

pp ky R4369/2*

LIKE, EQUAL TO (?) (cf pp k-)

[Scriptio plena for pp k- id?]

R4369/2: ^{c}lbn dky ^{c}šr 'mm "this ^{c}lb-land which is equal to (?) ten cubits"

KYB

v inf kybhmw C87/10*

PROTECT (cf GYB v id)

[See under GYB v.]

C87/10: may the god grant them children wl kybhmw bn nḍ^{c} wšṣy šn'm "and may He protect them from injury or evil eye of (any) enemy"

KYD

v pf kd J750/12; kydw J585/7-8*

LIE IN WAIT; BETRAY, TREACHEROUSLY ENDANGER

[Ar kāda (y) id.]

J750/12: hdym dkd 'fshmw "the guide who treacherously endangered their lives (by losing them in the desert)"; J585/7-8: kydw 'ḤBŠn hgzn grb 'bhmy "the Ḥabashites lay in wait to put an end to their father's life"

Note: BeJSS20/192 tr kydw J585/7-8 as aux, "they nearly put an end to...," cfing Ar kāda (w) "almost do."

ti pf ktd[w] R3992/6-7*

LIE IN WAIT FOR, AMBUSH (cf KYD v sim)

R3992/6-15: WHBDSMY thanks the god for favors, wktd[w] grbhw MS^{c}Dm ...whmd WHBDSMY xyl wmqm T'LB...[bd]t mt^{c}...^{c}bdhw WHBm bn hyt 'rxn dtkydw [b]nhw 'ysm MS^{c}Dm w[d]b^{c}mhw "and M. ambushed his life; and WHBDSMY praised the strength and power of (the god) T. because He saved His servant WHBm (son of WHBDSMY?) from that situation, (in which) that fellow M. and those who were with him had ambushed his (WHBDSMY's?) son"

tp pf tkydw R3992/13*

LIE IN WAIT FOR, AMBUSH (cf KYD v, ti)

R3992/13 quoted under KYD ti

KYL

n s kltn C570/1(+)

MEASUREMENT, AREA (?)

[Cf Ar kāla (y), Mh kiyôl "measure."]

C570/1: kwn lnxln...dt kltn "let the palmgrove have this measurement"; read also phps in R4233/10-1: ...]ztn dt tstmyn 'BWFY bkl.n bhgrn Š "the ... which is called A., in area (?), in the town Š."

Note: For 'kylm C548/12, see under 'KL

KYN

v pf kyn Ry502/4+

BE (= KWN v)

Ry502/4: gyš hmt S wdkyn kwnhmw bn '^{c}rbn "the troop of those S. and those who were (allied) with them among the beduins"; sim J601/10; R4138/7: xwm[m d]kyn bkl 'rdn "the sickness which was (present) in all the land"

KL--See under K (+ l), KYL, KLL

KL' I

n p 'kl'(n) J735/7+; 'kl'hw ib/5+
TERRACED FIELDS
[Cf Ar kala' "grass, pasture"; Dat kilā' "cultivated terrace or garden."]
J735/7: hmḥlt kl 'srr w'kl' M "all the valleys and terraces of M. became barren"; ib/15: hfsw mnfstn wdnm kl 'kl'n "the distributors and rain spread water out over all the terraces"; C11/3: bqln...'[ᶜ]nb w'kl' wynhmw "planted the vines and terraces of their vineyard"

KL' II

n adj: m kly Ir14/3+; var kl'y J557; f kl'ty J672/1
TWO, BOTH
[Ar kilā, f kiltā, m oblique kilay, Heb kil'ayim, Eth kal'ē id.]
J557: he dedicated kl blqhw...wkl'y mḥfdnhn "all its masonry and both towers"; J672/1: he dedicated kl'ty bḥtnhn "these 2 bḥt-offerings"; Ir14/3: may the god grant crops lkly mlkyhmw mlk ᶜTTR w'LMQH "in their 2 domains, that of A. and that of I."; J666/5: frsm wrkbhw kly dhbm "a horse and its saddle, both of gold" (or read 'ly, "which are of gold"?)

KLW

n s? klw J678/2; p klwt(n) R3913/3+
WATER DROP between aqueducts and palmgroves (or cf kl' "terrace")
[Cf Ar kallā' "bank of a river," Sq mukli' di-rího "dam" (Irv/204-5); also Eth kel'a "hold back, restrain."]
R3913/3: bny...ḥrtnhn dty šltn klwtn lnxlyhw "he built the 2 aqueducts of the three water drops for the 2 palmgroves"; F61/2-3: (')rbᶜn kl(w)tn mẓkkt [lnxl](h)w "four water drops, the distributors (of water) for his palmgrove"; R3943/6: mwqrn wklwt mzff "the rock cistern and the water drops of the sluices"
Note: In R4233/10-1 R restores bkl.n as bklwn, but prefers to read bkltn (see under KYL).

KLL

v pf/inf kl J842/3; var kll R3902b#130/2+
BRING TO COMPLETION
[Cf Aram šaklil, Akk šuklulu "finish," PBH kālīl "entire."]
J842/3: bny wkl fnwthw "he built and completed his canal"; R3902b#130/2: bnyy wkll ṭlf ḥrt "they built and completed the embankment of the aqueduct"

h <u>inf</u> hklln lr24*

GIVE IN MARRIAGE (?)

[Cf Ug klt "bride, marriageable girl," Heb kallāh "bride, daughter-in-law," Akk kallatu id.]

lr24: kystkmln wstwfyn lhw 'wln whkrbn whklln mr'tn "may (the god) succeed in allowing him to bring, offer and give in marriage this woman"

n[1] <u>s</u> klm J643/8+; kl R2695/6++; klhmw J665/22

ALL, EVERY; ALL OF, THE WHOLE (OF)

[Ar kull id.]

J550/1: he dedicated to the god kl tml' gn'n...wkl mǵbb...wkl wldhw "the whole fill of the wall and all the niches and all his children"; R2695/6: kl sṭrm kbrm f'w ṣǵrm "every document, great or small"; J665/22: 'śrhmw klhmw "he bound them, all of them"; J643/8: klm slmm mẓ'w "they arrived in all peace (completely at peace?)"

<u>compound</u> kl + <u>d</u> ALL THAT WHICH: R3966/7: kl <u>d</u>qny wb[c]l "all that he had acquired and possessed"; R4935/4: kl <u>d</u>lhw "all that he had"

Note: For kl<u>kdy</u> R2876/3, see under K.

<u>b + kl</u> IN ALL: J627/11: ysqyn...kl 'rḍhmw bkl 'brq d<u>t</u>' wxrf "(the god) will irrigate all their land with/in all the rainstorms of spring and autumn" AND OFTEN

<u>bn + kl</u> FROM ALL: R4193/11: the god allowed them tfrqn bn kl hwt 'gyš[n] "to be saved from all those troops" AND OFTEN

Note: For the form kly, see under KL' II.

n[2] <u>s</u> klm MüBilinguis/3+

EVERYTHING, ANYTHING, ALL

[Ar kull id.]

MüBilinguis/3: mr' smyn w'rḍn <u>d</u>br' klm "the Lord of heaven and earth, who created everything"; R5094/4: bly mrd'm bklm 'wnkrm "let there be no damage in anything (?)"

n[3] <u>s</u> kll C548/13-4*

COMPLETION > PAYMENT IN FULL

C548/13-4: wkll rẓ'n [c]ly kl 'nsn "and the full payment of the expenses (penalties for ritual offences) (is to fall) on every (guilty) man"

n[4] <u>s</u> klythmw C562/2+

ENTIRETY

[Ar kullīya[t] id.]

C562/2: SB' wFYŠN bklythmw "(the tribes of) S. and F. in their entirety"; R2726/4: mśwdn bklythmw "the assembly in their entirety"

n[5] <u>s</u> mkl R4646/9*

ENCLOSING WALL (?)

[Cf Ar kll <u>D</u> "enclose; crown."]

R4646/9: ...]mkl wmḥglm "enclosing wall (?) and enclosed land"

KLM--doubtful in C546/7 (before lacuna): [wl] yẓtlfn mṯlhw klm ḤLFN [... "let him refrain from (committing) the like of it (a certain ritual offence); ...? (the god) Ḥ...." Verb (cf Ar kallama "speak")? or *cj* k- with *pt* lm (negative); or compound of *pp* l-, sense unknown?

KLT--For *n* klt, see under KYL

KMW--For kmtt C654/2, see under KMT *v*

KMKM

n *s* kmkm C682 (on an incense burner)*

KIND OF RESIN used as incense

[Ar kamkām, Gr kángkamon, phps also Heb karkōm id (resin of the Pistacia lentiscus, according to RhASI/420).]

C682: rnd ḍrw kmkm qsṭ "nard, ḍrw-incense, kmkm-incense, costus"

KML

v *pf* k[ml]w C541/130-1*

COMPLETE (?)

[Ar kml *D* id.]

C541/130-1: k[ml]w mqḥhmw bṯmny[t wx]msy [y]m[tm] "they completed (?) their achievement (a building project) in fifty-eight days"

h *inf* hkmln J651/36*

COMPLETE (cf KML *v* id)

[Ar kml *h* id.]

J651/36: he made a thank-offering kkhlw whkmln bkl ḏwqhhmw mr'hmw "when they had succeeded in completing all that their lord had commanded"

st *pf* stkml C308/11; *ipf* ystkmln Ir24; *inf* stkmln J564/14+

COMPLETE, ACCOMPLISH (cf KML *v*, *h*)

[Cf Ar kml *ti*, *Lt* id.]

J564/14: he dedicated because stwfy wšrḥn wstkmln lmr'hmw...kl mngt wqhhmw "(the god) had granted successful completion (lit., granted and made successful and completed) for their lord all the affairs (concerning which) he had commanded them"; C308/4: bstkmln kl ṭyb wṣrf tnṭ^{c}w "in completing (the planting of?) all the ṭyb- and ṣrf-incense they planted"; ib/11: stkml h' 'xwnn bynhmw "he accomplished this alliance (or, this alliance was brought about) between them"

KMN--In obscure context Gl379/6: kmn ḥywn; for kmnw in CoRoC/169B, read kmn-mw; see under MN II.

KMNM(W)--For k-mn-m(w) GaAlON33/2, R3910/3, see under MN II.

KMS

h *inf* hkms(n) J574/13+

SUBDUE

[Cf Ar kamasa "frown," Syr kmas "let fade or languish; languish, wither," and also (or more likely), Ar kabasa "attack, raid."]

J574/13: wḍᶜ wṯbr whms whkms kl ḍrhmw "lay low, crush, break down and subdue their every foe"; C314/22: škr wṯbr wḍrᶜn whkms "defeat, crush, subjugate, subdue"

KMT

v pf kmtt C654/2*

EXTEND BEYOND something

[Cf Akk kamū "outside; that which is outside" (f ending -t has become part of root--BeDGESA/17:2).]

C654/2: w'l kmtt ḥrtn wṯn nxln "let this aqueduct not extend beyond the boundary of the palmgrove"

KN

av kn R3951/1+

THUS

[Cf Heb kēn id. Prob 'deictic' or prepositional k- + suffix -n (common with pps).]

R3951/1: kn ḥṯbw whḥr K...mlk SB' "thus ordained and decreed K., king of S."; sim R2726/1 and elsewhere

cj b-kn R4176/1++

WHEN, AT THE TIME WHEN (contrast k- cj)

[Pp b- + kn, analyzed above.]

R4176/1: ḥḥr T'LB...šᶜbhw...bkn styfᶜ bxrf 'A "(the god) T. ordained (for) His tribe, at the time when He was 'exalted,' in the year (named for) A."; J629/26: he thanked the god because hwšᶜ whwfyn ᶜbdhw...bkn sb'w lšwᶜn mr'yhmw "He had saved and protected His servant when they campaigned to furnish service to their 2 lords"

Note: Followed by pf verb except in C80/10 (bkn yfqln) and J702/6 (bkn yᶜdwn). A nuanced translation does not seem warranted by the contexts.

Note also the compound k-bkn-mw J647/11, apparently synonymous with bkn "when": xmrhw tb[š]rtm bms'lhw kbknmw [... "(the god) granted them a response through His oracle when (?)..."

For kn elsewhere, see under KWN.

KNN--Forms sometimes assigned to this root have been referred to KWN, q.v.

KNS

h pf hkns GaAntYem2/2*

CLEAN OUT silt from a canal

[Cf Ar kanasa and D "sweep."]

GaAntYem2/2: hkns mrhmw "cleaned out their channel"

KNF

n s knf J635/36+

BORDER, FRONTIER

[Cf Ar kanafa "fence in," kanaf "wing," Heb kānāp "wing, extremity."]

J635/36: yḥrbhmw bknf 'rḍ 'l "he fought them on the border of the land of l."; C407/22: bknf š'mt "on the north border"

KSW

n p 'kswthw C523/6; var 'kswtw ib/8 (HöASG/23)

CLOTHES, GARMENTS (cf root KŚW)

[Ar kiswa[t] "garment."]

C523/6: he confessed because y'd b'kswthw ǵrṭhr "he had dressed himself (?) in his clothes without purification"; ib/8: nḍx 'kswtw hmr "he spattered his clothes with semen"

Note: The use of s in this root (contrast kśwy "garments" J555/4) is phps a feature of the Harami dialect of this inscription. The suffix -w for -hw (3m.s) occurs twice in the inscription (cf also ḥrmw for ḥrmhw, l.3).

K^{c}D--For k^{c}d C376/15, read k-^{c}d "as in." Discussion of other possible trs BeSl/45-6.

KFḤ

n s kfḥ J635/45-6*

signs doubtful; UNEXPECTED ATTACK (?)

[Cf Ar kafaḥa "meet...face to face, suddenly, or unexpectedly" (Lane/2619C).]

J635/45-6: may the god protect them bn nḍ^c wšsy wtṯ^{c}t w^{c}bṭt wkfḥ šn'm "from injury, evil eye, abuse, compulsion and unexpected attack (?) of (any) enemy"

KFL

n s kfl J575/4*

NARROW PASS (?)

[Sq kaféleh "steep brink of a valley," Ar qafīl "narrow pass."]

J575/4: hḏrw hmt '^{c}ṣdn bn kfl ^{c}rn W "they scattered those warbands from the pass (?) of the citadel W."

KFR

v ipf ykfrn C539/1*

ATONE; EXPIATE a sin

[Ar kafara "cover, hide," Heb kippēr "cover over; atone for a sin."]
C539/1: ykfrn ḥbhmw wyqbln qrbnhmw "he expiated their sin and made their offering"

n s̲ kfr C597/3; p̲ 'kfrhw C308/9
   PART OF IRRIGATION APPARATUS, SLUICE (?)
   [Eth kanfar "side, bank"; cf phps also Ar kafara "cover."]
   C308/9: šr^c qšmtn w'hdrhw w'kfrhw "the irrigation of the orchard and its cisterns and sluices (?)"; also C597/3 in fragmentary context
   Note: For kfrn C600/5, R2724/5 reads kqrn and emends to wqrn, root WQR, q.v.

KRB 1

v pf/inf krb R3890#3*
   DEDICATE (?)
   [Cf Akk karābu, kitrubu "render homage," Eth mek^{w}rāb, Sab mkrb "temple." V̲ skrb frequent in Min, sim sense?]
   R3890#3: ...]'l wkrb ^{c}x [...]BḎ "...l., and he dedicated 15...[to the god ^{c}TTR dQ]BD"

ti ipf yktrbnnhw R4935/4*
   DEDICATE, OFFER (cf KRB v̲)
   R4935/4: kl dlhw yktrbnnhw "let them (?) dedicate to (the god?) all that is His (?)"

h inf hkrbn Ir24+
   DEDICATE, OFFER (cf KRB v̲, ti)
   Ir24: ^{c}ḏb whkrbn ǵlmt...'wln whkrbn whklln mr'tn "making expiation and offering the girl...leading and offering and giving this woman in marriage"

n^1 s̲ krbtm J567/22-3+
   BLESSING
   [Akk kerebtu id.]
   J567/22-3: may the god grant them n^{c}mtm wwfym whẓym wkrbtm "prosperity, health, good fortune, blessing..."; sim J692/10

n^2 s̲ mkrbn MüBilinguis/5+
   TEMPLE, SANCTUARY (specifically, SYNAGOGUE?)
   [Eth mek^{w}rāb "temple," esp Temple in Jerusalem or Jewish synagogue (Mü Bilinguis).]
   MüBilinguis/5: wkd̲'l yknn lm^{c}nhw wmknt mlkn lmkrbn 'A "and may nothing happen to his dwelling or the chapel of the king (belonging) to the temple A."; F60/3: h]šqrn (m)krbn B "completed the temple B." (F read bkrbn, Ry emended to (z̲)rbn); elsewhere in fragmentary contexts

n^3 s̲ mkrb C957+ (D prt?)
   COLLECTOR OF SACRED TAXES, title of Sab ruler referring to his function as collector and distributor of taxes for public works

[Cf KRB v "dedicate (property to a god)." For discussion of functions of the mkrb, see, e.g., BeJESHO15/264-5, HöWar?, RycSemAS4/24-5.]
C957: Y D mkrb S gn' 'A byt 'I ywm dbḥ ^{c}TTR whwṣt kl gwm "Y.D., the mkrb of S., built the wall of A., the temple of (the god) I., on the day he sacrificed to (the god) A. and legitimized the whole (Sabaean political) community"; R4177/2: Y...mkrb SB' qf qyf "Y., the mkrb of S., erected the altar stone"; AND OFTEN in sim building contexts; R3945/1: ['I]t hfṭn K...mkrb SB' bmlkhw I'LMQH wl SB' "The following (territories conquered in battle) has K., the mkrb of S., assigned to (the god) I. and to S., in his capacity as king"

KRB II

n s? krbn R3960/5+
LABOR (?), LABORERS (?)
[Cf Akk karābu "work the fields."]
R3960/5: ...]krbn mr^{c}ẓm "labor (?) (and) levies"; R3895/5: ...]t kr(b)n wmr^{c}(ẓn), same tr

KRW

n s krwm R4177/4+
RITUAL HUNT; or, FEAST, BANQUET
[Cf Ar karā "dig a pit (for snaring game)"; or Akk karū "entertain" > "feast," Heb kārāh "give a banquet" MüW/97, BeRitH/185).]
R4177/4: ṣyd ^{c}TTR wkrwm "the ritual hunt of (the god) A. and the krw-hunt/feast"; R3946/7: ṣd ṣyd krwm "he hunted the ritual hunt of the krw-hunt/feast"

KRY

n p 'kry C291/1*
RENTS (?)
[Ar kry h "rent, hire," Mh kôre "rent."]
C291/1: ṣrf w'kry wmgz^{c}t "expenses, rents (?) and payments"

KRKR

n p krkrm C540/95-6*
LOAD or MEASURE
[Cf Heb kikkār "talent," Ar kāra (w) "carry a burden on the back," kūr "camel saddle," kāra^{t} "burden to be carried on the back" (Irv/290).]
C540/95-6: ṯny w'rb^{c}y krkrm dbsm wxm'tm "forty-two loads/measures of honey and butter"

KR^{c}

n s kr^{c} J619/8*
KNEE

[Mh kurā^c "foot, or thinnest part between the knee and the foot of ovine and bovine animals," PBH kera^c "knee, leg."]
J619/8: dqt wdq ^cln 'blhw bh' byn kr^c 'blhw "the fall he took because of his camel, in which his camel's knee was dislocated"

KRF

n s krfm C107/2; var kryfm C40/3; p krf(m) C291/6+
CISTERN
[Himyaritic karīf id (Hamdānī, 69.19, 239.2, cited in CoRoC/171A).]
C290/2: hnklw 'rb^ct krfm wb'r "they paved four cisterns and dug wells"; C291/6: krf w'b'r "cisterns and wells"; C107/2: krfm...wm'glm bxlf hgrhmw "a krf-cistern and a m'gl-cistern outside their city"

KRR

v pf kr C548/10(+); krw Ry507/2
(1) RETURN to a campaign
[Ar karra "turn around and attack; return, come back."]
Ry507/2: wdkrw 'qwln l[... "and the tribal leaders had already (?) returned to the campaign..."
(2) REPEAT a religious offence
[Ar krr D "do again."]
C548/10: wdkr ntš ^cšt mḥrmn "and whoever repeats (the offence) must leave the community of the temple"; phps sim in obscure context R5094/5: whmw dkr sm^c fsfh hys^c bmqbrt

D inf krrhmw C313/6*
CAUSE TO RETURN to a campaign (said of a god) (cf KRR v sense[1])
C313/6: yh^cnnhmw wkrrhmw "may (the god) help them and return them (to the campaign)"

av krrm C308/9,10*
ALL TOGETHER
[Cf Ar karra† "whole, entirety."]
C308/9: kl mhwkbhmw krrm...wkl mwsṭ hyt mkntn krrm "all their estates, all together; and the whole interior of that chapel, all together"

KŚ'

v pf kś' R4194/2; ipf ykś'nn G1539/4
COMMAND, EXERCISE AUTHORITY
[Ḥaḍ kṯ' R2693/4 "command (said of a god)"--context parallels those of Sab wqh. Cf also Eth gz' in 'egzi' "lord"?]
R4194/2: 'nsm ḥškm kś' bbythmw "a man, a steward, who exercised authority in their household"; cf also G1539/4 (fragmentary context): ...]r wmzr kykś'nn[..., no tr

KŚW

n p kśwy J555/4*

CLOTHES, GARMENTS (cf root KSW)

[Ar kiswa†, p kasāwī id.]

J555/4: hwf' kl nṭc wkśwy...ḍb' "he provided all the tents (?) and garments for the campaign"

KŚḤ

h pf/inf hkśḥ R3945/5,14*

DEFEAT, DESPOIL, DESTROY

[Ar kasaḥa "destroy," ti "take everything"; cf Heb kāsaḥ "cut off."]

R3945/5: mxḍhw bW cd hkśḥ 'A "he defeated him in W. until he had despoiled (the kingdom) A."; ib/14: nš'...mnš'm...whkśḥ S wN "he mounted a campaign and destroyed (the man) S. and (the city) N."

KŠT

v pf kšthw G1218/9 twice*

REVEAL to s.o. (said of a god, in an oracle?)

[Eth kašata id (SoSoSEG4/22).]

G1218/9: kšthw...whwfynhw bm[s'lh]w ḥgn kšthw "(the god) revealed to him ...and granted to him in His oracle as He had revealed to him"

KTM--Prob n.pr in C550/10, J550/1. Discussion in Note to 'DN n3. For the proposed tr "gold-dust," cf Heb kétem "gold."

1-L

L

pp l- passim

(1) TO, TOWARD

[Cf senses of Ar li-: "to (a place); to (dative), for, on behalf of"; used to mark accusative and genitive; used with subjunctive "so that, in order that"; used with jussive, e.g., li-yaktub "let him write."] C547/5: ẓ^{c}nw lY "they journeyed to Y." AND OFTEN SIM; C555/3: l'rkn "to eternity = forever"; R3946/5: bn X l'wṯnh "from X. to its borders"

(2) FOR the purpose of

C314/17-8: stṣr...ldrm "summoned aid for war"; C74/4-5: wqh bny M lšym "commanded the b.M. to establish..."

(3) FOR the benefit of

Ham9/5: yxmrnhmw r'y lhmw "may (the god) grant them an oracular vision for their advantage"; R3946/1: hfṭn...l'LMQH "he assigned (these territories) to(the god) I."; C375/2: whṯb lhw...t'mnm "he rendered to (the god) a thank-offering"; phps also C539/4: lsm RḤMNn "for (?) the Name of (the god) R."

(4) marking genitive, BELONGING TO

Ist7627/1: wtfn...lḏS "this wtf-land belonging to ḏS."; C376/3: śxly w^{c}hd...lY...'lfm blṭm "acknowledge a thousand blṭ-coins (as belonging) to Y."; Sh31/10: mlk l'A "a king of A."; and often in dates, e.g., C448/6: the month ḏQ ḏbxrfn ḏl(396) "in the year of 396"

(5) WITH REFERENCE TO, CONCERNING

C375/1: ḏt tnb'hw lwldm "what (the god) had promised him concerning a child"; R3910/1-2: wqh...lkl š'mt "commanded, with reference to every purchase..."

(6) marking object after an infinitive

C74/13-4: wgtnnn lhmt 'srrn "and to harvest these valleys" (syntax somewhat obscure)

(7) introducing subjunctive senses (+ ipf)

C548/2-3: hn lyngsn slḥhw "if he should defile his weapons..."; R4176/4: land which lies along the highroad ^{c}dy lyrt^{c} śdn "so far as to lie opposite the dam"; and cf esp the exp l-dt SO THAT, IN ORDER THAT, e.g. Ir3: they dedicated because the god had protected him wldt yz'n...hwfyn "and so that He would continue to protect (him)" AND OFTEN SIM; other examples under DT

Note also l-dt in sense BECAUSE, e.g. NNAG12/1: hqny...ldt wqhhw "he dedicated because (the god) had commanded him"

(8) introducing jussive senses (+ ipf or inf)

R850/6: wdS lyz' mt^{c}n "and as for (the god) dS., let Him continue to save"; R4176/11: ^{c}šr...ly't ^{c}dy 'l "(as for) the tithe-money, let it come to I."; C546/9: wḤ ltwbn "as for (the god) Ḥ., let him reward"; R4190/9: wl s^{c}dhmw "and may (the god) grant them" AND VERY OFTEN SIM

Note: For the compounds k-l, k-l-k-dy, l-kd, l-k-dy, see under K.

L'--For l' R2865=C610/4, read 'l (normal Sab negative; reading confirmed by new photo, cf BeDGESA/56:4)

L'K

v pf l'k[t] C542/1*

SEND > DEDICATE (?) (but see Note)

[Eth la'aka "send"; cf Sab h'tw "cause to come > dedicate."]

C542/1: W š^{c}t S l'k[t nfsh?] "W., wife of S., dedicated [herself?]"

Note also Eth tale'ka "serve, administer to"; tr the Sab sim?

LB'

n s lb'n Ir21; d lb'nhn id+; lb'ynhn C312/5

LION

[Ar labu' "lion" (archaic), labu'a^{t} "lioness."]

Ir21: he asked kyhrgn lb'nhn h'tn ^{c}dy N "that he might kill the 2 lions which had been tracked (?) to N."; ib: gives thanks because hrg hwt lb'n bfgrt "he had killed that lion in a pit (?)"; Ry538/28: the god allowed him hrg lb'n wnmrn "to kill the lion and the panther"

LBB I

n^{1} s lb Ir24+; lbh J489A/8; lbhw J567/20+; p 'lbb(n) R4962/11+; 'lbbhmw J615/22+

HEART

[Ar libb id.]

J632/6: he returned from campaign bwfym...wǵnmm dhrdw lb mr'hw "with safety and booty which satisfied the heart of his lord" AND OFTEN SIM; Ir24: may the god grant them ḥẓy wrḍw lb mr'hmw "the favor and good will of the heart of their lord" AND ELSEWHERE SIM; C28/6: may the god grant them rḍwn 'lbbhmw "the satisfaction of their hearts"

n^{2} p lbbm C548/13*

CAKES (?)

[Cf Heb ləbībāh "cake (so called from heart shape?)."]

C548/13: šnnm wdbsm wlbbm "šnn (a dairy product), honey and cakes"

LBB II

n s lbt(m) C540/11,13,76*

CLOSE-LAID STONEWORK (but see Note)

[Cf PBH lābab "join closely, tie"--here, stones bound by transverse stones or by clamps (Irv/261).]

C540/11-13: mbr'm grbm wlbtm w'zyym frznm brrm mhbḏlm blbt 'zyyn "stonework (consisting of) rough stone and close-laid stonework and iron quoins, clamps (being) inserted into the close-laid stonework of the quoins"

Note: Irv cfs alternatively Phoen lbn, Akk labānu "laminate, flatten (metal)," tr phps "polished stone." Occasionally suggested is the tr "bricks," after Akk libittu, Heb ləbēnāh id.

LBN

n d lbnhn (< *lbnnhn, discussion BeDGESA/16:2) C338/8-9; p? lbnt R3945/11

FRANKINCENSE PLANTATION (?) (but see Note)

[Ar lubān, Heb ləbônāh "frankincense."]

C338/8-9: the mountain shoulder (on which stand) kwrn wlbnhn wmṣrbn wmqṭrnhn "the fire-altar (?), the 2 frankincense plantations (?), the incense altar and the 2 incense burners"; R3945/11: they conquered the whole territory w^{c}brt wlbnt kl 'hgrhmw "and the meadows and frankincense plantations (?) of all their towns"

Note: Considering the context in C338/8-9, lbn there may designate a kind of incense altar or burner (specifically for the burning of frankincense?). For n lbt in C540, see under LBB II. In R3945, ^{c}brt and lbnt may be nn.pr; the locale of this inscr is not in the incense country.

LBS

v pf lbst R3956/3*

PUT ON, WEAR a garment

[Ar labisa id.]

R3956/3: she confessed because lbst ^{c}ṭf ṭm'm wgzztm "she had worn a dirty, torn mantle"

LBT--For n lbt C540, see under LBB II

LG^c

n s lg^c D71/1*

CALF (?)

[Te lagā "bull-calf," Tña lag^{c}e "draw the first milk" (D/28-9).]
D71/1 (on a statuette of a female bovine): lg^{c} lṢBT "calf (?) of Ṣ."

LDN

n s ldn C685+ (all on incense burners)
KIND OF AROMATIC RESIN used as incense
[Ar ladan, Akk ladunu id (resin of Cistus creticus etc, CoRoC/172A-B).]
C685: rnd ldn ḍrw ḥdk "nard, ldn-incense, ḍrw-incense, 'pungent' incense" AND OFTEN SIM

LDT--See under L, DT

LHM--For lhm Ry510/4, lhmw J665/28, read ghm, ghmw; see under GHM

LWD--For n 'lwd, see under WLD n^{l}

LWH--In obscure context R2861/2: b' lyhb l[..]st mtbmdgb lw[h?] św^{c}ltn, no tr. Glaser emended to (g)w[lt], tr "the best parts"; Grimme read lw[h] and tr "to pawn."

LWṬ--MüW/100 cites n mlwṭ (p) "friends, companions (of the king)" in Pl24g, tr after Ar lāṭa (w) "stay in one's mind, hang on."

LWL

n d lwlyhmw J2110/6-7*
NIGHTS (cf lyl, lly id)
[See under LYL.]
J2110/6-7: tlt 'ywmm wlwlyhmw "three days and the 2 (intervening) nights"

LḤNMDYQTT^{c}--In R3119, full text of inscription. No tr

LXB--For lx[b] J750/15-6,13-4, see under LXY

LXY

n s lx[n] J750/15-6; var? l[xy]n ib/13-4
DISPUTE, QUARREL
[Ar laxâ "abundance of idle talk" (BeJSS14/230).]
J750/13-6: lh^{c}nnhmw 'LMQH bn l[xy]n dyknn bynhw wbyn 'tthw [km?] h^{c}nnhmw 'l bn hwt lx[n] b^{c}m 'tthw "may (the god) l. deliver them from (any further) quarrel between him and his wife, as l. delivered them from that quarrel with his wife"
Note: J restored as lx[b], l[xb]n, tr "slaps, contentions" after Ar laxaba "to slap."

LXM

n s lxmm J700/11*

BRAWL

[Ar laxama "strike, hit in the face," laxām "a slap" (IrvBSOAS30/288).]

J700/11: wsb bynhmy lxmm b^{c}ly hwt wldn "a brawl took place between the two over that child"

Note: Cf also mlxm R3077, only word in inscription. N.pr?

LYL

n s lyl(m) J649/33 twice; var llm C532/7-8

NIGHT, NIGHT-TIME; exp lyl lylm: ALL NIGHT LONG (cf lwl, lly "night")

[Ar layl "night-time," layla^{+} "a night," layl laylīl "long night." RycExp-Ast/523n13 analyzes the exp lyl lylm in J649 as an inf followed by cognate noun, tr "the duration of the night."]

J649/33: they fought ^{c}dy mqṭt šmsn wlyl lylm ^{c}dy šrq kwkbn ḏsbḥ "until sunset and all night long until the rising of the morning star"; C532/7-8: she confessed bḏt xṭ't bllm 'l bhn š^{c}rt w'l lm tš(^{c})r "because she had sinned at night (?), those (sins) of which she was conscious and those she was not conscious of" (for discussion see under BLL)

LKD

n s mlkdn Ist7632/2-3*

RESERVOIR

[Cf Heb lākad "capture," malkōdet "trap"--here, something which traps the water brought by the canal (BeFSTI/282-3).]

Ist7632/2-3: ^{c}s' whqḥ ḥrtn wmlkdn lmsqt nxlhw "built and prepared for use the canal and reservoir to the irrigation of his palmgrove"

LKḎ--For the cjs lkḏ, lkḏy, klkḏy, see under K

LLY

n s lly(n) J631/30+; p llt Ir28/1

NIGHT (cf lwl, lyl id)

[Syr lēlī id, < *laylay; cf Mh ḥallîu "night."]

Ir28/1: 'ty sb^{c}t ymtm bllt "to arrive in seven days and nights (lit., days with (corresponding) nights)"; C581/8: blly sdṯm "on the sixth night"; J631/30: b^{c}ww bllyn ḥyrt 'ḤBŠn "they attacked the Ḥabashite camp by night"; ib/24: yfṣn...^{c}dy hgrn...bn llyn "they went to the city during (?) the night"

LM

av lm C523/7+

NOT + ipf (Harami subdialect) (cf 'l id, under 'L III)

[Ar lam + jussive id.]

C523/7: ms 'nṯ ḥyḍ wlm yǵtsl "he touched menstruating women and did not wash himself"; C532/8-9: sins of which she was conscious w'l lm tš(^{c})r "and those she was not conscious of"; also in R3912/2 in fragmentary context

Note: For lm in verbs, see under LMM.

LMD

v <u>pf</u> lmdw C540/78*

COAT with plaster

[Cf Tña labada "coat with mud the inside of a clay bread oven to prevent the heat from dissipating," from a supposed basic sense "cover (s.th.) with mud or plaster" (lrv/287-8); cf also Syr lmad "join" (CoRoC/173A).]

C540/78: lmdw kl ᶜqlmn wnmryn wᶜwdn bgyrm ṣlwhmw w'r'shmw "they coated the whole diversion mole, control wall and settling basin with plaster, their sides and their tops"

Note: C read gmdw.

LMM

v <u>pf</u> lmw R3959/3+

ACQUIESCE IN, GUARANTEE (?)

[Cf Ar lamma "collect, assemble" > "act collectively"?]

R3959/3: lmw bny Ḥ ltwfyn 'rḏhmw bᶜlm ẓrbm "they guaranteed (for) the b.Ḥ. that (the latter) would pledge themselves to pay for their land by means of a title deed/contract"; R4134/5: wlmw ẓ()rb <u>d</u>'A lywfynn ẓ[r]bm "they guaranteed the contract of (the clan) A. to pay (the sum named in) the contract"

h <u>pf</u> hlmw R3960/5*

ACQUIESCE IN, GUARANTEE (cf LMM <u>v</u> id)

R3960/5: ...]krbn mrᶜẓm whlmw wqhw 'mr'hm[w... "laborers (?) and levies (?); and they guaranteed (what) their lords had commanded"

LMŠ--For lmšw J720/15, read l-mšw; see under MŠW <u>v</u>

LN

pp ln R3945/4+; before m, l- R4085/15

FROM

[Cf Ug l- "from," extended here by Sab <u>pp</u> suffix -n (BeDGESA/47:6).]

R3945/4: gb<u>d</u> W ln L ᶜd Ḥ "he plundered (the territory) W. from L. as far as Ḥ."; R4085/3: ln ǵylm ᶜdy šqrm "from the bottom to the top" AND SEVERAL TIMES SIM; J633/15: the god cured his disease ln tkwn <u>d</u>t hqnytn wl'xr "from the (date of the) making of this dedication and thenceforward"; J745/5-6: hqnyw...hqnyt šftw lnqdmm "they dedicated the offering they had promised from before, i.e. formerly (?)"; <u>with assimilation:</u> R4085/15: lmhyᶜ...ᶜd w<u>tn</u> "from the sanctuary to the boundary stone"

cj ln C338/4+; ln <u>d</u>- C95/1+; ln <u>d</u>t R4624/7

SINCE > WHEN

[Development from prepositional usage "from (the time when)" > "after, since" > "when."]

C338/4: kl mhy^{c} hḥdṯ T'LB...ln styf^{c} "every shrine he restored (for) (the god) T. when He was 'exalted'"; C95/1: ...]wfyhmw ln ḏṯ'wl ^{c}dy hgrn "protected them when he returned to the city"; R4624/7: šrḥ...ln ḏṯ fśl "he succeeded when he hewed out (the mountain road)"

Note: Read lnh' J584/7 as n.pr. In C126/12, read bn for ln with BeMus64/307? Passage reads: wy]^{c}zln sb^{c}t ywm[n] bn (ḏ)ymwtn ḏymwtn "there is a postponement of seven days so that he who is to die may not die (during those days)." C emended to ln, tr as negative after Ar lan "not."

LSN

n s lsn C86/9-10+; lsnhw J570/13+

(1) TONGUE

[Ar lisān id.]

J570/13: may the god šrḥ ydhw wlsnhw "protect his hand and tongue (or, protect with His hand and tongue, i.e. His oracle?)"; sim Ir28

(2) CALUMNY (?)

C86/9-10: may the god protect them from ḥry wlsn wm^{c}dw "harm, calumny and despite"

Note also 'lsnyhmw in obscure and fragmentary context R3232/3, prob to be compared to the v 'lśn, q.v.

L^{C}B

n s ml^{c}b C37/7+

FLOOD PLAIN

[Cf Ar la^{c}aba "emit a flow of slaver...from [one's] mouth" (Lane/2662A).]

C37/7: [wh]bhmw...ml^{c}b ^{c}brn ḏD "they gave them the flood plain of the riverside pasture D."; C356: ml^{c}b ḏ'rḍhw "the flood plain of his land"

L^{C}Z--In fragmentary context J763/3: ...wl^{c}zm w[..., no tr

L^{C}L

n? s l^{c}l C80/11*

HEIGHT (?); in exp l-l^{c}l: HIGHER, MORE

[Cf Eth la^{c}ala "be high," ultimately from root ^{C}LY "be high"; cf Sab pp ^{c}l(y) "upon."]

C80/11: yfqln 'rb^{c}y 'qdrn wbnh ll^{c}l "he harvested (or, the land produced) forty measures (of crops), and more than that"

LFY

v pf lfyw J576/6+; ipf ylfyhmw J577/12; ylfyw J576/4+

OBTAIN BLOOD REVENGE

[Cf Ar lfy h "find, get," Lt "obtain blood revenge on s.o." (BeNL7/542).]

J576/4: hǵrw wlfyw bn hnt hgrn mhrgtm wsbym wǵnmm d^{c}sm "they attacked/raided and obtained blood revenge from those towns, (consisting of) numerous slaughters, captives and booty"; J644/24: kl mhrg lfyw "every slaughter (which) they obtained (as) blood revenge"; J577/12: h]ǵrw b^{c}lyhmw...wylfyhmw "they attacked/raided them and obtained blood revenge upon them"

LFF

n s lf J584/3*

CROWD=PEOPLE (?)

[Ar liff "crowd, multitude" (JSIMB/91).]

J584/3: he dedicated to the god because mt^{c}hw dlf DMR "He of the people (?) of D. (a divine epithet?) had saved him"

LṢQ

v ipf ylṣqnn DJE10/4; inf lṣq ib/3

CATCH (?)

[Ar laṣiqa "cling to, hang on to, stick to," Eth laṣaqa "stick to, fasten to" (MüHaz/83).]

DJE10/3-4: lytlwnn wlṣq kl 'ns y'x[dn...]rn fl ylṣqnn w^{c}yr kl 'ns yxṭ'n bdt mqb[rtn... "let them pursue and catch (?) any man who takes (this burial place...); and let them catch and disgrace any man who sins in this burial (place)"

LQḤ

v ipf ylqḥnn F55/4; inf lqḥ R2724/9

TAKE, SEIZE > CAPTURE, ARREST

[Heb lāqaḥ, Ug lqḥ id.]

F55/4: gzmw...kdm ylqḥnn kl 'nsm... "they pledged themselves as follows: they will seize any man..."; in obscure context R2724/9: WDD^{c}L ^{c}lbnbyh blqḥ lrb^{c}, no tr

h inf hlqḥn C155/4+

CAPTURE, ARREST (= LQḤ v)

C155/4: [w]l tbr wh[t]lf[n w]hlqḥn wdr^{c}n "to crush, cause to perish, capture and defeat"; J601/9: ytbrw whlqḥn hmt 'š^{c}bn "they crushed and captured those tribesmen"

n p mlqḥtm J643b/4+ (D prt?)

THINGS CAPTURED, CAPTURES

J643b/4: they returned from campaign b[sḥ]tm wtbrm wmlqḥtm "with defeat and crushing (i.e., having defeated and crushed) and captures"; sim J643/32

LQṬ

v inf lqṭhw C84/4*

MAKE INCURSIONS ON (?)

[Cf Ar lqṭ ti "fall on a thing by chance," Syr lqṭ "pick up > capture."]

C84/4: h'xdw llqṭhw bbyt bn Ṣ "they began (?) to make incursions on him (?) in the fortress of the b.Ṣ."

st pf stlqṭ DJE13/7*

BE ABDUCTED (?)

[Cf Ar laqaṭa "take up, glean"--here, reflexive of the causative? (cf MüTa^{c}izz/98).]

DJE13/7: ǵlm stlqṭ bn MRB "the young man who was abducted (?) from M."

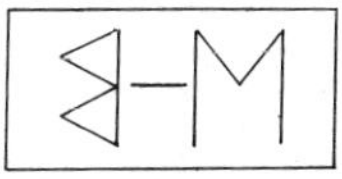

M I

ab m R3945/13+

SYMBOL FOR THE NUMBER ONE HUNDRED

[Initial of Sab m't "hundred."]

R3945/13: xms m't ▯ mmmmm ▯ "five hundred: 500"

Note also the symbol ◁ (half of the symbol m 𐩣), which stands for the number fifty; e.g., R2868: sdṯy šwḥṭ ▯ ◁ ^{c} ▯ "sixty šwḥṭ-units: 60"

M II

pt -m C84/6+; -mw R4194/2+

deictic particle, usually untranslatable, but sometimes indicating indefiniteness (cf var -my under M^{c}N)

[Cf sim particles in Ar (e.g., attached to prepositions; min + mā mimmā, bi + mā bimā) and Heb (e.g., bə + mô).]

enclitic on various parts of speech:

n.pr: R4194/2: M^{c}D'Lmw (name of a man); G1184: ḏ'BHYmw (name of a month)

v: R3946/4,6: wyśfmw ḥwhw...wyśfmw qnyhw "and he increased his clan ...his property"

pn: R3910/6: wmnmw ḏyš'mn "and whoever buys..."

adv:R2724/10: 'hnmw "when/wherever"

pp: N19/7: wbmw hwt xrfn "and in that year"; C84/6: bmhyt ^{c}ṣrn "in that calamity"; C975/7: bnm nxln "from the palmgrove"; R3951/5: wḥgm khḥrw 'mlk "and as the kings decreed"

M III

pp m-, short for mn "from" (see under MN I), has been proposed in R2740/9 (mmd, see under MDD n^I); R5055 (msbl, see under SBL); and C160/7 (m^{c}mhw, read b^{c}mhw and see under ^{c}M).

M'

n s m't J649/27-8+; d m'nhn G1533/7; m'tyn C540/85 (late Sab); m'tn ib/49; p m'(m,n) C413/1+ (early and middle Sab); var m'tm C325/5+ (late Sab)

(ONE) HUNDRED

[Ar mi'a^t id.]

J649/27-8: sb^{c}y wm't 'sdm "170 soldiers"; ib/39: 'rb^{c} m'tm sbym "400 captives"; J644/22: šlt m'n 'sdm "300 soldiers"; J576/15: xms m'nm w'lfm 'sdm "1,500 soldiers"; Ry507/8: ts^{c}y wtty m'tn "290"; Ry508/6: tmnyt wtty m'tn "280"; note also R4010/4: ...]n m' w'ḥd wsty wt[... "161 (?)"

Note: For m't C338/11, see under 'TW n^{2}.

M'L

n p m'yltn J655/17*

GARDENS, or MEADOWS

[Ar ma'la† "luxuriant garden, or meadow" (JSIMB/160).]

J655/17: may the god grant harvests bmlk m'yltn wxytmtn "in the property (consisting of) gardens/meadows and sown fields"

M'N

v ipf ym'n R2862/2-3,4*

context obscure; REFUSE (?)

[Cf Heb mi'ēn id.]

R2862/2-6: ...]ln dt (y)m'n ttmrn whm ym'n d(y)s'l tmrn ds'lhw... "until he refuses (?) to ...?; and if anyone who is asked (?) refuses (?) the crops (?) which are asked of him (?)..."

M'T--For n m't, see under M'

MG'--For n mg't J647/26-7, read ml't, see under ML'

MDD

n^{1} s? mmd R2740/8+ (prt?)

adj: PROLONGED, EXTENDED (?) (only in obscure exp tfd mmd)

[Ar madda and D, "lengthen, prolong."]

R2740/8: ^{c}sy dbḥn tfd mmd "he offered a sacrifice (for?) the prolonged harvest"; C516/18: tfdm m'tm mmd wwfd F mmd "harvest, a hundred (measures?), prolonged; and F. produced crops, prolonged"

n^{2} s mdt C541/96*

PERIOD OF TIME

[Ar mudda† id.]

C541/96: bmdt dD 'xrtn "in the latter period of (the month) dD."

MDY

n s mdyh R4176/4-5*

SETTLING BASIN; or, OVERFLOW from such a basin

[Irv/228 cites Q on Ar madī in both senses, also "small stream."]

R4176/4-5: the embanked land which lies opposite śdn H wmdyh "the dam H. and its settling basin/overflow"

MDF--For n mdfn C553/3, see under DFN

MDR

n s mdr R4231/5; p 'mdrn R3951/4

(1) EARTH, SOIL

[Eth medr id.]

R4231/5: kl b'xbb wmdr xdrn gwlm "everything in the niches and soil of the tomb, as private property"

(2) (RURAL) DISTRICTS

[Cf Eth medr id.]

R3951/4: bhgrn Ṣ wb kl 'mdrn "in the city Ṣ. and in all (its) (rural) districts"

Note: Cf also mdrtn R4054/3 in fragmentary context; n.pr?

MHN I

n p mhn Ry510/4*

OPERATIONS, COURSE (?)

[Ar mihna^{t}, p mihan "occupation, work" (RodConf'66-7/134).]

Ry510/4: commissioned this inscription ^{c}ly mhnsb'tm "during the operations/course (?) of the campaign"

Note: BeOr25/295 suggests reading mḥn, tr mḥnsb'tm "expeditionary camp," after Heb maḥăneh "camp."

MHN II

pn^{1} mhn J720/13+

indefinite and interrogative pn: WHAT, WHAT THING?

[Cf Ar man "who," mā "what, that which"; Min mhn "who."]

NNAG12/10-1: he sought a vision w'l mhn hr'yhmw 'LMQH "and there was nothing (lit., not what) (that) (the god) I. showed them"; J720/13: mrḍm... ḏ'l mn š^{c}r kmhn h' ḥlẓhw "a sickness (about) which no one knew what that disease of his was (lit., 'what is that disease of his?')"

pn^{2} k + mhn + mw J669/10+

deictic pt + indefinite pn + indefinite enclitic pt: WHATEVER > WHENEVER, IF (cf k-m^{c}n-mw id, under M^{c}N, and esp the Note there)

J669/10: šftw 'LMQHW kmhnmw yldn lhmw bnm...fyhqnynn "they promised (the god) I. that 'if a son should be born to them,' they would dedicate..."

AND ELSEWHERE SIM

MHR I

h pf hmhr F55/7*

FIX a date of payment

[Cf Ar mhr D "fix a dowry."]

F55/7: hmhr mlkn bnhmw gwz "the king has fixed the date of payment against them" n _s_ mhrthw C492/3+

PROPERTY; or GIFT

[Cf Ar mahr "dowry," Akk māru "send," tamīrtu "(missive,) gift" (BDB/555B).]

C492/3: he dedicated to the goddess kl wldhw wmhrthw "all his children and his property" AND ELSEWHERE SIM

MHR II

n _s_ mhrtm J752/10-1; mhrthw ib/9-10

FILLY

[Ar muhra† id.]

J752/5ff: hqnyw...frsm _dt_ _dhbm_ _dt_ šfthw lgrm mhrthmw kwldt mhrtm "they dedicated a gold mare which he had promised (to the god) for the life of their filly, when a filly was born"

Note: For mhrt R4069/5 read mḥrg (?), see under ḤRG

MHR III

n _s_ tmhrthw J665/12-3+

ELITE CORPS

[Cf Ar mahara "be skilled," Heb māhîr "practiced, expert."]

Ir32/2: 'sy...S...wtmhrthw ᶜbrn Q "he sent S. and his elite corps to Q."; J665/12-3: their lord commanded them lsb' wqdmnhmw wtmhrthw 'ᶜrb mlk S "to go on campaign and command (?) them and his elite corps, the beduins of the king of S."

MW--For enclitic _pt_ -mw, see under M II; for _n_ mw, see under MWY

MWY

n _s_ mw(m,n) J750/9+; _d_ mwnhn J635/37; _p_? mwy C338/7+; mw(y)hmw R4774/2

(1) WATER

[Cf Akk mū, Ar mā', ModḤaḍ muwayh id.]

R4815/2: fnwtm msb' mwn "a canal, a conductor of water"; C547/10: the god granted them in the spring and fall rainstorms mn mwm qllm "only a little water"; J750/9: lost in the desert, they obtained qll mwm _d_šrḥ 'fshmw "a little water, which saved their lives"; C570/7: mnḍḥt mwn "irrigation gods (lit., sprinklers of water)"

(2) NATURAL or ARTIFICIAL SOURCE OF WATER

J635/37: bknf 'rḍ 'l mgzt mwnhn "on the border of the land l., at the ford of the 2 streams"; C338/7: ᶜ_db_ byn msb' ᶜrn wᶜ_db_ mwn "he conducted repairs in the vicinity of the road to the fortress, and he repaired the water system"; R3945/16: stmxḍ mwy _d_Q "he confiscated the water systems of Q."

MWL--For _n_ mlt, see under MLY I

MWN

n s mwnn J2109/10*

FOOD

[Cf Ar mūna† "victuals, food" (DoJRAS'68/14).]

J2109/7-10: myt ǵyr qlt mwnn "he died for lack of (lit., without) a small quantity of food"

MWR

v pf mwrhmw C353/6*

ENCLOSE, SHUT IN

[Ar māra (w) "run about, go around."]

C353/6: tṣn^{c}w bhgrn Ḍ wmwrhmw bhw mlk...wẓwrhmw bhw "they fortified themselves in the city Ḍ and the king shut them in there and besieged them there"

n s mrm Ist7630/4; mrhmw GaAntYem2/2; var mwrt(n) C40/3+; mwrthmy C569/2; mwrthmw ib+; p mwwrt N26/2; var 'mwrtn C343/11

RETAINING WALL

[Cf MWR v "enclose" and Ar mawr "trodden road" (Lane/2443A).]

C40/3: kl mwrt wgn' wṣwbt mḥfdn "every retaining wall, (outer) wall and the substructure of the tower"; C343/11: kbr 'mwrtn [b]mšmthmw "enlarged the retaining walls in the fields"; Ist7630/4: krfm wmrm "a cistern and (its) retaining wall"

MWT

v pf mt R5045; mtw Ry507/5; var mwt J735/7; ipf ymtn C126/13+; ymt D65/a; var ymwtn C126/12; inf mwt Ry520/7

DIE (cf myt id)

[Ar māta (w) id.]

Ry520/7: may the god grant them ḥyy ḥyw ṣdqm wmwt mwt ṣdqm "to live a proper life and die a proper death"; J649/21: he and his horse were wounded whdr ktxd^{c}nn rglhw wymtn frshw "and he feared that his legs would be useless and his horse would die"; J735/7: mwt dbn '^{c}mdn bn ṣm'm "some of the naturally watered fields died of the drought"; C126/12-3: wy]^{c}zln sb^{c}t ywm[t] ln dymwtn dymwtn wl ymtn nfshw "let seven days be set aside before the one who is to die dies (after committing an offence); and (then) let his person die"; D65/a: ^{c}WBymt "let A. die!"

h pf hmt cited by MüW/102 in C588b/5 and N9/3--read prob as hmt demonstrative pn in both cases, see under HMT

st pf stmtw C353/8*

SEEK DEATH

[Ar mwt st id, also "fight desperately."]

C353/8: ẓwrhmw bhw ^{c}dy stmtw bs[b'tn?] "besieged them there until they sought death in b[attle?]"

n[1] s mwt(m,n) C557/6+; mwthw R3910/6
DEATH; in some contexts, phps MORTAL SICKNESS (cf mwtt)
[Ar mawt id.]
R3910/6: if a purchased animal dies within a specified period, fbr'm mhš'mn bn mwthw "the seller is not liable for its death"; MüBilinguis/2: mr' ḥyn wmwtn "Lord of life and death (epithet of God)"; C557/6: the god saved her bn ᶜws wmwtn kwn bkl 'rḍn "from the plague and death/mortal sickness which was in all the land"; C540/69: ḍllm wmwtm "illness and death/mortal sickness"

n[2] s mwtt J645/13*
DEATH, or MORTAL SICKNESS (cf mwt n[1])
[Ar mawta† "death," cf also mūta† "epilepsy."]
J645/13: the god saved His servant bn xwm wᶜws wmwtt kwn b'rḍn "from the pestilence, plague and death/mortal sickness which was in the land" (cf sim context with mwt, C557/6 quoted under MWT n[1])

MZN--In C541/23, read mznm prob as n.pr: 'xḏ MZNm hgn 'A "captured M., bastard of A."

MZR

n s mzrm C540/50*
BEER
[Ar mizr id.]
C540/50: ṯty m'tm ''blm mzrm ḏtmrm "two hundred camel (loads) of date-beer"
Note also mzr in fragmentary context Gl539/4, quoted under KŚ' v.

MḤK

n s mḥkm J576/11*
QUARREL
[Ar maḥaka "to quarrel."]
J576/11: nbl bᶜbrhmw Š...lmḥkm bḥblm "Š. sent to them concerning the quarrel in (i.e., which underlay?) the revolt"

MḤL I

h pf hmḥlt J735/6*
BE BARREN, ARID (land)
[Ar mḥl h id.]
J735/6: ybsw 'mṭrn whmḥlt kl 'srr "the rain-watered fields dried up and all the valleys were barren (because of the drought)"

n s mḥlm C539/6*
DROUGHT > FAMINE
[Ar maḥl id.]
C539/6: ᶜwsm wḍllm wmḥlm "plague, disease and famine"

Note: For n mḥlnn C542/5, p mḥl[lt] R4197/1-2, see under ḤLL I.

MḤL II

n s mḥlym Gl533/5*

OATH (?)

[Eth maḥala "swear," maḥalā "oath" (HöSEG8/31).]

Gl533/5: ^{c}hdy 'l[t] blṭn mḥlym "they pledged themselves (respecting) that money by oath"

Note: For mḥly in Gl142, 1143 read mxly, see under XLY.

MḤN I

v ipf ymḥn R2861/12-3*

TRY legally, EXAMINE (?) (context fragmentary)

[Ar maḥana id.]

R2861/12-3: wlymḥn (ǵ)br hgr(n) "let him try/examine (?) the befouler (?) of the city"

MḤN II

n s mḥn Ry443/2*

KIND OF CANAL (?)

[Sense from context.]

Ry443/2: nwyn wmḥn 'xdw 'wtn dṢ "the channel and ...? (kind of canal?) which enclose the boundaries of Ṣ."

Note: Ry took as the n.pr of the channel, WMḤN.

MḤR

n s mḥrtm C435/2; mḥr[Cl40/8*

SALE, DEED OF SALE (?)

[Cf Heb meḥîr "price," Akk maḫirānu "buyer."]

C435/2: yt^{c}lmnn bnḥltm wmḥrtm "they signed the deeds of gift and sale"; Cl40/8: hqnyw dn ṣl[mn] RMN sybhmw bn mḥr[... "they dedicated this statue to (the god) R. (as?) their gift (?) from the (proceeds of the) sale (?) ..." (context fragmentary)

Note: For n mḥr elsewhere, see under ḤWR n^2, ḤRR III.

MXḌ

v pf mxḍ R2650/2+

(1) BREAK UP stone, QUARRY

[Ug mxṣ, Akk maḫāṣu, Heb māḥaṣ "beat, break to pieces."]

R2650/2: mxḍ blq m'xdn "he quarried stone for the control-dam"; same exp R2651/2, R3943/5

(2) STRIKE, OVERTHROW an enemy

R3234/1: mxḍ [kl] wld ^{c}M wfrḥw "he overthrew [all] the children of (the god) A. (= the Qatabanians) and they fled"; R3945/19: mxḍ M w'A wkl 'š^{c}b M "he overthrew M., A. and all the tribes of M."; ib/18: mxḍ S...whb^{c}l kl mnhyhmw "he overthrew S. and took possession of all their collecting basins"

h ipf yhmxḍ R3945/17; yhmxḍw ib

GRANT, HAND OVER confiscated territory to a new owner

[Sense from context; cf MXḌ st.]

R3945/16-7: stmxḍ mwy dQ bn S...wyhmxḍ Y...wstmxḍ bn S...ḥrrtn dt M wyhmxḍ N...bn ḥrrtn dt M ln 'wtn wtn K "he confiscated the water system of Q. from S. and they/it was given over to Y.; and he confiscated from S. the canals of M. and gave (them) over to N., from the canals of M. to the borders established by K."

st pf stmxḍ R3945/4+

CONFISCATE property from a defeated enemy

R3945/16,17 quoted under MXḌ h; ib/4: mxḍ D...wŠ wwfṭ 'hgrhmw wstmxḍ ^{c}rhmw ...wmnhythmw...l'LMQH wl SB' "he overthrew D. and Š. and burned their towns and confiscated their fortress and collecting basins for (the god) I. and for S."; ib/11: stmxḍ K...qsṭhw w'nmh[w] "he confiscated K., its qsṭ-citizens (yeomen?) and its civilians"

n^1 s? mxḍm C570/2*

ADMINISTRATION; in exp 'mt mxḍm: CUBITS OF THE ADMINISTRATION, OFFICIAL/ADMINISTRATIVE CUBITS

[Cf uses of root MXḌ in Sab; Min smxḍ "cause s.o. to administer (land)."]

C570/2: 'rb^c 'mn wšlt šwḥṭ b'mt mxḍm "four cubits and three spans in administrative cubits"

n^2 s mxḍnm J555/4*

EXACTION, CONFISCATION > GIFT, TRIBUTE (cf MXḌ st)

J555/4: htb lhw S t'mnm wšr^{c}tm wmxḍnm "S. rendered to (the god) thank-offering, payment(s?) and a gift"

MXR

v ipf ymxrw C555/1; ymxrn C570/1; inf/maṣdar mxr(m) J575/6+

(1) FACE TOWARD

[Akk maḫāru "face; oppose"; Ar mxr st sim.]

C555/1: ymxrw 'ln 'wtnn nsr mšrqn "let these boundary stones face toward the east"; C570/1: 'wtn ymxrn Q "the boundary stones which face Q."

(2) OPPOSE, FIGHT (b^{c}ly s.o.) (?)

J575/6: t'wlw wḥrbw b^{c}A wh^{c}n ldmxrm b^{c}lyhmw ds'r bn hmt 'ḤBŠN "they returned and fought in A. and helped to oppose those who remained of those Ḥabashites"; J649/41: wldmxr hwt ywmn fšw^{c}w "in order to fight those battles they furnished aid..."

MṬW

v pf mṭww Ir32/24-5+; inf mṭw J635/10+

ADVANCE militarily (b^{c}ly against)

[Ar maṭā "quicken one's pace, hurry," Aram mṭā' "reach."]

J635/10: the campaigns and fights sb'w wd̲b' wmṭw wh^{c}nn b^{c}ly kl 'xms "(which) they undertook and (in which) they fought, advanced, and gave aid against all the armies"; Ir32/24-5: mṭww ^{c}mhmw 'sd Ṣ b^{c}ly 'b^{c}l Š "the soldiers of Ṣ. advanced with them against the citizens of Š."

n p mṭw R4138/4*

FORAYS, EXPEDITIONS

R4138/4: the god protected them b[kl] sby' wmṭw wḥryb...sb'w "in all the campaigns, forays, and battles they undertook"

MṬR

n s mṭrn C365/5; p 'mṭrn J735/6+

FIELD WATERED BY RAIN (phps also by wells)

[Zafari mṭîra "cultivated land on both sides of a canal arising in a well," Dat̲ meṭîreh "plot of land surrounded by a meter-high wall, dependent on well-irrigation." Cf Ar maṭar "rain." In C365/5, f.]

J735/6: in the drought ybsw 'mṭrn "the rain-watered fields dried up"; ib/13: the floodwaters arrived wml'w 'mṭrn "and filled the rain-watered fields"; C365/5: tws^{c}t d̲t mṭrn "this rain-watered field was ruined/captured (?)"; F71/8: '^{c}ḍdhw w'mṭrn "its palm-plantations and rain-watered fields"

Note: Cf also mṭwr, epithet of the god T'LB J2137/6: T RYMm ^{c}dy mṭwr 'HGRn "T.R. in (= of) the rain-watered fields (var p?) of A."

MẒ'

v pf mẓ' R3945/5+; mẓ'hmw J643/26; mẓ't Ir32; mẓ'y J629/22; mẓ'w J576/6+; ipf ymẓ'w J643/7

REACH, ARRIVE, COME TO (cf MḌ' v id)

[Eth maṣ'a "come"; cf phps Ar maḍâ "go away."]

J735/12: mẓ' d̲^{c}bn bl[l]yn "the floodwaters arrived in the night"; R3945/5: mxḍhw ^{c}d mẓ' bḥrn "he defeated him until he reached the sea"; Ir32: mẓ't ^{c}brhmw ^{c}ẓtm...^{c}(m)n mr'hmw "an order from their lord reached them"; J643/26: mẓ'hmw mnd̲rm "a spy/warning came to them"

h pf hmẓ' Gl572/3+

CAUSE TO ARRIVE, DELIVER > (1) MAKE AN OFFERING

[Eth 'amṣe'a "cause to arrive, allot, make over" (HöSEG8/29f).]

GaAlON33/6: wlyd̲bḥn wl yhmẓ'n ṣdqm "let him sacrifice and make offering(s) appropriately"

(2) CEDE property

Gl572=R3649bB/3: whmẓ' wṣdq...kl ml' wrbḥ "he ceded and granted all the yield and profit"; sim Gl533/1

Also in fragmentary context J681/2.

MY--For -my, var of enclitic -mw (M II) in the compound km^{c}nmy, see under M^{c}N

MYL--For n mlt see under MLY I

MYR

h For yhmrn R2860=C603a/3-4, read yhgrm, see under GRM h

n s myr(m,n) C73/8+; p 'mrn J627/5+; var 'mrt J615/18+; var 'myrt J623/14-5+
GRAIN; p GRAIN CROP, GRAIN HARVEST

[Ar mīra† "provisions < grain stores," māra (y) "supply with grain."]

C73/8: ṣrb...ḏbhw kwn myrn ṯmn brm "an autumn harvest in which (the price of) grain was eight br-measures (or, one-eighth of a br)"; J666/16: may the god grant fr^{c} 'myrt dṯ' wxrf...w'ṯmr ṣdqm "grain crops of the spring and autumn harvests, and satisrying crops" AND OFTEN SIM; J627/5: kbrn 'rḍhmw bn 'mrn ḏmlym "enlarged their lands after (?) the winter grain crop"

MYT

v pf myt J669/20+
DIE (= mwt)

[Aram mīt id.]

J669/20: wmyt byd bnhmw "he died at the hand of one of them"; J2109/7: myt ǵyr qllt mwnn "he died for lack of (lit., without) a little food"

MYṮ

n s myṯn R3104/4-5*
THAT WHICH SPRINKLES the earth with rain (?), epithet of the month dṮWR

[Ar māṯa (y) "soften, soak."]

R3104/4-5: altar on which the king sacrifices bywm ts^{c}m dṮWR myṯn bt^{c}mm "on the ninth day of (the month) dṮ. the Sprinkler; an announcement (?)"

Note: The month may be named for the god ṮWR (= 'LMQH), and the epithet may refer to the god.

MKR

n p mkrn R3951/2*
MERCHANTS, TRADESMEN

[Cf Heb mākar "sell."]

R3951/2: SB' nš'n w'š̌^{c}bn qsdn wmkrn wśl'n "the Sabaeans, military classes and tribesmen, 'yeomen,' tradesmen and tribute-paying classes"

ML'

v pf ml'w J735/13; ipf yml'n J618/6; inf ml' R4766/2+
(1) FILL

[Ar mala'a id.]

J618/6: the god agreed kyml'n mnxthmw...bṯny brqn "that He would fill their canals in two rainstorms"; J735/13: the floodwaters came wml'w 'mṭrn "and filled the rain-watered fields"

(2) COMPLETE

[Cf Eth mal'a "bring to completion, maturity."]

R4766/2: bnyw wml' qbrhmw "they built and completed their tomb"

h pf hml'hmw J631/20+; inf hml'n J557

(1) FILL IN

[Ar ml' h "cause to be full, fill s.th."]

J557: ml' tml' nṭ^c hml'n whwśqn "he filled in the fill of the nṭ^c constructions, filling in (?) and heaping up" (part of the construction of the outer wall of the great temple of Mārib)

(2) GRANT, FULFILL a request (said of a god)

[Cf esp Ar māla'a "assist" and Sab ML' v "complete."]

J631/20: they campaigned ḥgn hml'hmw šymhmw ^{c}TTR "as their patron deity A. granted to them"; J671/16: xmrhmw hml'hmw b'mrhw ky'fqn...d^{c}bn "(the god) agreed to grant them by His oracle that he would hold back the floodwaters"

st pf stml' J560/17+; stml'w C88/8+; stml'nn J565/10+; ipf ystml'n J590/18-9+; ystml'nn C88/8+; inf stml'n J567/19+

SEEK AN ORACULAR RESPONSE of the ml' ("fulfillment") type, IMPLORE (b^{c}m of the deity)

[Denom from ml' "fulfillment > oracular response promising fulfillment of a request."]

C88/8: the god granted kl 'ml' stml'w wystml'nn b^{c}mhw "all the oracle responses they have sought or will seek from Him"; Ir7: stml'w wšftn b^{c}mhw "they implored of Him with promises"

n[1] s ml' C407/10+; var ml't J647/26-7

(1) FULLNESS, DURATION of time; PERIOD

J647/26-7: hwsyhmw bml't sb^{c}t xryftm "he caused them to perform for the period of seven years"; C407/10: the disease he suffered bml' tmnt 'wrxm "during a period of eight months"

(2) CAPACITY

Ist7630/6: sṭrm dml'hw sb^{c}y wm' ḍ'nm "a tract of pasture land sufficient for (lit., of which the capacity is) 170 sheep"

n[2] s ml' G1572/3+; ml'h F30/3; ml'hw F30b/2-3+

(1) SUM, AMOUNT of money

[Cf Eth mal'a "be completed (a transaction)," Heb mālē', məlē'āh "fullness, full produce (of land)."]

F30b/2-3: ẓhrm...dml'hw tty m't(m) blṭm "a document, the sum of (= concerned in) which is two hundred blṭ"; sim F30/3

(2) YIELD of land

G1572/3: hmẓ'...kl ml' wrbḥ "he made over all the yield and profit"; sim G1547/8, GaAntYem2/2 (or tr after sense!, "all the sum and interest"?)

n[3] s ml' G934+933/2+; p 'ml' C343/10+

(1) "FULFILLMENT" of a request, KIND OF ORACULAR RESPONSE

[Cf ML' v "complete," h "fulfill a request."]

C343/10: kl 'ml' ṣdqhmw bms'lhw "all the oracular responses (the god) granted them in His oracle"; Gl934+933/2: they erected a cult-stone bml' wmᶜd ᶜTTR "by the oracular response and promise of (the god) A."; AND SEE THE COMMON EXPS quoted under ML' st

(2) ABUNDANCE (?)

J558/5: may the god save them from ml' wḥf šn'm "the abundance and encirclement/wrongdoing of (any) enemy"

n⁴ s tml' J550/1+

FILL of a wall

[Akk tamlû id (ADSA/231).]

J550/1: he dedicated to the god kl tml' gn'n ln ''wdn 'ly sṭrn ᶜd šqrm "the whole fill of this wall from the lines of this inscription to the top (of the wall)"

MLX--In R3077, mlxm only word in inscription. N.pr?

MLY I

v inf mly J649/40*

TAKE AS BOOTY

[Cf Sab ti, tp, st id; also Akk tamallâ "enjoy," Ar mlw D, Dt id, also "appropriate for one's own use"]

J649/40: ǵnmw wmly gmlm...šfqm "they acquired and took as booty numerous camels"

ti ipf ymtlyw J576/7; inf mtlyn J578/11+

TAKE AS BOOTY (cf MLY I v, tp, st id), TAKE POSSESSION OF

J631/9: hrg wsby wǵnm wmtlyn mhrgm wsbym wǵnmm dᶜsm "made killings, took prisoners, and took ǵnm- and mlt-booty"; J576/7: they captured all its children and women wymtlyw kl 'bᶜlhw "and took all its men as booty"; Ry502/3: nśfw wmtlyn h' gyšn "they overthrew and took possession of that troop"

tp pf tmly J635/3-4; tmlyw Ir13+

(1) ACQUIRE AS PROFIT from a business transaction

J635/2-4: he dedicated this gold statue dtmly bn qrytm wṭnfm ṭybm "which he acquired as profit from (the sale of) qryt- and ṭnf-incense"

(2) TAKE AS BOOTY (cf MLY I v, ti, st id)

J576/5: the god allowed them to hsḥtn hmt 'sdn...wtmlyw sby wqny hyt hgrn "destroy those soldiers and take as booty the captives and livestock of that town"

st inf stmly R3945/13*

TAKE AS BOOTY (cf MLY I v, ti, tp id)

R3945/13: ṯll wstmly kl b^c^rhmw "plundered and took as booty all their herds"

n s mltm J574/9+; mlthw Ir13; mlthmw C349/4+

BOOTY

[Usually referred to root MWL, cf Ar māl "property, wealth (esp in livestock"; assigned here on the basis of Ir13, quoted below.]

C349/4: they dedicated ḏn ṣlmn bn mlthmw bn 'rḍ M "this statue from their booty from the land of M."; Ir13: bn mlthw ḏtmlyw bn hgrn Š "from their booty which they took from the city Š."; J574/9: they returned from campaign with 'ḥllm wsbym wmltm wǵnmm "captured garments/weapons, captives, mlt-booty and ǵnm-booty" AND OFTEN SIM

Note: For ml[t]m C174/1, read ml[y]m "winter" (MLY II).

MLY II

n s mly(m,n) J615/19+

(1) WINTER; as adj, OCCURRING IN THE WINTER (?)

[Cf Ar malī "(long) period of time."]

C174/3: 'ṯmrm...^c^dy kl 'rḍt...bqyẓ wdṯ' wṣrb wmlym "crops in all the fields in summer, spring, autumn and winter"; J653/8: they asked that yxmrnhmw sqym mlym "(the god) would grant them winter irrigation waters"

(2) WINTER HARVEST

J615/19: 'mrt dṯ' wxrf ws^c^s^c^m wmlym "grain crops of the spring, autumn, summer and winter harvests" AND OFTEN SIM; J617/8: may the god grant xrf wdṯ' ws^c^s^c^m wmlym ^c^dy kl 'rḍthmw "autumn, spring, summer and winter harvests in all their fields"

MLK

h pf hmlkw Ir32/9*

CAUSE TO POSSESS, PLACE IN THE POSSESSION OF (?)

[Ar mlk h id.]

Ir32/9: they took with them 2 panthers (?) ḏhmlkw ḤḌRMWT "which they had placed in the possession of Ḥ."

n^1^ s mlk(n) J551+; d mlknhn J576/2+; mlky J565/12+; p 'mlk(m,n) J577/16+

KING (cf mlkt n^4^ "queen")

[Ar malik id; discussion of function BeJESHO15/260-65.]

C1/6: mr'hmw K...mlk SB' bn W mlk SB' "their lord K., the king of S., son of W., the king of S." AND OFTEN SIM; Ist7608b/7: 'mlkm lḤMYRM "kings of Ḥimyar"; J577/16: sb'w b^c^ly 'mlkm wxmsm "they campaigned against kings and armies"

n^2^ s mlk Ir18+; mlkhw R3945/1 (pt restored), 5

KING; OFFICE OF KING; KINGSHIP; phps also TERM AS KING, REIGN

[Cf Ar malik "king," mulk "kingship, reign."]

R3945/5: hkśḥ 'WSN wmlkhw MRTWm "he defeated (the land of) 'A. and its king M."; ib/1: ['l]t hftn K...mkrb SB' bmlkh[w] l'LMQH wl SB' "the following (conquered territories) has K., the mkrb of S., assigned, in his capacity as king, to (the god) I. and to S."; Ir18: mlk wnbtt w'tyt "kingship, descent, and (royal) arrival" (cf RycMus87/243); Gl689a/3: ršwthw bmlk Y "his term as priest in the reign of Y."

n^{3} p mlykym Ist7608b/4*

adj: ROYAL, BELONGING TO THE KING

Ist7608b/4: [']xmshmw mlykym wqylym "their armies, belonging to kings and tribal leaders (qayls)"

n^{4} s mlkt Ir13/7; p '[ml]ktm C609/7

QUEEN (cf MLK n^{1} "king")

[Ar malika† id.]

C609/7: 'l'ltm w'mlkm w'[ml]ktm w'[š^{c}b]m "gods, kings, queens (?) and tribes (?)"; Ir13/7: mr'thmw...mlkt ḤḌRMWT "their lady, the queen of Ḥ."

n^{5} s mlk J577/7+; mlkhw J608/13-4; mlkhmw J610/16+; d mlkyhmw Ir14/3; p 'mlk J816/9; var mlkt Ry507/11

PROPERTY, DOMAIN

[Ar mulk id.]

Ir14: kly mlkyhmw mlk ^{c}TTR w'LMQH "both their domains, the domain of (the god) A. and (that of) (the god) I." (these terms designate the lands around Mārib, those naturally vs. those artificially irrigated, supervised respectively by the gods ^{c}TTR and 'LMQH TWR B^{c}Lm, cf RycMus87/357, RycSemAS4/25); AND ELSEWHERE SIM; J655/17: summer and autumn crops (b)mlk m'yltn wxytmtn "in the property (consisting of) gardens and sown fields"; J608/13-4: lwfyhw wwfy mlkhw wxmshw "may (the god) protect him, his property (? or read as n^{1} "his king") and his army" AND ELSEWHERE SIM; Ry507/11: slm ^{c}ly mlkt ḤMYRm "(there is?) peace in the domain(s) of Ḥ."

MLT--For n mlt see under MLY I

MLT

v pf mlt C523/3*

HAVE SEXUAL INTERCOURSE WITH a woman (?)

[Cf Ar milt "one who does not become satiated with coitus"; v malata "soothe, tranquilize" (Lane/2731).]

C523/3: qrb mr'tm bḥrmw wmlt ḥyḍ "he approached a woman (sexually) at a forbidden time, and had intercourse with (?) a menstruating woman"

MN I

pp mn R3956/5+; mnhw C546/5; mnhm ib/6

FROM (Harami subdialect; corresponds to bn in standard Sab)

[Ar min id; and cf bn "from" (BN I), prob not etymologically related.]

R3956/5: she wore a soiled cloak fxb't mn 'mr'h "and (so) concealed it from her lords"; C548/8: ḏyndyn mr'm mn mḥrmn "whoever drives out a man from the temple..."; C547/10: fgr šrghmw...mn mwm "(the god) caused their watercourses to flow with (?) water"; C546/5: sr H...ḏmnhw "the district of H...those from it (i.e., its inhabitants)"; ib/6: ḏgdf mnhm lyḥḏrn "whoever is stubborn among them, let him beware"

MN II

pn mn C548/1+; mn l- + ipf R2861/29+; mn + pf R4088/2; mn ḏ- + ipf N74/11+; with enclitic pts, mn-m GaAlON33/2+; mn-mw R4091/2+; mn-mw ḏ- R3910/3+

indefinite pronoun: WHO, WHOEVER, ANYONE WHO

[Ar man "who, whoever."]

R4088/2: wṯn wmn ^{c}br yb'hw wl y'xḏ "(This is) the boundary! And whoever crosses to enter it, let him be seized"; J720/13: mrḍm...ḏ'l mn š^{c}r kmhn h' "a sickness (about) which no one knew what it was"; R2861/29: wmn lywḍ'n s^{c}m s[']l "and whoever gathers/exports fodder (illegally?) shall be held responsible"; C548/1: mn gr ḥm(y)m yḥrṭ slḥm "whoever visits the sanctuary bearing arms..."; N74/11: wmnḏ ḏy^{c}qwn (2nd ḏ dittography?)...wl yqtrn "and whoever commits an act of impiety, let him be punished"; sim R3197/5 (fragmentary context): mn ḏy[... "whoever..."; note also F64/6: wmn ḏnmn bš'mtm'[... "and whoever (?), by a (deed of) sale..."

with enclitics: GaAlON33/2: the god commanded kmnm 'ns ḏyḥẓr wlyḏbḥn "that whoever (is) a man who has been 'banned,' let him sacrifice..."; R4091/2: wmnmw yštrhw lyqm^{c}n ^{c}ṮTR "and whoever destroys it, may (the god) A. strike (him) down"; R3910/3: all sales and exchanges, kmnmw ḏyš'mn ^{c}bdm f'w 'mtm "(such) that whoever buys a servant or maidservant..." (note: CoRoC read kmnw, with Grimme)

Note: For C548/1: mn grḥ mnm, read mn gr ḥm(y)m.

MN III

n s mn J735/12*

PART OF THE TEMPLE

[Sense from context; also part of the temple in Min (R3427/2-3).]

J735/12: t'tww bn mn mḥrmn "they came away from the mn of the temple"

MNḎ--For ḏmnḏ J653/10, see under Ḏ; for mnḏ N74/11, see under MN II

MNX--For n mnxt, see under NXY

MNY

n s mnyt C581/19*

FATE (but see Note)

[Ar manīya† "fate," manâ "allot."]

C581/19: may the god save his lord bn b'stm wmnyt sw'm "from harm and ill fate"

Note: Phps a misreading of the more common mngt "fate, fortune" (root NGW)? Note the exp mngt sw'm "ill fortune" J564/23-4.

MNL--For n mnlt, see under NWL

MNM, MNMW--see under MN II

MN^{c}

v pf mn^{c}w C291/3; ipf ymn^{c}w R4815/6+; inf mn^{c} C573/5+

(1) REPEL

[Ar mana^{c}a id.]

C575/5: lwḍ^{c} wṯbr wmn^{c} w'xrn kl ḍrhmw "to lay low, crush, repel and drive back their every foe" AND ELSEWHERE SIM

(2) PREVENT

[Ar mana^{c}a id.]

R4815/6: f'l ymn^{c}w bny R...bn hy^{c} lhmw h' fnwtn "the b.R. shall not prevent this canal from providing water for their benefit (i.e., the benefit of the b.S.)"; sim exp C611/7-8

tp pf tmn^{c}hmw J643/23*

DEFEND ONE'S SELF AGAINST

[Ar mn^{c} Dt id.]

J643/23: w'dmhmw 'b^{c}l hmt hgrnhn...wtmn^{c}hmw "as for their clients, the citizens of those 2 cities, they defended themselves against them"

MNT--For n mntm C562/7, see under NMW

MSḤ

n s msḥḥw C541/2-3*

ANOINTED ONE, MESSIAH

[Loanword from Heb māšī^{a}ḥ, Syr məšīḥo id; cf Ar masīḥ id.]

C541/1-3: bxyl w[r]d' wrḥmt RḤMNn wmsḥḥw wrḥ[q]ds "by the might, help and mercy of (the god) R., His Messiah and the Holy Spirit"

Note: For ms[y]ḥ C609/3 read ms[m]ḥ (?) and see under SMḤ.

MSK

n s mskm R3203/1; d? msknhn R2859=A769/4

sense doubtful

[HöRel/263-4 discussing the title b^{c}l mskt (epithet of the god 'LMQH) suggests that mskt is a kind of incense, cf Heb mések "mixed wine, spiced wine." Ts on A769 suggests Heb méšek Jb 28:18, tr "jewel > bracelet (?)" (sense in Heb from context only).]

R2859=A769/4: mn lyh'yw ^{c}BDM ' d 's[m] s'l kl msknhn "whoever gives shelter to A., any man (?) claim both (his) ...s"; R3203/1 (fragmentary context): ...]m bmskm [...] mkntn w[... "with msk...the cella..."

MSS

v pf ms C523/6*

TOUCH

[Ar massa id.]

C523/6: he confessed hn ms 'nt ḥyḍ wlm yǵtsl "because he had touched menstruating women and not washed himself"

MSR

v pf msrw C540/72; inf msrn ib/28; msrhw C541/111; maṣdar msrm C540/73+

PACK IN earth

[Irv/255-7 cfs Amh.Te *msrt "lay the foundations," Te mäsar "axe, hoe." Cr also ModYem masar "dig or clean out silt from a well or canal" (RoVoc/307).]

C541/111: ḥrrw ^{c}rmn wmsrhw [wš]ṣnhw "they raked up earth (for) the dam, packed it in and faced it with stone"; C540/72-4: msrw ^{c}rmn...msrm wšṣnm b''bnm "they packed in earth (for) the dam, packing earth and facing with stones"

Note: For n msrt, see under SYR.

MSTL--For n mstl C541/67, see under SLY

M^{c}D

n s m^{c}dhmw J647/29*

PRODUCE, CROPS

[Cf Ar ma^{c}d "tender vegetables, fresh fruits or dates" (BeNL9/197).]

J647/29: kl mqblt wm^{c}dhmw...bd^{c}tn wsqyn "all the leased lands and their produce (consisting of) d^{c}t- and sqy-crops"

Note: For m^{c}d elsewhere, see under W^{c}D.

M^{c}W--Prob n.pr in R4204: ^{c}d mnxy M^{c}W "to the primary canal M."

M^{c}M--For m^{c}mhw C160/7, read b^{c}mhw, see under ^{c}M

M^{c}N

cj k + m^{c}n + mw J717/5-6+; var k + m^{c}n + my J2112/3-4+

WHENEVER, IF (cf kmhnmw id, under MHN II)

[The element m^{c}n in this compound seems to be a phonetic var (?) of mhn (indefinite pronoun "what, whatever").]

J717/5-6: she promised the god km^{c}nmw yxmrnhw ḥyw lhw wldm thqnynhw "that, if He would allow a child to survive for her, she would dedicate to Him ..."; J2112/3-4: ḏšft...km^{c}nmy y't'wln "which he promised, 'if he should return' (from campaign)"

Note: The k- particle in k-m^{c}nmw/y and k-mhnmw is not an integral part of the compound, but the k- introducing direct discourse; however, these forms never occur without it.

MṢ^C--For n̠ mṣ^cm C376/4, see under NṢ^C

MṢR
- v inf mṣrn R4176/6*
     EAT, FEED
     [Cf Eth maṣara id.]
     R4176/6: the god has prohibited 'rwyn bn nśg bn mṣrn kstnḥṣn "the mountain goats from being prevented from feeding, so that they may grow fat"
- n For n̠ mṣr, p̱ mṣyrt, see under ṢRR

MḌ'
- v inf mḍ' Ir9/3*
     REACH, ARRIVE AT (= MẒ' v) (?)
     [For another example of the exchange of ẓ and ḍ, cf mqyḍ for mqyẓ in Ir22.]
     Ir9/3: the god allowed him stwfyn wmḍ' wt'ysn bwfym ^cdy M "to reach and give aid (?) successfully, in safety, in M."

MḌW--For n̠ mḍwn C522/2, see under NḌW

MḌY
- v act.prt f.p mḍytm J649/19-20*
     PENETRATE; prt: PENETRATING
     [Ar maḍâ "penetrate, go deeper."]
     J649/19-20: zxn...xms zxnm mḍytm fx̱dyhw wrglyhw "he was wounded by five wounds penetrating his thighs and legs"

MQṬ
- n s̱ mqṭt J649/32-3*
     SETTING of a heavenly body
     [Akk maqātu "go out (said of the light of the sun or a planet." Note emphaticized ṭ in Sab in the vicinity of q (RycExpAst/523).]
     J649/32-3: they fought bn šf šrqm ^cdy mqṭt šmsn wlyl lylm "from the appearance of the rising sun until sunset, and all night long"

MQṢ--For n̠ mqṣm R4230/2, see under NQṢ

MQR--For n̠ mqr C438/4, C460/1, see under WQR

MR
- n s̱ mrn R4785/4; mrhm R4046/2; mrhmw GaAntYem2/2
     PART OF IRRIGATION SYSTEM, phps CHANNEL (?)
     [Contexts fragmentary. Phps connected with root RWY "irrigate, transmit water," q.v. Cf BeSM/396 on GaAntYem2.]

R4046/2: ...b]'rhmw [...] bmrhm/ [... "their well...in their ...?"; R4785/4: ...] (w)ḍ'm wr dʿb mrn xmrhmw [... "going out...the ...? (which) He granted them (?)"

For n mr elsewhere, see under MWR. For n mrt, see under MRT. For v mr, see under MRR.

MR'

n^1 s mr'(m) C548/7-8+; mr'hw J560/9+; mr'hmy J572/12+; mr'hmw J559/5++; d mr'yhw J579/9+; mr'yhmw J558/6+; p 'mr'hw J713/15; 'mr'hmw J565/6-7+

(1) MAN, PERSON (cf mr't n^2 "woman")

[Ar imra', al-mar' id.]

C548/7-8: ḏyndyn mr'm mn mḥrmn "whoever drives out a man from the temple ..."; C533/3: she confessed that qrbh mr' "a man had approached her (sexually)"

(2) LORD, divine or human (cf mr't n^2 "lady")

[Cf Syr mārē' "lord," Himyaritic marī id (Nashwān, Extr/100).]

divine lord: Ry534/2: mr' smyn w'rḍn "Lord of heaven and earth"; J670/5-6: hqnyw mr'hmw 'LMQH "they dedicated to their lord, (the god) I." AND VERY OFTEN SIM

human overlord: J669/21: ḏmr bʿmhmw mr'hmw...whḏll mʿbrn "their lord pronounced sentence in their presence and found against (them in) the trial"; J671/7-8: wqhhw mr'hmw...wbnhw...mlky SB' lqtdmn xmsn "their lord and his son, the 2 kings of S., commanded him to lead an army" AND OFTEN SIM; J566/8: may the god grant them ḥẓy wrḍw mr'hmw F "the favor and good will of their lord F." AND VERY OFTEN SIM; J578/5: they dedicated to the god bḏt hwšʿ whrd'n mr'hmw...mlk SB' "because He protected and helped their lord the king of S." AND OFTEN SIM

n^2 s mr't(m,n) Mü1/5+; mr'thw C558/3-4; mr'thmw C544/2+

(1) WOMAN, GIRL

[Ar imra'a^t id.]

C523/3: qrb mr'tm...wmlṯ ḥyḍ "he approached a woman (sexually) and had intercourse with (?) a menstruating woman"; J686/5: xmrhw wldm hyt mr'tn N "(the god) granted her a child, (namely) the girl N."; Mü5/1: qnyw xmst ǵlmm wmr'tm bn 'nṯthmw "they obtained five boys and a girl from their wives"

(2) LADY, divine or human

C544/2: mr'thmw 'MʿṮR "their lady, (the goddess) U."; Ir13/7: mr'thmw... mlkt ḤḌRMWT "their lady, the queen of Ḥ."

MRH--For n mrhm R4046/2, read mr-hm, see under MR

MRW--For n mrw R4194/1, R4197/11-2, see under RWY I n^6

MRY--For n mryt R4513, see under RWY I n^7

MRN--For n mrn R4785/4, see under MR

MR^{c}--For n mr^{c}t GI142/8, see under R^{c}Y n^4

MRḌ

v pf mrḍ J572/7+; mrḍt J706/6+; mrḍw J661/5+

SUFFER a sickness

[Ar mariḍa id.]

J731/6-7: the god saved his daughter bn kl 'mrḍ mrḍt "from all the sicknesses she suffered"; J661/5: the god saved them bn mrḍ wḍll mrḍw wḍlln "from the sickness and disease they suffered and were afflicted with" J706/6: may the god help His maidservant bn mrḍ mrḍt ^{c}ynhw "against the sickness her eye suffered"

n^1 s mrḍ(m,n) J720/12+; p 'mrḍ C343/6+

SICKNESS

[Ar maraḍ id.]

J613/14: ḥlẓm wmrḍm wmyqẓm "disease, sickness and sleeplessness"; J670/16-7: may the god protect grb ^{c}bdhw bn kl mrḍm wnkytm wb'sm "the body of His servant against any sickness, injury or harm"; J720/12: the god afflicted His servant stt 'wrxm mrḍm fš'm "(for) six months (with) an eruptive/contagious disease"; J702/12: nqm ^{c}bdhw...bmr(ḍ) '(ḍ)rshw "(the god) took vengeance on His servant with a sickness of his molar teeth" (J read bMRB)

Note: For mrḍ R4176/13, see under RḌY v

n^2 p mrḍyt J544/4*

SICK PEOPLE

[Ar marīḍ, p marāḍâ "sick person."]

J544/4: lxmrhmw ḥywm 'śḥmt wmrḍyt "may (the god) grant life (to) the oppressed and sick"

Note: For mrḍym C539/4, see under RḌY n^4.

MRQ--For n mrqhmw Ir22/I read mšrqhmw, see under ŠRQ

MRR I

v ipf ymrnhw J711/5*

HAPPEN TO, BEFALL

[Ar marra id.]

J711/5: may the god protect him bn ḥlẓ ḥqwnhn wḥlẓ ymrnhw drm bxrfm "from the disease of the hips and the disease which befalls him once a year"

Note: For n mr, see under MWR, MR; for n mrt, see under MRT

MRR II

n s mrrt N70/3+

MYRRH

[Ar murra^{t} id (cf HöRel/277).]

N70/3: WDm dmrrt "(the god) WD, (lord of) myrrh"; sim J496/3

MRT

n s mrtn F90/2*

CLAY, CLAYEY SOIL

[Eth marēt id.]

F90/2: m^{c}]rbt (w)śftn mrtn wṣhr[n... "squared stones, muddy soil, clayey soil and lead"

MŚR

n s mśr R3945/6*

REMOVAL

[BePESA/20 cfs Heb māsar "teach, hand down" and the sense development of Ar naqala "remove" > "transfer" > "hand down (a tradition)."]

R3945/6: he offered to the god xrš bythw...wmśr kl 'sṭr...bn bythw "the destruction of his house and the removal of all the inscriptions from his house"

MŠW

v pf/inf mšw J720/15*

GO, PROCEED (cf MŠY v sim)

[Ar mašâ (III-w or y) id.]

J720/15: wlmšw m^{c}rbtm bn dD wz'k šhn "and let one of (the tribe) dD. go to a place of sacrifice and offer the goat"

For n mšwn RycVase/2, see under NŠW.

MŠY

v pf/inf mšy C533/4*

GO (AWAY) (cf MŠW v sim)

[Ar mašâ id.]

C533/4: qrbh mr'...wmšy wlm yǵtsl "a man approached her (sexually) and went away and did not wash himself"

MT--see under MWT

MT^{c}

v pf mt^{c} C323/8-9+; mt^{c}hw J685/2+; mt^{c}hmw J567/16+; ipf y[m]t^{c} J586/21-2; ymt^{c}n J650/30+; ymt^{c}nhmw J736/16; inf mt^{c}(n) C407/12+; mt^{c}nhmy J652/18; mt^{c}nhmw J567/26+

SAVE; PROTECT, OFFER PROTECTION

[Cf Ar mt^{c} h "grant enjoyment (said of God); have the use, usufruct of s.th."]

J650/9: they dedicated because hwfy wmt^{c}n ^{c}bdhw...bkl sb't wḥryb sb'w "(the god) protected and saved His servant in all the campaigns and battles they undertook" AND OFTEN SIM; J558/4: yh^{c}nnhmw wmt^c 'LMQH bn b'stm wnkytm "may (the god) I. protect them from harm and injury"; C81/3: wqf lhw t̲wrm bkn mt^{c}hmw bn ^{c}ws "he made over a bull to (the god) when He saved them from the plague"; C407/12: the god agreed mt^{c}n grbhw bn hwt ḥlẓn "to protect his body from that disease"

h pf hmt^c R4998/3; ipf yhmt^{c}n G1364/6

PROTECT; or PROMISE TO PROTECT (?)

R4998/3: ywm hmt^{c}hw b'mrhw "when (the god) promised to protect (?) him in His oracle"; G1364/6: fl yhmt^{c}n whbrrn whṣḥḥn...whwfyn l'dmhw "may (the god) protect (?), make pure, make upright and preserve His servants"

n s R3945/2+

BENEFIT

[Cf Ar matā^c "enjoyment."]

R3945/2: wynš' 'sm lmt^c qnyhw "(each) man undertook (projects) for the benefit of his (own) property"

Note: Obscure in J664/17: wlmt^{c}nhmw bn mt^c wšṣy wtt̲^{c}t šn'm "and may (the god) save them from ...?, evil eye and abuse of (any) enemy." J cfs Ar matu^{c}a "be cunning, crafty" and tr "craftiness" (SIMB/169), but it seems likely that mt^c here is an error for nḍ^c "injury," which occurs very often in this context (dittography after mt^{c}n in same line?).

n^2 s mt^{c}tn C323/8-9*

PROTECTION

C323/8-9: wkwn h' mt^{c}tn mt^c bn hwt t̲yln bwrx Q "and that protection (which) (the god) offered (them) from that flood occurred in the month Q."

MTR--For n mtrm N66/2, see under TWR

MT̲B--For n mt̲bt, see under T̲WB

MT̲L

ti ipf ymtt̲lnn C380/5*

CONFORM (b^{c}m to a command)

[Ar mt̲l ti "follow an example, obey an order."]

C380/5: ...] lymtt̲ln b^c[mh]w wkwn d̲n wtfn... "let them conform to it. This deed was enacted..."

h pf hmt̲l G1533/14*

BE SIMILAR, BE A DUPLICATE (bn of s.th.)

[Cf Ar mat̲ala id.]

G1533/14: hmt̲l d̲n mṣdqn bn [mṣ]dq bhw t^{c}lm "this document is a duplicate of the document which he signed"

n s mt̲l(n) R3949/4+; mt̲lh C547/11-2; mt̲lhw C546/7; p 'mt̲ln J558/2

(1) LIKENESS, IMAGE

[Ar mit̲l id.]
R4669/3: they dedicated mt̲ln d̲dhbn lwfy bnhmy "a gold image for the well-being of their son" AND ELSEWHERE SIM

(2) LIKE, EQUIVALENT, DUPLICATE

[Ar mit̲l id; cf also Ar mit̲la pp "like, similar to."]
C546/7: lyḥd̲rn wl ynd̲rn [wl] yẓtlfn mt̲lhw "let him beware, vow penance, and refrain from (committing) the like (again)"; R3959/4: mt̲l d̲n wtfn bmḥrmn Š "a duplicate of this deed is in the temple Š."; F3/7: lyknn 'ln 'sdn...mt̲l wmknt 'dm d̲Ḥ "let these men (who are being adopted into the clan) be equivalent and interchangeable with the clients of d̲Ḥ"; sim F76/6,9

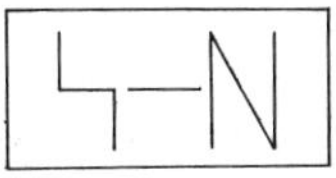

N I

ab n C570/2*

SYMBOL FOR "CUBIT"

[Reason for choice of symbol unknown.]

C570/2: 'rb^{c} 'mn wšlṯ šwḥṭ b'mt mxḍm ▯ IIInnnn ▯ "four cubits and three spans, in administrative cubits: IIInnnn"

N II

pt -n R2861/14*

ALSO (?) (context obscure; see Note)

[Cf Eth -ni id.]

R2861/14: wḥwr(n ḏxṭ') ()b^{c}mh(w) "and also (?) bring back him who sinned with him (?)"

Note: R reproduces Glaser's reading, but other editors omit this -n and read what follows differently.

N'D

n s n'd J564/20+; p? n'dm R4636/8+

(1) EXCELLENCE

[Akk nādu "exalt, praise; be lofty."]

J564/20: may the god grant n'd 'ṯmrm w'fqlm bn kl 'rḍthmw "excellence of crops and harvests from all their lands" AND OFTEN SIM; R4013/3: n'd dṯ' wqyẓ wṣrb "excellence of spring, summer and autumn harvests"

(2) as adj: EXCELLENT

[Akk nā'idu "high."]

R4636/8: 'ṯmrm w'fqlm n'dm whn'm "excellent and pleasing crops and harvests" AND ELSEWHERE SIM

N'K--For kt'k C540/68, see under T'K

NB' I

tp pf tnb' C83/3; tnb'hw J551+

ANNOUNCE, PROMISE

[Ar nb' D "inform," Dt "predict."]

J551: he dedicated because hwfyhw 'LMQH...d̲t tnb'hw "(the god) I. granted him that which He promised him"; J550/2: d̲t tnb'hw lwldm "that which He promised him concerning (?) a son"; C83/3: he dedicated this inscription d̲tnb' "which he had promised"

NB' II

n d̲ nb'n F74/2*

LEVEL, TERRACE of cultivated land

[Ar nabā "be high," nabâ "high" (RyET/47).]

F74/2: šr^cw bythmw...t̲ty nb'n d̲hbm "they supplied water for their house (from?) two terraces, irrigated land"

NBB

n s̲ nbt Gl547/4*

SPEECH, DECISION (?)

[Eth nababa "speak," nebat "counsel" (SchSEG7/42).]

Gl547/4: ...]m wqṭnm ln nbt Y bn by[... "(great?) and small, since the speech/decision (?) of Y., son of..."

Note: Cf the n̲ nbt listed under NBT

NBṬ

h p̲f̲ hnbṭ C399/2-3+

DIG DOWN TO WATER in making a well

[Ar nabaṭa "bubble forth," D̲, h̲, s̲t̲ "reach water by digging and bringing it to the light of day" (Irv/99-100).]

C399/2-3: hn[b]ṭ wḥfr b'rhw "he dug down to water and dug out his well"; sim in R4700/3, A773; C516/19-20: whnbṭ TǴB "and he dug T. (n̲.p̲r̲ of a well?) down to water"

NBL

v p̲f̲ nbl J576/11+; nblhw J631/11-2+; nblw J576/13+; i̲p̲f̲ ynblnhmw ib/13

SEND messengers, an embassy; SEND on a mission

[Eth tanbal "ambassador," tanbala "to be sent."]

J576/13: nblw...wwhbw bnyhmw...'wt̲qm "they sent (an embassy) and gave their sons as hostages"; ib/11: nbl b^cbr ^cA...lnṣrm "he sent to A. for help"; J631/11-2: the god helped His servant bkn nblhw mr'hmw ...^cdy 'rḍ Ḥ "when their lord sent him to the land of Ḥ."

n p̲? tnblt(m,n) Ir28+

MESSENGERS = EMBASSY

Ir28: wḥškhmw tnbltm b'rḍ Ḥ "he sent them (as) an embassy to the land of Ḥ."; J574/10: hdrkhmw tnbltm ^cmn G tdr^cm w^crbtm "an embassy overtook them from G. (to) surrender and (give) hostages"; C541/89: tnblt mlk F wrsl M "the embassy of the king of F. and the messengers of M."

NB^c

ti -- For ntb^{c}n J630/9, see under TB^c N̲

n s̲ nb^{c}n R4194/5*

ONE WHO CAUSES water TO FLOW/GUSH OUT, epithet of the god ^{c}ṮTR

[Ar naba^{c}a "bubble, gush out," nab^c "well" (HöRel/278n84).]

R4194/5: mnḍḥhmw ^{c}ṮTR nwbn wnb^{c}n "their irrigation god A., (he) who returns and causes water to flow"

NBT

tp p̲f̲ tnbth(m)w F74/1-2*

BE BROUGHT ABOUT, BE ACHIEVED (?)

[Ar nabata "sprout; grow up (said of plants and children)."]

F74/1-2: in that year tnbth(m)w w^{c}bm "the completion (of the building project) was brought about for them"

n^1 s̲ nbt(m) R4133/2+

(COLLATERAL) RELATIONSHIP, DESCENT (?)

[BeFSTI/278-9 suggests that this is a technical term of clan affiliation describing those not directly descended from the clan head--the direct descendants are the wldm--but who are members of collateral branches. The 'ys nbt (R4195/1) would be the paterfamilias of such a branch.]

R4133/2: bhṯ]m wqṭnm wḏnbtm ww[ldm?] "great and small, and those of collateral as well as (direct) descent"; R4195/1: 'A 'ys nbt bn byt bny N "A., head of a collateral branch of the b.N." (sim in Ist7630/1)

n^2 s̲ nbtt Ir18*

DESCENT, GENEALOGY (?)

Ir18: the god protected mr'yhmw mlk wnbtt w'tyt "the reign, descent (?), and (royal) entry of their 2 lords" (cf RycMus87/243)

NGB--For ygbnhmw Gl441/5, see under GYB v̲

NGD

n s̲ ngd Ir12/5*

HIGHLAND, PLATEAU

[Ar najd id. In Mus87/246 Ryc tr "mountain pass."]

Ir12/5: ngd M "on the plateau of M."

NGW I

v i̲p̲f̲ ygwnhw J567/8 (same form, broken context, C67/12)*

TELL, INSTRUCT through an oracular vision

[Ar najā "tell a secret" (MüW/104).]

J567/8: the god showed His servant (in a vision) ḏygwnhw klyhqnynn...ṯlṯt 'ṣlmn "(one) who told him that he should dedicate three statues"

NGW II

n s mngwn F71/9+; p mngwt J652/17+; mngyt J568/16+; mngt(n) J690/9+

OUTCOME, RESULT of an affair; FORTUNE; EVENT

[Ar najā "save one's self, come out (of danger)." Discussion BeRev/350B. Cfing Ar naja'a "injure by the evil eye," RycBiOr22/327 associates the form mngt with the results of magical practices undertaken by the dedicants or their enemies.--Note use of m.p demonstrative with mngt, Ir9/3.]

J690/9: may the god grant 'wldm wn^{c}mtm wmngt ṣdqm "children, prosperity, and satisfactory outcomes = good fortune" AND OFTEN SIM; J652/17: may the god grant them ''rx wmngwt ṣdqm bḍrm wslmm "satisfactory developments and outcomes in war and peace"; J564/23: may the god protect His servant bn b'stm wmngt sw'm "from harm and bad fortune"; J643/9: mngt ḥdṯw "events which took place"; Ir9/3: hmw mngtn 'ly kwnw bhmt xrfn "those events which took place in those years"

Note: Because of the similarity of OSA g and l, readings of mng(y)t and mnl(y)t are often confused. See also mnlt under NYL.

NGZ

v inf ngzn C522/1*

DAMAGE, DESTROY

[Ar najaza "perish, come to an end."]

C522/1: ...] yb's wngzn ḏnfsm "[punish anyone who?] injures or destroys what pertains to (?) the monument"

h inf hgzn J585/8+

PUT AN END TO s.o.'s life, EXECUTE

[Ar njz ẖ "deal the death blow" (BeJSS20/192).]

J585/8: kydw 'ḤBŠN hgzn grb 'bhmy "the Ḥabashites nearly put an end to the life of their father"; J644/17: they went on campaign lqdmn whgzn L "in order to fight and execute L."

NGY--For ngy R3946/2,5, read as n.pr

NGS

v ipf yngsn C548/3*

BE DEFILED, POLLUTED

[Ar najusa "be impure, soiled," D "soil, defile."]

C548/3: hn lyngsn slḥhw wdmwm bšy^{c}hw "if his weapons are defiled, there being blood on his garment...(let him pay a fine)"

NGF

tp inf tgfn G1537/8*

TEAR OUT, UPROOT

[Ar najafa "cut down, tear out," Eth nagafa "cut down, remove," ẖ "tear out" (SchSEG7/38).]

G1537/8: may the god grant them crops [wl]tgfn kl [š]n'hmw "and may He uproot their every enemy"

NGR--For mngr C547/1, see under MN pn, GWR v

n s ngrhmw R3967/2*

CULTIVATED LAND, or LAND CLEARED FOR CULTIVATION

[Daṯ najara "clear land with a pick or pointed stick" (Irv/209-10).]

R3967/2: 'nhr wfnwy w'nqb wmsqy ngrhmw "the conduits, canals, cuttings and irrigation system of their cultivated land"

NGŠ

v pf ngšw Ir32/8*

IMPOSE TRIBUTE UPON

[Ar najaša "rouse, bring forth game"; Heb nōgēš "ruler; exactor of tribute"; Eth nagša "reign."]

Ir32/8: wngšw kl hgr Ḥ wsrrn "and they imposed tribute upon all the towns of Ḥ. and the valley"

n s ngšyn J577/10+; p ngšt Ist7608b/3; var? 'gšm G1062/4 (HoAA2/142)

NEGUS = KING OF ETHIOPIA

[Ar.Eth naj/gāšī id.]

J577/10: lh^{c}nn ^{c}qb ngšyn "to aid the deputy of the Negus"; J631/15: kl blthmw ^{c}mn ngšyn "all their missions against the Negus"; Ist7608b/3: 'm]r'hmw ngšt 'KSMN "their lords, the Neguses/kings of Axum"; G1062/4 (obscure context): kšymn wk'gšm "as patron(s?) and kings (?)"

Cf also the title wld ngšyn "child (deputy?) of the Negus," J577/3+

ND--For ndn Ir28, see under NWD

ND'

h inf hnd'n J643/7*

TAKE UNAWARES

[Ar nada'a id.]

J643/7: wymẓ'w whnd'n Y wmṣrhw ^{c}dy xlf hgrn "Y. and his troop arrived outside the city and took (it) unawares"

NDB

v inf ndb C448/1*

WORK/CARRY OUT A PROJECT ZEALOUSLY (?)

[Ar nadaba "call, summon, rouse," Heb nādab "urge on, incite" (SchSEG7/57).]

C448/1: ^{c}ḏ]b wndb whqš[b... "repaired, worked zealously (?) and refurbished ..."

NDY

v ipf yndyn C548/7; inf ndynhmw Ry510/4-5

(1) PURSUE, HARRASS

[Cf Eth nad'a "drive animals, a flock, captives before one"; Heb nādāh "thrust away, exclude (from the community of worship)," in later Heb D.]

Ry510/4-5: in the course of the campaign, ghm d̲ndynhmw ^{c}rbn "when the Arabs harrassed them"

(2) DRIVE OUT

C548/7: d̲yndyn mr'm mn mḥrmn lyẓl^{c}n "whoever drives out a man from the (community of the?) temple, let him pay a fine"

NDF

v pf ndfw Ir13/9*

FLEE (?)

[Ar nadafa "gallop."]

Ir13/9: they slew them ǵyr...d̲ndfw ^{c}dy ṣnwq Š "except for those who fled (?) to the ... of (the town) Š."

n s? ndf J631/33*

LIGHT CAVALRY

J631/33: ytśbbnn b^{c}m 'ḤBŠN wb^{c}mhmw bn ndf M "they made an encircling maneuver around (?) the Ḥabashites, having with them some of the light cavalry of (the tribe) M." (tr after BeNL8/451)

ND̲H

pf tnd̲h J600/8*

DRIVE livestock (?)

[J cfs Ar nadaha id, citing StSESA/513 for SA d̲ = Sem d.]

J600/4-8: xmrhw stwfyn md̲ht mr'yhw...bkn tnd̲h bmwṯbn Y "(the god) granted protection to the herd (?) of his 2 lords when he (accidentally?) drove (?) (them) into the shrine Y."

n s md̲ht J600/4*

DROVE, HERD

J600/4 quoted under ND̲H tp

ND̲R I

v ipf ynd̲rn C546/6*

VOW PENANCE; phps specif MAKE A PENITENTIAL OFFERING

[Ar nad̲ara "bind one's self by a vow."]

C546/6: lyḥd̲rn wl ynd̲rn [wl] yẓtlfn mṯlhw "let him beware, vow penance, and refrain from (doing) the like (again)"

ti inf ntd̲r C547/2+

VOW PENANCE (= ND̲R v)

C547/2: [tn]xyw wntd̲r lḤ hn 'l hwfyhw mtrdhw "they confessed and vowed

penance to (the god) Ḥ. because they had not duly rendered to Him His
ritual hunt"

tp pf tnḏrt C568/2; inf tnḏrn C523/1-2+
    VOW PENANCE (= NDR v)
C523/1-2: tnxy wtnḏrn lḏS bhn qrb mr'tm "he confessed and vowed penance to
(the god) ḏS. because he had approached a woman" AND OFTEN SIM

n s tḏrm J720/5* (D inf?)
    PENITENTIAL OFFERING
[Ar naḏr "votive offering."]
J720/5: they dedicated ṣlmn ḏṣrfm tḏrm lqbly ḏxt'w "this bronze statue as
a penitential offering because they had sinned"

NDR II

n s mnḏrm J643/26-7*
    SPY or WARNING
[Ar munḏir id, naḏira "be on one's guard."]
J643/26-7: mẓ'hmw mnḏrm ᶜdy Y kyhṣrn bᶜlyhmw K "a spy/warning reached them
at Y., (saying) that K. had set out against them"

NHG

n s mnhg Ry506/6*
    WAY, ROUTE
[Ar nahaja "mark out a path," manhaj "well-marked path," Daṯ ma/inhağ id.]
Ry506/6: bwd bmnhg T "in the valley (?) on the route to T."
    Note: Correct reading may be mnhl, for which cf Ar manhal "watering
    place" (T. is such a place, BeOr25/302).

NHY

n s mnhythmw R3945/4; p mnhyhmw ib/18
    a) COLLECTING BASIN; or, b) DIVERSION BARRAGE
[a) Irv/206-7 quotes Q on Ar nihy "pool," TA on Ar tanhiya† "place where
water is held back from the wadi"--same sense of root in b), cf Ar nahâ
"forbid, restrain."]
R3945/4: stmxḏ ᶜrhmw...wmnhythmw "he overthrew their fortress and collecting
basin/diversion barrage"; ib/18: hbᶜl kl mnhyhmw "he took possession of all
their collecting basins/diversion barrages"
    Note: MNHYTM ib/15 is a n.pr

NHK

v pf nhk J620/6; ipf ynhkn R4090/2-3
    INJURE, INFLICT INJURIES
[Ar nahaka "wear out; grind down, crush."]
R4090/2-3: wlyqmᶜn ᶜTTR...ḏynhkn wštrhw "and may (the god) A. strike down

him who injures or destroys (the funerary stela)"; J620/6: the god helped His servant's body bn tšynt hšyn bn ''rx nhk ^{c}lyhmw šn'n "against the injuries he suffered from the troubles the enemy inflicted upon them"

NHL--For mnhl Ry506/6, see under NHG

NHM

n^{1} s̲ nhmt C541/59+

PECKED MASONRY

[MSA ḥajar manhūm "bright whitish unhewn building stone," Dat̲ nahama "strike vigorously" (Irv/300-301). For a description of Sab pecked masonry, see ADSA/287-95 and plates (pp209-14).]

C541/59: grbtm wbr'm...wnh[m]t...l^{c}d̲bn ^{c}rmn "rough stonework, masonry and pecked masonry to repair the dam"; R4772/2: bnt nhmt bn ^{c}lm "a tax on pecked masonry, according to the document(?)"

n^{2} s̲ mnhmt(m) C325/9+

PECKED MASONRY (= NHM n̲^{1})

C325/9: mnhmtm wgrbm "pecked masonry and rough stone"; sim F74/1

NHḌ

tp p̲f̲ tnhḍ(w) F121*

BE TRIBUTARY (t̲ḥtn to)

[Ar nhḍ "impose tribute" (RyET/73).]

F121: 'dmh(w) 'lw tnhḍ(w) tḥtn byt X "his clients who were tributary to the clan X."

NHR

n p̲ 'nhr R3967/2+

CONDUITS

[Ar nahr "stream"; MSA "type of canal" (Dozy).]

R3967/2: 'nhr wfnwy w'nqb "conduits, canals and cuttings"; C308/6: kl 'nhr wbqlt "all the conduits and vegetable gardens"

NWB

h p̲f̲ hnbw J560/13*

REPLACE (?)

[Ar nāba (w) id.]

J560/13: they rescued their allies whnbw rkbhmw "and replaced (?) their riding animals"

n s̲ nwbn R4194/5*

ONE WHO RETURNS, epithet of the god ^{c}T̲TR

[Ar nāba (w) "return from time to time" (HöRel/278n84).]

R4194/5: ^{c}T̲TR nwbn wnb^{c}n "(the god) A., (he) who returns and causes water to flow"

NWD

n s ndn lr28*

WIND

[Dat nawd, ModYem nowd id (RycMus88/201,203).]

lr28: f'fq ndn sb^{c}t 'wrxm bbḥrm "so (the god) restrained the wind seven months on the sea (?)"

NWX--For ynxhw C464/7, see under NXX v; for mnxthmw J618/6, see under NXY n

NWY

n s nwy(m,n) C516/20+; nwyhw ib/13-4

a) WATERING PLACE; or, b) CHANNEL (?)

[a) Irv/82-3 cfs Te newat id. Cf also PBH nāweh "marked-off place, circle, dwelling," Heb "pasturage." b) Ar nawâ "intend, purpose" may suggest a channel or means of directing the flow of water.]

C516/20: hnbṭ T wnhlhw Y nwym lḤ "Y. dug (the well?) T. down to water and gave it as a watering place (?) to Ḥ."; ib/13-4: ...w[kl] nwyhw Ḍ "and all its watering place (?) Ḍ."; Ry443/2: nwyn wmḥn 'xdw 'wtn dS "the channel (?) and ... which enclose the borders of dS."

Note: For nwyn N72/3 read 'wyn, see under WYN n

pp nwyt R3943/3

IN THE DIRECTION OF

[Ar nawâ "aim at, go toward," nawâ^{n} "destination."]

R3943/3: he burned R. wkl 'hgr nwyt R "and all the towns in the direction of R."

NWL

h pf h(nw)lhw J584/11*

LEAD, GUIDE (?)

[Cf Heb nhl D id. J's reading is an emendation; he does not quote the original text (JSIMB/91).]

J548/11: xmrhw h(nw)lhw h' w'xyhw "(the god) granted to him to lead (?) him and his brother"

NWM

v pf nm GaAlON33/37*

NEGLECT, OMIT

[Heb nām (w) "be indolent, sleepy."]

GaAlON33/37: kmnm 'ns dyhẓr wl yḏbḥn...f'w y'xrn ršwn ḥẓrhw "when a man neglects to request to make a sacrifice, or the priest rejects his request ..."

For wynm C522/2,3, see under WYN n

NWF

h pf hnfhmw R4148/5*

ENRICH (?)

[MüW/107-8 cfs Ar nāfa (w) and h "be raised, pass over, surmount."]

R4148/5: hwfyhmw Ḥ whnfhmw Ḥ wF ṯny ḥllyn "(the god) granted them (the territory?) Ḥ. and enriched (?) them (with the territories?) Ḥ. and F., the two pieces of (land taken as) plunder (?)"

NWQ

n s nqt J665/44*

SHE-CAMEL

[Ar nāqa^{t} id.]

J665/44: they took from the enemy kl gwdm frsm wnqt "every swift horse and she-camel"

NWR

v ipf ynr R3945/1* (read phps hnr, cf NWR h)

MAKE A BURNT OFFERING (?)

[Ar nār "fire," nūr "light," nāra (w) "shine."]

R3945/1: he sacrificed three times to the god wynr btr[ḥ] "and made a burnt offering (?) by way of recompense"

h pf hnrhw Ry585+

MAKE A BURNT OFFERING (cf NWR v)

[Ar nwr h "light (a lamp)."]

Ry585: he held a ritual banquet for the god whnrhw btrḥ "and made Him a burnt offering by way of recompense" AND SEVERAL TIMES in this dating formula

n s mnrt C276/2*

ALTAR (for burnt sacrifice?)

[Cf NWR v, h and Min mnwrt R2869/5 id.]

C276/2: mḥ[r]mhmw...[w]mnrt ḏqdmhw "their temple and the altar which is in front of it"

NZḤ

n p nzḥt Ham4/3+

n.pr of a social or political group, tr phps THE OUTLANDERS

[Ar nazaḥa "be distant." BeJRAS'54/53 identifies these as a group of Sabaeans settled in an outlying area, organized into a "tribe" having its own kabīr-magistrate.]

Ham4/3: kbr nzḥt "kabīr-magistrate of the Outlanders"; J707/4: 'dm nzḥt "clients of the Outlanders"; R3951/1: nzḥt w^{c}hrw F w'rb^{c}n wḥśrw "the Outlanders, the nobles of (the clan) F., the clansmen and the indigents"

NZL

n *s* nzlm Ry509/6*

GOING DOWN, DESCENDING (*maṣdar*? or tr as *adv*, DOWNWARD)

[Ar nazala "dismount; go down."]

Ry509/5-6: sb'w whllw 'rḍ M dmw nzlm bn 'š^{c}bhmw "they campaigned and destroyed the land of M., some of the tribes sending raids down"

NZ^{c} I

v *pf* nz^{c}w J610/20; *inf* nz^{c} J577/8

(1) FIGHT for booty

[Ar naza^{c}a "rob," nizā^{c} "fight."]

J616/20: nz^{c}w gyšhmw whbryw ^{c}wfhmw "their troop fought (for booty) and 'liberated' their prey"

(2) with ydm, REBEL (*bn* against)

[Ar naza^{c}a yadahu min al-ṭā^{c}a^{t} "he drew back his hand from obedience = he rebelled," nāzi^{c} "deserter."]

J577/8: qsdw wnz^{c} ydm bn 'mr'hmw "they revolted and rebelled against their lords"

NZ^{c} II

n *s* nz^{c} R4188/10*

INJURY caused by an enemy (late *var* of nḍ^{c})

[See under ND^{c} *n* I.]

R4188/10: may the god protect them bn nz^{c} wšẓy šn'm "against the injury or evil eye of (any) enemy" (phonetically aberrant inscr)

NḤB I

v *pf* nḥbw J576/6,14*

TRAVEL/MARCH SWIFTLY

[Ar naḥaba "hasten; travel swiftly."]

J576/14: nḥbw hyt hgrn "they marched swiftly (to) that city"; sim ib/6

NḤB II

v *inf* nḥb J629/27*

BESIEGE (?)

[Sense from context, syn of ẒWR *v* "surround"; and cf NḤB II *tp*.]

J629/27: wẓwrw wnḥb hgrn "they surrounded and besieged the city"

tp *pf* tnḥbw Ir32*

PRESS CLOSE (*^{c}m* around?), BESIEGE (?) (cf NḤB II *v*)

Ir32: they attacked the town and its defenses wtnḥbw ^{c}mhmw "and besieged them" (cf RycMus88/213)

NḤL

v *pf* nḥlhw C516/20*

GIVE

[Ar naḥala id.]

C516/20: hnbṭ T wnḥlhw Y nwyn lḤ "y. dug (the well?) T. down to water and gave it as a watering place to Ḥ."

h pf hnḥlhw C350/10*

GIVE = PUT AT s.o.'s DISPOSAL (troops)

C350/10: hnḥlhw...'frshmw wbmw nḥl[th]mw fhrg ṯny nmrn "he put their cavalry at his disposal and on their mission he killed two panthers"

tp pf tnḥlw Ga3/4*

BE GIVEN, GRANTED

Ga3/4: tnḥlw wxtmrn "were given and granted"

n s nḥl(n) J665/33+; p/coll nḥl ib/37

(1) TROOP COMMANDER

[Cf military sense of NḤL h and nḥlt (n^2, sense^2). The nḥl was the "grantee" of the privilege of commanding (private?) nḥl-troops (BeNL8/452).]

J665/33,36: 'A...nḥl rkbn...G nḥl 'fṛsn "A., commander of the camelry; G., commander of the cavalry"

(2) TROOPS

J665/37: sb^{c}y w'rb^{c} m'tm 'sdm nḥl 'qwlm wmr's Ḥ "four hundred seventy men, nḥl-troops of the tribal leaders and chiefs of Ḥ."

n^2 s nḥlt(m) R2695/6+; nḥl[th]mw C350/10

(1) GIFT; USUFRUCT

[Ar niḥla^{t} "gift."]

Gl547/2: š'mt w'ṯwb wnḥlt wrdyt "purchases, payments, usufructs and rents"; R2695/6: xmrnm wnḥltm "grant and gift"

(2) military MISSION

C350/10 quoted under NḤL h

NḤṢ

st pf (f.p) stnḥṣn R4176/6*

GROW FAT

[Ar naḥiṣa "be fat (said of a she-camel)."]

R4176/6: the god has prohibited the mountain goats bn nśg bn mṣrn kstnḥṣn bnslm "from being prevented from feeding, that they may grow fat with offspring"

NḤT

n s nḥtm J650/32+

BEATING (maṣdar?)

[Ar naḥata "beat, strike with a staff or stick."]

J650/32: may the god protect them bn h'stm wnkytm wnḥtm "from harm, injuries and beating"; sim J2109/12

NXX I

v ipf ynxhw C464/7*

CAUSE TO KNEEL

[Ar naxxa, nwx h "cause (a camel) to kneel" (BeOracle/223).]

C464/7: let him turn himself toward this boundary stone once, wl ynxhw [š]lt ᶜynm "and let (the priest) cause him to kneel three times turning himself about"

NXX II

n s nx[thw] R2861/23*

FUNDS, ASSETS (?) (reading doubtful)

[Ar naxxa† "gold dinars."]

R2861/23: wl yᶜly bn nx[thw...wl] (y)nq(d)n mwḍ'hw "to raise (tax-money?) from his assets (?); (so let him?) pay his tribute"

NXY I

ti pf ntxy C678/2*

CONFESS

[Cf Eth tanāḥaya id. MüW/104 tr the Sab form "take consolation through confession of sins."]

C678/2: ...h]w ntxy [... "his..., he confessed..."

tp pf tnxy C523/1+; tnxyt C532/2+; tnxyw C546/1+

CONFESS (= NXY I ti)

C523/1: tnxy wtndrn ldS bhn qrb mr'tm "he confessed and vowed penance to (the god) dS. because he had approached a woman (sexually)"; C532/2: tnxyt wtndrn...bdt hxṭ't "she confessed and vowed penance because she had sinned"

n s tnxtn C547/15; var tnxyt(n) C546/1+

CONFESSION

C546/1: tnxyt tnxyw tmnytn "the confession made by eight (men?)"; C547/15: wkwnt dt tnxtn b'mr Ḥ "this confession was (made) by order of (the god) Ḥ."

NXY II

n s mnxy R3946/6+; p mnxthmw J618/6

PRIMARY CANAL

[Cf phps Heb nāḥāh "lead," Ar naḥâ "take, follow a direction" (MüW/104); or Ar nawwaxa "compel" > "guide, direct water"? (RycHim2/480n15).]

R3946/6: the cistern wmzfh mnxy Y "and its exit channel, the primary canal of Y."; J618/6: the god granted kyml'n mnxthmw...btny brqn "that He would fill their primary canals with two rainstorms"

NXL

n s nxl(m,n) R4172/4+; nxlhw J555/3+; nxlhmy R4907/3+; nxlhmw R3687+; d nxlnhn R4627/5+; "early Sab dual" (BeDGESA/29:7) nxlhn R4781/1; nxlyhw

R3913/3; nxlyhmw R4194/4; p 'nxl(n) R3911/4+; 'nxlhw J550/1+;'nxlhmy R3893/2+; 'nxlhmw R3686/1+

PALMGROVE

[Ar naxl (coll) "palm trees."]

R3902b#131/3: his control dyke ḏysqyn nxlhw "which irrigates his palmgrove"; R2876/4: 'rḍtn w'nxln w'^{c}nbn "the fields, palmgroves and vineyards"; R4626/1: mḥmt wmsqt 'nxlhmw "the embankment and canalization systems of their palmgroves"

NṬ^{c} I

tp pf tnṭ^{c}t C179/7; tnṭ^{c}w Ir18+; inf? tṭ^{c}n C308/19

(1) PLANT

[Heb nāṭa^{c} id.]

C308/4: kl ṭyb wṣrf tnṭ^{c}w whqšbw "all the ṭyb and ṣrf incense they planted and prepared"

(2) BEHAVE IN A HOSTILE MANNER; BEGIN A MILITARY ACTION

[Development from basic sense of Sem root "fix firmly (plants or tent pegs)" > "adopt a stubborn attitude" (cf HöWZ43/86, RyET/69).]

C179/7: she dedicated a statue [bk]n tnṭ^{c}t l'lhh "when she had behaved hostilely toward her god"; Ir18: tnṭ^{c}w...qblt sw'm "they began a campaign, a treacherous war (against their own lords)"; C308/19: bdr hšt'w wtṭ^{c}n "in the war they initiated and began"

st For stṭ^{c}w C401/8, see under ṬW^{c} st

n^{1} p? nṭ^{c} J555/4*

TENTS (?)

[PBH nāṭa^{c} "pitch a tent"; Ar.Daṯ naṭ^{c}, ModYem naṭā^{c}ah (RoVoc/307), "leather mat."]

J555/4: hwf' kl nṭ^{c} wkśwy...ḏb' S "he provided all the tents (?) and garments for the campaign of S."

n^{2} s nṭ^{c}t(n) R4663/3+; p? nṭ^{c} J557

PART OF A SANCTUARY associated with the god ^{c}ṮTR ŠRQN

[Related to nṭ^{c} "tent"?--or cf root sense "planted firmly in the earth" > "rampart, bastion" or the like?]

R4663/3: hwṯrw wbr' nṭ^{c}t ^{c}ṮTR...mšrqy hgrn "they laid the foundation for and built the nṭ^{c}t of (the god) A. east of the city"; J557: ml' tml' nṭ^{c} hml'n...gn' 'WM "he filled in the fill of the nṭ^{c}t-constructions, filling in the wall of (the temple) A."; C40/4: gn'n bhyt nṭ^{c}tn "the wall at that nṭ^{c}t (= bastion?)"

NṬ^{c} II

n s nṭ^{c} F119/12+

INJURY caused by an enemy (var of nḍ^{c})

[See under NḌ^{c} n^{1}.]

F119/12: may the god protect them bn nṭ^{c} wšṣy wxṭṭ [š](n)'m "from injury, evil eye or sand-magic of (any) enemy" (parallel contexts have nḍ^{c})

NṬF

h pf? hnṭf C338/5*

CAUSE blood TO FLOW (?)

[Heb nāṭap "drip," Ar nuṭfa^{t} "drop of liquid" (BeOracle/216).]

C338/5: h'tw mḥr hnṭf bd̲n ẓrn "he offered a sacrifice (whose blood) he caused to flow on this mountain"

n s mṭftn C460/6; mnṭftn ib/8+

ALTAR for blood sacrifice

C464/8: wb^{c}ly mnṭfṭ[n ysd s]'rt dm ṭlyn "on the sacrificial altar [he shall pour out] the whole of the blood of 2 lambs"; other contexts more fragmentary

NṬŠ

v pf nṭš C548/10*

LEAVE

[Cf Heb nāṭaš id, Ar naṭīš = ḥaraka^{t} "movement" (IrvJRAS'64/30n5, quoting Q).]

C548/10: wd̲kr nṭš ^{c}št mḥrmn whwfy...t̲wrm "and he who repeats (the offence) must leave the community of the temple and pay a bull (as a fine)"

NẒM--For hẓmn see under WẒM h

NẒF--For nẓf C338/1 read mnṣf with G1209, see under NṢF n

NẒR

v pf nẓrhw C353/5; nẓrw J577/10; inf nẓr J564/11+

(1) PROTECT, GUARD

[Ar naẓara id; also "have in mind" (cf sense[2]).]

J564/11: wqhhmw lnẓr wtnṣf qhthw bhgrn "he ordered them to protect and maintain his authority in the city"; C353/5: nẓrhw bkn hrgw qrn 'ḤMRN "(the god) protected him when they killed the Ḥimyarite guard"

(2) BETHINK ONE'S SELF OF, REMEMBER

J577/10: nẓrw mw^{c}d 'GRN ltṣryn b^{c}br mr'hmw "they remembered the promise of the Najranites to protect (them) against their lord"

n s nẓr C352/14; p nẓr J616/22; nẓrhw J651/11; nẓrhmw C541/101

(1) PROTECTION, CARE

[Ar naẓar id.]

C352/14: may the god grant them ḥẓy wrḍw...š^{c}bhmw...wnẓr mr'hmw "the favor and good will of their tribe and the protection of their lord"

(2) (ROYAL) OFFICIALS (overseers, ministers?)

[Ar nāẓir, p nuẓẓār, id.]

C541/101: 'qwln 'lht knw ^{c}m mlkn wnẓrhmw "tribal leaders who were with the king and their officials"; J616/22: men from their tribe wbn nẓr mlkn "and from (among) the king's officials"

NYL

n s? mnlt R4029/2+; var mnlyt R4138/9

PROPERTY (?) (but see Note)

[Ar nāla (y) "obtain, acquire," manāl "acquisition."]

R4029/2: may the god grant n^{c}]mtm wwfym w'ḏnm wmnlt ṣdqm "prosperity, safety, health and satisfying property (?)" AND ELSEWHERE SIM

Note: All contexts parallel those of mng(y)t "events, fortune." Considering the similarity of the OSA characters l and g, it seems likely that many, if not all, instances of mnl(y)t should be read mng-(y)t (root NGW), esp since the form mnlyt cannot be justified by the proposed etymology.

NKY

n^{1} s? nkym J563/14+

INJURER(S) (act.prt?)

[Ar nakâ "cause damage, injure."]

J563/14: may the god protect them bn b'stm wnkym wnḍ^{c} wšṣy šn'm "from harm, injurer(s), magic and evil eye of (any) enemy" AND OFTEN SIM; C82/10: bn b'stm wnkytm wnkym "from harm, injury and injurer(s)"; R3972/3: kl nkym wmhb'sm "any injurer or damager"

Note: Phps nkym should be interpreted as a var or p of nkytm (NKY n^{2}) "injury (-ies)."

n^{2} s nkytm R4938/24++

INJURY

[Ar nikāya† id.]

R4938/24: may the god protect them bn b'stm wnkytm wbn nḍ^{c} wšṣy šn'm "from harm, injury, magic and evil eye of (any) enemy" AND OFTEN SIM; cf also C82/10 quoted under NKY n^{1}

NKL

v pf nkl C648/4; nklw Ir19

INLAY with pebbles

[ModYem nakl "pebbles" (RoVoc/307), Ar mankal "rocks" (RycMus87/504).]

C648/4: nkl kl ṣdqm "he inlaid (it) all satisfactorily (??)"; Ir19: nkl wmqḥ...nklw "the pebblework and paving (which) they laid down"

h pf hnklw C230/2+

INLAY with pebbles (= NKL v)

C230/2: hnklw 'rb^{c}t krfm wb'r "they inlaid with pebbles four cisterns and a well" n s nkl R4050/2+; nklhmw R4194/6+

(ORNAMENTAL?) PEBBLEWORK, PAVING

Ir19: nkl wmqḥ "pebblework and paving"; R4050/2: hḥd]ṯw kl nkl qdm ḏqn "they restored all the pebblework in front of the oratory"; C373/3: zlt nkl gwbn "fortification of pebbled stonework"

NKM--For nkm C40/3 read nkl n

NKS--For nks C540/84, cited in CoRoC/187B, read nśk and see under NŚK

NKF

n s nkfm J576/14+

MILITIA (?)

[Daṯ.ModḤaḍ nkf "muster, mobilize (in military sense)."]

J576/14: fxrhmw lSB' wṯhbhmw nkfm "he gathered (troops) together for S. and brought them back as a militia (?)"; also in J643/9 after lacuna

Note: BeNL10/414 tr "[he] returned them an answer rejecting [cf Ar nakafa ʿan "reject"] the idea of his resuming peaceful relations..."

NKR

v pf nkr J720/11+; ipf ynkrn C380/6; inf nkrn R4646/17+; act.prt nkrm C29/5

PUNISH; pass BE AFFLICTED, PUNISHED, FINED

[Ar nkr h "censure, disapprove."]

C81/6: nkr bʿlyhmw ḏyftḥn bythmw "he punished them in that their house was destroyed"; C380/6: fl ynkrn xms rḍyn "let him be fined five current (coins)"; J720/11: nkr ʿbdhw...mrḍm "(the god's) servant was afflicted (with) a disease"

tp pf tnkrhw C405/8; inf tnkrn ib/7

BE AFFLICTED WITH, SUFFER a disease

C405/7-8: ḏmrḍ tnkrn ʿrqm...wtnkrhw 'sm "who was sick (and?) afflicted with a sweating sickness, and (another?) man was afflicted with it"

h inf hnkrnhw J562/21; var hkrnh J558/7; prt mhnkrm C449/4+; var mhkrm R4660/3+

ALTER an inscriptional offering

[Ar nakir "unknown," nkr D "disguise."]

J558/7: they dedicated their offering for its protection bn hkrnh w'xrnh "against altering it or removing it"; J562/21: bn hnkrnhw bn brṯ()hw "from altering (?) it from its place"; C449/4: bn mhnkrm wmhb'sm "against an alterer or injurer"; R4660/3+ sim formula with mhkr(m)

n^I s nkrm G1533/11*

ANOTHER, AN UNKNOWN PERSON (?)

[Ar nakir "unknown," nakira^t "unknown person."]

G1533/11: byt ḏḤ w'qyn Ṣ wnkrm "the (vassals of) the house Ḥ., or the

qyn-officials of Ṣ., or anyone else" (tr HöSEG8/32f)
n^2 s̱ nkr(m) R5094/4+
   ALTERATION, DAMAGE
   R5094/4: mrd'm...'w nkrm "damage or alteration (of monuments in a cemetery?)"; R2860/4: wmn lyh(g)rm nkr qntm "and whoever is guilty of damage (to) a storage pit..."
n^3 s̱ tkrm NNAG12/18-9; var tnkr(m) C546/4+
   FINE, REPARATION
   NNAG12/18-9: to dedicate to the god d[n sl]mn tkrm lqbly d... "this statue as a fine/reparation because..."; C546/4: zl^{c}m wtnkrm "fine and reparation"

NKŚ--For nkśm Ry535=J576/14, read nkfm, see under NKF

NKṮ
 v inf nkṯhw Ir25/3*
   BREAK OFF
   [Cf Ar nakaṯa "break (a contract)."]
   Ir25/3: they placed it under the god's protection bn 'ys...h'xrnhw wnkṯhw bn 'shw "against (any) man who would remove it or break it off its base"

NL, NLY--For n̲ mnl(y)t, see under NYL

NM--See under NWM, NMW, NMM

NMW
 v pf nmw J702/1*
   INCREASE
   [Ar namā (III-w or y) "grow, multiply" (MüW/106).]
   J702/1: knmw T "that T. may increase" (hope expressed in the erection of the stela)
 n as adj: m.s mntm C562/7*
   FAT, RICH (said of curds) (?)
   [Cf Ar muntami^n "fat, satiated" (MuW/106).]
   C562/7: bn qrśn 'fyn 'w ṯwr mntm "part of (?) a qrś-measure of baked goods, or rich curds"

NML
 n p̱ nmln C380/6*
   CALUMNIES (?)
   [Ar namala "utter calumnies".]
   C380/6: wdyx[dl wnm]l nmln fl ynkrn "and whoever is neg[lectful] or [utters] calumnies (?), let him be fined"

NMM
 v pf n()mw IrApp2/1*

PLOT, CONTRIVE (?)

[Text reads n^{c}mw, but RycMus88/216n3 cfs Ar namma "tell tales in order to injure s.o. or to cause quarrels."]

IrApp2/1: bkn n()mw 'b^{c}l hgrn...xys b^{c}br ḤḌRMWT "when the citizens of the town plotted to act treacherously for the sake of Ḥaḍramawt"

NMR I

n s nmrn Ry538/28,31; d nmrn C350/12

PANTHER, LEOPARD

[Ar namr id. Discussion against the suggestion that Sab usage is metaphorical ("adversary" or the like), RycMus87/507-8.]

C350/12: bmw nḥl[th]mw fhrg ṯny nmrn "on their mission he killed two panthers"; Ry538/28: xmrhw...hrg lb'n wnmrn "(the god) allowed him to kill the lion and the panther"; sim ib/31

Note: Sometimes n.pr (NMRN 'WKN, C429/6+)

NMR II

n s? nmry(n) C541/20+; p 'nmr C329/2+; '[n]mrhw (?) J576/13

CONTROL WALL

[Irv/269-70 suggests a dissimilation from root MRW/Y, originally *mmryn? (Cf Sab mrw "fertile field.")]

C329/2: 'nmr wfnw "control walls and canals"; C541/20: nmryn dqdm 'rmn "the control wall which is in front of the dam"; J576/13: kl mḥfdt kwnw '[n]mrhw "all the towers which were its control walls" (for another interpretation see under 'MR n^{2})

Note: In R3943/6 n.pr.

NS'

v pf ns'w C547/7*

PUT OFF, POSTPONE

[Ar nasa'a id (Lane/2785B).]

C547/7: ns'w mṭrdn ^{c}d d^{c}A "they put off the ritual hunt until (the month) dA."

NSL

n s nslm R4176/6*

OFFSPRING of animals

[Ar nasl id.]

R4176/6: the god prohibited the mountain goats from being prevented from feeding kstnḥṣn bnslm "that they may grow fat with offspring"

NSM

v ipf yn[s]mn C612/3*

sense doubtful; BLOW (?)

[Ar nasama id.]
C612/3 (context fragmentary): d̲yn[s]mn tkbym "whoever blows (?) burning incense (?)"

NSR

pp nsr R3943/5+; nsrn R3945/16+

TO, TOWARD, IN THE DIRECTION OF

[Cf Ar yasara "be easy," Heb yāšar "be smooth, straight" (HöASG/155).]
R3945/16: šfthmw nsrn 'l'ltn "their dedication to the gods"; C555/3: ymxrw 'ln 'wt̲nn nsr mšrqn wnsr m^{c}rbn "these boundary stones shall face toward the east and toward the west"; R3943/5: the control dyke d̲nsr blq mnxy Y "which is in the direction of the opening of the primary canal of Y."; C553/1: bn nsrn T "from the direction of T."

N^{c}B

n s n^{c}bm C352/16*

ENEMY, ILL-WISHER (lit., RAVEN, CARRION BIRD) (?)

[Ar na^{c}aba "caw (of a raven)," na^{cc}āb "cawing; ill-boding."]
C352/16: coercion and hatred mr'm wš^{c}bm wn^{c}bm "of any man, tribe or enemy"

N^{c}M

v pf n^{c}m G1773b/4+; n^{c}mt C79/12+; ipf yn^{c}m C547/13; tn^{c}mn C79/12+

PLEASE, BE PLEASANT; impersonally, GO WELL (l- with)

[Ar na^{c}ama "live in prosperity; be happy."]
C79/12: they dedicated so that the god would grant them such and such wld̲t n^{c}mt wtn^{c}mn lbny 'A "and in order that it may have gone well and will go well with the b.A." AND OFTEN SIM; G1773b/4: hšb^{c} SB'...wn^{c}m SB(')N "(the god) satisfied Saba and pleased the Sabaeans"; C547/13: lyt̲wbnhmw t̲wb yn^{c}m "let him reward them with a reward (which) will be pleasing"

Note: For n^{c}mw IrApp2#1/2, read phps nmw, see under NMM v.

n^{1} as adj: f.s n^{c}mtm G1533/3*

GOOD, VALID, STANDARD (of coins)

[Ar na^{c}ama "be happy, confident."]
G1533/3: ['r]b^{c} m'n blṭm n^{c}mtm "four hundred standard blṭ-coins"

n^{2} s n^{c}m C683*

SWEET INCENSE

[Ar na^{c}īm "gentle, pleasant."]
C683 (on an incense burner): rnd d̲hb n^{c}m qsṭ "nard, golden incense, sweet incense, costus"

n^{3} s n^{c}mtm J563/7++

PROSPERITY, HAPPINESS

[Ar ni^{c}ma^{t} "blessing; wealth."]
J563/7: may the god grant them n^{c}mtm wwfym wmngt ṣdqm "prosperity, health

and good fortune" AND OFTEN SIM; R3956/6-7: fl yśwbnh n^{c}mtm "may (the god) restore her to happiness (= divine favor?)"

NF--see under NWF

NFX

n s? mnfxthw C570/4*

PART OF IRRIGATION APPARATUS

[Ar nafaxa "blow; pump," manfaḥ "bellows," Eth menfax "pump-like contrivance."]

C570/4: he bartered for one seventh of ḥrthw wmnfxthw "its canal and mnfxt-apparatus"

NFY--For nfm J576=Ry535/3, see under NQM

NFL

v pf nflhmw G1217/6; nflw Ir13

FALL UPON an enemy, MAKE AN ATTACK (?)

[Heb nāpal id.]

Ir13: dnflw xlf bytn "those who made the attack outside the fortress" (tr "those who fell, i.e. were killed" is also possible here); G1217/6: the god saved him bn nflt nflhmw "from (being injured in) the attack he made on them"

n s nflt G1217/6*

ATTACK

G1217/6 quoted under NFL v

NFM--For nfm J576=Ry535/3, see under NQM

NFS

h pf hfsw J735/15*

CAUSE water TO SPREAD OUT

[Ar nfs Dt "spread out, flow out."]

J735/15: hfsw mnfstn wdnm kl 'kl'n "the distributors and rain spread water out over all the pastures"

n[1] s nfs R2706/1+; nfshw R4043/3+; p 'fshmw J750/9+; 'fshmy C544/5; var 'nfshmy C355/4; 'nfshmw J558/3

(1) SELF, SOUL, LIFE (usually f)

[Ar nafs "soul, self."]

R4011/8: the god helped him wfrqnfsh[w] "and saved his life"; R4043/3: [hq]ny nfshw [ww]lthw "he dedicated himself and his daughter (?)"; R4558/2-3: whm (')l t'xd fhlt nf[s]hw ldyhrgnh(w) "and if he does not give himself up, his life is forfeit to (anyone) who may kill him"

Note: In C126/13 nfs takes a masculine verb: lymtn nfshw "let his soul die (?)"--contrast R4558/2-3 above.

(2) STELA, esp FUNERARY STELA, GRAVESTONE

[Phoen npš, Eth nafes id.]

R2706/1: nfs wqbr X "gravestone and grave of X." AND OFTEN SIM; R4176/10: the god prohibited disputation on a certain day wḥẓrnh nfsm "and its ban is (written on?) a stela"

n^2 s nfsm C523/4*

WOMAN IN THE PERIOD OF UNCLEANNESS FOLLOWING CHILDBIRTH

[Ar nafsā', ModYem nēfis (RoVoc/307), id.]

C523/4: he confessed because bh' ^{c}ly nfsm "he approached (sexually) a woman unclean after childbirth" (other sexual faults are listed)

n^3 s m(n)fs F70/1; mnfshw G1327/2; p mnfstn J735/15

WATER DISTRIBUTOR or DISTRIBUTION SYSTEM

[ModYem manfas "opening in a canal or the wall of a house" (Irv/218).]

F70/2: he built the control dyke, mḥmt wm(n)fs "the embankment system and the water-distribution system"; see also J735/15 quoted under NFS h

NF^c--For hf^c J651/53, see under HF^c

NFṢ

v pf nfṣ Ir13; nfṣw Ir32/15+

GO/COME, in military context

[Cf Heb nāfaṣ, Eth nafṣa "disperse, be scattered," Ar nafaḍa "shake."]

Ir32/4: wnfṣw ^{c}dy mḥrmn dyǵrw "they went to the fortified camp which they had provisioned"; ib/15: w'l n(f)ṣw ǵyr kbn SB' "but no one went except from S."

NFQ

v pf (n)fq G1574/8; inf nfq C581/11

BE INDEBTED (bn to)

[Cf Ar nafa/iqa "be spent, used up (money)."]

G1574/8: k(n)fq bnhw ^{c}A bṣnqm bbrtm "when A. was indebted to him for a debt in reparation (?)"; C581/11: wnfq bnhw "(they were) indebted to him"

n^1 s nfqm G1533/7+

as adj: BINDING

[Ar nafaqa "go out," parallel to Heb yāṣā' "go out; be promulgated (laws, judicial decisions)."]

G1533/7: t^{c}lm...b'd[m] wnfqm wšṣsm kl ẓhr "he signed every document as public, binding and prohibitive"; R3951/4: nfqm wśxlm "binding and obligatory"; R2724/6: ḥqqm wnfqm "legally obligatory and binding"

n^2 s mnfqn R2724/12*

OBLIGATION

R2724/12: kwn dn mnfqn bwrx... "this obligation (went into effect) in the month..."

NṢB

v pf nṣb R3894A/2+; nṣby RyGraf/p563

ERECT

[Ar naṣaba "set up."]

R3894A/2: byt WD dnṣb "the house of (the god) W. which he erected"; also R5009/2, fragmentary context

n¹ s nṣb C443/1+

(1) FUNERARY STELA

[Ar naṣb id (also nṣb in Phoen.Aram.Nab); Heb neṣîb "statue, pillar."]

C443/1: nṣb K...wlyqm^cn ^cTTR...dyš'nhw "(This is the) funerary stela of K., and may (the god) A. strike down him who takes it away"

(2) LABOR (?)

[Ar naṣaba "fatigue, wear out" (cf BeSM/399).]

GaMosna^c/10-11: nṣb wmnṣf "the labor (?) and labor force (used in constructing the roads)"

n² p mnṣbt F127/2+

PILLARS

[Akk minṣabu "pillar," cf Heb maṣṣēbāh "stela" (RyET/79).]

F127/2: bn[y]w...mnṣbt wmḥrm 'lhhmw "they built the pillars and temple of their god"; sim ib/4, partly restored

NṢḤ

ti ipf ytṣḥ cited in P132 (RyNE4/152); may be tp of ṢYḤ

n¹ s nṣḥt C538/1*

GOOD ADVICE, COUNSEL

[Ar naṣTḥa^t id.]

C538/1: ...] wrdw wnṣḥt h[... "and good will and counsel..."

n² p? mnṣḥ R3951/4-5; var? mnṣḥtm ib/3

REQUISITION, DEMAND

[Ar naṣaḥa "advise," semantic development > "state one's needs" > "requisition"?]

R3951/4: kl xrṣ wšrk wmnṣḥ wmṯbt w'rzm "all assessments, partitions, requisitions, ordinances and commandeerings (concerning the harvest)"

NṢ^c

n s mṣ^cm C376/4*

GOOD (COIN), OF LEGAL STANDARD

[Ar naṣa^ca "be pure" = "up to standard" (IrvJRAS'64/20).]

C376/4: 'lfm blṭm mṣ^cm HY'LYTm "a thousand good ḥy'lyt-coins"

Note: Sometimes derived from root ṢW^c, cf Ar ṣāǵa "melt, cast in a mold," Heb ṣa^căṣu^cîm "things fashioned by casting = images." For another conjecture cf IrvJRAS'64/25.

NṢF

v pf nṣfw N74/3*

PERFORM A RELIGIOUS RITE

[Ar naṣafa "serve."]

N74/3: nṣfw khyf^{c}t ḏt B. wz^{c}mh bysṭ mḥrmn "they had performed the rite at the time when (the goddess) ḏt B. was 'exalted,' and had invoked Her in the temple"

tp inf tnṣf(n) Ir12+

MAINTAIN ORDER

[Cf Ar nṣf h "see that justice is done, treat without discrimination," Dt "demand justice."]

Ir12: gzy ltnṣf wqrn "he performed his commission to maintain order and guard"; J564/11-2: lnẓr wtnṣfn "to protect and maintain order"

n s mnṣf(m) C338/1+; p? mnṣf Ir13/11; var mnṣftm R4176/5

(1) CELEBRANT of a religious rite; MINISTER

C338/6: tšm T'LB M mnṣfm ym styf^{c} "(the god) T. appointed M. as celebrant the day He was 'exalted'"; R4176/5: wqwlnhn...wmnṣftm lykwnw b^{c}ly mb^{c}l T'LB "as for the 2 tribal leaders and the ministers, let them be in charge of the property of (the god) T."

(2) SERVICE or LABOR FORCE (?)

GaMosna^{c}/10-11: nṣb wmnṣf "the labor and labor force (used in constructing the roads)" (cf BeSM/399); Ir13/11: hrgw...ḏbn 'nṯ...wmnṣf wkbw bbytn "they killed some of the women and laborers who were performing (tasks) in the fortress"

NṢR

v ipf yṣrnn Ry508/10; inf nṣr J640/4+

HELP, PROTECT (b^{c}ly against)

[Ar naṣara id.]

J640/4: ḍb' lh^{c}nn wnṣr...mlk Ḥ "he fought to aid and help the king of Ḥ."; Ry508/10: w''lhn...lyṣrnn mlk Y b^{c}ly kl šn'hw "and may the gods help the king Y. against all his enemies"

h inf hnṣrnhmw C308/20*

HELP (= NṢR v)

C308/20: they sent S. to ḏR. lhnṣrnhmw lḍrm b^{c}ly 'mr'hmw "to help them in the war against their lords"

st pf stṣr C314/17; stṣrhmw J577/3; stṣrw J575/6

ASK FOR HELP

[Ar nṣr st id.]

C314/17: they submitted b^{c}d ḏstṣr Š...'ḥzb ḤBŠT lḍrm b^{c}ly 'mlk SB' "after S. had asked the help of the warbands of Ḥabashat for the war against the kings of S."

n^1 s nṣr R4069/11+

HELP

R4069/11: brd' wnṣr RḤMNN "with the aid and help of (the god) R."; C540/31: bmqm wnṣr "by the power and help of..."; J576/11: nbl b^{c}br ^{c}A...lnṣrm b^{c}ly 'mlk S "he sent to A. for help against the kings of S."

n^2 p/coll nṣr(m) J647/22+; nṣrhmw J577/11

"HELPERS" = AUXILIARY TROOPS (?); or "PROTECTORS" = GUARDS (?)

[Ar naṣara "help, protect."]

C287/10: mqtt nṣrm "officers of the auxiliary troops/guards (?)"; R5085/9: nṣrhmw wṣydhmw "their auxiliary troops/guards (?) and their hunters (scouts?)"; cf also J576/11, quoted under NṢR n^1

NḌW

v pf nḍw R3945/15; ipf yḍwn C522/3

INJURE; DEMOLISH walls

[Ar naḍā "take off (a garment)," cf Eng "dismantle"; Heb nāṣāh "fall in ruins."]

C522/3: wd̲yḍwn wynm [... "and whoever injures a vineyard..." (context obscure); R3945/15: wnḍw gn' hgrhw...^{c}d hšrshw "he demolished the wall of his town to eradicate it"

n s mḍwn C522/2*

INJURY

C522/2: ...] mḍwn wynm bn d̲ysrqn mḥrmhw [... "injury (to) a vineyard on the part of someone who is robbing his (?) temple (to which the vineyard belongs?" (context obscure; cf ib/3 quoted under NḌW v)

ND̤H̤

n^1 p 'd̤h̤m C540/45*

WATER-CARRYING CAMELS

[Ar nad̤īh̤ id (Irv/279).]

C540/45: 'd̤h̤m w^{c}d̤wdm "water-carrying camels and transport (food-carrying?) camels"

n^2 s md̤h̤ C211/2; md̤h̤hmw C41/3+; var mnd̤h̤hmw R4194/5+; d mnd̤h̤yhmw R3958/9; p mnd̤h̤t R4775/4+; mnd̤h̤thmw R4197b/3

WATER/IRRIGATION GOD (m and f) (a class of patron deities)

[Ar nad̤ah̤a "water, sprinkle."]

R4194/5: mnd̤h̤hmw ^{c}T̲TR...nb^{c}n "their irrigation deity A. who causes water to flow"; R4775/4: 'sms wmnd̤h̤t 'mlk SB' "the sun goddesses and irrigation gods of the kings of S."; C194/3: mnd̤h̤hmw b^{c}l bythmw "their irrigation god, the lord of their house/family"

n^3 s? mnd̤h̤t C570/7*

OUTFLOW, OUTLET (?)

[Cf mnd̤h̤ (ND̤H̤ n^2) and Ar mind̤ah̤a$^+$ "watering can" and other derivatives

naming arrangements for sprinkling liquids.]
C570/7: ^{c}brn N 'wṯnn mnḍḥ[t] mwn wm'kly ṯmrm "toward N. the boundaries (are to be) the outflow (?) of water and the 2 storehouses for crops"

NḌX

v pf nḍx C523/7-8+
(1) SPRINKLE, SPATTER
[Ar naḍaxa id.]
C523/7-8: he vowed penance because nḍx 'kswthw hmr "he had spattered his garments with semen"
(2) LET FLY a shower of arrows; ATTACK with arrows (?)
[Ar naḍaxa id.]
Ry507/4: wkw[rd...wn]ḍx R...whrg "that he went down (?) and attacked R. with arrows (?) and killed..."

NḌ^c

v pf nḍ^{c}w NNAG12/27; ipf yḍ^{c}n C612/2
LITIGATE, ARGUE a legal case (?)
[Cf Ar nṣ^c h "rouse up strife, seek a quarrel."]
NNAG12/27: l'rx nḍ^{c}w b^{c}br 'LMQH "concerning the litigation they had argued before (the god) I. (?)"; C612/2 (context obscure): wḏyfdnhw wyḍ^{c}n ^{c}ynm "and whoever continues to litigate (concerning ownership of?) the spring..."

tp pf tnḍ^c J657/4+; tnḍ^{c}hw J816/5; ipf yḍ^{c}n (< *ytḍ^{c}n < *ytnḍ^{c}n?) J657/10+; inf tḍ^{c}n R4150/4+
(1) SEEK A QUARREL
Ir18/2: the god granted that štkrn 'sd tnḍ^{c}w b^{c}ly mr'yhmw "the men who sought a quarrel with their 2 lords were defeated"
(2) ASK (b^{c}m of the god) TO BRING ABOUT HARM for one's enemies
J657/10: lyz'n xmrhw ḏyḍ^{c}n b^{c}mhw "may (the god) continue to grant him that (harm) which he asked Him to bring about"; sim Ir30; R4150/4: kl 'ml' stml' wtḍ^{c}n b^{c}mhw "all the favors and injuries he sought and asked of Him" AND OFTEN SIM
Note: For tḍ^{c}n J581/8, see under WḌ^c ti.

n^{I} s nḍ^c J609/11-2++
INJURY caused by an enemy (cf NZ^c II n, NṬ^c II n)
[A more precise tr is difficult to suggest. "Hostility" is proposed from the sense of Ar nṣ^c h "seek a quarrel." BeRitH/187-8 considers this tr too abstract, and tr "magical song or incantation" from contexts paralleling nḍ^c with šṣy "evil eye" and ml' "oracular response."]
J609/11-2: kl 'ml' wnḍ^c yz'n stml'n wtḍ^{c}n b^{c}mhw "all the favors (for himself) and injury (for his enemies) he will continue to seek and ask of (the god)"; C87/10: wl kybhmw bn nḍ^c wšṣy šn'm "and may (the god) protect them from the injury and evil eye of (any) enemy" AND VERY OFTEN SIM

n^{2} s mnḍ^{c} R4818/6*

INJURY caused by an enemy (= NḌ^{C} n^{1})

R4818/6: may the god keep away hyl [w']ṭly wmnḍ^{c} šn'm "assault, insult and injury of (any) enemy"

n^{3} s tnḍ^{c}tm C571/7*

sense doubtful

[Phps connected with a proposed "magical" sense of nḍ^{c} n^{1}. A kind of ritual? Discussion BeRitH/187-8.]

C571/7: hmt ymtn d̲tnḍ^{c}tm "those days of the ..."; cf ib/3-4: yṣdn lh tnḍ[^{c}tm] "celebrate for (the goddess) a ritual hunt accompanied by a ..."

NQ--For n nqt see under NWQ

NQB

v pf nqbw R4069/8; inf nqbn C518/2

CUT CHANNELS in the side of an aqueduct

[Ar naqaba "pierce, bore"; ModḤaḍ neqāba "cisterns; chambers excavated in the clay subsoil" (lrv/176).]

C518/2: ẓrb wnqbh Y "he acquired and cut channels in it (for) Y." (reading uncertain); R4069/8: they repaired the irrigation system wnqbw nqb tb^{c}t [...] 'mtm "and cut a channel, [the length of which] amounted to ... cubits"

h For hqb C149/1, see under QBB h

n s nqb R4069/8; p 'nqb R3967/2; var nqbt R4194/3+; nqbthw R3958/3; [n]qbthmw R2732P/1 (?)

CUTTING, CHANNEL

R4194/3: qrwt wnqbt wm'tt "canals, cuttings and channels"; R3958/3: kl nqbthw w'šṣnhw w'b'rhw "all its cuttings, revetment walls and wells"

NQD

v ipf (y)nq(d)n R2861/24*

PAY (?)

[Ar naqada "pay in cash."]

R2861/24: wl y^{c}ly bn nx[thw...wl](y)nq(d)n mwḍ'hw "to raise (taxes?) from his assets (?)...so let him pay (?) his tribute..."

NQD̲

h pf hqd̲w J665/37; hqd̲hmw C353/12; ipf yhqd̲w J586/22; inf hnqd̲(n) J643b/2+

(1) RESCUE

[Ar naqad̲a, h and st "save from danger."]

J560/12: [st]wkbw whnqd̲n w'xd̲ hmt 'sdn 'ṣ[ḥb]hmw "they escorted, rescued, and (re-)captured those soldiers, their allies"

(2) "LIBERATE" = CAPTURE as booty (specifically, riding animals)

J586/22: xmrhmw...hrg...wyhqd̲w rkbhmw "(the god) allowed them to kill (the enemy) and 'liberate' their riding animals"

st pf stqdw J665/39+; inf stnqdhmw J644/20

"LIBERATE" = CAPTURE as booty (= NQD h)

J644/20: yhrg(n)hmw wstqḥn bhmw wstnqdnhmw kl 'frshmw wrkbhmw "they killed them, conquered them and 'liberated' all their horses and riding camels"

n p nqydm J665/45-6*

THINGS CAPTURED, BOOTY (specifically, riding animals)

[Ar naqīda+ "horse taken from the enemy in combat."]

J665/45-6: their army returned from campaign with 'xydtm wnqydm 'frsm wrkbm "prisoners and booty (consisting of) horses and riding camels"

NQZ

v inf nqz(n) C20/2+

EXCAVATE, DIG OUT; phps also a stage in preparing land for cultivation

[Cf PBH nāqaz "puncture," Ar nuqz "well," ModYem mangaz "small well" (RoVoc/308).]

C20/2: ᶜs'w wnqzn mqbrhm "the acquired and excavated their tomb"; C158/2: ṣyḥn wnqz whqš[b] "leveling, digging out and preparing (prob land)"

NQY

ti ipf [y]tqynn R4784/5*

PURIFY ONE'S SELF

[Ar naqiya "be pure," D "purify."]

R4784/5: ...y]tqynn lᶜZYN "they shall purify themselves for (the goddess) ᶜU."

NQL I

v pf nql R4635/4+

PROVIDE STONE for a building project

[Ar naqil "rocky (place)," naqal "stone and plaster remains of a ruined house."]

R4635/4: ywm nql lmbny m'lmt "when he provided stone for the construction of the banquet hall"; R4228/7: nql lḥḏr "he provided stone for the forecourt"

n s mqln J576/6; p mnqltn C418/1+; mnqlthw R2633/7

MOUNTAIN ROAD or PASS in the living rock

[ModḤaḍ, Dat manqal "road through mountains," Ar naqīl "mountain pass."]

C418/1: kl mnqltn wkl msb' "all the mountain passes and every road"; J576/6; fśmkw mqln dY "and they went up the mountain road/pass dY."

NQL II

n p mnqlm R3951/3*

TRANSFERS, DELIVERIES

[Ar naqala "move from its place, transfer; deliver."]

R3951/3: kl mnṣḥtm wgzfm wmnqlm "all requisitions, wholesale purchases and deliveries (of provisions)"

pp mqly C541/29*

TOWARD

[Cf Eth ba-mangala id.]

C541/29: wrdw mqly SB' "they went down toward S."

Note: C tr "they descended the mountain pass [should be dual?] of S.," referring the form to NQL I n m(n)ql.

NQM

v pf nqm J702/11; inf nqm J577/4+

TAKE VENGEANCE UPON (b- for)

[Ar naqa/ima id.]

J577/4: lnqm bḥrbt ḥrbw...b^{c}d gzm wslm "to take vengeance for the battle they fought after the oath and peace (treaty)"; J652/20: lnqm wwqm 'LMQH "may (the god) I. take vengeance and treat harshly"; J702/11: nqm ^{c}bdhw... bmr(ḍ) '(ḍ)rshw "(the god) took vengeance on His servant by means of the disease of his molars"

h ipf yhqm R3945/18*

AVENGE

R3945/18: bḍ^{c}...śl'm...wnqm yhqm ḥr SB' "he imposed a tribute and a penalty (= payment of blood money) such as should avenge the freemen of S."

Note: For hqm elsewhere see under QWM h.

n s nqm R3945/18*

PENALTY, specifically PAYMENT OF BLOOD MONEY

[Cf Ar niqma^{t} "revenge; punishment."]

R3945/18 quoted under NQM h

NQṢ

h inf hnqṣn R2695/1*

DIMINISH

[Ar nqṣ h id, naqaṣa "decrease; be deficient or faulty."]

R2695/1: the 2 kings of S. xmry whnqṣn w'xrn "granted, diminished and restrained (i.e., they granted a diminishment and restraint)"

n s mqṣm R4230C/2+

DAMAGE, DECREASE

R4230C/2: ly'xrn (qlmm) wmqṣm wbrdm "may (the god) keep away insect pests, damage (to crops) and cold"; Ir25/3: b'stm wḍr^{c}tm wmqṣm "harm, defeat and damage"

NQR

n s nqrm J2109/13-4; p nqrm J1028/7

ADVERSARY, ENEMY (SOLDIER)
[Ar nāqara "quarrel," Yem naqr "dispute" (RodBiOr26/30B).]
J2109/13-4: šn'm wmhb's...wnqrm "(any) enemy, evil-doer, or adversary";
J1028/7: ᶜrbn wnqrm "beduins and enemy soldiers"

NR, see under NWR

NŚG

v inf nśg R4176/6*
PREVENT
[Cf phps Eth našaga "to bar"?]
R4176/6: the god prohibited the mountain goats bn nśg bn mṣrn kstnḥṣn "from being prevented (?) from feeding, that they may grow fat"

NŚK

n s nśkm C540/84*
EXPENDITURE
[Cf Heb nāsak "pour out" (Irv/288-9).]
C540/84: d̲rz'w...xrṣm l'šᶜbn...wnśkm lfᶜln "what they spent, by estimation for the tribal (laborers) and in (actual) expenditure for the (non-tribal) workers"

NŚF

v pf nśfw Ry502/3*
OVERTHROW
[Ar nasafa "overthrow, destroy" (SchSEG7/16).]
Ry502/3: wnśfw wmtlyn h' gyšn "they overthrew and took possession of that troop"

NŚR

n s mnśrt J631/29+
DETACHMENT of troops
[Ar mansir, minsar "advance troops."]
J631/29: ybrrn d̲bn D̲ wmnśrt xmsn "some of (the tribe) D̲. and a detachment of the army made a sortie"; Ir12: qtdmn mnśrtm bn xmsn "(he) took command of a detachment of the army"

NŠ'

v pf nš' J643/5+; ipf ynš' R3945/2+ (in R3958/2 read prob wnš' for ynš'); yš'nhw C443/4; inf? nš' R4176/7
(1) UNDERTAKE a project, esp a military action
[Phps D? Ar nš' D̲ "cause to grow," h̲ "start, organize."]
J643/5: mnš' wšt' wmṣr nš' whšt' whṣrn "the military campaign, skirmish and expedition he undertook, carried out, and set out on"; R3945/2: ynš'

'sm lmtᶜ qnyhw "(each) man undertook (projects, prob not military) for the benefit of his (own) property"

(2) TAKE, TAKE AWAY

[Eth naš'a "remove."]

C443/4: this is the funerary stela of K., wlyqmᶜn ᶜTTR...ḏyš'nhw "and may (the god) A. strike down (any)one who takes it away"; R4176/7: hṣr bḥrmt 'A wnš' ḏM qsdn "setting out (from?) in the sanctuary A., the governor of M. taking away the yeomen"; R4815/2: fnwtn...ḏt tnš'n mwn bn ḏhbn "the canal which takes water from the irrigated land"

(3) BANK UP a terraced field

[Ar naša'a "raise," Daṯ manšiya "earth thrown up by the plow on each side of the furrow" (lrv/52-3).]

R3958/2: ḥyf (w)nš' wwdn wḥrr...kl ḥrt "revetted, banked up, prepared for flooding and raked up earth for every aqueduct"

ti *ipf* ytš'n (< *ynťš'n) C308/13*

UNDERTAKE a military action (cf NŠ' *v* sense^1)

C308/13: their war and peace will be mutually undertaken bᶜly kl ḏytš'n bᶜbrhmw "against anyone who undertakes a military action against them"

tp *pf* tnš' J577/17; tnš'w J576/1+; *ipf* ytnš'n Ir14/4; *inf* tnš'n J589/11

UNDERTAKE a military action, a war (cf NŠ' *v* sense^1 and *ti*)

J576/1: kl 'xms w'šᶜb tnš'w bᶜlyhmw ḏrm "all the armies and tribesmen who undertook war against them"; J644/11: bmnš' wqblt tnš'w wqtbln "in the campaign and fight they undertook and fought"

n^1 *s?* nš'n R3951/2*

MILITARY CLASSES (?)

[Cf military senses of NŠ' *v*, *ti*, *tp*.]

R3951/2: 'šᶜbn wSB' nš'n w'šᶜbn "the tribes and Saba (= the Sabaeans?), military classes (?) and tribal (contingents?)"

n^2 *s* mnš'm R3945/14+; mnš'hw R2861/25; mnš'hmw R3945/1

(1) TRIBAL LEVIES > MILITARY EXPEDITION, CAMPAIGN

[Cf Ar naša'a "raise" (in sense of "raising, mustering" forces?), Sab NŠ' *v* sense^1 "undertake a project, esp military."]

R3945/1: y'tmmw wyḥtẓyw mnš'hmw k'ḥd bᶜsy ṣdqm "their tribal levies were led forth and succeeded communally in doing well"; ib/14: he overthrew, burned and plundered b'ḥd mnš'm wywm nš'ṯnym mnš'm... "on one campaign, and when he undertook a second campaign..."; J644/4: mnš' wqblt tnš'w wqtbln "the campaign and fight they undertook and fought"

(2) KIND OF TAX

R2861/25: (y)nq(d)n mwḏ'hw wmnš'hw "let him pay his tribute and tax"

NŠW

n *s* mšwn RycVase/2* (on a bronze vase)

PERFUME-VASE (?)

[Ar našā "smell good" (RycVase/145).]

RycVase/2: hqnyw...mšwn "they dedicated this perfume-vase"

NŠṢ

v <u>pf</u> nšṣ R3945/6*

sense doubtful; indicates some destructive act

R3945/6: mśr kl 'sṭr...wnšṣ[... "he obliterated all (his enemy's) inscriptions and ...ed ..."

NT, NTM--For mntm C562/7, see under NMW <u>n</u>

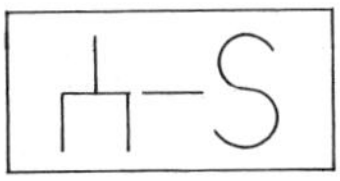

S

p s- Ist7608b/6(+?)

assimilation of pp swn: TO, TOWARD

[See under SWN pp.]

Ist7608b/6: ...]m smlkn 'l "...to the king l."; RodConf'69-70/173 reads also in C541/78: wṣḥw [s]mlkn "they reached the king"

S'L

v pf s'l C318/4+; s'lhw J721/4+; s'lhmy R3902b#130/3; s'lhmw R4626/2+; ipf (y)s'l R4781/3+; y(s)'(l)n R4768/2

(1) ASK FOR, LAY CLAIM TO a piece of property

[Ar sa'ala "ask, request, claim."]

J721/4: she dedicated to the god dn ṣlmn ds'lhw bṣdǵhw "this statue which He had asked of her in His manifestation"; sim C79/2-3: s'l...bms'lhw "He asked in His oracle"; C318/4: 'l s'l xdrn "let no one lay claim to the tomb" AND OFTEN

Note: In Ry507/6 read phps lys'lnn bnhmw rhnm "to claim hostages from them" (Ry read lyh^{c}lnn, see under ^{c}LN h).

(2) QUESTION s.o.'s right or title (b- to a piece of property); CALL s.o. TO ACCOUNT

[Ar sā'ala "interrogate, call to account."]

R3902b#130/3: w'l 's s'lhmy bḥrthmw "let no one question their right to their aqueduct" AND OFTEN SIM; R3951/2: 'l s'lw 'sd mlkn [... "let the king's soldiers not be called to account..."

ti ipf yst'ln C76/5-6*

ASK, BEG a response from an oracle

[Ar s'l Dt "beg."]

C76/5-6: may the god grant ms'l yst'ln b^{c}mhw "the oracle-response he asks from Him"--phps passive sense, "the response which is asked," but parallels suggest active tr

tp pf ts'l C80/3*

ASK, BEG a response from an oracle (= S'L ti)

C80/3: wqhhw...bms'lhw bkn ts'l b^{c}mhw "(the god) commanded him in His oracle when he asked (a response) from Him"

h pf hs'l C570/7*

LAY CLAIM TO (cf S'L v sense^{1})

C570/7: w'l hs'l nxln "and let no one lay claim to this palmgrove"

st inf sts'ln C609/4*

BE RESPONSIBLE FOR, HONOR documents

[Ar su'ila id.]

C609/4: t^{c}lm wyt^{c}lmn wsts'ln S...hmw 'strn "S. has signed and will sign and honor those documents"

n^{1} s s'l(m) R4815/4+; p s'wlt(n) C609/5+

(1) REQUEST; CLAIM, OBLIGATION

[Ar su'āl "request, demand, claim."]

R4815/4: 'l s'lw s'lm bny S "let the b.S. not lay claim by (means of) a claim"; J877/6: wqhhmw bms'lhw s'lm b^{c}ly ṣrythmw "(the god) commanded them in His oracle (with) a request in addition to their oracular response"; Gl533/5: fdy N...bn s'l b^{c}ly 'bhhw "N. was redeemed from the obligation (lying) upon his ancestors"; ib/8: ^{c}lmy bhw s[']lm "they both acknowledged it as an obligation (a debt)"

(2) DOCUMENT stating a claim or obligation

C609/5: 'sṭr wš'mtn w^{c}lmnhn ws'wltn "documents, deeds of sale, ^{c}lm-documents and claims"; R2726/7-8: kl s'wlt w'sm^{c} w'zhd "all claims, attestations and renunciations"

n^{2} s ms'lm J551; ms'lhw C397/5-6+

PLACE OF REQUESTS = ORACLE > ORACULAR RESPONSE

[Cf Akk muštālu "he who decides," a divine epithet; ms'l in Sabaean is prob n.loc.]

C397/5-6: xmrhw 'LMQHW bms'lhw "(the god) I. granted him by means of His oracle..."; J626/5: they dedicated this statue to the god ḥgn wqhhmw... bms'lhw "as He had commanded them in His oracle" AND OFTEN SIM; C80/11: kwn dn ms'ln wṣrytn bxrf... "this oracular response and decision (were given) in the year..."

S'R

n s s'r J575/6+; var s'rt R3910/7

THAT WHICH REMAINS, THE REST; phps in some cases ALL

[Ar sā'ir in both senses.]

J575/6: gave help to the tribe b^{c}lyhmw ds'r bn hmt 'ḤBŠN "against those who (were) the remainder (or tr as v, those who remained) of those Ḥabashites"; C315/10: 'mr'hmw 'mlk S...ws'r 'mlkn "their lords, the kings of S., and the rest/all of the kings"; R3910/7: yhwḥbn wrqm wd^{c}tm...f'w s'rt ṭmrm "giving (?) greenstuff and d^{c}t-crops or any other/remaining (kind of) security/property"

SB--See under SBB

SB' I

n adj: m.s SB'Yn J756/2+; f.s SB'YTn J706/1; d 'SB'yn J693/2; p 'SB'N J562/8+

SABAEAN

[Nisba from SB' "Saba."]

J693/2: R...wbnhw R [b]nw ᶜA 'SB'yn "R. and his son R., of the b.A., the 2 Sabaeans"; J706/1: 'A SB'YTn bt X "A. the Sabaean, daughter of X."; J562/8: 'dmhw 'SB'N w'qwln wxmsn "His servants, the Sabaeans, the tribal leaders and the army"

Note: The form SB' is often used in a collective sense for "Sabaeans" (e.g. R3951/2: SB' nš'n w'šᶜbn "the Sabaeans, military classes and tribesmen"). Note also that JSIMB/40+ tr 'SB' consistently as "warriors" after SB' v, which he tr "fight."

SB' II

v pf sb' J750/4+; sb'y J578/10+; sb'w J650/20+; ipf ysb' J586/15+; ysb'n J590/15+; ysb'nn J650/26+; inf sb' J651/29+

(1) SET OUT on a journey; UNDERTAKE A PROJECT, esp a military campaign [Cf Ar sub'a[†] "long journey" and phps saba'a "seize, grasp" (cf Lane/1286-C).]

J750/4: sb' ᶜ[dy] 'rḍ Ḥ bltn 'dnhw ᶜ[dy] [h]ᶜyw bmsb'n "he traveled to the land of Ḥ. without (the god's) permission until they went astray on the journey (or, road)"; J651/29: wqhhmw mr'hmw...lsb'wqtdmn xms SB' lhᶜn wlbr' 'gn'...hgrn "their lord commanded them to undertake and be in charge of the Sabaean army to help and build the walls of the city"; J650/20: the god protected him bkl sb't wḥryb sb'w wšwᶜn mr'hmw "in all the campaigns and battles they undertook and furnished aid (in for) their lord" AND OFTEN SIM

(2) "PRESENT ONE'S SELF" (bᶜbr before the deity, to obtain a benefit) [Development of sense[1] "go on a journey" suggested in BeNL9/194-5.]

J735/7-8: sb'w kl šᶜbn SB'...bᶜbr 'LMQH "all the tribe S. 'presented themselves' before (the god) I. (to ask for the end of a drought)"; J647/13: dedicant asked for a child and was directed (?) by the oracle lsb' bᶜbrhw '[nt]t[hw] "that his wife should 'present herself' before (the god)"; NNAG12/16-7: asked of the god sb' ḥrbn lḥrb "(that) the (ritual) 'fighter' might 'present himself' to 'fight' (i.e., perform the ritual of incubation in the temple)"

D? pf sb' C418/1; ipf ysb'n R3910/5; inf sb'nhw F30/1-2

(1) LEAD, BRING

[Cf SB' v "go on a journey," and exp msb' mwn "conductor of water = canal."]

F30/I-2: whbyhw wsb'nhw wwfynhw...kl bl(ṭ) "they gave, brought and paid to him all the money"; C418/I: kl msb' sb' ln...^{c}A ^{c}d...M "every road which leads (one) from A. to M."

(2) WORK (b^{c}ly with? an animal) (?)

[Cf SB' v "undertake an activity," and phps Ar saba'a "injure" (RycHim2/448n38).]

R3910/5: whoever returns a hired animal flyhbn ^{c}śbhw ś^{c}tn ḏysb'n b^{c}lyhw "shall pay its hire for the period (during) which he worked it"

tp pf tsb'w A452/5; inf tsb'n C289/7

BE COMPELLED

[Cf SB' D "work (an animal)."]

A452/5: the clients of S. and F. tsb'w wtwfyn kl [r]z' wḥly "are compelled and under obligation (regarding) all expenses and gifts"; in fragmentary context C289/7: ...] tsb'n wṯhbthw kl [...

n^{1} s sb't(n) J560/8+; d sb'tnhn J629/39; sb'ty J601/4-5; p sb't(m) J581/6+; var sbt F1655/I; var sby'(n) J577/16+

PROJECT, esp MILITARY CAMPAIGN

A788/4-5: kl sb't ysb'n bḍrm wslmm "all the projects he undertook in war and peace"; C332/2: kl sb't sb'w bqht 'mr'hmw "all the projects/campaigns they undertook in obedience to their lords" AND OFTEN SIM; J581/6: they returned in safety bn kl sb't wḍby' wtqdmt "from all the campaigns, fights and battles" AND OFTEN SIM

Note hwt sb'tn (m?) Ir8/2--an error? (with f modifiers elsewhere)

n^{2} s msb'(n) J750/4+; p msb' J665/20; msb'hmw R4624/5

(I) ROAD, including exp msb' mwn WATERCOURSE ("conductor of water")

[Ar masba' "mountain road."]

J750/4: sb'...^{c}[dy h]^{c}yw bmsb'n "he set out on a journey until they went astray on the road"; ib/10: m[ẓ']w msb'n wmwn "they reached the road and water"; C418/I: kl mnqltn wkl msb' "all the mountain passes and every road"; R4815/2: fnwtm msb' mwn "the canal, the watercourse"

(2) TROOPS IN THE FIELD, EXPEDITIONARY TROOPS (?)

[Connected with SB' v "undertake a military campaign"--participle?]

J665/20: the king sent men l'xḏ lhw 'xḏm bn msb' hgrnhn "to make captures for him among the troops of the 2 cities"; R4624/5: ywm šrḥ SB' wmsb'hmw bḍr "the day He (?) protected S. and their troops in the war of..."

n^{3} p tsb'tn Ry507/8*

EXPEDITIONARY TROOPS (cf msb' sense^{2})

Ry507/8: 'qwln w'^{c}rbn wtsb'tn "tribal leaders, beduins and expeditionary troops"

SBB I

v pf sbt J700/15*

CUT, SLASH

[Ar sabba id.]

J700/15: sbt yd S b^{c}lm R "S.'s hand was slashed by the mark (inflicted by) R."

SBB II

v pf sb J700/10*

COME ABOUT, TAKE PLACE

[Cf Ar sbb D "bring about, cause to arise."]

J700/10: wsb bynhmw lxmm "a brawl took place between the 2"

SBḤ

n s sbḥ GI369/5*

JOURNEY (?)

[Ar sabaḥa "make a long journey" (SoSoSEG4/42).]

GI369/5: [s]tyd^{c}w T'LB kl ''rx sbḥ "they asked (the god) T. to make known all the ways of the journey"

SBṬ

v pf sbṭhmw J665/34,42; ipf ysbṭ(n) J700/12+; ysbṭw Ir32; inf sbṭ J578/6

STRIKE, BEAT DOWN

[Akk šabāṭu "smite, slay"; Heb šébeṭ "rod."]

J700/12: wysbṭ S R bqḍbn "and S. struck R. with a stick"; J665/34: sbṭhmw whrgw bnhmw "they beat them down and killed some of them"; Ir32: wytqdmw b^{c}mhmw...wysbṭw dG wgšhw mhrgtm "they confronted them and beat down dG. and his army with slaughters"

tp pf tsbṭ J669/19*

CONTEND (b^{c}m with), FIGHT

J669/19: ^{c}dw...^{c}dy 'rḍhmw wtsbṭ b^{c}m 'wldhmw "he invaded their land and contended with their children"

n p sbṭm C380/6*

LASHES, STROKES of the whip or stick (?)

C380/6: fl ynkrn xms rḍym f'w xmsy sbṭm "let him be fined five current (coins) or fifty lashes"

Note: J considers sbṭhmw J665/34,42 a n "their executioners"; IrvRev/132 tr "drovers." But these are prob finite verbs (see under SBṬ v).

SBY

v pf sbyw J575/6+; inf sby R3943/2+; sbyhmw R3945/3+; maṣdar sbym ib/6

CAPTURE, TAKE CAPTIVE

[Ar sabâ id.]

R3943/2: hrghmw...wsby 'wldhmw sdṯy wšlṯṯ 'lfm "slew them and captured their children (to the number of) three thousand sixty" AND OFTEN SIM;

J576/7: the god granted to them hb^{c}ln hyt hgrn...wylfyw bhw mhrgtm wysbyw kl 'wld w'nthw "to take possession of that city and take blood revenge there and capture its children and women"; R3945/6: ^{c}tbhw hrgm wsbym "(the Sabaean conqueror) destined (the Awsanian nation) to slaughter and captivity"

n   p̱ sby(m) J665/26+; sbyhmw C353/12+; var 'sby(m) C79/6+
    CAPTIVES (contrasted with 'xyd̲t "prisoners")
    [Ar sabī, p̱ sabāyā id.]
J665/26: lfyw mhrgtm w'xyd̲tm wsbym w''blm w'twrm "they took blood revenge and prisoners, captives, camels and bulls"; J577/14: t̲ny wsty wxms m'nm 'sbym "five hundred sixty-two captives"; J649/39: 'rb^c m'tm sbym "four hundred captives"
    Note: For contrast of sby and 'xyd̲t, see discussion under 'XD̲ n^1.
    Cf exp specialized use of Ar saby for "captured and enslaved women" (Lane, s.v.).

SBL

n   s̲ msbl R5055*
    ROAD
    [Ar sabīl "way, road."]
R5055 (in full): tr^c msbl "he turned aside (from) the road"

SB^c I

n^1 cardinal number: f sb^c J577/15+; m sb^{c}t J647/26+
    SEVEN
    [Ar sab^c, sab^{c}a^t id.]
J577/15: sb^c wts^{c}y 'b'rm "ninety-seven wells"; J665/15: xmsy wsb^c m'tm 'sdm "seven hundred fifty soldiers"; J647/26: bml't sb^{c}t xryftm "in a period of seven years"; R4176/7: bywm sb^c d̲S "on day seven (= the seventh day) of (the month) d̲S."
    Note also sb^{c}n^{c}šrwn C975/2-3 ("twenty-seven"?), prob n.pr.

n^2 s̱ sb^c C570/3+
    ONE-SEVENTH
    [Ar sub^c id.]
C570/3-4: qyd...bsb^c N wsb^c hrthw "exchanged for one-seventh of (the palm-grove) N. and one-seventh of its aqueduct"

n^3 s̱ sb^c(m,n) Ir26/1+
    SEVENTH (ordinal)
    [Ar sābi^c id.]
Ir26/1: xrf M...sb^{c}n "the year (named for) M., the seventh (year of his eponymate)"; R3910/6: if a purchased animal dies wygzn sb^{c}m ywmm fbr'm mhš'mn "and the seventh day has passed (since the sale), the seller is not liable"

n^{4} cardinal number: sb^{c}y C540/91+; sb^{c}hy R4197b/4

SEVENTY

[Ar sab^{c}ūn id. The form sb^{c}hy shows Min influence.]

J665/16: sb^{c}y 'frsm "seventy horses"; ib/36: sb^{c}y w'rb^{c} m'tm 'sdm "four hundred seventy soldiers"; R4197b/4: ṯny wsb^{c}hy wm't xryftm "the year 172"

SB^{c} II

v pf sb^{c} J578/28; sb^{c}w Ir32/24-5+; inf sb^{c}(n) Ry548/4+

SUBJECT, CONQUER, SACK; pass SUBMIT, ADMIT DEFEAT (l-, tḥt to)

[Ar saba^{c}a "strike, hit; steal, pillage."]

C353/14: sb^{c}w kl mḥfdt R wkl mṣn^{c} 'A "they conquered all the towers of R. and the fortifications of A."; J576/13: sb^{c}w hyt hgrn...fhṣrw "they sacked that city and then advanced..."; J578/28: sb^{c} wtḍr^{c}n K...tḥt mr'hmw "K. submitted and humbled himself to their lord"; Ir32/24-5: wb^{c}dhw fsb^{c}w lhmw "and after that, they submitted themselves to them"

h pf hsb^{c}w J668/11; ipf yhsb^{c}w J576/7; inf hsb^{c}n J576/4+

SUBJECT, DEFEAT (cf SB' v)

J576/4: ṯbrw whb^{c}ln wqm^{c} whsb^{c}n byt ḏŠ "they crushed, took possession of, subdued and subjected the house of Š."; J629/30: the god helped him bhsb^{c}n wwḍ^{c} hgrn M "in defeating and laying low the city M."

n s sb^{c} Ir24*

DEFEAT

Ir24: may the god protect bn b'stm wsb^{c} wšṣy wtṯ^{c}t šn'm "from harm, defeat, evil eye and abuse of (any) enemy"

Note: J restores ['s]b^{c}m "pillagers" (his tr) in J586/19 (fragmentary context).

SGD

n s msgdn MüAf024p153*

PLACE OF PRAYER

[Ar masjid "place of prostration = mosque."]

MüAf024p153: Amen, amen, wḏbytn msgdn "and this house is the place of prayer" (on a pillar originally from a synagogue)

SD--see under SYD

SD'--For sd' Ry507/7, read k-d' and see under D(')

SDY

n s sdy[m] C464/4*

(BLOOD) POURED OUT, SHED

[Ar sadā "dew," Syr šədā "cast on the ground (tears or leaves)" (BeOracle/222).]

C464/4: f[l y]'mrn hy^{c}m sdy[m] "and let him proclaim 'an offering (of) (blood) poured out'"

SDL

n s sdlm C540/86*

FINE (WHEAT) FLOUR

[Cf Eth sendalē < Gk semídalis id (compare Ar samīd, samīḏ id).]

C540/86: 1200 (measures of) sdlm wṭḥnm ḏbrm "fine flour and wheat meal"

SDM

n s sdm(m) J619/12+

AFFLICTION (phps name of a specific disease)

[Ar sadam "sadness, affliction."]

J619/12: the god saved him wkl 'ḥṣnhw...bn sdm wmrḍ mrḍ "and all his dependents from the affliction and disease they suffered"; Ir20/2: t'wlw bn mrḍm wsdmm "they recovered from the disease and affliction"

SDṮ

n^{1} cardinal number: f sdṯ J644/25; m sdṯt(n) R3945/4+

SIX (cf stt, sṯt)

[Eth seds id, cf Ar saddasa "make sixfold."]

J644/25: sdṯ m'n 'ḥllm "six hundred garments (taken as booty)"; R3945/4: sdṯt ^{c}šr 'lfm "sixteen thousand"; J855/3: sdṯtn 'ṣlm[n] "these six statues"

n^{2} s sdṯ(m) Ry538/22-3+

SIXTH (ordinal)

[Cf Ar sādis id.]

Ry538/22-3: bmw sdṯ hwt ywmn "on the sixth (day) of that expedition"; C581/8: blly sdṯm "on the sixth night"; R4646/21: xrf M...sdṯn "(in) the year (named for) M., the sixth (year of his eponymate)" AND ELSEWHERE SIM

n^{3} cardinal number: sdṯy R2868/4+

SIXTY

R2868/4: he extended N sdṯy šwḥṭ "sixty šwḥṭ-units (in length)"; R3943/12: sdṯy wšlṯt 'lfm "three thousand sixty"

SHL

n s shln C405/13; shlhw Ry508/4

PLAIN > SURROUNDING TERRITORY

[Ar sahl "plain."]

Ry508/4: ḥrb kl mṣn^{c} Š wshlhw "fought all the fortresses of Š. and its plain/surrounding territory"; C405/13: [ywm wr]dhmw bshln "[the day he sent] them down into the plain"

SHF--Read shfn R3923 prob as n.pr

SW'

n <u>s</u> sw'm J564/23-4+

EVIL, ILL; often used in construct phrase as modifier ADVERSE, MISFORTUNATE

[Ar sā'a (w) "be evil; be adverse (fortune)," sū' "evil; misfortune." Note parallel uses in construct phrases in Ar.]

R3957/6-7: she had rendered her clients ritually impure fgzm sw' <u>dS</u> ᶜly ršdh "and (the god) <u>dS</u> decreed an ill (i.e., decreed adversely) against her conduct"; J564/23-4: may the god protect him bn b'stm wmngt sw'm "from harm and adverse fortune" AND ELSEWHERE SIM; J567/17-8: mwtm wnkytm wḥlẓ sw'm "death, injury and misfortunate disease"; J644/14: qblt wmnš['] sw'm "adverse battles and campaigns"

SWG

n <u>s</u> msgthmw J649/17*

BODYGUARD (?)

[Ar siyāj "enclosure," Syr syōgto "enclosure, stronghold" (JSIMB/152).]

J649/17: sb'...wstbrw bmsgthw ᶜly šᶜbn Ḥ "he campaigned and attacked, with his bodyguard (?), the tribe Ḥ."

SWD I

v <u>inf</u> swd Ry509/10*

BE CHIEF, LEADER (?)

[Ar sāda (w) id. Tr of RycIHS/328; Ry took as <u>n</u>.<u>pr</u>.]

Ry509/10: wswd wwgh wh[... "and be the chief and surpass in dignity and... (?)"

n¹ <u>p</u> sdt C597/2*

CHIEFTAINS

[Ar sayyid, <u>p</u> sāda^t, sādāt id.]

C597/2: w'wlw sdt ᶜMNM [... "the chieftains of A. returned..." (context fragmentary)

n² <u>d</u> 'swdyhmw J665/31*

CHIEFTAIN

[Ar 'aswad "very great in respect of rank, dignity, etc," and cf Sab mśwd "council of clan-heads" (BeNL8/451-2).]

J665/31: 'sdm rkbm w...'frsm w'swdyhmw "soldiers--cameleers and horsemen --and their 2 chieftains"

Note: RycBiOr25/6 connects with root 'SD (see <u>n</u>²). Cf also J513/5: they dedicated to their lord <u>d</u>smym 'swd b[... "<u>dS</u>. (<u>n</u>.<u>pr</u>?) ...?" (J tr "the greatest of...," cfing Ar 'aswad cited above.

SWD II (?)

n <u>d</u> msw[dhn] C26/6*

ALTAR (cf mśwd) (?)

[Connection with mśwd conjectural, based on restoration of final d. StSESA/523 cfs Heb yāsad "set up," yĕsōd "foundation (of a building, an altar)."]

C26/6: ...]mqṭrm wṯwrm wmsw[dnhn w]mṯkḥnhn "incense burner, bull, 2 (?) altars (?) and 2 tablets" (apparently a list of offerings)

SWM--For smy C613/4, see under SMY I

SWN

pp sn R4159/1+; snhmw Ir32; var swn C608/8+

TO, TOWARD, IN THE DIRECTION OF (cf s-, sn)

[MüW/64 cfs Akk sūnu "lap; hipbone; thigh." On relationship between sn and śn, cf BeDGESA/8:8. Prob related to Ar sanna "follow the path."]

C325/2: dsn mśwdn "which is in the direction of the altar"; Ir32: 'sdn... d'(s)yw snhmw qrnm "the soldiers who were sent to them as a guard"; R4159/1: ...]tm bsn šr[qn "...in the direction of the east"; C608/8: swn mšrqn "toward the east"

Note: For tsn C45/4 (in fragmentary context), cf phps t-śn C540/16+ "which (t-) is in the vicinity of" (see under ŚNN). For wtsn Ry507/4, read (q)lsn, see under QLS.

SW^c--For s^c N62, see under S^{c}Y

SWQṬ--For n swqṭm F120/18 (in fragmentary context), cf phps Ar sawāqiṭ "merchants who go to the Yemen to bring back dates" (RyET/72).

SWR

h pf hsr C396/5*

ERECT a wall (for another etymology, cf under YSR h sense 2)

[Ar swr D "enclose, wall in," sūr "wall," ModYem swār "wall of a reservoir" (MüW/63).]

C396/5: hsr gn' hgrn "he erected the wall of the city"

SḤT

v pf sḥt J578/8; sḥt[w] C541/20; ipf ysḥtw P135a/2

DESTROY; EXTIRPATE (bn from a place)

[Ar saḥata "extirpate," Akk šētu "destroy."]

C541/20: sḥt[w] mṣn^{c}t K "they destroyed the fortress of K."; J578/8: tqdmw ...wsḥt K...bn ^{c}rn "they fought and extirpated K. from the fortress"

h pf/inf hsḥthmw R4988/2+; inf hsḥtn J575/7+

DESTROY (cf SḤT v)

J575/7: ḥsm whrg whsḥtn "cutting to pieces, killing and destroying"; R4988/2: tqdmw whsḥthmw "they attacked and destroyed them"; J576/9: hsḥthmw mqdmthmw ^{c}dy ḥmlhmw hgrn "their vanguard destroyed them until (they) drove them (into) the city"

n s sḥt(m) J643b/4+

DESTRUCTION, DEFEAT (maṣdar?)

J643b/4: the god helped him bškr wsḥt wḥsm mlk Ḥ "in the defeat, destruction and cutting to pieces of the king of Ḥ."; Ir32: w^{c}dww bsḥtm hgrhmw wṣn^{c}hw "they invaded their city and its fortification with destruction (= to destroy them)"; J578/21: they returned from campaign 'ysm ^{c}brhw sḥtm "as a man to whom is defeat (i.e., like defeated men)"

SXL--In C609/5, sx[ln] is misprint for śx[ln]; see under ŚXL

SXM

n p sxmm R4176/12*

RESENTMENTS, DISPUTES

[Ar saxīma† "hatred, resentment."]

R4176/12: w^{c}qb sxmm lyrt^c ḏ'A "and as for any subsequent disputes (lit., consequences and disputes), let the governor of A. set (them) right"

SXN

n p msxnn R3951/1+; var msxntn C337/11; msxnt[h]w C418/2

LANDOWNERS > ASSEMBLY OF LANDOWNERS (?)

[Etymology doubtful. Cf phps Samaritan msḥn "owner."]

C69/3: kl 'sdn w'nṯn wmsxnn "all men, women, and landowners"; R3951/1: thus decreed K.; wSB' msxnn ^{c}d'l dstqr[']...bh'w "and (as for) Saba, the assembly of (its) landowners--to that which he proclaimed they have conformed"; sim exp C563/1; C418/2: mr'hw...wmsxnt[h]w w[^{c}]hr[w] F "his lord and his assembly of landowners and the chiefs of (the clan) F."

SXR--For s[x]r C86/10, read sḍr; see under SḌR

SṬW

h pf hsṭw R4964/12* (new readings in HöSEG8/49)

AGREE, GRANT

[Eth 'asṭawa "agree, answer, grant."]

R4964/12: hsṭw gḏm[n] bnhw "(the god) agreed to save his son (because of his incessant prayers)"

SṬR

v pf sṭr R2635+; sṭry C613/4+; sṭrw Ry506/2+; inf sṭr R4009/3

(1) INSCRIBE, WRITE

[Ar saṭara id.]

R2635: M bn 'A sṭr smh "M., son of A., wrote his name"; Ry506/2: mlkn 'BRH ...sṭrw ḏn sṭrn "the king A. wrote (p.maj) this inscription"; Gl772/3: sṭr ywm ršw ᶜTTR "he wrote (this) the day he served (the god) A. as priest"

(2) DRAW a boundary line

R2865/2: bḥg sṭr wtwṯn sṭr wwṯn "according to the boundary line and boundary which he drew and fixed"

tp pf tsṭr Ry512/5; tsṭrw Ry508/2+

CAUSE TO WRITE/BE WRITTEN; RECORD

J1028/6: tsṭrw dn msndn "they caused this tablet to be written (?)" Ry508/2: tsṭrw bḏt msndn "they caused (this) to be written on this tablet"; Ry512/5: he fought with his ally and his lord bkl ḏtsṭr "in all that (the latter?) has recorded (or, in all that has been recorded)"

h pf hsṭr Ry507/9*

CAUSE TO BE WRITTEN (cf SṬR tp)

Ry507/9: hsṭr dn msndn qln Š "the chief of Š. caused this tablet to be written"

n s sṭr(m,n) R2695/6+; p 'sṭr(n) C609/5+; '[s]ṭrhmy R2726/16

(1) INSCRIPTION, DOCUMENT

R2695/6: deed of transfer, concession, wkl sṭrm kbrm f'w ṣǵrm "and every document large or small"; J551/1: he dedicated the construction of this wall ln ''wdn 'ly sṭrn ᶜd šqrm "from the lines of this inscription (carved on the wall) to the top" AND ELSEWHERE SIM

(2) BOUNDARY LINE

R2865/2 quoted under SṬR v sense 2

(3) TRACT of land, enclosed by a boundary

Ist7630/6: fdy sṭrm dml'hw sbᶜy wm' ḍ'nm "they acquired a tract of (pasture) land sufficient for 170 sheep"

SYB I

n s syb J567/28+; p? sybhw DJE12/3-4

(1) FLOOD, ASSAULT of enemies (?)

[Ar sāba (y) "flow, stream (water)."]

J567/28: may the god protect them bn nḏᶜ wšṣy wsyb wtṯᶜt "from injury, evil eye, assault (?) and abuse"; sim Ir9/6

(2) ENTRENCHMENT(S), FORTIFICATION(S) (?)

[Ar sīb "channel where water flows," Om sībe, p sieb "entrenchment" (MüTaᶜizz/94).]

DJE12/3-4: sṯt 'sqfm bsṯt bḥwrm wsybhw ṯny bḥrn "six roofs with six floors (= six stories), and its fortification(s) (?), two floors"

SYB II (?)

n s sybhmw C140/8*

GIFT (?) (but see Note)

[Ar sayb id.]

C140/8: hqnyw dn ṣl[mn] R sybhmw bn mḥr[... "they dedicated this statue to (the god) R. (as?) their gift (?) from the (proceeds of the sale (?)..." (context fragmentary)

Note: MūTa^{c}izz/94 calls this a "ghost word," reading s^{c}dhmw, but GaAlON-33/431,432 continues to read sybhmw after a new photograph.

SYḤ--For ms[y]ḥ C609/3, read ms[m]ḥ (?); see under SMḤ

SYṬ

n p 'syṭ J735/14*

PONDS OF STANDING WATER

[Ar sawṭ, p 'aswāṭ "place where water collects and stagnates;...water pond" (Lane/1467B).]

J735/14: after the long drought, rain came wsqy kl 'nxln...šfqm 'syṭm ^{c}smm "and watered all the palmgroves abundantly (with) numerous ponds of standing water"

SYR I

n s sr(n) C546/4+; srhmw ib/10-1; var syr(n) C518/2+; d syrnhn C376/9

DISTRICT surrounding a city, phps enclosed by walls

[Ar sūr "(city) wall"; and cf Sab SWR "erect a wall." Alternatively, cf Ar sāra (y) "pass along"; the Sab sr might be seen as the area held in common where animals "go about freely."]

C546/2: syr wmfr hgrn H "the district and country (around) the town H."; C506/3: sr wmwfr "the district and country"; C518/2: built channels bqlḥ syr hgrn H "in the cultivated land of the district of the town H."; R4775/2: they built their control dam bsyrn 'A "in the district A."

Note: For sr elsewhere, see under SRR.

SYR II

n s msrt(n) R4788/1+

WATERCOURSE, CANAL

[Ar sāra (y) "go, travel; flow (water)," masīra^{t} "road, course"; cf Eth fenot "road" and Sab fnwt "canal" (StSESA/525).]

R4788/1: wkwnt msrtn lY "this canal was (established) for Y."; C645/6: ...] msrt hgr[... "the canal of the city ...?"

Note: For msr elsewhere, see under MSR.

SKB--For n mskb G1365/1 (in fragmentary context), SoSoSEG4/44 cfs Ar sakaba "pour out, flow" (context is agricultural).

SKN

n p mhsknm J576/15* (h prt)

WRETCHED persons > DEFEATED soldiers (?)

[Ar skn h "render or be poor, miserable"; cf Ar miskīn "poor, miserable"

(JSIMB/76).]

J576/15: śmkw bn ḥyrthmw mhsknm w'frshmw b'A "the defeated and their horses (or, horsemen) went up from their camp into A."

Note: For msknhn R3203/1, see under MSK.

SKR

v ipf yskr C568/5*

BE QUIET, APPEASED

[Ar sakara "(the wind) grew quiet after a violent blast" (CoRoC/195B).]

C568/5: she confessed bḏt st^{c}ḏrthw kyskr "because she asked (the god's) pardon, that He might be appeased"

Note also n (?) skrn R4069/9: ...]'mtm skrn wbr'w...ḥrthw[... "cubits (?) ...? and they built their aqueduct..." (first word in the line may be incomplete).

SLḤ I

v pf slḥt R3957/5*

AFFLICT WITH A RITUAL IMPURITY (?)

[Cf Ar salaḥa "void excrement."]

R3957/5: she confessed bhn slḥt ḏ'ḏnh fgzm sw' ḏS ^{c}ly ršdh "because she had afflicted her clients (?) with ritual impurity (?) and (the god) ḏS. had decreed adversely against her conduct"

SLḤ II

n s slḥm C548/1; slḥhw ib/3

ARMS, WEAPONS

[Ar silāḥ id.]

C548/1: mngr ḥm[y]m yḥrṭ slḥm "whoever visits the sanctuary bearing arms ..."; ib/3: hn lyngsn slḥhw wdmwm bšy^{c}hw "if his weapons are defiled, there being blood on his garment...(let him pay a fine)"

SLṬ

n p? slṭm NNAG12/7-8*

ARROW(S)

[Cf Ar silṭa^{t}, p silaṭ id, and the pre-Islamic practice of rhabdomancy (istiqsām) (RycMancie/269).]

NNAG12/7-8: w'l ḥrb bhwt wrxn ^{c}ln ḏ'l tqr^{c} slṭm "but he did not perform the ḥrb-ritual in that month because he had not drawn (favorable) arrow(s)"

SLY

n s mstlh C541/67*

MONASTERY

[Cf Syr šli and eštli "live a retired life," šelyā "the ascetic or eremitical life." Sab word is n.loc (BeNL9/188).]

C541/67: qdsw b^c^t M kbhw qṣṣm 'bmstlh "they held Mass in the church of M., for in it is a priest, abbot of (the church's) monastery"
Note: For the sense cf also phps ModYem mastal "luogo di riunione" (RoVoc/308).

SLK--In obscure context R3605b=Ry547/1: snt t̲ntn slk (or slf?) mlk' (because of its many errors, this insc is considered a forgery). Ry tr "the second year of MLK''s supervision," after Ar silk "organization, body."

SLM

v pf slmw C308b+
MAKE PEACE
[Ar slm D id, denom from salām (Sab slm) "peace."]
C308b: slmw wsm^c^n qhtm "they made peace and submitted to (his) authority"; Ir12: ^c^dy d̲t slmw 'ḤBŠN "until the Ḥabashites made peace"; R4137/6: fr' kslmw wt['wlw] "now they have made peace and re[turned] (from campaign)"

h pf hslm C315/10*
MAKE PEACE (= SLM v)
C315/10: he reconciled the kings lhwt slmn whslm w'tm...byn 'mlkn "to that peace, and made peace and concluded an agreement among the kings"

n¹ s slm(m) J576/3+; slmhmw C308/12
(1) PEACE
[Ar salām "peace; soundness, health."]
C308/12: tgzmw kwḥd d̲rhmw wslmhmw "they vowed that their war and their peace should be in unison"; J576/3: gzm wslm gzmw "the oath and peace they swore"; C314/15: he sent an embassy lslmm b^c^br mr'yhmw "for peace (or, to make peace, maṣdar of SLM v?) to their lords"
(2) SOUNDNESS, HEALTH
Ir28: the god allowed them 'tw bwfym w'wln bslmm "to arrive in safety and return (from campaign) in health"; sim C375=J550/2

n² s? slmtm C541/82*
PEACE (?) (cf slm)
C541/82: the king w'qwln 'lht knw [s]lmtm "and the tribal leaders who were (in? at?) peace (?)"

n³ s mslmn F124+; var? [m]slmt C692
INCENSE ALTAR or LIBATION TABLE
[Cf Heb šélem, sacrifice connected with a ritual meal. GaAION33/33-7 distinguishes two types of mslm: incense burners and libation tables (with drainage channels).]
F124 (an incense burner): hqnyw 'LMQH...mslmn "they dedicated to (the god) I. this incense altar" C338/8: mslmn d̲dhbn "this incense altar of gold (or, for d̲hb-incense?)" (cf Heb mizbeaḥ hazzāhāb Ex 37:38+); C692 (a tablet or altar): [m]slmt YF^c^N "incense altar (?) of Y."

SL^{c}

n p 'sl^{c}m C548/8-9*

KIND OF COIN

[Cf the Nabataean sl^{c}yn, a coin corresponding in Talmudic writings to the Heb šéqel.]

C548/8-9: dyndyn mr'm mn mḥrmn lyẓl^{c}n xms 'sl^{c}m "whoever drives a man from the temple, let him be fined five sl^{c}-coins"

Note: IrvJRAS'64/32 cfs Daṯ sul^{c} "damages; blood money," Tña and Te associations of the root with "salary." He tr "specified sums of money" or "quantities of bullion," phps used in making large payments; or, "a forfeit."

SLF

n^{1} s slf(n) C329/2,4*

LEVELED AREA (?)

[Cf Ar maslūf "leveled ground." Cf also discussion BeStI/93.]

C329/2: kl nkl slf w'nmr wfnw "all the paving of the leveled area (?), the control wall and the canals"

n^{2} s mslf C67/14; mslfhw C40/4

GLACIS (?)

[Cf SLF n^{1}; tr "glacis" from context.]

C40/4: gn'n bhy nṭ^{c}tn...wmslfhw "the wall of this nṭ^{c}t-fortification and its glacis"; C67/14: he restored for the god (?) mslf dn ^{c}hrn "the glacis of this fortified town"

SM--see under WSM, SMY

SMH--In R3945/5, SMHT prob name of a goddess. Passage reads: ^{c}tbhw 'r's mśwd 'WSN lSMHT w^{c}tbhw hrgm wsbym "the chiefs of the assembly of A. had destined him (or, it) for (the goddess) S. (?), but he destined (A.) for slaughter and captivity." The deity SMHT is otherwise unknown. Other proposed trs include "glory" (cf Eth sem "fame") and "fraud, falsehood" (cf Ar summahâ "lie, futility")

SMHR

h pf hsmhr R5065*

BE BRAVE

[Ar ismaharra (quadriliteral, IXth form) "be vehement in fight" (Lane/1433 B).]

R5065 (in full): hsmhr K "K. was brave"

SMḤ

n s ms[m]ḥ C609/3* (act.prt)

ONE WHO ACCEPTS, ASSENTS (?)

[Ar sāmaḥa "show kindness, tolerance," Daṯ smḥ "agree" (RhGr/30).]
C609/3: kl ms[m]ḥ bynn f'w y'tmnn bhyt š'mtn "anyone who accepts (?) publicly (?) or agrees to this purchase..."
Note: G read ms[y]ḥ bynn, tr "liberalis regionis," from Ar msḥ (better syḥ) "flow" and byn "district."

SMṬ

n d smṭnhn R4085/4*
OUTLET, SLUICE
[Cf Heb sāmaṭ "let drop, fall," Ar samaṭa "hang," D "release" (cf Mü Beitrage/315).]
R4085/4: the stone construction for the palmgroves wḏfnwtm wsmṭnhn "and that of the canal and the 2 outlets" (R took fnwtm and smṭnhn as nn.pr)

SMY I

n s sm R3904/16+; smh R2635; smhw Ry548/3
NAME
[Ar ism, Heb sēm id.]
R2635: M bn 'A sṭr smh "M., son of A., wrote his name"; R3904/16: bsm RḤMNN "in the name of (the god) R."; Ry548/3: 'blṭn ḏt smhw... "the she-camel whose name is..."; C539/4: mrḍym lsm R "propitiation/thanks to the name of (the god) R."

v ipf ysmyn C605/6; ysmynn C435/3+; inf smy F3/6+; pf smy J705/4
NAME; pass BE CALLED by a name; BE NAMED in a document
[Ar smy D "name, designate (by a name)," denom in Sab from sm "name."]
J705/4: bnhmw Ḍ ḏsmy 'LMQH 'WS'L "their son Ḍ., whom (the god) I. named 'WS'L (?) (or, who is called I.A.?)"; C605/6: ḏn mšmn ḏysmyn M "this field which is called M."; F3/6: those men 'lw sṭrw wsmy bḏn wtfn "who wrote and are named in this deed of transfer"; C613/4: sṭry wsmy whśnn b'ṯwbt "they (two) wrote, are named in and prescribed the repayments"

ti pf? stmyn R4505/2; ipf ystmyn J655/9-10+; tstmyn Ir24+; ystmynn R3960/3+
BE NAMED/CALLED
[Ar smy Dt id.]
R4505/2: H bn Ḫ ḏstmyn bn T "H., son of Ḫ., who was/is called the son of T." (read prob ḏ(y)stmyn); Ir24: mr'tn ḏtstmyn T "the woman who is called T." (cf R4233/10: ḏt tstmyn); R3960/3: 'sdn w'nṯn 'ly ystmynn N "the men and women who are called (the clan) N."

SMY II

n s smyn C540/82+
HEAVEN (only in divine epithets)
[Eth samāy, Ar samā' id.]
C540/82: 'lhn b^{c}l smyn w'rḍn "(the) God, Lord of heaven and earth" AND

ELSEWHERE SIM; C542/7: [R]ḤMNN dbsmyn "(the god) R. who is in heaven"; also C543/1

Cf also the deity named dSM(W)Y, C536/8+.

SM^c

v pf sm^c J643/25+; ipf ysm^{c}n R4109/1+; inf sm^{c}n C308/25+

(1) HEAR (bn about), LISTEN (l- to)

[Ar sami^{c}a "hear, listen" (li- to).]

J643/25: sm^c mlk Ḥ bn hyt ^{c}ntn "the king of Ḥ. heard about that auxiliary force"; J2138/4: hqny 'l fsm^c lh "I. dedicated, so let (the god) listen to him!"

(2) OBEY, SUBMIT

[Cf Heb šāma^c ləqôl "hear the voice of > obey."]

C308b/25: slmw wsm^{c}n qhtm "they made peace and submitted to (the king's) authority"

n s sm^c(m,n) Ist7626/6+; p 'sm^c R2726/8; var? sm^c(m) R4123/1+; sm^{c}h C570/9

(1) WITNESS

[Ar sāmi^c id.]

R4123/1: bḥg rwthmy dt sm^c yqmn ^{c}A wH "according to their report, (to) which serve as witnesses A. and H."; C570/9: mtbt sm^{c}h yqmn H w'lw b^{c}mhw "the decree (to which) serve as its witnesses H. and those with him"; R2726/19: sm^{c}m dt^{c}lm "the witnesses who signed (were): (list follows)"

(2) KIND OF LEGAL DOCUMENT = ATTESTATION

R2726/8: kl s'wlt w'sm^c "all claims and attestations"; Ist7626/6: dn sm^{c}n wgzytn "this attestation and definition"; G1572/3: sm[^{c}]m d^{c}mdm "document attesting a loan (or, gift)"

SMR--In fragmentary context R2682/2, n msmrn (kind of land or construction?): ...]r kl msmrn gw[lm "all/every ...?, as pr[operty]"

SMT--see under WSM

SN

n s snt Ry547/1*

YEAR (?)

[Ar sana^t id.]

Ry547/1: snt tntn slk M "the second year of M's supervision (?)"

Note: R3605b/1 (same inscr) read ḥnt for snt. For sn elsewhere, see under WSN, SWN, SNN.

SND

n s msnd(n) Ry508/2+

INSCRIBED VOTIVE TABLET (= mśnd, mtnd)

[Ar musnad "Old South Arabic script," cf sanada "be propped" (reference to the inscribed stelae?). Form mśnd more common in Sab. Note use with both m and f modifiers.]

Ry508/2: dt msndn dšmw "this tablet which they set up"; sim ib/11; Ry510/3: hwrw wwtf dn msndn "(he) displayed and commissioned this tablet"

SNḤ

h inf h(s)nḥn F74/6*

BE FAVORABLE, TREAT FAVORABLY (said of a god)

[ModAr sanaḥa and L "be favorable" (RyET/49).]

F74/6: (l)h(s)nḥn RḤMNN "may (the god) R. be favorable"

n s snḥ R5068*

GOOD LUCK

[Ar sanḥ id.]

R5068 (in full): snḥ "Good luck!"

SNN

tp pf tsn J720/11*

DECREE

[Cf Ar snn ti id and Sab root ŚNN.]

J720/11: wtsn nkr ^{c}bdhw...stt 'wrxm mrḍm "and (the god) decreed that His servant should be afflicted (for) six months (with) a sickness"

n s snt R2876/6+

LAW

[Ar sunna^{t} "custom, law."]

R2876/6: wtrdn sntn 'rḍtn w'nxln "the law will take effect on these lands and palmgroves"; also in F76/8: [.]sdw sntn "they ...ed the law"

Note: For sn elsewhere, see under WSN, SWN, SN.

SSL

n s sslt Ry508/8+

CHAIN, BARRIER (= sślt)

[Ar silsila^{t} "chain."]

Ry508/7-8: the king remained to guard against Ḥabashat wlṣn^{c}n sslt MDBn "and to fortify the 'chain' (of fortifications) of al-Mandab"; sim J1028/6-8

S^{c}--For n s^{c} N62, see under S^{c}Y; for n s^{c}m R2861/30, see under S^{cc} II

S^{c}D

v pf s^{c}d J559/7+; s^{c}dhmw J559/4+; ipf ys^{c}dn F9/5-6; ys^{c}dnhw J643b/8; ys^{c}dnhmy J572/14; ys^{c}dnhmw J642/7; inf s^{c}d J559/11+; s^{c}dnh J727/19; s^{c}dhw J571/4+; s^{c}dhmy J594/6+; s^{c}dhmw R4198b/5+; s^{c}dhn Ir34

FAVOR s.o. with, GRANT

[Ar sa^{c}ada "be happy," L "support, favor"; ModYem sa^{c}ad "grant a request" (GoTY/87).]

R4039: hqnyw dt B ls^{c}dhmw 'tmr "they dedicated to (the goddess) dt B. so that (She would) favor them with/grant them crops"; J559/4: they dedicated because s^{c}dhmw 'LMQH wfy mr'hmw "(the god) I. had granted them the well-being of their lord"; J587/10: lxmrhmw ḥz̤y...mr'yhw...wls^{c}dhmw n^{c}mtm "so that (the god) would bestow on them the favor of his lords and grant them prosperity" AND VERY OFTEN SIM

n s s^{c}d F123/6+

SUPPORT, FAVOR

F123/6: '(m)r ws^{c}d 'LMQH "by order and favor of (the god) I."; J2107/17: may the god grant 'fqlm hn'm ws^{c}d ṣdqm "pleasing harvests and satisfying favor"; C535/7-8: may the god grant them rḍw lbhw ws^{c}d ymnhw "the good will of His heart and the support of His right hand"

S^{c}Y

n s s^c N62*

COURSE, AREA MARKED OUT by an inscription (?)

[Cf Ar sa^{c}â "run," sa^{c}y "run, course."]

N62 (fragment): (built the wall?) bn s^c 'sṭrn ^{c}dy ḍqrm "from the course (?) of these inscriptions to the top (?)"

Note: MüW/64 tr "stone" (root SW^c) after J.Aram su^{c}ā'.

S^{c}L

n s s^{c}lm Ry507/6*

COUGHING (?)

[Ar su^{c}āl "a cough" (Lane/1365C) (cf DrNote/103).]

Ry507/6: d'syw...bn ḥšym ws^{c}lm "what they encountered of bronchial trouble and coughing"

S^{c}S^c

s s^{c}s^{c}m J615/19+

SUMMER; SUMMER HARVEST

[Ar sa^{c}sa^{c}a "pass away (month)"; cf also Ar saw^c "period of time," sā^{c}a^t "hour" (Lane/1467C).]

J615/19: 'mrt dt' wxrf ws^{c}s^{c}m wmlym "grain harvests of spring, autumn, summer and winter" AND ELSEWHERE SIM; J617/8: the god granted xrf wdt' ws^{c}s^{c}m wmlym ^{c}dy kl 'rḍthmw "autumn, spring, summer and winter harvests in all their lands"

S^{cc} I

h pf hs^{cc} N19/4*

INCREASE, MULTIPLY (?)

[Tr of RyNE4/162; sense from context? Cf also S^{cc} II, for a sense connected with agriculture.]

N19/4: [f]hs^{cc} ḏṯ'n ṯmrn wxrfn "may (the god) multiply (?) the spring harvest, (its) crops, and the autumn harvest"

S^{cc} II

n s s^{c}m R2861/30*

FODDER (?)

[R cfs Ar su^{cc} id.]

R2861/30: wmn lywḍ'n s^{c}m s[']l "and whoever exports/gathers fodder (?) (illegally?) shall be held responsible"

S^{c}Ḍ

v ipf ys^{c}ḍw J586/24*

FIGHT WITH SPEARS (?)

[IrvRev/132 cfs Ar sa^{c}aṭa "spear s.o. in the nose."]

J586/24: ysb'...lwḍ[^{c}...] wys^{c}ḍw bmq[... "he went on campaign in order to lay low...and they fought with spears (?) in..."

SFH

v pf sfh R5094+; sfhw J643/19; ipf ysfhn C140/12; ysfhnn J2109/22-3

sense doubtful; in some instances, DESPISE, TREAT WITH SCORN (?) (l- or b^{c}lw s.o.)

[Cf Ar safaha "be unwise, witless," L "act foolishly" (Lane/1376A,C). Sense might be (D?) "consider/treat s.o. as witless or negligible."]

C140/12: k'l ysfhn lhw w[y]rt'yn š[w]ftm "let him not despise (the god), and he will experience protection (from Him)"; J2109/22-3: bn kl mngt w''rx sw'm ḏysfhnn wḏ'l ysfhnn "(protection) against all adverse outcomes and fortunes, those they despise (= consider negligible?) and those they do not despise"; J643/19: they set out on campaign ksfhw b^{c}(l)whmw K... wmsrhw "because K. and his force had treated them with scorn (= revolted against their overlordship?)"; prob sim ib/28-9: he set out against them wsfh mlk Ḥ 'tmn b^{c}lwhw mṣrnhn "and the king of Ḥ. treated them with scorn (?), collecting (? syntax doubtful) 2 forces"

Cf also the obscure passage R5094: whmw ḏkr sm^{c} fsfh hys^{c} bmqbrt "and as for those who repeat (a ritual offence) ... (doubtful) ... in the cemetery"

SFḤ

v pf sfḥ J578/22; sfḥw J735/8-9

ORDER

[Eth safḥa "spread" > "publish" > "decree, order" (RycRite/385).]

J578/22: blt K...t^{c}rbm wsfḥ ^{c}qbthw tḥt mr'yhmw "K. sent a pledge of submission and ordered his governors (to submit) to their lords"; J735/8-9: sfḥw rqthmw wt^{c}rbn lmr'hmw "they ordered their sorceresses to give pledges of submission to their Lord"

SFL I

n s sfl(m,n) C540/9+; sflhw R3958/5+; p sflthmw R3966/10; var sfylt J585/14

(1) BEDROCK

[Cf Syr šəpûlay ṭûrā' "roots of mountains" (Irv/257-8), Ar safala "be low."]

C540/9: ^{c}d̲bhw bn sfln bn wdyn Ṭ "repaired (the dam) from the bedrock of the wadi Ṭ. (upward)" (but cf J616 quoted below)

(2) LOW-LYING LAND (contrasted with ^{c}ly "highlands"), LOWER PART of a tract of land

[Ar 'asāfil "lower or lowest parts of valleys," Heb šəpēlāh "lowland."]

R3966/10: bn 'ẓrbhmw ^{c}lyhmw wsflthmw 'fql[m] "harvests from their fields, high-lying and low-lying"; J616/26: ḥrbhmw bsfl 'wdytn "fought them in the lowland of the wadis"; R3958/5: all the vegetable gardens in the valley bnmw ^{c}lyhw ^{c}d sflhw "from its upper to its lower part"

SFL II

v pf sflt R4151/5*

ASK a favor of a deity (?)

[Sense from context.]

R4151/5: sflt wxwdn 'm(h)hw...ktldn bnm "(the god's) maidservant asked (?) and sought that she might bear a son"

SFN

n p sfnm Ir13*

BOATS

[Ar safīna^{t}, p sufun id.]

Ir13: ^{c}dww wdhr ^{c}sm sfnm bḥyqn Q "they occupied and burned a number of boats in the cove (?) Q."

SFR I

n s sfrt C570/5-6*

MEASURE, LENGTH

[Eth safara "measure," sefrat "measure (n)," masfart "length."]

C570/5-6: bn sfrt nxln...yḍ'n tḥrw byn nxlnhn "along the length of the palmgrove N. the delimitation between the 2 palmgroves will be established"

SFR II

n p sfrtm R3945/3*

GOATS

[Akk sappāru "goat."]

R3945/3: bḍ^{c} b^{c}lhmw b^{c}m ś́l'hmw bqrm wsfrtm "imposed on them, in addition to their tribute, cattle and goats"

ṢD^{c}--In fragmentary context R4201/1: ṣd^{c} l/ bn ḥ (inscr in full, no tr)

SḌR

n s sḍr C86/10*

INJURY (?)

[Sense from context. Cf phps Eth šaḍara "split"?]

C86/10: may the god protect them bn ḥry wlsn wmʿḍw whrm wsḍr "from harm, calumny, despite, suffering and injury (?)"

Note: Praetorius read s(x)r, tr "mockery" after Ar suxrīya† id.

SQ'

v pf sq' C554/1*

IRRIGATE (cf SQY v id)

[See under SQY v.]

C554/1: l''nf 'rʿw sq' ''nfhn "for the near sides of the pastures (whose) near sides irrigate (?)" (water moves through canals to the extremities of the pastures?)

SQH

n s sqh J603/5-6*

CISTERN (?)

[Cf Ar siqqāya† id.]

J603/5-6: br'w...sqh wmśwd wṣrḥt bythmw "they built the cistern (?), the shrine, and the upper chamber of their house"

SQṬ

v pf sqṭ R4581/1-2*

ARRIVE

[Ar saqaṭa "fall; reach."]

R4581 (in full): sqṭ ḤLSm "Ḥ. has arrived"

Note: For n swqṭm F120/18, see under SWQṬ.

SQY

v pf sqy G1779/4-5+; sqyw J735/13; ipf ysqyn J627/5+; ysqynhmw J735/11; tsqynhw C657/3; inf sqy J735/4+; act.prt m.p? sqym C540/47+

(1) WATER with rain (said of a deity)

[Ar saqâ "give to drink; irrigate."]

G1779/4-5: wsqy ʿṮTR SB' wgwm xrf dṯ' "(the god) A. watered (with rain) S. and the community in autumn and spring" AND OFTEN SIM

(2) IRRIGATE; PROVIDE WITH WATER

C657/3: fnwthw ḏt tsqynhw "its canal which irrigates it"; C540/56: sqyw bnhw 'rḍn bn ḏhb dṯ'n "they irrigated the land from it (the dam) from the spring flood"; J735/13: mẓ' ḏʿbn...wsqyw kl 'srrn "the flood came and all the valleys were irrigated"; C540/47: ''blm sqym "water-providing (i.e., water-carrying) camels" ti pf stqy R4040/2; ipf ystqynn Ir13+

(1) SLAKE ONE'S THIRST with water

[Ar sqy ti id.]

Ir13: 'l lhmw bhw kl mwm dystqynn "there was no water for them there (with) which they might slake their thirst"; ib: wystqynn qllm sqym "and they slaked their thirst (with) a little drink"

(2) WATER with rain (?) (cf SQY v sense[1])

R4040/2: wstqy SM^c d^c[... "and (the god) S. watered (with rain) (?)"

n[1] s sqy(m,n) C610/4+

(1) IRRIGATION (prob maṣdar of SQY v sense[2])

[Ar saqy "watering, irrigation."]

C610/4: ṯmrm 'l sqy "crops (grown) without irrigation" (or read as passive v "crops not irrigated"?); C611/4: a canal which carries water lsqy mṯ^{c}d "for the irrigation of the estate"

(2) specifically, IRRIGATION WATERS

C562/3-4: 'l s'lw...sqy kl msqym "let them not claim the irrigation waters of any irrigation scheme"; F71/4-6: the god granted bbrq dṯ'n sqym mhšfqm bM "in the spring rainstorm(s) abundant irrigation waters in M."; J653/12: the god granted ḏnmm wsqym "rain and irrigation waters"

(3) DRINK

Ir13 quoted under SQY ti

n[2] p? sqy(m,n) J691/10+

CROPS cultivated by artificial irrigation (opposed to d^{c}t, see under D^{cc})

[Ar saqī "watered (a tree, etc)." Discussion RycMus87/514-6 and n4.]

J691/10: may the god grant 'ṯmrm šfqm d^{c}tm [ws]qym "abundant crops, both d^{c}t and sqy (varieties) (i.e., both naturally and artificially irrigated)"; Ir24: qlmt ḥb(l)tn wṯmrn wsqyn "vermin on vines, fruits/crops, and sqy-crops"; J670/26: 'fqlm sqym wbrm wš^{c}rm "harvests (consisting of) sqy-crops, wheat and barley"

n[3] s? sqyt R2734F/2 in fragmentary and uncertain context; sim in R3687; read [m]sqyt?

n[4] s? msqy(m,n) C563/2+; msqyhmw C308/5; msqyhmy R3911/4-5; var msqt(m) R4626/1+; msqthw R3958/4; var msqyt(m,n) R3915/2+; msqythmw R3958/4

(1) LAND IRRIGATED BY CANALS (msqy only)

[Cf ModHaḍ sāqiya[†] "canal."]

C563/2: offerings bn 'wdwn wmsqyn "from the wadis and canal-irrigated land"; C562/4: sqy kl msqy "irrigation of all the canal-irrigated land"; C308/5: kl mhwkbhmw wkl msqyhmw "all their plantations and canal-irrigated land"

(2) CANALS, CANALIZED IRRIGATION SCHEME; or, IRRIGATION in general (includes varr msqt, msqyt, prob originally ps)

R3958/4: their valley wkl nqbthw w'šsnhw w'b'rhw wmsqthw "and all its channels, revetments, wells and canals = canal scheme"; C584/2-3: bny ḥrthw lmsqt nxlhw "he built his aqueduct for the canal scheme of his palmgrove"; R4069/6: ʿḏbw...msqy 'r[ḍ]hmw "they repaired the canal scheme of their land"; R4626/1: mḥmt wmsqt 'nxlhmw "the embankment and canal schemes of their palmgroves"

n[5] s mstqyn C308/7* (ti prt)

(LAND) IRRIGATED BY CANALS

C308/7: kl 'hdr mstqyn wmštrʿn "all the channels of the canal-irrigated and lifting-gear-irrigated (i.e., well-irrigated) lands"

SQF

v inf sqf C434/2*

ROOF OVER a building

[Ar sqf D "provide with a roof."]

C434/2: bnyw wsqf mḥrm "they built and roofed over the temple"

n[1] s sqf(m) C40/3+; sqfhmw Māriyal/2; d sqfyn GaAlON31p303; p 'sqf R4919/4

(1) ROOF > STORY of a building (?)

[Ar saqf "roof."]

GaAlON31p303: mḥfdthw ḏtny sqfyn wḏsqfm "his towers of two stories (?) and of one story (?)"

(2) ROOFED VESTIBULE (?)

[Ar saqīfa^t "vaulted entrance chamber or hall" (BeSM/400).]

C40/3: sqf kwn bhyt nṭʿtn "the vestibule which was in this nṭʿt-building"; Māriyal/2: hwṯ]r whšqr wḥẓyn sqfhmw "founded, completed and 'inaugurated' their vestibule"

n[2] d msqfn C132/2-3; p msqftn R4461+

ROOFED PASSAGE, PORTICO

[Cf Ar masqūf "roofed."]

C132/2-3: ṯny msqfn mšrqy wmʿrby hyt ṣrḥtn "two porticoes, east and west of that upper chamber"

SR--see under SWR, SYR, SRR

SRW

n p srwtn C541/78; srwthmw ib/33-4; var srwytn ib/53+

TROOPS, ARMY

[Eth sarāwit id.]

C541/78: wṣḥw mlkn ʿm srwtn 'lht hḏkyw lqrnhmw "the king arrived with the troops whom he had sent to fight them"; ib/40-1: hʿdhmw ydhw qdmy ḏkyn srwytn "he had rebelled against them before the sending of the troops"

SRS

n s srys C550/1*

EUNUCH (?) (but see Note)

[Ar sarīs, Heb sārîs id (if the correspondence is correct, prob a loanword

in Sab).]
C550/1: ^{c}BDŠMSm 'ṢLM srys b^{c}ln tb^{c} ŠRḤB'L mlk SB' "A.A., eunuch of the lord T.Š., king of S."
Note: C finds line 1 very doubtful, and emends to ^{c}A 'A bn 'B^{c}T̲TR wŠRḤB'L...

SRQ

v pf srq C398/11+; ysrq R3247; ysrqn C522/2
STEAL; ROB
[Ar saraqa id.]
C30/4-5: they dedicated an incense burner bḥr mqṭr srq bn mḥrmn "in place of the incense burner (which) was stolen from the temple"; C522/2: the god allowed him to obtain it bkn srq ^{c}[...] ^{c}bd bn M mḥrm b^{c}l 'w^{c}ln "when he robbed A. servant of the b.M. (in the) temple of the Lord of Mountain Goats (= the god 'LMQH)"; ib: ḏysrqn mḥrmhw "whoever robs His temple..."

SRR

n s sr(n) Ry340/6+; srhw R3945/9+; srhmw R3958/3+; d srnhn J577/11+; sryhw F71/6+; sryhmw J627/7; p 'srr(n) J615/10+; 'srrhw R3910/2+; 'srrhmw J561b/21+; var srrn Ir31+
SLOPE, (side of a) VALLEY on either side of the wadi, subject to cultivation; CULTIVATED LAND in general
[Ar sirr "good land," 'asirra^{t} "good land in the middle of a wadi"; ModYem sirr "better part of the wadi" (RoVoc/308).]
Ry340/6: bsr ^{c}mqn "on the slope of the valley"; R3958/3: srhmw M wkl nqbthw w'šṣnhw w'b'rhw w...kl bql kwn wsṭhw bnmw ^{c}ln ^{c}d sflhw "their valley M. and all its channels, revetments, wells, and all the vegetable gardens (which) are in it, from its upper to its lower part"; F71/6: MRB wsryhw "M. and its 2 valleys (on each side of the wadi)"; R3910/2: hgrn MRB w'srrhw "the city M. and its valleys"; Ir31: kl hgrn wsrrn ḤḌRMWT "all the settled and cultivated land (called) Ḥ."; J564/21: harvests bn kl 'rḍthmw w'srrhmw w'ǵylhmw wmfnthmw "from all their fields, valleys, stream- and canal-irrigated lands"

n^{2} p srwrm C308/5+
UNITS OF SURFACE MEASURE
[Related to sr "valley"?]
C308/5: the ṣrf-incense they planted, m't srwrm ṣrfm "one hundred srwr-units of ṣrf-incense (size of the plantation?)"; sim ib/8

ŚSL

n s śslt Ry507/10*
CHAIN, BARRIER (= sslt)
[Cf Ar silsila^{t} "chain," phps Heb sansinnîm "fruit-stalk of date" (BeDGESA/

8:8 holds that the expected OSA form would be *śślt).]

Ry507/10: wyṣn^{c}n sślt MDBn "and he strengthened the 'chain' (of fortifications) of al-Mandab"

STY

n s msty C563/2*

DRINK-OFFERING, LIBATION

[Eth satya, Heb šātāh "drink."]

C563/2: ...]kl 'kl wmsty wtfṯ yh'twn šw^{c}n "all the food- and drink-offerings and lustrations the priest shall offer"

STL--For n mstl C541/67, see under SLY

STR

h pf hstr C126/5*

PROTECT

[Ar satara "cover, protect." Cf BeMus64/308.]

C126/5: he is proclaimed an outlaw from the highland of F. and bḏ hstr '[L]MQH "in (the territory) which (the god) I. protects (i.e., all Sabaean territory)"

STT

n^{1} cardinal number: f st G1533/2*

SIX (cf sdṯ, sṯ id)

[Ar sitt, sitta^{+} id.]

G1533/2: 'ly st 'qyn Ṣ "those belonging to the six administrators of Ṣ."

Note: BeNL10/409 remarks on the lack of nunation of st and suggests relating it here to Heb šātôt (e.g., Is 19:10), phps "persons of high social standing," and tr "those who are possessed of the same authority as the qayns"

n^{2} cardinal number: sty R5085/11*

SIXTY (cf sdṯy, sṯy id)

[Ar sittūn id.]

R5085/11: ḏlsty wxms m'tm "in (the year) 560"

SṮṮ

n^{1} cardinal number: f sṯ C325/5+; m sṯt(n) C315/3+

SIX (cf sdṯ, st id)

[Ar sitt, sitta^{+}; Heb šēš, šiššāh id.]

J577/4: sṯ w^{c}šry 'frsm "twenty-six horses"; C325/5: bxrfn ḏlts^{c}t wsṯy wsṯ m'tm "in the year 669"; C315/3: sṯtn 'ṣlmn "these six statues"; J649/37-8: sṯt w'rb^{c}y 'sdn "forty-six soldiers"

n^{2} cardinal number: sṯy J577/14+

SIXTY (cf sdṯy, sty id)

[Ar sittūn, Heb šiššîm id.]

J577/14: tmn wsty hgrm "sixty-eight towns"; C540/53: xrfm dl'rb^c^t wsty wxms m'tm "the year 564"; R4010/4 (fragmentary): m' w'ḥd wsty wt[... "one hundred sixty-one ...s"

n3 cardinal number: stm'tm R2633/10*

SIX HUNDRED

[St (n1, f modifier) + m'tm "hundreds."]

R2633/10: dl'rb^c^y wstm'tm xrftm "the year 640"

n4 cardinal number: stt^c^šr R4196/4*

SIXTEEN

[Ar sitta^t^ ^c^ašar id.]

R4196/4: d stt^c^šr wtlt m'tm xryftm "the year 316"

Note: Cf stt ^c^šr J576/15, st w^c^šrm J649/39, same sense.

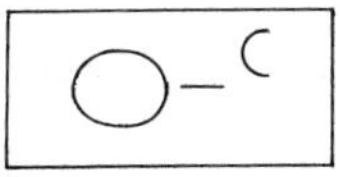

c

ab ^{c} R2868+

SYMBOL FOR NUMBER 10

[Initial of Sab ^{c}sr "ten."]

R2868: sdty šwḥṭ ▯ n^c "sixty spans (?): 60"; R3943/2: 'ḥd šlty 'lfm ▯ ^{ccc}' ▯ "thirty-one thousand: 31"; R4922/4: ^{c}x "15"

^{c}BD

v pf ^{c}bdhn C69/4*

REDUCE TO SERVITUDE, ENSLAVE (?)

[Ar ^{c}bd D id, denom from ^{c}abd "slave."]

C69/4 (context somewhat obscure): msxnt KLB ^{c}bdhn 'l "the council of K. (n.pr?), whom l. enslaved (?)"

tp ipf yt^{c}bdnn Ist7608b/8*

SUBMIT ONE'S SELF

Ist 7608b/8: yt^{c}bdnn l'mlk 'A "they submitted themselves to the kings of A."

n s ^{c}bd(m,n) J723/1+; ^{c}bdhw J643/12+; d ^{c}bdy R4967/2; ^{c}bdyhw J568/7+; coll? ^{c}bdhw R3945/6

SERVANT, SLAVE (of individual, tribe or god); CLIENT (of king--i.e., member of a politically subordinate group)

[Ar ^{c}abd "slave; servant (of man or God)."]

R3910/3: whoever buys ^{c}bdm f'w 'mtm "a manservant or maidservant"; J643/23: wqh ^{c}bdhw N...lh^{c}nn "he commanded his servant N. to give (military) aid"; J711/1: ^{c}bd KBRXLL "servant of the Leader of X."; J741/2: ^{c}bd dt N "servant of (the clan) N."; R3945/6: wld 'LMQH wgwm ḥrhw w^{c}bdhw "the children and community of (the god) I., His freemen and His slaves"; J560/18: lwz' 'LMQH s^{c}d ^{c}bdhw...n^{c}mtm "may (the god) I. continue to grant His servant prosperity"; J723/1: ^{c}bd mlk SB' "client of the king of S."

Note: The p of ^{c}bd in all its senses is supplied by 'dm ('DM II), q.v. Note also the sequence ^{c}BDMMQT' in R4763/1 in fragmentary and unintelligible context.

^{c}BṬ

n s ^{c}bṭ(m) J567/27+; var? ^{c}bṭṭ(m) J635/45+

EXACTION, COMPULSION

[Eth ^{c}abaṭa "force s.o. to do (s.th.)."]

J567/27: to deliver them from kl b'stm wnkytm w^{c}bṭm "all harm and injury and compulsion"; J615/27: bn b'sm wnkytm wnḍ^{c} wšṣy wtṯ^{c}t w^{c}bṭ wǵbṭ šn'm "from harm, injury, incantation, evil eye, abuse, compulsion, or envy (?) of (any) enemy" (^{c}bṭṭ in sim contexts)

^{c}BY--t^{c}byḏd, R3116 (in full): no tr.

^{c}BR

v pf ^{c}br R4088/1; ipf y^{c}brn C87/5+

(1) PASS, CROSS

[Ar ^{c}abara "cross, pass over."]

R4088/1-3: tqṣw ^{c}brm wṯnn wmn ^{c}br yb'hw "Beware of crossing! (This is) the boundary! And whoever crosses, entering it..."

(2) DEDICATE (?)

[Cf Heb he^{c}ĕbîr "offer to a god."]

C87/5: they dedicated lqbly 'ṣf y^{c}brn fr^{c} lǵlm yldn "for the maidservants (who) dedicate (?) firstfruits, in recompense (?) for the children they will bear"

pp ^{c}br J652/21-2; ^{c}brn R4815/3+; ^{c}brhw J578/21; ^{c}brnhw J643/15; b-^{c}br C398/7+; b-^{c}brhw C308/10+; b-^{c}brhmw J576/11; l-^{c}br J700/10; l-^{c}brhw J633/11; ^{c}brhmw Ir13

(1) TO, TOWARD; "CHEZ"

^{c}br, ^{c}brn: Ir13: mẓ't ^{c}brhmw ^{c}ẓtm "an order came to them"; R4815/3: msb' mwn ^{c}brn QTBN "a means of conducting water toward Q."; J578/21: 'ysm ^{c}brhw sḥtm "a man toward whom is defeat = a defeated man"; b-^{c}br: C308/10: nbl wbltn b^{c}brhw "dispatched and sent to him"; J735/8: they made a procession b^{c}br 'LMQH ^{c}dy mḥrmn "to (the god) I. in the temple"; J577/12: tḍr^{c}m b^{c}br mr'hmw "in submission to their lord"; l-^{c}br: J700/10: bh' l^{c}br R S "S. came to R."; J633/11: to ask the god for help l^{c}brhw "for himself"

(2) AGAINST

J652/21-2: ḏyxrgnhmy ^{c}br mr'hmy "whoever incites them against their lord"; J656/11: ḍr hšt' b^{c}br mr'hmw "the war he began against their lord"

(3) INCUMBENT UPON (in exp b^{c}br wb^{c}ly)

C609/2: 'l b^{c}br wb^{c}ly kl 'bwthmw "those (things) which were incumbent upon all their forefathers" (cf sim exp b^{c}rb wb^{c}ly, under ^{c}RB)

cj k-^{c}brn-mw J628/7*

TO THE END THAT, SO THAT

J628/7: wkbw flythmw k^{c}brnmw 'l...kwn xdg 'tw sqym "they obtained (the object of) their supplication, to the end that (the god) I. would allow the irrigation water to return" n[1] s ^{c}br(m,n) R4088/1+; p ^{c}brt C376/7-8; ^{c}brthw J555/3; ^{c}brthmw J617/5; p? '^{c}br[... R3916/1

(1) CROSSING (maṣdar)

R4088/1 quoted under ^{c}BR v.

(2) CULTIVATED BANK OF CANAL OR RIVER = MEADOW

[Cf Heb ^{c}éber "region across or beyond," Akk ebertum "further bank" "field," East Yem ^{c}abr, p 'a^{c}bar "land cultivated in terraces."]

J623/17: 'rḍthmw wmfnthmw...w^{c}brthmw wmšymthmw "their lands, canal-irrigated lands, meadows and fields" AND OFTEN SIM in lists of kinds of cultivated land

(3) (LARGE) CANAL

R4351/1: ^{c}brn...dyws^{c}n 'srrn "the canal which waters the valley lands..." (seven valleys are named, suggesting the ^{c}br is large) (same sense in R4514/2)

n[2] s m^{c}brn J669/22*

EXAMINATION or TRIAL (to determine responsibility)

[Cf Ar ^{c}abara "he examined (coins) to determine their weight and quality." IrvHom/280n17 compares the MSA biš^{c}a or trial by ordeal.]

J669/22: he died at the hand of one of them wdmr b^{c}mhmw mr'hmw...whdll m^{c}brn "and their lord pronounced a ban against (?) them and found against them in the trial"

pp b-m^{c}br C611/6*

TOWARD (= ^{c}br?), IN THE DIRECTION OF

C611/6: all the cultivated lands ykwnn bh bm^{c}br mt^{c}d S d^{c}brn Ẓ "which are in it in the direction of the cultivated plot S., which is in the direction of Ẓ"; in R4815/2 m^{c}br Ẓ, ib/5-6 b-m^{c}br; restored in fragmentary context R3912/[3]

n[3] s t^{c}br C949/1* (D inf?)

DELIMITATION, FIXING (of boundaries)

C949/1: mšr^{c}m bt^{c}mm bt^{c}br wtnn "Regulation regarding announcement of the delimitation of this boundary"; NNAG4/2-3 same formula

^{c}GD

n s ^{c}gdm C562/6*

GRAPES (?)

[Ar ^{c}ujd "grape."]

C562/6: ^{c}gdm xbṭm wdblm "pressed grapes and pressed figs" (context somewhat obscure)

^{c}GL (?)

n s ^{c}g(l)tm (text has ^{c}gmtm) R3167/1

CALF (?)

[Ar ^{c}ijl id.]

R3167/1 (in full): dm ^{c}g(l)tm "generous gift (?) of a calf (?)"

^{c}GLM

n s? ^{c}glmn C540/75+; p? ^{c}glmtn ib/14+

DIVERSION MOLE

[Eth ^{c}agl "wall," Yem ^{c}ijlama "small rock wall to divert floodwaters" (RoVoc/308). Discussion Irv/263-5.]

C540/61: ṯbr ^{c}glm[tn] wnmryn w^{c}wdn "the diversion moles, the control wall and the settling basin broke"; ib/75: br'w ^{c}glmn wnmryn ḥrṣm bgrbm wlbtm "they constructed the diversion mole and the control wall carefully with rough stone and close-laid stonework"

Note: BeESACD/46n95 suggests reading ^{c}llmtm for ^{c}glmtn and tr "foundations (?)" from Heb ^{c}lm "be concealed, hidden."

^{c}GM--For ^{c}gm, C548/9, read ^{c}l-m (?), pp, see under ^{c}LY; for ^{c}gmt, R3167/1, read ^{c}glt (?), see under ^{c}GL.

^{c}GR

n s ^{c}gr G1218/14*

HARM

[Ar ^{c}ajārī "evil," ^{c}ujrīy "liar, evil, very critical position" (BiKa); cf also ^{c}ajara "he made an assault, attack upon him with the sword" (Lane/1958B).]

G1218/14: bn n[ḍ^{c}] w^{c}gr wšṣyt šn'm "from magic and harm and the evil eye of an enemy"

^{c}D, pp--see under ^{c}DY. k-^{c}d, C376/15, see under ^{c}DY

^{c}D'L, pp + rl, see under ^{c}DY

^{c}DD

n s ^{c}dd C571/10* (or read bdd, q.v.)

NUMBER, RECKONING

[Ar ^{c}idād id.]

C571/10: drm drm b'ḥd xrfm l^{c}dd xrfnhn "one a year, to the number of 2 years"

For k-^{c}d, C376/15, see under ^{c}DY. For ns m^{c}d, m^{c}dt see under W^{c}D.

^{c}DW

v pf ^{c}dw J577/3+; ^{c}dww ib/1+; ipf y^{c}dwn J576/4+; y^{c}dww Ir13; t^{c}dwnhmw Ir14/4

(1) ENTER, often ENTER IN WAR > INVADE, MAKE A RAID, AN INCURSION

[Heb ^{c}ādāh "progress, advance"; Ar ^{c}adā, Eth ^{c}adawa "pass through, cross"; Syr ^{c}dā "invade."]

J702/6: bkn y^{c}dwn dmqmtn bbt 'LMQH "when the supervisor enters the temple of (the god) I."; C289/14-5: t'wlw w^{c}dww ^{c}dy hgrn "they returned and entered the city"; J585/15: ^{c}dw bḍrm wtškr h' 'sn "he invaded with war and that fellow (= the enemy) was defeated"; Ir13: ^{c}dw whb^{c}ln wxtršn wdhr hgrn "they invaded, conquered, destroyed and burned the city"

(2) BREAK a law, TRESPASS boundaries

C563/5: dy^{c}dwn b^{c}ly dn mḥrn "whoever breaks this law..."; R4646/12: wmnmw dy^{c}dwn...bhwt srn "and whoever trespasses in this valley..."

D for ^{c}dw D, Ry533/12, cited by MüW/78, see under ^{c}WD.

h pf h^{c}dw Ist7626/8; inf h^{c}dwn C570/8

REMOVE boundary stones, or TRESPASS, VIOLATE boundaries (cf ^{c}DW v)

C570/8: 'l bf 'l...h^{c}dwn 'wtnn "nor by the authority of (the god) I. shall the boundary stones be removed/violated"; Ist7626/8: ...[w]r' kh^{c}dw "he did indeed trespass (?)"

n^{1} s ^{c}dw R4646/7* (inf? maṣdar?)

TRESPASS

[Cf Eth ^{c}edwat "transgression."]

R4646/7: bn ^{c}dw kl 'snm lx[d^{c}] wḥsm wštr kl mšym "against trespass (by) any man, to let go to waste or damage or upset any field"

n^{2} s ^{c}dwthmw Ir13*

PENETRATION, (FORCIBLE) ENTRY

Ir13: ^{c}dwthmw "their forcible entry" into the fortress

For '^{c}dwn, C563/2, read 'wdwn, see under WDW.

^{c}DY

v pf C541/65*

ENTER (cf ^{c}DW v)

C541/65: ^{c}dyw hgrn M wqdsw b^{c}t M "they entered the city M. and held mass in the church of M."

pp ^{c}d C418/2+; ^{c}dy R4176/11+; ^{c}dyhw J628/6; ^{c}dyhmw J561b/10-11

(1) AS FAR AS, UP TO

[Heb ^{c}ad, ^{c}ǎdê id; Ar ^{c}adā "except for." Discussion BeDGESA/50:1.]

C418/2: ^{c}d xlf MRYB "as far as the vicinity of (the city) M."; R4176/11: ly't ^{c}dy Ẓ "to come as far as Ẓ."

(2) IN, AT

R4190/10: fr'...^{c}dy kl 'srrhmw "produce in all their valleys"; R3884/9: sb'y...^{c}dy 'rḍ Ḥ "they campaigned in the land of Ḥ."; frequent in divine epithets, e.g., 'LMQH ^{c}dy MRB "I. in (the temple of) M.," R4176/1-2.

p + rl ^{c}d'l d- R3951/1

AS FOR, TO THAT (WHICH)

R3951/1: thus ordained K. and the Sabaean freemen--^{c}d'l dstqr[' wx]ll bh'w dwmm "to that which he publishes and determines have they conformed forever--" (sim formula R2726/2) cj ^{c}dy C407/22; ^{c}dy ḏ- J576/16; ^{c}dy ḏt ib/9; ^{c}dy l- R4176/4

UNTIL

[Heb ^{c}ad "until." Cf also phps Ar ḥattâ id, pp and cj.]

C407/22: ^{c}dy ḥmlhmw bḥrn "until he drove them into the sea"; J576/9: hsḥthmw mqdmthmw ^{c}dy ḏt ḥmlhmw hgrn "their vanguard destroyed them until it drove them to the city"; R4176/4: which runs beside the high road ^{c}dy lyrt^{c} śdn "until it is opposite the dam"

^{c}DN

h *pf* h^{c}dn R2745/5+

BESTOW WELL-BEING

[Heb ^{c}dn *Dt* "enjoy luxuries," Ar ǵadan "dainties."]

R2745/5: MTBNṬYN h^{c}dn "(the god) M. (who) bestows well-being"--cf the title of M., C514/4+, ẓwr ^{c}dn: tr "rock of well-being"?

For ^{c}dn *n*? C541/92, see the proposed emendation quoted under RYD *tp*.

In C504/5 ^{c}dn phps *n.pr.*

^{c}DQ

n *s* ^{c}dqm Ir31+

PERSECUTION (?)

[Cf PBH ^{c}ădaq "stick to" (JSIMB/27).]

Ir31: bn b'stm wnkytm w^{c}dqm wšṣy šn'm "against harm and injury and persecution (?) and evil eye of an enemy"; J558/5 sim

^{c}ḎB

v *pf* ^{c}ḏbhw C540/8+; ^{c}ḏbw R4069/5; *ipf* y^{c}ḏbn N74/13; y^{c}ḏbnn R2877/4; *inf* ^{c}ḏb(n) C541/60+

(1) BE PUNISHED, FINED

[Ar ^{c}ḏb *D* "punish."]

N74/13: he committed such and such offenses, wl y^{c}ḏbn ^{c}šry bl[ṭm] "so let him be fined twenty blṭ"

(2) REPAIR

[Daṯ ^{c}aḏḏab "cut and hew to give s.th. the desired shape (LaGD/2247); Heb ^{c}āzab "repair."]

C541/60: l^{c}ḏbn ^{c}rmn..wmṯbrtn "to repair the dam the the breach"

h *pf* h^{c}ḏb R3945/1+; *ipf* yh^{c}ḏb (?) R2860/5-6; *inf* h^{c}ḏb R3951/5

RENEW; REPAIR (cf ^{c}ḎB *v* sense[2])

R3945/1: h^{c}ḏb m^{c}šrt SB' "he renewed/reinaugurated the tribal assembly of the Sabaeans"; J542/2: h^{c}ḏb wkll kl ḥwdn "he repaired and completed the whole cistern"

st *ipf* yst^{c}ḏbhw C563/5; *inf* st^{c}ḏbn C326/1

PUNISH (cf ^{c}ḎB *v* sense[1])

C563/5: whoever breaks this law, wl yst^{c}ḏbhw "let him (?) punish him"

n^1 s ^{c}ḏb(m) C504/3+; p? ^{c}ḏbth C563/5

(1) EXPIATION, PUNISHMENT

C504/3: she dedicated this inscription ^{c}ḏbm bḏt... "in expiation, because..."; C563/5: 'rb^{c}m wś^{c}tn ǵwytm ^{c}ḏbth "fourfold (compensation) and a period of 'sin' are his punishments (?)"

(2) DYKED LAND

[Ar ^{c}aḏaba "restrain," ^{c}aḏib(ah) "the ridge of earth that surrounds a sown piece of ground to retain the water for irrigation"; here, land provided with such embankments (Irv/222).]

R3945/15: stmxḍ ^{c}ḏb Ẓ w^{c}ḏb Ḥ "he confiscated the dyked land of Ẓ. and the dyked land of Ḥ."

Obscure in R2747/2, context fragmentary

n^2 s? ^{c}ḏbt(m) R4388+

REPAIR

R4388 (in full): ...]^{c}ḏbt hḥḏṯ b[... "the repairs he made"; prob same exp in R4276/1, context fragmentary

^{c}ḎB II

st ipf yst^{c}ḏbn R4176/6*

MOVE FREELY, WANDER (?)

[Cf phps Heb ^{c}āzab "forsake, set free."]

R4176/6: a prohibition bn hwḍ'n 'śrm ḏyst^{c}ḏbn kḥrm "against driving out the herds that wander (?) (there), for they are sacred"

^{c}ḎR II

v inf ^{c}ḏrn C308/22+

HELP

[Heb ^{c}āzar id, Ar ^{c}aḏara "forgive."]

C308/22: some of the tribes set out on campaign l^{c}ḏrn b^{c}mhmw bhwt ḍrn "to help them in that war"

st pf st^{c}ḏrthw C568/4*

ASK FOR HELP or FORGIVENESS

[Cf Sab st^{c}n "ask for help," ^{c}nt "help."]

C568/4: she confessed bḏt st^{c}ḏrthw kyskr "because she had asked (the god) for help/pardon, that He might be appeased"

n s ^{c}ḏr(m) J740/12+; '^{c}ḏr C601/6+; '^{c}ḏrhw R4197b/2; '^{c}ḏrhmw R2695/2+; '^{c}ḏrhn F76/5-6

HELP, PROTECTION; in exp ḏ-'^{c}ḏr: THOSE (UNDER) S.O.'S PROTECTION (cf ḏ-'mnt sim) = PROTEGÉ(S), DEPENDENT(S)

F76/5-6: hnt 'nṯn..w'wldhn wḏ'^{c}ḏrhn "those women and their children and their dependents"; J740/12: may the god s^{c}dhmw wldm w^{c}ḏrm "grant them children and dependents (or, help?)"

^{c}ḎR II

n s m^{c}ḏrn Gl175+I130+I134/2*

GLACIS

[ModYem ma^{c}ḏar "small wall to protect fields" (RoVoc/309); ModḤaḍ id, "rock-hewn passage for waters in a dam"; and see the discussion in Hö3PW/40.]

Gl175+I130+I134/2: he dedicated mbny ṣ[lw]t m^{c}ḏrn "the construction of the front of the glacis"

^{c}HD I

v pf ^{c}hdy Gl533/5; inf ^{c}hd C376/1

MAKE A COVENANT, PLEDGE ONE'S SELF

[Ar ^{c}āhada id.]

Gl533/5: w^{c}hdy 'l[t] blṭn bmḥlym "both (treaty-partners) have pledged themselves regarding those blṭ (i.e., that sum of money) by oath";
C376/1: wśxly w^{c}hd H...wḤ "Now H. and Ḥ. bound themselves and covenanted";
sim ib/5

ti ipf y^{c}thdn J716/7*

TAKE CARE OF

[Ar ^{c}hd Dt id.]

J716/7: the god promised them ky^{c}thdn brwyhmw "that He would take care of his 2 sons"

n^{1} s ^{c}hdn C541/47*

CHARGE, COMMISSION

[Ar ^{c}ahd id.]

C541/47: after the dam broke, wṣḥhmw ḏn ^{c}hdn "this commission reached them"

n^{2} d m^{c}hdy J554; p? m^{c}hdt R4424

DEPUTY (?)

[Cf Ar ^{c}ahida "delegate, authorize."]

J554: X and Y, m^{c}hdy qyn 'LMQH b'WM "the 2 deputies of the administrator of (the god) I. in (the temple of) A."; R4424 (in full): ...] m^{c}hdt q[... "deputies of the ad[ministrator?]"

^{c}HD II

n s ^{c}hdtn J651/18*

RAIN AT THE BEGINNING OF SPRING

[Ar ^{c}a/ihda† id.]

J651/17-20: wḏnm ḏnmn bywm ts^{c}m ^{c}hdtn "and rain fell on the ninth day, a spring rain"

^{c}HR I

n s ^{c}hrn C67/3,13*

(FORTIFIED) TOWN

[Cf Sab ^{c}r id, root ^{c}RR; Heb ^{c}ir "town."]

C67/14: mslf ḏn ^{c}hrn "the glacis of this fortified town"; ib/3: [Ḥ] Q b^{c}l ^{c}hrn T[... "(the god) Ḥ.Q., lord of the town T."

^{c}HR II

n p ^{c}hrw C601/3+

PRINCES, CHIEFS (?)

[Sense from context. Cf phps Ar ^{c}āhil "sovereign, prince," Min ^{c}hr Jauss 19/3 syn of kbr (?).]

C601/3: ^{c}hrw FYŠN wNZḤT w'rb^{c}n w'ḥśrn wmśwdn bklythmw "the chiefs of (the clan) F. and the Outlanders and the clans and the indigents and the assembly in its entirety"; sim R3951/1

^{c}WD

v ipf y^{c}dw Ry533/12*

as aux, DO ULTIMATELY or AGAIN (?)

[Ar ^{c}āda "return, come back; do again." For use as aux cf BeJSS20/192, who quotes Ibn al-Dawādarī: ^{c}ādati l-Aḥsā'u madīnatu l-Baḥrayn "ultimately, al-A. became the capital of B."]

Ry533/12: wy^{c}dw [q]m^{c} QRYTNHN "ultimately (or, again) they subdued Q."

D pf ^{c}wdt C533/5; inf ^{c}wdnhw J643/9

CAUSE TO RETURN > sense[1]: BRING BACK

J643/9: ...]nkfm bn ^{c}wdnhw slmm "in good order from his bringing back peace"

sense[2]: REPULSE

C533/5: a man approached her sexually w^{c}wdt mr' "but she repulsed the man"

h pf h^{c}dhmw C541/39; h^{c}dw ib/51+

in exp h^{c}d yd: TAKE BACK, WITHDRAW one's HAND (from obedience) = REBEL

[Caus of ^{c}WD v in sense "go back." Cf Ar 'axraja yad, naza^{c}a yad min al-ṭā^{c}a^{t}, id.]

C541/51: klhmw h^{c}dw 'ydhmw wrhnhmw "all of them who had rebelled and (then) given pledges of obedience to them"; ib/79: the army they sent to fight them, wh^{c}dw 'ydhmw "they having rebelled"

n s ^{c}wdn C540/25+

SETTLING BASIN

[Discussion Irv/272-4. Phps place where water "returns" to purity?]

C540/25: ^{c}ḏbw ^{c}wdn ḏmbr'm wqyrn "they repaired the settling basin of (with?) masonry and large stones"; ib/62: ṯbr ^{c}glm[tn] wnmryn w^{c}wdn "the diversion moles, control wall and settling basin broke"

^{c}WK--for ^{c}tk, t^{c}tk see under ^{c}TK

^{c}WL

n s ^{c}lhmw C379/1*

FAMILY

[Ar ^{c}āla (w) "nourish," ^{c}ayyil "family (= those dependent on one for nourishment)," Šx ^{c}el = family."]

C379/1: R w^{c}lhmw bn S...hqny "R. and their family, the clan S., dedicated ..."

^{c}WM I

v pf ^{c}m Ry507/10*

PROCEED, MARCH

[Cf Ar ^{c}āma (w) "swim, sail; proceed (like a camel)" (RyMus66/294).]

Ry507/10: k^{c}m mlkn bM bn Ḥ "when (an army) marched against the king at M., from Ḥ."

^{c}WM II

n^1 s ^{c}wm C575/8*

YEAR

[Ar ^{c}ām, Eth ^{c}āmat id.]

C575/8: b^{c}wm 'ḥd "in one year" (context fragmentary)

n^2 s t^{c}m Ry416/3*

DURATION, LENGTH OF TIME; l-t^{c}m: FOREVER

Ry416/3: Y tḥbb ^{c}A lt^{c}m "Y. attests his love for A. forever"

n^3 d t^{c}mtn NNAG12/6*

ASTROLOGICAL or NOCTURNAL PERIOD

NNAG12/2: lḥrb byn t^{c}mtn "to fight (ritually) between 2 nocturnal (?) periods"

^{c}WN I

h pf h^{c}n J572/5+; h^{c}nhw J583/8+; h^{c}nhmw J750/10+; h^{c}nw J629/33+; ipf yh^{c}n C282/5; yh^{c}nnhmw J558/4+; yh^{c}nw J577/5; inf h^{c}n(n) J567/15-6+; hnn C535/8; h^{c}nnhw J587/12+; h^{c}nhmw C350/18; h^{c}nnhmw R4188/9-10+; h^{c}nhn Ir34

HELP, SAVE

[Ar ^{c}wn L and h "aid, support," Mh awîn "help."]

C82/6: he made an offering ldt h^{c}n wmt^{c}n 'LMQH ^{c}bdhw...bn zxnt zxn "because (the god) I. saved him from the wounds he suffered"; C350/18: wlh^{c}nhmw T'LB bn nḍ^{c} wšṣy šn'm "and may (the god) T. save them from the magic or evil eye of an enemy"; J750/12-3: wlh^{c}nnhmw 'LMQH bn l[xy]n "may (the god) I. save them from dispute"; J629/33: h^{c}nw whdrkn b^{c}d 'ḤḌR "they gave help and pursued the Ḥaḍramis"

st inf st^{c}nnhw J633/11*

ASK FOR HELP

[Ar ^{c}wn st id.]

J633/11: the god commanded him lst^{c}nnhw drm bxrfm "to ask Him for help once a year"

n^{1} s ^{c}nt(m,n) J670/11+; ^{c}nth[... R4969/5

(1) AID

J670/11: the god saved His servant wh'wl bnhw b^{c}ntm "and brought back his son by aid (which the god granted)"; R4969/5: ...] lysm^{c}n b^{c}nth[mw?... "let him (a god?) concern Himself with helping them (lit., with their aid)"

(2) AUXILIARY FORCE, AUXILIARY (MILITARY) OPERATION

J577/5: wyh^{c}nw b^{c}lyhmw dbn 'ḤBŠN...wyhdrkhmw ^{c}nt hmw 'ḤBŠN "and some of the Ḥabashites gave aid against them, and the auxiliary force of those Ḥabashites pursued them"; J635/20: kl 'brt wḍby' w^{c}nt sb'w "all the campaigns, battles and auxiliary operations they undertook"

n^{2} s m^{c}wnhmw C646/5* (h prt? or cf ^{c}WN II)

HELPER (?)

C646/5: ...m^{c}wnhmw hṣlḥ... "their helper (?) who made successful..." (fragmentary context)

^{c}WN II (?)

n s m^{c}nhw MüBilinguis/5*

DWELLING (cf mgwn sim, under GWN)

[Ar ma^{c}ān, Heb mā^{c}ôn id; cf MüBilinguis/122.]

MüBilinguis/5: wkd'l yknn lm^{c}nhw wmknt mlkn "and that it shall not happen to his dwelling and the king's cella"

Also in Gl593/5 (SchSEG7/48); phps in R4204 m^{c}w[n?], fragmentary.

^{c}WS

n s ^{c}ws(m) J645/13+

PLAGUE

[Sense chiefly from context, but cf ModYem ^{c}ws "dislocation, sprain," Ar ^{c}āsa (w) "wear one's self out (for the support of one's family)."]

J645/13: xwm w^{c}ws wmwtt "pestilence, plague and death"; C541/72: ḍllm w^{c}wsm "disease and plague"

^{c}WF I

n s ^{c}wfhmw J616/21*

PREY, BOOTY (?)

[Cf Ar ^{c}awf "prey, profit."]

J616/21-2: their army fought for booty whbryw ^{c}wfhmw "and 'liberated' their prey (?)"

^{c}WF II

n s ^{c}wfyn C575/11; p '^{c}wf NNAG11/32

FAMINE or PESTILENCE; or, EVIL OMEN (?)

[Ḍof ^{c}awf "famine, dearth"; cf Ar ^{c}awf "bird's-eye view"--connection with augury?--or ^{c}āfiya^{t} "health," phps a euphemism (MüW/83).]
C575/11 (context obscure): bn hwt ^{c}wfyn "from that famine (?)"; NNAG11/32: nḍ^{c} wšṣy wšft w'^{c}wf "magic and evil eye and adverse oracular decree and evil omens (or, famines) (?)"

^{c}WR I

n ^{c}rt C547/13*
(IN) EXCHANGE (FOR)
[Ar ^{c}wr L, h, Lt, st "lend; borrow."]
C547/13: may the god reward them with ṯwb yn^{c}m ^{c}rt tnxytn "a pleasing reward (in) exchange (for) this confession"

^{c}WR II

n s ^{c}rthw C548/17*
DEFECTIVENESS, FAULT (?)
[Ar ^{c}awra^{t} id.]
C548/17: after committing certain sacrilegious acts a man shall pay fines, but ^{c}rthw dmtn "his defectiveness (?) is permanent (?)"--but context is damaged and first word may be incomplete.

^{c}WR III

n s m^{c}rn Gl368/1*
TOMB (?)
[Cf Heb mə^{c}ārāh "cave (including cave used for burial)."]
Gl368/1: bny w^{c}sy m^{c}rn gwlm "he built and constructed the tomb (?) as (his own) property" (parallel contexts often with qbr)

^{c}ZZ

v pf/inf ^{c}zz R2865/1*
ESTABLISH, CONFIRM
[Ar ^{c}zz D id.]
R2865/1: hgdd w^{c}zz...hrwḥt trwḥ "he determined and established the enlargement (of boundaries) he had brought about"

h pf/inf h^{c}zz R4176/14*
ESTABLISH, CONFIRM (= ^{c}ZZ v)
R4176/14: hgddw wh^{c}zz mḥr ḥḥr "he determined and established the law he passed"

n s ^{c}ztm J559/12+
STRENGTH
[Ar ^{c}izza^{t} id.]
J559/12: may the god grant n^{c}mtm wwfym w^{c}ztm wbry ''ḏnm wmqmm "prosperity, health, strength, and soundness of mental and physical faculties"; sim

in C326/3 and J561/12

^{c}ZY

v pf ^{c}zhmw F55/6*

ASSIGN to s.o. AS PROPERTY

[Ar ^{c}azâ id (RyET/32), Min ^{c}z R3202/3.]

F55/6: ^{c}zhmw...wrqhmw "he has assigned to them their vegetables (?)"

^{c}ZL

v ipf [y]^{c}zln C126/12*

POSTPONE, SET ASIDE a period of time

[Ar ^{c}azala "set aside, separate."]

C126/12: wy]^{c}zln sb^{c}t ywm[t] ln (d) ymwtn dymw[t]n "let seven days be set aside before the one who is to die dies" after committing an offense

h pf? h^{c}zl J516/7; inf [^{c}]zln R4178/[1]

REMOVE

R4178/1: w'l śn h^{c}]zln whr'šn bn ṣrf "it is not lawful to remove or take away any of the ṣrf-incense"; also in J516/7 in fragmentary context.

n ^{c}zly, C541/4-5--see under ^{c}LY ti

^{c}ZM--inf or n in J763/3: wl^{c}zm w[...; context too fragmentary for tr

^{c}ṬW--y^{c}ṭnn R4176/1--see under ^{c}ṬN

^{c}ṬN

v ipf y^{c}ṭnn R4176/1*

NEGLECT, ABSTAIN (bn from)

[Cf Ar ^{c}aṭṭala id. The form has also been compared, less satisfactorily, with Ar ^{c}ṭy L "give."]

R4176/1: lkd 'l y^{c}ṭnn S bd'A bn hḥḍrn 'LMQH ^{c}dy M "that (the tribe) S. shall not neglect in (the month) dA. to present themselves before (the god) I. in (the city) M."

^{c}ṬF

n^{1} s ^{c}ṭf R3956/3*

MANTLE

[Ar ^{c}iṭāf "coat, cloak."]

R3956/3: lbst ^{c}ṭf ṭm'm wgzztm "she wore a dirty, torn mantle"

n^{2} p? ^{c}ṭwfhn J735/9*

(AT THE) SIDE (OF)

[Ar ^{c}iṭf "side (of the body)."]

J735/9: the sorceresses gave pledges of submission w'ntn ^{c}ṭwfhn "the (other) women being at their side"

^{c}ẒM

D? inf ^{c}ẓm C318/6*

ENLARGE (?)

[Ar ^{c}ẓm D id.]

C318/6: 'l 's s'l w^{c}ẓm xdrn "let no one lay claim to or enlarge (?) this tomb (to add more occupants?)"

^{c}ẒN

v pf ^{c}ẓn Ir32/3*

SEND A CALL FOR, SUMMON

[Sense from context.]

Ir32/3: mẓ't ^{c}brhmw ^{c}ẓtm wṭbytm ^{c}ẓn mr'hmw "the summons and appeal (which) their lord sent reached them"

n s ^{c}ẓtm C541/56+

COMMAND, SUMMONS

C541/56: mlkn dky ^{c}ẓtm ^{c}ly 'š^{c}bn "the king sent a command concerning the tribes"; Ir32/3 quoted under ^{c}ẒN v

^{c}ẒT, n--see under ^{c}ẒN

^{c}YD--for ns m^{c}d, m^{c}dt see under W^{c}D

^{c}YY

h pf [h]^{c}yw J750/6*

LAG BEHIND

[Ar a^{c}yā "he was fatigued, tired or wearied in walking"; a^{c}yā bihi ba^{c}īruhu "his camel became jaded and lagged behind with him."]

J750/6: he made a journey without the god's permission ^{c}[dy dh]^{c}yw bmsb'n "so that they lagged behind on the road"; cf also ...]h^{c}y[... F108, isolated in fragmentary context

^{c}YL--for ^{c}ylt R3958/10, epithet of the goddess ŠMS, read ^{c}lyt "the High" (see under ^{c}LY)

^{c}YN

h ipf yh^{c}ynn C464/4*

TURN ONE'S SELF TOWARDS

[Cf Ar ^{c}yn L "face towards, survey" (BeOracle/222).]

C464/4: yh^{c}ynn...^{c}ynm wbdlh šlṯ '^{c}ynm "let him turn himself toward (the altar) one turning, and then three turnings"; cf also ...]h^{c}y[... F108, isolated in fragmentary context

n^1 s ^{c}ynm C464/4; p '^{c}ynm ib

ACT OF TURNING, FACING

C464/4 quoted under ^{c}YN h

n^2 s ^{c}ynm C612/2; ^{c}ynhw J706/7; p '^{c}ynn J665/28

(1) EYE

[Ar ^{c}ayn "eye; spring of water."]

J706/7: dedicant thanks the god for helping 'mthw N bn mrḍ mrḍt ^{c}ynhw "from the disease (which) her eye suffered"

(2) SPRING OF WATER

J665/28: ḥrbw bsfl '^{c}ynn X "they fought in the lowlands of the springs of X."; C612/2: wḏyfdnhw wysḍ^{c}n ^{c}ynm "and whoever continues to neglect the spring (?)"--context obscure

^{c}YR I

v inf ^{c}yr J644/10+

INSULT (?), BRING DISGRACE UPON

[Mh awêr "wound, injure," cf Ar ^{c}wr D "make one-eyed," Ar.Eth ^{c}ayyara "reproach, insult."]

J644/10: they dedicated because tškrw w^{c}yr hw' 'ysn wš^{c}bn "that fellow and (his) tribe were defeated and disgraced"; DJE10/4: fl ylṣqnn w^{c}yr kl 'ns yxṭ'n bḏt mqb[rtn] "let them harrass and bring disgrace upon every man who commits a fault in this cemetery"

^{c}YR II

n s ^{c}rn RyGraf/p561*

CARAVAN

[Ar ^{c}īr id.]

RyGraf/p561: hdy ^{c}rn ymnytn wš'mytn "he guided the caravan (to) southern and northern parts"

For ^{c}r elsewhere, see ^{c}WR and ^{c}RR

^{c}YŠ

n s ^{c}št(n) C548/10+

(1) WAY OF LIFE > COMMUNITY

[Ar ^{c}āša (y) "live." ^{c}īša^{t} "way of life."]

C548/10: wḏkr ntš ^{c}št mḥrmn "whoever repeats (the offense) must leave the community of the sanctuary"

(2) FOOD, PROVISIONS, PRODUCE

[Ar ^{c}ayš "nourishment," Mh áyś "food."]

Sh18/2: w^{c}štn b'mṭrn "and the produce of (lit., in) the fields"; F63/2: sqy ^{c}št 'LMQH "irrigated the produce of (the god) I."

^{c}KR

v pf ^{c}kr C376/15+; ^{c}krw C609/6; ipf y^{c}krn Robin al-Mašamayn/9; inf ^{c}krn R3197/3

CONTRADICT, RAISE OBJECTIONS

[Ar ^{c}kr id, ti "show opposition, hostility."]
C376/15: they acknowledged (the debt of) this sum, 'hnn ^{c}kr "when/wherever it may be denied"; R3560 (in full): ^{c}kr lyr[dn] wyf^{c} h' [^{c}]lm "(For anyone who) raises objection, let this document be set down (?) and recorded"

Note: Another sense in C581/9? khmy ^{c}kr wš'm hyt [ṣ]lmtn

ti ipf y^{c}tkrnn G1574/17*

ACT IN A HOSTILE MANNER

[Ar ^{c}kr ti id.]
G1574/17: ^{c}tlhw wstml'n b^{c}mhw bkl dy^{c}tkrnn "besieging (the god) (with prayers) and beseeching Him against all who act with hostility"

^{c}KŚ

n s t^{c}kś C405/15* (D inf?)

UNHAPPINESS, TROUBLE

[Ar ^{c}ks D "render unhappy."]
C405/15: mr]dn wt^{c}kś wnḍ[^{c}] "disease and trouble and (harmful) magic"

^{c}LB I

n p '^{c}lb R3958/4+

^{c}ILB-TREES, POANTATIONS OF ^{c}ILB-TREES

[A well-known southern Arabian tree, Zizyphus (or rhamnus) spina Christi, providing shade, fodder, and timber (cf, e.g., Lane/2126B).]
R3958/4: bql w'^{c}lb w'bwn "vegetable gardens and plantations of ^{c}ilb- and ban-trees"

^{c}LB II?

n s/coll ^{c}lb(m,n) R2865/3+; p '^{c}lb R4085/2+

ARTIFICIALLY IRRIGATED LAND, contrasted with ^{c}md, q.v.

[Cf Ar ^{c}alaba "it was, or became, hard, or firm," ^{c}alb "a rugged and hard place of the earth, which, if rained upon for a long time, will not give growth to any green thing"--such land, to be fertile, must be artificially irrigated. Discussion Irv/211-2.]
R4085/2: ṣyḥ wtbqlt '^{c}md w'^{c}lb "leveled and planted land, naturally and artificially irrigated"; R2865/3: ^{c}md w^{c}lbm w'l htmr "naturally and artificially irrigated land, and (all) that produces crops"

Note: ^{c}lb in R4176/7 is prob n.pr, cf BeSI/80. For another derivation of ^{c}LB II, cf BeNL8/446-7: the type of arable plot called ^{c}lb may derive its name from ^{c}ilb-trees [^{c}LB I] which shade it.

^{c}LW

pp ^{c}lwhw C325/8; b-^{c}lwhw J643/29

ABOVE; AGAINST (cf ^{c}ly, pp)

[Cf the frequent Sab ^{c}ly; ^{c}lw is more common in Qat.]

C325/8: ṯlṯt flśtm ^{c}lwhw "three tops of columns above it"; J643/29: 'tmn b^{c}lwhw mṣrnhn "the 2 forces coming to an agreement against him"

n ^{c}lwm C325/6

as adv: ABOVE

C325/6: 'rb^{c}t flśtm ^{c}lwm "four tops of columns, above"

^{c}LY

v ipf (y)^{c}l R2861/[11]; y^{c}ly ib/24

(1) BE HIGH, PRE-EMINENT (?)

[Ar ^{c}alâ id.]

R2861/[11]: fḏ[š']m l(y)^{c}l qwm[m w]dwrm "and whoever was appointed to be pre-eminent (? over) peoples and groups..." (R emends from w^{c}l)

(2) EXACT, IMPOSE taxes or the like (?)

[Ar ^{c}ly L id.]

R2861/24: wly^{c}ly bn nx[thw] "to impose (? taxes) from his assets (?)"

Note: Both contexts of this verb are dubious.

N ipf tn^{c}ly R4829A/2*

BE EXALTED (of a deity)

[Cf Heb na^{c}ăleh id, Ps 47:10, 97:9.]

R4829A/2: ^{c}ZYN...ltn^{c}ly "(the goddess) ^{c}Uzzay, may She be exalted!"

ti pf ^{c}tly C541/4-5*

as royal epithet: HIGHNESS

[G read ^{c}zly, F ^{c}tly. Cf Ar ^{c}ly ti "be enthroned, exalted"; for use as a title, cf Ar jalāla^{t} al-malik "His Majesty the king," and ta^{c}ālâ (tp pf), epithet of Allah.]

C541/4-5: ['BR]H ^{c}tly mlkn 'G^{c}ZYN "A., His Highness the king of the Ethiopians"

tp pf t^{c}ly J540/2+; t^{c}lyhw C596/3

BE VIOLATED (a boundary) = BE CARRIED AWAY (a boundary stone)

[Cf etym under ^{c}LY h.]

J540/2: w'l t^{c}ly l'wṯnh "and let not its boundaries be violated"; J541/6: w'l t^{c}ly wkwn lhḏkwt 'ln 'wṯnn "let not these boundaries be violated, and let them be established"; in damaged contexts C596/3,8 (transitive use?) R4158/10

Note: J tr the phrase 'l t^{c}ly as "(the god) 'Il, the Most High" after Ar Allah ta^{c}ālâ "God, may He be exalted." This interpretation is discussed and rejected in LuMus76/207-9, on the basis of parallels with ^{c}LY h, q.v.

h pf h^{c}ly NNAG4/5+; h^{c}lyt R4627/4

BE VIOLATED, INFRINGED UPON (a boundary, rights of ownership)

[Eth ^{c}alawa "transgress, break (a law)" (Irv/45-7).]

NNAG4/5: w'l h^{c}ly dn 'tbn "let not this boundary be violated";

R4627/4: w'l h^{c}lyt dt ḥrtn dR "let not this canal belonging to (the tribe) R. be infringed upon"

pp[1] ^{c}l C69/2+; ^{c}l-m C548/9; ^{c}l-n R4176/13+; ^{c}lnhmw Ir14/4; ^{c}ly J649/17+; ^{c}lyhmy C376/13; ^{c}lyhmw J620/6+ (for b-^{c}ly pp see next item)

(1) ON, UPON, ABOVE

[Ar ^{c}alâ "on, over > to the detriment/benefit of > according to, on the basis of." Cf also Heb ^{c}al, Eth la^{c}la.]

R3945/10: cities 'lt ^{c}ly bḥrm "which are on the sea (i.e., on high land overlooking the sea)"

(2) INCUMBENT UPON

C599/2: bn w^{c}ln š^{c}bhmw "(that which is) obligatory for and incumbent upon their tribe"; R3951/4: bn ^{c}ly mśwd "incumbent upon the assembly"

(3) CONCERNING; exp TO THE DETRIMENT OF, AGAINST

R3957/7: gzm sw' dS ^{c}ly ršdh "(the god) dS. decided adversely concerning/against her conduct"; J620/6: ''rx nhk ^{c}lyhmw šn'n "troubles the enemy inflicted to their detriment"; C376/13: a document of indebtedness, śxlm [wnfqm] ^{c}lyhmy "effective (and binding) against them"; C548/9: w^{c}lm bd'n lywfyn ẓl^{c}m "and concerning the first occasion (of sin), let him pay a fine"

(3a) FOR THE BENEFIT OF (?)--but see Note

J601/17-8: wl'xrn 'LMQH ^{c}ln 'dmhw...b'stm "and may (the god) I. repel harm for the benefit of His servants"

Note: Tr phps "keep away harm (from) upon His servants." Or cf the prepositional uses of ^{c}ln quoted under ^{c}LL I.

(4) ACCORDING TO

R4176/13: ^{c}ln ḥgr T'LB "according to the sacred disposition of (the god) T."

pp[2] b-^{c}lhmw R3945/3+; b-^{c}ly J550/2+; b-^{c}lyhw C352/5+; b^{c}lyhmw J575/6+

(1) ABOVE, UPON, TOWARD (cf senses of ^{c}ly pp)

[Cf ^{c}ly pp.]

R4196/2: they built their cisterns b^{c}ly wynhmw "above (=further up the hillside than) their vineyard"; R3945/3: he doubled their tribute wbḍ^{c} b^{c}lyhmw "and imposed a (new) tribute upon them"; J576/8: yt'wlw b^{c}ly hgrn "they returned toward the city"

(1a) IN ADDITION TO, "ON TOP OF"

Ir10: he offered a statue wb^{c}lyhw kbtm "and in addition a cup"

(2) FOR THE SAKE OF (= ON THE SIDE OF? AGAINST?--see Note)

J635/10: the campaigns and battles they undertook and fought b^{c}ly kl 'xms wš^{c}b tn̮š'w ḍrm b^{c}ly mr'hmw "for the sake of (against?) all the armies and tribes who initiated war for the sake of (against?) their lord" AND OFTEN SIM

Note: In contexts describing wars, b^{c}ly is often ambiguous, like

English "with": "he fought with the tribes" = "for" them or "against" them? As in English, the sense must be determined from context in individual instances. The tr "against" seems preferable in most cases, and is sometimes clearly indicated, as in J574/5: yḍb'...mlk SB'...b^{c}ly 'ḥzb ḤBŠT "the king of S. fought against the warbands of Ḥabashat."

(3) UNDER THE AUTHORITY OF (?)

R4781/3: a palmgrove b^{c}ly ['']xhw "under the authority of (? =owned by?) his brother"

(4) DURING (?)

[Cf Ar ^{c}alâ ^{c}ahdihi "in its time" (BeOr25/297).]

Ry507/6: ḏ^{c}syw b^{c}ly msb'hmw "which they did during (?) their campaign"

Note: For the expression b^{c}br wb^{c}ly "obligatory for and incumbent upon" (cf sense^1 above), see examples quoted under ^{c}BR.

n^1 s ^{c}lyt R3958/10 (f.adj)*

(THE) HIGH, EXALTED (ONE) (epithet of a goddess)

[Ar ^{c}alī, f ^{c}aliyya^t id.]

R3958/10: ŠMS ^{c}lyt "(the goddess) Š., the Exalted One"

n^2 s ^{c}lyhw R3958/5+; ^{c}lyhmw R3966/10; p ^{c}lt(m) J585/14+; ^{c}lthmw C67/18

(1) HIGH(ER) PART

R5085/7: they built it bn ^{c}lyhw ^{c}dy sflhw "from its higher part to its lower part"

(2) HIGHLAND(S)

J585/14: ^{c}ltm wsfylt bḥrm wybsm "highlands and lowlands of sea(coast?) and (dry) land"; C67/18: all their territory, ^{c}rqhmw w^{c}lthmw "their lowland(s) and their highland(s)"

Note also J560/3: w^{c}lt 'A "and the highlands of A."--J took from root W^{c}L.

n^3 s ^{c}l[y]n C539/3*

BURNT OFFERING (?)

[Heb ^{c}ôlāh id.]

C539/3: šym ^{c}l[y]n wbšrn "he arranged for a burnt offering and a flesh offering"

n^4 s m^{c}lhw Gl100/2*

HIGH(ER) PART (cf ^{c}ly n^2 above)

[Ar mu^{c}āl^{in} id.]

Gl100/2: the irrigation of nxlhw M wm^{c}lhw "his palmgrove M. and its higher part"

n^5 s? mh^{c}ltm R4672A*

UPPER PART, UPPER STORY of a building (?) (cf m^{c}l n^4 above)

R4672A (in full): ...]m mh^{c}ltm "..., an upper story (?)"--part of a building inscription?

^{c}LL I

h inf h^{c}lln Ir13/12*

aux: CONTINUE TO DO

[Ar ^{c}alla "do something a second time."]

Ir13/12: xmr whwš^{c}n wh^{c}lln ^{c}bdhw...mhrgt "(the god) granted and bestowed and continued (to grant) to His servant slaughters..."

pp ^{c}ln J619/7-8; ^{c}ln ḏ- J702/14-5

BECAUSE OF

[Cf Ar ^{c}illa^{+} "cause" (cf RycMancie/265,269).]

J619/7-8: bn dqt wdq ^{c}ln 'blhw "from a fall which he took because of (?) his camel" (or, if from ^{c}ly pp "on," tr phps "a fall he took (from) on his camel"); J702/14-5: ^{c}ln ḏśf ḏwkb wh' fl śyf ḥwlm "because he has given (the god) what he obtained, may He give a dream..."; phps also in J601/17-8, quoted under ^{c}ly pp sense 3a

^{c}LL II

n s ^{c}ln Ir29/2+

NAME OF A SEASON and A MONTH

[ModYem ^{c}Allān "rainy season, September" (RycMus88/206n10; BeNewL/2-3).]

Ir29/2: n'd qyẓ wṣrb w^{c}ln "products of summer, autumn, and ^{c}ln"; unpub text quoted by Be: [wrxh]w ^{c}LN ḏbxrfn ḏlxmst w[... "(published in the month) A. in the year five..."

^{c}LL III

n s ^{c}ll C351/9*

DISEASE

[Ar ^{c}alla "be sick," ^{c}illa^{+} "disease."]

C351/9: ^{c}ll rglyh[w] "disease of his feet" (parallels have mrḍ)

^{c}LM I

v pf ^{c}lm R4772/3?; ^{c}lmy G1533/8+; ^{c}lmw F3/9

SIGN > ACKNOWLEDGE, RECOGNIZE

[Cf Ar ^{c}lm D "make a mark," tp "inform one's self, take notice."]

F3/9: ^{c}lmw ḏḤ lywfyn "(the clan) Ḥ. signed so that (the document) might be valid"; G1533/8: w^{c}lmy bhw s[']lm "they acknowledged it as a debt/obligation"

tp pf t^{c}lm C74/16+; t^{c}lmy F30/4+; ipf yt^{c}lmn C609/3; yt^{c}lmnn C435/1,2; inf t^{c}lmn Ir27

(1) TAKE COGNIZANCE OF, RECOGNIZE an obligation (cf ^{c}LM v)

F30/4: ^{c}lm wšnqt ḏbhw t^{c}lmy "the document/acknowledgment of debt which they recognized"; Ir27: ḏšft wt^{c}lmn 'A kyhqnynhw "which A. promised and recognized as an obligation to dedicate to (the god)"

(2) INSTRUCT by means of oracular "signs"

[Cf Ar ^{c}lm D "teach."]

C74/16-7: yhwfyn bḥg ^{c}lm bhw t^{c}lm "let (the god) protect (him) according to the oracular sign by which he was instructed" n s ^{c}lm J700/15+; ^{c}lmhw R2876/3; var ^{c}lmnhw C609/5,7

(1) MARK indicating blood guilt

[Ar ^{c}alam "mark, badge."]

J700/15: sbt yd S b^{c}lm R "the hand of S. was marked with the sign of (his victim) R."

(2) DOCUMENT, WRITTEN ACKNOWLEDGMENT

F30/4 quoted under ^{c}lm tp; R2876/3: š'mthw w'ṯwbthw w^{c}lmhw wṯq[t]hw "its purchase deed, payment, written acknowledgment, and guarantee"

(3) ORACULAR SIGN from a deity

C74/16-7 quoted under ^{c}LM tp sense^{2}

^{c}LM II

n s ^{c}lm(n) C539/2+

WORLD

[Ar ^{c}alām id.]

C539/2: b^{c}lmn b^{c}dn wqrbn "in the world, far and near"; Ry508/11: wtrḥm ^{c}ly kl ^{c}lm RḤMNN "May (the god) R. show compassion to the whole world (?)"

^{c}LN I

v? pf ^{c}ln Gl446/2*

OPPRESS (?)

[Ar ^{c}ln id (TsSEG6/17).]

Gl446/2-3 (context obscure): N b'ḥd ^{c}ln ḏ/nwb 'ḥd ^{c}ln N,no tr--cf phps ^{c}ln ḏ- "because of," under ^{c}LL I.

^{c}LN II

h ipf yh^{c}lnn Ry507/6*

NOTIFY, BRING S.O.'S ATTENTION TO (but see Note)

[Ar ^{c}ln h id (RyMus66/291-2).]

Ry507/6: in 2 missions to N. lyh^{c}lnn bnhmw rhnm "to bring its attention to a pledge from them"

Note: Read phps ys'lnn "ask for."

n as adj, m.p. ^{c}lnyn R4818/5*

NOTABLE

[Ar ^{c}ln L "indicate, make known."]

R4818/5: may the god grant them ['wld]m '(ḥ)rrm 'ḏkrwm ^{c}lnyn "freeborn, male, notable children"

^{c}LṢ I

n s m^{c}lṣ(n) C197/5+

BATTLE

[Cf Ar ^{c}lṣ L "wrestle, struggle with s.o." (HaAED/486).]

C197/5: s^{c}dhw m^{c}lṣ ṣdqm "(the god) granted him a satisfying battle";

C352/7: the god allowed him 'tw bwfym bn m^{c}lṣn "to come back safely from the battle"

^{c}LṢ II

n s m^{c}lṣhw C408/5; p m^{c}lṣtn ib/11-2

WHEATFIELD

[Ar.Eth ^{c}alas "kind of wheat," here with s > ṣ in the vicinity of ^{c}]

C408/5-12: ...]d̲n t̲wrn wm^{c}lṣhw[...] xmr...hyhr wfr^{c} bm^{c}lṣtn "this bull, and his wheatfield (description of offering?)...(the god) granted (him) hyhr-grain and crops from the wheatfields"

^{c}M

pp ^{c}m(n) C609/7+; ^{c}mnhmw Ir12/3; b-^{c}m(n) R4727/5+; b-^{c}mhw J560/6+; b-^{c}mhmy J629/9; b-^{c}mhmw R4727/5+

(1) IN ASSOCIATION WITH

[Cf Heb ^{c}im "with." Discussion BeDGESA/51:6.]

R4727/5: 'sd b^{c}mhmw "those who are in association with them"; J700/9: bnhw ^{c}mn 'shw "her son by her husband"; R4782/3: lyt̲bn b^{c}m š^{c}bn "to return to (association with) the tribe (after paying a fine)"

(2) in military contexts, AGAINST

C350/7: tqdmw b^{c}m ḤBŠT "they made an attack against Habashat" AND OFTEN SIM

(3) in buying, FROM; regarding a deity, FROM WITH = AUTHORIZED BY

C37/5: d̲qny w^{c}sy ^{c}mn 'A "which he acquired and bought from A."; C609/7: š'mtn ^{c}mn kl 'l'ltn "a contract of sale authorized by all the gods"; C88/8: stml' b^{c}mhw "to seek an oracular response authorized by (the god)" AND OFTEN SIM; R4085/5: he built ^{c}mnhw [w]bydhw "on his own authority (?) and at his own expense (?)"

Note: Obscure in C581/7: b^{c}mn 'sm "(in association) with (?) a man."

^{c}MD I

pp b-^{c}md R4176/2*

in exp b-^{c}md ^{c}dy: STRAIGHT TO, DIRECTLY TO

[Ar ^{c}amada 'ilâ "he intended it, he directed himself, or his course...to it" (Lane/2151A).]

R4176/2: srn nsrn N b^{c}md ^{c}dy R "the valley towards N, directly to R."

^{c}MD II

n s ^{c}md R2865/3; p '^{c}md(m,n) R4085/2+

NATURALLY IRRIGATED LAND (contrasted with ^{c}lb, q.v.)

[Ar ^{c}amada "it became moistened by rain and compacted, layer upon layer (of earth)," ^{c}amid "earth moistened by rain" (Irv/211-2).]

R4085/2: ṣyḥ wtbqlt '^{c}md w'^{c}lb "leveled and planted land, naturally and artificially irrigated"; J735/7: mwt d̲bn '^{c}mdn bn ṣm'm "some of the naturally irrigated lands have died from drought"

^{c}MD III

n^1 p '^{c}mdm J577/15+

VINE- PROPS, as a measure of plundered territory

[Cf Ar ^{c}amūd (albi'r) "one of the two posts supporting the bucket-rope of a well." Ryc, in BeNL8/446, rejects the tr "naturally irrigated field" (^{c}MD II) here because of the large numbers of '^{c}md cited.]

J577/15: ygbḏ[w...s]ṯy ''lfm '^{c}mdm "they plundered sixty thousand vine-props"

n^2 s ^{c}mdm GI572/3+

KIND OF DEED or DOCUMENT

[Ar ^{c}amada "support, sustain"--deed establishing an endowment? (Cf HöSEG 8/36).]

GI572/3: he ceded all the profit by virtue of sm[^{c}]m ḏ^{c}mdm "an ^{c}md-deed"; F30b/2: ẓhrm ḏ^{c}mdm "an ^{c}md-document"

^{c}MHN, J722/a--in fragmentary context, phps incomplete: ...]^{c}mhn 'LMQH [.] (b')xmsm... "...? (the god) I....with the armies (?)"

^{c}MY

tp ipf yt^{c}myn C542/2*

MAKE PUBLIC (or, BE PUBLISHED)

[Root ^{c}MY doublet of ^{c}MM, q.v.? (Irv/131).]

C542/2: tbšrt ḏbhw yt^{c}myn w[y]^{c}nw(n) "an oracular response which will be made public and attended to"

^{c}ML

v pf ^{c}ml J527/2*

WORK land

[Ar ^{c}amila id.]

J527/2: ^{c}ml bmḥgr ṣyḥ "he worked in the enclosed land (which) he had leveled"

Note: Regarding ^{c}ml in Ry507/6, RyMus66/291 tr "vicinity," cfing Ar ^{c}aml "land, province." But the m, written on its side, probably marks the middle of the inscription and should be ignored: Ry507/6: ḏky ṯny b^c[m]ly N "two missions to (the city) N."

^{c}MM I

n s ^{c}mhw Sh22; p '^{c}mmhw C37/6; '^{c}mmhmw R4018/2

PATERNAL UNCLE

[Ar ^{c}amm id.]

C37/6: 'bhhw w'^{c}mmhw "his fathers and his fathers' brothers (i.e., his ancestors and paternal relatives?)"; Sh22: N w^{c}mhw Y mlky SB' "N. and his paternal uncle Y., the 2 kings of S."

^{c}MM II

h inf h^{c}mmn J627/10+; prt mh^{c}mm Ir24/2; var mh^{c}mmn Ir22/1

CAUSE TO SPREAD OUT (irrigation waters); prt: AMPLE

[Ar ^{c}amma "spread."]

J627/10: the god promised kysqyn whšfqn wh^{c}mmn m'xḏhmw "that their control dam would irrigate and make (water) abundant and spread (it) out"; same formula J628/11-2; Ir22/1: ḏnm w'ḏ^{c}bn mhšfqn wmh^{c}mmn "rains and floods, abundant and ample"; Ir24/2: mhšfqm wmh^{c}mm "abundant and ample"

n^{1} s ^{c}mthmw C562/3*

PEOPLE

[Ar ^{c}āmma^{t} "the people, the masses."]

C562/3: [Ik]brhmw w^{c}mthmw wṯkmthmw "for their kabir, people and subjects"

n^{2} s t^{c}mm R4514/1-2+ (D inf?)

PUBLICATION, ANNOUNCEMENT

[Ar ^{c}mm D "make public." Irv/60-61 tr "(for) public usage."]

R4514/1-2: mšr^{c}m bt(^{c})mm bwṯn "Regulation regarding announcement of the boundary"; C949/1-2 sim: mšr^{c}m bt^{c}mm bt^{c}br wṯnn "Regulation regarding announcement of the delimitation of this boundary"

^{c}MQ

n s ^{c}mqn Ry340/6+; p ^{c}mqt N49/1

(CULTIVATED) VALLEY

[Ar ^{c}amuqa "be deep," Heb ^{c}ēmeq "valley," Šx ^{c}enqot "enter the valley," Sq ^{c}amiqoh "graze."]

N49/1: b^{c}mqt wbytm bhgrn "in the valleys and settlements in (i.e., belonging to) the city"; Ry340/6: bsr ^{c}mqn "on the slope/side of the valley" (same exp R5085/6)

^{c}MR

n p/coll? ^{c}mrh R4230A/3*

(a) COLONISTS, or (b) A CERTAIN BUILDING

[Ar ^{c}amara "live long, inhabit." (a) BeSI/86 quotes Rh: "Ar ma^{c}mar is explained as a place with much water and pasturage...the verb ^{c}mr may best be translated 'colonise.'" (b) Cf Ar ^{c}imāra^{t} "building, edifice."]

R4230A/3 (on an incense altar): bym kwn ^{c}qbm bbt bn Ṯ ḏS w^{c}mrh "when he acted as steward in the house of (the clan) Ṯ., of (the city) S. and its colonists/^{c}mr-building (?)"

n^{2} s m^{c}mr R3966/3*

TOMB

[From root sense "live long, inhabit" > "place of long abiding, tomb." Esp common in Qat "memorial monument (in a cemetery);" discussion RycMus 66/360-64.]

R3966/3: they restored and prepared for use m^{c}mr mwlgm "the tomb of mwlg-stone"

^{c}N

pp ^{c}nhw J570/6*

AWAY FROM

[Šx ^{c}an id (MüRev/105B).]

J570/6: ...] wǵwy ^{c}nhw "and he went away from him" (context fragmentary)

Note: For ^{c}n elsewhere see under ^{c}WN.

^{c}NB

n p '^{c}nbn C604/3; '^{c}nbhmw J620/12+

VINEYARD

[Cf Ar ^{c}inab "grapes."]

J620/12: harvests from '^{c}nbhmw w^{c}brthmw "their vineyards and meadows";
G1441/3: '^{c}nbhmw wḥblthmw "their vineyards and vines"

^{c}ND

n s? ^{c}ndm R3902b#133; ^{c}ndhmw R4638/1

obscure in both contexts

R3902b#133 (in full): ...q w^{c}ndm w...[b^{c}]TTR wb 'L[MQH...; R4638/1: ...FM qwl Y ^{c}ndhmw "..., chieftain of Y., ...?"

Note: In R4638 ^{c}NDHMW may be n.pr as in R4555.

^{c}NW I

v pf ^{c}nw C523/9+; ^{c}nwt R3957/8-9; inf ^{c}nw C568/7+

BE HUMBLE, ABASE ONE'S SELF

[Ar ^{c}anā "be humble, lowly."]

R3957/8-9: she confessed fhḍr^{c}t w^{c}nwt wxṭ't "and submitted herself and abased herself and made a sin-offering"

^{c}NW II

v ipf [y]^{c}nwn C542/2*

ATTEND TO

[Ar ^{c}aniya "take trouble about." ti "take pains to, take charge of" (Irv/131). Cf also ^{c}NY v.]

C542/2: tbšrt dbhw yt^{c}myn w[y]^{c}nw(n) "an oracular response which will be made public and be attended to"

^{c}NZ

n p/coll ^{c}nzm Ry508/6*

GOATS

[Heb ^{c}ēz, Ar ^{c}anza^{+} "goat."]

Ry508/6: ''blm wbqrm w^{c}nzm "camels, cattle and goats"

^{c}NY

v pf ^{c}ny R3162/1*

sense doubtful

[Cf phps Ar ^{c}aniya "take trouble about," ^{c}anâ "have in mind," ti "take care of, worry about" (as in Qat and Min); Sab ^{c}NW v "attend to."]

R3162 (in full): w^{c}ny t^{c}nthmw...'ydwhmw w...bn ṣby wbn... "he ...ed their ...; ...their hands and...from an impurity (?) and from..."

n s t^{c}nthmw R3162/1*

sense doubtful

R3162/1 quoted under ^{c}NY v

^{c}NMWM--n.pr? R5048, to the left of the torso of an engraved human figure (the word YMṢ on the right)

^{c}NN

v pf ^{c}nn C542/7*

MANIFEST ONE'S SELF (of a deity)

[Cf Ar ^{c}anna "appear to s.o."; Heb ^{c}ônēn "cause to appear," used esp of divination and raising of spirits (Irv/107-8).]

C542/7: [bR]ḤMNN dbsmyn hn ^{c}nn "by (the god) R. who is in heaven, when He manifests himself"

^{c}NT--n ^{c}nt, see under ^{c}WN; n t^{c}nt, see under ^{c}NY

^{c}S'

v pf ^{c}s' R4088/4+; ^{c}s't DJE10/1; ^{c}s'y R4626/1+; ^{c}s'w R4627/2+

MAKE, CONSTRUCT

[Prob a simple doublet of ^{c}SY, q.v. Some authors, notably HöWZ43/88-9, tr specifically "make in stone, hew from stone," chiefly from contexts. He cites Ar 'a^{c}sā' "hard [hollows, or cavities, in stone, or in rugged ground, that retain the water of the rain]" (Lane/2048A), but Lane assigns this to the root ^{c}SW "be thick, coarse, or rough" (the ' is not radical).]

R4627/2: ^{c}s'w wbny whwtr wšqr ḥrtn "they constructed, built, laid the foundations of and completed the aqueduct"; C20/2: ^{c}s'w wnqz mqbrhm "they made and dug out their tomb"; R4085/4: br' w^{c}s'...'rb^{c}t 'hlm "he built and constructed four cisterns"

h pf h^{c}s' R3967/1; inf h^{c}s'n R4714

CAUSE TO BUILD/BE BUILT (?)

R3967/1: h^{c}s' m'xdhmw "he caused their control-dyke to be built"; R4714: bnyy wh^{c}s'n dqnn "they built and caused to be built (?) the oratory"

n s m^{c}s' R4127/2+

CONSTRUCTION, BUILDING

R4127/2: they dedicated kl m^{c}s' wmbn "all the construction and building";

R4630: m^{c}s'...d̲^{c}s' lhw "the building which he made for himself"; R4085/3: ln ǵylm ^{c}dy šqrm m^{c}s' blqm "from the foundation to the roof, a construction of blq-stone"

^{c}SY

v pf ^{c}sy R3954/1+; ^{c}syy R3994/1-2; ^{c}syw Ry507/6+; inf ^{c}sy G1379/2-3+

(1) MAKE, CONSTRUCT

[For this and sense[2] cf Heb ^{c}āśāh "make; obtain," despite the unexpected ś in the Heb verb (š would be expected). Semantic development phps ultimately from Ar ^{c}asā (w) "be, become strong" > "be able" > "make, construct" > "make for one's self" > "make one's own" > "acquire." Cf discussion HöWZ43/89.]

R3954/1: ^{c}sy wbny rb^{c} qbrm "he made and built one quarter of the tomb" AND OFTEN with bny and in tomb-building contexts

(2) ACQUIRE, BUY

G1693/5 (Sab portion): qny w^{c}sy wš'm "obtained, acquired and bought" AND OFTEN with š'm; G1379/2-3: their tomb bn ^{c}sy wh^{c}syn "(acquired?) through buying and selling" (same formula C318/2)

(3) PRESENT AN OFFERING

[Eth ^{c}asaya "repay, give thanks," prob related to root sense[1].]

R2740/8: ^{c}sy d̲bhn tfd mmd "he offered a sacrifice (for?) the prolonged harvest (?)"

Note: The expression d̲^{c}syw b^{c}ly msb'hmw follows a lacuna in Ry507/6. Ry tr "which they did during their campaign" (var of sense[1]). RycPCH/14 emends to 'syw "they sent." Note also that ^{c}sy cited by MüW/79 in R4176/3, h^{c}sy ib/7, h^{c}syn ib/3 do not exist.

h inf h^{c}syn G1379/2-3+

CAUSE TO BUY = SELL

G1379/2-3 quoted under ^{c}SY v

n^{1} s ^{c}sym J669/7*

as adj: VERIFIED, CORRECT (or phps name of a weight)

[Ar ^{c}ās^{in} "proper, fitting."]

J669/7: this statue and a bronze inscription, wmdlthmy ^{c}sym "their weight being verified (or, weighing one ^{c}sy)"

n^{2} s m^{c}sm C640/4*

CONSTRUCTION (cf m^{c}s')

C640/4: ...] m^{c}sm gwlm [... "a construction, as property" (fragmentary context includes building and irrigation terms)

Note: C assigns to root ^{c}SM, tr "kitchen"; cf under ^{c}SM III.

^{c}SM I

v pf ^{c}sm Ry506/6*

COVET or DESIRE (?)

[Ar ^{c}asima "covet," ti "get one's wish."]
Ry506/7: wmnmw d̲^{c}sm wmxḍ mlkn "and whomever the king desired (?), he defeated"

Note: RyMus66/282-3 tr "flee" after Freytag, after Qāmūs: ^{c}asama "throw one's self among men not caring whether a fight will begin" "throw one's self into flight."

h pf h^{c}smw J577/9; ipf yh^{c}sm C429/7; yh^{c}smn Ir33

aux: DO S.TH. REPEATEDLY, ON NUMEROUS OCCASIONS

[Denom from ^{c}sm n "large number" (BeJSS20/192).]
Ir33: lyh^{c}smn 'LMQH mt^{c}n 'dymthw "may (the god) I. continually aid His servants"; J577/9: h^{c}smw hxṭ'n "they sinned repeatedly"

n s ^{c}sm(m) Ir7++; d̲-^{c}sm J576/14++

AN INDEFINITE, or LARGE, NUMBER; SEVERAL, MANY

[Cf etym of ^{c}SM v; BeNL9/188-9 cfs English "as many as you like."]
Ir7/2: rain had been lacking ^{c}sm xryftm bqdmy d̲t hqnytn "for several years previous to this dedication"; C397/10-13: the god granted ^{c}sm sbym wmltm "a large number/amount of captives and goods"; J576/14: mhrgtm wsbym wǵnmm d̲^{c}sm "a large number of slaughters, captives, and booty" AND OFTEN SIM in lists of spoils of war; J735/14: watered the palmgroves 'ṣytm ^{c}smm "(with) numerous ponds of standing water"; C350/14-5: the god allowed him to beget ^{c}sm ǵlmm "many sons"

^{c}SM II

n s ^{c}sm J585/10*

STIFFNESS, SCLEROSIS

[Ar ^{c}asima "be, become distorted (hand or foot)."]
J585/10: ^{c}sm ḥlẓ wmrḍ mrḍ "the sclerosis which he suffered and the illness he had"

^{c}SM III

n s ^{c}smym C660/3*

PART OF THE mwt̲b CULT-BUILDING (the KITCHEN?)

[Cf phps, with CoRoC/210B, Haḍ m^{c}sm "kitchen."]
C660/3: ^{c}smym wmḥmym wmḥḍrtn lmknt mwt̲bn "an ^{c}smy, a sanctuary, and the shrines of the cella of the mwt̲b-building"

^{c}SN

v pf ^{c}sn C338/12+

(1) DIG OUT, HEW OUT

[Akk esēnu "vault, cave"; Aram ^{c}ǎsan "be substantial, strong." V in Min (R2916/2) "dig and build the foundations."]
C338/12: ^{c}sn wḍrk brktn "dug out and faced with stone (?) the cistern"; A752a: bny w^{c}sn mḍrf F "he built and dug out the channel F."

(2) DIG FOUNDATIONS FOR (?)

C338/13: ^{c}sn kwr T'LB "he dug foundations for the fire-altar of (the god) T."

n^{1} s ^{c}sn(n,m) R3946/6+

UNDERGROUND STORAGE CHAMBER or CISTERN

R3946/6: bny...^{c}snn T. wmzfn mnxy Y wbny m^{c}sn Y wmzfhw mnxy 'A "he built the ^{c}sn-cistern T. and the exit channel, the primary canal Y.; and he built the m^{c}sn cistern Y. and its exit channel, the primary canal A."; C553/3: mdfn ^{c}snn "underground chambers of the cistern"; C337/8: ^{c}snm ^{c}dy šqr "underground chamber (= foundations) to roof"

n^{2} s m^{c}sn R3946/6*

CISTERN (cf ^{c}SN n^{1})

R3946/6 quoted under ^{c}SN n^{1}

^{c}FR

n s ^{c}frm C570/9*

TIME (?)

[Sense from context; or phps connected with Ar ^{c}afar "dust" > "ground," "place" or the like (?), synonymous with 'rk.]

C570/9: bn kl ^{c}frm w'rkm "through all time (?) and space = for ever, everywhere" (at end of inscription establishing boundaries)

^{c}FŠ

n s h^{c}fšn N74/10*

ACT OF SACRILEGE

[Sense from context.]

N74/10: wl ḥtmyn wstwfn bn h^{c}fšn w^{c}qwtn "may (the goddess) give protection and deliver from [the consequences of? repetitions of?] this act of sacrilege and impiety"

^{c}ṢD

n p '^{c}ṣd(n) J574/3+; '^{c}ṣdhmw ib/5-6

BAND, HORDE of enemy troops

[Ar ^{c}aṣwada "fight," qawm ^{c}aṣāwīd "band of men rushing altogether, for instance in a hand to hand fight" (JSIMB/62).]

J574/5-6: he fought b^{c}ly 'ḥzb ḤBŠT w'^{c}ṣdhmw "against the warbands of Ḥ. and their hordes"; J575/4: they came down b^{c}ly '^{c}ṣd dllw lhmw whḏrw hmt '^{c}ṣdn "upon the bands (who) were pointed out to them (by scouts) and scattered those bands"

^{c}ṢM

n s? ^{c}ṣmm C290/5*

KIND OF TRIBUTE/OFFERING (?)

[Cf the phrase ^{c}ṣm WDM "offering (to?) (the god) W." in Qat (RhQatTI/14).]
C290/5: kl ^{c}ṣmm ḏy'tyn lM "every offering (?) which they offer at (the sanctuary?) M."

^{c}ṢR

tp pf t^{c}ṣrw J700/13*

STRUGGLE

[Cf Ar ^{c}aṣara "press, squeeze."]
J700/13: t^{c}ṣrw bynhmw bšzbn wtlf R "they struggled between them with the dagger and R. was struck dead"

n s ^{c}ṣrn C84/6-7*

TROUBLE, CALAMITY (?)

[Cf esp Eth ^{c}aṣāri "tormentor," also Ar ^{c}nṣr "calamity."]
C84/6-7: stml' b^{c}mhw bm[h]wt ^{c}ṣrn "he sought an oracle from (the god) in this trouble"

^{c}Ḍ

n s ^{c}ḍhw J557*

WOOD, WOODWORK

[Cf Ar ^{c}iḍḍ "small thorn tree," Mod Sa^{c}udi Ar ^{c}uḍ "fragrant wood burned before guests," Eth ^{c}eḍ "wood."]
J557: the wall of the temple, kl blqhw w^{c}ḍhw "all its masonry and woodwork"; reconstructed in R3918/[2], [^{c}ḍm wt]qrm "wood and stone," after R2774/2 Min.

Note: BeStI/97 suggests tr "footing courses" of the wall for ^{c}ḍ, as originally having been constructed of brushwood.

^{c}ḌD

v pf ^{c}ḍd R4781/5*

WORK land COOPERATIVELY (?)

[Ar ^{c}ḍd v, D, L "help, aid"; Lt "give mutual aid, cooperate."]
R4781/5: 'tm w^{c}ḍd 'A ḏt byn ḥrtn wbyn wṯn[n] "he acquired title to and worked A. cooperatively between the aqueduct and the boundary"

n^1 p '^{c}ḍdhw Sh18/2+

(1) DIVERSION MOLES (?)

[Ar ^{c}aḍada "support," ^{c}aḍada^t "side of a door, doorpost" (LuMus86/183-4).]
Sh18/2,4: 'A w'^{c}ḍdhw w^{c}rmn wḏ'fn "A. and its diversion moles (?), and the dam and canals"

(2) PLANTATIONS OF PALM TREES (?)

[Ar ^{c}aḍud, ^{c}aḍīd(a^t) "row of palm trees" (Irv/53-4); cf also Eth ^{c}aṣad "field."]
F71/6-8: stwfyt 'A w'^{c}ḍdhw w'mtrn "A. and its palm-plantations and rain-watered fields were protected"

n^2 p ^{c}ḍwd C540/45*

TRANSPORT CAMELS (?), phps carrying food

C540/45: 'd̤hm w^{c}ḍwdm "(water-carrying?) camels and (food-carrying?) camels"

^{c}ḌW

n s m^{c}ḍw C86/9-10*

HARM, DESPITE

[Ar ^{c}aḍḍa "bite," Eth ^{c}aḍaḍa "do harm to."]

C86/9-10: ḥry wlsn wm^{c}ḍw whrm wsḏr "harm, calumny, despite, suffering, injury"

^{c}QB

v pf ^{c}qb C516/7-8; ^{c}qbhmw J577/12; ipf y^{c}qb C375/2+; y^{c}qby BeGlean/42,l.5; inf ^{c}qb J2109/6-7+

ACT AS GOVERNOR or DEPUTY

[Cf ^{c}qb n "deputy," of which this is denom.]

J550/2: Y. established him in authority wy^{c}qb bkbtn "and he acted as (his) deputy during the campaign"; Sh31: his lord ordered him l^{c}qb bhw 'rb^{c}t xryftm...wxmrhw 'LMQH...slmm bkl xryft ^{c}qb bhw "to act as governor in (a certain city) four years, and (the god) I. granted him peace in all the years he acted as governor there"; J2109/6-7: l^{c}qb wtnṣf [b]hgrn "to act as governor and protect the city"

h pf/inf h^{c}qb(n) C448/3-4+

(1) RESTORE a building

[Cf Ar ^{c}qb D "do again, do by turns."]

C448/3-4: hdbwhw wh^{c}qbn [...] lxlfhw mṣr^{c}tm "they fortified it and restored, outside it, (its) gates"

(2) GIVE IN EXCHANGE FOR, PURCHASE

[Ar ^{c}qb h "exchange s.th. for, recompense, requite."]

C570/2-4: qyḍ wh^{c}qb...bḥg qyḍhw w^{c}qbnhw "he exchanged and purchased according to (the terms of) its exchange and purchase"

n^{1} s ^{c}qb(m) J577/10+; ^{c}qbhw C571/9; p ^{c}qbt J619/2-3+; ^{c}qbthw J578/22; ^{c}qbthmw Gl547/7; '^{c}qbthmw ib/3

(1) GOVERNOR, DEPUTY

Ir13: ^{c}qbt wmr's w'b^{c}l "governors, dignitaries and citizens"; J577/10: ^{c}qb ngšyn bhgrn N "deputy of the Negus in the city N."; J619/2-3: ^{c}qbt mlkn bhgrn N "deputies of the king in the city N."; C571/9: wl yṣdn...f'w ^{c}qbhw "let him or his deputy perform the (ritual) hunt"

(2) STEWARD, MAJORDOMO

R4230A/2-3: he dedicated an altar bywm kwn ^{c}qbm bbt bn Ṯ "when he was steward in the house of (the clan) Ṯ."

n^{2} s ^{c}qb C548/12; var? ^{c}qbnhw C570/2

PURCHASE

[Cf ^{c}QB h.]

C570/2-4 quoted under ^{c}QB h; C548/12: he must pay 'kylm w^{c}qb šnnm "(for) the meal, and the purchase of the šnn"

n^{3} p? ^{c}qb R4176/12*

CONSEQUENCES

[Ar ^{c}uqb "consequence."]

R4176/12: w^{c}qb wsxnm lyrt^{c} ḏ'ḥdqhn "(as for any) consequences and disputes = subsequent disputes, let the governor set (them) right"

n^{4} s ^{c}qbt(n) J649/31+

WATCHTOWER

[Eth ^{c}aqaba "guard," Ḥaḍ ^{c}qbt R2687/2+ "watchtower."]

J649/31: they attacked b^{c}qbtn ḏR "at the watchtower of R."; R3958/6: ^{c}M... b^{c}l ^{c}qbt W "(the god) ^{c}M, lord of the watchtower W."

n^{5} p? m^{c}qbthmw R5085/10*

GUARD, GUARDIAN (cf ^{c}QB n^{1}, n^{4})

R5085/10: with the aid of nṣrhmw wṣydhmw...wm^{c}qbthmw "their auxiliaries, 'hunters' and guards (various military branches?)"; cf also C44/3 bm^{c}qbh, no context

^{c}QD

n^{1} s ^{c}qdm J577/12*

CONTRACT, OATH (?)

[Ar ^{c}aqd "pact, contract," ^{c}aqada "take an oath."]

J577/12: yhrgw bn hmt 'GRN mhrgm ḏ^{c}qdm "they slaughtered some of those Nagranites, a slaughter according to (their) oath (?)"

n^{2} s m^{c}qdn R3156/3*

CONTRACT (?) (cf ^{c}QD n^{1})

[Ar ^{c}qd L "establish by contract"; this may be the pass.prt.]

R3156/3: wkwn lwṯnn m^{c}qdn "let the boundary be established by contract (?)"

^{c}QW

ti ipf y^{c}tqwn N74/11*

COMMIT a certain impious act

[Ar ^{c}aqā "(the affair) became bitter and increased in bitterness"; Heb ^{c}qh "oppression, tyranny" (BeNL4/142); more specifically, cf Ar ^{c}aqā "defecate" (RycConf/4).]

N74/11: wmnḏ ḏy^{c}tqwn...bysṭ mḥrmn wl yqtrn "and whoever commits an impiety in the temple, let him be punished"

tp pf t^{c}qw N74/1*

COMMIT a certain impious act (= ^{c}QW v)

N74/1: bn ^{c}qwt t^{c}qw...bysṭ mḥrm[n] "as a result of the impious act (which) H. committed in the temple"

n s ^{c}qwt(n) N74/1+ (only this inscription)

ACT OF IMPIETY

N74/10: may the goddess give protection bn h^{c}fšn w^{c}qwtn "from [the consequences of? repetitions of?] this act of sacrilege and impiety"

^{c}QL

n p/coll ^{c}q[l] R4158/[3]*

CHIEFS

[Ḥaḍ ^{c}uqqāl = Ar šayx "chief" (LaH/97).]

R4158/[3]: ...'q]wlhw 'b's w^{c}q[l... "its leaders, (common) men and chiefs"

^{c}QM

n s m^{c}qmn C540/15-6*

OVERFLOW LEDGE

[Ar ^{c}aqama "obstruct," ^{c}uqma† "embankment of a field," ma^{c}qam "a dam designed to make water flow onto fields"; cf also Himyaritic ma^{c}āqim "threshholds" in *Iklil* (Irv/265-6).]

C540/15-6: ^{c}glmtn tbšnf m^{c}qmn "the diversion moles which abut on the overflow ledge"

^{c}QR I

n s/coll ^{c}qrhw R4069/10 (restored ib/6-7)*

DAM WALL, or WALLED FIELDS

[Ar ^{c}uqr "back part of a reservoir"; ModYem ^{c}āgir "a barrier of stones at the bottom of a stream to raise the level of water"; or cf ^{c}aqqar in ModYem: "field watered by rain and requiring no artificial irrigation"--phps so called because walled (Irv/174-5).]

R4069/6: ś́ḥb kl [^{c}]q[rhw w]mbr'hw wmdl^{c}hw "eroded all its dam wall/walled fields, stonework and revetting walls"; ib/10: mdl^{c}hw w^{c}qrhw "its revetting walls and dam wall/walled fields"

^{c}QR II

n s m^{c}qrn Ir12/3*

PURSUIT

[Ar ^{c}aqara bil-ṣayd "he pursued game" (RycMus87/246 and n7).]

Ir12/3: ydrkhmw bllyn ṯntn bm^{c}qrn ḏšrḥtn "they pursued them on the next night in a successful (or, secret) pursuit"

^{c}RB I

v pf? ^{c}rb R3890#5+; ^{c}rbw C537/6; ipf y^{c}rb R4767/5; y^{c}rbn R4773/1+; inf ^{c}rbn Robin al-Mašamayn/3

OFFER A SACRIFICE (as a pledge of future conduct?); DEDICATE

[Akk erābu "bring"; Ar ^{c}rb D, h "give a pledge"; Heb ^{c}ārab "pledge one's self."]

R3890#5: ...s w^{c}rb mṯ^{c}y W["and offered incense to (the god) W."; C537/6: ^{c}rbw wstqfw "they offered sacrifices and erected qyf-stones"; Robin al-

Mašamayn/3: yḥgrnn w^{c}rbn...IN "set apart and dedicate to (the god) N."

tp pf t^{c}rbw C308b+; inf t^{c}rbn J735/9

GIVE PLEDGES in token of submission > SUBMIT

C308/23-4: t[^{c}]rbw lmr'hmw...ṯny rbbn "they gave in pledge to their lord two hostages"; C308b: t^{c}rbw wstḏr^{c} lmr'hmw "they gave pledges of submission and humbled themselves to their lord"

n^1 s? ^{c}rbn C461/5; p? ^{c}rbtm J574/11

PLEDGE, HOSTAGE; OFFERING SACRIFICIAL VICTIM

J574/11: an embassy tḏr^{c}m w^{c}rbtm "(offering) submission and hostages"; C461/5: 'twhw ṯnym t'twm ^{c}rbn "offered (the god), a second time (?), the offering"

pp b-^{c}rb R2724/7+

INCUMBENT UPON (lit., what one is pledged to do)

R2724/7: 'l b^{c}rb wb^{c}ly bny B "(These are) those (things) which are incumbent upon the b.B." (cf the sim exp b^{c}br wb^{c}ly under ^{c}BR); R2876/1: 'l b^{c}rb kl [']nsm...w'l b^{c}rb kl 'rḍt "(These are) those (things) which are incumbent upon all men (regulations concerning landed property), and upon all territories"

n^2 s m^{c}rbtm J720/15-6*

PLACE OF SACRIFICE

[Cf ^{c}RB v.]

J720/15-6: lmšw m^{c}rbtm bn dD wz'k šhn "that a member of (the clan) D go to a place of sacrifice and offer the goat"

n^3 s t^{c}rbm J578/22*

PLEDGE of submission (cf ^{c}RB tp and n^1)

J578/22: blt K...t^{c}rbm wsfḥ ^{c}qbthw tḥt mr'yhmw "K. sent a pledge of submission and ordered his governors (to submit) to (the authority of) their 2 lords"

^{c}RB II

n^1 s m^{c}rb(n) C555/4+; d m^{c}rby R4773/2

(1) SUNSET > WEST

[Eth ^{c}araba, Ar ǵaraba "go down, set."]

Ir12/2: bm^{c}rb Ḥ "on the west of Ḥ."; Ir20/1: sb' m^{c}rbn "he campaigned in the west"; C555/4: 'wṯnn nsr mšrqn wnsr m^{c}rbn "the boundary stones toward the east and toward the west"

(2) ENTRANCE

[Akk erēbu "enter, go in."]

R4773/2: m^{c}rby mṣr^{c}y...mḥwl "the 2 entrances of the double doors of the encircling wall"

n^2 adj: m.s m^{c}rby C132/2*

ON THE WEST, WESTERN

C132/2: t̲ny msfqn mšrqy wmᶜrby hyt ṣrḥt "the two arcades on the west and east of this upper chamber"

ᶜRB III

n p/coll ᶜrb J629/33; ᶜrbn Ry510/5+; ᶜrbnhmw Ry507/1; p 'ᶜrb(n) C353/10+

ARABS = BEDUINS, NOMADS (?)--a social and military class

[Ar ᶜurb, ᶜarab id; dialectal Ar p ᶜurbān.]

C541/8: mlk SB' wd̲R wḤ wY w'ᶜrbhmw ṭwdm wthmt "king of S., d̲R., Ḥ., and Y., and their beduins of highland and coastland" AND OFTEN SIM; J629/7-8: kl 'ns w'ᶜrb "all men (city-dwellers?) and beduins"; Ry507/1: 'qlhmw wmr'shmw [w]ᶜrbnhmw "their leaders, dignitaries, and beduins"; C79/9-10: tqdm qdm bᶜm ᶜrbn "the expedition he made against the beduins"; J561b/12-3: 'rḍt ᶜrbn 'ᶜrb xṭ'w b'mr'hmw "lands of the beduins, beduins (who) sinned against their lords"

ᶜRB IV

n¹ p? mᶜrbt R4069/7*

SQUARED STONES, SQUARED MASONRY

[ModYem mᶜrb, Dat̲ taᶜarīb id; named as a building material in Ḥaḍ and Min (Irv/175-6). Cf phps root RBᶜ "four" > "four-sided."]

R4069/7: ś́ḥb kl [ᶜ]q[rhw w]mbr'hw wmdḷᶜhw bn mᶜrbt "eroded all its dam wall, stonework, and revetting walls of squared masonry"

n² s? tᶜrbn R4779/2* (D inf?)

SQUARED MASONRY (?) (cf ᶜRB IV n¹)

R4779/2 (context fragmentary and obscure, but concerns building a water distributor (?) ...'wbtᶜrbn [... "of ...? or of squared masonry (?)"

ᶜRGL

n p/coll ᶜrglm J610/8*

KIND OF (MIGRATORY?) LOCUST

[Cf Akk ergilu "a migratory locust?" (v.Soden, AHw/240); Heb ḥargol, Syr ḥargəlā "kind of locust"; also Ar ᶜirjul "large troop of men on foot" (RycHim2/479).]

J610/8: the god protected them bn brdm w'rbym wᶜrglm wbn kl qlmtm "from hail and non-migratory (?) and migratory (?) locusts and from all noxious insects"

ᶜRHN--n.pr? R3121 (in full): ᶜrhn bn 'ᶜl (read ᶜLHN?)

ᶜRW--for ᶜrwtn, C320/2, read wrwtn, see under WRW

ᶜRM

v pf G1364/3; inf ᶜrm Ir14/2

ENCLOSE, SURROUND (?)

[Daṯ ^{c}arama "shut up"; Ar ^{c}arim, ^{c}arima† "any barrier separating two things."]

Gl364/3: ḥgn k^{c}rm w'xḏ kl hwt byt "so that he surrounded and took prisoner all that house"; Ir14/2: lwḍ^c wṯbr w^{c}rm w'xrn "to lay low and crush and surround and repel"

n _s_ ^{c}rm(n) C541/43+; _p_ '^{c}rmhw C432/4

(1) DAM, DAM WALL of earth and stones (esp the great dam at Mārib)

[Ar ^{c}arm, Yem ^{c}arīm "dam." BeBSOAS17/155n2 cfs also Ar ^{c}arama† "heap (of grain)"--a dam is thus a heap or pile of masonry.]

C541/43: ṯbr ^{c}rmn w^{c}wdn "the dam (wall) and settling basin broke"; C540/6: ^{c}ḏbw ^{c}rmn...^{c}dy wṣḥw qdm ^{c}brn "they carried out repairs on the dam until they reached the front of the opposite side"

(2) CAIRNS marking boundary

[Cf esp Ar ^{c}urum id.]

Gl142/10: ^{c}rmhwt mrbḍn kl tśnnthw "the cairns of that sheep-pen along all its boundaries"

^{c}RMK--_n.pr_? R3584 in unreadable context

^{c}RF

n _p_ '^{c}rfhm C24/5*

CHAMBERS (?)

[Cf Ar ǵurfa† "room, chamber."]

C24/5: ...]'^{c}rfhm rzḥ[... (context concerns building an aqueduct)

^{c}RḌ

n _s_ ^{c}rḍ C540/74*

FACE, SURFACE of a wall

[Ar ^{c}arḍ "width," ^{c}urḍ "a lateral, or an outward part or portion = jānib ('side')."]

C540/74: they packed in earth for the dam wšmw ^{c}rḍ r'shw "and prepared the face of its upper area (i.e., the area above the level of wadi silt, Irv/287)"

^{c}RQ I

n _s_ ^{c}rq Ry510/4; _p_ ^{c}rqhmw C67/18

LOWLAND, COASTAL PLAIN

[Ar ^{c}irq "land near the sea"; cf also ^{c}arq "dune."]

C67/18: all their territory, ^{c}rqhmw w^{c}lthm[w] "their lowlands and their highlands"; Ry510/4: sb'tm b^{c}rq K "campaigns in the coastal plain of K."

Note: In Ry510 ^{c}rq may be a misreading of ^{c}rf; cf here Ar ^{c}arūf "source, spring" (RyMus66/309).

^{c}RQ II

n s ^{c}rqm C405/7*

SWEATING SICKNESS (?)

[Ar ^{c}araq "sweat."]

C405/7: ḏmrḍ tnkrn ^{c}rqm "who was sick (and) afflicted with a sweating sickness (?)"

^{c}RR

n s ^{c}r(n) C540/21+; d ^{c}rnhn J626/22+; p '^{c}rr(n) R3945/8+

(1) BEDROCK; ROCK, HILL

[Daṯ, Had ^{c}urr "mountain."]

C540/21: they went up to the dam and dug ṯw wṣḥw ^{c}rn wb^{c}lw ^{c}rn lhwṯrn ^{c}[w]dn "until they reached bedrock; and they excavated the bedrock to lay the foundation of the settling basin"

(2) FORTRESS ON A HILL, CITADEL

[Cf Heb ^{c}ir, p ^{c}ārim "city," Yem ^{c}urr "hill fortress."]

C74/4: 'LMQH b^{c}l 'WM ḏ^{c}rn 'LW "(the god) I., lord of (the temple) A. of the citadel of A." AND OFTEN in epithets of deities; R3945/4: he burned their towns wstmxḍ ^{c}rhmw "and took over their fortress"; R4624/4: brṯ msb' ^{c}rn "he leveled the road to the (hill) fortress"

(3) INHABITED AREA, VILLAGE (opposed to sr "cultivated area"; sometimes difficult to distinguish from sense^{2})

R3945/8: N w'hgrhw w'ḏhbhw w'^{c}rrhw w'srrhw "N. and its towns, fields, inhabited and cultivated lands" AND OFTEN with 'srr

Note: ^{c}rrtm in R4904/2 prob n.pr. Note also ^{c}rrw (n?) in fragmentary context R4046/1, phps (part of?) a building.

For ^{c}r elsewhere see under ^{c}WR, ^{c}YR

^{c}RR II

n p/coll ^{c}rrm R4907/7-8*

CYPRESSES

[Ar ^{c}ar^{c}ar "cypress."]

R4907/7-8: ...] ṣwd ^{c}rrm mdrrm[... "a hillside (plantation) of flourishing cypresses (?)"

^{c}RŚ

n p '^{c}rśn C308/6*

YOUNG PLANTATIONS

[BeNL9/56 cfs Ar ǵars "seedling." The often-cited Ar ^{c}arš "support," leading to trs such as "pillars," is not satisfactory.]

C308/6: '^{c}mdn w'^{c}rśn "naturally irrigated lands and young plantations"

^{c}RT, n--see under ^{c}WR

^{c}ŚB I

v inf ^{c}śbhw C603b/5*

HIRE

[Ar ^{c}asaba "hire (a stallio)," Eth ^{c}asaba "hire."]

C603b/5: lyš'm bn ^{c}bd'sm w^{c}śbhw "to buy the son of a man's slave (?) and hire him"

n s ^{c}śbhw R3910/5; p ^{c}śbthmy R4194/4

(1) HIRE-PRICE

[Eth.Ar ^{c}asb "hire."]

R3910/5: flyhbn ^{c}śbhw ś^{c}tn dysb'n b^{c}lyhw "he shall pay the hire-price for the time he worked it (the hired animal)"

(2) HIRED LANDS

R4194/4: the well provided irrigation bqrw bn ^{c}śbthmy "in the direction away from their hired lands"

^{c}ŚB II

n s? ^{c}śbn C320/2; p? ^{c}śbt C544/10

FODDER; or OFFSPRING (?)

[Akk ešēbu "be green," Heb ^{c}éśeb, Ar ^{c}ušb "plants." For tr "offspring" (Be2SAIn/78) cf Ar ^{c}asaba (^{c}ŚB I) "cover a female (said of stallions and camels); beget offspring," ^{c}asb "offspring" (Lane/2041).]

C320/2 (fragmentary context): ^{c}śbn šwbn "fodder of various types (?)"; C544/10 (context fragmentary): ...] ^{c}śbt b^{c}rhmw "fodder/offspring (?) of their camels"; phps also in C661/2

^{c}ŠQ

n s? ^{c}šq(n) R4194/3+; p ^{c}šqt R4230C/1

CULTIVATED LAND, phps LAID OUT IN STRIPS, suited for vineyards

[Cf Qat ^{c}šq "excavate; plow, work land." Irv/164-5 suggests basic sense "mark out, divide up (foundations, land, etc)." Cf Akk es/šēqu "scratch, incise."]

R4194/3: after a list of parts of an irrigation system, wkl ^{c}šq 'ywnhmw w'rḍhmw "and all the strip-cultivated land of their vineyards and fields"; ib/4: hqḥ kl dn ^{c}šqn "he set in order all the strip-fields"; R4230C/1: 'ywnm dkwn b^{c}šqt "vineyards which are in the strip-fields"

^{c}ŠR

D? pf ^{c}šrhw J615/9+; ipf y^{c}šrnhw Ir22; t^{c}šrnhw N14/6; y^{c}šrnn J650/4; y^{c}šrnnhw C342/6

PAY/OFFER AS A TITHE

[Heb ^{c}iśśēr "pay a tithe," cf Ar ^{c}ašara "collect a tithe" (denom from ^{c}šr "tenth, tithe").]

J615/9: they dedicated a statue d̲^{c}šrhw bn sqy wd^{c}t fqlw "which they offered as a tithe from the sqy- and d^{c}t-crops they had harvested"; N14/6: she dedicated bn ^{c}šr t^{c}šrnhw "part of the tithe she offered to (the god)"; Ir22: he dedicated ṣlmn bn ^{c}šr y^{c}šrnhw "a statue from the tithe he offered Him"

h pf h^{c}šr C516/27*

OFFER AS A TITHE (= D?)

C516/27: ...]wh^{c}šr d̲hwrt̲hw "he offered as a tithe (?) what he had acquired"

n^1 cardinal number: f ^{c}šr(m,n) R4176/13+; m ^{c}šrt ib/12+

TEN

[Ar ^{c}ašr, ^{c}ašara† id.]

R4922/3: kwn mrwḍh sdt̲t̲ ^{c}šr '[mm] "its length was sixteen cubits"; R4624/9: ^{c}šrn wm'tn lM "the hundred and ten of (the tribe) M."; J649/37: ^{c}šrm wm't 'sdm "one hundred and ten soldiers"; ib/39: st̲ w^{c}šrm wt̲lt̲ m'tm rkbm "three hundred and sixteen riding camels"; R4176/13: b^{c}šr d̲'A "on the tenth (lit., the Ten) of (the month) d̲A."; ib/12: ^{c}šrt xrfn "ten years"; R4196/4: st̲t̲^{c}šr wt̲lt̲ m'tm xryftm "year three hundred and sixteen"; R3910/4: ^{c}šrt ymtm f'w ^{c}šry "ten days or twenty"

Note: For another sense, see Note to ^{c}ŠR n^3.

n^2 s ^{c}šr C369/2+

(1) TENTH (fraction)

[Ar ^{c}ušr id.]

C369/2: 'ḥt 'sb^{c}m bn t̲ty yd ^{c}šr qbrm "one finger out of two hands, (i.e.) a tenth of the tomb"

(2) TITHE(S)

[Ar ^{c}ušr id.]

OFTEN IN FORMULA hqny ṣlmn bn ^{c}šr d̲^{c}šrhw "he dedicated this statue (as) part of the tithe he offered Him (the god)," J615/9+; R4176/4: lyqny T'LB ...^{c}šr B "(the god) T. shall receive the tithe(s) of B."; ib/8: lyf^{c}l T b^{c}šr 'lm "T. shall hold a banquet (using) the tithes"

n^3 cardinal number: ^{c}šrnhn C573/2-3+; ^{c}šry R3910/4+

TWENTY

[Ar ^{c}išrūn, Eth ^{c}ešri id; the Sab form is a true dual of ^{c}šr "ten."]

C573/2-3: 'rb^{c}tn w^{c}šrnhn 'ṣlmn "these twenty-four statues" (elsewhere always construct form ^{c}šry, but see Note); J577/14: 'rb^{c}t w^{c}šry wts^c m'nm 'sdm "nine hundred and twenty-four soldiers"; ib/4: st̲ w^{c}šry 'frsm "twenty-six horsemen"; R3910/4: ^{c}šrt ymtm f'w ^{c}šry "ten days or twenty"

Note esp J653/13: ywm ^{c}šrm d̲^{c}šrnhn bmw hwt wrxn "the tenth day, which is the twentieth (lit., the Twenty) of this month." Ryc (in BeRev/352A) tr "the 2 decades = periods of ten days," taking ^{c}šrnhn as the dual of a presumed ^{c}šr "decade."

n^4 s? ^{c}šrt J616/24+; p? ^{c}šr ib/12+

CLAN, TRIBAL GROUP organized on a genealogical, not territorial basis (contrasted with š^{c}b)

[Ar ^{c}ašīra$^+$, _p_ ^{c}ašā'ir "family, subdivision of a tribe."]

J616/12: 'š^{c}b w^{c}šr X G "the š^{c}b- and ^{c}šrt-tribes of (the community) X.G."; ib/24: ḥrb bn ^{c}šr D ^{c}šrt 'A w'A wḤ "there fought of the clans of (the tribe) D. the clan (or clans?) A., A., and Ḥ."; J635/34-4: lḥrb ^{c}š[r] Y 'sd kwnw kwn bny Y "to fight the clans of Y., those who were with the b.Y."

n^5 _s_ m^{c}šrt(m) R3945/1+

TRIBAL ASSEMBLY for the transaction of communal business

[Cf ^{c}ŠR _n_^{4} and Ar mu^{c}āšara$^+$ "social intercourse" (BeNL3/128n8).]

C19/6-7: bkn stml' b^{c}mhw bm^{c}šrtm "when they sought an oracle from (the god) in the assembly"; R3945/1: h^{c}ḏ[b] m^{c}šrt SB' wy'tmmw...mnš'hmw "(the king) reinaugurated the tribal assembly of the Sabaeans so that their tribal levies were led forth"

^{c}ŠT, _n_--see under ^{c}YŠ

^{c}T, _n.pr_ (?), phps incomplete, C548/16.

The other words in the line seem to be _nn.pr_.

^{c}TB

v _pf_ ^{c}tb R3945/6+; ^{c}tbhw ib/5+; ^{c}tbhmw C516/8

CONSIGN, DESTINE; ORDER

[Eth ^{c}ataba "sign, seal, design"?]

R3945/5: ^{c}tbhw 'r's mśwd 'A lS w^{c}tbhw hrgn "the chiefs of the mswd-assembly of A. had destined him (or it) for (the goddess) S., but he destined him (or it) to slaughter"; ib/6: kl 'sṭr ^{c}tb K "all the inscriptions (which) K. ordered/indicated"; ib/16: ^{c}tbhw xrš bythw "he ordered (concerning) it (?) the destruction of its palace"

^{c}THYT, R4979/3 in fragmentary context: ...'tlt ^{c}thyt[...

^{c}TK

pp ^{c}tk R4194/4; ^{c}d ^{c}tk R3945/3

(IN) THE DIRECTION OF

[Cf Q: ^{c}āka ^{c}alayhi "turn toward it, draw near it" (Irv/167), with by-form ^{c}ataka.]

R4194/4: their field t^{c}tk nxlyhmw "which is in the direction of their 2 palmgroves"; R3946/3: 'A ^{c}d ^{c}tk W...wkl ḏqny bB "(the territory) A. (which lies) in the direction of W, and all that he possessed in B."; restore phps in ib/3 where R reads ^{c}d [^{c}tb]

^{c}TL

v _inf_ ^{c}tlhw Gl574/16*

ASSAULT, BESIEGE a deity with prayers

[Ar ^{c}atala "push, press," here "oppress, besiege" (HöSEG8/50).]

GI574/16: the god agreed to save the dedicant's son lqbly d̲'l yẓbnn ^{c}tlhw "because he (the dedicant) did not refrain from besieging Him (with prayers)"

^{c}T̲R--For h^{c}t̲r Ry9/1-2, read hwt̲r, see under WT̲R h̲

𐩶 - Ǵ

ǴBB

n[1] For l-ǵbt C657/3, read as n.pr LǴBT

n[2] s mǵbt R4794+; mǵbthmw Ist7628/2; d mǵbtn n J556; p? mǵb R3980/2 (fragmentary context); var mǵbb J550/1+; mǵbbhmy J557

RAMPART, DYKE

[Cf Ar ǵbb D "turn away; prevent."]

J550/1: kl mǵbb wmḥfdt dn mhy^{c}n "all the ramparts and towers of this sanctuary"; J557: mḥfdnhn...wmǵbbhmy ^{c}d šqrm "the 2 towers and their ramparts, to the top (of them)"; Ist7628/2: B wK wmǵbthmw "B. and K. and their rampart (= defensive wall)"; R4794: mbny mǵbt W "construction of the dyke (?) of W."

ǴBṬ

n s ǵbṭ J615/27+

ENVY (?) (note rhyming use with ^{c}bṭ)

[Ar ǵibṭa[†] id, ǵabaṭa "regard with a wish for the like of [s.o.'s] condition" (Lane/2225-6.]

J615/27: may the god protect bn b'sm...w^{c}bṭ wǵbṭ šn'm "from harm and coercion or envy (by any) enemy"; sim Irl8/5

ǴBR

n s ǵbrm Gl532/1* (maṣdar)

BLOCKING OFF (?) (but see Note)

[Cf Ar ǵabara "delay, hold back" (HöSEG8/25).]

Gl532/1: [']l śn ǵbrm lqbl 'ln 'wtn "blocking off (of this canal) is not lawful in front of these boundary stones"

Note: Hö also suggests, as a plausible alternative, Ar ǵabara "go away," D "remove"--tr would be "removal is not lawful, (i.e.) the shifting (of) these boundary stones."

ǴWY

v pf ǵwy J570/6*

MISLEAD (?) or COVET (?) (^{c}n + object) (context fragmentary)

[Cf Ar ǵawâ "lose one's way; mislead, tempt," ǵawiya "covet," D "mislead, tempt."]
J570/6: yr'yn dśfhw bk[...] wǵwy ᶜnhw "he saw what (the god?) had bestowed (?) on him (another man?), and he misled him (or, coveted it)"

n[1] s ǵym J651/51-2*
TRANSGRESSION
[Cf Ar ǵawâ "go astray, err," ǵayy "trespassing, transgression."]
J651/51-2: may the god save them bn b'stm...wǵym wndᶜ...kl šn'm "from harm, transgression and injury (by) any enemy"

n[2] s ǵwyt C563/5*
SIN > PUNISHMENT FOR SIN, EXCOMMUNICATION (?)
[Cf Ar ǵayya† (root ǴWY) "error, sin."]
C563/5: lystᶜdbhw 'rbᶜm wśᶜtn ǵwytm ᶜdbth "let him punish him: (a) four-fold (compensation) and a period of 'sin' (= excommunication?) are his punishments"

ǴWN

n s mǵwnhmw J577/12*
DWELLING-PLACE (?) (cf mᶜn sim (?), under ᶜWN II)
[Cf Ar maᶜān ("place of help"?), Heb māᶜôn "refuge > habitation" (cf JSIMB/81, who cfs Ar maᶜān "place, spot, space").]
J577/12: h]ǵrw bᶜlyhmw bn mǵwnhmw dsrn R "they raided them from their dwelling-place (?) of the valley R."

ǴWR I

v pf ǵrw Ir32/4; ipf yǵrw J643/32+
PROVISION, PROVIDE WITH FOOD SUPPLIES
[Cf Ar ǵāra (w) id (RycMus88/213n9).]
J643/32: mẓ'w ᶜdy mḥrm dyǵrw "they arrived at the fortified camp which they had provisioned"; sim ib/34-5, Ir32/4

ti ipf yǵtwrw C74/10-1*
PROVIDE ONE'S SELF WITH SUPPLIES (cf ǴWR v)
[Ar ǵwr ti "he procured (provision of corn, or wheat)" (Lane/2307C).]
C74/10-1: they are to reap (?) certain areas wl yǵtwrw bnhw...wl ydbḥw bn mšmnhn "and provide themselves with supplies (specifically, grain?) there-from and make an offering of some of (the produce of) the 2 fields"

ǴWR II

h pf hǵrw J576/4+
RAID, ATTACK
[Ar ǵāra (w), L and st id.]
J576/4: hǵrw wylfyw bn hnt hgrn mhrgtm "they raided and took as blood revenge from those cities slaughters (and other booty)"; J616/23: hǵrw

wṣbḥn wḥrb bn ᶜšr D "they attacked and made morning raids on and fought some of the clans of D."

st inf s(t)ǵrn Ir32/19-20*

RAID, ATTACK (= ǴWR II h)

[Ar ǵwr st id.]

Ir32/19-20: wysb'n wstǵrn hgrn Ṣ "he set out for and attacked the city Ṣ." (Ir's text reads sǵrn)

Note: For st[ǵ]rw Ry507/7, read phps st[q]rw and see under WQR st. Ry read in Ry507/7: when the hostages had already been given, wst[ǵ]rw ᶜlhmw mgrmtm "they attacked them criminally."

ǴZW

v inf ǵzw J739/9+

CARRY OUT A MILITARY EXPEDITION, RAID (= ǴZY v)

[Ar ǵazā id.]

J739/9: the god protected him bn kl sb't sb' wǵzw "from (harm in) all the campaigns he undertook and carried out"; J758/7-8: sb'w wḏb' wǵzw ᶜdy 'rḍ R "they campaigned, waged war, and raided in the land of R."

n s ǵzwhmw C541/116; p? ǵzw C26/4; var? ǵzwy J577/14+; var ǵztm J586/15+; var ǵzwt(m,n) Ry506/3+

(1) UNDERTAKING, PROJECT; esp MILITARY EXPEDITION, RAID

[Ar ǵazw "raiding," ǵazwa† "raid."]

C541/116: ḏrz'w bn ywmn ḏbhw yfᶜw [l]ǵzwhmw... "what they spent since the day on which they went up for their project (i.e., the repair of the dam) was: (figures follow)"; J586/14: he returned safely from kl sb't wǵzw(y) w'(ḏ)[b'] sb' "all the campaigns, raids and battles he undertook" (J emends to ǵzw(y) from ǵzwt and tr as dual); ib/15: ysb' ǵztm b'rbᶜ(y) 'sdm ᶜdy xlf S "he undertook raids with forty men outside S."; sim ib/19; Ry506/3: kǵzyw M ǵzwtn rbᶜtn bwrxn dT "when (the tribe) M. made (its) spring raids in the month dT."

(2) p only= RAIDERS

C26/4: 'gyš wǵzw "troops and raiders" (reading of HöWZ40/11); J577/14: 'gyš wǵzwy "troops and raiders" (J tr as dual "2 raiding-corps")

Note also (ǵ)zwtm in obscure context C405/12, quoted under HḌG. (C emended from bzwtm.)

ǴZY

v pf ǵzyw Ry506/3*

CARRY OUT RAIDS (= ǴZW v)

[Cf Ar ǵazā id.]

Ry506/3: ǵzyw M ǵzwtn rbᶜtn "(the tribe) M. carried out (its) spring raids"

ǴY--For n ǵym J651/52, see under ǴWY

ǴYL

tp ipf [y]tǵln J618/18-9*

FLOW with water (?) (said of streams, 'ǵyl)

[Denom, cf Ar ǵayl "water running in rivers or rivulets, or streamlets for irrigation" (Lane/2319A), Mh ǵayl "mountain torrent (bed)" (MüW/88).]

J618/18-9: may the god grant them wfy kl 'ǵyl yf^{c}w [wy]tǵln b'rḍ "the well-being of all the streams which rise and flow (?) in the land"

n s ǵylm R4085/3; var ǵlhmw R5085/5-6; p 'ǵyl J618/18+; 'ǵylhw J555/3+; 'ǵylhmw J564/21

(1) STREAM; STREAMBED (cultivated)

[Cf Ar.Mh ǵayl mentioned under ǴYL tp.]

J564/21: kl 'rḍthmw w'srrhmw w'ǵylhmw "all their fields, valleys and streams (or, streambeds)"; R3899: bn ^{c}snm ^{c}dy 'ǵylhw "from the cistern to its streams (i.e., its sources)"; sim R4797/1; J670/29: may the god allow them hgb'n lhmw 'ǵylhmw "to lease out (?) to them their streambeds"; R5085/5-6: hq̣šbw wgrb ǵlhmw bsr ^{c}mqn "they prepared for use and terraced their streambed in the slope of the valley"

(2) BED or BOTTOM of a well

R4085/3: b'rn...ln ǵylm ^{c}dy šqrm "the well, from (its) bottom to (its) top"

Note: Also the n.pr of the lefthand channel of the northern sluices of the Mārib dam (Irv/267-8), e.g. C540/17: ǴYLn.

ǴYR

pp ǵr C523/5+; var ǵyr C532/6-7+; ǵyr k- Ir32/15; b-ǵyr C619/4+

(1) WITHOUT; UN-/IM- + n

[Ar ǵayr "not, no, un-."]

C619/4: b^{c}lmn wbǵyr ^{c}lmn "with or without a document"; C532/6-7: wḍ't ^{c}dy mwṭnn ǵyr ṭhrm "she went out into the forecourt (of the temple) without purity/purification (= in a state of impurity)"; sim C523/6; C86/14: bǵyr ṣdqm "unlawfully"

(2) EXCEPT

[Ar ǵayra id.]

Ir32/15: 'l n(f)ṣw ǵyr kbn SB' "none came except from S."; J665/49: 'l tfqd bn gyšhmw ǵyr 'sm "no one was missing from their troop, except one man"

ǴYṮ

h inf hǵṯn J735/10*

WATER WITH RAIN (said of a deity)

[Ar ǵāṯa (y) id.]

J735/10: may the god grant sqy whǵṯn M w['m]ṭrn w'srrn "(that He will) provide irrigation waters for and water with rain M. and the [rain-] watered fields and the valleys"

ǴL--See under ǴYL, ǴLL

ǴLB

n s ǵlbn Ist7608b/16*

adj: VICTORIOUS one

[Cf Ar ǵalaba "conquer."]

Ist7608b/16: bsm RḤMNn wbnhw KRŚTŚ ǵlbn "in the name of (the god) R. and His son K., the Victorious One"

ǴLY

n s ǵlyt C352/16+

HATRED (cf ǴLL v sense^1 "be filled with hatred")

[See under ǴLL I v.]

C352/16: may the god protect bn rǵm wǵlyt mr'm "against the coercion or hatred of (any) man"; sim R4011/12, J664/18; Ir9/4-5: the god granted restitution and security bn ǵlyt...fqd wǵll "from the hatred (to which) He had given vent and (with which) He was filled"

ǴLL I

v ipf yǵln R4176/5; inf ǵll Ir9/4-5

(1) BE FILLED WITH HATRED (ǵlyt)

[Ar ǵalla id.]

Ir9/4-5: ǵlyt wtnkr fqd wǵll wnkrn 'LMQ̣H "the hatred and affliction which (the god) I. gave vent to, was filled with, and used as a punishment"

(2) DAMAGE or EMBEZZLE (?)

[Cf Ar ǵll h "defraud."]

R4176/5: ḏyǵln bn mb^{c}l T'LB lyt^{c}lmn T "whoever damages/embezzles (?) the property of (the god) T., let T. take cognizance of (it)"

h ipf yhǵllnhmw F71/9-10*

DAMAGE (cf ǴLL v sense^2 sim)

F71/9-10: (m)ṯbrm wmngwm ḏyhǵllnhmw "the breach and occurrences which damaged them (crops and fields)"

ǴLL II

h ipf yh(ǵ)lln Sh18/2

PRODUCE crops

[Ar ǵll h id.]

Sh18/2: yh(ǵ)lln hyt brqn "(crops) which are produced in that rainy season"

ǴLM

n s ǵlm(m,n) C19/7-8+; p ǵlm(m) Mü1/5+

CHILD, BOY, YOUTH

[Ar ǵulām "boy, youth," Heb ^{c}élem "young man."]

C19/7-8: ǵlm wldthw M "the boy M. bore (to) him"; J2109/9: ǵlmm d̲krm "a male child"; Mül/5: qnyw xmst ǵlmm wmr'tm bn 'nt̲thmw "they acquired five boys and a girl from their wives"

Note: In Mus87/512, Ryc quotes a passage in which the f̲ ǵlmt "girl" appears, stating that the passage occurs in Ir24; the citation is incorrect. (For the passage, see under KRB h̲.)

ǴMM

n p̲ ǵmmm C674/3+

CLOUDS (?) or n.pr (in a divine name)

[Ar ǵamma "cover, veil," ǵamām "clouds," ǵumma -l-hilāl "the new moon was covered by clouds" (HöRel/280).]

C674/3: mdbḥt bny d̲M ld̲ǴMMm "altar of the b.M. to (the god) Him of the Clouds (or, Him of Ǵ.)"; sim R3627/3

ǴNM

v pf̲ ǵnm J631/9+; ǵnmw J641/4+; Inf̲ ǵnmnhmw C349/6

(1) PLUNDER, TAKE AS BOOTY

[Ar ǵanima id.]

J713/11: xmrhw hrg wsby wǵnm bsb't sb' "(the god) allowed him to kill and take captives and booty in the campaigns he fought"; J649/40: ǵnmw wmly gmlm "he took as booty and captured camels" AND OFTEN

(2) GIVE s.th. to s.o. AS BOOTY

[Cf Ar ǵnm h̲ id.]

C349/6: may the god yz'n...ǵnmnhmw "continue to give them booty"

n s̲ ǵnmm J574/9+; ǵnmhmw J641/4+; p̲ ǵnmt J561b/8+

BOOTY

[Ar ǵunm id; cf also ǵanam "small cattle" (most valuable plunderable property, HöSEG8/55).]

J574/9: they returned from campaign bwfym wḥmdm w'ḥllm wsbym wmltm wǵnmm d̲ᶜsm d̲hrḍwhmw "with health, praise, spoils, captives and much plunder and booty, which satisfied them" AND OFTEN SIM; C407/28: the god granted him mhrgm wǵnmm 'hnmw ysb'nn "slaughters and booty wherever they campaigned"; J641/4: they dedicated ṣlmn bn ǵnmhmw d̲ǵnmw bn Q "this statue from their booty which they took from Q."

ǴSL

ti ipf̲ yǵtsl C523/7+

WASH ONE'S SELF as a ritual purification from uncleanness

[Ar ǵsl t̲i̲ id.]

C523/7: he confessed because ms 'nt̲ ḥyḍ wlm yǵtsl "he had touched menstruating women and not washed himself"; C533/5: she confessed because qrbh mr'...wmšy wlm yǵtsl "a man had approached her (sexually) and went away and did not wash himself"

ǴḌR

n s ǵḍrn C573/2+

ABUNDANCE, PROSPERITY (?) or n.pr, in name of a goddess and epithet of the goddess ŠMS

[Cf Ar ǵaḍira "be rich, abundant."]

C573/2: šmshw TNF b^{c}lt ǵḍrn "his sun goddess T., the Lady of Abundance"; sim C132/4: and several times ḏt ǵḍrn alone, e.g. J550/1: ršw ḏt ǵḍrn "priest of (the goddess) She of (= Dispenser of?) Abundance"

ǴR--See under ǴWR, ǴYR

ǴRB I

v pf ǵrbw J651b/54 twice*

KNOW (bn of s.o.)

[Mh ǵarōb id, cf Ar ^{c}arafa id.]

J651b/54: kl šn'm ḏrḥq wqrb ḏbnhw ǵrbw wḏbnhw 'l ǵrbw "any enemy, far or near, of whom they know or of whom they don't know"; cf parallel contexts under D^{c} v

ǴRB II

n s ǵrbn C149/2-3*

WEST (?) in epithet of the god ^{c}ṮTR

[Ar ǵarb id; cf Sab m^{c}rb id.]

C149/2-3: ...^{c}ṮTR ŠR](Q)n wǴRBn "[A. of the Eas]t and West (?)"

ǴRBB

n p ǵrbbm C540/48+

KIND OF GRAPE (black?)

[Ar ǵirbīb "kind of good black grape" grown at eṭ-Ṭā'if (Lane/2242-3).]

C540/48: ''blm sqym ǵrbbm wfṣym "camels carrying drink (made from) black (?) and white (?) grapes"; same exp C541/128

ǴRḌ

v ipf yǵrḍw R4176/3' inf ǵrḍ ib

HOLD A FEAST (?)

[Cf Ar ǵrḍ D "eat fresh meat" (Lane/2248A).]

R4176/3: ḥgr srn lǵrḍ bhw wyǵrḍw S bsrn...sb^{c} m't qnym b'ḥd ywmm "(the god) set apart the valley as sacred for holding feasts (?) in, and (the tribe) S. held a feast (?) in the valley, seven hundred slaves (or, phps, sheep--as the main course?) on one day"

ǴṮ--For v hǵṯ J735/10, see under ǴYṮ h

◊—F

F I

cj f- passim

(1) AND, SO (introducing predicate; connecting narrative clauses) [Ar fa- "and; then."]

C314/13: wbm d̲n xrfn fnbl Š "and in this year, Š. sent..."; R3956/5-8: she wore a mantle fxb'ṭ "and concealed..." flyśwbnh n^{c}mtm "so let her be restored to favor..." fhḍr^{c}t "and she humbled herself"; R4194/2: fgrbw wśw^{c} wḥrr "so they revetted and leveled and embanked"

(2) in apodosis, THEN

R4088/4-5: hm 'l t'xd̲ fḥlt nfshw "if he does not give himself up, (then) his life is forfeit"; R3910/6: b'n ymtn b^{c}rm...fbr'm mhš'mn "if an animal dies(after a specified period of time), then the seller is not liable"

compounds with f-

f + 'w, OR: C74/14-5: bn M f'w d̲yqhn "the b.M. or whoever commands (in their place)"; C571/8-10: wl yṣdn...f'w ^{c}qbhw "let him or his deputy perform the hunt"; C599/6: kl sṭrm kbrm f'w ṣgrm "every document, large or small"

f + 'l, LET NOT: R4815/4: f'l s'lw s'lm bny S bnkl 't̲mr "let the b.S. not lay a claim to any produce"; ib/6: f'l ymn^{c}w bny R "and let the b.R. not hinder..."; R852/6f: wbnw S w'wldhmw f'l ymn^{c}w "and (as for) the b.S. and their descendents: let them not hinder..."

f + h' (introducing second section of document): G1532: [']l śn ǵbrm... fh' lyh^{c}n msb' SB' "removal (of boundary stones) is unlawful; and (as for) that (canal), let it flow (as) the canal of S." (tr HöSEG8/27)

f + l AND, SO (introducing jussive sense): R3956/5-6: she confessed her sin, fl yśwbnh n^{c}mtm "so let (the god) restore her to favor"; C547/11: they sinned and were punished, fl hd̲rn "so let (them) beware"

f + r' AND NOW, AND INDEED--see under R'

F II

n s̲ f R3945/3+

MOUTH > COMMAND, AUTHORITY

[Cf Ar fū "mouth"; Heb peh id, cf also bəpî, ^{c}al pî "according to, in accordance with."]
R3945/3: wbf K wdy wt'w zm "and by command of K. the waters flowed and gathered together"; C570/8: 'l bf 'l...h^{c}dwn 'wt̲nn "no one, by command of l., may remove these boundary stones"; R4052/4: lf hr'yt hr'y "by command of/on the authority of the vision (the god) showed them"

F'Y--For v hr', see under FY' h

F'L

n s f()'lhw F119/14* (act.prt?)

ONE WHO WISHES s.th. ILL

[Ar fa'l "omen, prediction (good or bad)" (cf RyET/69).]

F119/14: rt̲dw...bn t̲brhw wf()'lhw "they placed (it) under the god's protection against (any)one who would break (it) or wish it ill"

FG--In obscure context C608=R659/7; read wfym for wfg? Passage reads: bn dn ṣtrn lš'm wbnyt wf(ym) kbrhw swn (read SWN?) mšrqn "built/erected this inscriptional stela as a dedication (?) and pious construction (?) (for) his great one/lord/patron (?), toward the east (or, if n.pr, for SWN the Eastern--phps a god)."

FGM--For n fgmm R4230C/2=Cant5/10, read qlmm; see under QLM I

FGR I

v pf fgr C88/5-6*

DESTROY (?)

[Cf Aram pgr id.]

C88/5-6: 'ns fgr bythmw "the men whose house was destroyed (?)"

FGR II

v pf fgr C547/8-9; fgrw Ir13/12

(1) CAUSE water TO FLOW

[Ar fajara "he broke open a dam...that the water might break...through" (Lane/2340B).]

C547/8-9: ffgr šrghmw...mn mwm qlm "and (the god) made their watercourses flow with little water"

(2) MAKE A SORTIE

Ir13/12: mfgrt fgrw b^{c}lyhmw "the sortie they made against them"

n s mfgrt Ir13/12*

SORTIE

[Cf FGR II v sense^{2}. Discussion of military context, RycMus87/249.]

Ir13/12 quoted under FGR II v

Note: Prob n.pr in J665/16: rqyw bn MFGRTn "they went up from M."

FGR III

n s fgrt Ir21*

PIT (?)

[Cf Yem fagīr "cistern lined with masonry"; for discussion of the capture of lions in pits, cf Encyclopedia of Islām, 2.ed, vl, p682 (article Asad) (RycMus87/250n10).]

Ir21: hrg hwt lb'n bfgrt "(he) killed that lion in a pit (?)"

FDW--For v yfdw Gl520/5,7, see Note to FDY v

FDY

v pf fdy Ist7630/6+; fdyhw C967/3+; fdyt N27/4; fdyw GaAntYem2/2

REPAY s.o.; PURCHASE s.thl. REDEEM s.o.

[Eth fadaya "pay"; Ar fadā "he bought back a slave at a price"; Heb pādāh "redeem."]

Ist7630/4-5: fdy yynhmw ^{c}mn bny ^{c}A "they purchased their vineyard from the b.A."; GaAntYem2/2: fdyw wqṣṣ wbrṯn kl ml' "they acquitted themselves of, repaid and discharged the whole sum"; Gl533/4: ['r]b^{c} m'n blṭm...bḏfdy N "four hundred blṭ-coins with which he repaid N."; N27/4: hqnyt...nfsh wbnh...ywm fdyt mwklh "she dedicated herself and her sons when she redeemed her obligation" (but RobAtt/61 reads ywm fdyth mwlkh "when (the goddess) released her from her vow")

esp common in eponym formulas, e.g. C967/3: fdyhw bn kl 'bythw "(the god) redeemed him from (service in) all His temples (after the completion of his service as eponym)" AND OFTEN SIM

Note: MüW/88 cites the ipf yfdw Gl520/5,7, without context; he tr "be obtained, earned" and cfs FDY v.

ti inf ftdyn Robin al-Mašamayn/9*

BE USED AS FIDĀ' (ransom)

Robin al-Mašamayn/9: wdy^{c}krn ftdyn qnyhw [ly]š'mnhw "and whoever refuses (to allow) his animal to be confiscated as fidā', let him sell it"

FDFD--For n fdfdt, see under WFD

FW^{c}

n s tf^{c} Ry416/3*

BEGINNING (?)

[Cf Ar fay^{c} "beginning," faw^{c}a^{t} "prime" (MüW/91).]

Ry416/3: Y...ltf^{c}...Y tḥbb ^{c}A lt^{c}m "Y. for the beginning (?)...Y. attests his love for A. for the duration = forever"

FḤM

n p? fḥm R3234=C924/3*

INCENSE ALTARS (?) (word phps incomplete)

[Ar fḥm "place where charcoal is burned." PirenneGloss lists also under mfḥm, as a "correction." Cf Min R3327/6 mfḥmnyhn "2 incense altars (?)"]
R3234/3: wfrhw w/fḥm lYT^{c}'MR 5 "and they fled (?), and [lacuna?] incense altars (?) for Y., five"

FXḎ

n s fxḏm R4782/2; d fxḏyhw J649/20
THIGH
[Ar faxiḏ id.]
J649/20: zxn...xms zxnm mḍytm fxḏyhw wrglyhw "he received five wounds which penetrated his thighs and legs"; R4782/2: let him offer to the god fxḏm wmqdmn "a thigh and the 2 forequarters (of the sacrificial beast)"

FXR I

v pf fxrhmw J576/14; fxrw J577/2+
GATHER TOGETHER (said of troops; both transitive and intransitive usages?)
[JSIMB/76 cfs Akk paḫāru D "gather together, muster," Ẓofāri fóxra "together."]
intransitive? J577/12: fxrw hmw 'GRN tḍr^{c}m b^{c}br mr'hmw "those Nagranis gathered together in submission to their lord"; ib/2: fxrw b^{c}br Š...wmsrhw "they gathered together against Š. and his expeditionary force"
transitive (D?) J576/14: yhwkbnn bhw mqtt...lšrḥhw wfxrhmw lSB' "they mustered the officers there to reinforce him, and gathered them together for S."

FXR II

n p fxrm C314/15*
GIFTS (?) sent as peace offerings
[Cf phps Ar faxara "boast"; fāxir "precious, magnificent, splendid."]
C314/15: tnbltm wtḍr^{c}m wfxrm "embassies, submission and gifts (?)"

FṬN

h pf hfṭn R3945/1+; hfṭnhw J2856/4; ipf yhfṭnn C413/3
INITIATE A LEGAL PROCEEDING; specif ASSIGN, ORDAIN ownership of conquered territory
[Cf Ar faṭana "understand"; Sab causative originally "proclaim" or the like.]
J2856/4: w'l hfṭnhw kl fṯḥm "let no legal proceeding be initiated against him"; R3945/1: ['l]t hfṭn K...l'LMQH wlSB' "these (territories) did K. (their conquerer) assign to (the god) I. and to S."; R3946/1: 'lt 'hgrm w'bd^{c}m gn' whfṭn K l'LMQH wl SB' "these are the towns and districts (which) K. walled and assigned to I. and to S."; C413/3 in fragmentary context

FẒR

n s mfẓr VanLessen 7/4*

EXTENT (?)

[Sense from context, BeNL10/422).]

VanLessen 7/4: the dimension of the whole territory mṯmn wmfẓr "in value and extent (?)"

FY'

h pf hf' Ry507/8; inf hf'n J1028/5

INFLICT DAMAGE, or CAPTURE AS BOOTY

[Cf Min sf'y R3022/4+ "inflict damage" (root F'Y; BeOr25/299); or cf Ar fā'a (y) "take as booty," fay' "booty."]

Ry507/8: gm[c] ḏhf' mlkn...14,000 mhrgtm "the total of the damage inflicted (on the enemy)/the booty taken by the king was 14,000 killings (i.e., 14,000 slain)"

FYḤ

n s? fyḥ Ry507/7*

TROOP OF HORSEMEN = TRIBESMEN (?) (reading uncertain)

[Ar fayāḥ "troop of horsemen."]

Ry507/7: kl fyḥ ymn whbw ([c]l)n m'tm rhnm "all the tribesmen (?) of the south gave over a hundred hostages" (tr BeOr25/299)

Note: RodConf'65-6/136 cfs Ar fwḥ D "give off an odor," h "shed blood," and suggests the passage deals with an oath (ymn) sworn by means of incense or blood.

FYṢ

v ipf yfṣn J631/22*

LEAVE FOR, GO TO ([c]dy a place)

[Ar fāṣa (y) "go away to a place" (JSIMB/133).]

J631/22: wyfṣn Q...[c]dy hgrn Ẓ "then Q. left for the city Ẓ."

FYŠ

n[1] s fyšm R4401*

WATER DISTRIBUTOR (?)

[Cf Ar fšy "spread out (intransitive)." R comments that the inscription is written on what seems to be "un kiosque distributeur d'eau."]

R4401: bny fyšm fnwt mḥrm "he built a water distributor (?) in front of the temple"

n[2] s? tfyšn R4779/2* (or phps tp inf?) Context obscure: ...ktwṯm w'qtfyšn wsth..w'bt[c]rbn[..., no tr

FKL--For n 'fklt, see under 'FKL

FLW--For v tflw, see under FLY tp, FLL tp

FLY

tp pf tfl J633/9-10; tflw Gl441/3+

SEEK or OBTAIN AN ORACLE (b^cm from a god); BE COMMANDED by oracle

[Assigned here to root FLY because of the derived n flyt, below. Cf Eth fāl (Ar fa'l) "omen," tafāwala "consult omens" (HöRev/425).]

Gl441/3: tflw b^cm T'LB lxybt "they sought an oracle from (the god) T. regarding the drought"; J628/4-5: the god commanded them bkn tflw b^cmhw "when they sought an oracle from Him"; NNAG12/3: he dedicated this statue ḥgn ktflw b^cm 'LMQH "as they had been commanded by oracle from (the god) I."

n s flytn R4009/7+; flythmw J628/7

ORACULAR RESPONSE; ORDINANCE (established by oracle?)

J628/7: tflw b^cmhw...wwkbw flythmw "they sought an oracle from (the god) and obtained their response"; C74/5: lšym flyt 'srrhmw "to establish the ordinance (or, consult the oracular response?) (pertaining to) their valleys"; R4009/7: ...kwnt flytn... "this ordinance was enacted..." (prob to be followed by date of ordinance)

FLK

n p 'flkm Ry533/9*

FELUCCAS

[Ar falūk (from Gk ėphólkion) id.]

Ry533/9: forty-seven 'ś́dqm w'flkm "ferry-boats and feluccas" (part of the booty of a coastal town)

FLL I

tp pf tflw J576/6*

FLEE

[Ar falla "flee"; cf also phps Eth tafalawa "separate (transitive)" (JSIMB/72).]

J576/6: tflw mṣr dR w'l qdmhmw "the expeditionary force of dR. fled and did not oppose/fight them"

FLL II

h inf hflln CI1/2+

CUT CHANNELS

[Cf Ar falla "notch the edge of a sword" and Sab MFLL, n.pr of the right-hand channel of the northern sluices of the Mārib dam (Irv).]

CI1/2: whflln $šr^ct$ "and cut water channels"; also in fragmentary context R4299/3

n s fltn C380/4; p 'fl ib

CHANNEL, DYKE separating fields

C380/2-4: lbrktn...fltn lywfyn fnwhw wkl mḥmyn f'l śn qšbn mḥmyn wb^{c}d 'fl ṣrb[n] lbrktn "for the cistern...this dyke, to make safe his channels and all the embanked land: so it is not lawful to clear the embanked land or remove (extend?) the dykes of the autumn-crop field for the cistern"

FLQ

n s mflq(m,n) R4626/2+

SYSTEM OF IRRIGATION by dispersion of water by means of inflow cuts

[Cf Ar falq "fissure," Daṯ "river." Irv/217 refers this word to the "common practice of cutting a hole in the earthen wall of a canal to let the water through to flood a field." This is described (p.218) as a temporary process as opposed to mnfs, a permanent stone structure.]

R4626/2: w'l's s'lhmw mḥmtm wṣ^{c}tm wmflqm "let no one challenge their possession of the embankment system, the diversion system, or the dispersion system"; same exp R3686A, F70; J550/1: A, B and C (names of palm-groves) mflqn wX...mḥmyn "(irrigated by) inflow cuts, and X. (another palmgrove), (irrigated by) embankments"

FLŚ I

D pf flśw C334/11; inf flś NNAG13-4/3

EXPEL

[Eth fallasa id.]

C334/11: flśw š^{c}bn R...bn ḥrtn "they expelled the tribe R. from the camp"; NNAG13-4/3: [s]b'w wflś b[n ']rḍ w'wyn ḏR "they fought and expelled (them) from the land and vineyards of ḏR"

FLŚ II

n p flśtm C325/6,8*

TOPS OF COLUMNS (?), on which the beams of a roof rest

[Te falāša "top of a column" (CoRoSab/27-8). Cf Sq fls "discover," Heb pālas "observe" (from supposed conspicuousness of column-tops)--BePESA/12.]

C325/6: 'rb^{c}t flśtm ^{c}lwm w'rb^{c}t mḥwlt "four tops of columns above, and four pillars"; ib/8: wṯlṯt flśtm ^{c}lwhw "and three column-tops above it"

FNW

n[1] s fnwt(m,n) C1/3-4+; fnwthw C657/3; var/p fnw(n) C40/2; p fnwy R3967/2

(1) ROAD, ENTRANCE PASSAGE (?)

[Eth fenot, p fenāw "road, direction," fenā "in the direction of"; Sq fane "road, way"; Yem fāniya "canal." For root sense "face, confront, oppose," cf esp Heb pānāh.]

R4773/2: m^{c}rby mṣr^{c}y wfnwt mḥwl "the entrances of the double doors and the entrance passage of the encircling wall (?)"; C1/3-4: šmw mṣr^{c}y fnwt ṣrḥthmw "they set up the double doors of the entrance passage (?) of their upper chambers (or, in front of their upper chambers, cf sense[3] below?)"; Ir13: hsḥthmw bn xlf fnwt hwt bytn "exterminated them from the vicinity of the entrance passage of that fortress"

(2) secondary CANAL

C657/3: fnwthw d̲t tsqynhw "its canal which irrigates it"; C329/4: slfn w'nmrn wfnwn "glacis, control walls and canals"; R3967/2: 'nhr wfnwy "streams and canals"; R4815/2: fnwtm msb' mwn "the canal, the watercourse"

(3) adverbially, and with pp b-: IN THE DIRECTION OF, IN FRONT OF

R3943/6: bny m'xd̲n...fnwt 'A "he built the control dyke in the direction/in front of A."; C518/4: 'rḍ ytlwn lmlk bfnwn W "land tributary to the king in the direction of W."; C37/5: fnwt syr Ḥ "in the direction/in front of the common land of (the city) Ḥ."

n[2] p mfnt J615/10-1+; mfnthmw J564/21+; var mfnythmw J645/25

LAND IRRIGATED BY CANALS

[From n fnwt sense[2] "canal."]

J615/10-1: fqlw bn kl 'srr wmšymt wmfnt "they harvested from all the valleys, fields and lands irrigated by canals" AND ELSEWHERE in lists of kinds of cultivated land

Note: Cf also n mqny (QNY n[6]), phps a misreading of this word.

FNY--For n mfnyt J645/25, see under FNW n[2]

FS--For v hfs J735/15, see under NFS h

FSD

v pf fsd C541/9+; fsdw Ry506/3 (or read qsd, qsdw; see under QSD)

REBEL

[This v and the related n below are emended in the passages cited from a previous reading qsd by BeOr25/295,302, who cfs Ar fasād "rebellion." However, PiMus69/178n42 confirms the reading with q at least in Ry506.]

Ry506/3: ǵzwtn...kfsdw (?) kl bny ʿA "the raid...when the b.A. rebelled"; C541/9,13 quoted under QSD v

n s fsdm Ry510/5* (or read qsdm)

REBELLION

Ry510/5: ghm d̲ndynhmw ʿrbn fsdm "when the beduins fought against them (in) rebellion"

FSḤ

h pf hfsḥ J618/11*

ENLARGE, BUILD ADDITIONS TO

[Cf Ar fasuḥa "be large, spacious," fasaḥa "enlarge."]

J618/11: the god allowed him to complete their control dyke (?), fhfsḥ "so he built additions..."

n p mfsḥthw J618/17*

ENLARGEMENTS of cultivated area; or INCREASES of harvest obtained by enlarged irrigation system

J618/17: may the god grant [w]fy...m'xd̲thw wmfsḥthw "the well-being of his control dyke and its (or his) enlargements (or, the increases of harvest made possible by his additions to the irrigation system)"

F^c--See under FW^c

F^cL

v ipf yf^cl R4176/8*

MAKE, PREPARE

[Ar fa^cala id.]

R4176/8: lkd̲ lyf^cl T'LB b^cšr 'lm "that (the god) T. may prepare a banquet (by means of) the tithes"

n p f^cln C540/84*

LABORERS; phps SKILLED LABORERS, CRAFTSMEN

C540/84: expenditure lf^cln wlzfn "for the craftsmen and unskilled laborers (on the dam-repair project)"

F^cM

? f^cm J730/5*

sense doubtful

[JSIMB/209 unconvincingly tr "solid," after Ar fa^cm "full." The exp "statue of clay" preceding this puzzling word is also unique, though the inscription otherwise follows standard formulas.]

J730/5: hqnyw...ṣlmn d̲ṣly f^cm ls^cdhmw...n^cmtm "they dedicated this statue of clay ...? so that (the god) might grant them prosperity"

FṢ--See under FYṢ

FṢY

n p fṣym C540/48*

KIND OF GRAPE (white?)

[Ar faṣâ "grape seed"; Akk piṣû "white, sound, pure"; used in contrast to ǵrbbm, "black grapes."]

C540/48: ''blm sqym ǵrbbm wfṣym "camels carrying drink (made of) black and white (?) grapes"

FQD

v pf fqd J651/26; fqdw NNAG15/4-5

(1) LOSE; pass BE LOST, MISSING

[Ar faqada id.]

J651/26: 'l d̲fqdw bn '$šr^c$hmw "nothing was missing from their articles of booty"

(2) LOOSE, GIVE VENT TO (hatred, etc)

lr9/4-5: ǵlyt wtnkr fqd wǵll wnkrn 'LMQH "the hatred and affliction (which) (the god) I. gave vent to, was filled with, and used as a punishment"

tp pf tfqd J665/48-9*

BE REPORTED MISSING (cf FQD v sense[1])

J665/48-9: they returned from campaign in safety w'l tfqd bn gyšhmw ǵyr [']sm "and no one was reported missing from their army except one man"

n s fqdh J525/2*

LOSS, THING LOST (?)

J525/2: she humbled herself before the god, wh' lyṣḥ bn fqdh "so let Him make restitution (?) for her loss(?)"

FQḤ

v pf fqḥ R3945/15+; fqḥy C289/3; inf fqḥhw C372/2

OPEN > RELEASE; esp RELEASE water by opening sluices, or OPEN OUT, LAY OUT a channel or the like

[Cf Heb pāqaḥ "open (the eyes)," Ar fuqqāḥ = ittisāᶜ "extending, spreading out" (LA).]

C372/2: 'śrhw wfqḥ[hw] "binding him and releasing [him]"; R3945/15: fqḥ ṯᶜd mlk "he watered (or, opened out channels for) the irrigated land of the king"; C540/29: fqḥ mḍrft "he opened the channel"

n s fqḥ(m) R3112/1+

(1) SYSTEM OF CHANNELS (?)

R3112/1: ᶜsy wbny fqḥ R "he constructed and built the channel-system of R."

(2) OVERSEER, INSTRUCTOR

[Here cf also Syr pwqḥ' "counsels."]

R4176/9: šm T'LB Y 'ḥdfqḥm "(the god) T. appointed (for) Y. one (person) as instructor (or, overseer)"; in ib/12 for 'ḥdqḥn read same or tr as n.pr: as for subsequent disputes, lyrtᶜ ḏ'ḥd(f)qḥn (or, ḏ'A) "let someone (appointed by?) that one instructor settle (them) (or, let the governor of A. settle them)"

(3) INTEREST

[Cf Te faqḥā "lease out; lend money at usurious interest," fəqaḥ "interest" (SoSoSEG4/37).]

G1361/2: ...]b fqḥm wṯlṯ blṭm ḏrdym "...interest, and three current blṭ-coins"

FQL

v pf fqlw J615/10; ipf yfqln C80/10; yfqlnn J730/8

PRODUCE or HARVEST RICH CROPS

[Ar fql h "be fruitful (land)"; Yem fagal/yifgil "thresh grain."]

J615/10: sqy wdᶜt fqlw bn kl 'srr "crops they harvested from all the valleys"; C80/10: yfqln 'rb^{c}y 'qdrm "he harvested (or, it produced) forty qdr-measures of rich crops"; J730/8: lṭ^{c}mn lhmw 'fql yfqlnn "that (the god) may allow them to taste the harvests they shall harvest".

n s fqlm J727/10; p 'fql(m) J730/8+; 'fqlhmw J656/24

HARVEST, CROPS

J727/10: ls^{c}dh wldm wfqlm "to grant him children and a harvest"; J656/24: wfy grybthmw w'ṯmrhmw w'fqlhmw "the safety of their persons, crops and harvests"; AND OFTEN in the formula 'ṯmr w'fql ṣdqm "satisfying crops and harvest" (J561b/20-1+)

FRD

n s frdm F74/3*

adj: SOLE, UNIQUE; as adv, SOLELY, UNIQUELY

[Ar fard "alone, single, sole."]

F74/3: šr^{c}w bytyhmw lhmw frdm "they provided water for their two houses, for themselves solely"

FRH

v pf frhw R3234/2*

FLEE (?)

[Cf Ar farih "lively, nimble."]

R3234/2: mxḍ [kl] wld ^{c}M wfrhw "he overthrew [all] the children of (the god) A. (= the Qatabanians), and they fled (?)"

FRZN

n s frznm C540/12+

IRON

[Akk parzillu, Heb barzel id.]

C540/12: 'zyym frznm "iron quoins (or, sills)"; cf also the n.pr of part of a fortress, ZLT FRZNM "the Iron Glacis" C40/4

FRṬ--In J660/17, read frṭn prob as n.pr: 'xḏhmw...bFRṬn "he captured them in F."

FRY

tp pf tfry lr19+; ipf ytfrnn ib+

CULTIVATE

[Cf Eth faraya, Heb pārāh "bear fruit."]

lr19: kl 'rḏhmw ḏtfry wytfrnn bnw G "all their lands which the b.G. have cultivated and will cultivate"; NNAG11/17-8 sim exp; lr24/2: crops, 'hnmw ytfrnn wxtdmn "wherever they are cultivated or grown"

Note: HoASG/22 assigns tfr R4176/7 here, but see under WFR tp.

FRS

n^{1} s frs(m,n) J745/6+; frshw J577/1+; d frsnhn J745/8-9; p 'frs(m) J584/1+;

'frshmw J643b/2+

HORSE, MARE (m and f)

[Ar faras "horse, mare." For modern Central Arabic, cf Rwala/372: "A thoroughbred mare is called faras,...and as, with but few exceptions, only mares are bred, the word faras has come to mean horses regardless of sex."]

J745/1-9: 'tlwt 'frs mlkn hqnyw...frsn wrkbhw ḏdhbn...bḏt stwfy frs mlkn ...bḏt mt^{c} frsnhn...bkn rkby bn srn bryn "the equerries of the king's horses dedicated this horse and its trappings of gold because (the god) had preserved the king's horse, because He saved the 2 horses when they were ridden out of the healthy valley"; J649/21-2: he and his horse were wounded and he feared that ymtn frshw "his horse would die"; J752/7: hqnyw ...frsm ḏt ḏhbm "they dedicated a mare of gold"; J665/44: kl...frsm wnqt "every horse/mare and she-camel"

n^{2} p 'frs(m,n) J576/15+; 'frshw ib/4+; 'frshmy Ir19/1; 'frshmw J574/8-9+

HORSEMEN, CAVALRY

[Ar fāris "horseman."]

J665/37: hqdw bn 'frshmw xms w'rb^{c}y 'frsm "they plundered from their horsemen 45 horses"; J576/15: 'lfm 'sdm w'rb^{c}y 'frsm "a thousand soldiers and forty horsemen"; J576/4: 'qwlhw wxmshw w'frshw "his tribal leaders, his infantry and his cavalry"

FR^{c} I

v pf fr^{c}hw R4930; fr^{c}y R4578; fr^{c} R2740/6

PAY/RENDER TRIBUTE OF FIRST-FRUITS

[Cf Ar fara^{c} "firstling offered to the gods"; phps also (for this and tp) fr^{c} D "put forth branches," far^{c} "sprout, shoot"; Syr pra^{c} "bear fruit."]

R2740/6: ywm fr^{c} M "when he rendered tribute of first-fruits to (the god) M."; R4578: fr^{c}y b^{c}l b[ythmy] "they rendered tribute to their clan-deity"; R4930: hqny...bn fr^{c}t fr^{c}hw "he dedicated (it)...from the first-fruits he had rendered to (the god)"

tp ipf ytfr^{c}nn C352/13+

BE CULTIVATED, BE CAUSED TO GROW (crops)

Ir24: fr^{c} 'myrt...'hnmw ytfr^{c}nn wxtdmn "first-fruits of grain, wherever they are cultivated or grown"; sim C352/13 quoted under fr^{c} n^{1}

h For hfr^{c} C19/5, read hqrw; see under QRW h

n^{1} p fr^{c}(m) C352/11+; var fr^{c}w J615/18; var fr^{c}t R4930

CROPS; specifically, FIRST-FRUIT

R4930 quoted under FR^{c} v; Ir24 quoted under FR^{c} tp; J623/14: may the god grant them fr^{c} ḏt' wxrf "crops of the spring and autumn harvests" AND OFTEN SIM; C352/13: fr^{c} w'ṯmr 'hnmw ytfr^{c}nn "first-fruits and crops wherever they are cultivated"; J735/11: 'mrm fr^{c}m "cereal crops, first-fruits"; C87/5: 'ṣf y^{c}brn fr^{c} lǵlm yldn "women (who) offer first-fruits for the children they will bear"

Note: Obscure in J649/12: mhrgt ṣdqm wḏfr^{c}m b[...] gyšn "satisfying killings and ...? in/with...the army." In R2678, read FR^{c} as n.pr: kbr ḥśrn FR^{c} "chief of the Indigents of F." (For Rh's tr "chief of the collectors of first-fruits," see under ḤŚR.)

n^{2} p? mfr^{c}n G1361/3*

FIRST-FRUITS (?) (= fr^{c})

G1361/3: yḥmln wrqn mfr^{c}n "he will pay (as tribute) vegetables, first-fruits"

FR^{c} II

n s tfr^{c}(m) C569+; tfr^{c}hw C325/4

SUMMIT, SUPERSTRUCTURE of a building

[Cf Ar fara^{c}a "excel," far^{c} "top."]

C569: bn mwṯrm ^{c}dy tfr^{c}m "from the foundation to the summit/superstructure"; R3946/5: tfr^{c} bythw...ln ẓwrm "the superstructure of his house from the pillars (upward)"

FRQ

v pf frq R4193/5-6+; inf frqn J567/16

SAVE (s.o.'s life), DELIVER from danger (said of a god)

[Syr praq "rescue," Eth farāqi "savior," ferqān "safety."]

R4193/5-6: ḥmdm bḏt frq ^{c}bdyhw...bn ḍ[w^{c}] ḍ^{c}w "in praise because (the god) saved his servants from the trouble they suffered"; R4011/8: frq nfsh[w] "(the god) saved his life"; J567/16: h^{c}nn wmt^{c}n wfrqn grybt 'dmhw "helped, rescued and saved the lives of His servants"

tp pf tfrqw J644/22+; inf tfrqn R4193/11

LEAVE, ESCAPE, DESERT (?) (phps ultimately < BE DELIVERED)

[Cf Ar frq Dt "disperse, become separated."]

J644/22: 'sdm ḏtfrqw bn hgrn M "soldiers who left/escaped/deserted from the town M."; J660/13: to pursue them bkn tfrqw bn ḏḤ "when they left/escaped/deserted from (the tribe) Ḥ."; R4193/11: the god allowed them tfrqn bn kl hwt 'gyš[n] "to escape from all those troops"

FRŚ

n p mfrśtn R3945/7*

a) WEIR, SPILLWAY; or, b) DAM

[a) Cf Heb prš Pual "be divided," h "separate" (MüBeitrage/313). b) Cf Heb prs "break," Akk parāsu "block (the road), check, hold back" (StSESA/524).]

R3946/7: ^{c}sy mfrśtn 'l mḥmyn "he acquired the weirs/dams which belong to the embankment system"

FRŠ

n s fršt J574/7*

FIELD

[Cf Ar farš "field...covered with plants and herbs" (JSIMB/62).]
J574/7: they fought bkdnn d̲W wW wfršt L "in the 2 plowed fields of W. and W. and the field of L."

FŚL

v _pf_ fśl R4624/7*
CUT, HEW stone (?)
[Cf Aram pəsal "cut, hew."]
R4624/7: ln d̲t fśl w[... "when he hewed out (the mountain road) (?)"

FŠ'

n _s_ fš'm J720/12-3*
adj: SPREADING, ERUPTIVE; or, CONTAGIOUS (a disease)
[Cf Ar fašā "spread," _D_ "spread wider (epidemic)."]
J720/12-3: mrd̲m fš'm d̲'l mn š^c^r kmhn h' ḥlẓhw "an eruptive/contagious sickness, (about) which no one knew what that disease of his was"

FŠḤ

h _inf_ hfšḥn Sh31/13*
GLADDEN, FILL WITH JOY (?)
[Cf Eth astafaššeḥa 'emenna id, causative of tafaššeḥa "rejoice."]
Sh31/13: xmrhw 'LMQH 'tw bwfym whfšḥn b[n] kl d̲blthw mr'hw "(the god) I. allowed him to return in health and gladdened him (?) in all that his lord sent him (to do)"

FTḤ

v _pf_ ftḥhmw J643/20; _ipf_ yftḥn C81/7
CONQUER, LAY WASTE
[Ar fataḥa "open; conquer."]
J643/20: mẓ'w ^c^dy xlf hgrn Y wftḥhmw "they arrived in the vicinity of the town Y. and conquered them (or phps tr, and (someone) opened (to) them)"; C81/7: nkr b^c^lyhmw d̲yftḥn bythmw whd̲lln qnyhmw "(the god) punished them (in) that their house was laid waste and their property was ravaged"

h _pf_ hftḥw F76/8; _inf_ hftḥn R3959/1
LEAVE THE DECISION TO s.o., AUTHORIZE (?)
[Eth ftḥ _h_ "make s.o. decide or give judgment"; Ḥimyaritic fataḥa "give judgment" (Nashwān Extr/82).]
R3959/1: ...] hftḥn ^c^A w'xyh[w...wb]^c^b[r] wb^c^ly 'A [w]'xyh[w] "authorized (?) ^c^A. and his allies...it is obligatory for and incumbent upon 'A and his allies..."; F76/8: sṭrw bd̲n wtfn lqblyd̲t hftḥw b^c^m bn ^c^A "they wrote (in) this document because of what they have authorized concerning the b.A."

n _s_ ftḥ(m,n) F4907/6+
(1) AUTHORIZATION = DECREE (cf FTḤ _h_) (?)
R4907/6: bftḥm "by decree" (context fragmentary; may be an irrigation term

like fqḥ)

(2) LAWSUIT

[Eth fətaḥ id (BeJSS14/229).]

J750/11: h^{c}nhmw '[LM]QH bn ftḥm d̲kyn "(the god) I. helped them in the lawsuit which took place"

FTX

n s̲ ftxm C325/1*

ENGRAVED stone (?)

[Heb ptḥ D̲, Qat ftx "engrave."]

C325/1: rb^{c}tm mwl[g]m wftxm "squared masonry, (of) mwlg-stone and engraved (stone) (?)"

Note: For ftxn N66/1, read ftḥn (RyNE4/167).

FTY, FTT--For n̲ mftt Ry535/4, read mqtt; see under QTW n̲

𐩮—Ṣ

Ṣ'L--For tṣ'ln R4964/5, read tṣl'n; see under ṢL' *tp*

ṢB'

v *ipf* yṣb'w J576/6*

FIGHT, WAGE WAR (cf ḌB' *v* sim)

[Heb ṣābā' id; cf Ar ṣaba'a "go forth." See also under ḌB' *v*.]

J576/6: the troop went away and did not oppose them, wb^{c}dhw fyṣb'w b^{c}ly 'rḍ M "and afterward they fought against the land of M."

ṢBB

n *p*? ṣbbm R4772/4*

adj: PAID DOWN (a sum of money)

[Ar ṣabba "he paid down a price or sum of money" (IrvJRAS'64/32n4).]

R4772/4: blṭm r(ḍ)ym ṣbbm rmym "current coin, paid down as interest"

ṢBḤ

v *inf* ṣbḥn J616/23*

MAKE A MORNING RAID

[Ar ṣabaḥa id (Lane/1640C).]

J616/23: hǵrw wṣbḥn wḥrb bn ^{c}šr D "they raided, made a morning raid and fought some of the clans of D."

n *s* ṣbḥn J649/34+

(1) MORNING

[Ar ṣubḥ, ṣabāḥ id.]

J649/34: they fought all night long ^{c}dy šrq kwkbn ḏṣbḥn "until the rising of the morning star (lit., star of morning)"

(2) EAST (figurative, from sense^{1})

C652/3-4: ^{c}brn m^{c}[rbn w^{c}brn] ṣbḥn "toward the we[st and toward] the east"

Note: ṢBḤm C418/4 prob *n.pr*.

ṢBY I

n *p* ṣb[y]m Ry544/6*

GAZELLES (cf ẓby sim)

[See under ẒBY, and cf Heb ṣəbî id.]

Ry544/6: he killed 2000 'w^{c}lm wṣb[y]m "mountain goats and gazelles"

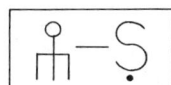

ṢBY II

n s ṣby R3162/3*

UNCLEANNESS

[Cf ModYem ṣbā "be soiled (garment)" (MüW/71).]

R3162/3: ...]'ydwhmw w[...] bn ṣby wbn[... "their hands and...of uncleanness and..."

ṢBN

v pf ṣbnw J720/7-8*

REMOVE, TURN AWAY

[Ar ṣabana id.]

J720/7-8: hxṭ'w...k'l ṣbnw wṯb bmḥrmn wystṣyn bn ḏfr'n "they sinned because they did not turn away the person who sat in the temple stinking of ill-smelling plants"

ṢB^c

n s 'ṣb^{c}m C369/1+; p 'ṣb^c R3112/2

FINGER

[Ar 'iṣba^c id.]

C369/1: ^{c}sy 'ḥt 'ṣb^{c}m bn ṯty yd ^{c}šr qbrm "he built one finger out of two hands, (i.e.) one-tenth of the tomb"; R3112/2: bny...'ṣb^{c}m bn ṯmny 'ṣb^c "he built one of the eight fingers (i.e., one-eighth?)"

ṢD'

n s mṣd'(n) Ry362/1+

AGENT, OFFICIAL

[Cf Ar ṣd', ṣd^c, ṣdy Dt "be concerned, charged with" (BafIns/59).]

Ry362/1: mṣd' 'mr'hw "agent of his lords"; BR-Yanbuq 49/1-2: M...mṣd'n "M., the agent"

ṢDǴ

n s ṣdǵ NNAG12/12,26; ṣdǵhw J721/4+

MANIFESTATION of a deity

[Cf Ar ṣada^{c}a "split, manifest, bring to light"?]

J721/4: he dedicated this statue to the god ḏs'lhw bṣdǵhw "which He had asked of him in His manifestation"; NNAG12/26: wxwdhmw 'LMQ̣H bṣdǵ hwt 'sn "(the god) I. granted to them (what they wished) in the manifestation (to) that man"; R4151/6: the god granted? ...b]ṣdǵhw ktldn bnm wwldt "[in] His manifestation that she would bear a son, and she did"

Note: RycMancie/270 cfs Ar ṣadaǵa "become very weak," tr "weakness" in NNAG12, less plausibly.

ṢDQ

v pf ṣdq R3945/2+; ṣdqhmw C343/10+; ṣdqw Gl136/2; inf ṣdq J627/12+

GRANT, FULFILL an obligation

[Ar ṣadaqa "be upright, just; pay debts, fulfill obligations."]

R3945/2: ywm ṣdq ^{c}_T_TR w'LMQH ḥghmy wyh_t_b mwy _d_hbhw "the day when (the gods) A. and I. fulfilled their obligations and sent water (for) his land"; J627/12: fl yz'n ṣdq whwfyn ^{c}bdhw...bkl 'ml' stml'w "and may (the god) continue to grant and bestow on His servant all the oracle responses they have asked"; C343/10: ḥmdw T'LB bkl 'ml' ṣdqhmw "they praised (the god) T. for all the responses He had granted them"; G1572/2: whmẓ' wṣdq...kl ml' wrbḥ "he ceded and granted all the yield and profit"

ti _inf_ ṣtdqn C429/11*

KEEP FAITH WITH (?)

[Cf Ar ṣadaqa "keep one's promises."]

C429/11: may the god protect him wṣtdqn wn^{c}m lhw bn kl b'stm "and keep faith with (?) and show favor to him against any harm (which might befall him)"

h _inf_ hṣdqn G1364/6+

GRANT (cf ṢDQ _v_ sim)

Ir20/2: may the god continue hṣdqn whwfyn ^{c}bdhw...bkl 'ml' to grant and bestow on His servant all the oracular responses"; G1364/6: fl yhmt^{c}n whbrrn whṣḥḥn whṣdqn whwfyn l'dmhw "may (the god) save and make upright and sound (?) and grant and bestow on His servants..."

n^1 _s_ ṣdq(m) R3945/1-2++

(1) RIGHT, DUE

[Cf Ar ṣdq _D_ "sanction, legalize."]

R3945/1-2: yḥtẓyw mnš'hmw k'ḥd b^{c}sy ṣdqm "their tribal levies succeeded together in doing (what was) right"; G1574/10 (re-edition of R4964): wr' kxmrhw 'LMQ(H) hgb'n l'A ṣdq "and now (the god) I. has agreed to restore to A. (his) due"; C86/12: bǵyr ṣdqm "illegally"

(2) _adj_: PROPER, APPROPRIATE > "HAPPY," FORTUNATE, SATISFYING

C2/15: may the god grant 'fql w'_t_mr ṣdqm ^{c}dy 'rḍhmw "appropriate/satisfying harvests and crops in their lands" AND OFTEN SIM; J561b/8: the god granted to the campaigner mqyht wmhrgt wǵnmt ṣdqm "appropriate/satisfying victories, slaughters and booty" AND OFTEN SIM; J563/8: may the god grant n^{c}mtm wwfym wmngt ṣdqm "prosperity, health and happy outcomes" AND OFTEN SIM; J567/23: may the god grant 'wldm hn'm 'ly kwkbt ṣdqm "pleasing children of happy fortune (lit., stars)" AND OFTEN SIM

n^2 _s_ ṣdqm J567/11,12*

TRUTH, REALITY (?)

[Ar ṣidq "truth, candor."]

J567/11-2: they asked the god khmy bṣdqm whkn hwt ḥlmn wwkbw b^{c}m 'LMQH kbṣdqm whkn hkn hwt ḥlmn "that these 2 (bulls seen in a vision) might (exist) in reality and that He would bring to pass that dream; and they obtained of I. that (it existed) in reality and He brought to pass the realization of that dream"

n[3] s msdq(m,n) R2695/6+

GRANT; DOCUMENT attesting a grant or loan

R2695/6: wtfm wmṣdqm wxmrnm wnḥltm "deed of transfer, grant, concession and gift"; C376/16-7: t^c lm Y bdn mṣdqn "Y. signed this document"

ṢHB

n s ṣhbn C527/3,6*

adj: SHINING (?), phps epithet of a god (fragmentary context)

[Cf Ar ṣahīb, Heb ṣāhōb "reddish, golden."]

C527/3: ...]w ṣhbn wḥmd [... "...shining (?); and he praised..."; ib/6: ...] ṣhbn "...shining (?)"

ṢHR

n s ṣhr(m) C541/60+

CLAMPING TOGETHER with lead clamps (maṣdar); phps also CLAMPS (?)

[Irv/301-2 cfs Ar ṣahara "melt, or liquefy," ṣuhāra† "what is melted, of fat or the like." Basic sense of root "amalgamate, flow together" > "be joined together," here by clamps?]

C541/60: ḥrrtm wmsrm wgrbtm...wṣhrm l^cdbn ^crmn "heaping up and packing in of earth, stonework and clamping together to repair the dam"; F90/2: śftn wmrtn wṣhr[n... "mud, clay and clamping together (means of joining masonry) (or, clamps)"; also in fragmentary context R4761/2

ṢWB

n s ṣwbt(n) C40/3+; ṣwbthw C448/3

GLACIS (?)

[Cf Ar ṣāba "it sloped down," ṣūba† "quantity collected together of dust or earth" (Lane/1740A, 1741C).]

C40/3: kl mwrt wgn' wṣwbt mḥfdn "all the retaining walls, the defensive wall and the glacis of the tower"; C448/1: wśfw wrymw kl gn'hw wṣwbt [... "extended and raised all its wall and glacis"

ṢWD

n s ṣwd R4907/7*

SIDE OF A VALLEY or HILL (?)

[Cf Ar ṣadd id.]

R4907/7: ...] ṣwd ^crrm mdrrm "a hillside (plantation) of flourishing cypresses (?)"

ṢWY

v ipf yṣwynn J577/9*

MAKE WEAK, WEAKEN (?)

[Cf Ar ṣawâ and D "dry up, wither" (JSIMB/81).]
J577/9: kyṣwynn ʾmrʾhmw...kh^{c}smw hxṭʾn "when they weakened (?) their lords, when they repeatedly rebelled"

Ṣw^{c}

n[1] s ṣw^{c}m C343/13*
GRANT, CONCESSION
[Cf Ar ṣāʿa (w) "disperse," N "retreat, yield" (Lane/1746-7).]
C343/13: kwn[t] ḏt hqnytn bwrx...ḏxrf S bn H ṣw^{c}m "this deed of dedication was (enacted) in the month...of the year (named for) S., son of H., as a concession" (for syntax cf use of sm^{c}m C601/9)

n[2] s ṣ^{c}tm R3686A=R4626/2*
SYSTEM OF IRRIGATION by diversion of water through canals
[Ar ṣāʿa (transitive), Dt (intransitive) "scatter" > "disperse (by channels)," MSA ça^{c}jèh "wall about one span high surrounding plots of land" (Irv/216-7.)]
R3686A/2: wʾlʾs sʾlhmw mḥmtm wṣ^{c}tm [w]mflqm "let no one challenge their possession of the embankment system, the diversion system or the dispersion system"

n[3] For n mṣ^{c}m C376/4, see under NṢ^{c}

ṢWF

n s ṣf C338/5-6; var ṣwf C40/3
STONE FACING of a building (?)
[Cf Eth ṣafṣafa "lay with stones," Ar ṣaffa "put in a row."]
C40/3: kl nkl wṣwf wṣll wṯḥẓt sqf "all the paving, stone facing (?), stonework (?) and inauguration (??) of the roof"; C338/5: ṣf RḤBT "stone facing of R. (?)"
Note: G1209, parallel text to C338, reads ḥrt RḤBT "aqueduct of R."

ṢWR I

n s ṣwr(n) C720+
IMAGE, STATUE
[Ar ṣūra† id.]
C720: ṣwr wnfs H "image and funerary stela of H." AND OFTEN simply ṣwr + n.pr; C705: ṣwr wnṣb "image and funerary monument"; F119/2-3: he dedicated ḏ[n ṣ]wrn ḏhbn "this image of gold"

ṢWR II

n p? ṣwrt(n) C308/6,7; ṣwrthw ib/9
EMBANKMENTS
[Cf Heb ṣwr "contain, enclose," māṣôr "rampart"; Ar ṣawr "riverbank, embankment," ModYem ṣawrah "wall of a well" (MüW/73).]

C308/6: kl msqyhmw [wkl] ṣwrt w'rfd ʿdy 'ʿmdn "all their irrigated land [and all] the embankments and supports (?) as far as the ʿmd-land"; ib/9: qšmtn w'hdrhw w'kfrhw wṣwrthw "the orchard and its cisterns, sluices and embankments"

ṢWR III

v inf ṣwr G1369/2*

SEPARATE one's self > LEAVE

[Ar ṣāra "separate, disperse (transitive)," N "become cut, divided" (Lane/1745BC).]

G1369/2: xdg wḥẓmn wṣwr "he left, departed (?) and separated himself"

ṢḤB

v pf ṣḥbw J560/11*

ASSOCIATE, BE(COME) ALLIED (?)

[Ar ṣaḥiba id.]

J560/11: lstwkbn [whn]qd̲n 'ṣḥb ṣḥbw xlfn hgrn M "to escort and 'liberate' the enemies (?) who had joined the (enemy) alliance outside the city M."

n p 'ṣḥb J560/11; 'ṣḥbhmw ib/12-3

ENEMIES (?)

[Dat̲ ṣaḥīb "enemy" (cf Ar ṣaḥīb "ally"--specifically, member of an enemy alliance?).]

J560/11 quoted under ṢḤB v; ib/12-3: st]wkbw whnqd̲n w'xd̲ hmt 'sdn 'ṣ[ḥb]h-(mw) "escorted and 'liberated' (i.e., took from the enemy as plunder) and took prisoner those soldiers/men, their enemies"

ṢḤḤ

v pf ṣḥḥw J525/4; ipf yṣḥ ib/2; inf ṣḥḥ(n) C305+

RESTORE; MAKE RESTITUTION

[Ar ṣḥḥ D id, also "restore to health."]

C305: hḥd̲tw wṣḥḥn wbnyn ṣrḥthmw "they repaired, restored and (re)built their upper chamber"; Ir9/4-5: xmr ṣḥḥ wḥẓmn bn ǵlyt "(the god) agreed to restore and deliver them from hatred"; J525/2: she humbled herself wh' lyṣḥ bn fqdh "so let (the god) make restitution (?) for her loss (?)"

h inf hṣḥḥn G1364/6*

MAKE HEALTHY, SOUND

[Cf Ar ṣaḥḥa "be healthy."]

G1364/6: fl yhmtʿn whbrrn whṣḥḥn whṣdqn whwfyn l'dmhw "may (the god) save and make upright and sound and grant and bestow upon His servants"

n[1] s ṣḥ(m) R4962/11+

(1) TRUTH, HONESTY

[Ar ṣiḥḥa† id, also "health."]

R4962/11: may the god grant ḥẓy wr[ḍ]w wṣḥ 'lbb mr'yhw "favor, good will and honesty of heart (from) his 2 lords"; sim J567/19-20; C308/13: bṣḥm w'mnm yt'xwnn "they made an alliance in honesty and security"

(2) HEALTH

R4671/3: w]fy wṣḥ mqymthmw "well-being and health of their physical faculties"; also with wfy J650/8, J651/39

n² s ṣḥḥm C392/9*

adj: HEALTHY

[Ar ṣaḥīḥ id.]

C392/9: ydbḥn...[db]ḥm ṣḥḥm 'nṯym f'w d[k]rm "(let him) sacrifice a healthy animal, female or male"

ṢḤF

v inf ṣḥf C314/9*

WRITE

[Eth ṣaḥafa id; cf Ar maṣḥaf "book."]

C314/9: the god agreed to protect them b'mr wṣḥft [...] R wW lṣḥf b[... "by means of the command and rescript [they entrusted to their officers] R. and W. to write (on their behalf)"

n s ṣḥft(n) C314/8,11*

RESCRIPT, DOCUMENT

C314/8 quoted under ṢḤF v; ib/11: wwkbw bhyt ṣḥftn 'ml' ṣd[q]m "and they obtained by means of this rescript fortunate oracular responses"

ṢYD

v pf ṣd R4177/3-4; var ṣyd Ry544/3; ipf yṣdn C571/3,8

HUNT; specifically, PERFORM A RITUAL HUNT

[Ar ṣāda (y) id. Discussion of the Sab ritual hunt BeRitH.]

R4177/3-4: ywm ṣd ṣyd ᶜṮTR wkrwm "the day he hunted the ritual hunt of (the god) A. and (performed) the krw-hunt/feast"; R3946/7 and Ry544/3 sim; C571/8: wl yṣdn...hmt ymtn f'w ᶜqbhw "let him or his deputy perform the ritual hunt on those days"

n¹ s ṣd R4176/7; var ṣyd Ry544/3

(1) (RITUAL) HUNT

[Ar ṣayd id.]

R4177/3 quoted under ṢYD v; R3946/7: ṣd ṣyd krwm "he hunted the krw-hunt (or, performed the hunt of the krw-feast)"

(2) GAME, HUNTED ANIMALS (not always distinct from sense¹)

[Ar ṣayd id.]

R4176/7: 'l śn S hxbn ṣd T'LB "it is illegal for (the tribe) S. to allow the game (animals) of (the god) T. to starve"

n² p ṣydhmw R5085/10+

"HUNTERS," name of a branch of the military (SCOUTS?)

[Cf Ar ṣayyād "hunter."]

R5085/10: brd' nṣrhmw wṣydhmw...wm^{c}qbthmw "with the help of their auxiliary forces, 'hunters' and guards"; Ry509/9: mqtwthmw w'tlyhmw wṣydhmw "their officers, equerries and 'hunters'"

ṢYḤ

v pf ṣyḥ J821A/3+; inf? ṣyḥn C158/2

LEVEL land for cultivation

[Eth ṣēḥa "level, make smooth."]

J821A/3: '[n]xl wtbqlt ṣyḥ wbqln "the palmgroves and plantations he leveled and planted"; R4920/2: bny bmḥgr ṣyḥ[... "he built in the enclosed field he had leveled..."; C158/2: ...]ṣyḥn wnqz whqš[b] "leveled (?) and dug a well and prepared for use" (C took as n.pr)

h pf hṣ[y]ḥw R4069/9; inf hṣ[y]ḥn ib/5

PREPARE FOR USE (?) (but see Note)

[Cf ṢYḤ v "level > prepare land for cultivation"; sense here more abstract.]

R4069/5: ^{c}dbw whṣ[y]ḥn msqy 'r[ḍ]thmw "they repaired and prepared for use the irrigation system of their lands (after the dam wall broke)"; ib/9: br'w whṣ[y]ḥw ḥrthw "they built and prepared its aqueduct for use"

Note: These forms might phps be restored as hṣ[ḥ]ḥw, hṣ[ḥ]ḥn--cf ṢḤḤ v "restore a building," h "make sound."]

n[1] s? ṣyḥ R4085/2*

LEVELED GROUND

R4085/2: tqdm lmr'hw...kl ṣyḥ wtbqlt '^{c}md w'^{c}lb "he took charge for his lord of all the leveled and planted ground, naturally as well as artificially irrigated"

n[2] s mṣyḥm R4176/4*

HIGHROAD; or, LEVELED GROUND (cf ṣyḥ) (?)

[Cf Eth maṣyāḥ "highway," maṣyāḥt "leveled ground"; MSA maṣyāḥ "courtyard of a mosque" (Irv/227-8).]

R4176/4: m[ḥ]mytn drt^c mṣyḥm ^{c}dy lyrt^c śdn "the embanked land which lies along the highroad/leveled ground so far as to lie opposite the dam"

ṢYY

st ipf ystṣyn J720/8-9*

SMELL BAD, STINK

[Cf Eth ṣē'a id (HöASASühne/108).]

J720/8-9: they sinned because 'l ṣbnw wtb bmḥrmn wystṣyn bn dfr'n wbn bṣln "they did not remove the person who sat in the temple stinking of ill-smelling herbs and onions"

ṢYN--For stṣyn J720/8-9, see under ṢYY st

ṢYR

v pf/inf ṣyr R3945/7*

WALL, EMBANK (?)

[Cf Dat ṣīra† "stone fence," Sq ṣer "divide, hold back."]

R3945/7: gn' 'hgr S wṣyr 'dhbhw "he walled the towns of S. and embanked (?) its fields"

Note: For n mṣr, p mṣyrt, see under ṢRR.

ṢYT

n s ṣythw J702/5*

(GOOD) REPUTATION (?)

[Ar ṣīt, ṣawt id.]

J702/5 (obscure context): l(ḥd)rn kl ršym d'l yšrḥn ṣythw "let every priest (?) beware (?) who does not protect his reputation"

ṢL--For n ṣlt, see under WṢL, ṢLW, ṢLL

ṢL'

tp inf tṣl'n R4964/5*

PROCLAIM

[Prob var of root ṢLW "pray, entreat > declare solemnly."]

R4964/4-5: dmr wtṣl' dmrw wtṣl'n "the edict and proclamation (which) they ordained and proclaimed"

Note: R's reading tṣ'ln is apparently an error.

n s tṣl' R4964/4* (D inf?)

PROCLAMATION

R4964/4 quoted under ṢL' tp

ṢLW I

n p? ṣlt MüBilinguis/3; ṣlthmw J866

PRAYERS

[Ar ṣly D "pray," ṣalā(w)† "prayer."]

MüBilinguis/3: with the help of his Lord (God) wbṣlt š^c^bhw...wbmqm mr'hw "and the prayers of his community and the power of his (human) lord"; J866: wlysm^c^n ṣlthmw "may (the god) hear their prayers"

ṢLW II

n s ṣlwt C553/2+; p ṣlwhmw C540/79

FACE or SIDE of a construction

[Ar ṣalāya† "front," ṣalā "backbone, small of the back"; Dat ṣly "face, be opposite."]

C553/2: let the boundary be b^c^br smt sṭr bṣlwt Ǵ dt nsr T "according to the mark inscribed on the face of Ǵ. which is toward T."; sim C554/1-2; C540/79: lmdw kl ^c^glmn wnmryn w^c^wdn bgyrm ṣlwhmw w'r'shmw "they plastered all the diversion mole and control walls and settling basin with plaster--their sides and their tops"; C434/5: they built the temple bn dt hwrtn ^c^dy ṣlwt byn dn mḥrmn wmbsln "from this cistern to the side (?) between this temple and the altar" (syntax of pp byn doubtful here)

ṢLḤ

v ipf yṣ[lḥ]n C74/8; inf? ṣlḥ(n) R4919/9+

(1) MAKE SUCCESSFUL (l- s.o.)

[Ar ṣalaḥa "be well, thrive," h "make thrive or prosper; put in order."]

R4919/9: ...RḤM]Nn b^{c}l smyn wrxhw dS lṣlḥn lhm[... "(by the god) R., lord of heaven. (This document's) month (was) dS. May (the god) make them successful!"

(2) PUT IN ORDER, MAINTAIN ORDER

Ist7608b/9: [ks]txlhmw lz^{c} bḥrn wlṣlḥ Ḥ "when he had appointed them to defend the sea and maintain order (in) Ḥ."; C74/8: lyṣ[lḥ]n Q wZ "to maintain order (?) in Q. and Z."

h pf? hṣlḥ[C646/5*

MAKE SUCCESSFUL (?) (cf ṢLḤ v sense[1] id)

C646/5 (fragmentary): wlṣlḥ [...] m^{c}wnhmw hṣlḥ[... "and to make successful ...their helper (?) (who) made successful (?)"

n s ṣlḥ(m) C538/2+

(1) PEACE, PROSPERITY (?)

[Ar ṣulḥ "peace," and cf ṢLḤ v.]

C538/2 (fragmentary context): ...] RḤMNn ṣlḥm by[... "...(the god) R. Peace in (?)..."; also in Gl194/10 (fragmentary context): ...wṣlḥ...; phps v

(2) adj: PIOUS

[Ar ṣāliḥ id.]

Ry520/8: may the god grant him wldm ṣlḥm sb'm lsmRḤMNn "pious children (or, a pious child?), campaigning for the name of (the god) R."

ṢLY

n s ṣly J730/4*

CLAY (?)

[Cf Ar ṣalla^{+} "dry ground," ṣaliya "burn," D "warm, heat" (cf JSIMB/209).]

J730/4-5: they dedicated ṣlmn dṣly/ f^{c}m ls^{c}dhmw n^{c}mtm "this statue of clay (?) ...? so that (the god) might grant them prosperity"

Note: J's tr of f^{c}m "full > solid" is not convincing. Aside from this unique expression the inscription follows standard formulas.

ṢLL

v pf ṣllw C660/2,3; inf/maṣdar ṣll C40/3

PAVE, LAY STONES

[Cf Eth ṣalala "cover," ModḤaḍ ṣlāl "layer of stone slabs" (CoRoC/224B), ModYem maṣlūl "paved with large stones" (RoVoc/310).]

C40/3: kl nkl wṣwf wṣll...sqf "all the pebble paving, stone facing (?) and stonework (?) of the roof"; C660/2-3: bnyw...mhẓllm...wṣllw bnwthmw...wṣllw mwṯbhmw "they built roofed porches and paved their buildings and paved their shrine"

Note: For ṣllm C62/1, read ẓllm (so BeSM/396).

n s ṣlt DJE12/2+; ṣlthw C325/2

CONSTRUCTION IN STONE

C325/2: grbm wrb^{c}tm...ṣlthw dsn mś́wdn "stonework and squared masonry for (?) the stone construction which is in the direction of the sanctuary"; DJE12/2: br'w...ṣlt bythmw "they built the stone construction of their house"

For n ṣlt elsewhere, see under WṢL, ṢLW I

ṢLM

n^1 s ṣlm(n,m) J650/4++; d ṣlmn J610/4+; ṣlmnhn J559/3+; ṣlmynn J574/2; p 'ṣlm(m,n) J689/2+

STATUE

[Heb ṣélem id; cf Ar ṣanam "image, idol."]

J689/2-3: he dedicated 'rb^{c}tn 'ṣlmn wṣlmtnhn lwfy bnyhw "four statues and two statues representing women for the well-being of his children (six nn.pr follow)"; J650/4: hqnyw 'LMQH...ṣlmn ddhbn bn ^{c}šr y^{c}šrnn l'LMQHW... ḥgn kwqhhmw 'LMQH...bms'lhw wlwfy mr'hmw "they dedicated (to the god) I. this statue of gold out of the tithes they paid to I. as He commanded them in His oracle, and for the well-being of their lord" AND VERY OFTEN SIM

n^2 s ṣlymn R4674/4*

STATUETTE (?)

[Diminutive of ṣlm (n^1 above), cf Ar form fu^{c}ayl, or merely plene writing?]

R4674/4: he dedicated to the god ṣlymn [d]šfthw "this statuette which he had promised Him"

n^3 s ṣlmt(m,n) J569/4-5+; d ṣlmtn J742/8; ṣlmtnhn J689/2-3; ṣlmtynn R4659/4

STATUE representing a woman (cf ṣlm)

J742/8: dedicated 'rb^{c}t 'ṣlmm wṣlmtn dšftt lbnyhw "four statues and 2 statues representing women which she had promised (to the god) for her children (six nn.pr follow)"; cf J689/2-3 quoted under ṢLM n^1; all contexts parallel those of ṣlm (n^1)

ṢM'

n s ṣm'm J735/7*

DROUGHT (cf ẓm' "thirst")

[Heb ṣāmā' "thirst," ṣimmā'ôn "parched ground."]

J735/7: ybsw 'mṭrn...wmwt dbn '^{c}mdn bn ṣm'm "the rain-watered fields dried up and some of the naturally irrigated fields died because of the drought"

ṢN^c

v ipf yṣn^{c}n Ry507/10; yṣn^{c}w Ir13/10; yṣn^{c}nn J1028/8; inf ṣn^c(n) Ir13/7+; ṣn^{c}hw Ir32/6

FORTIFY

[Cf Eth ṣan^{c}a "be strong," 'aṣne^{c}a "make strong"; ModYem ṣāni^c "wall" (RoVoc/310).]

Ry508/8: wmlkn hrzy bmqrnt Ḥ wlṣn^{c}n sslt MDBn "as for the king, he remained on guard against Ḥ. and in order to fortify the 'chain' (of fortifications) of al-Mandab"; Ry507/10: yṣn^{c}n sslt MDBn "he fortified the 'chain' of al-Mandab"; Ir13/7: lṣn^c hwt bytn "to fortify that fortress"

tp pf tṣn^{c}w C541/77+; inf tṣn^{c}n J644/6

FORTIFY ONE'S SELF

C541/77: wrdw 'qwln 'lht tṣn^{c}w bK "the tribal leaders came down who had fortified themselves in K."; C353/6: tṣn^{c}w bhgrn Ḍ "they fortified themselves in the city Ḍ."

h pf hṣn^{c}w J585/6*

CAUSE TO FORTIFY > BESIEGE

[Cf Heb ṣinnē^c "restrain," Eth 'aṣne^{c}a "keep, retain."]

J585/6: hṣn^{c}w 'bhmw...'ḤBŠn bhgrn Ś brqm wṯny xrfm "the Ḥabashites besieged their father in the city Ś. for one rainy season and two years"

st pf stṣn^{c}w R2633/8*

FORTIFY ONE'S SELF (cf ṢN^c tp id)

R2633/8: they repaired the fortress kstṣn^{c}w bhw kgb'w bn 'rḍ Ḥ "when they had fortified themselves in it after they had returned from the land of Ḥ."

n^1 s ṣn^{c}hmw Ir32; p 'ṣn^{c}m R4158/6

FORTIFICATION(S)

Ir32: ^{c}dww bsḥtm hgrhmw wṣn^{c}hmw "they attacked their town and its fortification(s) to destroy (them)"; R4158/6: ...b'ṣn^{c}m wsr[wtm "with fortifications and tr[oops]"

n^2 p ṣn^{c}wyhmw Ir22/2*

FIELDS IRRIGATED BY ṣn^c-BARRAGE

[Cf Ar ṣanā^c "wooden barrage to hold back water" (RycMus87/511 and n6).]

Ir22/2: 'rḍhmw wmšymthmw wmqyḍhmw wṣn^{c}wyhmw bmšrqhmw w^{c}lthmw "their lands, fields, summer-crop fields and ṣn^c-barrage fields in their eastern and highland territories"

n^3 s mṣn^{c}t(n) C155/2+; mṣn^{c}thmw BeGleanp42/4; p mṣn^c(m) C353/14+

FORTRESS

[Cf ModḤaḍ maṣna^{c}a^t id (CoRoC/224-5).]

J629/30: bhsb^{c}n...kl hgr wmṣn^c š^{c}bn 'A "in destroying all the towns and fortresses of the tribe A."; C155/2: ẓwrw 'ḤMRn bmṣn^{c}tn "they besieged the Ḥimyarites in the fortress"; C353/14: sb^{c}w kl mḥfdt...wkl mṣn^c "they destroyed all the towers and fortresses"

ṢNQ

n^{1} *s* ṣnq(m,n) C81/8+

DISTRESS, esp economic (?)

[Cf phps Ar ḍanuka "be narrow, strait," zanaqa "tighten," *D* "be stingy."]
C81/8: yftḥn bythmw whḏlln qnyhmw wmḥškn ^{c}dy ṣnqn "their house was laid waste and their property ravaged, and (they were) afflicted, in distress"; G1574=R4964/8: k(n)fq bnhw ^{c}A bṣnqm bbrtm "when A. claimed money from him in (his) distress"; also in fragmentary context in R4773/2

n^{2} *s*? ṣnwq Ir13/9*

sense doubtful

Ir13/9: they destroyed them, ǵyr...ḏndfw ^{c}dy ṣnwq Š "except for those who fled to the ...? of (the town of) Š."

Ṣ^{c}--For *n* ṣ^{c}t R3006A/2, see under ṢW^{c}; for *n* mṣ^{c}m C376/4, see under NṢ^{c}

ṢǴR

n *s* ṣǵrm R2695/6; ṣ(ǵr)hmw C575/12-3; *p*? ṣǵrt R4919/3; *var* 'ṣ[ǵ]rt Ry509/7-8 (*p* of comparative)

adj: SMALL, UNIMPORTANT

[Ar ṣaǵīr id.]
R2695/6: kl sṭrm kbrm f'w ṣǵrm "every document, great or small"; Ry509/7-8: 'ṣ[ǵ]rt 'qwlhmw "the lesser of their tribal leaders"; in C575/12-3 read phps ḏR (kb)rhmw wṣ(ǵr)hmw "(the tribe) R., its great and small (members)"

ṢF--see under ṢWF

ṢṢR--For ṣṣyr R2740/9-10, read 'ṣyr; see under 'ṢR

ṢR--see under NṢR, ṢRR

ṢRB I

n *s* ṣrb(m) C174/3+

(1) AUTUMN; AUTUMN HARVEST

[ModYem ṣorāb "autumn harvest," ṣarab/yuṣrub "reap, harvest" (RoVoc/310). Cf also Sab month-name ḏṢRBn.]
C174/3: abundance of crops bqyẓ wdṯ' wṣrb wmlym "in summer, spring, autumn and winter" AND OFTEN SIM; R4013/3: n'd dṯ' wqyẓ wṣrb "abundance of spring, summer and autumn harvests" AND OFTEN SIM; C73/7: they dedicated because hwfyhmw 'LMQH ṣrb šfthmw "(the god) I. had granted them the autumn harvest He had promised them"

(2) FIELD for autumn-harvest crops (cf mqyẓ, "field for summer crops")
C380/4: 'l śn qšbn mḥmyn wb^{c}d 'fl ṣrb[n] lbrktn "it is not lawful to clear the embanked land or remove (extend?) the dykes of the autumn-crop field to the cistern"

n[2] s ṣrbt GaMosna^{c}/6,10*

COLLECTIVE ENTERPRISE (?)

[Cf Ar ṣaraba "collect, amass"--here, a labor force? (BeSM/399-400).]

GaMosna^{c}/6: mnqltn ṣrbt xṣbw "these roads (were) the collective enterprise (?) which they cut"; ib/10: nṣb wmnṣf ṣrbt wtṯwb "the labor and labor-force (used in) the repeated collective enterprise (?)"

ṢRB II

n s mṣrb(n) C337/9+

ALTAR for burnt sacrifices, prob of incense

[Cf Heb ṣrb N "be burnt," ṣārāb "burning"; Min mṣrb mrtn (R2869/5) "altar for myrrh."]

C337/9: fh]qny T'LB mṣrbn [... "he dedicated this incense altar to (the god) T."; C338/9: mṣrbn wmqṭrnhn "the incense altar and 2 incense burners"

ṢRḤ

h inf hṣr[ḥ] C648/4* (?)

BUILD UPPER CHAMBERS (ṣrḥt) in a building (but see Note)

[Denom from n ṣrḥ, below.]

C648/3-4: mdqnt wmśwd [w]ṣrḥt wmẓllt bythmw...f^{c}dbw whẓl whṣr[ḥ] "(as for) the oratory, sanctuary, upper chambers and roofed porch of their house, they repaired and roofed and built (them)"

Note: Sometimes restored as hṣr[y], phps less plausibly. See under SRY h.

n s ṣrḥn C338/3; var ṣrḥtn C648/3; p ṣrḥthw C339b/2+; ṣrḥthmw C1/4+

UPPER CHAMBER, UPPER STORY of a building

[Eth ṣerḥ "upper story of a building," Ar ṣarḥ "lofty structure."]

C648/3 quoted under ṢRḤ h; C132/2-3: ṯny msqfn mšrqy wm^{c}rby hyt ṣrḥtn "two porticoes, east and west of that upper chamber"; C1/4: šmw mṣr^{c}y fnwt ṣrḥthmw "they set up double doors in front of their upper chamber"; C338/3: mhy^{c} ṣrḥn R "the sanctuary of the upper story of R."

ṢRX

v pf ṣrx J665/40*

CALL for help, SUMMON (l- s.o.)

[Ar ṣaraxa "call for help."]

J665/40: ṣrx lhmw kh^{c}n...wh^{c}n dG "he summoned them to help, and (the tribe) G. helped..."

h pf hṣrx Ir21*

INFORM (l- s.o.) (?); or, CALL for help (= ṢRX v)

[Ar ṣaraxa, Eth ṣarxa "cry out" (cf RycMus87/505).]

Ir21: whṣrx lhw bn lb'n wh^{c}n b^{c}lyhw "he informed/called to him for help (?) concerning the lion, and he helped against it"

n s ṣrxn C541/24*

SUMMONS

[Ar ṣarxa† "cry for help."]

C541/24: wṣḥhmw ṣrxn "the summons reached them"

ṢRY

v pf ṣry C74/19+; ṣryhw C430/3+; ṣryhmw C575/5; ipf yṣryhw R4009/4; yṣrynhmw J577/9; inf ṣry J633/13

(1) PROTECT

[Ar ṣarâ "cut (off); protect."]

C74/19: w'LMQH...fṣry hmt 'srrn...bn brdm "and as for (the god) I., may He protect those valleys from cold"; J577/9: they repeatedly rebelled ww^c^dhmw kyṣrynhmw mlk Ḥ b^c^br 'mr'hmw "and the king of Ḥ. promised them that he would protect them against their lords"

(2) DELIVER A favorable ORACULAR RESPONSE or DECISION

[Ar ṣarâ baynahum "decide" (MüW/72).]

J633/13: šft wh'mnn wṣry wtbšrn "(the god) promised/decreed, gave assurance, decided and announced oracularly"; C461/9: ṣry S btḥty ^c^T̲TR "S. delivered an oracular response by the inspiration of (the god) A."; J560/7-8: he dedicated bd̲t stwfy ṣry bnhw 'A "because (the god) granted an oracular decision to his son A."; AND ESP IN EPONYM FORMULAS, e.g. J589/1-5: Y 'A dṣryhw 'A wbnyhw H dṣryhw M (etc)...hqnyw "Y.A., to whom (the eponym) A. delivered an oracular decision, and his son H., to whom (the eponym) M. delivered an oracular decision, have dedicated..." (for the eponym's function of delivering oracles, see RycER8/283; phps the oracles in question here concerned the appointment of the succeeding eponym.

ti ipf yṣtrynn Ir14/2; inf ṣtryn J616/9,34

SEEK AN ORACULAR DECISION (cf ṢRY v sense 2)

J616/9: kl 'ml' wtbšr wṣry stml'w wtbšrn wṣtryn b^c^mhw "all the oracular responses, announcements and decisions they asked, requested and sought from (the god)"

tp pf tṣryw J877/7; inf tṣryn J577/9,10

(1) PROVIDE PROTECTION (cf ṢRY v sense 1)

J577/9: w^c^dhmw š^c^bn N...ltṣryn b^c^br 'mr'hmw "the tribe N. promised them to provide protection against their lords" (cf ib quoted under ṢRY v sense 1)

(2) SEEK or OBTAIN AN ORACULAR DECISION (?) (cf ṢRY v sense 2)

J877/7: wqhhmw bms'lhw s'lm b^c^ly ṣrythmw bkn tṣryw b^c^mhw "(the god) commanded them through His oracle (in) an oracle response concerning their oracular decision when they had sought/obtained (the latter) from Him"

h pf hṣry C466/6; hṣryy N75/5; phps inf hṣr[y] C648/4

CAUSE the god TO GIVE AN ORACULAR DECISION > SEEK/OBTAIN AN ORACULAR DECISION

C466/6: yd̲qṭn M whṣry T "M. offers sacrifice (?); T. obtains the oracular decision"; N75/5=C28/1: he (?) dedicated to the god because stwfy ṣry hṣryy "He had granted the oracular decisions they 2 had sought" (scribal error for hṣry "he had sought"?)' C648/4: ^{c}d̲bw whẓl whṣr[y] wḥẓyn tḥẓyt "they repaired, roofed, sought oracular decisions (concerning) and cast the horoscope of (the building)" (or read hṣr[ḥ], q.v. under ṢRḤ h̲)

n s̲ ṣryt(m,n) C80/12+; ṣrythmw C401/4+; p̲ ṣry R3992/5+

(FAVORABLE) ORACULAR RESPONSE/DECISION

C80/12: d̲n ms'ln wṣrytn "this oracular response and decision"; R3992/5: kl 'ml' wṣry wtbšr stml' b^{c}mhw "all the oracle responses, decisions and announcements he asked of (the god)"; C282/5: ṣdqhw bkl 'ml' stml' b^{c}mhw ṣrytm "(the god) granted him, in all the oracular responses he asked of Him, a favorable response"

ṢR^c

n d̲ mṣr^{c}y R4773/2+; p̲ mṣr^{c}t(m) J576/16+

GATES, DOORS, LEAVES of a door

[Ar miṣra^c id.]

R4773/2: m^{c}rby mṣr^{c}y wfnwt mḥwl "the 2 entrances, the 2 gates and the road of the encircling wall"; J576/16: ḥmlhmw mṣr^{c}t hgrn "drove them to the gates of the city"; C448/4: h^{c}qbw lxlfhw mṣr^{c}tm "they repaired, outside it, the gates"

ṢRF I

n[1] s̲ ṣrf(m,n) J669/6+

SILVER

[Ar ṣarīf id; cf ṣirf "pure, unmixed" and Heb ṣārāp "smelt, refine."]

J669/6: he dedicated ṣlmn wmśdm ṣrfm wmdlthmy ^{c}sym "a statue and an inscriptional plaque of silver, their weight (being) (one) ^{c}sy-unit"; J703/3: ṣlmn d̲ṣrfm wxmst 'ṣlmm d̲hbm "a statue of silver and five statues (of) gold"

n[2] s̲ ṣrf(m) C308/4+

KIND OF AROMATIC GUM used as incense = "SILVER" INCENSE (?)

[Phps so called from color, cf ṣrf "silver" and d̲hb "gold; 'golden' incense." Or cf Heb ṣārāp "smelt, refine metal by fire."]

R4178/1 (fragmentary): it is not lawful hr'šn bn ṣrf [...] bn mḥrmn "to remove any 'silver' incense from the temple"; C308/4: ṭyb wṣrf tnṭ^{c}w "the ṭyb- and ṣrf-incense(-producing plants) they planted"; ib/5: m't srwr ṣrfm "a hundred srr-measures of 'silver' incense (prob, of land planted with 'silver' incense)"

ṢRF II

n p̲ ṣrf C291/1*

EXPENSES

[Ar ṣarafa "spend, expend (money)," ṣarfīyāt "payments, disbursements."]

C291/1: ṣrf w'kry wmgz^{c}t "expenses, rents (?) and payments"

ṢRR

h pf hṣr J643/21; hṣrw J577/2+; ipf yhṣr J576/7; yhṣrn J576/8+; yhṣry J629/8; yhṣrw J576/14+; inf hṣr(n) J631/21+

(1) ADVANCE (on), LAUNCH AN ATTACK (said of a military expedition)

[Cf Ar ṣarra^{+} "rage, tumult (of a battle)," Sq ṣer(r) "throw."]

J576/5: hṣrw ^{c}dy dt mẓ'w ^{c}dy brrn dD "they advanced until they reached the plains of D."; J577/4: ḥrbt ḥrbw whṣrn b^{c}d gzm wslm "the battle they fought and launched after the oath and peace-treaty"; J631/21: ^{c}dw whṣrn B...wmṣr 'ḤBŠn ^{c}dy hgrn "B. and the Ḥabashite expeditionary force invaded and advanced on the city"

(2) ENACT A RITUAL PROCESSION (?)

[A ritual enactment of a military maneuver? Cf month-name dṢRR, "of the ṣrr-ritual"?]

R4176/7: bywm sb^{c} dṢRR ltfr qsd T'LB ^{c}dy T w^{c}dy 'l whṣr bḥrmt 'l "on the seventh day of (the month) dṢ., (let) the 'yeomen' of (the god) T. journey to (the shrines) T. and l. and enact the hṣr-procession (?) in the sanctuary l."

n s mṣr(m) J643/5+; mṣrhw J577/2+; mṣrhmw J578/21; p mṣyrt J576/15+; mṣyrth[w] C334/5+; var 'mṣrhw J512/5

(1) EXPEDITIONARY FORCE/TROOPS

[Cf ṢRR h "advance, attack."]

C308/12: stkml h' 'xwnn bynhmw wbyn G wmṣr 'ḤBŠn "that alliance was concluded between them and G. and the Ḥabashite expeditionary force"; J578/7: kl mṣr w'š^{c}b wxms Ḥ "all the expeditionary troops, tribesmen, and army of Ḥ."; J643b/2: hrg bn mṣr mlk ḤDRMWT ṯny 'lfn 'sdm "killed, of the expeditionary force of the king of Ḥ., two thousand men"; J512/5: he dedicated lwfyhw wwfy[...]w w'mṣrhw "for his own well-being and that of his [...] and his troops (?)"

(2) EXPEDITION

J643/5: mnš' wšt' wmṣr nš' whšt'n whṣrn "the campaign, uprising and expedition he undertook, started and launched"

Note: I have been influenced by the context in J643/5 in assigning mṣr (in both senses) to this root. The root has also been interpreted, both by scholars and by Old South Arabs, as ṢYR (cf the p mṣyrt) and as MṢR (cf the apparent p 'mṣr).

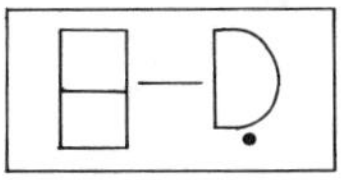

ḌʼN

n *coll* ḍʼnm J1028/6+

SHEEP

[Ar ḍaʼn (*coll*) id.]

J1028/6: ʼblm wbqrm wḍʼnm "camels, cattle and sheep"; Ist7630/7: sṭrm ḏmlʼhw sb^{c}y wmʼ ḍʼnm "a tract of pastureland sufficient for 170 sheep"

ḌBʼ

v *pf* ḍbʼ J555/4+; ḍbʼy J578/24; ḍbʼw J658/14; *ipf* yḍbʼ J574/4; yḍbʼn J577/8+; *inf* ḍbʼ J577/14+

WAGE WAR, FIGHT (cf ṢBʼ *v* sim)

[Eth ḍabʼa, Heb ṣābāʼ id; cf Ar ḍabaʼa "come forth unexpectedly" (Lane/1763A). Cf also Sab ṣbʼ "fight, wage war" prob a by-form of this root.]

J577/14: wʼgyš̌...hysr lḍbʼ b^{c}lyhmw wyhrgw bn š̌^{c}bn N "and as for the armies he sent to wage war against them, they killed (some of) the tribe N."; J581/6: they returned safely bn kl sbʼt wḍbyʼ wtqdmt sbʼy wḍbʼ wtqdmn "from all the campaigns, engagements and battles they undertook, fought and took part in" AND OFTEN SIM; J758/7: sbʼw wḍbʼ wǵzw ^{c}dy ʼrḍ R "they campaigned and waged war and raided in the land of R."

n^1 *s* ḍbʼ C516/5-6+; *p* ḍbʼt(n) J636/6-7+; *var* ḍbyʼ(n) J581/6+; note also possible *varr* ʼ(ḍ)[bʼ] J586/14, ḍbyʼtn Ir13/4 (Ir transliterates ḍbʼtn, which may be the correct reading)

BATTLE, ENGAGEMENT, FIGHT; WAR

C516/5-6: hqdmhw...ḍbʼ ʼWSN "he put him in charge of the war (with the kingdom) A."; J636/6-7: tʼwl mrʼhmw bn hnt ḍbʼtn bwfym "their lord returned from those wars in safety"; C137/1: the god granted them mqyḥt ṣdqm bḍbʼt "satisfying victories in the battles (they fought)"; and cf J581/6 quoted under ḌBʼ *v*

n^2 *p* ḍbʼt J635/24*

FIGHTERS, SOLDIERS (?)

J635/24: sbʼw...^{c}dy S b^{c}ly ʼA...w^{c}dy xlf hgrn N [b^{c}l]y ḍbʼt ʼḤBŠ̌n "they campaigned at S. against A. and outside the city N. against the Ḥabashite soldiers (?)"

ḌBḤ

n _s_ ḍbḥ R4176/2* (_inf_ or _maṣdar_)

TAXATION, LEVYING OF TAXES (?)

[Cf Eth ṣabāḥt, Qat ṣbḥt id, Eth ṣabḥa "pay taxes."]

R4176/2: ḥẓr T'LB qsdm bn ḍbḥ bbḍ^{c}hw "(the god) T. has prohibited the qsd-citizens from levying taxes (?) in His district"

ḌB^c

h _pf_ hḍb^c R3945/13*

ATTACK, STRIKE

[Ar ḍaba^{c}a "stretch forth the arm for the purpose of striking" (Lane/1766-A).]

R3945/13: hḍb^c _d_'mnt K wqtlhmw "he attacked those under the protection of K. and killed them"

ḌGM--For hḍgm C405/12, see under HḌG

ḌW--For _v_ yḍwn, _n_ mḍwn C522/3,2, see under NḌW

ḌW^c

n _s_ ḍw^c Ry538/44; _p_ 'ḍw^{c}w R4193/13-4

BATTLE (?) (cf ḌY^c _v_ "fight")

[See under ḌY^c and also, phps, under ṬW^c.]

Ry538/44: may the god protect them bn ḍw^c wnḍ^c wšṣy wt_t_^{c}t šn'm "from battle, injury, evil eye and abuse of (any) enemy"; R4193/13-4: mt^{c}hmw bn kl 'ḍw^{c}w mr'hmw "(the god) saved them from all the battles (?) of their lord (i.e., all those they fought for him?)"; cf also ib/6-7, quoted under ḌY^c _v_

ḌYM

v _pf_ ḍmw Ry509/6*

COMMIT CRIMES, SEND RAIDS (?) (but see Note)

[MüW/76 cfs Ar ḍāma (y) "injure; do wrong," Mh haḍayûm "do damage to s.th."]

Ry509/6: ksb'w wḥllw 'rḍ M ḍmw nzlm bn 'š̌^{c}bhmw "they campaigned and destroyed the land of M., some of their tribes sending raids down"

Note: Ry read as _n.pr_.

ḌY^c

v _pf_ ḍ^{c}w R4193/6-7*

FIGHT (cf ḍw^c _n_ "battle (?)")

R4193/6-7: the god saved His servants bn ḍ[w^c] ḍ^{c}w bxlf Z wbhwt [ḍw^c]n f'sw "from the b[attle] they fought outside A., for in that [battle] they were at a disadvantage"

Note: For w-ḍ^{c}n J647/14, read wḍ^{c}n (?); see under WḌ^c _n_^{2}.

ḌYF--In R2633/5, ḍyftn in list of <u>nn.pr</u>--prob a <u>n.pr</u>. MüW/75 cfs Ar ḍyf <u>Lt</u> "be narrow (a valley)," ḍīf "side of a valley"; tr "defile"

ḌLL

v <u>pf</u> ḍll J670/10; <u>inf</u> ḍlln J661/5

SUFFER GRAVE ILLNESS

[Cf Ar ḍalla "go astray," ḍull "state of perishing" (Lane/1796-7).]

J661/5: the god saved them bn mrḍ wḍll mrḍw wḍlln "from the sickness and (grave) illness they had and suffered"; J670/10: He saved him bn ḍllm ḏḍll "from the (grave) illness he suffered"

n <u>s</u> ḍllm C539/6+

(GRAVE) ILLNESS

C541/14: dny (or xny) ḍlln ^{c}ly 'š^{c}bn "the illness approached (or, was severe) among the tribesmen"; C539/6: ^{c}wsm wḍllm wmḥlm "pestilence, (grave) illness and famine"; C540/69: ḍllm wmwtm "illness and mortal sickness"

ḌL^{c}

n <u>p</u> mḍl^{c}hw R4069/7,10*

REVETTING WALLS, or TERRACES

[Cf ModḤaḍ ḍala^{c}(a) "support," maḍla^{c}a "rock slope (forming a terrace); terrace," Daṯ ḍāli^{c} "dam" (Irv/175).]

R4069/7: hṯbrt wśḥb kl [^{c}]q[rhw w]mbr'hw wmḍl^{c}hw "all its dam wall, stonework and revetting walls/terraces were broken and eroded"; sim ib/10

ḌM--For <u>v</u> ḍmw Ry509/6, see under ḌYM <u>v</u>

ḌMD

v <u>inf</u> ḍmd C315/5*

YOKE > UNITE

[Ar.Eth ḍamada id.]

C315/5: the god helped them bhslmn wḍmd w'tm Y...byn 'mlk "in Y.'s making peace, uniting and joining the kings"

n <u>p</u> ḍmdm C540/35*

YOKES, PAIRS of oxen (or camels?)

[Heb ṣémed id.]

C540/35 (fragmentary context); in repairing the dam they used camels (?) and ṯty m'tm [w'lf]m ḍmdm ḥ[rrm] "1200 yokes of oxen/camels for heaping up earth" (tr after Irv/276-7)

Ḍ^{c}--See under WḌ^{c}, NḌ^{c}, ḌY^{c}

Ḍ^{c}R--For <u>n</u> ḍ^{c}rtm R3945/2, read ṯ^{c}rtm; see under Ṯ^{c}R

ḌFW I

v <u>pf</u> ḍfwt C657/3*

OVERFLOW (a canal), SUPPLY WATER

[Ar ḍafā "become full, overflow (watering trough)" (Lane/1796B).]

C657/3: fnwthw d̲t tsqynhw bn ḥrtn L d̲t ḍfwt bʿly mḥm[yt] "its canal which waters it from the aqueduct L. which supplies water over the embanked land"

ḌFW II

n s̲ ḍfw C449/2+

(VOTIVE) TABLET (cf tf id, under TFF)

[Cf Ar ḍafā' "side," prob from Akk (and Sumerian) ṭuppu/duppu "tablet."]

C449/2 (fragmentary): ...m]śwtm wḍfw zlth "the fire-altars (?) and the votive tablet of their (?) zlt-building"; C70/1 (fragmentary; on a bronze tablet): he dedicated d̲n ḍf[wn] "this tablet"

ḌFR

v inf ḍfr R4700/3+

CASE a well WITH STONE

[Cf Ar ḍafara "build a house of stones without mortar," ModḤaḍ ḍafra "stone casing fitted into the top of a well after it has been dug" (cf BoOr19/477, Irv/101).]

R4700/3: hnbṭ wḍfr b'r(h) "dug and cased his well with stone"; R4198/2: hbḥr wḍfr wšrʿn b'rhmw "excavated, cased with stone and supplied with lifting gear their well"

Note: For ...]nḍfr at end of inscription R4807 read phps hḍfr = ḍfr v̲ (Irv/101).

ḌQR

n s̲ ḍqrm J62*

TOP of a wall (?) (cf šqr id)

[BeDGESA/9:7 suggests an unusual use of ḍ for š in the common šqr, q.v. for similar contexts.]

N62 (fragment): (built the wall?)...bn sʿ 'sṭrn ʿdy ḍqrm "from the course (?) of these inscriptions to the top (?)"

ḌRW

n s̲ ḍrw C682+ (all on incense burners); d̲ ḍrwnhn C439/2

(1) AN AROMATIC RESIN or FRUIT used as incense

[Cf Ar ḍāra "bleed," ḍa/irw "fruit of the gum tree" (Pistacia lentiscus) (MüW/75); ModYem ḍa/orw "aromatic shrub" (RoVoc/311).]

C682: rnd ḍrw kmkm qsṭ "nard, ḍrw-incense, kmkm incense, costus" AND SEVERAL TIMES SIM

(2) INCENSE BURNER (specifically for ḍrw-incense?)

C439/2: tqdm mhyʿ ḍrwnhn wmhyʿ Q "he took charge of (the building of) the sanctuary of the 2 incense burners and the sanctuary of Q."

ḌRY

v inf ḍrynh J558/8*

HIDE s.th.

[JSIMB/28 cfs Ar ḍara'a "be hidden, hide one's self."]

J558/8: they placed their offering under the god's protection bn hkrnh w'xrnh wḍrynh "against (any) injuring, removing or hiding (of) it"; cf sim context with dśś J703/12

ḌRK

v inf ḍrk C338/12*

a) STRENGTHEN; or, b) FACE WITH STONE (?) (but see Note)

[a) Irv/225 cfs Ar ḍurāk, cited in LA as a name of the lion as the strongest of beasts. b) Cf phps Ar ḍarasa "case a well with stones" (Lane/1785B)?]

C338/12: he repaired the gates of Ḥ. and ^{c}sn wḍrk brktn "reinforced and strengthened/cased with stone (?) the cistern"

Note: Reading d 𐩵 as b 𐩨 would produce a denom v brk meaning, phps, "build a cistern (brkt)."

ḌRS

n p 'ḍrshw J702/12,13-4*

MOLAR TEETH

[Ar ḍirs, p 'aḍrās id.]

J702/12: mr(ḍ) '(ḍ)rshw wṯnhw "the disease of his molars and incisors"; ib/13-4: t'hrn 'ḍrshw wṯnyhw "the inflammation of his molars and incisors"

ḌR^{c}

v inf ḍr^{c}(n) C2/18+

HUMBLE, SUBJUGATE, DEFEAT an enemy

[Cf Ar ḍara^{c}a "be humble," ti and Dt "humiliate s.o."]

C2/18: may the god allow them wḍ^{c} wṯbr wḍr^{c}n kl ḍrhmw "to lay low, crush and defeat their every foe" AND OFTEN SIM

tp inf tḍr^{c}(n) J578/28+

HUMBLE ONE'S SELF, SURRENDER

J578/28: sb^{c} wtḍr^{c}n K...tḥt mr'yhmw "K. submitted and humbled himself under the authority of their lords"; C314/18-9: the god granted to their lords tḍr^{c}n Š "the surrender of (their enemy) Š."

h pf hḍr^{c} J577/13+; hḍr^{c}t R3957/8+

HUMBLE, DEFEAT s.o.; pass HUMBLE ONE'S SELF (l- to s.o.)

[Ar ḍr^{c} h id.]

J577/13: tg^{c}r kl dhḍr^{c} bn hgrn Ṣ "all whom he had defeated from the city Ṣ. were called together"; R3957/8: fhḍr^{c}t w^{c}nwt wxṭ't "so she humbled herself, submitted herself, and made a propitiatory offering" AND SEVERAL TIMES SIM; C523/8: hḍr^{c} w^{c}nw wyḥln "he humbled himself, submitted himself and paid a fine"; J525/2: hḍr^{c}t lhw "she humbled herself to (the god)"

st inf stḍr^{c}n C308b/23-4*

HUMBLE ONE'S SELF, SURRENDER (cf ḌR^{c} tp id)

C308b/23-4: ft^{c}rbw wstḍr^{c}n "they gave pledges of submission and surrendered"

n^{1} s ḍr^{c}[n] C350/13-4; var/p ḍr^{c}tm Ir25/3

SURRENDER or DEFEAT

C350/13-4: this inscription ḏbhw hṯqf...ḍr^{c}[n] ḏX "by which he announces the defeat of (the tribe) X."; Ir25/3: may the god protect them bn b'stm ...wḍr^{c}tm wmqṣm "from harm, defeat(s) and damage"

n^{2} s ḍr^{c}(m,n) R4626/1+

WEST

[Cf Ar ḍarra^{c}at al-šams "the sun approached the setting" (Lane/1787A) and Eth ḍer^{c} "Greeks," i.e., "westerners" (CoRoC/227-8).]

R4626/1: their palmgroves 'ly bḍr^{c}n M "which (lie) to the west, (toward) M."; C342/7-8: the tithes they assessed him lmšymthmw ḏḍr^{c}m "for his western fields"

Note: For C342, C cfs Yem ḍrw^{c} "kind of grape."

n^{3} s tḍr^{c}m J577/12+ (D inf?)

SUBMISSION, SURRENDER, DEFEAT (= ḍr^{c} n^{1})

Ir9/6: may the god protect them bn b'stm wtḍr^{c}m "from harm and defeat"; J577/12: fxrw hmw 'GRN tḍr^{c}m b^{c}br mr'hmw "those Nagranis assembled (in) submission to their lord"; C314/15: fnbl Š...tnbltm wtḍr^{c}m "and Š. sent embassies and submission (i.e., embassies to surrender)"; sim J574/10-1

ḌRF

n s mḍrf(n) J671/12+; p mḍrft C540/29+

REVETMENT of a canal, MOLE

[Cf Ar maṣrif "drainage canal," ModYem maṣraf "dam in a streambed" (RoVoc/311), maḍraf "dam" (GoJem/87, #580).]

C540/29: fqḥ mḍrft ḏ[']fn "he opened (sluices in) the revetments of the canals"; sim C541/44; J671/12: ṯbr kl mḍrfn ḏbynn Ḥ wR "the whole mole which separates Ḥ. and R. broke"; J651/32: lšym lhw mḍrfn swn T "to construct for him a mole in the direction of T."

ḌRR

v pf ḍrw Ry506/5; var ḍrrw Ir12+

FIGHT

[Eth ḍarara "be hostile," Ar ḍarra "hurt, injure."]

Ir12: ḍrm ḍrrw "a war they fought"; Ry506/5: wmxḍw [w]ḍrw qdmy gyšn "they overthrew (enemies) and fought at the head of (?) the army"

n s ḍr(m,n) C547/5+; ḍrhmy J581/8; ḍrhmw R4190/17+; p 'ḍrr(m) J585/13+; var? 'ḍrhmw C575/12 (but see Note)

(1) WAR

[Cf Ar ḍurr "harm."]

C547/5: bḍr ḤḌRMTm "in the war (against) Ḥ."; R4962/18: bslmm wḍrm "in peace and war" AND ELSEWHERE SIM; C308/19: ḍr hšt'w...b^c^br 'mr'hmw "the war they began against their lords"

(2) FOE, ENEMY

[Eth ḍarr id.]

R4190/17: ḍr^c^n drhmw wšn'hmw "to subjugate their (every) foe and enemy"; J581/8: _t_bry wtḍ^c^n ḍrhmy "they crushed and laid low their foe"

Note: For 'ḍrhmw C575/12, read phps (kb)rhmw; passage quoted under ṢǴR

ḌTR

ti _inf_ ḍttrn G1321/3*

WAGE WAR

[Prob a development from *ḍtr, _ti_ of root ḌRR "fight."]

G1321/3: ḍb]'w wḍttrn lmr'hmw "they fought and waged war for their lord" (cf SoSoSEG4/34)

𐩤-Q

QBB

h *inf* hqb C149/1*

CONSTRUCT DOMES (?)

[Cf Ar qubba† "dome."]

C149/1: [br]'w whqb wqy[f]n "they built and constructed domes and erected qyf-stones"

n *s* hqbm C462/6*

sense doubtful; OFFERING (?)

[BeOracle/221 cfs *v* hqb (QBB *h*?), but fragmentary context for both *n* and *v* make translation difficult.]

C462/6: ṯny šmlm wš[ṣym] bhqbm "a second evil omen or e[vil eye], with an offering (?)..."

QBY

n *s/d*? mqbyhmw C542/2*

DRINKING CISTERN

[Ar qubba† "building covered with a dome or cupola," cf modern siqāya† frequently a domed building. Cf also Daṯ qabû "vault, cellar," MSA gābiyen "reservoir fed by hotsprings," maquba "subterranean chamber cistern" (Irv/131-2).]

C542/2: mqby[hmw] wḥṣrh[m]w wb'ryhmw "their drinking cistern, its enclosing wall, and their 2 wells"

QBL

v *ipf* yqbln C539/1*

ACCEPT, RECEIVE

[Ar qabila id.]

C539/1: ykfrn ḥbhmw wyqbln qrbnhmw "he expiated their sin and (the god) accepted their offering"; prob also in F76/7: f[y]qbl[n] ḏtqwmw "may (the agreement) be accepted (by) those who witnessed (it)"

ti *inf* qtbln J644/4+

FIGHT

[Ar qbl *L* "be, stand opposite s.o. or s.th.; confront"; Akk muqtablu "fighter."]

J644/4: mnš' wqblt tnš'w wqtbln "the campaign and battle they undertook and fought"; Ir18: dyntš'n wqtbln "whoever went on campaign or fought"

D? pf qblw R2876/6; ipf yqblnn YM281/3 (BeNL9/97); inf qbln R2876/2

LEASE OUT LAND

[Aram qabbēl "contract, agree; esp lease, rent (a field)"; Ar qabāla† "annual leasing of lands."]

R2876/2: mqblt qnyw wqbln 'mlk "leased estated (which) the kings possessed and leased out"; YM281/3: 'rḍn F dyqblnn "the territory F. which they leased out..."

tp pf [t]qblw R2876/5-6*

LEASE LAND, HOLD LAND ON CONDITION OF PAYING RENT (cf QBL D)

R2876/5-6: t]qblw wwrd wwxr "they leased (lands); and (if? they?) neglect (their care) or delay (rent-payment)..."

h ipf yhqbln C376/11*

BE ABUNDANT (a crop)

[Ar qbl h id.]

C376/11: hgb'y l'LMQH hyt 'rḍn wl yhqbln l'LMQH "they leased out this land to (the god) l.; and may (its crop) be abundant for l."

st pf stqbl Gl365/12+

FIGHT (cf QBL ti)

Gl365/12: bn qblt stqb[l... "from the battle he fought..."; J762/4: [bw]rx stqbl[... "in the month (when) he fought..."

pp l-qbl Gl532+; l-qbly J671/24+

(1) IN FRONT OF

[Ar qubl "fore part, front," qabla "before, prior to."]

Gl532: [']l śn ǵbrm lqbl 'ln 'wtn lmšrqm "it is not lawful to block off (this canal?) in front of these boundary stones on the east side" (HöSEG8/26 takes as D verb "to shift")

(2) BEFORE, PRIOR TO

J671/24: hᶜnw hwt mtbrm lqbly tltt 'wrxm "they repaired that breach before (i.e. within) three months"

(3) FOR THE SAKE OF, BECAUSE OF

C87/5: they dedicated this tablet lqbly 'ṣf yᶜbrn frᶜ "for the sake of the maidservants who are offering firstfruits"; J840/5: he dedicated this statue lqbly ḥlẓ ḥlẓ rglyhw "because of the disease (which) afflicted his feet"

cj l-qbl dt C79/2-3+; l-qbly d- R4938/5-6+; l-qbly dt Ry375/2+

(1) BECAUSE (followed by pf)

[Cf pp l-qbl(y) sense[3] "for the sake of, because of," Aram loqŏbēl d↑ "because."]

C79/2-3: he dedicated lqbl dt s'lhw 'LMQH "because (the god) l. asked for it (the offering)"; C344/5: lqbl d[t] hᶜnhw wmtᶜhw bn t'r "because He helped him and saved him from blood-revenge"; J669/8: they dedicated lqbly ḏwld lhmw bnm "because a son was born to them"; Ry375/2: he dedicated lqbly ḏt 'l ḥyw lhmw wldm "because no child had survived for them"

(2) SO THAT (followed by l- + subjunctive)

R4142/6: he dedicated lqbly ḏlyz wrk bn[hmw] "so that (the god) would continue to support their son"

n^1 s qblt Gl365/12+

FIGHT, BATTLE

[Cf Akk qablu, qabaltu id, Sab QBL ti, st "fight."]

Gl365/12: bn qblt stqb[l "from the battle he fought"; J644/4: qblt wmnš' sw'm "disastrous battle and campaign"; ib/4 quoted under QBL ti

n^2 s qbltn C439/2*

KIND OF INCENSE (?)

[Cf Syr qublā matricaria chamomilla L. and m. Parthenium L. (RhAST2/185n6).]

C439/2: mhy^c ḍrwnhn wmhy^c qbltn "shrine of the 2 (offerings of) drw-incense and shrine of qblt-incense"

n^3 p 'qblm VanLessen 7/5--see below at n^5

n^3 s mqblhmw J574/12*

GUARANTEE (?)

[Cf Ar qabāla^t "contract, agreement; guarantee."]

J574/12: fwhbw 'wṯqm wmqblhmw "and they gave pledges and their guarantee"

n^4 p? mqblt(n) R2876/4+

LEASED LAND(S) (cf QBL D)

R2876/4: 'rḍtn w'nxln w'^{c}nbn wmwhtn wmqb(l)tn "fields, palmgroves, vineyards, wine-presses and leased lands"; ib/2: mqblt qnyw wqbln 'mlk "leased lands which the kings possessed and leased out"

n^5 s tqbl VanLessen 7/4*

SIZE, DIMENSION (?)

[Apparently related to 'qblm (n^3) in the same passage, which seems to be a unit of measure (BeNL10/420).]

VanLessen 7/4: wkwn tqbl kl 'rḍn...sb^{c}t w^{c}šry 'qblm "and the dimension (?) of the whole territory...is twenty-seven 'qbl-units"

QBḌ

n p qbḍhmw Ry509/9*

"SEIZERS," branch of the military forces

[Ar qabaḍa "seize, arrest; oppress"; Syrian, Lebanese Ar qabaḍāy "bodyguard" (Wehr/739).]

Ry509/9: mqtwthmw w'tlyhmw wṣydhmw wqbḍhmw "their officers, grooms, 'hunters' (scouts?) and 'seizers'"

QBR

ti inf qtbrn C619/3*

BE BURIED

[Ar.Eth.Heb etc qbr "bury."]

C619/3: w'l bn 'dm w'mh bny M qtbrn bqbrhmw "and none among the servants and maidservants of the b.M. is to be buried in their tomb"

n^{1} s qbr(n) R2706/1+; qbrhmw F72/3-4

TOMB, GRAVE

[Ar qabr id.]

R2706/1: nfs wqbr ^{c}A "grave stela and grave of A." AND OFTEN SIM; C984: wgr wqbr "tumulus and grave"; R3954/2: bny rb^{c} qbrn Y "he built a quarter of the tomb Y."; F72/3-4: hwṯrw wbr' whšqrn mḏqntn lqbrhmw "they laid the foundation for, built and completed the oratory for their tomb"

n^{2} s mqbr R4536/1+; mqbrhmw R4050/3+; p mqbrtm R3431+; mqbrthmw R3947/2

TOMBS, GRAVE (= qbr); in p, also BURIAL GROUND, CEMETERY

[Ar maqbar, maqbura^{t} "tomb, burial ground."]

R4536/1: mqbr D "tomb of D." AND ELSEWHERE SIM; R3431: grbw mqbrtm "they walled up their burial ground"

QBŚ--R2881 (in full); d qbśn w(ṣ)dq w, no tr

QDH

v pf qdh C350/12*

sense doubtful; REPEAT, RECORD (?)

[Cf Ar qdy ti "imitate, copy."]

C350/12: on that mission he killed 2 panthers wkl dqdh bḏn mṯkḥn "and (achieved) all that is recorded (?) on this inscriptional tablet"

QDḤ

n s mqdḥ(m,n) R2740/7+

BOWL, CUP (for divination?)

[Ar qadaḥ "cup." Associated with divination by means of arrows? Cf GrOLZ 9/col259.]

R2740/7: fr^{c} M mqdḥm ḏrbm 50 "he brought tribute to (the god) M., (consisting of) a bowl (with a capacity of) 50 rb-units"; R3247: may the god destroy d ysrq mqd(ḥ)n "anyone who steals this bowl"

QDM

v pf qdmhmw J665/21; qdmthmw R576/13

PRECEDE, GO BEFORE (sometimes indistinguishable from QDM D "confront, fight")

[Ar qadama id.]

J665/21: qdmhmw mqdmthmw "their advance troops preceded them"; J576/13: wqdmthmw ḥyrthmw ^{c}dy xlf [... "and their camp (?) preceded them to the vicinity of..."

tі pf qtdm R4085/5+; qtdmhmw C434/7-8+; inf qtdmn J635/33

TAKE COMMAND OF, BE IN CHARGE OF

[Cf Ar qdm Dt "be at the head; order, commission."]

Ir12: qtdm mnśrt "he took command of a detachment"; J635/33: his lord sent him lsb' wqtdmn ḏbn X...lḥrb "to go on campaign and take command of part of (the tribe) X., to fight"; sim J651/29-30, J671/10; R4085/5: qtdm lmr'hw "he took charge of...for his lord"

D pf qdm C461/7+; qdmhmw C352/8+; ipf [y]qdm C465/6; inf qdmn J665/9+; qdmnhmw ib/12

(1) PRESENT an offering (?); pass, RECEIVE an oracular response (?)

[Ar qdm D "send forward, offer."]

C461/7: qdm xlf B wh'twhn "he presented (offerings) outside B. and offered them..."; C465/6: whm [y]qdm bnh bn tḥty ^{c}ṮTR "and if he receives (a response) from it/her by the inspiration of (the god) A..." R4830/2: 'mr 'LMQH qdm wšw^{c} K "by command of (the god) I., K. presented an offering and sacrificed"; sim R4831/2

(2) COMMAND, esp LEAD A MILITARY EXPEDITION

[Ar qdm Dt "order"; ModYem tagaddam "go to war" (RoVoc/311), and cf QDM tp.]

C352/8: b'hnmw ḏqdmhmw wblthmw 'mr'hmw "when/wherever their lords commanded them and assigned them missions"; C309/4: ywm qdm š^{c}bhw...bmbny Ḍ "at the time when he commanded his folk in the construction of Ḍ."; C79/9: the god saved His servant btqdm qdm b^{c}m ^{c}rbn "in the expedition he led against the Arabs"; J665/12: lsb' wqdmn "to go on campaign and lead an expedition"

(3) CONFRONT, FIGHT

J576/6: tflw mṣr ḏR w'l qdmhmw "the troop of ḏR. went away and did not confront/fight them"; J644/17: they continued to campaign lqdmn whgzn L "so as to fight and execute L."

tp pf tqdm Ry507/11+; tqdmw J631/5+; ipf ytqdmw J576/5+; ytqdmn R4646/15; inf tqdm(n) J649/30+

(1) UNDERTAKE A PROJECT; specifically A MILITARY EXPEDITION > OPPOSE MILITARILY, FIGHT

[See under QDM D senses^{2,3}.]

J576/5: ytqdmw b^{c}mhw...wxmrhmw 'LMQH hsḥtn hmt 'sdn "they fought with him, and (the god) I. allowed them to destroy those soldiers"; Ir32/24: tqdmw whtrgn "they fought together and killed one another"; ib/20: they attacked the town Ṣ., wytqdmw b^{c}mhw 'b^{c}l Ṣ "and the citizens of Ṣ. opposed/fought them"

(2) UNDERTAKE A BUILDING or AGRICULTURAL PROJECT

Ry507/11: wtqdm wsṭr ḏn msndn "he undertook (the construction of) and wrote this inscription"; C338/3: ym tqdm hšqr kwrn "when he undertook to complete the cistern"; R4085/1: tqdm lmr'hw kl ṣyḥ "he undertook all the leveling (of land) for his lord" h pf hqdmhw C516/5; hqdmw C541/48

SEND FORWARD

[Cf Ar qdm D id.]

C541/48: hqdmw brdnn brt ydnn "they sent forward a courier (to) the place they were approaching"; C516/5: hqdmhw Y ḍb' 'A wḍb' "Y. sent him forward to fight A., and he fought"

n^{1} adj: m qdmn R4646/19; f qdmtn C547/14+; p 'qdmn C541/113+

FORMER, PRECEDING

[Ar qadama "precede," qadīm "old, ancient."]

R4646/19: wrx dN qdmn "the month dN., the Former"; sim C547/14: ḥyn dM qdmtn "at the time of dM., the Former"; C541/94: bʿẓthmw qdmtn "ac- to their former summons"; Ry548/6: he conquered bxr[q]hw [']qdmn "in his preceding attacks (?)"; C541/113: they repaired the channel ǵyr 'qdmn "without (undertaking) preliminary (works) (?)" (or cf QDM n^{2} "commanders, supervisors"?)

n^{2} s qdmhmw R3232/1; p 'qdm J547/2-3

CHIEF, COMMANDER (?)

[Cf Ar qadama "precede."]

R3232/1: [kb]rhmw wqdmhmw "their kabir and their commander (?)"; J547/2-3: 'qdm...šʿb dH "chiefs (?) of the tribe dH."

pp qdm R4174b/9+; b-qdm J649/18-9+; b-qdmy R3951/5+; b-qdmyhmw J575/3

BEFORE

[Eth qedma, qedmē- id.]

local: R4174b/9: db qdm Ẓ "which is in front of/before (the temple) Ẓ."; R4050/2: they repaired kl nkl qdm dqn "all the paving in front of the oratory"; J575/3: ysrw bqdmyhmw dlwlm "they sent guides before them"

temporal: R3951/5: bqdmy w'tr dt mtbtn "before and after this edict"; J735/6: the god had caused irrigation water to be lacking bqdmy dt brq "before that rainstorm" (or, noting lack of nunation, tr as cj: "before He thundered, i.e. sent a rainstorm"?)

Note also in J745/5-6: hqnyt šftw lnqdmm "an offering which they had promised previously (?)" reading ln + qdmm "up to before"?

n^{3} s tqdm(n) C79/9+; p tqdmt J581/6+ (D inf)

EXPEDITION

C79/9: the god saved His servant btqdm qdm bʿm ʿrbn "in the expedition he led against the beduins"; J581/6: kl sb't wḍby' wtqdmt sb'y wḍb' wtqdmn "all the campaigns, battles and expeditions they undertook, fought and led"

n^{4} d mqdmn R4782/2*

FOREQUARTER of an animal

[Cf Ar qadam "foot."]

R4782/2: wl yhbtn l'lhn fxdm wmqdmn "let him offer to the god a thigh and 2 forequarters (of the beast killed in the ritual hunt)"

n[5] s mqdmt(m,n) J665/17+; mqdmthmw ib/21+
ADVANCE TROOPS, VANGUARD
[Ar muqaddima[†] id.]
J665/17: ḏkww ṯlṯy rkbm...mqdmtm "they sent thirty cameleers as advance troops"; ib/21: qdmhmw mqdmthmw "their advance troops preceded them"

QDS

v pf qdsw C541/66; inf qds C541/117
HOLD A RELIGIOUS SERVICE/HOLD MASS IN a church
[Christian Ar qds D "say Mass" (cf BeNL9/187).]
C541/66: qdsw b^{c}t M "they held Mass (in) the church of M. (after repairing it)"; ib/117: they went up for a raid wqds b^{c}tn "and held Mass (in) the church"

n adj: s qds C541/3+
HOLY
[Ar qudsī, Heb qādôš id.]
C541/3: RḤMNN wmsḥhw wrḥ[q]ds "(the god) R., His Messiah and the Holy Spirit"; Ist7608b/1: (mn)fs qds "the Holy Spirit"

QDR

p 'qdr(m) R2747/2+
UNIT OF MEASURE
[Ar qadara "be capable of (doing s.th.)"; Ḥaḍ "estimate how much is necessary (to do s.th.)"; Ar qadr and miqdār "measure; extent; amount"; and cf phps such Ar terms as qidr "cooking pot," qadara[†] "small bottle" as possible units of measure. BeNL10/409 suggests, alternatively, a tr "x-fold," where x is a number.]
R2747/2: ^{c}ḏbn 'qdr [... "repairing, ...measures" (context fragmentary); C80/10: yfqln 'rb^{c}y 'qdrn "it produces crops (to the amount of) forty qdr-measures (or, forty-fold)"

QḌ, see under NQḌ

QH--for ns qh, qht, and v tqh, see under WQH

QHL

n[1] s qhl(m,n) C352/15+
(1) ASSEMBLY, GROUP of men or (?) animals
[Cf Heb qāhāl "congregation."]
C352/15: kl qhl šn'm "every assembly of enemies"; C563/3: ṯwrm ybḥr bn qhln "a bull which will be chosen from the group (or, phps, in the place of/to represent the Assembly?)"
(2) specifically, ASSEMBLY, COUNCIL of tribes
C570/9: SB' gwy qhlm "Saba, the community (of associated tribes) in assembly"

n² s qhlt C973/6-7*
ASSEMBLY, COUNCIL (?) (cf QHL n¹ sense²)
[Cf Heb qəhillāh = qāhāl; Min qhl(t) ᶜTTR "assembly/'college' of A."]
C973/6-7: tḥty qhlt SMᶜ "by authority of the council (?) of (the god) S."

QWḤ

v pf qḥw C566/2*
SWEEP CLEAN > SET IN ORDER
[Ar qāḥa (w) "sweep, scour, sweep clean."]
C566/2: qḥw m'xdn "they set the control dyke in order"
Note: For qḥ in C516/17, read fqḥ with C; but context is obscure and fragmentary.

N? pf nqḥt R4369/1*
BE SET IN ORDER, BE MADE READY FOR USE (?) (but see Note)
R4369/1: hšhr [...]nqḥt [... "has allocated for public use (?)...has been set in order (?)"
Note: Read phps as a noun, of uncertain meaning.

h pf hqḥw C653/2+; var hqwḥ C40/2+; inf hqḥ R4194/4+
SET IN ORDER, MAKE READY FOR USE, COMPLETE, in building and agricultural contexts (cf QWḤ v)
C40/2: br'w whwṯr whqwḥ whšqrn nṭᶜthmw "they built, laid the foundation for, made ready, and completed their nṭᶜt-construction"; R4197/1: hš]qr whqḥ mrw "completed and made ready the irrigated field"; R4194/4: hzrfw whqḥ kl dn ᶜšqn "they improved and made ready all this strip-cultivated land"; Ist7632/2: ᶜs' whqḥ ḥrtn "he built and made ready this aqueduct"

st inf stqḥn J559/8+
COMPLETE, ACHIEVE > ACHIEVE SUCCESSES, VICTORIES
J559/8: the god allowed him stqḥn mqyḥt ṣdqm bkl 'brṯ hwṣl lbytn S "to achieve satisfying successes in all the enterprises in which he joined with the house S."; same formula J561/8; J644/19: tqdmw...wyhrg(n)hmw wstqḥn bhmw "they fought and killed them and achieved (a victory) over them"

n¹ p? qḥn R4176/12*
in exp d'ḥdqḥn: HE WHO IS (APPOINTED AS) FIRST OF THE CULTIVATORS (?) (but see Note)
[Development from sense of QWḤ v: "prepare (land for cultivation)"; this would be act.prt?]
R4176/12: ᶜqb wsxmm lyrtᶜ d'ḥdqḥn lR "subsequent disputes are to be settled by him who is first of the cultivators on behalf of R."
Note: 'ḥdqḥn can be taken as a n.loc; tr d'ḥdqḥn "he of/the governor of 'A." It seems likely, however, that the expression is an error for 'ḥdfqḥn, tr "overseer" or the like (?), which occurs in l.9 of the same inscr (see under FQḤ n).

n[2] s mqḥ(m,n) R3911/2+; mqḥhmw C541/131; var mqyḥ C448/4; p mqyḥt(m) J559/8+; mqyḥthmw R4648/6+

(1) ACHIEVEMENT > FINAL STAGE OF BUILDING (cf QWḤ h); specifically phps LEVELING, PAVING

R3911/2: m^c]s' wmqḥ m'x̱dhmw "the construction and completion (or, paving?) of their control dyke"; R4648/6: rṯdw mqyḥthmw ^cTTR "they placed their completed works (or, pavings?) under the protection of (the god) A."; C28/2: mqḥ wnk(l) "leveling and paving"; C448/4: mbr' wmqyḥ "stonework and paving"

(2) SUCCESS, (military) VICTORY (cf QWḤ st)

J559/8 quoted under QWḤ st; J561b/7: mqyḥt wmhrgt wǵnmt ṣdqm bkl 'brṯ "satisfying victories and slaughters and booty in all the campaigns"; C598/1: mqḥ ṣdqm bkn tqdmw "a satisfying victory when they fought"

QWY--For n mqtwy, see under QTW

QWL

h pf hqlhw C642/7*

APPOINT AS RULER (?) (but see Note)

[Denom from n qwl, q.v.]

C642/7: ym hqlhw "when (the god) appointed him as ruler/qawl (?)"

Note: Context is unhelpful; assign phps to root QLL?

n[1] s ql(n) C394/2+; qlhmw J559/15+; var qwl C645/3+; d qwlnhn R4176/5; p 'qlhmw Ry507/1; var 'qwl(m,n) J561/1+; 'qwlhw J574/5; 'qwlhmw ib/8

TRIBAL LEADER, CHIEF of a subject tribe (cf qyl)

[Ar qayl, p 'aqyāl, 'aqwāl title of South Arabian princes (MüW/94). For root sense cf Heb qôl "voice," Ar qāla (w) "speak" > "command" (cf development of root 'MR, Heb "speak," Ar 'amīr "prince"). Discussion RyQayl.]

R4771/1: 'l'ltm w(')mlkm w'qwlm w'š^cbm "gods, kings, tribal leaders and tribesmen"; R3990/9: bytn R w'b^clhw wqlhmw "the house R. and its inhabitants and their chief"; R2633/9: mlk ḤMYRM w'qwlhw 'ḤMRN w'RḤBN "the king of Ḥ. and his Ḥimyarite and Raḥabite tribal leaders"; C41/1: 'ršw ^cA 'qwl š^cbn M "the priests of A., chiefs of the tribe M." (specifically religious function of the 'qwl?); J665/37: 'qwlm wmr's "tribal leaders and dignitaries"; J578/18: 'qwlhw wxmshw w'š^cbhw w'frshw "his chiefs, army, tribal military contingent, and cavalry"

n[2] p mqwlhmw J577/17*

TRIBAL LEADERS, CHIEFS (= qwl)

[Ar miqwal, p maqāwil "kinglet (among the Himyarites)" (JSIMB/83).]

J577/17: M wṢ wN wkl mqwlhmw "(the cities) M., Ṣ. and N. and all their tribal leaders"

n[3] p? mqwlthmw J647/27*

OFFICIAL DUTY or ACTIVITY

[Cf sense "command" underlying n qwl "chief" (BeNL9/97n2).]
J647/27: kl mqwlthmw wsythmw "all their official activities and projects"

QWM

v ipf yqmn C570/9-10+
with sm^c, SERVE as witness
[Cf Heb qām (w) "rise, stand," used of serving as witness Pr 27:12, Job 16:8; sim usage in Ar.]
C570/9-10: mṯbt sm^{c}h yqmn "the edict to which serve as witnesses...(list of names follows)"; R4123/1: rwthmy ḏt sm^c yqmn "their report (to) which serve as witnesses...(list of names follows)"
Note: For qm elsewhere, see under NQM, QMM

D? pf qwm R4635/2+; ipf yqwm Gl520/4
ERECT a qyf-altar > ESTABLISH, LAY OUT BOUNDARIES by means of qyf-stones
[Ar qāma (w) "stand," D "erect."]
R4635/2+: qwm bny qyf ^{c}ṮTR "he erected (and) built a qyf-altar (for) (the god) A."; Gl520/4: 'l yqwm kl ^{c}lbm bfnwtn "let him establish the boundaries of no ^{c}lb-land by this canal"

tp pf tqwmw F76/7*
SERVE as witness (?) (cf QWM v)
F76/7: f[y]qbl[n] ḏtqwmw "may (the agreement) be accepted (by) those who witnessed (it) (?)"

h pf hqm R4357/1+; hqmhw Ry526/2; inf hqm(n) R3946/6+; pf hqmw C537/7
(1) ERECT a building (cf QWM D)
R3946/6: bny whqm 'bny Y "he built and erected the buildings of Y."; C537/7: hqmw bythmw "they erected their house"
(2) PUT IN ORDER
[Ar qwm h id.]
R4646/16: fl ytqdmn whqmn xfrt mr'hmw "let him take charge of and put in order the enclosed field of their lord"; J557: hqm 'qnyt 'bhhw "he put in order the dedicated property of his forefathers"
Note: For hqm elsewhere, see under NQM h

n^1 s qwm[m] R2861/11*
PEOPLE, COMMUNITY
[Ar qawm "kinsfolk; tribe, people."]
R2861/11: ḏ[š']m lw^{c}l qwm[m w]dwrm "he who was appointed to rule over the community and the people"

n^2 s qwm Cl94/2*
STAND, SUPPORT (?) of an incense-burner
[Ar qāma^t, qawām id.]
Cl94/2: she dedicated qwm hyt mqṭrn "the stand (?) of this incense-burner"

n^3 s mqm(m,n) J633/6+; p mqmt(m,n) J712/13-14+; var mqymt(m) R3972/2+; mqymthmw

C315/20+

(1) PLACE; phps esp SACRED PLACE

[Ar maqām "place," and cf sense "sacred place" of Heb māqôm.]

J633/6: ln d'tw bn mqmn dL "until he came from the place of L."

(2) ABILITY, FACULTY (specifically "physical," contrasted with 'dn "mental faculty"?); POWER

[Cf Ar qawām "strength, vigor."]

C76/9: may the god grant him bry 'dnm wmqmm "health of mental and physical faculties" AND OFTEN SIM; when dedicants are plural, ''dnm wmqymt, e.g. J658/30; R3992/11: xyl wmqm T'LB "might and power of (the god) T." AND OFTEN SIM; R3972/2: they built it brd' wmqymt 'mr'hmw "by the aid and powers of their (human) lords"

(3) PROPERTY (p only?)

[Same sense in Qat, e.g. R3566/12,20 (BeOr19/442).]

J702/6-7: y^c dwn dmqmtn bbt 'LMQH "the supervisor (= person in charge of property) entered the temple of (the god) I."

Note: J takes as n.pr. Be sees this sense also in contexts here assigned to sense².

QWF

h? pf hqwf J541/8*

FIX BOUNDARIES, DELIMIT by means of boundary stones (cf QYF D) (?) (but see Note)

[Doublet of root QYF, q.v.?]

J541/8: kl hqwf b'dbnn d'db brhmw "all that he delimited by means of the 2 boundary stones which delimit their land"

Note: For an alternate interpretation cf BonVar/333n.j, who reads (prob without re-examining the actual text) kl hqwf w'dbnn d'db, and tr "all the fences and boundary stones which delimit." He identifies the root HQF with SQF, Sab and Ar "cover with a roof," cf esp Sq héqef "barrier."

QWR

v pf qwr VanLessen 7/3*

ENGRAVE

[Ar qāra and D "cut holes in s.th." (BeNL10/420).]

VanLessen 7/3: qwr t^c lmn "the document has been engraved"

QḤN--For n qḥn in R4176/12, see under QWḤ n¹

QḤF

n p qḥfm C464/10*

STREAMS

[Ar sayh^un quḥāf^un "rapidly flowing torrent" (BeOracle/223).]

C464/10: dm ṭlyn [...] wdyn bqḥfm "the blood of a lamb, flowing in streams"

QṬṬ

v? pf/inf? qṭṭ Gl188/3*

CUT, HEW OUT (?)

[Cf Ar qaṭṭa "cut."]

Gl188/3: lm qṭṭ...m^cs' wm...[m]qbrtm "...hew out (?)...construction... graves"

QṬY--For mqṭt J649/32-3, see under MQṬ

QṬN

n[1] s qṭnm R2876/1+

SMALL (but see Note)

[Cf Heb qāṭôn, Eth qaṭin id.]

R2876/1: kl [']nsm bhṯm wqṭnm "every man, great or small" AND ELSEWHERE SIM

Note: BeStI/89 suggests comparison with Ar qaṭana "reside," and trs "transient and resident."

n[2] p qṭntm C541/124-5+

SMALL CATTLE = SHEEP, FLOCKS

C541/124-5: ḏbyḥm wbqrm wqṭntm "sacrificial animals, cattle and sheep"; Gl142/9: prohibit any herdsman bn ḥmlhmw qṭntm "from driving flocks"

n[3] p [m]qṭnhmw R3563B/3*

COMMON PEOPLE (?)

R3563B/3: mśwdhmw wmr'shmw [w...]hmw [wm]qṭnhmw "their councillors, dignitaries, ...s and common people (?)"

QṬR

v inf qṭr C948/5*

BURN INCENSE, MAKE AN INCENSE OFFERING

[Cf Heb qṭr D id, denom from Heb qəṭóret "incense"; cf Ar qāṭir "resin."]

C948/5: wqṭr bhgrn "and burned incense in the city..."

n s mqṭr(m,n) R4230A/1+; d mqṭrnhn C338/9; p mqṭrtn C338/8

INCENSE BURNER; INCENSE ALTAR

[Ar miqṭar, Heb miqṭéret id.]

R4230A/1 (on an incense burner): hqny mqṭrn wṯmrm l^cTTR "he dedicated an incense burner and crops to (the god) A."; C338/9: mṣrbn wmqṭrnhn...wmslmn "the mṣrb altar, the 2 incense altars and the mslm altar"

QẒ'

n s qẓ't F90/1*

DISTANCE (?)

[Cf Ar qaṣā/qaṣiya "be far away," qaṣā^n "distance"; Ḥaḍ qẓ' R2693/3 "complete" (RyET/59).]
F90/1: ...]ym bnhw ḥmym wqẓ't [... "from it an embankment (?), and the distance (?)..."

QY--For [y]tqynn R4784/5, see under NQY

QYHR

n s qyhrn C308/7*
KIND OF PULLEY (?), or n.pr (?)
[Tr suggested from context; Rh, Conti Rossini take as place name.]
C308/7: kl] ṣwrt w'r̤fd ʿdy 'ʿmdn...wkl ṣwrtn ḏqyhrn "all the embankments (?) and supports as far as the naturally irrigated land, and all the embankments (?) of (the?) QYHRN"

QYW

v pf qyww Ir32/5*
STRENGTHEN, REINFORCE
[Ar qwy D id.]
Ir32/5: qyww kl 'gyšhmw "and they reinforced all their armies"

QYḤ--For n mqyḥ(t), see under QWḤ n[2]

QYṬ--For n mqṭt J649/32-3, see under MQṬ

QYẒ

n[1] s qyẓ(m,n) C174/3+
(1) SUMMER
[Ar qayẓ "hottest part of the summer"; Yem gayẓ or giyaẓ "time of the last rain, summer harvest." Cf Sab qyṣ "summer; summer harvest."]
C174/3: n'd 'ṯmrm...bqyẓ wdṯ' wṣrb wmlym "abundance of crops in summer, spring, autumn and winter"; R4013/3: dṯ' wqyẓ wṣrb "spring, summer and autumn"; cf also C323/9: wrx qyẓ "the month of Summer"
(2) SUMMER HARVEST
J651/48: n'd qyẓm wṣrbm ʿdy kl 'rḍhmw "abundance of summer and autumn harvests in all their fields"

n[2] p mqyẓhmw J631/40-1+
FIELDS PLANTED WITH SUMMER CROPS (cf mqyḍ id)
[Cf Ar maqīẓ "summer residence" (JSIMB/123).]
J631/40-1: abundance of summer and autumn crops ʿdy 'rḍhmw w'srrhmw wmqyẓhmw "in their fields, valleys and mqyẓ-fields" AND ELSEWHERE in lists of types of cultivated land

QYL

n[1] s qyl(n) C314/2+; d qyly N15/4; qylyhmw Ry 538/30-1

TRIBAL LEADER, CHIEF of a subject tribe (= qwl)
[See etym under QWL n^1.]
C314/2: R.Y., qyl š^{c}bn B "chief of the tribe B."; R4196/1: F.Y., qyl š^{c}bnyhn Q wM "chief of the 2 tribes Q. and M."; ib/2: wynhmw dqyln wdy D "their vineyard belonging to the tribal leader and to the 2 (chiefs of) D."; C259/2: bt qyln "the fortress of the tribal leader"

n^2 adj: p qylym Ist7608b/4*
BELONGING TO A QAYL (= TRIBAL LEADER)
Ist7608b/4: [']xmshmw mlykym wqylym "their armies belonging to kings and to qayls"

QYN

tp For [y]tqynn R4784/5, see under NQY

n s qyn J555/1+; d qyny J556; p 'qynm C140/2+
ADMINISTRATOR of a god or king; GOVERNOR of a town
[Ar qayn, qinn "slave; smith"--phps originally in Sab "slave (of the god)."]
J554: qyn 'LMQH "administrator of (the god) I."; J556: qyny HWBS w'LMQH "the 2 administrators of (the gods) H. and I."; J552/1: qyn Y B wY W "administrator of (the 2 kings) Y.B. and Y.W."; J555/1: qyn MRYB "governor (?) of (the city) M."
AND OFTEN in exp kbr 'qynm (C140/2+), kbr'qynm (C399/1+) and its p 'kbrw'qynm (R2695/2+), "chief/tribal leader of the Aqyān"--originally phps a clan of artisans or smiths? Cf R2695/2: 'kbrw'qynm 'qwl š^{c}bn B "the chiefs of the A., tribal leaders of the tribe B."

QYF

v pf qf C390/1+; qfhw C393/2-3; qfhmy Ry591/2; var qyf R4635/2+; qyfw NNAG19/1-2; ipf yqfnn G1142/6; inf qy[f]n C149/1
(1) ERECT AN ALTAR of the type called QYF
[Prob denom from QYF n^1, q.v.]
C149/1: [br]'w whqb wqy[f]n bṢ "they built, raised domes and erected qyf-altars in Ṣ." R4177/3: qfw qyf šmshmw "they erected the qyf-altar of their sun goddess"; C390/1-2: qf whḥdt mqf qf Y "he erected and renewed the mqf-altar (which) Y. had (formerly) erected"; C393/2-3: qfhw wtnn "he erected (for?) (the god) this boundary stone"
(2) FIX BOUNDARIES, DELIMIT by means of qyf-stones
G1142/6: yqfnn wḥgr mrbdn kl r^{c}y "they shall delimit and prohibit this sheepfold to every herdsman"

st pf stqfw C537/6*
ERECT QYF-STONES (?) (cf QYF v)
C537/6: w^{c}rbw wstqfw "they offered sacrifices and erected qyf-stones (?)"

n^1 s qf G1520/2+; var qyf J618/35+; qyfhw C19/5; p 'qyf Ry591/1
KIND OF ALTAR or CULT STONE, sometimes used to mark boundaries

[The qyf-stone was probably used in rituals of circumambulation. Cf Heb nāqap, hiqqîp "go around" (ultimately from root QWP), təqûpāh "circuit"; Aram qûpā "stake, grapevine"; ModYem mugwaf "upright standing stone to support grapevines."]

R3958/11: ŠMSM bᶜlt qyf W "(the goddess) Š., lady of the cult stone of W."; C19/5: he dedicated this statue bqyfhw d̲hqrw "at His cult stone which he offered"; Gl520/1: ᶜd qf wt̲n Ḥ "up to the cult stone, the boundary stone of Ḥ."

n² s̲ mqf(n) C180/3+; v̲a̲r̲? mqyftn DJE21/2

KIND OF ALTAR or CULT STONE (cf q(y)f, id)

C180/3: d̲n mḥrmn wmqfn "this temple and cult stone"; C390/2: qf whḥdt̲ mqf qf Y "they erected and renewed the cult stone (which) Y. had erected"; DJE21/2: [hqnyw...d̲t] ḤMY wŠMS d̲n mqyftn "[they dedicated to (the goddesses) d̲t] Ḥ. and Š. this cult stone"

n³ s̲? mhqftn R3114*

context fragmentary; related to n̲s̲ qyf, mqf?

R3114 (in full): tn mhqftn, no tr

QYṢ

n s̲ qṣ J594/10; v̲a̲r̲ qyṣn C448/6

SUMMER; SUMMER HARVEST (= qyẓ)

[Cf etym under QYẒ n̲¹.]

C448/6: wrxn d̲qyṣn "the month of Summer"; J594/10: n'd qṣ wṣrb "abundance of summer and autumn harvests"

QYḌ I

v p̲f̲ qyḍ C570/2*

BARTER, EXCHANGE

[Ar qāḍa and L̲ qāyaḍa id; ModYem gayẓ and mugāyaẓah "exchange of goods."]

C570/2: qyḍ whᶜqb...bᶜl nxln...'A "the owner of the palmgrove exchanged and bartered with A."

tp i̲n̲f̲ qtḍ Ir13*

BREAK, ROUT an enemy

[Ar qāḍa (y) "break, split," t̲p̲ "rout," N̲ "collapse, be routed" (RycMus87/248 and n2).]

Ir13: t̲br wqtḍ wht̲(lᶜ)n wwḍᶜ "crushed, routed, broke and laid low (the enemy)"

For qtḍn J616/14, see under QḌY t̲i̲

tp p̲f̲ tqyḍw C11/2*

CUT FROM ROCK, EXCAVATE (for a well or cistern)

[Cf esp Ar qāḍa (y) "dig a well in the rocks," bi'r maqīḍa⁺ "a well... having been hollowed out, or cleft."]

C11/2: cut water channels for their land w'qyḍ tqyḍw "and (for) the cisterns they excavated"

st inf stqḍn R3910/3*

PAY, GIVE IN EXCHANGE (cf QYḌ v)

R3910/3: kl š'mt w'qyḍ yš'mnn wstqḍn bn 'nsm w'b[l]m "all purchases and payments they may make or give in exchange for a man or camel"

n s qyḍ[h]w C570/4; p 'qyḍ C11/2+

(1) ROCK CISTERN (cf QYḌ tp)

C11/2 quoted under QYḌ tp

(2) EXCHANGE, PAYMENT (cf QYḌ v, st)

C570/4: bḥg qyḍ[h]w w^{c}qbnhw "according to (the terms of) its exchange and sale"; R3910/3 quoted under QYḌ st

QYḌ II

n p mqyḍhmw Ir22/1,2*

FIELDS FOR SUMMER CROPS (= mqyẓ)

[Phonetic variant of mqyẓ, see under QYẒ n^2; and cf mḍ' for mẓ' "arrive" in Ir9/3.]

Ir22/2: 'rḍhmw wmšymthmw wmqyḍhmw "their land, fields, and summer-crop fields"

QYR

n s [t]qrm R3918/2*

OVERLAY (?) of plaster, or the like

[Common in Min, usually with blq, 'bn ("stone") or ^{c}ḍ ("wood"). Usually tr "dressed stone," cf Ar waqara "split stone." However, Irv/342n125 cfs PBH yəqîr "asphalt, pitch" (Ar qīr, Eth qar); Akk qâru "gold ornamentation on an offering dish." Assignment to root WQR would be equally valid.]

R3918/2: kl m^{c}s' wmb[ny...^{c}ḍm wt]qrm "the whole construction and building [in wood and o]verlay"

QL--see under QWL, QYL, QLL

QL'--For n ql't C74/20, see under QLM

QLD

n s mqldhw R4197b/2+; p mqldtm C338/11

BASIN, STORAGE CISTERN

[Eth maqlad "basin," cf Ar qalada "collect (water, milk, wine) in a receptacle."]

R4197b/2: [br'] mqldhw...yhzḥ lhw "[he built] his storage cistern (which) overflows for him"; C338/11: m't mqldtm "the water channel of the cisterns"

QLḤ

n s qlḥ(n) C518/2,3*

CULTIVATED LAND

[ModYem qlḥ "cultivate land," mqlḥ "rod used to measure furrows" (C on C518).]

C518/3: bqlḥ syr hgrn...[w]ḏhw bydn ḏqlḥn "in the cultivated land of the territory of the city...which is near the cultivated land"

QLY--In Ry390/4 read as place-name? (as in Qat R3550/4)

QLL

n s qll(m) J750/9+; var? qllt J2109/10

A LITTLE, A SMALL QUANTITY

[Ar qill "small quantity." qalīl "small."]

J750/9: wwkb[w] qll mwm "they obtained a little water"; Ir13: ystqynn qllm sqym "they quenched their thirst (with) a little drink"; J2109/10: ǵyr qllt mwnn "without (even?) a small quantity of food (?)"

QLM I

n s qlmtm C74/20+ (C read ql'tm); p/coll qlmm R4230C/(2) (Rh read fgmm)

NOXIOUS INSECT, VERMIN (cf qmlt, id)

[Syr qalmā "harmful insect," qlmwtā "lice, fruit-worms." With metathesis, cf Ar qaml (coll) "lice."]

J610/9: bn...'rbym wʿrglm wbn kl qlmtm "from 'rby-locusts, ʿrgl-locusts, and from every noxious insect"; R4230C/(2): may the god drive away (ql)mm wmqṣm "noxious insects and loss (of crops)"; Ir24: may the god protect them bn qlmt ḥb(l)tn wṯmrn wsqyn "from vermin of vines, crops, and sqy-crops"

QLM II

n s qlm R3853*

KIND OF INCENSE = CALAMUS

[Gk kálamos = calamus odoratus, a sweet-smelling plant (GrohmSüdar/116-7).]

R3853 (on an incense altar): qlm qsṭ rnd ḍrw "calamus, costus, nard, ḍrw-incense"

QLS

n s qlsn Ry508/3+

CHURCH

[Ar qalīs, Gk ekklēsía id.]

Ry508/3: dhrw qlsn "they burned the church"; in Ry507/4 read qlsn for wtsn in the same exp, followed by whrgw 'ḤBŠN "and killed the Ḥabashites"

QM--see under QWM, QMM, NQM

QML

n s̲ qmltm C174/4* (C read qm^c tm)
    NOXIOUS INSECT (cf qlmt, QLM I, id)
    [Cf Ar qaml (coll) "lice," and etym under QLM I n̲.]
    C174/4: may the god protect them bn kl qmltm "from every noxious insect"

QMM

n s̲ qmm C338/13*
    SUMMIT
    [Ar qimma^t id.]
    C338/13: msb' ^c rn d̲M bn rydhw [^c]dy qmm "the mountain road of the citadel d̲M. from its ridge to the summit"

QM^c

v pf qm^c w J576/12+; ipf yqm^c w ib/8; yqm^c n R4090/2+; inf qm^c J576/4+
    SUBDUE, SUBJUGATE; STRIKE DOWN (said of a god)
    [Ar qama^c a "restrain, subdue."]
    J576/12: they leveled all their wells wqm^c w hgrn Q "and subjugated the city Q."; ib/4: t̲brw whb^c ln wqm^c whsb^c n byt "they crushed, seized, subjugated and plundered the fortress"; Ry533/12: wyd^c w [q]m^c Q "ultimately, they subdued Q."; R4090/2: wlyqm^c n ^c TTR...dynhkn wštrhw "and may (the god) A. strike down anyone who seizes or destroys it (a grave stone)" AND OFTEN SIM

n For qm^c t C174/4, read qmlt, see under QML

QMT--For n̲ qmt J558/5, see under WQM

QNY

v pf qn R3945/15; qny C37/5+; qnyy J734/5; qnyty R4653/1; qnyw C94/5-6+;
  ipf yqny R4176/4; tqny R3696B/3; yqnyn C535/10+; yqnynhw R4730/4; yqnynn C94/6+; inf qny R3994/2
    POSSESS; ACQUIRE
    [Ar qanâ, Heb qānāh, Eth qanaya id.]
    R3966/7: kl d̲qnyw wb^c l "all that they possessed and owned"; C94/6: 'qnyhmw d̲qnyw wyqnynn "their property which they possessed and will possess (or, which they have acquired and will acquire)"; R4994/2: qnyw wbr' bythmw "they acquired and built their house"; C37/6: a canal d̲qny w^c sy "which he acquired and bought"; Mül/3: kyhmdnn mqmhw bkn yqnynn 'wldm "let them praise (the god's) might when they acquire children"; J855/5-6: qnyhw ^c A d̲qny "his slave A. whom he acquired"

D? inf qnyn F3/1*
    CAUSE TO POSSESS > HAND OVER
    F3/1: xmr wqnyn wbrgn wb^c ln wz̲rbn l'dmhmw "(the kings) granted, handed

over, repaid, caused to own and confirmed possession to their vassals"
Note: CoRoC assigns to this v qnyhw R3945/8, but see under QNY n[1] sense[3].

h pf hqny R3620+; hqnyt J706/2+; hqnyy J556+; hqnyw R3990/3+; hqnytw J686/2-3; hqnythw J584/10; ipf yhqnynhw C336/9; thqnynhw J717/7; yhqnynn J567/8-9+

CAUSE TO POSSESS > DEDICATE an offering to a god (with 2 accusatives; rarely l- with 1st object)

R4187/3: hqnyw šymhmw "they caused their patron deity to possess" (no 2nd object) AND ELSEWHERE SIM; J579/4: hqny 'LMQH...ṣlmn d̲d̲hbn ḥmdm bd̲t... "he dedicated to (the god) I. a statue of gold, in praise because..." AND OFTEN SIM; SIM with other persons of the pf; J669/11-2: they promised the god that if a son should be born, fyhqnynn ṣlmm "they would dedicate a statue"; J717/7: she promised the god that if He would grant her a child thqnynhw "she would dedicate him (or, dedicate to Him?)"; C336/9: he promised yhqnynhw ṣlmm "he would dedicate to Him a statue"

n[1] s qny(m,n) C550/3+; qnyhw J844/5-6; p qny(m) J705/7+; qnyhw J550/1+; qnyhmw R3943/2+; p 'qnyhmw C94/6+; var qnwym R4176/2

(1) SLAVE (p 'qny)

[Eth qenuy id.]

C550/3: 'xhw M qny mlk bnw W "his brother M., slave of the king of the b.W."; J844/5-6: qnyhw ^{c}A d̲qny "his slave A. whom he acquired"; C609/2: 'qnyhmw w'dymthmw w'mhhmw "their slaves, servants and maidservants (or, slaves and male and female dependents)"

(2) p qny, LIVESTOCK, phps including slaves

[Cf Heb miqneh "cattle (including cows, sheep, goats)," Ar qunwa^{t} "property in livestock."]

R3943/2: t̲ll qnyhmw ''blm wbqrm "took as booty their livestock: camels and cattle"; J576/5: tmlyw sby wqny hyt hgrn "they took as booty the captives and livestock of that city"; J553/3: he dedicated to the god kl wldhw wqnyhw "all his children and livestock (or, slaves?)"; J558/3-4: for their own safety and that of bnyhmw w'wldhmw wqnyhmw "their sons, their children and their livestock (or, slaves)"

(3) specifically, SHEEP AND GOATS (?)

R3945/19: t̲ll b^{c}rhmw ''blm wbqrm wḥmrm wqnym "took as booty their herds: camels, cattle, asses, sheep and goats (?)" AND ELSEWHERE SIM; cf also R4176/2: the god prohibited a certain place bn ẓlf qnwym "from the cloven hoofs of sheep and goats (i.e., from having these animals driven through it) (?) " (alternative tr "from beating slaves"); cf also ib/3 quoted under ǴRḌ v

n[2] s qnt(m) R2860/2+

STORAGE PIT (?)

[Ar qina†, qutna† "pit; silo for grain."]

R2860/1-4:]m wf()r(ᶜ)m wkl myrm (b)qnt xlfn wmn lyh(g)rm nkr qntm... "...and first fruits and all cereals in the storage pit of (by?) the gate; and whoever is guilty of damaging a storage pit..."

Note: BeNL6/319 tr this word "official responsible for collection of market-dues or sales taxes," but gives no consecutive tr or convincing eytmology.

n3 s 'qnyt(n) J557+

(1) OFFERING, DEDICATED PROPERTY

[Var of hqnyt, QNY n4.]

J557: hqm 'qnyt 'bhhw "he put in order the dedicated property of his (fore)-fathers"; C95/3: wbn dt 'qnytn "and from this (piece of) dedicated property"

(2) DEED or ACT OF DEDICATION of property

C343/12: wkwn(t) d(t) 'qnytn bwrx dD "and this deed/act of dedication was enacted in the month dD."

n4 s hqnyt(m,n) J745/5+; hqnythw J664/8; hqnythmw J558/7+

(1) OFFERING, THING DEDICATED (cf 'qnyt sense1)

[Derived from hqny (QNY h) "offer, dedicate."]

J745/5: hqnyw...frsn...ddhbn hqnyt šftw "they dedicated this horse of gold, the offering they promised" AND OFTEN SIM; J664/8: hwfy lmr'hmw hqnythw dšfthw "he bestowed on their lord his offering which he promised Him"; J562/20: rtdw hqnythmw ᶜTTR ŠRQN "they placed their offering under the protection of (the god) A.Š." AND OFTEN SIM; J626/16-7: wkwnt dt hqnytn ldt nᶜmt wtnᶜmn lY "and this offering was (made) so that it may have gone well and will go well with Y" AND ELSEWHERE SIM

(2) DEED OF DEDICATION (cf 'qnyt sense2)

R4133/3: k]wn wtfn whqnytn b[wrx... "this deed of transfer and dedication (of property) was enacted in [the month...]"

Note: Obscure in Gl773b/3: wsqy ᶜTTR hqnyt "and (the god) A. provided irrigation for the offering (?)"--phps n.pr, or tr "property dedicated (to a god)." Parallel texts have sqy ᶜTTR SB' "A. provided irrigation for Saba."

n5 s mqn Ry507/11*

LORD, MASTER (context doubtful)

[Copy has bxfrt/ mqn w'rḍn; RyMus66/295 reads bxfrt/ [s]myn w'rḍn; RycPCH/50 quotes as bxfrt mqn (smyn) w'rḍn, which, though questionable, yields the most plausible translation. If a genuine word, prob a var of *mqny (cf mbn for mbny). Cf Sq qaninhín "Lord, Master (God)" LeLS/378; Heb qōnēh šāmáyim wā'āreṣ (Gen 14:19,22); Phoen 'l qn 'rṣ (Karatepe 3/18).]

Ry507/11: bxfrt mqn (smyn) w'rḍn "under the protection of the Lord of heaven and earth" n^6 s mqny R3958/13; p mqnythmw NNAG9/25

POSSESSION, PROPERTY (but see Note)

R3958/13: wkwn dn srn ẓrb wmqny bny M "and let this valley be the rightful possession and property of the b.M."; NNAG9/25: 'rḏthmw w'srrhmw wmqnythmw "their fields, valleys and property"

Note: J645=NNAG9 reads mfnythmw, root FNW, q.v. Very possibly, owing to the similarity of the characters for Q and F, both citations above should be referred to this root.

QN^c

tp pf tqn^{c}w J564/4+; tqn^{c}hw J562/7

SATISFY; RECONCILE, CAUSE TO ACQUIESCE (l- in)

[Ar qn^c D and h "satisfy"; Dat qana^{c}a "be satisfied with."]

J562/7: tqn^{c}hw 'dmhw..'SB'N "his servants the Sabaeans satisfied Him"; J564/4: stwfy mngwm dbhw tqn^{c}w wstyd^{c}n 'SB'N "(the god) granted an outcome with which the Sabaeans were satisfied and (which) they had sought"; C315/8: tqn^c...'mr'hw...lhwt slmn "he reconciled his lords to that peace"

n^1 s qn^{c}m J643/10*

SATISFACTION; adv qn^{c}m: SATISFACTORILY (?)

[Ar qana^c id.]

J643/10: mngt hdtw...hgrn ḤNN qn^{c}m lhysrn b^{c}brhw bn 'SB'N "the outcome which (the king) brought about (at) the city Ḥ., satisfactorily, to send him some of the Sabaeans (?)"--or n.pr?

n^2 s mqn^c F80*

ADEQUATE SUPPLYING

F80: šr^{c}tm lmqn^c bthmw "water channels for the adequate supplying of their house"

QNT--For n qnt R2860/2,4, see under QNY n^2

QNTN

n s qntn C541/122*

UNIT OF MEASURE (HUNDREDWEIGHT?)

[Cf Ar qinṭār "hundredweight (100 raṭl)" = Latin centenarium, Gk kentēn-árion.]

C541/122: 50,806 dqqm w26,000 tmrm bqntn Y "50,806 (measures of) flour and 26,000 (measures of) dates, by the measure (hundredweight?) of Y."

QSB

v pf qsb F120/6+

context fragmentary; sense doubtful

[RyET/72 cfs Ar qsb "be hard," Heb hiqšîb "be attentive to, consider."]

F120/6: ...] qsbtm dqsb R... "the ... which R. ...ed"; ib/14: ...]rd

^{c}lhmw qsb R ḥšd [... "upon them, R. ...ed ..."

n _s_? qsbtm F120/6*

sense doubtful; see under QSB _v_

F120/6 quoted under QSB _v_

QSD I

v _pf_ qsd C541/9-10+; qsdw J577/8; _maṣdar_ qsdm Ry510/5

REBEL

[Cf Ar qiswadd "extremely obstinate person" (Irv/370n131, after LA). BeOr-25/302 wished to read _fsd_, phps in all occurrences, but PiMus69/178n42 confirms the reading of _q_ in Ry506 from photos, and _fsd_ is not attested except as an alternative reading to _qsd_.]

C541/9-10: kqsd whxlf bgzmn "when he rebelled and assumed the function of xalīfa/governor by (swearing) an oath"; J577/8: qsdw wnz^{c} ydm bn 'mr'hmw "they rebelled and withdrew (their) hand (= revolted) from their lords"; Ry510/5: (y)ndynhmw ^{c}rbn qsdm "the beduins were harrassing them in rebellion"

n _s_ qsdt(n) J577/13+

REBELLION

J577/13: 'sd hb'sw whšt'w qsdtn "those who evilly raised the rebellion"; J667/8: ḥbl wqsdt kwn bhgrn "the revolt and rebellion which existed in the city"

QSD II

n _p/coll_ qsd(m,n) C356/4+; qsdhmw C601/6-7

A CLASS OF CIVILIANS (small landed proprietors?), distinguished from the client class; "YEOMEN" or "FREE PEASANTS" (cf qsṭ, sim)

[Identical with qsṭ? See this for possible etymology. For the conjectured role of this class cf BeSI/69,74, RycERI/272.]

C601/6-7: mśwdhmw wqsdhmw w'dwmthmw "their assembly, their qsd-class and their clients"; C356/4: 'sdm wqsdm "soldiers and 'yeomen'"; R3951/2: 'š^{c}bn qsdn wmkrn wśl'n "the tribes, (i.e.) the qsd-class, the traders (?) and the tribute-paying serfs"; Robin al-Mašamayn/3: qsdhmw wrglhmw w'dmhmw "their free peasants and soldiers and clients"

QSḤ

n _s_ qsḥ C82/7-8*

VIOLENCE, HARSHNESS

[Ar qasaḥa "be hard, firm"; Heb hiqšāh "treat roughly."]

C82/7-8: the wounds he suffered bqsḥ 'sdn "through the violence of the soldiers"

QSṬ I

n _p/coll_ qsṭ(n) R3945/12+; qsṭhw ib/11

A CLASS OF CITIZENS (cf qsd "YEOMEN")

[Cf Ar qisṭ "share, allotment," taqsīṭ "payment in installments." Phps this class of citizens was characterized by the payment of a certain kind of tax. Discussion RycERI/272.]

R3945/11: ḥṯb Y wqsṭhw w'nmhw wbḍ^{c}hw w'^{c}rrhw "he made over [to the Sabaean state] Y. and its qsṭ-citizens and civil population, its district and fortresses"; ib/12: kl qsṭ K ḥrhw w^{c}bdhw "all the qsṭ-citizens of K., its freemen and its servants"; R4134/2: qstn 'SB'N "qsṭ-citizens, Sabaeans"

QSṬ II

n s̲ qsṭ C682/4+ (all on incense burners)

KIND OF INCENSE = COSTUS

[Gk kóstos, Latin costus, id.]

C682/4: rnd ḍrw kmkm qsṭ "nard, ḍrw-incense, kmkm-incense, costus"

QSM

n s̲ mqsmm C548/2*

ORACLE SHRINE

[Heb qāsam "practice divination," Heb miqsām, Min mqsm (R3700/2) "oracle by lot."]

C548/2: whoever visits a sanctuary k'xḏ bmqsmm "in order to obtain (an oracle) in the oracle shrine..."

QSS

n s̲ qssm C541/67*

PRIEST

[Ar qasīs, Syr qaššîš, id.]

C541/67: they held mass in the church of M., kbhw qssm 'bmstlh "for there is a priest in it, the abbot of its monastery"

QSR

n s̲ mqsr(m,n) R4584/2+

BONDMAN

[Ar qasara "force, compel, constrain," here a person bound to pay certain tribute or perform certain work? (R on R4583/2).]

R4584/2: R bn mqsr(m) B "R., son of the bondman B."; R4585B: 'A mqsrn hw^{c} "A., the bondman, made an offering"

QFD

n s̲ mqfdtm R4652/1*

FOUNDATION

[Sense from context. In Ar qafada = "tie a knot," ModḤaḍ "roll one's self up"--reference may be to a foundation constructed in a particular way.]

R4652/1 (fragmentary): ...bn] mqfdtm ^{c}dy š[qrm... "[from] the foundation to the r[oof]"--this formula is common with mwṯr "foundation" and other synonyms

QFL

v pf qflw Ry506/8+

RETURN FROM A JOURNEY

[Ar qafala id.]

J1028/9: qflw 'bthmw "they returned to their houses"; Ry506/8: wqflw bn Ḥ [b]xyl RḤMNN "and they returned from Ḥ. (by) the power of (the god) R."

Note: Irv reads wqf[lw] in C541/132; C read wqš[bnm], Be wq^{c}[dw].

QṢ--For n qṣ, see under QYṢ, QṢṢ; for n mqṣm, see under NQṢ

QṢW

v imv m.p tqṣw R4088/1*

BEWARE OF, HOLD ALOOF FROM

[Ar qaṣā, qaṣâ "be, go far away."]

R4088/1: tqṣw ^{c}brm "beware of crossing (the boundary)!"

QṢ^{c}

v pf qṣ^{c}w C325/8*

CUT DOWN

[Ar qaṭa^{c}a "cut," Heb hiqṣi^{ac} "scrape."]

C325/8: qṣ^{c}w ḥṣmhw "they cut down its wood"

QṢṢ I

v inf qṣṣ GaAntYem2p540/2*

REPAY, SETTLE a debt

[Ar qāṣaṣa "settle accounts, be quits."]

GaAntYem2p540/2: fdyw wqṣṣ wbrṯn kl ml' "they acquitted themselves of, repaid, and discharged the whole sum"

QṢṢ II

n s qṣm R5085/7*

PLASTER

[Ar jiṣṣ, Sq qaṣ id.]

R5085/7: he prepared it for use bgyrm wqṣm "with lime and plaster"

QṢR

v pf qṣr C204/4*

BRING IN THE HARVEST

[Heb qāṣar id.]

C204/4: kqṣr bn wrd ḏnmn "when he brought in the harvest, away from the fall of rain"

QḌB

n *s* qḍbm J700/12*

STICK, STAFF

[Ar qaḍīb id.]

J700/12: wysbṭ S R bqḍbm "and S. struck R. with a stick"

QḌY

ti *inf* qtḍn J616/14*

BE CALLED UP for military service

[Ar qḍy *ti* "require, demand" (BeNL7/543).]

J616/14: t'tmw wqtḍn kl 'š^{c}b w^{c}šr X "all the tribes and clans of X. assembled and were called up"

For qtḍ Ir13, see under QYḌ *ti*

QḌN--For qtḍn J616/14, see under QḌY *ti*

QR'

v *ipf* yqr'nhw J570/7; yqr'nhmw C581/9

CALL UPON, SUMMON (contexts doubtful)

[Heb qārā' "call, proclaim; summon."]

J570/7: ...]ysr tny 'sn wyqr'nhw k[... "sent two men, and he called on him..." (fragmentary context); C581/9: yqr'nhmw khmy ^{c}kr wš'm hyt ṣlmtn "he (the god?) summoned them when they ... (?) and set up this statue" (context obscure)

Note: In C581/9 the *v* is phps to be construed with what precedes: btrm[.] yqr'nhmw "in the ... (?) which befell them"--cf Heb qārāh (and qārā') "meet, befall."

st *pf* stqr' R2726/2+

(1) PROCLAIM, or SEEK TO HAVE PROCLAIMED

R2726/2: thus ordained the king of S., w^{c}d'l dstqr' wxll bh'w dwmm "and to that which he proclaims and settles have (his subjects) conformed forever"; sim in C976/3, R3951/1

(2) MEET (?)

[Ar qarâ, Heb qārāh/qārā' "meet."]

R2659 (in full, context obscure): ...] hwṯbt mḥwlm wḏstqr' ṯt(y)[... "it was established as the encircling wall, and that which the two ...s meet..."

QRB

v *pf* qrb C523/2; qrbh C533/3; qrbw J643/31+; *inf* qrb IrApp2#3/12

BE or DRAW NEAR (sometimes with sexual implication); APPROACH; ARRIVE

[Ar qari/aba "be, come near."]

IrApp2#3/12: he sent him to the city lqrb lḥḏr "to be near for the pilgrimage"; J643/31: mr'hmw...w'sd qrbw b^{c}mhw "their lord and those who drew near/arrived with him"; C523/2: he confessed bhn qrb mr'tm bḥrmw wmlṯ ḥyḍ "because he approached a woman (sexually) at a forbidden (time) and had intercourse (?) with a menstruating woman" (sim in C533/3)

D pf qrb Ir2I+

BRING, BRING NEAR

[Ar qrb D id.]

Ir2I: 'sd ḏqrb bśnhw "men whom he brought with him"; sim J649/28

n¹ s qrb(n) J578/4I+; p? qrbt R4157/4

adj: NEAR (l- to)

[Ar qarīb id.]

J578/4I: may the god preserve them bn nḍᶜ wšṣy...šn'm ḏrḥq wqrb "from injury and evil eye of (any) enemy who is far or near" AND OFTEN; J737/4-5: šn'm rḥqm wqrbm "(any) enemy, far or near"; IrApp2/2: šn'm...ḏqrb lhmw "(any) enemy who is near to them"; C539/2: bᶜlmn bᶜdn wqrbn "in the world, far and near"; R4157/4: ...]'qbrt bn sb' w[... "those near Saba (or, those near the expedition?)"; C540/6-7: bn qrb R "from near R."; Ir12/8: expeditions he sent them to command bqrbm wrḥqm "near and far"

n² s qrbnhm[w] C539/I*

OFFERING

[Ar qurbān, Heb qorbān id.]

C539/I: ykfrn ḥbhmw wyqbln qrbnhm[w] "he expiated their sin and (the god) accepted their offering"

QRW

h pf hqrw C19/5*

OFFER, DEDICATE (?)

[MüW/9I tr "dedicate" cfing Ug qry "offer" and Eth 'aqāraya; cf phps Ar qarâ "collect water in a reservoir" (reference to pouring out of libations?), cited by R on Min R3610/6 (qrw in sim sense).]

C19/5: the god commanded him through His oracle bqyfhw ḏhqrw bhgrn M "at His altar which he dedicated in the city M." (presumably the dedicant of the inscription also dedicated the qyf-altar)

Note: C read ḏ.qrw but emended to ḏhfrᶜ

pp b-qrw R4194/4*

IN THE DIRECTION OF

[Ar qarw = qaṣd "aim, direction" (Q, cited in Irv/167a).]

R4194/4: b'rn T bqrw bn ᶜśbthmy "the well T. in the direction away from their hired fields"

n p qrwt R4194/3*

SECONDARY CANALS

[Ar qarī "channel for water in a garden (or) cistern"; al-miqrâ(†) "place where rainwater collects from every side" (LA, cited in Irv/163-4).]

R4194/3: qrwt wnqbt wm'tt "canals, cuttings and channels"

QRẒ

n p qrẓm C540/43*

MERINO SHEEP (?)

[Cf Te qərṭ̌ī "a kind of black, steatopygous Merino sheep to be found in the Abyssinian highlands," phps same as "Aden sheep"? (Irv/278, who also cfs Ar 'ibil qaraẓīya† "camels which eat the qaraẓ tree").]

C540/43: ḏbyḥm wqrẓm wbqrm "sacrificial animals, Merino sheep (?) and cattle"

QRY I

ti ipf yqtrn N74/12*

BE PUNISHED

[Cf Ar qry ti "make diligent search," Dt "pursue fugitives" (Dozy2/349).]

N74/12: wl yqtrn bmḥrmn [w]l yh[b]ṭn wlyʿḏbn ʿšry bl[ṭm] "let him be punished in the temple, let him be beaten, and let him be fined twenty blṭ"

QRY II

n d qrytnhn Ry533/12*

SETTLED AREA, RURAL DISTRICT (or n.pr?)

[Cf Ar qarya† "village." Discussion RyMus68/305.]

Ry533/12: yʿdw [q]mʿ qrytnhn "ultimately, they subdued the two rural districts (or, Q.)"

For qryt J635/4, see under QRT

QRM

n p qrm Ry508/7*

TRIBAL LEADER, CHIEFTAIN

[Ar qarm, p qurūm, id.]

Ry508/7: the king sent him to fight ʿly N bn qrm bn 'Z'N "against N., one of (?) the chieftains among the Yaz'anites"

QRN

v pf qrn J643/22; qrnw C541/54; inf qrn Ry508/6+; masdar? qrnm J1028/7

(1) FIGHT

[Eth taqārana "be opposed, combat."]

C541/54: srwytn ḏhḏ[kyw]...qrnw 'qwln 'lht qsdw "the troops whom they sent fought the chiefs who had rebelled"; Ry508/6: ḏkyw mlkn lqrn ʿly N "the king sent (them) to fight against N."

(2) GUARD

[Ar qarana "be s.o.'s companion; guard." Discussion RycMus88/212.]

J662/12: their lord commanded them lqrn wnẓr bhgrn "to guard and keep watch in the city"; Ir12: lšrḥ wqrn b'wṯn "to give protection and guard on the frontiers"; J1028/7: bʿm mlkn qrnm "the king was on guard"

n¹ s qrnm J576/13+; p 'qrnm J660/17; var? qrn J576/14

GUARD

J660/17: 'wlhmw b'qrnm b^{c}br mr'hmw "he sent them back with guards (= under guard) to their lord"; J576/14: mqtt w'rgl wqrn ysr Š lšrḥhw "the officers, foot-soldiers and guards Š. sent to reinforce him"

n^2 s mqrn J578/39+; var mqrnt Ry508/8

GUARD DUTY

J578/39: wherever their lords command them (to go) lbltm wmqrnm wqhtm "for mission(s), guard duty or service"; Ry508/8: wmlkn hrzy bmqrnt Ḥ wlsn^{c}n sslt MDBN "as for the king, he remained on guard (duty) of (= against) Ḥ. and fortifying the 'chain' of al-Mandab"

QR^c

tp pf tqr^c NNAGI2/7-8*

DRAW (slṭm "arrows," as a means of divination)

[Cf Ar qr^c Lt "draw lots," and the practice of divination by lances, istiqsām (RycMancie/269).]

NNAGI2/7-8: w'l ḥrb bhwt wrxn ^{c}ln ḏ'l tqr^c slṭm "but he did not 'fight' (ritually) in that month because he had not drawn (favorable) arrows"

QRF

n ḏ qrf[n] C614/2*

sense doubtful (fragmentary context)

C614/2: Ḥ]Y'LYm wṯny qrf[n... "[ḥ]y'l-coins and two ...s"

QRḌ

n s qrḍ R4813/1*

AGENT (?)

[Ar qaraḍa "lend money; conduct business."]

R4813/1: Y Y qrḍ Y "Y.Y., agent (?) of Y."

QRR

n s qrhmw J574/4*

SETTLEMENT

[Ar qarr id, qarra "stop and stay...in a place" (JSIMB/61).]

J574/4: ḥrbt ḥrbw bqrhmw bsrn "the battle they fought in their settlement in the valley"

QRŚ

n s qrśn C562/7*

A DRY MEASURE (?)

[Cf Eth qoros, a dry and liquid measure corresponding to Heb kōr.]

C562/7: 'rb^{c}t dblm wbn qrśn 'fym "four fig-cakes and part of (?) a qrś-measure of baked goods"

QRŠ

n <u>s</u>? qršt R4664/1; <u>d</u> qršty BR-Yanbuq 28/1-2
sense doubtful; CATTLEHERD (?)
[Cf Yem qâriša/qurâš "animal; <u>p</u> cattle" (LaGD, cited and discussed in BafIns/39-40).]
R4664/1: ...] llt qršt [..., no tr; BR-Yanbuq 28/1-2: ᶜA wG qršty B "A. and G., the 2 cattleherds (?) of B."

QRT

n <u>s</u> qrytm J635/4*
KIND OF MUSK
[Ar qarīt "excellent musk," qārit "light and of higher quality (musk)" (Dozy2/324).]
J635/4: qrytm wṭnfm ṭybm "musk and sweet-smelling ṭanūf"

QŚM

n <u>s</u> qśm R4176/13*
SHARE, PORTION
[Ar qism id.]
R4176/13: the god commanded mrḍ <u>t</u>l<u>t</u> lqśm 'qwl "the grant of a third as the portion of the tribal leaders"

n^2 <u>s</u> qśmtm Gl379/5*
SHARE, ALLOTMENT (cf qśm)
[Ar qisma⁺ id.]
Gl379/5 (= C318): 'l s'l xdrn <u>t</u>ᶜdtm wqśmtm "let no one lay claim to this grave, for a cultivated plot or as a share (i.e., let there be no claim to a share in the communal tomb)"

QŠB

v <u>inf</u> qšb C380/4*
CLEAR land
[Ar qašaba "free from rust"; here, free from obstructions?]
C380/4: f'l śn qšbn mḥmym "it is not lawful to clear (?) embanked land (i.e., remove the embankments?)"

h <u>pf</u> hqšbw C325/7+; <u>inf</u> hqšb(n) C308/4+
(1) CLEAR land (cf QŠB <u>v</u>)
C308/4: kl ṭyb tnṭᶜw whqšbn "all the incense plantations they planted and cleared" (or tr as sense² below, "incense plants...they prepared for use"?)
(2) BUILD, (RE)FURBISH, RENOVATE; PREPARE FOR USE (building works)
C325/7: št'hw bn mw<u>t</u>rhw whqšbw bh[w sf]lhw "they raised it from its foundations and built in [it] its [lo]wer part"; Ist7630/4: yqṭ wgyrn whqšbn krfm "dug, plastered, and prepared for use the cistern"; R3966/1: hḥd<u>t</u>w whqšb "they repaired and renovated"

n s qšbnm C541/104-5*
CONSTRUCTION; specifically, STONEWORK (?)
[Irv/316-7 cfs Sq qáśbub "stone," and Sab QŠB h.]
C541/104-5: dwz'w bqdm ᶜwdn qšbnm "that which they extended in front of the settling basin as a stone construction (or, in stonework)"

QŠD

n s qšdn C282/6,10*
sense doubtful (a kind of evil or injury)
[No etymology; conjectures in C.]
C282/6: lhᶜnnhmw bn qšdn bbrq dt' "may (the god) protect them from ... in the spring stormy season"; ib/10: ṣdqhmw ml'hw...wqšdn 'l r'yw "He granted them His oracle-response and they did not experience the ..."

QŠM

n s qšmtn C308/9*
ORCHARD
[Cf Eth qašama "gather fruit," qašām "apple harvest"; Ar qšmt in Iklīl "fruits."]
C308/9: kl mhwkbhmw krrm wšrᶜ qšmtn w'hdrhw w'kfrhw "all their estates altogether, and the irrigation of the orchard and its hdr- and kfr-cisterns"

QTW

n s.m mqtw(n) Ry513/1+; var mqtwy J579/1+; mqtwyhmw J577/7; d mqtwyy J578/2-3+; mqtwyyhmw J577/10; p mqtt J576/14+; mqtthw IrApp2#3/20+; var mqtwthmw Ry509/8; var mqtythmw J577/7; var mqtwyt C289/6+; s.f mqtwyt N14/2-3+
ROYAL OFFICER or OFFICIAL (civil and military)
[Ar maqtawī "servant of the king" (Muᶜallaqa of ᶜAmr ibn Kultūm/56), qatā "he served well and was in the service of kings and chiefs"; Eth 'aqtawa "impose (tribute), bind, oblige."]
J579/1: D bn T mqtwy...mlky SB' "D., son of T., official of the 2 kings of S." AND OFTEN AS EPITHET OF DEDICANTS; J576/14: mqtt w'rgl wqrn Y. "the officers, foot-soldiers, and guard(s) of Y."; C308/17: kl 'qwl wmqtt "all the tribal leaders and officials"

QTL

v inf qtl J2107/8-9; inf/pf qtlhmw R3945/3+
KILL
[Ar qatala id.]
R3945/3: wfṭ kl 'hgrhmw wqtlhmw šltt 'lf[m] "burned all their towns and killed them (to the number of) three thousand"; sim ib/4,13; J2107/8-9: škr wnqm wqtl whtlᶜn "defeating, taking vengeance upon, killing, breaking (the enemy)"

QTḌ--see under QYḌ _ti_, QḌY _ti_

Q_T_RY--In R2628, only word in inscription; _n.pr_?

)-R

R'

pt r' + pf C376/10+; r' + k- + pf C397/10+; k- + r' + k- + pf J616/19

NOW; INDEED

[Prob derived from root R'Y "see, look," phps frozen use of imv m.s ("behold!") Optionally followed by deictic k-.]

J693/7: he promised the god an offering if a son should survive, wr' xmr 'LMQH...^{c}bdhw...ḥyw bnhw "and now (the god) I. has granted His servant the life of his son"; J706/7: she promised the god an offering to help her ailing eye, wr' kh^{c}nhw "and now He has helped her" AND OFTEN SIM with both r' and r' k-; C581/14: wr' kwqh [l]hqnynhw hyt ṣlmtn w'LMQH [f]l yšrḥn... grb mr'hw "now he has ordered the dedication to (the god) of that statue, so let (the god) I. protect the life of his lord"; C376/10: w'A wY r' hgb'y ...'rḍn "and as for A. and Y., they have now/indeed leased out this land"; J567/12: wr' khqnyw dt hqnytn ḥgn kwqh 'LMQH "they have now/indeed dedicated this offering as (the god) I. commanded"

R'B

h ipf yhr'bn R3910/7+; yhr'bnn F55/6; inf hr'bn C291/9

ENTER AN AGREEMENT, AGREE UPON

[Cf Ar ra'aba "bring/come together" (Irv/170).]

R3910/7: wmnmw dyhr'bn wyhwḥbn wrqm "whoever enters an agreement and ...s greenstuff..."; sim C291/9; F55/6: wdmw yhr'bnn b^{c}ly (ẓ)hrn "and whoever enters an agreement concerning this document..."

n s r'b DJE14/1*

"MEDIATOR," name of a royal official

[Ar ra'b "a chief who rectifies, or amends, the affair...of a people," ra''āb "a man who affects reconciliation or makes peace between people" (Lane/993-4, quoted in MüTa^{c}izz/99).]

DJE14/1: R r'b mlkn "R., the king's 'mediator'"

R'Y

v pf r' C74/4; r'yw C541/73+; ipf yr'yn J643/15+; yr'ynh C456/2-3; yr'ynhw J567/7-8

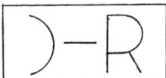

SEE > EXPERIENCE

[Ar ra'â id.]

C74/14: ^{c}lm r' bmḥrmn "the (oracular) sign he saw in the temple"; C541/73: kl r'yw kdny ḏlln ^{c}ly 'š^{c}bn 'd̲nw lhmw "when they saw that the disease was approaching the tribesmen, they dismissed them"; C456/2-3: wd̲hrghw w'bhw lyr'ynh ^{c}T̲TR "as for the one who killed him and his father, may (the god) A. see (and punish) him!"; C282/10: they made an offering wqšd̲n 'l r'yw "and did not experience the qšd̲ (an agricultural calamity they had asked the god to prevent)"

Note: For the exp r' (k-), see under R'.

ti ipf [y]rt'yn C140/12-3*

SEE > RECOGNIZE, EXPERIENCE (?) (cf R'Y v)

[Cf Ar r'y ti "consider, have an opinion."]

C140/12-3: k'l ysfhn lhw w[h]rt'yn bhw š[w]ftm "let him not despise (?) (the god), and he will experience in Him protection"

h pf hr'y C357/10-1; hr'yhw R3929

CAUSE TO SEE > SHOW, specifically an oracular vision

J567/5: ḥgn d̲t hr'y 'LMQH...^{c}bdhw bwsṭ snthw "according to what (the god) I. had shown His servant in his sleep"; C357/10-1: hr'yt hr'y lhmw "the vision (the god) showed them"; sim R4052/4

Note: For yhr[']n Ry3=R3910/7, read yhr['b]n, see under R'B h.

n^{1} s r'y Ham9/5*

ORACULAR VISION

Ham9/5: yxmrnhmw r'y lhmw "may (the god) grant them an oracular vision (propitious) to them"

n^{2} s hr'yt R4052/4+

ORACULAR VISION (cf r'y and R'Y h)

R4052/4: the god commanded them by means of the oracle, wlf hr'yt hr'y "and according to the oracular vision He showed (them)..."

R'S

n s r's C5/21+; r'shw R3951/4+; r'shm C371/3; r'shmw R4226/2; p 'r's R3945/5; 'r'shmw C540/22

(1) HEAD

[Ar ra's "head; chief; top."]

J577/7: he defeated that fellow w'wlw r'shw "and they brought back his head"

(2) CHIEF

R3945/5: 'r's mśwd 'A "the chiefs of the council of A."

(3) TOP

C540/2: they repaired various parts of the dam bn mwt̲rhmw...[^{c}]dy 'r'shmw šqrm "from their foundation(s) to their tops, (i.e.) the top of the walls"

(4) SELF

[Cf Ar bi-ra'sihi "in a class by itself," Eth ra'sa reflexive pn.]
R4226/2: hqnyw 'LMQH r'shmw "they dedicated themselves to (the god) I." (parallels have nfs); R3951/4: 'sm lr'shw "an individual (acting) for himself"

n[2] p mr's(n) Ir13+; mr'shmw R3563/3+
DIGNITARIES
[Ar mar'ūs "subordinate," cf ra'īs "chief."]
Ir13: ᶜqbt wmr's w'bᶜl "governors, dignitaries and citizens"; Ry507/1: 'qlhmw wmr'shmw [w]ᶜrbnhmw "their tribal leaders, lesser chiefs and beduins"; J576/2: mr's w'kbrt KDT "lesser chiefs and clan-heads of Kinda"

R'Š

h pf hr'šhmy R2724/4; ipf yhr'šn R3910/7; inf hr'šn C400/1+
(1) REMOVE, TAKE AWAY
[Sense from context.]
C400/1: w'l śn hᶜzln whr'šn bn kl ṣrf...bn mḥrmn "it is not lawful to remove or take away any of the ṣrf-incense from the temple"; same formula R4178/1
(2) SET ASIDE > PAY DOWN as a deposit (?)
R3910/7: wmnmw...yhr'šn z'dm f'w s'rt "and whoever pays down extra as a deposit (?) or any other security..."; R2724/4: hr'šhmy lhwṯqn "he paid them down as a deposit (?) to assure..."

st pf str'š C607/4*
BE TAKEN AWAY (pass of R'Š h sense[1])
C607/4: ...]hw ṣrf str'š bn R w[... "...srf-incense (which) was taken away from R...."

RBB

v pf rb Gl143/1*
BE THE OWNER OF, POSSESS
[Ar rabba "be lord, have possession of."]
Gl143/1: rb T'LB...kl brrn "(the god) T. is the owner of all the open country (pasturage)"

h pf hrbbhmy J716/6-7*
TAKE/HOLD AS HOSTAGE (?)
[Cf Sab rbb "hostage," below.]
J716/6-7: the god protected His 2 servants bkn hrbbhmy šᶜbn S "when the tribe S. took/held them hostage" (they were later returned to their own tribe, 1.8)

n[1] s rbm R2740/7+; in compounds rbYHD C543/2; rbHD J1028/12; rbHWD Ry515
(1) LORD (divine title)
[Ar rabb "lord, master."]
C543/2: 'lhhmw rbYHD "their god, the Lord of the Jews"; Ry515: rbHWD bRḤMNN "Lord of the Jews. By (the god) R."; sim J1028/12; cf also Gl062/4 (obscure

context): xm]st w^{c}šry rbm kšymn "twenty-five lords (?) as patrons (?)" (cf HoAA2/142)

(2) MEASURE OF VOLUME, "GREAT" UNIT (?)

R2740/7: mqdḥm drbm [] 50 [] "a vessel of (which the capacity is) 50 rb-units"

n^{2} d rbbn C308/24-5; p 'rbb(n) C608/5+; var 'rbbw R4176/12

(1) SERVANT; CLIENT

[Cf Ar rabīb "foster-son; ally." Note also rbb, rbbt frequent elements in nn.pr.]

Gl180/1: ['[rbb S '[qwl] š^{c}bn S "the clients of S., leaders of the tribe S."; R4176/12: a slave was killed, so lyhrd' mr' 'rbbw "let the master of the slaves be compensated (for his loss)"

(2) HOSTAGE (cf RBB h)

C308/24-5: t^{c}rbw lmr'hmw...whysrw ṯny rbbn "they gave pledges of submission to their lord and sent (him) two hostages"

RBW

v ipf yrbwn R4646/18*

CAUSE TO GROW > CULTIVATE

[Ar rby D "make or let grow, cause to sprout."]

R4646/18: fl yz'n nkrn b^{c}ly xfrthw dyrbwn "let the cultivator continue to be held responsible concerning his enclosed field"

RBḤ

n s rbḥ Gl572/2; p? rb()ḥt Gl547/8 (copy has rbnḥt)

ACCUMULATED INTEREST, PROFIT

[Ar rabiḥa "obtain monetary gains as a result of commercial transactions" (cf BeSM/396).]

Gl572/2: they repaid and discharged kl ml' wrbḥ "the whole sum, with accumulated interest"; Gl547/8: bnml' wrb()ḥt hmt 'sṭrn "from the yield and profits of these documents"

RBX

v inf? rbx C544/5*

MAKE TRANQUIL > CONTENT s.o. (?)

[Ar and ModYem rabax(a) "rest" (cf RoVoc/311).]

C544/5: the goddess granted them children wrbx 'fshmy bhmt 'wldn "and contented their souls with those children" (or read as n, "granted them children and contentment of their souls")

Note: BeDGESA/5:2 cfs Ar rabaḥa "profit from."

n^{1} s rbs(m) J633/4+

(1) RELIEF

J633/4: as for the god, fšft...^{c}bdhw brbx wḥyw bn hwt ḥlẓn "he decreed (for) His servant relief and cure from that disease"

(2) REST(ING PLACE) (?)

N51/3: šmy...mqbrhmw rbxm "they established their grave (as) a resting place" (or phps n.pr here and in sim contexts)

n^2 s mrbxm C21/3+

PLACE OF REST, RESTING PLACE (cf rbx, sense^2)

C20/3: ^{c}s'w...mqbrhm [m]rbxm "they constructed their grave (as) a resting place"; C21/3: ...] mqbrhn mrbxm ^{c}ṮTR "[they entrusted?] their grave, a resting place, (to?) (the god) A." (read phps as n.pr?)

RBNḤT--For rbnḥt G1547/8 read rb()ḥt, see under RBḤ

RB^c

tp pf trb^c J586/23*

TAKE for one's self A FOURTH PART OF THE BOOTY

[Ar raba^{c}a "take a fourth part of s.o.'s property or possessions, a fourth part of the spoil" (Lane/1015A), denom from rb^c n "fourth part, quarter."]

J586/23: yhqḏw rkbhmw wḥṣqhmw ḏtrb^c mr'yhmw "they 'liberated' (the enemy's) riding animals and baggage train which their lords had taken for themselves (as their share of a quarter of the booty)"

n^1 cardinal number: f 'rb^c(m,n) R4143/2+; m 'rb^{c}t(n) R3958/14+

FOUR; as adv, 'rb^{c}m: FOURFOLD

[Ar 'arba^c, 'arb^{c}a^t "four."]

R4143/2: 'rb^{c}n ''bln ḏhbn "these four gold camels"; J653/9: bywm 'rb^{c}m ḏF "on the fourth day (lit., day four) of (the month) ḏF."; R3958/14: ḏl'rb^{c}t w'rb^{c}hy wm't xryftm "in the year 144"; C573/2: 'rb^{c}tn w^{c}šrnhn 'ṣlmn "these twenty-four statues"; C563/5: yst^{c}ḏbhw 'rb^{c}m "let him punish him fourfold"

n^2 cardinal number: 'rb^{c}y R3943/2+; var 'rb^{c}hy R3958/14

FORTY

[Ar 'arba^{c}ūn, id. Form 'rb^{c}hy shows Qat or Min influence.]

R3943/2: 'rb^{c}y wxms[t 'lf]m ▯ 5040 ▯ "five thousand forty: 5040"

Note: In all attested cases, followed by mimated n.

n^3 cardinal number: 'rb^{cc}šrhw J577/11*

FOURTEEN

J577/11: Ḥ...w'rb^{cc}šrhw 'frsm "Ḥ. and his fourteen (men), horsemen"

Note: Cf 'rb^{c}t ^{c}šr "fourteen," C541/109.

n^4 s rb^c(n) R3954/1+; rb^{c}hmw C398/20+

(1) QUARTER, FOURTH

[Ar rub^c id.]

R3954/1: bny rb^c qbrn "he built a quarter of the grave"; C371/2: rb^c kl šlṯ mbḥr[hw] "a fourth of every third (= a twelfth) of his tomb"; F64/4: whbhw rb^{c}n "he gave him a quarter (of it)"

(2) MOON IN THE FIRST QUARTER, epithet of a deity

C398/20: b^{c}ṮTR šymm wrb^{c}hmw wšmshmw "by (the god) A. the Patron and by their quarter-moon god and their sun goddess"; cf also FI19/2: RB^{c}n YH^{c}N "the Helpful Quarter-Moon"

n^5 s rb^{c}n C95/6; var rb^{c}yn Ir17/1; p 'rb^{c}w J650/2; 'rb^{c}whmw Ir22/1; var 'rb^{c}n R2726/3+

DIVISION of a clan; phps PEOPLE of a town

[Ar rub^c "division of a clan," rab^c "people of one's clan" (BeNL9/189-92).]

C95/6: š^{c}bhmw B rb^{c}n d^{c}A "their tribe B., the division of (clan) A."; J650/2: š^{c}bn D H 'rb^{c}w dS "the tribe D.H., divisions of (clan) S."; Ir22/1: š^{c}bn Ǵ w'rb^{c}whmw "the tribe Ǵ. and (its) divisions"; R2726/3: ^{c}hrw F... w'rb^{c}n w'ḥśrn wmśwdn "the nobles of (clans) F., the clansmen, the indigents, and the council"; sim R3951/1; R2726/25: mlk 'rb^{c}n dB "king of the clan-divisions of B." (BeNL9/92 takes as d, "the townsfolk of ṢRWḤ and MRB")

n^6 adj: m.s rb^{c}n C435/3-4+; f.s rb^{c}tn Ry506/3

FOURTH (ordinal)

[Ar rābi^c id.]

C435/3-4: bxmsn rb^{c}n "in the fourth fifth"; Ry506/3: ǵzwtn rb^{c}tn "the fourth raiding expedition" (BeESACD tr "spring raiding expedition," after Ar rabī^c "spring"); F71/15: xrfm M...rb^{c}n "the year (named for) M., the fourth (year of his eponymate)"

n^7 s rb^{c}m C562/4*

YOUNG ANIMAL (camel? lamb?)

[Ar rabā^c "young animal which has lost its first teeth."]

C562/4: bdbḥ rb^{c}m "with the sacrifice of a young (camel or lamb)"

n^8 s rb^{c}tm C325/1*

SQUARED MASONRY

[Ar tarbī^{ct} "square; square tile," Heb merubbā^c "squared (architectural term)."]

C325/1: [g]rbm wrb^{c}tm mwl[g]m wftxm "grb-masonry and squared masonry (of?) mwlg-stone and engraved (stone?)"

RBḌ

n^1 s mrbḍn GI142/7; [m]rbḍnhmw ib/12

(1) SHEEPFOLD, PEN for grazing animals

[Ar marbiḍ id.]

GI142/7: yqfnn wḥgr mrbḍn kl r^{c}y "they shall delimit and prohibit this sheepfold (to) every herdsman"

(2) RIGHT or PRACTICE OF PENNING flocks in a fold (?)

GI142/12: xmrhmw [m]rbḍnhmw 'mr'hmw "their lords granted them their right to pen flocks (?)" (or tr as sense^1?)

n^2 s mhrbḍm J650/13*

adj: SATISFACTORY (?) (but see Note)

[Cf Ar rbḍ h "satisfy thirst; manage the expenses of one's family"

(Lane/1012A; cf JSIMB/154).]
J650/13: the god may grant fr^{c} 'mrt dṯ' wxrf...mhrbḍm "excellent cereal crops of spring and autumn harvest, satisfactory (crops)"
Note: It is tempting to interpret the sequence bḍ (Π 日) as a dittography, reading mhrḍm and connecting with root RḌY "satisfy" (cf mrḍym "satisfactory").

RBQ

ti ipf yrtbqnh[w] R4730/2*
LAY SNARES FOR, CONSPIRE AGAINST (?)
[Cf Ar ribq "lasso," ribqa^{+} "noose."]
R4730/2: he placed it under the god's protection, (namely?) hgrn H bnkl yrtbqnh[w] "the city H., against anyone (who) might conspire against it (?)"

h inf hrbqn C429/6*
LAY SNARES FOR, AMBUSH (?)
C429/6: that fellow N., ḏyf^{c} whrbqn l'l'ltn wl'nsn "who rises against and lays snares for (?) the gods and men"
Note: RoVoc/312 cfs ModYem rabag/yirbig "shout" (like an attacking bandit?).

RGL

n^{1} s rglhw R3991/7; d rglyhw J583/7+; var? rglhw J649/21
FOOT, LEG
[Ar rijl, f, id.]
J840/8: ḥlẓ rglyhw "disease of his feet/legs"; J583/9: mrḍ rglyhw "sickness of his feet/legs"; R3991/7: the god saved him from tšyn šyn rglhw "the injury which affected his foot"; J649/20-1: zxnm mḍytm fxḏyhw wrglyhw...wḥḏr ktxd^{c}nn rglhw "wounds (which) pierced his thighs and legs, (so that) he feared his legs would be useless"

n^{2} s? rgly J566/1-2; p/coll rglm J577/5+; rglhmw Robin al-Mašamayn/3; p 'rgl J550/2
FOOTSOLDIER
[Cf Ar rājil "(one who goes) on foot," rajul "man."]
J550/2: 'sm rkbm wṯlṯt rglm "(one) mounted man and three footsoldiers"; J576/14: mqtt w'rgl wqrn "officers, footsoldiers and guards"; J556/1-2: R...rgly mlkn w'xyhw hqnyw "R., the king's footsoldier, and his brother dedicated"; J577/5: ytqdmw b^{c}mhmw rglm "footsoldiers fought with them" Robin al-Mašamayn/3: qsdhmw wrglhmw w'dmhmw "their free peasants, footsoldiers and clients"

RG^{c}

n s (rg)^{c}m Ry508/2*
RETURN (?) (but see Note)

[Ar rijā^c id.]

Ry508/2: tsṭrw...ḏšmw bsb'tm...khm (rg)^{c}m mr'hmw "their lord recorded (p. maj) those (things) which he had accomplished on campaign, likewise those of (his) return"

Note: The first two letters, which Ry restores as rg, have been hammered out. Omitting them, tr phps "when they (were) with their lord (khm ^{c}m mr'hmw)."

RD' I

v pf rd' RevSem'08p299 (cited in CoRoC/238A)*

DEDICATE, OFFER (?)

[Cf phps Ar rada'a "support, prop up."]

RevSem'08p299: rd' l'ṮRT ts^{c}n bḥtn "he dedicated (?) to (the goddess) A. these nine votive objects"

h pf hrd' C543/2; hrd'hmw C434/13; inf hrd'n J576/1+

HELP, AID

[Cf Ar rada'a "support" and Eth 'arde'a "give help."]

J576/1: they dedicated to the god because hwš^c whrd'n ^{c}bdhw...bškr kl 'xms "He had helped and aided His servant in defeating all the armies"; sim J578/5,15; C434/13: hrd'hmw šfr W "the labor force of W. helped them"

n s rd' R3958/5+

HELP, AID

[Ar rid' id.]

R3958/5-11: they built the aqueduct brd' wmqm ^{c}ṮTR...wbrd' mr'hmw 'l...wbrd' mnḍḥthmw...wbrd' šmshmw...wbrd' wxyl š^{c}bhmw "with the aid and might of (the god) A. and with the aid of their (human) lord I. and with the aid of their irrigation gods and with the aid of their sun goddess and with the aid and strength of their tribe"; C41/4: brd' wtḥrg mr'hmw "by the aid and command of their lord"

RD' II

h ipf yhrd' R4176/12*

COMPENSATE for a loss

[Cf Amh arädda "apply for compensation" (IrvBSOAS30/284n3). Phps related ultimately to RD' I.]

R4176/12: a slave was killed, wlyhrd' mr' 'rbbw "so let the master of the slaves be compensated (for his loss)"

RD' III

n s mrd'm R5094/4* (act.prt)

ONE WHO DOES HARM

[Cf Ar radī' "evil, vile."]

R5094/4: bly mrd'm bklm 'wnkrm "without/against any (sort of?) harmer or injurer"

RDY

n <u>s</u> rdy R2862/1-2; <u>p</u> rdyt R3439/2

INTEREST, PROFIT

[Eth radaya "pay interest," cf Ar radiya "increase, propagate (cattle)."]

R2862/1-2: ...] <u>d</u>lhw bn rdy ln <u>d</u>t (y)m'n "...what belongs to him of the profit, until he refuses to (pay?)"; R3439/2: kl 'sṭr wš'mt w'<u>t</u>wb wnḥlt wrdyt "all documents, deeds of sale, payments, usufructs, and profits"

RDF

v <u>pf</u> rdf R5044*

PURSUE (?)

[Ar radafa id.]

R5044 (in full): L rdf "L. has pursued (?)" (accompanying picture shows a camel whose rider carries a rope)

RHM

h <u>ipf</u> yhrhm C338/2*

(HE WHO) CAUSES RAIN TO FALL (?), epithet of the god T'LB

[Ar rhm <u>h</u> "rain lightly and continuously."]

C338/2: T'LB RYMm YHRHM "T.R., (he who) causes rain to fall"

Note: HöWdM/543 reads yhrxm, tr "he who brings good fortune" after Ar raxama "be gracious." She also cites (without giving a reference) the title of the goddess ŠMS b^{c}lt mrxmm "Lady of Graciousness," or the like.

RHN

v <u>pf</u> rhnw Ry506/7; rhnhmw ib/8+

GIVE PLEDGES or HOSTAGES in sign of surrender

[Ar rahana "pawn, deposit as security."]

C541/52: kklhmw h^{c}dw 'ydhmw wrhnhmw "when all of those who had rebelled had given them pledges of submission"; Ry506/7: wrhnw wb^{c}dnhw $wś^{c}$hw "they gave pledges (of submission), and then he gave them his guarantee"; ib/8: rhnhmw bnhw "he gave them his son as a hostage"

n^{1} <u>s</u> rhnm Ry507/7; <u>p</u>? rhnn ib

HOSTAGE

[Ar rahn id.]

Ry507/7: wkd' whbt rhnn wst(q)rw ^{c}lhmw mgrmtm "when they had already given hostage(s), they imposed on them a monetary penalty"; ib: whbw wln m'tm rhnm "they gave as many as (?) one hundred hostages"

n^{2} cf also rhnt R3199/4 (fragmentary context): ...] rhnt bny [..., no tr; context mostly <u>nn.pr</u>.

RWḤ

h <u>pf</u> hrwḥ R2865/1-2+

WIDEN, ENLARGE

[Ar rawiḥa "be wide."]

R2865/1-2: hgdd...hrwḥt hrwḥ 'wd hgrn N 'bhw "he determined the enlargement (by which) his father had enlarged the boundary of the city N."; R4369/2: hrwḥ ᶜlbn d̲ky ᶜšr 'mm "he enlarged the ᶜilb-tree plantation equal to (?) ten cubits"; R2868: hrwḥ N ᶜd 'ln 'wt̲nn "he enlarged N. to these boundaries"

st pf st[r]ḥ[t] C334/13*

BE AT PEACE, BE SAFE/SAVED

[Ar rwḥ st id.]

C334/13: ḥrt mr'hmw...wwfyt wst[r]ḥ[t] "(as for) the camp of their lord, it was saved and at peace"

n[1] s rḥ P123/2; in a compound: rḥ[q]ds C541/3

(1) SPIRIT

[Loan translation: cf Ar rūḥ al-qudus from Heb ruᵃḥ qōdeš, Syr rūḥā də-qudšā "Holy Spirit."]

C541/3: RḤMNN wmsḥhw wrḥ[q]ds "(the god) R., His Messiah and the Holy Spirit"

(2) PLATEAU (?)

[Cf Ar rāḥa† "palm of the hand."]

P123/2: d̲r'w mḥql rḥ "they sowed the fields of the plateau (?)"

n[2] s hrwḥt R2865/1*

ENLARGEMENT, WIDENING

R2865/1 quoted under RWḤ h

RWY I

h ipf yhrwy[n] R4781/3*

PROVIDE WITH IRRIGATION

[Ar rwy h "give to drink; water (plants)."]

R4781/3: nxlm Z bᶜly [']xhw wd̲yhrwy[n] "the palmgrove Z. is the responsibility of (?) his brother and the (person who) provides (it?) with irrigation"

n[1] s rwym C652/2+

(1) WELL, WATERING PLACE

[Ar rawâ "give to drink"; riyy, rayy "irrigation."]

A773a+b+798/2: hnbṭ wdfr rwym "dug and walled with stone a well"

(2) PROVIDER OF IRRIGATION (often plausibly taken as n.pr)

C652/2: ḥrtn rwym l'nxlhmw "the aqueduct, provider of irrigation for their palmgroves"; C399/3: b'rhw rwym bnxlhw "his well, a provider of irrigation in his palmgrove"; sim R4085/3; R3687: ...] rwym [ms?]qytm lnxlhmw "a provider of irrigation, a canalized irrigation scheme for their palmgrove"

n[2] s rwthmy R4123/1*

REPORT, ACCOUNT

[Ar rawâ "report, inform," riwāya† "report."]

R4123/1: bḥg rwthmy d̲t smᶜ yqmn ᶜA "according to their report, (to) which A. bears witness"

n[3] p? rwthmw J665/43*

WATER-CARRYING ANIMALS, TRANSPORT ANIMALS (?)

[Ar rāwiya† "camel, mule...any beast upon which water is drawn" (Lane/1196).]
J665/43: stqdw kl rwthmw wrkbhmw "they 'liberated' all (the enemy's) transport and riding animals"

n[4] For rw[yt] R4556/1 read prob rw[ym], cf RWY n[1] sense[2]

n[5] s rt(m,n) Gl573/1+; var ryt(m) J564/10+

OBLIGATION, CLAIM; also, DOCUMENT STATING A CLAIM

[Ar rawīya† "a want, the reminder of a debt or the like" (Lane/1196). Cf also Min ryt "penitential offering" (an obligation rendered to the god?).]

Gl573/1: tᶜlmw bᶜmhw brtm dbdm ḤY'LYm "they signed with him the (document stating the) claim, with regard to a compensation in ḤY'l-money"; ib/4: twfyw bhyt rtn "they pledged themselves to pay by this claim-document"; J564/10: gzyw bhgrn...bn ryt mr'hmw "they performed a commission in the city under obligation to (i.e., under the orders of?) their lord"; also in R4010/3 (fragmentary context)

n[6] s mrw R4197/1; mrwhmw R4194/1; var mrwym P147

SWEET WELL

[ModAr marwâ id (PMidian/36); cf Ar rawâ "water (plants)."]

R4194/1: br'w mḥfdhmw Y wmrwhmw T "they built their tower (part of the irrigation scheme) Y. and their sweet well T."; R4197/1: hš]qr whqḥ mrw wmh[lt] "completed and prepared for use the well and (its) outflows"

Note: Irv/158-9 tr "irrigated field," cfing (less plausibly) Akk marû "fat (said of animals)," Ar amrâ tamara†an "more productive," Daṯ al-'arḍ marīya† "the land is fertile." Cf also mryt (n[7] below) and the fragmentary texts cited under MR.

n[7] s mryt R4513/3*

SWEET WELL (?) (cf mrw n[6] above, id)

R4513/3: ᶜsy rbᶜ mryt "he constructed a quarter of the well (?)"

RWY II

n p 'rwyn R4176/6*

MOUNTAIN GOATS (sacred animals, cf wᶜl id)

[Ar 'arwīya† id; Sab p takes f verb.]

R4176/6: ḥẓr T'LB s'r 'rwyn bn nś́g bn msrn kstnhṣn bnslm "(the god) T. has prohibited the rest (or, all) of the mountain goats from being prevented from feeding, that they may grow fat with young"

RWK--For mhrkm F119/8, see under HRK

RWS--For rwsy C352/5, read rsyw and see under RSY v

RWḌ

n s mrwḍh R4922/3*

EXTENT, WIDTH

[Cf Ar rwḍ h "lie down, stretch out; extend."]
R4922/3: wkwn mrwḍh sdṯt ᶜšr '[mm] "and its width was sixteen cubits"

RWT--For n rwt, see under RWY I n[2,3]

RZ--For n rzm, see under RZM

RZ'

v pf rz'w C540/82+
SPEND, PAY OUT
[Ar raza'a "deprive," pass "suffer loss."]
C540/82: w[d]rz'w ᶜlyhw xrṣm l'šᶜbn...wnśkm lfᶜln... "and what they spent on (the project), by estimation for the tribal (workers) and in (actual) expenditure for the (non-tribal) laborers, (amounted to): (figures follow)"; sim ib/36 (fragmentary), prob also C541/115

n[1] s rz'n C548/13*
EXPENSE, COST; or, HARM
C548/13: wkll rz'n ᶜly kl 'nsn "and the completion of the cost (i.e., payment in full) is to (fall) upon every man," or, "reparation of the harm (done) is to (fall) on every man (responsible for it)"--in a text prescribing penalties for ritual offences

n[2] s trz' C546/5*
INJURY, LOSS
C546/5: fyẓtlfnn ḏmnhw ltrz' 'hlhtn "so let them refrain from whatever (tends) to the injury of the clans"

RZY

h pf hrzy Ry508/7-8*
REMAIN, STAY
[Daṯ 'arzà "stay in a place, remain immobile," Om marzà "place where one stays and is secure" (RodConf'66-7/129).]
Ry508/7-8: wmlkn hrzy bmqrnt ḤBŠT wlṣnᶜn sslt MDBn "as for the king, he remained on guard (against) Ḥabashat and to fortify the 'chain' of al-Mandab"

RZM

n s rzm R3951/3; p 'rzm ib/5+
REQUISITIONING, COMMANDEERING; ACT OF REQUISITIONING (maṣdar?)
[Ar razama "collect together, wrap up" (Lane/1077B).]
R3951/3: xrṣ wšrk wrzm bᶜmhmw wrqm "assessing, distributing and requisitioning from them greenstuff"; ib/5: kl xrṣ wšrk wmnṣḥ w'rzm "all assessments, distributions, demands and requisitions"; R2726/8: kl s'wlt w'smᶜ w'zhd... w'rzm "all claims, attestations, renunciations and requisitions"

RḤB

n^{1} *s* rḥbm C541/109-10*

WIDTH

[Ar ruḥb id.]

C541/109-10: xms wṯlṯy 'mm rymm w'rb^{c}t ^{c}šr 'mm rḥbm "thirty-rive cubits in height and fourteen cubits in width"

Note: RḤBm C540/6 is *n.pr*.

n^{2} *s* rḥbtn C540/68+; *p*? rḥybm R4229/6

PLAIN, FLATLAND or LOWLAND

[Ar raḥba^{t} "wide place, open country, plain."]

C540/68: hwqlw 'š^{c}b rḥbtn dllm "the lowland tribes were in confusion (?) (because of) the disease"; R4229/6: they dedicated for the health of b^{c}rhmw rḥybm "their herd (in) the lowland (pastures?)"

RḤL

n *s*? rḥlm J651/26-7; *p* rḥlhn J649/40+

CAMEL SADDLE

[Ar raḥl id.]

J649/40: their booty included 316 rkbm brḥlhn "riding camels with their saddles"; sim J665/39; phps also J651/26-7: 'l ḏfqdw bn 'šr^{c}hmw kbr rḥlm "nothing was missing from their booty (?) of the size of (i.e., not so much as) a camel saddle" (J takes as *n.pr*)

RḤM

tp *pf* trḥm Ry513/3-5+; *inf* trḥm C926/4; *act.prt* mtrḥ(m)n F74/3

HAVE MERCY (^{c}*ly* upon)

[Ar raḥima, *D* and *Dt* id.]

Ry513/3-5: wtrḥm ^{c}ly 'bny M...RḤMNn "May (the god) R. have mercy upon the sons of M."; F74/3: RḤMNn mtrḥ(m)n "R., the merciful"; Ry508/11: trḥm ^{c}ly kl ^{c}lm...rḥmk "may Your mercy (?) have mercy upon all the world"

n *s* rḥmk Ry508/11 (but see Note); *var* rḥmt C541/1-2

MERCY

[Ar raḥma^{t} id.]

Ry508/11 quoted under RḤM *tp*; C541/1-2: bxyl w[r]d' wrḥmt RḤMNn "by the power, aid and mercy of (the god) R."

Note: It has been suggested that the form rḥmk in Ry508/11 is a unique example of the Sab second person (*m.s*) perfect verb, as in Eth; tr "You have had mercy" or "You are merciful."

Note also the name of the god RḤMN(n), "the Merciful One" (cf Ar ar-Raḥmān "the Merciful," title of Allāh, and the Rabbinic epithet raḥămānā'), cf esp C541/3: RḤMNn wmsḥhw wrḥ[q]ds "R., His Messiah and the Holy Spirit."

RḤḌ

n s rḥḍ Robin al-Mašamayn/6* (maṣdar)

WASH

[Ar raḥaḍa id (Rob/Att/52).]

Robin al-Mašamayn/6: prevent anyone bn sqy bdṯ brktn qnym f'[w]-rḥḍ bhw "from watering animals from this cistern or from washing in it"

RḤQ

n s rḥq(m) R3929/13+

adj: FAR (bn from)

[Eth reḥqa, Heb rāḥaq "be far," Heb rāḥôq "far."]

R3929/13: may the god protect them from b'stm...šn'm ḏrḥq wqrb "harm of (done by) an enemy who is far or near" AND OFTEN SIM; J737/4: šn'm rḥqm wqrbm "an enemy, far or near"; IrApp2#2/15: šn'm ḏrḥq bnhmw "an enemy who is far from them"; R4962/18: kl b[rṯm] qrbm wrḥqm "every project, (carried out) near or far"

RḤŚ

v inf? rḥś C428/2*

OFFER incense by sprinkling on a fire

[Eth reḥsa "sprinkle moisture."]

C428/2: ...w]rḥś wᶜrb mṯ[ᶜt "sprinkled and offered in[cense]"

RḤT

n p 'rḥthw MüBilinguis/5*

KINSMEN, FELLOW-CLANSMEN

[Ar raht "group of people less than ten; a man's immediate and closest kinsmen" (BeSM/395).]

MüBilinguis/5: bmqm [bny]hw w'rḥthw "by the strength of his sons and kinsmen"

RXM--For proposed instances of this root, see under RḤM

RYD I

tp pf tryd C541/92*

ABATE (a disease)

[Daṯ rāda "go hither and thither" (Irv/312).]

C541/92: wkbᶜdn ḏtryd ḏlln "and after the disease abated..." Obscure in R4158/9 (fragmentary context): ...] wtryd mḏrᶜm w[...

RYD II

n s ryd C338/8; rydhw R4624/4+; rydhmw R4774/2

MOUNTAIN SHOULDER, RIDGE

[Ar rayd "ledge of a mountain" (Lane/1199C).]

C338/12: he built the road to the hill-town bn rydhw [ᶜ]dy qmm "from its (the road's?) (lower) ridge up to the summit"; same R4624/4; C338/8: mqṭrtn ḏryd kwrn "the incense altars of the ridge of (i.e., on which stands?) the fire altar"; F72/4: šdwn Ḍ wrydhw "the hillside Ḍ. and its ridge"

Note: Cf also ryd in R4635/5: nql lmbny m'lmt S wmbny ryd wwśq. J ANET/507 tr the last two words "he planned and made strong," but this is implausible syntactically. Tr prob with R "he provided stone for the construction of the banquet hall of S. and the construction of RYD and WŚQ," reading as nn.pr.

RYM

v pf rymw C448/2*

MAKE HIGHER, RAISE

[Cf esp Heb rwm "be high"; cf Ar rāma (y) "(rise up and) go away."]

C448/2: wśfw wrymw kl gn'hw "they enlarged and raised all its wall"

Note: For rymn Ry3=R3910/1 read ryśn, see under RYŚ. For ḏyrm R3945/2, see under ḎYR.

tp pf trymw C596/8*

TAKE AWAY

[Cf Ar rāma (y) "go away, move, leave."]

C596/8: ...]trymw xẓf wtᶜlyh[... "they took away the booty (?) and carried it off"

n¹ s rym(m) C541/108+

HEIGHT; adv rymm: UPWARD, HIGHER

C541/108: xms wṯlṯy 'mm rymm w'rbᶜt ᶜšr 'mm rḥbm "thirty-five cubits (in) height and fourteen cubits (in) width"; J557: he built the wall ln ḏn 'wdn ḏsṭrn wrymm "from this line of the inscription and upward"; R3946/5: he built the superstructure of his house ln ẓwrm wrymm "from the pillar(s) upward"

n² s rym(m) C973/3+

adj: EXALTED, in divine epithets (esp of T'LB)

C973/3: SMᶜ rym "(the god) S., the Exalted"; J561b/24: T'LB rymm "(the god) T., the Exalted" AND VERY OFTEN

n³ s rmt C660/4*

RAISED DEVICE, phps a tank

[Prob to be connected with root RYM "be/make high."]

C660/4: the provided water for the whole oratory wrmt hwr šdwhmw "and the raised (tank?) of the basin of their font (or, the raised (tank?) of the cistern of their hillside terrace)"

Note: An overhead cistern was found in the Mārib temple, cf ADSA/225-6.

n⁴ s mrym(n) R4107/3; mrymhw C448/3+; p? mrymhw DJE12/4

TOP, HIGHEST POINT; ROOF or TERRACE of a building

[ModYem rēm "flat roof, terrace" (MüW/59-60).]

C448/3: bn mrymhw ^{c}dy ṯrthw "from its roof to its foundation" AND ELSEWHERE SIM; DJE12/4: kl gnwzhw wmrymhw "all its storerooms and terraces" (cf MŭTa-^{c}izz/95)

RYS--For rys R3910, C126, read RYŚ, q.v.

st pf strsw J561b/9*

BE CHIEF, SERVE AS CHIEF

[Cf Ar r's ti id.]

J561b/9: kl 'brṯ bhmw strsw b'ḍrr "all the campaigns in which they served as chiefs in the wars"

RYŚ

v ipf [y]rśn C460/5-6; yr[y]śn C126/3+; inf ryśn R3910/1+

DECREE (with oracular force?), PROCLAIM

[Cf Ar ra'asa, rāsa (w) "be the head > preside, direct."]

R3910/1: [kn] wqh wryśn whknn whḥrn mlkn "thus the king ordered, decreed, established and commanded"; C460/5-6: [y]rśn bmṭftn "proclaim at the sacrificial altar"; C126/3: mn ḏlhw yr[y]śn SB' stwḍ' "anyone with respect to whom S. makes a decree, so that (thereby) he is proclaimed an outlaw"; sim ib/11,15

RYT--For n ryt, see under RWY I

RKB

v pf rkbhw J745/7; rkby ib/9-10

RIDE a horse

[Ar rakaba id.]

J745/7: the god protected the king's horse bkn rkbhw ^{c}dy S "when he rode it to S."; ib/9-10: and He saved frsnhn...bkn rkby bn srn "the 2 horses when they were ridden out of the valley"

n^{1} s rkb(m,n) J665/23+; p rkb(m,n) ib/16+; rkbhw J577/15

RIDER, specifically CAMELEER; p CAMELRY

[Ar rakkāb id.]

J665/23: saved from the enemy 'sm rkbm wṯlṯ rglm "one man, a rider (i.e., one mounted man), and three footsoldiers"; J577/15: xmshw w'frshw wrkbhw "his army (i.e., his infantry), his cavalry and his camelry"; J665/16: (700) 'sdm rkbm w(70) 'frsm "seven hundred men, cameleers, and seventy horsemen"; ib/33: 'A...nḥl rkbn "A., commander of the camelry"

n^{2} p/coll rkb(m,n) J576/3+; rkbhmw J665/43+; p rkbt(n) Ir32+

(1) RIDING ANIMALS

[Ar rakūb id.]

Ir32: 'sdm 'tlwt rkbt 'frsm "men, equerries of the riding animals, (specifically) the horses"; sim J715/2

(2) specifically, RIDING CAMELS

[Ar rakūb id, Mh rikīb, p rikōb "female camel" (MüRev/107B).]

J665/43: rwthmw wrkbhmw "transport camels and riding camels"; ib/46: 'frsm wrkbm wǵnmm "horses, riding camels and booty"

n[3] s rkbhw J745/4+

SADDLE or other TRAPPINGS of a horse

[Cf Ar rikāb "stirrup," Heb rékeb "chariot."]

J745/4: they dedicated frsn wrkbhw ddhbn "this gold horse and its saddle/trappings"; sim C306/5

Note: On C306 the editors comment that this tr agrees better with the accompanying picture than another proposed tr "and its rider" (cf Ar rākib, Sab rkb n[1]).

RKL

ti pf [r]tkl R4624/7-8*

SET OUT, GO ON A JOURNEY

[Cf Heb rākal "go about (for trade)," Ar rakala "kick (a horse, to make him go)."]

R4624/7-8: he dedicated (?) on the day fśl w[ywm r]tkl 'rxhw "he hewed out (the mountain road); and on the day he set out on his road"

RM--see under RYM; for n dyrm R3945/2, see under DYR

RMY

v ipf yrmyn J539/4-5*

EXCEED, LIE BEYOND (?)

[Ar rmy h "exceed" (Lane/1162C); Lt "be vast, extend into the distance" (Bon3T/30n4).]

J539/4-5: from this inscription w[l] sṭrnhn yrmyn b'rn (50) "to the 2 inscriptions (which) lie beyond the well (are) fifty (cubits)"

n s rmym R4772/4*

INTEREST

[Cf Ar ramā' "interest, usury" (IrvJRAS'64/32n4).]

R4772/4: blṭm rḍym ṣbbm rmym "current coin, paid down as interest"

RMT--For n rmt, see under RYM

RND

n s rnd C683+ (all on incense burners)

AN AROMATIC PLANT used for incense = NARD

[Ar rand id; cf Heb nērd, Gk nárdos, Artemisia pontica or abyssinica.]

C683: rnd dhb n^{c}m qsṭ "nard, golden incense, sweet incense, costus"

RS--see under RYS, RSY, RSS

RSY

v pf r(syw) C352/5* (C reads rwsy)

DIRECT AT, PREPARE FOR a person

[Eth rsy D id, also "do (ill) to a person."]

C352/5: he dedicated because mt^{c}hw bn kl ''rx rsyw b^{c}lyhw "(the god) saved him from all the troubles they had prepared for him"

Note: HöASG§84 considers rwsy an abstract n from root R'S > RWS, tr "command, leadership," but this seems contextually unlikely.

h pf hrs J550/2; ipf yhrs R3951/4

(1) PERFORM MILITARY SERVICE

[Cf Eth rsy Dt "be armed."]

J550=C375: bkl xrfy hrs bkbtn b^{c}ly S "during the whole year he performed military service in the hostilities on behalf of S."

(2) PROVIDE goods

[Eth rsy D "prepare, provide."]

R3951/4: requisitions and wholesale purchases must be agreed upon for the buyer (?) wl 's yhrs bhgrn "and for the individual who provides (the goods) in the city"

Note: This v has also been referred to root HRS, tr "fight; take up arms" (cf Heb hāras "destroy; invade," Ar harasa "bruise, crush"); and to root RYS, tr "be in command" (with more plausibility).

RSL

n p rsl C541/90,90-1*

MESSENGERS

[Ar rasūl, p rusul "messenger."]

C541/90-1: wṣḥhmw mḥškt mlk R tnblt mlk F wrsl M wrsl Ḥ...wrsl 'A "there reached them the emissaries of the king of R., the embassy of the king of F., and the messengers of M., Ḥ., and A."

RSS

v pf rsty (f.d?) R3232/3*

sense doubtful

R3232/3: ...]mn wl'ś[m]w 'lsnyhmw rsty l() (s)myn w'rḍn w[... (context obscure and fragmentary)

R^cW

n p 'r^{c}w C554/1*

PASTURES (?) (cf mr^c(y)t id, under R^cY)

[Cf Sab R^cY ti "graze" and related ns.]

C554/1: l''nf 'r^{c}w sq' ''nfhn "for the near sides (?) of the pastures (?), whose near sides irrigate" (i.e., water moves through canals from side of the pastures near the primary canal, and then outward?)

R^{c}Ẓ

h pf hr^{c}ẓhmw C540/67,70*

COMMAND, SUMMON

[Cf Ar ra^{c}aḍa "move, set in motion, disturb"; Heb rā^{c}aṣ "shatter."]

C540/67: 'š^{c}bm dd' ḥr ^{c}lyhmw tqh...dr^{c}zm hr^{c}ẓhmw "the tribes on whom it was already incumbent to bring (the repair project) to completion, (the king) having (already?) sent a summons to them"; ib/70: wkhr^{c}ẓhmw...dwrd... ^{c}šry ''lfm "and when he summoned them, those (?) who came down were twenty thousand (in number)"

n^1 s r^{c}ẓ(m) C540/67+

COMMAND, SUMMONS

C540/67 quoted under R^{c}Ẓ h; R2740/10: śl' M...br^{c}ẓ WD w'l'lt H "he dedicated to (the god) M. By command of (the god) W and the gods of H." AND ELSEWHERE SIM

n^2 s? mr^{c}ẓ(m,n) R3960/5+

LEVIES, workers summoned to carry out a project (?) (cf mnš' sim)

R3960/5: krbn mr^{c}ẓm whlmw wqhw 'mr'hm[w... "laborers (?) and levies (?), and they guaranteed (what) their lords had commanded"; sim R3895/5; also in fragmentary context F96/2

R^{c}Y

ti ipf yrt^{c}nn J745/10*

GRAZE

[Ar r^{c}y ti id.]

J745/10: the god protected the 2 horses bkn rkby bn srn bryn yrt^{c}nn ^{c}dy xbtn "when they had been ridden out of the healthy valley (to) graze in unhealthy pasturage"

n^1 s r^{c}y G1142/7*

SHEPHERD, HERDSMAN

[Ar rā^{c}i^n id.]

G1142/7: yqfnn wḥgr mrbḏn kl r^{c}y "they shall delimit and prohibit their sheepfold (to) every herdsman"

Note also r^{c}ym R4010/6 in fragmentary context, and cf C745: S [r]^{c}y 'l ḤNQm "S., shepherd (?) of the clan Ḥ." (Ry takes as n.pr).

n^2 s r^{c}yn F74/6*

CARE, PROTECTION

[Ar ra^{c}y id.]

F74/6: they built their house with the help of their lords wbn[ṣr] wr^{c}yn '(x)wthmw "and with the help and care of their brothers"

n^3 s r^{c}t C561/4*

FLOCK, HERD (?)

[Ar ra^{c}īya^t id.]

C561/4: hqny r^{c}t "he dedicated a flock/herd (?)" (C takes as n.pr) n[4] s mr^{c}t Gl142/8; var mr^{c}yth R3945/10+; mr^{c}ythmy R3946/5; mr^{c}ythmw ib/3; p mr^{c}yhw R3945/8; mr^{c}yhmw C546/11; var mr^{c}yt R3946/8; mr^{c}ythw R3945/9+; mr^{c}ythmy ib/10; mr^{c}ythmw ib/11

PASTURE, PASTURE-LAND (for grazing, not agriculture) (cf 'r^{c}w id, root R^{c}W)

[Ar mar^{c}â id.]

Gl142/8: wṯmt wmr^{c}t ^{c}rn "wasteland and pasture-land belonging to the hill-town"; R3945/11: 'hgrhmw wmḥrṯthmw wmr^{c}ythmw w'srrhmw "their towns, plowed lands, pasture-lands and valleys" AND ELSEWHERE SIM in lists of kinds of land

Note: On Gl142/8, HöTPK/35 cfs Ar mara^{c}a "be rich in grass and fodder" (phps a denom in Ar from mar^{c}â "pasture").

R^{c}L

h inf hr^{c}ln[n] J735/13-4*

MOVE FORWARD (of waters) (?)

[Cf Heb rā^{c}al "quiver, shake."]

J735/13-4: the floodwaters came and watered the valleys, wwz'w hr^{c}ln[n] wsqy kl 'nxln "and continued to move forward (?) and water all the palm-groves"

R^{c}L II

n s? r^{c}ltm R4760A/2*

PALMGROVE (?)

[Ar ra^{c}la^t "very tall palm tree."]

R4760A/2: ...]bs r^{c}ltm š'mh šlṯy r[... "a palmgrove (?) (which) he bought (for?) thirty..."

RǴM

n s rǵm C352/16*

COERCION

[Ar raǵama "force, compel, coerce," raǵm "coercion, dislike, hatred" (Lane/1114B).]

C352/16: may the god protect them bn rǵm wǵlyt mr'm wš^{c}bm "against coercion or oppression by an individual or a tribe"

RF'

v inf rf' J700/16*

HEAL, or FAVOR

[Heb rāpā' "heal," Ar rafa'a "mend, repair"; Ar L "treat with gentleness; abate..the price, or payment (in selling)" (Lane/1117C).]

J700/16: and as for the god, lz'n h^{c}n wrf' wh^{c}n ^{c}bdhw "may He continue to help and heal/favor and help (?) His servant"

Note: Cf also rf'n epithet of the god ᶜTTR R3978/1; tr "the Healer (?)" or "He who Shows Favor (?)."

RFD

n s rfd F74/3+; d rfdyhw R3911/2; p? rfdt C40/3-4; var 'rfd C308/6

(1) SUPPORT, HELP

[Cf Ar rafada "prop up (a wall)."]

F74/3: they built their house bnṣr wrd' RḤMNn...wbnṣr wrfd mr'hmw "with the help and aid of (the god) R., and with the help and support of their lord"

(2) REVETMENT

R3911/2: their control-dyke wḥrty brfdyhw "and the 2 aqueducts at its 2 revetment (walls)"; C40/3-4: kl mwrt wgn' wṣwbt mḥfdn...ᶜdy rfdt hy' mwrtn wgn'nn "all the retaining wall, (outer) wall and substructure of the tower as far as the revetments of this retaining wall and (outer) wall"; C308/6: kl msqyhmw [wkl] ṣwrt w'rfd "all their irrigated land and all the embankments and revetments"; also in fragmentary context (rfd bythmw) C643/1

RFQ--n or n.pr in fragmentary context R4199/2: ...] wb rfqtn ▯ x ▯ [...; dimensions of something named RFQT?

RḌW

v pf rḍwhmw J586/7-8; ipf yrḍwnhmw J691/10

SATISFY, CONTENT (cf RḌY h id)

[Cf Ar rḍy D id.]

J586/7-8: the god granted that they returned from campaign bwfym wḥmdm wbdtrḍwhm[w] "with safety, praise, and those (things) which contented them (or, and because He had contented them, but parallel contexts suggest the first tr)"; J691/10: may He grant them 'tmrm šfqm...dyrḍwnhmw "abundant crops which will satisfy them"

h For hrḍw, see under RḌY h

n s rḍw J561b/18++; p/var rḍwn C28/6

GOOD WILL, SATISFACTION (cf rḍy id)

[Ar riḍâ id.]

J561b/18: wlsᶜdhmw ḥẓy wrḍw mr'hmw "may (the god) grant them the favor and good will of their lord" AND VERY OFTEN SIM; C28/6=N75/10: may the god grant them mngt ṣ[dqm w]rḍwn 'lbbhmw "happy fortune and the satisfaction of their hearts"

RḌḤ

v inf? rḍḥ J647/15*

WEARY a deity with prayers (?)

[Sq riḍah "be weary," Ar raḍaha "break, bruise, crush" (BeNL9/195).]

J647/15: ...] rḍḥ wstydᶜn wwfyn [... "wearied with prayers (?), besought and paid (?) (the god)" (context obscure and fragmentary) ti inf rtḍḥn R3884/5+

SLAY, FIGHT (b^c^m with)

[Cf esp Heb rāṣaḥ "murder, slay."]

J631/5: tqdmw wrtḍḥn b^c^m 'mlk "they opposed and fought with the kings"; R3884/5: t'tmw wrtḍḥn bbrrn ḏH "they gathered together and fought in the plain of Ḥ."; J575/5: y'ttmw wtqdmn wrtḍḥn "they assembled, opposed (each other) and fought"

RḌY

v ipf yrḍyn Ry507/9; inf/maṣdar? mrḍ R4176/13

(1) BE WILLING, CONSENT

[Ar raḍiya "consent, agree."]

Ry507/9: ṯw yqhn mlkn ḏyrḍyn w'xwthw wgrhmw "until the king commanded those who were willing (= a volunteer force?) and his allies (formally bound to obey the king) and their clients" (tr after BeOr25/300)

(2) CONCEDE, GRANT (?)

R4176/13: ḥgr T'LB 'śwrhw wmrḍ ṯlṯ lqśm 'qwl "(the god) T. commanded His produce and the grant of a third (of the tithes) (to be) the portion of the tribal leaders"

h pf hrḍhw C407/26; hrḍhmw J703/4; hrḍw J577/16+; hrḍwhw J581/11+; hrḍwhmy J632/7; hrḍwhmw J574/9-10+; var 3.m.s hrḍyhmw C397/12-3+; ipf yhrḍynhw J613/21; yhrḍyn J571/5+; yhrḍynhmw J623/15-6+; var yhrḍwn J615/22+; yhrḍw C333/9-10; yhrḍwnhmw J610/15+; inf hrḍwn J650/23-4

SATISFY, CONTENT (cf RḌW v id)

[Ar rḍy h id.]

C397/13: the god granted him ^c^sm sbym wmltm ḏhrḍyhmw "numerous captives and (much) booty which contented them" AND OFTEN SIM; J615/22: may the god grant n'd 'ṯmrm...ḏyhrḍwn 'lbbhmw "abundance of crops which will content their hearts" AND OFTEN SIM

n[1] s rḍy C81/10+

GOOD WILL (= rḍw)

[Ar riḍâ "satisfaction; good will."]

C81/10: may the god grant them 'ṯmrm w'wldm 'ḏkrm wrḍy 'mr'hmw "crops, male children, and the good will of their lords"

n[2] p rḍy(m,n) C73/9+

adj: ACCEPTABLE, CURRENT (coin); also used as a UNIT OF WEIGHT

[Ar raḍī "agreeable, good"; cf also Heb rāṣāh "pay a debt."]

C73/9: ṯmn brm ḏḏhbn bblṯm rḍym "eight br-units of gold in current coin"; C380/6: fl ynkrn xms rḍyn "let him be fined five current (coins)"; J608/6: ṣlmn ḏsrfn ḏmdlthw 'l(f)n rḍym "this silver statue whose weight is one thousand rḍy"

n[3] For mrḍ R4176/13, see under RḌY v sense[2]; elsewhere, see under MRḌ n[1]

n[4] s mrḍym C539/4* (D prt?)

SATISFACTION (?); or tr as adj: SATISFYING, SATISFACTORY (?)

C539/4: ...]wmrḍym lsm RḤMNn "and (it is?) satisfying to the name of (the god) R. (or, satisfaction to the name!) (?)"

Note: For mrḍyt J544/4, see under MRḌ n^2

RḌ^c

v pf/inf rḍ^c R3945/13*

SLAY (?)

R3945/13: he captured their children wrḍ^c 'nmhmw ṯny 'lfm "and slew (?) their civil population (to the number of) two thousand"

RḌF

n s rḍfm J572/4* (but see Note)

UNIT OF WEIGHT

[JSIMB/60 cfs Ar raḍf (coll) "stones reddened by fire."]

J572/4: ṣlmn ḏsrfn ḏmdlthw ṯlṯ m'nm rḍfm "this statue of silver of which the weight is three hundred rḍf-units"

Note: It is likely that this form is an error for rḍym (see under RḌY n^2 for parallel context), a better-known unit of weight.

RQB

n p? rqbn Ry554/2*

SERFS

[Ar raqba† "serf, slave."]

Ry554/2: ...] rqbn wbkln kl[... "serfs and subjects, all..."

RQD

v pf rqdw Ry509/4*

INSCRIBE, WRITE (?)

[Sense from context, but RyMus66/306 cfs Ar musnad "pad, cushion; Old South Arabic inscription" with marqad "bed"--inscription is seen as "stretched out," reclining along the rock?]

Ry509/4: the kings of S. rqdw ḏn mrqdn bwdyn M "wrote (?) this inscription (?) in the wadi M." (parallel contexts have root STR)

n s mrqdn Ry509/4*

INSCRIPTION (?)

Ry509/4 quoted under RQD v

RQY I

v pf rqyw J665/16*

GO UP

[Ar raqiya id.]

J665/16: tg^{c}r...kl gyšhmw...wrqyw bn M wḏkww...mqdmtm "their whole troop was called together and they went up from M. and sent (forward) a vanguard"

RQY II

n p rqthmw J735/9*

SORCERESSES

[Ar raqâ "use magic, incantations," raqqā' "sorcerer."]

J735/9: to end a drought brought on by sorcery (?) sfḥw rqthmw wt^crbn lmr'hmw 'LMQH w'nṯn ᶜṭwfhn "they commanded their sorceresses to give pledges of submission to their lord (the god) I., the (other) women (being) at their side"

RQT--For n rqt J735/9, see under RQY II

RŠD

v pf ršdw F55/7*

CONCLUDE, ARRANGE an agreement

[Ar ršd D, h "guide well, direct."]

F55/7: ršdw (ᶜ)lm[n] byt ᶜA lyfynn...dn wtfn "the house/family A. have concluded (the agreement represented by) this document so that this deed of transfer may be valid"

D pf ršd C398/10*

GUIDE

[Ar ršd D id.]

C398/10: wršd ᶜA w'sdhw bdt xmrhw ['LM]QHW wkbhw b'rḍ X "(the god) guided A. and his soldiers because I. granted him His help in the land of X"; also ib/6 in fragmentary context

n s ršdh R3957/7-8*

(GOOD) CONDUCT; or, GUIDANCE, DISCIPLINING

[Ar rušd "proper conduct"; cf also ršd h "instruct, guide."]

R3957/7-8: slḥt ḏ'ḏnh fgzm sw' ḏS ᶜly ršdh "she had (ritually) soiled her clients, and (the god) ḏS. decided adversely concerning her conduct (or, concerning disciplining her)"

RŠW

v pf ršw C607/4+

(1) OFFER, DEDICATE (?)

[Ar rašā "give the price; obtain s.o.'s favor by gifts."]

C607/4: wršw dn wtfn K[... "and he dedicated (?) this wtf-land..."

(2) SERVE a god AS PRIEST (or phps COMPLETE ONE'S TERM as priest)

Gl766/3: ywm ršw ᶜTTR wfdyhw bn kl 'bythw "the day he served (the god) A. as priest, and He redeemed him from (service in) all His temples" AND OFTEN SIM in eponym texts

h pf hršw R3943/4*

SERVE a god AS PRIEST (cf RŠW v)

R3943/4: when he built the temples of certain gods wbyt ḏbR whršw ḏb R "and the temple of Him who is in R., and he served Him who is in R. as priest" n^1 s ršw(m,n) J550/1+; p 'rš R3303/2; var 'ršw C41/1; var 'ršww(n) C548/5+; var 'ršwt C563/4+; s.f ršwt J122/5; ršwth[w] R4935/2 (?)

PRIEST; PRIESTESS (cf RŠY n sense^2 id)

J550/1: T ršw dt Ǵ qyn S "T., priest of (the goddess) dt Ǵ., administrator of S." GaAION33/4: kmnm 'ns dyḥzr wl ydbḥn...f'w y'xrn ršwn ḥẓrhw "whenever (there is) a man who has been 'banned,' let him sacrifice, or let the priest remove his ban"; R3303/2: kbr 'rš M "chief of the priests of (the god) M."; C548/5: lyẓl^{c}n l'lt ^{c}TTR w'ršwwn "let him pay a fine to those of (the god) A. and the priests"; R4935/2: ...] ^{c}M bdt hwfy ršwth[w... "(the god) A., because He protected (or, granted to) His priestess (?)" (but cf ršwt n^2 below)

n^2 s ršwt(m) C555/8+; ršwthw R3655/2+

PRIESTHOOD, TERM AS PRIEST (= YEAR OF EPONYMOUS OFFICE)

C555/8: bwrx dD dršwt W "in the month dD. of the priesthood/year of office of W."; R3655/2: bkl ršwthw "in his whole term as priest"

RŠY

n s ršy(m,n) J702/4+; p ršt C289/9; var ršyt J718/9

(1) GIFT, OFFERING

[Cf RŠW v and Ar rišwa^t "gift; bribe."]

J718 isolated in fragmentary context; R4762/3: he offers this to the god bdltn wršyn "as a recompense and offering"

(2) PRIEST (?) (cf ršw id)

J702/4 (obscure context): l(hd)rn kl ršym d'l yšrḥn ṣythw "let every priest (?) beware who does not protect his reputation" (tr doubtful)

RT--For n rt, see under RWY n^5

RT^c

v pf rt^c J576/7+; rt^{c}hw Ham9/9; rt^{c}w Ir13; ipf yrt^c R4176/4; inf rt^c J658/11-2+

(1) DECLARE (?)

[Cf Eth rat^{c}a "tell the truth."]

Ham9/9: he was granted a child [h]g krt^{c}hw b[m]s'lhw "as (the god) had declared to him in His oracle"

(2) DISPOSE, ARRANGE, SETTLE, ESTABLISH; pass BE DISPOSED ALONG, LIE OPPOSITE

[Eth rat^{c}a "be rightly disposed, arranged," and cf Eth retu^c "opposite."]

J576/7: yt'wlnn ^{c}dy hgrn N wrt^c b^{c}mhw dbn xmshmw "they returned to the city N. and disposed some of their army around it"; sim Ir13; R4176/12: w^{c}qb wsxmm lyrt^c d'A IR "and (as for) subsequent disputes, let the governor of A. settle them for R."; J658/11-2: his lord commanded him lrt^c šrḥtm bhgrn Ṣ "to establish security in the city Ṣ."; R4176/4: m[ḥ]mytn drt^c

mṣyhm ʿdy lyrtʿ śdn "the embanked land which is disposed along the highway so far as to lie opposite the dam"

Note: For yrtʿnn J745/10, see under RʿY *ti*

n *s* mrtʿ R4176/8*

DISPOSITION, ARRANGEMENT

R4176/8: wkwn mrtʿ 'lmn xmst b'ḥd xrf "and the disposition of the ritual banquets was: five in every year..."

RṮD

v *pf* rṯd J727/5+; rṯdhw F56; rṯdhmy J683/5; rṯdy C330/3; rṯdty R4653/3; rṯdw J558/7; *inf* rṯd R4992/2-3+; *pf* rṯdh R3634

PLACE s.th. UNDER THE PROTECTION OF a deity > DEDICATE

[Sense from context.]

R4992/2-3: hqny wrṯd S bnhw "he dedicated and placed his son under the protection of (the god) S."; R3634: mḏbḥt...wrṯdh 'LMQH "an altar...and he placed it under the protection of (the god) I."; C20/4: rṯdw mqbrhmw ʿṮTR...bn mhb'sm "they placed their grave under the protection of (the god) A. against (any) injurer" AND OFTEN SIM

ti *inf* rtṯdn J716/11+

CARE FOR, PRESERVE from harm

J716/11: may the god continue šr[ḥ] wšwf wrtṯdn grybt ʿbdyhw "to protect, care for and preserve the lives of His 2 servants"; sim J572/8, J586/10

tp *pf/inf* trṯd C359/6-7*

PLACE UNDER THE PROTECTION OF a deity (or phps *pass* sense) (cf RṮD *v*)

C359/6-7: tqdm lhw wtrṯd T'LB ḏn mhdrn "he undertook (its construction) for Him and placed this tomb under the protection of (the god) T. (or, it was placed under T.'s protection?)"

h *pf* hrṯdw Ist7608b/4+

PLACE s.th. UNDER THE PROTECTION OF a deity (cf RṮD *v*, *tp*)

Ist7608b/4: khrṯdw wšrḥn "when they were placed (?) under (the god's) protection and (were) protected (?)"; F123/11: hrṯ(d)w tb[q]lthmw 'LMQH "they placed their plantations under (the god) I's protection"

n[1] *s* rṯdt N20/8-9*

PROTÉGÉ

N20/8-9: lwfy brwhmw rṯdt T'LB "for the well-being of their son, the protege of (the god) T." (final t in rṯdt may be dittography)

n[2] *s* mrṯd R4043/2+ (*D* *prt*?)

THING DEDICATED > PROTÉGÉ (cf rṯdt id)

R4998/1: Ḥ bn 'A mrṯd T'LB "Ḥ., son of A., protege of (the god) T."

RṮY

n *s* rṯyw R4176/5*

PLACE OF JUDGMENT, part of the temple (or *n.pr*?)

[MüW/54 cfs Ar raṯâ "complain."]
R4176/5: ḏyǵln bn mb^{c}l T'LB lyt^{c}lmn T brṯyw "whoever steals from the property of (the god) T., let T. take cognizance of it in the place of judgment"

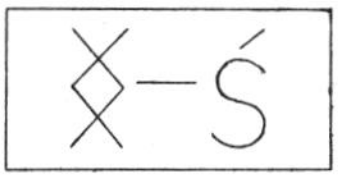

Ś'D--In J576/9,10 the exp ś'd ykl' is prob a place-name. J tr "the prince of Y" after Ar *sā'id > sayyid "lord." Passages read "drove (the enemy) to Ś.Y.," "they reached Ś.Y."

ŚBB I

v <u>inf</u> śb J702/8-9*

BLASPHEME (?)

J702/8-9 (context obscure): l(ḥḏ)rn kl ršym d'l yšrḥn ṣythw...hxṭ' wśb "let every priest (?) beware (?) who does not protect his good reputation (?) (regarding) sinning and blaspheming (?)"

ŚBB II

tp <u>ipf</u> ytśbbnn J631/32; <u>inf</u> tśbbn ib/34

SURROUND (<u>b^{c}m</u> an enemy)

[Heb sābab id.]

J631/31-4: they made a sortie wytśbbnn b^{c}m 'ḤBŠn...wyhrgn bn 'ḤBŠn btśbbn wgb'w bnhmw 'ḤBŠn ḥyrthmw "and surrounded the Ḥabashites, and he killed some of the Ḥabashites in surrounding (them), and they returned from those Ḥabashites to their camp"

ŚDD

n <u>s</u> śdn R4176/4*

DAM

[Ar sadd id, sadda "block the way." Discussion of function Irv/225-8.]

R4176/4: land lying along the highroad ^{c}dy lyrt^c śdn H wmdyh "so far as to lie opposite the dam H. and its overflow"

ŚDQ

n <u>p</u> 'śdqm Ry533/9*

(FERRY) BOATS

[Cf Ar ṣunduq "box, chest"? RycER2/154A suggests de-emphaticization of ṣ before n (as in Sq, cf LeLS/35-6), followed by assimilation of n: 'ṣndq > 'sndq > 'sdq, realized in Sab as 'śdq.]

Ry533/9: 'śdqm w'flkm "(ferry) boats and feluccas" (part of the booty of a coastal town)

ŚWB

D? ipf yśwbnh R3956/7*

GRANT (= ṮWB v)

[See under ṮWB. Substitution of ś for ṯ as a feature of the Harami dialect, discussion BeDGESA/18:3.]

R3956/7: she confessed, fl yśwbnh nᶜmtm "so let (the god) grant her prosperity (or, phps, restore her to favor)"; cf C568/7-8 quoted under ṮWB D, parallel text

ŚWD I

n p śwwdt C376/8*

PASTURE LANDS

[ModḤaḍ swād "a rich pasture"; cf Ar 'aswad "black" referring to soil?]

C376/8: 'rḍ wᶜbrt wśwwdt "land, meadows and pasture lands"

Note: C read śwwdt, Rh read ḏwwdt, q.v. under ḎWD.

ŚWD II

n p mśwd(n) R4176/14+; mśwdhmw R2726/6+; var mśwdt J2115/2-3

(1) CLAN-HEADS, SAYYIDS (not always distinct from sense 2)

[Cf Ar sāda (w) "be lord," L "discuss, arrange secretly"; sayyid "lord"; ModḤaḍ musawwad "lord" (MüW/65). BePESA/18 cfs rather Heb sōd "council."]

R4176/14: 'qwl wmśwd wqsd šᶜbn S "the chiefs and clan-heads and qsd-citizens of the tribe S."

(2) COUNCIL/ASSEMBLY of clan-heads

R3951/2: kbr Ṣ...wmśwd Ṣ "the chieftain of (the tribe) Ṣ. and the council (of clan-heads) of Ṣ."; ib/3: mśwd Ṣ wšᶜbn Ṣ "the council and tribe of Ṣ."; ib/4: śxlm bn ᶜly mśwd Ṣ "obligatory upon the council of Ṣ."

(3) COUNSELORS

J2115/2-3: 'dm wmśwdt mlkn "servants and counselors of the king"

ŚWD III

n s mśwd(n) C648/3+; mśwdhw Ry520/9+; mśwdhmw R3564/2; p? [m]śwtm (for *mśwd-tm?) C449/2

FIRE-ALTAR, HOUSE SHRINE (cf mswd id)

[Cf Eth soda "set fire to," maswad "incense burner."]

R2860/6 (obscure context): wl yh(b) ḏb mś(w)dn "let him give that which is on the altar"; R3564/2: mwṯ]rn mśwdhmw wmḏqnthmw "laid the foundation for their fire-altar and oratory"; J603/6: mśwd wṣrḥt bythmw "the shrine and upper chambers of their house"

ŚWK

v pf śwk R3943/3; śwkt R3945/14

(1) ENCLOSE, FENCE IN

[Heb swk "hedge or fence about, shut in," Syr sāk "become bounded, narrow" (MüW/66).]

R3945/14: ygn' gn'm ḏbhw śwkt N "he built a wall by which (the city) N. was enclosed"

(2) BESIEGE

[Development from sense "fence in."]

R3943/3: wśwk Y wgbḏ ḏhby [y] "besieged Y. and plundered/laid waste the 2 cultivated territories of Y."

ŚW^c I

v inf św^c R4194/2,3*

LAY OUT, LEVEL ground

[Irv/162 cfs Ar sy^c D "plaster (a wall with mud and chopped straw)," Aram šu^{ac} "be smooth, soft; plaster" šu^{c}a' "smooth rock." MüW/66 cfs Ar ṭā^{c}a (w) "flow (water)," tr "irrigate."]

R4194/2: grbw wśw^c wḥrr "they revetted, leveled and embanked"; ib/3: bql wśw^c wṯ[^{c}d] "planted, leveled and irrigated (?)"; cf also phps ś^c J570/8, in fragmentary agricultural context

ŚW^c II

n s ś^{c}tn R3910/5+

TIME, PERIOD OF TIME

[Ar sā^{c}a^t "(short) time; hour."]

R3910/5: when a man hires an animal flyhbn ^{c}śbhw ś^{c}tn ḏysb'n b^{c}lyhw "let him give/pay its hire-price (for) the period (during) which he worked it"; C563/5: lyst^{c}ḏbhw 'rb^{c}m wś^{c}tn ǵwytm ^{c}ḏbth "let him punish him: (a) fourfold (compensation) and a period of 'sin' (= excommunication?) are his punishments"

ŚW^{c}L--For św^{c}ltn R2861/3, read ḏwwdt (?); see under ḎWD

ŚWF

n s śftn F90/2*

CLAY, MUDDY SOIL

[Ar sā'if "soft soil" (RyET/59).]

F90/2: m^c]rbt (w)śftn mrtn wṣhr[n... "[squared ma]sonry, muddy soil, clayey soil and clamps"

ŚWR

v inf śwrhw C463/5; act.prt śwrm Ir13/15

SET APART, REMOVE

[Cf Heb swr h "remove, put aside."]
C463/5: he shall offer an oblation on a certain day wśwrhw "and set it apart (?)"; Ir13/15: they placed it under the god's protection bn kl mhkrm wśwrm wm'xrm "against anyone who would injure (it), set (it) aside, or remove (it)" (cf n² below, sense¹)

n¹ For n 'śwr R4176/13, see under 'ŚR

n² s mśwrm J703/12* (D prt?)
ONE WHO REMOVES (cf ŚWR v "remove")
J703/12: they placed it under the god's protection bn m'xrm wmśwrm wdśśm "against (any)one who would take away, remove or hide (it)"; cf sim context with śwrm quoted under ŚWR v

ŚWR II

n s mśwrh R4781/1; p? m[ś]wrtn R4040/6 (fragmentary context)
DYKE or REVETMENT
[Cf Ar swr "enclose, fence in," sūr "wall"; and cf Sab śwr h "erect a wall."]
R4781/1: mśwrh lsqy 'ln nxlnhn "its dyke for the irrigation of these 2 palmgroves"

ŚḤB

v inf śḥb R4069/6*
LAY WASTE or ERODE
[Cf Ar saḥaba "pull down to the ground," MSA saḥb "plow(share)" (cf Irv/174); Ḥimyaritic saḥaba "hoe the ground" (RabAncWar/27).]
R4069/6: bᶜdn ḥṯbrt wśḥb kl [ᶜ]q[rhw w]mbr'hw "(they repaired the irrigation system of their land) after all its dam wall and masonry were broken and eroded (by flood waters)"

ŚḤM

n p 'śḥmt J544/3*
HEALTHY people
[Cf Ar saḥīm "fat" > "robust"? (Bon2T/134-40n8). Correspondence of Sab ś: Ar š unusual.]
J544/3: lxmrhmw ḥywm 'śḥmt wmrḍytm "to grant them life, (both) the healthy and the sick"

ŚḤR

n s śḥr C695/1*
MAGICAL PROTECTION (?)
[Akk saḫāru "turn, encircle, surround," Heb sāḥar "go around," Ar saḥr "incantation." Note also ŚḤRm Qat divine name--the moon in its circuit? (HöWZ43/216).]

C695/1 (on a small tablet): śḥr 'l w'xhw "magical protection (?) for l. and his brother"

ŚXL

v pf śxly C376/1*

BIND ONE'S SELF, ACKNOWLEDGE ONE'S RESPONSIBILITY

[Sense from context.]

C376/1: śxly w^c hd...lY...'lfm blṭm "they bound themselves and contracted (regarding) one thousand blṭ-coins (owed) to Y."

n s śxlm C376/12-3+

(1) OBLIGATION

F76/8: dn wtf śxlm "this deed (and) obligation > obligatory deed"; C376/12-3: ẓhrn dhzhr...śxlm bn ^c lyhmy "this document which attests an obligation incumbent upon them"

(2) adj: BINDING, OBLIGATORY

R2726/4-5: śxlm wnfqm bn^c ly 'dmhw "binding and obligatory upon his clients"; sim R3951/4

Note: Read śx[ln] C609/5, where C erroneously prints sx[ln].

ŚYF

v inf śf J702/14-5; śfhw J570/5; var śyf J702/15-6

GIVE, GRANT

[Prob var of root WŚF/YŚF "increase > grant."]

J702/14-6: ^c ln dśf dwkb wh' fl śyf ḥwlm "because he gave (to the god) what he had obtained, may He give an oracular dream"; in fragmentary context J570/5 and F120/15

ŚYQ

v inf śyq J702/9*

DRIVE cattle

[Ar sāqa (w) id.]

J702/9: 'l śnyw śyq bwsṭ mḥrm gnztn "they are forbidden to drive (cattle) through the midst of the cemetery"

ŚL'

v pf śl' R2740/4+

PAY > OFFER as tribute, DEDICATE

[Ar sala'a "pay"; cf Heb sl' Pual "be weighed."]

R2740/4: śl' M...ywm fr^c M "he dedicated to (the god) M. on the day he made an offering of first-fruits to M."; A716a,b/1: N...śl' Š "N. dedicated to (the god) Š." (cf TsSEGI I/24)

n¹ s śl'(m,n) R3945/16+; śl'hmw ib/3 twice

TRIBUTE

R3945/3: bḍ^c b^c lhmw b^c m śl'hmw bqrm "he imposed on them, in addition to their tribute, (a payment of) cattle"; ib/16: bḍ^{c} bẓhr N śl'm 'fklt "he imposed tribute (for?) the priests on the back of (the city) N."; ib/20: bḍ^{c} b^{c}ly M śl'm l'LMQH wl SB' "he imposed on M. tribute for (the god) I. and for S."

n^{2} p śl'n R3951/2*

TRIBUTE-PAYING CLASS

R3951/2: SB'...qsdn wmkrn wśl'n "the Sabaeans, 'yeomen,' merchants and the tribute-paying class"

ŚLB

v pf ślbt C504/4*

CARRY OFF, ABDUCT (?)

[Ar salaba id.]

C504/4: he dedicated because ślbt bth...bn mbḥr ^{c}A w'l ẓyt "his daughter had been abducted from the rock-dwelling A. but was not held captive (?)" (for an alternate tr, see under ẒYW v)

ŚLL

h inf hśln J576/7*

ROB (?) (but see Note)

[Cf Ar salla "pull out; take, steal," h "steal" (Lane/1396A).]

J576/7: yhsb^{c}w whśln hgrn 'A "they plundered and robbed the city A."

Note: Conceivably this form, like other instances of hśl, should be assigned to WŚL h "offer (to a deity)"; cf h'tw in R3945/6, apparently of offering conquered property to a god.

ŚL^{c}

v pf śl^{c}w C211/2*

LAY THE FOUNDATION of a building

[Cf Heb sela^{c} "rock, crag," Ar sal^{c} "fissure in rock" > "establish on a foundation of rock" (MüHāz/78).]

C211/2: śl^{c}w w^{c}ḏbn whg[... "they laid the foundation and repaired and..." (reading of MüHāz; C read śl^{c}w w[^{c}ḏ]b whš[qrn...)

ŚMK

v pf śmkw J576/6+; yśmkw ib/3; yśmkn ib/14

GO UP (?) or VEER, TEND (toward a place) (?)

[Cf Ar samaka "be high." Or cf basic sense "lean on" of Eth h below.]

J576/6: śmkw mqln ḏY "they went up the pass of Y."; ib/3: yśmkw bn hgrn M ^{c}dy hgrn Ṣ "they went up from the city M. to the city Ṣ."

D? inf śmk C314/12*

RAISE or SUSTAIN

[Eth smk h "prop up, support."]

C314/12: 'ml'ṣd[q]m...lśmk wtyf^{c}n mr'yhmw "fortunate oracle responses to raise (or, sustain) and exalt (or, support) their 2 lords"

ŚN--See under ŚNY, ŚNN

ŚND

v <u>inf</u> śnd N74/7*

ERECT an inscriptional plaque (mśnd)

[Ar snd <u>D</u> "support, prop s.th."]

N74/7: yqht <u>d</u>t B...lśnd <u>d</u>n mśndn "(the goddess) <u>d</u>t B. commanded (them) to erect this inscriptional plaque"

n <u>s</u> mśdm J669/6,12; <u>var</u> mśndn R2633/6+

INSCRIPTION; VOTIVE PLAQUE or TABLET bearing an inscription (cf msnd, m<u>t</u>nd id)

[Cf ŚND <u>v</u> and Ar musnad "Old South Arabic script."]

R2633/6: sṭrw <u>d</u>n mśndn b^{c}rn M "they wrote this inscription on the rocks of M."; J669/6: they dedicated to their lord ṣlmn wmśdm ṣrfm "this statue and an inscriptional plaque of silver"; C73/4: they dedicated to their patron deity mśndn ḥg <u>d</u>t wqhhmw "this inscription as He had commanded them" AND SEVERAL TIMES SIM

ŚNY

v <u>pf</u> śnw C225/2; <u>var</u> śnyw J702/9

BE ALLOWED to do s.th., in exp 'l śny "(he) is not allowed/is forbidden (to)" (cf 'LŚN <u>v</u> id)

[Verbalization of the phrase 'l śn "it is not lawful (to do s.th.)"; see under ŚNN <u>v</u>.]

J702/9: 'l śnyw śyq bwsṭ mḥrm gnztn "they are forbidden to drive (cattle) through the midst of the cemetery"; C225/2 (fragmentary context): ...]w'l śnw bnw [... "the b. ... are not allowed to..."

ŚNN

v <u>pf</u> śn C400/1+; śnhmw G1573a/1

BE LAWFUL for s.o. to do s.th., in exp 'l śn "it is not lawful, it is forbidden" (cf 'LŚN <u>v</u>, ŚNY <u>v</u>, and root ŚNN)

[Cf Ar sanna "enact a law or custom," sunna† "customary procedure or action."]

C400/1: w'l śn h^{c}zln...bn [k]l ṣrf...bn mḥrmn "it is not lawful to remove any of the ṣrf-incense from the temple"; C617/1: w'l śn hy^{c} msb'n 'nsm wb^{c}rm "it is not lawful for this watercourse to provide drink for man or beast"; G1573a/1: (fragmentary context): <u>d</u>kr bnw <u>d</u>Ḥ ...k'l śnhmw [... "the b.Ḥ. have announced that it is not lawful for them..."

Note: For śnw C225/2, see under ŚNY <u>v</u>.

h <u>inf</u> hśnn C613/4*

PRESCRIBE, ENACT a legal proceeding

[Ar snn h id.]

C613/4: sṭry wsmy whśnn b'ṯwbt "they wrote, decreed and prescribed the repayment"

n[1] s śn C540/16+; śnhw J576/7+

(1) BOUNDARY

[Cf ŚNN h "prescribe," Min n 'śnn synonym of 'wṯn "boundaries" (cf BeBSOAS 17/155).]

C540/16: k'bt Ǵ tśn ^cglmtn "the buttress of Ǵ., which is the boundary of the diversion mole"; sim ib/19; prob also in fragmentary context R3912/3: śn wm^cb[r] "boundary and delimita[tion]" or the like?

(2) AREA enclosed by a boundary, VICINITY; note esp the exp b-śnhw "in his vicinity," i.e., "with him"

J687/8: ...bśn byt h[... "in the vicinity of the house..."; J576/7: 'sd qrbw bśnhw "the men who came with him"; sim Ir21

Note also R4787/4 (fragmentary context): dt śn lsn.

n[2] p tśnnthw Gl142/10-1*

BOUNDARIES (cf śn n[1] sense[1])

Gl142/10-1: ^crmhwt mrbḍn kl tśnnthw "the boundaries/cairns of that sheep-fold (along) all its boundaries"

Ś^c--v in fragmentary context J570/8: ...] lgtnn l'LMQH kś^c y[... "to harvest for (the god) l. when he (or, He?)...?" Cf phps ŚW^c I v "level (land)." For n ś^ct, see under ŚW^c II.

ŚF--For vs, see under WŚF, ŚYF. For n śftn F90/2, see under ŚWF

ŚFM--For v yśfmw R3946/4,6, read yśf-mw; see under WŚF

ŚQT--In doubtful context C581/8: mẓ' wwgr bythmw blly sdṯm śqt btrm[.] C tr "a man who came and built their house in six nights. It fell (cf Ar saqaṭa, with doubtful correspondence of t and ṭ) in an earthquake (?--doubtful)." GressAOT/468 tr: "a man who had come and caused much (śqt, cf Ar wasq "camel load") disturbance (btrm[.], no etymology) on the sixth night."

ŚRM

n p 'śrm R4176/6*

HERDS (?)

[Cf Ar sirba[†] "group (= flock, herd) of partridges, horses, donkeys, gazelles, or wild oxen" (Lane/1342B).]

R4176/6: the god prohibited the districts bn hwḍ'n 'śrm...kḥrmw "from driving out the herds (of mountain goats), for they are sacred"

Cf phps 'śwr ib/13, under 'ŚR.

Σ–Š

Š'M I

v *pf* š'm C435/4+; š'mh R4760A/2; *ipf* yš'm R2861/4; yš'mn R3910/3+; yš'mnn ib/2; *inf* š'm C37/4+; *act.prt* š'mn J2856/3

BUY (^{c}mn from)

[Akk šāmu id; cf Mh śêm, Sq śíom "sell."]

C37/4: ḥqlm whgrm...d^{c}sy wš'm Y ^{c}mn B "cultivated and settled land which Y. acquired and bought from B."; R2861/4: mn lyš'm bn ^{c}bd'sm w^{c}śbhw "whoever buys the son of a man's slave and hires him out..."

Note: For fš'm J720/12-3, see under FŠ'.

h *pf* hš'mhw R3946/8; hš'mhm[w] J734/2 (context fragmentary); *inf?* hš'm G1447/2; *act.prt* mhš'mn R3910/6; mhs'mhw J2856/3

CAUSE TO BUY = SELL

R3946/8: wyśf ḥwhw F 'dm hš'mhw Ḥ "he increased his clan F. with the clients (whom) Ḥ. sold him"; R3910/6: if a purchased animal dies within a specified period, fbr'm mhš'mn bn mwthw "the seller is not liable for its death"

n *s* š'mtm C609/3+; *p* š'mt(m,n) R3910/2+

PURCHASE or SALE; also, DEED OF SALE

R3910/2: kl š'mt w'qyḍ yš'mnn wstqḍn "all purchases and exchanges they may make or carry out"; R3439/3: 'ḥt š'mtm b[n]xln "one purchase/deed of sale for (?) the palmgrove"; R3439/2: hmt 'sṭrn wš'mtm w'ṯwbn wnḥltn "those documents, deeds of sale, and (contracts regarding) payments and gifts"; R4771/1: 'myntn wš'mtn "the deposit and deed of sale"

Note: A possible *var* š'm occurs in fragmentary context in R3197/3: ...]^{c}krn š'm [... "disputed purchase (?)"

Š'M II

v *pf* š'mw C541/29-30*

TURN TO THE LEFT or NORTH

[Ar ša'ama id, and cf Sab š'm "left," š'mt "north" below.]

C541/29-30: š'mw bn Ṣ ^cly N ^cdy ^cA "they turned left/north from Ṣ. over N. to A."

n¹ s š'm C608/6-7*

LEFT

[Ar šimāl, ša'māl "left," and cf ša'm (Sab š'mt) "north."]

C608/6-7: bn dn sṭrn lš'm "from this inscription, to the left"

n² s š'mt J577/18+

NORTH

[Ar ša'm "north, northern region."]

J577/18: bn š'mt wymnt wbḥrm wybsm "from north and south and sea and land"; C407/22: hwkbhmw b^cly ^cA bknf š'mt "he pursued them over A. on the north border (lit., border of the north)"

n³ p š'mytn RyGrafp561*

NORTHERN PARTS, PLACES LYING TO THE NORTH

RyGrafp561: hdy ^crn ymnytn wš'mytn "he guided the caravan to southern and northern parts"

Š'M III

n s š'mn C432/6*

STATUTE

[Derived from v ŠYM "establish, appoint."]

C432/6: he forbade [d]yhš'mln w...yhymnn bn dn š'mn "anyone who might go to the left or right of (i.e., deviate from) this statute"

Š'ML

h ipf yhš'mln C432/6*

GO TO THE LEFT = DEVIATE (bn from)

[Cf Ar šimāl, ša'māl "left," Heb hiśmī(')l "turn to the left."]

C432/6 quoted under Š'M III n

ŠBM

n s šbm R2861/10*

STRANGLING (as a form of execution?)

[Cf Ar šabama "place a piece of wood crosswise in the mouth of a kid, in order that it may not suck its mother" (Lane/1499).]

R2861/10: lkdkbr dwqr hḏrn bšbm "so that whoever opposed what is inscribed (namely, a law) (let him?) beware of strangling (?)" (context obscure)

ŠB^c

h pf hšb^c Gl773b/4*

SATISFY, SATE (specifically, with water for irrigation)

[Ar šb^c h id.]

Gl773b/4: sqy ^cTTR...whšb^c SB' "(the god) A. provided irrigation water for and satisfied S."

Note: Tr phps as aux: "satisfactorily provided irrigation."

n s šbᶜm C967/4*

SATIETY, SATISFACTION

[Ar šabᶜ id.]

C967/4: wsqy xrf wdṯ' SB'...šbᶜm "(the god) provided irrigation for S. in autumn and spring, (to) satiety"

ŠDW

n s šdw(n) R4169/2+; šdwhmw C660/4

HILLSIDE, TERRACED HILLSIDE (and see Note)

[Cf Akk šadû "mountain," Heb śādeh "field."]

R4169/2: bn srrn wšdw[... "from the valleys and the hillside"; F72/4: qbrhmw...bšdwn Ḏ "their grave on the hillside Ḏ."; C660/4: rmt hwr šdwhmw Ḏ "the raised tank of the cistern of their hillside terrace Ḏ."

Note: If the context of C660/4 is to be interpreted as cultic, tr phps "the raised tank of the basin of their font (?) Ḏ," after Ar ṯadiya "become moist" (Irv/199-200).

ŠH--For n šh, p šhw, see under ŠHW

ŠHD

n s šh[d]hw C40/2-3*

SIGHT, VIEW; b-šh[d]: WITHIN SIGHT OF, OPPOSITE

[Ar šāhada "view, observe."]

C40/2-3: ḏt bfnw hwr mḥfdhmw...wbšh[d]hw kryfm "...which is in front of the hwr-cistern of their tower, and opposite it is the kryf-cistern"

ŠHW

n s šhn J720/16-7; p? šhw C694/1-2

SHEEP or GOAT

[Ar coll šā', p šiyāh "sheep," Heb śeh "sheep, goat," Daṯ šāh "goat."]

C694/1-2 (on an altar): mḏbḥt šhw "sacrificial altar for sheep/goats."; J720/16-7: lmšw mᶜrbtm...wz'k šhn "let him go to a place of sacrifice and offer the sheep/goat"

ŠHR

v pf [š]hr C333/6*

DECLARE, PROCLAIM (said of a god speaking through an oracle)

[Ar šahara id.]

C333/6: š]hr T'LB wtbšr[n "(the god) T. proclaimed and announced"

h pf/inf hšhr R4369/1*

ALLOCATE FOR PUBLIC USE (?)

[Cf ŠHR v "publish, proclaim" and Min šhr (R2827A/10) "be given over to public use."]

R4369/1 (fragmentary): hšhr ᶜ[...]nqḥt [... "has allocated for public use (?)...has been set in order (?)"

n[1] s [š]hr C290/6*

PROCLAMATION, RESPONSE of a god through an oracle

C290/6: wkwn [š]hr 'A bṯnyn bthḥrbn "the oracle-response (to) A. occurred on the second (occasion), in a vision"

n[2] s šhrm J651/19*

NEW MOON

[Ar šahr id.]

J651/19: bywm šhrm wywm ṯnym ḏnm ḏᶜsm "on the day of the new moon and the second day it rained heavily"

Cf also C30/2: WD šhrn "(the god) W., the New Moon (?)"

n[3] s šhrm C713/2*

adj: FAMOUS

[Ar šahīr id.]

C713/2: nṣb Q...ḥrbm šhrm "grave-stela of Q., a famous fighter"

n[4] s mšhrm C83/3-4* (D prt?)

PUBLIC ANNOUNCEMENT (?)

[Cf Ar šhr ẖ "proclaim," išhār "announcement."]

C83/3-4: hqny...ḏn mśndn ḏtnb' mšhrm "he dedicated this inscription which he had promised as a public announcement (?)"

ŠWB

n s? šwbn C320/2*

MIXED, (OF) VARIOUS KINDS (?)

[Cf Ar šāba (w) "mix, mingle" (MüW/68).]

C320/2 (fragmentary): ᶜśbn šwbn wṯwrn "fodder of various kinds (?) and a bull" (description of an offering?)

Note: C cfs Ar šawb "honey."

ŠWḤṬ

n s šwḥṭt J539/1-2; p šwḥṭ(m) R2868/4+

UNIT OF MEASURE = SPAN (?) or a larger measure

[Cf ModYem šayz "distance between the points of the thumb and index finger" (RoVoc/312). Bon3T/30n2, on J539, equates the šwḥṭt with the Gk pléthron = 65 cubits; he offers no etymological justification for this identification.]

J539/1-2: ln ḏn sṭrn šwḥṭt bḏ xms 'mm ᶜd wsṭ b'rn "from this inscription one šwḥṭt-unit, which is (?) five cubits from the middle of the well"; R2868/4: hrwḥ N ᶜd 'ln 'wṯnn sdṯy šwḥṭ "he extended N. to these boundaries: sixty šwḥṭt-units"; J671/13-4: ṯbr bn ᶜrmn sbᶜy šwḥṭm "seventy šwḥṭt-units broke off from the dam"; C570/2: 'rbᶜ 'mn wšlṯ šwḥṭ "four cubits and three spans (?)"

Šw^c I

v <u>pf</u> šw^c J586/13; šw^{c}hw J564/8-9; šw^{c}hmy Ir5/3; šw^{c}y J658/8; šw^{c}w J656/8+; <u>ipf</u> yšw^{c}nn J623/5+; <u>inf</u> šw^{c}n R4842/3+

FURNISH AID or SERVICE (usually military)

[Cf Ar šāwa^{c}a "help," šī^{c}a$^+$ the "partisans" of ^{c}ALĪ. Root in Sab prob a doublet of WŠ^c with metathesis (so BePESA/16, denied by HöSEG8/58f).]

J656/8: the god allowed them to return from campaign bkn šw^{c}w mr'hmw "when they had furnished aid/service to their lord"; R4842/3: kl 'br<u>t</u> bhw sb' wḍb' wšw^{c}n mr'hm[w] "all the expeditions on which he campaigned and fought and aided their lord" AND OFTEN SIM; J586/13: tqdmt bhmw šw^c mr'yhmw "the battles in which he aided their 2 lords"

n^1 <u>s</u> šw^{c}hw J629/26+; šw^{c}hmw J631/14

FOLLOWERS, ALLIES (cf š^{c}y id)

J629/26: the god helped His servant w'sd wmqtt šw^{c}hw bkn sb'w lšw^{c}n mr'yhmw "and the soldiers and officers of his followers when they went on campaign to furnish aid to their 2 lords" (tr as <u>v</u> "soldiers and officers who aided him" is also possible); J631/14: the god brought his son back from campaign, hw' wkl šw^{c}hmw "him and all their followers"

n^2 <u>s</u> š^{c}t C542/1+; š^{c}thw C6/1

(1) AID (?) (cf tš^{c}t ŠW^c <u>n</u>^{3} id?)

R4106/1: brd' 'mr'hmw 'mlkm wbš^{c}t [... "with the help of their lords the kings and with the aid (?) of..."

(2) WIFE

[Cf ŠW^c <u>v</u> "aid, help" and Akk še'ū, <u>f</u> še'itu "friend" (cf MüW/68).]

C6/1: ^{c}A wš^{c}thw 'A bt 'I "A. and his wife A., daughter of I."; C542/1: W š^{c}t S...wb'th "W., wife of Š., and her house(hold)"

n^3 <u>s</u>? tš^{c}t C308/17*

a) AID (cf š^{c}t <u>n</u>^{2} sense^1); or, b) PRESENTATION, GIFT (?)

[a) Cf ŠW^c <u>v</u> "aid," Heb təšū^{c}āh "deliverance." b) Cf Sab Š^{c}W <u>tp</u> "take for one's self, acquire."]

C308/17: kl tš^{c}t wzbd ysrw 'ysm l'xhw "all the aid/presentation(s) (?) and gift(s) which (each) man sent to his ally"

Šw^c II

v <u>pf/inf</u> šw^c R4830/3+

SACRIFICE

[Cf Ar šy^c <u>D</u> "burn s.th.," Eth šaw^{c}a "offer" (MüW/69).]

R4830/3: 'mr 'LMQH qdm wšw^c K "by command of (the god) I., K. presented an offering and sacrificed"; same exp R4831/3

n <u>s</u> šw^{c}n C563/2*

PRIEST who offers sacrifices

[In Min in same sense.]

C563/2: kl 'kl wmsty wtfṯ yh'twn šw^{c}n "all food and drink (offerings) and lustrations (which) the priest shall offer"

ŠWF

v *pf* šf R3991/6,9; *inf* šwf C82/8+

WATCH OVER, PROTECT (*bn* against)

[Cf Ar šāfa (w) "see, look at" > "watch over."]

C82/8: wlwz' 'LMQH šwf wmt^{c}n ^{c}bdhw "may (the god) I. continue to protect and save His servant"; C429/5: h^c[nn] wšwf bn šṣyt "help and protect against the evil eye"

Note: In J584/7, ŠWF ḏt LNH' is a *n.pr.f.*

n *s* šwftm J686/6+

CARE, PROTECTION

J686/6: may the god grant them šwft grybthmw "protection (for) their bodies/persons"; C43/6: may He grant them [n^{c}m]tm wšwftm w'ml' "prosperity, protection and (favorable) oracle responses"

ŠWR

v *ipf* yšrn C460/8*

DECLARE (?)

[Ar šwr h̲ "show, indicate, state" (cf BeOracle/219).]

C460/8: yšrn ^{c}d mnṭftn "declare (?) at the sacrificial altar"

ŠZB

n *s* šzb(n) J700/13,14*

DAGGER (?)

[Cf Ar mišḏab "pruning hook" (IrvBSOAS30/288,292).]

J700/13-4: xrṭ R šzb S bn ḥqwyhw wt^{c}ṣrw bynhmy bšzbn wtlf R "R. drew S.'s dagger from his hips, they struggled between them with the dagger, and R. perished"

ŠḤṬ--For *n* šwḥṭt, *p* šwḥṭ, see under ŠWḤṬ

ŠḤK

n *p* mšḥkn C81/8*

AFFLICTED

[Cf Eth sḥk "be harsh, rough, rude," ma/osḥag "grief."]

C81/8: yftḥn bythmw whḏlln qnyhmw wmšḥkn ^{c}dy ṣnqn "their house was laid waste and their property ravaged, and (they were) afflicted, in distress"

ŠḤM--In C548/16, read ŠḤM as *n.pr*

ŠẒY

n *s* šẓy R4188/10*

EVIL EYE (= šṣy)

[See under ŠṢY v and n[I].]
R4188/10: may the god help them bn nz[c] wšẓy šn'm "against injury or evil eye of (any) enemy" (inscription phonetically aberrant)

ŠYH--For n šh, p šhw, see under ŠHW

ŠYḤ

n s? or elative adj 'šyḥ C540/64*
DRYNESS; or, if adj: VERY DRY
[Daṯ šîḥ "dryness," Ar šiyāḥ "year of drought" (Irv/281).]
C540/64: w[c]rmn bn sflhw 'šyḥ "and as for the (broken) dam, from its foundation (outwards was) dryness (or, it was very dry)"

ŠYM I

v pf šm R4176/9+; var šymhw R4845b; šmy R4708/1+; šmty C389/4; šmw Ry508/2+; ipf yšmn J611/16-7+; inf šym J651/32+
(1) SET UP, PREPARE, ESTABLISH
[For most senses cf Eth šēma "put," Heb śy/wm "put, set; establish (a law); appoint (a person)."]
C382/1: šm mdbḥtn "he set up an altar"; J651/32: lbr' 'gn'...hgrn M wlšym lhw mḏrfn "to build up the walls of the city M. and to set up for it a revetment wall"; C540/74: msrw [c]rmn...wšmw [c]rḍ r'shw "they packed in earth (for) the dam and prepared the face of its upper part"; R4708/1: mlky S... šmy mxmry m'dbthmy "the 2 kings of S. established 2 concessions (for) their clients"
(2) APPOINT s.o. to an office
R4176/9: šm T'LB Y 'ḥdfqhm "(the god) T. appointed (for) Y. one (person) as overseer"; C496/5: ywm šymhw Y b[c]ly K "when Y. appointed him (to rule) over K."
(3) CONFIRM, PROTECT
[Development of sense "establish" > "make secure, protect."]
J611/16-7: flyšmn wfy grb [c]bdhw "so that (the god) might protect the health of the body of His servant"; C349/6: yz'n...šym wfyhmw "may He continue to protect their safety/health"
(4) ASSURE OF, PROMISE
J750/6: he was dying of thirst wšm I'LM[QH] (t)'d'm bhbtn "and he promised to (the god) I. a payment, consisting of this gift (now being dedicated)"
(5) GO TO WAR, GO ON CAMPAIGN
[Cf Ar šāma (y) "carry out a military attack." (cf Lane/1634C).]
Ry508/2: šmw bsb'tm...mr'hmw "their lord went on campaign (p.maj)"; J576/13: kl qrn šym bhw dR "every fighter/guard with whom dR. had gone to war"; C314/13: wšmw dn xrfn fnbl Š... "and they went to war (?) in this year, so that Š. sent..." (but read phps bmw "in this year, Š. sent..."--so RyCS/239n1)

(6) CONSULT omens or oracular visions

[Cf Ar šāma (y) "observe (lightning) to see if it will rain; be on the lookout" (RycMancie/268).]

R4632/2: šmw tḥrb(n) lwfyhm "they consulted tḥrb-visions for (the sake of) their well-being"; sim R4633; phps also C74/5: wqh...lšym flyt 'srrhmw "(the god) commanded (them) to consult the oracle responses regarding their valleys"; phps also NNAG12/1: the god commanded him lšym ḥrbm "to consult (?) the ḥrb-ritual" (or tr after sense[1], "prepare the ḥrb-ritual"?)

tp <u>pf</u> tšym C337/5; <u>var</u> tšm C338/6

APPOINT FOR ONE'S SELF

[Cf ŠYM <u>v</u> sense[2] "appoint s.o. to an office."]

C338/6: bkn tšm T'LB M mnṣfm ym styf[c] T "when (the god) T. appointed M. for himself as minister, on the day T. was 'exalted' (i.e., M. performed the ritual of 'exaltation'?)"; C337/5: ...] ywm tšym T [...] ywm styf[c] T [... "on the day T. appointed for himself...on the day T. was 'exalted'"

n <u>s</u> šym(m) R3945/1+; šymhmw R3990/3+; <u>d</u> šymyhmw J578/43; <u>p</u>? šymn G1062/4

PATRON DEITY (class of deity contrasted with 'l "god")

[Phps <u>act.prt</u> of <u>v</u> ŠYM in sense "appoint"; cf the cultic usage of ŠYM <u>tp</u> (cf HöWar?/81-2). Frequently-used title of the god T'LB.]

R3945/1: kl hwm <u>d</u>'lm wšymm wdḥblm wḥmrm "every community (owing allegiance to) a god or patron deity, and (bound by) an alliance or treaty" AND ELSEWHERE SIM; R3990/3: hqnyw šymhmw T'LB "they dedicated to their patron deity T." AND OFTEN SIM; G1062/4 (obscure context): kšymn wk'gšm "as patron(s?, patron deities?) and kings (?)"

ŠYM II

n <u>s</u> mšm(n) C605b/6+; mšmhmw C352/12; <u>d</u> mšmnhn C74/12; <u>p</u> mšmthmw J650/14+; <u>var</u> mšymt J615/10+; mšymthmw J613/22+

CULTIVATED FIELD

[Cf Ar šayām "plain," and phps also sawwāma[†] "arable field."]

C605b/6: dn mšmn...wkl tlhw wkl 'ṯlhw "this field and all its palms and tamarisks"; C343/12: kbr 'mwrtn [l]mšmthmw w[c]brthmw "he enlarged the retaining walls belonging to their fields and meadows"; C74/12: ydḇḥw bn mšmnhn "let him offer sacrifices (of the crops?) from the 2 fields"

ŠYN

v <u>pf</u> šyn R3991/7+

SUFFER an injury

[Cf Ar šāna (y) "disfigure, deform," Daṯ tšyyn "become ugly" (MüW/71).]

R3991/7: tšyn šyn rglhw "the injury his leg suffered"; J578/34: kl tšynt šyn "all the injuries he suffered"

h <u>pf</u> hšyn J620/6*

SUFFER an injury (= ŠYN <u>v</u>)

J620/5-6: the god saved His servant bn tšynt hšyn bn ''rx nhk ^{c}lyhmw šn'n "from the injuries he suffered from the troubles the enemy inflicted upon them"

n s tšyn(n) R3991/7+; p tšynt J578/34+ (D inf?)
INJURY
R3991/7, J578/34 quoted under ŠYN v; J620/5 quoted under ŠYN h

ŠY^c

n s šy^{c}hw C548/4*
GARMENT (?) (but see Note)
[Cf phps Eth šu^c "linen" > "garment."]
C548/4: hn lyngsn slḥhw wdmwm bšy^{c}hw "if he has defiled his weapons or there is blood on his garment (?)..."
Note: Another possible tr might be "attendants, suite" after šw^c "followers" (ŠW^c I n^1).

ŠKR

v pf škr J585/14; inf škr J576/1+
DEFEAT
[Cf phps Heb sikkēr "give into s.o.'s power" Is 19:4.]
J2107/8-9: škr wnqm wqtl whṯl^{c}n whsḥtn "defeating, taking vengeance on, killing, crushing and destroying"; J576/1: the god helped His servant bškr kl 'xms "in defeating all the troops"; Ir18/2: may the god continue škr wḍr^{c}n whkmsn "to defeat, subjugate and overthrow (the enemy)"

ti inf štkrn Ir18/2*
BE DEFEATED (or phps active, DEFEAT)
Ir18/2: the god granted that štkrn 'sd tnḍ^{c}w b^{c}ly mr'yhmw "the men were defeated who had sought a quarrel with their 2 lords"

tp pf tškr J585/15; tškrw J644/10+
BE DEFEATED (cf ŠKR ti)
J644/10: tškrw w^{c}yr hw' 'ysn...wš^{c}bn "that fellow and (his) tribe were defeated and disgraced"; J585/14-5: škr 'sn G...bkn ^{c}dw bḍrm wtškr h' 'sn "he defeated that fellow G....when he invaded in war and that fellow was defeated"

ŠLW--In fragmentary context R4784/2: ...]^{c}lt šlwn wlm[..., no tr. MüW/68 cfs Ar šilw "limb (of a sacrificial animal)."

ŠLṮ

n^1 cardinal number: f šlṯ(m,n) Ir34+; m šlṯt(n) J604/1-2+
THREE (cf later Sab ṯlṯ)
[Eth šalastu, Ar ṯalāṯ, ṯalāṯa† id.]
J604/1-2: šlṯtn 'ṣlmn "these three statues"; Ir34: šlṯn ṣlmtn "these three (f) statues"; R3945/1: šlṯt 'ḏbḥm "three sacrifices"; R3154/2: šlṯm ḏF

"the third day (lit., day three) of (the month) _d_F."

n[2] _s_ šl_t_n R4190/9+

ONE THIRD, THIRD PART OF (cf _t_l_t_ id)

[Ar _t_ul_t_ id.]

R4190/4,9: s͗ᶜbn SMᶜY [š]l_t_n _d_HGRm...ws͗ᶜbhmw YRSm šl_t_n _d_HGRm "the tribe S., one third of (the larger tribe) _d_H...their tribe Y., one third of _d_H."

n[3] _cardinal number_: šl_t_y R3943/2+

THIRTY (cf _t_l_t_nhn, _t_l_t_y id)

[Ar _t_alā_t_ūn id.]

R3943/2: _t_ll qnyhmw...'ḥd wšl_t_y 'lfm "plundered their livestock (to the number of) 31,000"; R4760A/2: š'mh šl_t_y r[... "he bought it (for?) thirty r..."

av šl_t_t'_d_ C366/2+

adv: THREE TIMES (?)

[Ug _t_l_t_'_d_ "three times"; cf for suffix -'_d_ Ar yawma'i_d_in "(on) that day."]

C366/2: hᶜ ḥrmtm šl_t_t'_d_ whwṣt kl gwn "he sacrificed in the sanctuary three times (?) and legitimized the whole community"; sim exp G1677

ŠM--See under ŠYM (for _n_ mšm, under ŠYM II)

ŠML

n _s_ šmlm C462/5*

EVIL OMEN

[Ar šamāl "evil omen" (BeOracle/220), cf šimāl "left hand."]

C462/5: _t_ny šmlm wš[ẓym] "a second evil omen or (injury caused by?) the e[vil eye?]"

ŠMS

n _s_ šms J761/4+; šmshw J853A/2; šmshmw J629/47+; _d_ šmsyhmw J664/20-1+; _p_ 'šms R4775/4+; 'šmshmw R4197b/3+

(1) SUN

[Ar šams id.]

J649/33: they fought bn šf šrqm ᶜdy mqtt šmsn "from the appearance of the rising sun until the setting of the sun"

(2) KIND OF PATRON DEITY = SUN GODDESS

[Cf also the _n.pr_ of a goddess, ŠMS (TNF), e.g. J854/4+.]

J761/4: bšms mlkn TNF "by the sun goddess of the king, T. (her _n.pr_)"; contrast J854/4: ŠMS TNF bᶜlt ǴḌRn "(the goddess) S.T., lady of Ǵ."; C40/5: brd' wmqmt...'šmshmw wmndḥt 'bythm[w] "by the help and power of their sun goddesses and the water gods of their families" AND ELSEWHERE SIM; C332/7: [']šms ''bwhmw "the sun goddesses of their (fore)fathers"

ŠMT

n _s_ šmt J581/18+

JOY IN OTHERS' MISFORTUNE, SCHADENFREUDE

[Ar šamāt id.]

J581/18: may the god protect them bn b'stm wnkytm wnḍ^{c} wtṯ^{c}t wšmt šn'm "from harm, injury, injury, abuse or Schadenfreude (on the part of any) enemy" AND ELSEWHERE SIM

ŠN'

n s šn'(m,n) R3991/16++; šn'hmy J652/20; šn'hmw R5099/2+

ENEMY

[Cf Heb śōnē' id, Ar šana'a "hate."]

R3991/16: may the god save His servants bn b'stm wnkym wnḍ^{c} wššy šn'm "from harm, injurer(s), injury or evil eye of (any) enemy" AND VERY OFTEN SIM; R5099/2: wl wḍ^{c} ḍrhmw wšn'hmw "and may (the god) lay low (any) foe or enemy of theirs" AND ELSEWHERE SIM

ŠNN I (?)

h inf hšnn C613/4* (but read more probably hśnn with C)

ESTABLISH (b- object)

[Cf Ar sanna "enact, establish (a law or custom)."]

C613/4: sṭry wsmy whšnn b'ṯwbt wgb'n "they wrote, are named in and established (the document prescribing) repayments and refunds"

ŠNN II

n s šnnm C548/12*

A MILK PRODUCT

[Ar šanīn "pure milk upon which cold water has been poured...any milk, whether fresh or collected in a skin...upon which water is poured" (Lane/1602C). Alternatively, cf modern Central Arabic shenna "skin of dates" (Doughty2, Index s.v.).]

C548/12: šnnm wdbsm wlbbm "šanīn, honey and cakes"

ŠNM

v pf šnm R5053/1; ipf yšnmn R3966/8

(1) BE PROSPEROUS

[Cf Ar snm Dt "rain copiously or abundantly (said of clouds)," sanim "(water) rising high" (Lane/1446-7). R on R3966 tr Ar snm "be raised; increase."]

R5053/1 (in full): šnm 'Y "'Y is prosperous (or, may 'Y be prosperous!)"

(2) CAUSE TO PRODUCE CROPS (said of a deity) (?)

R3966/8: wlḏt yšnmn lgrybthmw "and so that (the god?) may cause their terraced fields to produce crops"

ŠNF

n s šnf C540/15*

OPPOSITION; b-šnf: OPPOSITE, BESIDE, ABUTTING ON
[Cf Ar šanafa "look in a state of opposition, or resistance (at a thing)" (Irv/265).]
C540/15: ^cglmtn tbšnf m^cqmn "the diversion moles which abut on the overflow ledge"

ŠNQ

n[1] s šnqm F124/9*
AFFILIATED GROUP
[Cf Ar šaniqa "love, become attached to" (Lane/1607A, cf RyET/76).]
F124/9: dqhlm wšnqm "a member of the community or an affiliated group"

n[2] s šnqt(m,n) F30/3,4,5*
INDEBTEDNESS, AMOUNT OWED
[Cf Ar šanaq "blood price, in excess of the sum fixed by law" (Lane/1607C).]
F30/4: ^clm wšnqt dbhw t^clmy "document and indebtedness (= document recognizing indebtedness) which they signed"; ib/3: ^clmm wšnqtm; ib/5: ^clmn wšnqtn

Š^c--see under ŠW^c I

Š^cB

n s š^cb(n) J559/1+; š^cbhw J649/13+; š^cbhmw J558/7+; d š^cbnhn J555/3+; š^cbnn J716/3; š^cbnyhn R4196/1; š^cbynhn C326/1+; š^cbynhyn C40/1; š^cbyhmy Ir5/3; š^cbyhmw C40/6; p 'š^cb(m,n) J577/16+; 'š^cbhw J578/8+; 'š^cbhmy ib/31; 'š^cbhmw J643b/8; var? š^cb J635/11
TRIBAL GROUP organized on a political and territorial (not genealogical) basis (contrasted with ^cšrt), PEOPLE, COMMUNITY; p often TRIBESMEN
[Ar ša^cb "people, nation, tribe." Discussion of function in Sab society BeJESHO15/258).]
R4013/2: lwfy bythmw wš^cbhmw "for the well-being of their family and tribe"; R3958/12: they completed the work brd' wxyl š^cbhmw "with the aid and strength of their tribe"; R3951/3: mśwd ṢRWḤ wš^cbn ṢRWḤ "the assembly of Ṣ. and the tribe Ṣ."; R3910/2: š^cbn SB' 'b^cl hgrn MRB "the tribe S., citizens of the city M."; MüBilinguis/3: brd'...mr'hw...wbṣlt š^cbhw YŚR'L "with the aid of his Lord and the prayers of his (or, His?) community Israel"; Ir5/2: 'sd w'š^cb kyn kwnhmw "the soldiers and tribesmen who were with them"; J635/12: kl 'xms wš^cb "all the troops and tribesmen (?)"

Š^cW

tp pf tš^cww C308/8*
TAKE FOR ONE'S SELF, ACQUIRE (?) (but see Note)
[Cf phps Ar š^cw h bi- "watch upon" = "look after, take care of" (?) (HaAED/321).]
C308/8: kl ṣwrtn dQ...tš^cww ^cdy š'mt "all the palms of Q. (which) they had acquired (?) in the north"

Note: Alternatively, BePESA/16 cfs Ar ša^{cc}a "be split," ša^{c}ā "be scattered" and tr "irrigate" (taking ṣwrt in this case as "canals"). For n tš^{c}t C308/17, see under ŠW^{c} I.

Š^{c}Y

n s š^{c}y R3951/4*

FOLLOWERS, ALLIES (cf šw^{c} id under ŠW^{c} I)

[Prob connected with root ŠW^{c} I, q.v. (cf the Ar noun pattern fa^{c}lâ).]

R3951/4: all requisitions, wholesale purchases and transfers (of provisions) b^{c}m š^{c}y SB' bmsb'n "(effected) with the allies of S. on the road (i.e., in the field)"

For n tš^{c}t C308/17, see under ŠW^{c} I.

Š^{c}M

ti ipf yšt^{c}mhw R4970/2*

context fragmentary; RECONCILE (?)

[R cfs Ar š^{c}m id.]

R4970/2: ...] lyšt^{c}mhw b^{c}s[... "let him reconcile (?) him with..."

Š^{c}R I

v pf š^{c}r J720/13; š^{c}rt C532/8; š^{c}rw C429/7+; ipf tšr C532/9

KNOW, BE AWARE/CONSCIOUS OF

[Ar ša^{c}ara id.]

C429/7: men d̲bnhw 'l d^{c}w wš^{c}rw "of whom they did not know and were not aware"; C532/8-9: she committed sins 'l bhn š^{c}rt w'l lm tš(^{c})r "those of which she was conscious, and those she was not aware of"; J720/13: mrḍm ...d̲'l mn š^{c}r kmhn h' ḥlẓhw "a sickness (about) which no one knew what that disease of his was"

n s š^{c}rhmw J745/11*

KNOWLEDGE

[Ar ši^{c}r id.]

J745/11: the god protected the 2 horses bkn rkby...bl[t] š^{c}rhmw "when they were ridden without (their caretakers') knowledge"

Š^{c}R II

n s š^{c}rm J670/26-7+

BARLEY

[Ar ša^{c}īr id.]

J670/26-7: may the god grant them 't̲mrm w'fqlm sqym wbrm wš^{c}rm "crops and harvests (of) sqy-crops, wheat and barley"; also C540/40,87, fragmentary

ŠǴL

n p? šǵlm Ry509/8*

WORKERS (?)

[Cf Ar šaǵala "work."]
Ry509/8: 'ṣǵrt 'qwlhmw wšǵlm [wkl] mqtwthmw "their lesser chiefs, their workers (?), and all their officials"

ŠF--See under ŠWF, ŠFW

ŠFW

n <u>s</u> šf J649/32*
APPEARANCE, RISE of a heavenly body
[Ar šafā "appear (said of the new moon)."]
J649/32: they fought bn šf šrqm ^{c}dy mqṭṭ šmsn "from the appearance of the rising sun until sunset"

ŠF^{c}

n <u>s</u> šf^{c} J651/53*
INVASION (?) (note rhyming use with hf^{c})
[JSIMB/157 cfs Syr šfa^{c} "pour forth, overflow," šif^{c}o "flood."]
J651/53: may the god protect them from šf^{c} whf^{c} wṭw^{c} kl šn'm "invasion (?) and ...? and constraint of any enemy"

ŠFQ

h <u>pf</u> hšfq J665/27; hšfqhw R2861/20; <u>inf</u> hšfqn Sh18/2+; <u>pass</u>.<u>prt</u> mhšfq(m) Ir19+
ENRICH; as <u>aux</u>, DO ABUNDANTLY; <u>prt</u> mhšfq: ABUNDANT
[Cf Heb śāpaq "suffice."]
J665/27: they took as booty prisoners and livestock ḏhšfq gyšhmw "which enriched their army"; R2861/20: hšfqhw ṯmrn "(the god) enriched him with crops"; Sh18/2: wsqy whšfqn M "(the god) watered M. abundantly"; F71/17: sqym mhšfqm "abundant irrigation water"; Ir19: 'ṯmr ṣdqm hn'm mhšfqm "satisfying, pleasing, abundant crops"

n <u>s</u> šfqm J649/41+
ABUNDANCE; as <u>adv</u>, ABUNDANTLY
J649/41: ǵnmw...gmlm wbqrm wḍ'nm šfqm "they took as booty camels, cattle and sheep, an abundance (i.e., an abundance of camels, etc)"; J691/9: wl [s]^{c}dhmw 'ṯmrm šfqm "may (the god) grant them crops, an abundance (i.e., an abundance of crops)"; J735/14: sqy kl 'nxln...šfqm "(the god) watered all the palmgroves abundantly"

ŠFR

n <u>s</u> šfr C434/9+; šfrhw ib
LABOR FORCE, CORVÉE FORCE (?)
[Cf Ar šifra† "servant," Akk šapartu "security for a debt" (CoRoC/251B).]
C434/6-14: qtdmhmw N...qdmn bšfrhw wšfr W...w'A...wN whrd'hmw šfr W "N. was in charge of them, commanding his own labor force (?) and the force(s)

of W., A. and N.; and the labor force of W. aided them"; R2747/3: šfr Ḥ bn 'dm bn Š "the labor force of Ḥ., (composed) of the clients of the b.Š."

ŠFT

v <u>pf</u> šft J698/9+; šfthw J582/6+; šfthmw C73/6-7+; šftt J743/6+; šftthw J717/4; šftw J641/7-8+; <u>inf</u> šft(n) J627/9+

(1) PROMISE; of a god, phps DECREE of the like

[Prob denom from the biradical <u>n</u> *šft "lip" (not attested in Sab, but cf Ar šafa†, Heb śāfāh, Sq ŝebeh id).]

J698/9: he dedicated this statue ḥgn šft 'bhw "as his father had promised"; J717/4: šftthw 'mthw...km^c^nmw yxmrnhw ḥyw lhw wldm thqnynhw "His maidservant promised (the god) that if He would allow a child to survive for her, she would dedicate"; C333/14-6: wT'LB fyz'n šft wtbšrn ^c^bdhw...[mng]t ṣdqm "as for (the god) T., may He continue to promise/decree and announce to His servant happy outcomes"; C73/6-7: hwfyhmw 'LMQH ṣrb šfthmw "(the god) I. granted them the harvest He had promised/decreed (for) them"

(2) SEEK an oracular response or decree

Ir14/1: 'ml'...stml'w wšftn b^c^mhw "the oracular responses they asked and sought from (the god)"; sim ib/2

n <u>s</u> šft R3945/14+; šfthmw ib/16

(1) PROMISE, oracular DECREE

R3945/14: ygn' gn'm...bšft ^c^T̲TR "he built the wall by the decree of (the god) A."; N15/18-20: kl ṣry wtbšr wšft wtxwd ṣry wšft wxwdn wtbšr "every decision, announcement, promise and favor which (the god) took, promised, granted and announced"; in a pejorative sense, NNAG11/32: nḍ^c^ wšṣy wšft w'^c^wf wṭw^c^ šn'm "injury, evil eye, adverse oracular decree (?), pestilences and subjection (brought about by) an enemy"

Note: RycMancie/271-2n2 tr "conspiracy, plot" after Ar šfh <u>L</u> "confer, have an interview with s.o."

(2) STATE OF BEING PROMISED = DEDICATION (?)

R3945/16: 'l wḍ't šfthmw nsrn 'l'ltn "those whose dedication to the gods (i.e., those who had been promised to the gods?) was allotted"

ŠṢY

v <u>ipf</u> yšṣyn C2/18-9+; yšṣynn C313/4+

INJURY BY MEANS OF THE EVIL EYE (<u>b-</u> s.o.)

[Ar šaṣâ "stare fixedly," Central Ar šaẓâ "attack" (MüW/67).]

C2/18-9: kl ḍrhw [wšn'h]mw <u>d</u>yšṣyn bhmw "any foe or enemy of theirs who may injure them by means of the evil eye"

n <u>s</u> šṣy R3991/16+; <u>p/var</u> šṣyt C411/8+ (contexts same as for šṣy)

EVIL EYE, INJURY CAUSED BY THE EVIL EYE (cf šẓy, <u>var</u> spelling)

[Cf Ar šaṣw "hardship, distress, adversity" (Lane/1548B) and ŠṢY <u>v</u>.]

R3991/16: may the god save His servants bn b'stm wnkym wnḍ^c^ wšṣy šn'm "from harm, injurer(s), and the injury or evil eye of (any) enemy" AND OFTEN SIM; J747/18 (context fragmentary): may the god injure (?) their enemies bšṣy sw'm "by the dire evil eye (?)"

ŠṢN

v <u>inf</u> šṣnn C540/28; [š]ṣnhw C541/III-2; <u>maṣdar</u> šṣnm C540/8,73

FACE WITH STONE

[Cf Dat maššan "stone parapet at the end of the primary irrigation canal," šaṣna "mole" (Irv/255-7).]

C540/8: ᶜdbhw msrm wšṣnm "repaired it, packing earth and facing with stone"; ib/73: msrm wšṣnm b''bnm "packing earth and facing with stone"; C541/III-2: ḥrrw ᶜrmn wmsrhw [wš]ṣnhw "they raked up earth for the dam and packed it and faced it with stone"

n <u>p</u> 'šṣnhw R3958/3

STONE FACING or REVETMENTS

R3958/3: they built all the aqueduct of their valley wkl nqbthw w'šṣnhw w'b'rhw "and all its channels, revetments and wells"

ŠṢṢ

n <u>s</u> šṣṣm F30/6+

<u>adj</u>: PROHIBITIVE

[Ar šṣṣ <u>L</u> "forbid, prohibit" (RyET/22).]

G1533/7: tᶜlm...b'd[m] wnfqm wšṣṣm kl ẓhr "signed as public, binding and prohibitive each document"; F30/6: wl yknn h' ᶜlmn...x(y)dm wbdlm whqqm wšṣṣm wxdᶜm "let this document be restrictive and conceding, legally binding, prohibitive and constraining"

ŠQR

v <u>inf</u> šqr R4627/2+

BUILT TO THE TOPS OF THE WALLS, COMPLETE a building

[Cf Akk šaqāru, zaqāru "erect a wall," ModYem mušgurī "flower wreath worn on the head" (RoVoc/313). Last stage of building, contrasted with hwtr "lay the foundation."]

R4627/2: ᶜs'w wbny whwtr wšqr ḥrtn "constructed, built, laid the foundation for and completed the aqueduct"

Note: In all complete examples the object is ḥrt "aqueduct," except F61/2, which parallels G1100/1 except for the omission of ḥrt.

h <u>pf</u> hšqrw J671/17; <u>inf</u> hšqr(n) R4196/2+

BUILD TO THE TOP > COMPLETE a building (cf ŠQR <u>v</u>)

R4196/2: br'w whwtr whšqr m'glyhmw "they built, laid the foundation for and completed their 2 cisterns" AND OFTEN SIM; J671/17: y'fqn lhmw dᶜbn ᶜdy hšqrw nklhmw "(the god) restrained the floodwaters until they had completed their paving" n[1] s šqr(m,n) C374+

TOP of a construction, esp a wall

C374: he dedicated kl tml' gn'n ln 'wdn dsṭrn ᶜdy šqrm "all the fill of the wall from the line (marked by) this inscription to the top"; R4626/1: they built their control-dyke bn mwṯrm ᶜdy šqrm "from the foundation to the top" AND OFTEN SIM

n[2] s tšqr C338/3* (D inf?)

COMPLETION

C338/3: he dedicated himself ym tqdm tšqr kwrn wmhyᶜ "on the day he took charge of the completion of the fire altar and sanctuary"

ŠR--See under ŠWR

ŠRG

n p šrghmw C547/9*

WATERCOURSES

[Ar šarj "place where water flows," ModYem šarīg "canal" (RoVoc/313).]

C547/9: fgr šrghmw mn mwm qllm "(the god) made their watercourses flow with little water"

ŠRḤ

v pf šrḥ R4624/5+; šrḥhw J576/14; ipf yšrḥn J702/5+; inf šrḥ(n) N15/6+

MAINTAIN IN GOOD SHAPE > PROTECT, SAFEGUARD, SAVE

[Eth šarḥa "cause to succeed; prosper"; ModYem and Ḥaḍ šaraḥ "protect, guard; deposit (money)" (RycMancie/265n1).]

R4624/5: ywm šrḥ SB' wmsb'hmw bdr "the day (the god) protected S. and its expedition in the battle"; N15/6: hᶜn wšrḥ wmtᶜn "helped, protected and saved"; J670/15: may the god continue to šrḥ grb ᶜbdhw bn kl mrḍm wnkytm "safeguard the body of His servant against all sicknesses and injuries"

ti pf štrḥt C334/13; inf štrḥn J564/13

KEEP SAFE, PROTECT (cf ŠRḤ v)

C334/13: ḥrt mlkn...wwfyt wštrḥt "as for the king's camp, it was kept safe and protected"; J564/13: they dedicated because stwfy wštrḥn wstkmln lmr'hmw...kl mngt wqhhmw "the god granted and kept safe and brought to completion for their lord all the matters (wherein) he had commanded them"

n[1] s šrḥtm J658/12+

PROTECTION, SECURITY

J658/12: their lord commanded them lrtᶜ šrḥtm bhgrn "to establish security in the city"; NNAG13-4/1: lšrḥt mlkhmw bywm hšt'...bᶜlyhmw "for the protection of their domain when he began hostilities against them"

Note also C350/8 (fragmentary context): tqdm šrḥt [...] ᶜrbn "fought in safety (?) against the beduins"?

n[2] p šrḥthmy R2726/17*

EXPLICATION, EXPLANATORY DOCUMENT

[Ar šarḥ id.]
R2726/17: ywfyn š'mtm w'ṯwbtm ḥg '[s]ṭrhmy wšrḥthmy "to pay the purchase (prices) and payments according to their documents and explications"

ŠRY

v inf? šry Gl366/4*
SAVE (?)
[Cf Eth šaraya "cure."]
Gl366/4 (fragmentary context): ...] wšry xrfn q[... "and saved (?) the autumn harvest..."

h inf hšryn C313/3*
CURE, KEEP HEALTHY > SAVE, PROTECT (cf ŠRY v)
C313/3: h^{c}n wmt^{c}n whšryn bn hwt 'nsm "helped, saved and protected from that man" (context fragmentary)

ŠRK

v pf šrkw R3951/5; inf šrk ib/3
(1) SHARE OUT, APPORTION
[Ar šarika "share, be a partner."]
R3951/3: xrṣ wšrk wrzm b^{c}mhmw wrqm wd^{c}tm "assessing, apportioning and commandeering from then greenstuff and fodder"; ib/4-5: kl xrṣ wšrk wmnṣḥ ...bhmw šrkw wxrṣ "all assessments, apportionments and demands whereby they apportion and assess (the foodstuffs)"
(2) ASSOCIATE WITH (?)
[Cf esp in this context the Islamic doctrine of širk "polytheism," the "associating" of partners with the One God.]
C539/3: let him make an offering wbn šrk lmr'm bb'sm "and (?) against anyone who associates (partners?) with the Lord, maliciously"

n p šrk R3951/4*
APPORTIONMENT
R3951/4 quoted under ŠRK v

ŠRM

n p 'šrm[t]n C380/3-4*
CHANNELS, GUTTERS (?)
[Cf Ar šarama "split, cleave," šarm "cleft; small bay, inlet."]
C380/3-4: lbt[h]mw wl brkthmw lywfyn 'šrm[t]n lbrktn "for their house and for their cistern, to keep safe the gutters (?) for the cistern" (context fragmentary)

ŠRS

h inf/pf hšrshw R3945/15-6*
ERADICATE, RAZE

[Cf Heb šērēš "root up/out."]
R3945/15-6: nḍw gn' hgrhw N ^{c}d hšrshw "he demolished the wall of his city N. until he had razed it"

n s šrsm R4799; šrshmw R4126/2+

(1) BEGINNING

[Ar širš "root," Min 'šrs "foundations (of a building)" (R3022/1).]
R4126/2: b]n šrshmw [... "(at) the beginning of their (eponymate)"

(2) FOUNDATION (?)

R4799 (fragment): ln šrsm "to the foundation (?)"

Note: RycER3/285, discussing LuDopol, cites this form from a list of eponyms.

ŠR^{c}

v pf šr^{c}w C660/3-4+; inf šr^{c}n R4198/2

(1) ERECT buildings

[Cf Ar šr^{c} ẖ "lift, raise," ModḤaḍ šarī^{c} "high."]
C660/3-4: wšr^{c}w kl mḏqn 'bythmw "they erected all the oratories of their houses" (or tr as sense², as in F74 below)

(2) PROVIDE a well WITH LIFTING GEAR > PROVIDE WATER FOR a settlement

[Cf MSA tešrū^{c}ah "apparatus for raising water from a well" (HuZfA26/224) and Ar šarī^{c}a^{t} "water hole."]
R4198/2: hbḥr wḍfr wšr^{c}n b'rhmw "excavated, cased with stone and provided with lifting gear their well"; F74/2: wz'w šr^{c}w bythmw...ṯty nb'n ḏhbm wkl ḏhbn ḏšr^{c}w bytyhmw "they continued to provide water for their house (from) 2 terraces, irrigated land, and all the irrigated land (from) which they provided water for their 2 houses"

n¹ s šr^{c}hw R3910/6+; p šr^{c} Ir12/3; var šr^{c}tm J555/4; var 'šr^{c}hmw J651/26

(1) JUST DUE, (JUST) PAYMENT

[Eth šer^{c}at, Ar šar^{c} id.]
R3910/6: if a purchased animal dies, the seller is not liable; wl yfyn lmhš'mn šr^{c}hw "and let (the buyer) pay to the seller his just due"; C291/5: they refused to pay an increase in tribute, fl yxbn bn šr^{c}hw "so let it be lacking from (H.'s) just payment"; J555/4: hṯb lhw S t'mnm wšr^{c}tm wmxḍnm "S. rendered to (the god) a thank-offering and payments and a gift"

(2) PORTION, ARTICLE of booty (?)

[Extension to articles which belong to the soldier by "right" of conquest? (Cf proposed connection of 'ḥll "booty" with Ar ḥalāl "legitimate.")]
J651/26: 'l ḏfqdw bn 'šr^{c}hmw kbr rḥlm "they missed nothing from their articles of booty of the size (?) of a camel saddle"; Ir12/3: ^{c}sm šr^{c}...tmlyw "a number of articles of booty which they took"

n² s šr^{c}t(m) C308b/5+; p šr^{c} C308/8-9+

SMALL WATER CHANNEL

[Cf Ar šarī^{c}a^{t} "watering place."]

C308/8-9: wk[l mhw]kbhmw krrm wšr^{c} qšmtn w'hdrhw w'kfrhw wṣwrthw "and all their estates all together and the channels of the orchard and its cisterns, sluices and ṣwrt-equipment"; C308b/5: kl 'nhr wbqlt ^{c}dy šr^{c}t '^{c}mdn "all the channels and vegetable gardens as far as the šr^{c}t-channels of the irrigated lands"; F80: šr^{c}tm lmqn^{c} bthmw "a channel to supply their house (with water)"

n^{3} s mšr^{c}(m,n) C949/1+; mšr^{c}hmw J650/16

REGULATION, or CULTIVATED (i.e., IRRIGATED) LAND

[Cf Ar šara^{c}a "enact laws"; or, if mšr^{c} indicates a kind of land, phps it is derived from an original sense "legally defined (territory)." Otherwise, cf ŠR^{c} v and mštr^{c} below.]

J650/16: 'rḍhmw mšrqm w^{c}ltm wmšr^{c}hmw "their land, eastern and highland, and their cultivated land"; C949/1: mšr^{c}m bt^{c}mm bt^{c}br wṯnn "(This is) a regulation (or, a piece of land subject to regulation), regarding the announcement of the delimitation of this boundary"; sim R4514/1

n^{4} s mštr^{c}n C308/7*

LAND WATERED BY ŠR^{c} (lifting gear, i.e. wells)

C308/7: kl 'hdr mstqyn wmštr^{c}n "all the channels of the canal-irrigated and well-irrigated lands"

ŠRQ

n^{1} s šrq(m) J649/32,33*

(1) RISING of a star; (2) RISING SUN

[Ar šaraqa "rise (a heavenly body)," šurūq "(sun)rise," šarīq "rising sun."]

J649/32-3: they fought bn šf šrqm ^{c}dy mqṭt šmsn wlyl lylm ^{c}dy šrq kwkbn ḏsbḥn "from the appearance of the rising sun until sunset and all night long until the rising of the morning star"

n^{2} s šr[qn] R4159/1*

EAST

[Ar šarq, mašriq "east; eastern land."]

R4159/1: ...]tm bsn šr[qn "in the direction of the ea[st] (?)"

Note: Cf also the common epithet of the god ^{c}ṮTR, ŠRQN (J559/20++).

n^{3} s mšrq(m,n) J650/16+; mšrqhmw Ry502/2; p mšrqt J576/7 twice; mšrqthmw Ir22

EAST, EASTERN TERRITORY; phps also a technical term for a kind of (low-lying?) cultivated land, contrasted with ^{c}lt "highland"

J650/16: 'ṯmr...^{c}dy kl 'rḍhmw mšrqm w^{c}ltm "crops from all their lands, eastern and highland"; also with ^{c}lt Ir19,22; C555/3: ymxrw 'ln 'wṯnn nsr mšrqn wnsr m^{c}rbn "let these boundary stones face toward the east and toward the west"; Ry502/2: sb'w...^{c}dy mšrqhmw "they campaigned in their eastern territory (or, east of their own land?)"

n^{4} adj: m.s mšrqy C132/2+; f.s mšrqytn C572/2-3; f.p? mšrqytn J629/27

EAST OF, EASTERN; f.p POINTS EAST, EASTERN TERRITORIES (?)

[Ar mašriqī "eastern."]

X-T

T I

ab t R4172/5*

ABBREVIATION FOR THE NUMBER FOUR

[Usage derives from the shape of OSA character t: X ; sim in Nab.]

R4172/5: the palmgrove d[...] sz ▯ t ▯ ᶜ[... "which...4, 10 (?)"

T II

rl t- R4194/3+

relative pn, f.s and p: (THAT, THOSE) WHICH

[Cf the element -t- in Ar 'allati "that (f) which" and other f pns.]

R4194/3: 'rḍhmw tbsrn Ẓ "their land which is in the valley Ẓ."; ib/4: ᶜśbth]my tᶜtk nxlyhmw "their [hired fields] which are in the direction of their 2 palmgroves"; C540/14-5: ᶜglmtn tbšnf mᶜqmn "the diversion moles which abut on the overflow ledge"

T'--For v yt'nn F123/9-10, see under W'Y ti

T'W--For v t'w R3945/3, see under 'WY tp

T'K--Doubtful exp kt'k C540/68. Many analyses have been proposed, none very satisfying; e.g., some havé taken this form as a tp of the root N'K, cf Eth ne'ka, Heb nā'aq "moan, groan," but this reading would be syntactically confusing. The passage reads: rᶜẓm hrᶜẓhmw kṭ'k hwqlw 'šᶜb "the command he gave them when...(?) the tribes were in confusion."

T'L--For v t'l R4176/12, see under 'WL tp

TBᶜ

v pf tbᶜt R4069/8*

BE̜ COMPLETED, or AMOUNT TO (?)

[Cf Ar tbᶜ L "he made (his work) sound, or free from defect," or Aram təbaᶜ "demand." According to Irv/176-7, the subject is a word for "length."]

R4069/8: nqbw nqb tb^{c}t [... "they cut a channel, (the length of which) amounted to..."

N inf ntb^{c}n J630/8-9*

aux, DO INCESSANTLY or INSISTENTLY

[Cf Ar tb^{c} ti, tp "pursue incessantly, ask insistently," Lt "repeat, do s.th. incessantly" (RycHim2/484).]

J630/8-9: bkl 'ml' ystml'n wntb^{c}n b^{c}mhw "all the oracle responses (which) they ask of (the god) incessantly"

Note: J read as tp of root NB^{c}, tr "to express" after "Semitic" nb^{c} "spring, gush" (SIMB/131).

n s mtb^{c}m R4133/5*

SUFFECTUS, substitute who fills out the term of an office vacated by a death or resignation (?)

[Ar tabi^{c}a "follow, succeed." Discussion BeESACD/33-4.]

R4133/5: xrf N bn 'A [bn...] mtb^{c}m ṯnyn "the year (named for) N., son of A., [son of ...], the suffectus, the second (year of his eponymate)"

Note: Be suggests alternatively that the second year of N.'s eponymate may here be described as "following" immediately upon his first, cf Ar mutatābi^{c} "coming in uninterrupted succession."

TBR--For n mtbrm R2861/[2], see under BRR I n^{2}

THM

n^{1} d thmy R4626/1*

LOW-LYING FIELDS at the foot of the hills on the two sides of a wadi

[Cf etymology under THM n^{2}.]

R4626/1: msqt 'nxlhmw wthmy 'ly bḍr^{c}n "the irrigation of their palmgroves and the 2 low-lying fields which (lie) on the west"

n^{2} s thmt R3193+

COASTAL PLAIN = the Tihāma

[Ar Tihāma^{t}, the coastal plain along the southwestern and southeastern shores of the Arabian peninsula. Etymologically, cf phps Akk tiamtu, Heb təhôm "(the) deep; abyss" > "low-lying lands"?]

R3193: 'hl thmt wṭwdm "people of the coastal plain and the hill-country/ highlands"; C540/6: '^{c}rbhmw ṭwdm wthmt "their beduins of the highlands and the coastal plain" AND SIM FORMULAS ELSEWHERE

TWR

n^{1} p twrthw C308b/7*

OUTLETS (?)

[Cf Ar tāra (w) "flow (of water)" (Lane/322B).]

C308b/7: šr^{c} qšmtn wtwrthw "the irrigation system of the orchard and its outlets (?)"

Note: MüW/33 cfs Egyptian twr "repel" and supposed cognates, and translates "rampart."

n[2] s mtrm N66/2*

CISTERN or DRINKING-TROUGH (?)

[Cf Ar tawr "drinking vessel of brass or stone" (Lane/322C; cf RyNE4/167).]

N66/2: hwṯry whšqrn mtrm [... "they laid the foundation for and completed a cistern/drinking-trough (?)"

TWṮM--For twṯm R4779/1, cf tw[.]m R3440/1 (same inscription)--context obscure, no tr. Read phps, with R, t^c lm.

THT

pp tḥt J578/22+; tḥtn F121; tḥty C973/6+; b-tḥty C461/9-10+; bn tḥty R3945/12-3; bn tḥt C971/1

(1) UNDER

[Cf Ar taḥta, Heb taḥtay id.]

C971/1: bn tḥt ḏn wṯnn "below this boundary stone"

(2) UNDER or BY THE AUTHORITY OF; ON THE INITIATIVE OF

J578/22: tdr^cn...tḥt mr'yhmw "to submit under their lord"; F121: tnhḍ(w) tḥtn byt X "they were under the authority of (= tributary to?) the clan X."; C461/9-10: ṣry S btḥty ^cṮTR "S. delivered an oracle response by the authority/inspiration of (the god) A."

n[1] For n tḥyt C40/3, read tḥẓt; see under ḤẒY

n[2] adj tḥtyn R3955/3+

LOWER, LOWEST

R3954/2: bny rb^c qbrn...ḥwln ḏbynn ḏtḥtyn "he built a quarter of the tomb, the tiers of loculi of the interior chamber: namely that which is the lowest (tier)"; sim context R3955/3

TYM--For n tymm C126/4, see under TMM

TL

n p tlhw C605b/6*

KIND OF PALM, phps YOUNG PALM

[Cf Akk tālu "palm shoot," J.Aram tā'lā' "kind of palm," Ar tāl Borassus flabellifer, "Palmyra palm" (MüW/33).]

C605b/6: this field wkl tlhw wkl 'ṯlhw "and all its tl-palms and tamarisks"

Note: For n tlt C373, see under TLL.

TLW

v ipf ytlwn C518/4+; ytlwnn DJE10/3; inf NNAG1/10

(1) FOLLOW; as aux, CONTINUE to do

[Ar talā, Eth talawa id.]

DJE10/3: lytlwnn wlṣq kl 'ns "let them follow and seize any man who ...";

NNAGI/10: lwz' 'LMQH hwfy...wl tlwn h^c^nnhw "may (the god) l. continue to protect and continue to help him"

(2) PAY TRIBUTE to, BE TRIBUTARY to (but see Note)

[Cf Ar tlw h "transfer a debt from one to another," tulāwa† "residue of a debt" (Irv/69).]

C518/4: 'rḍ ytlwn lmlk SB' "land tributary to the king of S."; C588b/6: wl ytlwn ^c^TTR bmrtd "let him pay tribute to (the god) A., consisting of the offering"

Note: For these contexts, another possible etymology is from Ar waliya "administer," Dt "be appointed to an office, concern one's self with," ti "have under one's direction." The tr would be "administer" or the like; C518/4 "the land he will administer for the king of S.," C588b/6 "let A. concern himself with/take charge of the offering." BeStl/96 tr "lands [cf Ar 'araḍi] which belong" after Ar Dt "take possession."

n s tly J584/l; p 'tly Ry509/8-9; tlwt C743/l; 'tlwt J745/2+

FOLLOWER > SERVANT > OFFICER; phps specifically GROOM, EQUERRY

[Cf Ar talā "follow." When horses are specifically mentioned, cf phps also Te talāy "herdsman, of horses" (HöRev/425).]

Ry509/8-9: mqtwthmw w'tlyhmw "their officials and their officers"; J584/l: tly 'frs mlkn "officer (in charge of)/equerry of the king's horses"; same title, p, J745/2; Ir32: 'tlwt rkbt 'frsm "equerries of the mounts of the cavalry"

TLY--For ns tly, 'tly, see under TLW n

TLL

n s tlt C373* (C emended to zlt)

RUBBISH DUMP (?)--but read prob zlt, see under ZLL

[Cf Heb tēl "rubbish heap" (MüBeitrage/316).]

C373: hḥdty tlt nkl gwbn "they restored/rebuilt the rubbish dump (?) (or, fortification) (with) pebbled stonework"

TLF

v pf tlf J700/14*

PERISH, BE STRUCK DEAD

[Ar talafa "perish, pass away."]

J700/14: t^c^ṣrw bynhmw bšzbn wtlf R bn ydyhw "they struggled back and forth with the dagger and R. was struck dead on the spot"

h inf htlfn F71/19+

CAUSE TO PERISH

F71/19: lwḍ^c^ whtlfn kl ḍrhmw "to lay low and cause to perish their every foe"; C155/4: wl tbr wht[l]f[n w]hlqḥn wḍr^c^n "to crush, cause to perish, capture and defeat" n s tlftm J567/27+

LOSS, LOSS OF LIFE (?)

[Cf Ar talaf "loss, ruin," Heb talpiyôt "deadly things."]

J567/27: may the god save them from b'stm wnkytm...wtlftm wxybtm "harm, injury, loss and famine"; sim context J636/18, J739/18

TLT--For n tlt C373, see under TLL

TMM

n s tymm C126/4*

PERPETUITY; as adv, IN PERPETUITY (?)

[Cf Ar tāmm "complete" and other derivatives of the root tmm; BeMus64/308 describes this as a fay^{c}al form (i.e., both ms are radical).]

C126/4: mn dlhw yr[y]śn [S]B' wstwḍ' tymm "anyone with respect to whom S. makes a decree (so that thereby) he is proclaimed an outlaw in perpetuity (or, completely) (?)..."

TMS--Read tms in C40/2 prob as n.pr, as in R3946/1. HöWZ41/87 associated this word with Heb ms, tr "corvée," but the context is unhelpful and the sibilant is incorrect.

TMR

n p/coll tmrm C541/121+

DATES

[Ar tamr (coll) id.]

C541/121: tmn m'tm wsdtm dqqm wstt w^{c}šry ''lfm tmrm "806 (measures) of flour and 26,000 dates"; C540/40-1: thn[m...] wbrm wš^{c}[rm wt]mrm "flour... wheat, barley and dates"; ib/50-1: mzrm dtmrm "date-beer"

TNX--For n tnxtn C547/15, see under NXY I n

TS^{c}

n^{1} cardinal number: f ts^{c}(m,n) R3104/3-4+; m ts^{c}t C325/5

NINE

[Ar tis^{c}, tis^{c}a^{t} id.]

R3104/3-4: bywm ts^{c}m dT "on the ninth day (lit., Day Nine) of (the month) T"; C325/5: xrfn dlts^{c}t wsty wst m'tm "the year 696"

Note: For ywm t(s)^{c}m R3101/[1]-2, BeESACD/38 reads the n.pr [Y]F^{c}m.

n^{2} s ts^{c}n J735/5*

NINTH

[Ar tāsi^{c} id.]

J735/5: xrf T...ts^{c}n "the year (named for) T., the ninth (year of his eponymate)"

n^{3} cardinal number: ts^{c}y J577/15+

NINETY

[Ar tis^{c}ūn id.]

J577/15: sb^c wts^{c}y 'b'rm "ninety-seven wells"; C448/6: xrfn d̲lst̲t wts^{c}y m'nm "the year 396"

T^{c}BYD̲D--In R3116, only word in inscription, no tr

T^{c}TK--For t^{c}tk R4194/4, see under 'TK

TFL--For v tfl, see under FLY tp, FLL tp

TFT̲

n p? C563/2* tft̲

KIND OF OFFERING, LUSTRATION (?)

[Cf Ar tafat̲ "one of the rites and ceremonies of the pilgrimage" (Lane/308A), but described variously by the Arab lexicographers.]

C563/2: kl 'kl wmsty wtft̲ yh'twn "all the food, drink and lustrations (?) they will offer"

TQH--For v tqh, see under WQH ti

TQY--For v [y]tqynn R4784/5, see under NQY ti

TQR--For n tqr, see under QYR

TRD--For v trdn R2876/6, see under WRD tp

TRḤ

n s trḥ Ry585+

REDEMPTION, RECOMPENSE for favors received from the god

[Cf Ug trḫ "pay a bride's dowry; marry" (RycER2/155). Discussion of the date formula in which this word appears, RycRepas/328.]

Ry585: ywm 'lm ^{c}T̲TR...whnrhw btrḥ "the day he held a ritual banquet for (the god) A. and made him a burnt offering by way of recompense"; same formula R4129, R4906/2, and phps elsewhere

TRX

h pf htrx J2834/1

FIX/DRAW A BOUNDARY-LINE

[Ar taraxa "make a light incision" (JaCM/12).]

J2834/1: whtrx d̲n wt̲n[n] b^{c}ly wt̲n nxln "and this boundary-line was drawn along the boundary of the palm grove"

TRM--For btrm C581/8, see under BTRM

TR^c

v pf tr^c R5055+

TURN ASIDE (?)

[Cf Ar tara^{c}a "avert, turn (s.o.) back" (Lane/303B). The Sab usage is presumably intransitive.]

R5055 (in full): tr^c msbl "he turned aside on/from the road"; R5056 (in full): tr^{c}h' "that one (?) turned aside"

TRF

v ipf ytrfn C975/6*

REMAIN

[Eth, Tña tarafa id.]

C975/6: nxlm dT ^{c}brn Ẓ wbyn dytrfn lG "the palmgrove of T. toward Ẓ. and the surrounding district which remains (in the possession of) G."

TŠ'--For v ytš'n C308/13, see under NŠ' ti

T$\underline{T}^c$--For n t$\underline{t}^c$t, see under $\underline{T}^c$Y n I

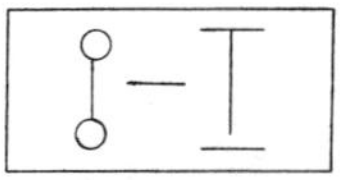

Ṯ'R

v pf ṯ'r C344/7+; ṯ'rhw J725/8

WREAK VENGEANCE, TAKE BLOOD REVENGE

[Ar ṯa'ara id.]

J725/7-8: zxn w'ṯ['r] twṯbhw wṯ'rhw "the wounds and acts of vengeance he inflicted (?) and wreaked on him"; C344/7: the god saved him bn ṯ'r ṯ'r "from the revenge he took (i.e., from being killed in retaliation for the revenge he took?)"; same exp C347/7

n s ṯ'r Ry405/1-2+ p 'ṯ['r] J725/7-8

(1) ACT OF VENGEANCE

J725/7-8, C344/7 quoted under Ṯ'R v

(2) REPLICA, IMAGE

[Phps sense derives from the idea of vengeance as a "reply" to a previous act.]

Ry405/1-2: ṯ'r wnfs "image and funerary stela"

ṮB, see under WṮB, ṮWB

ṮBN--For hṯbn see under ṮWB h

ṮBR

v pf ṯbry J581/8; ṯbrw J576/4; ipf yṯbrw J601/9; pass.pf ṯbr J671/12,13; ṯbrt ib/11; inf ṯbr R3884/4+; ṯbrh R3945/5; prt ṯbrhw F119/14

BREAK s.th.; CRUSH an enemy

[Heb šābar "break," Ar ṯabara "destroy, ruin."]

R4775/3: mṯ]br[n] ḏt ṯbr wxd^{c}n hwt m'xḏn "the breach which broke and injured that control dam"; J671/11-2: ṯbrt ^{c}rmn...wṯbr kl mḍrfn...wṯbr bn ^{c}rmn sb^{c}y šwḥṭm "the dam was broken and all the revetment was broken, and seventy spans were broken off the dam"; F119/14: they placed it under the god's protection bn ṯbrhw wf()'lhw "against (any)one who would break it or wish it ill"; C573/5: lwḍ^c wṯbr wmn^c w'xrn kl ḍrhmw "to lay low, crush, repel and drive back their every foe" AND SEVERAL TIMES SIM; R3945/5: mxḍ T wṯbrh wwfṭh "he overthrew T. and broke it and burned it"

h pf hṯbrt R4069/6*

BREAK, DESTROY (cf ṮBR v)

R4069/6: they repaired the irrigation system b^{c}dn hṯbrt wśḥb kl [^{c}]q[rhw] "after all its dam wall was broken and eroded"

n^1 s ṯbrm J643b/4*

DESTRUCTION, DEFEAT of the enemy = VICTORY (maṣdar of ṮBR v?)

J643b/4: they returned from campaign [b..] wṯbrm wmlqḥtm "(with) ... and victory and captives (?)'

n^2 s mṯbr(m) C334/11-2+; p mṯbrtn C541/61

(1) BREACH

C541/61: to repair the dam wmṯbrtn ḏb MRB "and the breaches which were in M."; F71/9: the area A. was saved bn kl [m]ṯbrm wmngwm ḏyhǵllnhmw "from any breach or event which might have injured them"; and cf R4775/3 quoted under ṮBR v

(2) DEFEAT (cf ṮBR n^1)

C334/11-2: they expelled the tribe from the camp sḥtm wmṯbrm "(with) destruction and defeat"

ṮBT

n s? 'ṯbt N52/4+

PERMANENCE, or n.pr; or, as adj: ENDURING (?)

[Ar ṯābit "firm, enduring"; ṯabāt "permanence."]

N52/4: [šm]y mqbrhmw 'ṯbt "they established their tomb (as a place of?) permanence (?)"; C468/2: [mqbr]hmw rbxm 'ṯbt "their (tomb), (a place of) rest (and?) permanence"

Lack of mimation makes 'ṯbt syntactically difficult.

ṮHB

v pf ṯhbhmw J576/14+; ṯhbw J631/14; inf ṯhbhmw J616/15+

BRING BACK

[Var of root ṮWB, cf Ar ṯāba (w) "return, come back"?]

J576/14: he gathered (troops) together wṯhbhmw nkfm "and brought them back as a militia"; sim J643/8; J631/14: ṯhbw mr'hmw...bkl blthmw ^{c}mn ngšyn mṯbt ṣdqm "they brought back (to?) their lord, in all their missions to the Negus, a satisfactory compensation"

ṮHW

n s ṯhwn J565/3-4++; var ṯwn J664/18-9

SPEAKER, ONE WHO SPEAKS (through oracles?), epithet of the god 'LMQH

[Ar ṯhy "speak" (JP/63-4n20).]

J565/3-4: 'LMQH ṯhwn b^{c}l 'WM "I., the Speaker, lord of (the temple) A.";

J664/18-9: 'LMQHtwnb^{c}l'WM "I., the Speaker, lord of (the temple) A."

TW

cj tw Ry507/9+

UNTIL

[Sq tio, tu, tiu "when; as" (Irv/306); ModYem taw "in front" (RoVoc/313).]

Ry507/9: qrn b's^{c}b dH...tw yqhn mlkn "he fought with the tribes of H. until the king commanded..."; C541/68: wbnhw yf^{c}w ^{c}rmn whfrw tw wshw ^{c}rn "then they raised the dam and dug until they reached bedrock"

TWB

v ipf ytbn R4782/3; [y]tbhw C581/13-4

(1) RETURN (?)

[Ar taba (w) id.]

R4782/3: let him offer a gift to the god lytbn b^{c}m š^{c}bn "so that he may return (?) to the tribe"--but see also WTB v

(2) RESPOND, ANSWER (?) (cf ŚWB v)

C581/13-4: stml't b^{c}m 'LMQH wh' [y]tbhw "she asked a response of (the god) I. and He answered (?) her"

For ytb elsewhere see under WTB v.

D? pf twbhw R2633/7; ipf ytwbn C523/9; ytwbnh C568/7-8; ytwbnhmw C547/12-3; inf twbn C546/9+

(1) RETURN s.th. > RENDER, BESTOW (cf ŚWB v)

[Causative of TWB v "return," here "return an equivalent" > "compensate, bestow."]

J703/4: xmr wtwbn 'dmhw...'wldm "(the god) granted to and bestowed on His servants children"; C568/7-8: she confessed to the god, fl ytwbnh n^{c}mtm "so let Him bestow on her prosperity"

(2) RESTORE, REPAIR

[Causative, "return to a former condition" > "repair."]

R4107/2: br' wtwbn bthw "he built and repaired his house"; R2633/7: twbhw gn'thw wxlfhw "he repaired it, its wall and its gate"

h pf htb R3946/2+; htbh[mw] R3943/1; htbw R3991/10; ipf yhtb R3945/2+; inf htbn R4775/2

(1) RENDER to a deity, OFFER (cf TWB D? sense[1])

R4782/3: wl yhtbn l'lhn fxdm "let him offer to the god a thigh (of the sacrificial animal)"; R3991/10: htbw lšymhm[w...] t'mnm "they rendered to their patron deity a thank-offering" AND SEVERAL TIMES SIM

(2) SEND BACK

R3946/3: whtb wld ^{c}M ^{c}d 'hgrhmw "he sent the children of (the god) A. (= the Qatabanians) back to their towns"

(3) REPAIR (cf TWB D? sense[2])

R3945/2: yhtb mwy dhbhw "he repaired the water (system) of his field";

C24/4: hṯbw wbr' ḥrt "they repaired and constructed the aqueduct"

(4) DECREE

[Cf Heb hēšîb "reply"?]

R3951/1: kn hṯbw whḥr "Thus (the king, *p.maj*) decreed and enacted"

st stṯwbn C291/7*

SEEK A REWARD or PAYMENT (?)

C291/6-7 (fragmentary context): kfr w'b'r yš'm[...st]dbrn wstṯwbn "cistern and wells he bought, ...? and sought payment (?)"

n^1 *s* ṯwb C546/10+; *p* 'ṯwb R3439/2+; *var* 'ṯwbt R2726/15+; 'ṯwbthw R2861/17-8

COMPENSATION > REWARD, PAYMENT

[Ar ṯawāb "requital, recompense, reward."]

C546/10: may the god ṯwbn š^{c}bhw...ṯwb yn^{c}mn lhmw "bestow on His tribe a reward which will be propitious for them"; C613/4: 'ṯwbt wgb'n "(re)payments and refunds"; R2726/15: š'mtm w'ṯwbtm "purchases and payments"; R3439/2: 'sṭr wš'mt w'ṯwb wnḥlt "documents, purchases, payments and usufructs"

For *n* 'ṯbt see under ṮBT

n^2 *s* ṯbt G1367+

RESERVOIR

[Ar ṯuba^t "place where the water collects in a valley or low ground, so called because the water returns to it" (SoSoSEG4).]

G1367: ṯbt...ḏhqšb 'A "the reservoir which A. prepared for use"; R4127/2-3: kl m^{c}s' wmbn ṯbt "the whole construction and building of the reservoir"

For ṯbt elsewhere see under WṮB *n*^{1}

n^3 *s* mṯbt(n) R3951/5+

(1) ANSWER, or COMPENSATION

[Cf *v* sense^2 and *n*^{1}, and Ar maṯwaba^t "requital, recompense."]

C37/8: gdyt wmṯbt hṯb "the concession and compensation he rendered"; J631/16: they brought back to their lord from their missions to the Negus mṯbt ṣdqm "a satisfactory answer"; J643/14: mṯbt mngyt "a fortunate compensation"

(2) DECREE (cf ṮWB *h* sense^4)

R3951/5,6: bqdmy w'ṯr ḏt mṯbtn...wkwnt ḏt mṯbtn bF "before and after this decree...and this decree was (enacted) in (the month) F."

n^4 *s* tṯwb GaMosna^c/10* (*D inf?*)

(SOMETHING) UNDERTAKEN REPEATEDLY (?)

[Ar taṯwīb "repeatedly summoning people to prayer or to other things" (BeSM/399-400).]

GaMosna^c/10: nṣb wmnsf ṣrbt wtṯwb "the labor and service of the repeatedly undertaken collective enterprise (of building a road)"

ṮWY

n? s yṯw J564/29+

a) SPEAKER, i.e. ORACLE (?); or, b) DWELLER, in epithet of 'LMQH

[a) Phps a prefixed form of a root ṮWY or the like, related to the root ṮHW of 'LMQH's epithet ṯhwn of the same meaning, q.v. b) MüW/37 cfs Ug ṯw, Ar ṯawâ "dwell."]

J564/29: 'LMQH b^{c}l MSKT wyṯw BR'N "(the god) I., lord of M. and oracle of (or, dweller in) B."

ṮWR

n s ṯwr(m,n) R3104/2-3+; ṯwrhw C82/5; var ṯr(m) C405/4+; d ṯwrn J669/14+; ṯwrnhn IrAppII#2/2; ṯrnhn J567/8+; p 'ṯwr(m,n) J665/26+

BULL

[Ar ṯawr id.]

R4193/5: they dedicated ḏn ṯwrn "this bull"; R3104/2-3: mḏbḥt bh yḏbḥn mlkn ṯwrm "altar on which the king sacrifices a bull"; R3910/4-5: 'blm f'w ṯwrm f'w b^{c}rm "camel, bull or head of cattle"; J567/8: a vision in his sleep kyr'ynhw byn ṯrnhn ḏxlf mṣr^{c}y Q "when he saw (the god) between the 2 (sculptured?) bulls outside the gates of Q."

as a divine epithet: Ry394: SM^c ṯwr 'bḍ^{c}m "(the god) S., bull of the rural districts"; J733/3-4: 'LMQH ṯhwn ṯwr b^{c}lm "(the god) I., the Speaker, bull of the naturally irrigated land"; cf C581/4: 'LMQH ṯhwn wṯwr b^{c}lm "I., the Speaker, and the Bull of the b^{c}l-land"

ṮWR II

n s ṯwr C562/7*

CURDS (?)

[Ar ṯawr "portion of curdled milk" (MüW/37).]

C562/7: bn qrśn 'fym 'w ṯwr mntm "part of (?) a qrś-measure of baked goods or rich curds (?)"

ṮYL

n s ṯyln C323/3,5-6*

FLOOD, SAYL (?)

[Ar ṯāla (w) "pour out"; cf Ar sayl "flood, torrential stream."]

C323/3-6: 'tw h' ṯyln ^{c}dy 'rḍ M wḥmdw š^{c}bn mqm T...bḏt mt^c mḥrmthmw whgrhmw bn hwt ṯyln "that flood came to the land of M. and this tribe praised the might of (the god) T. because He saved their temples and towns from that flood"

ṮKḤ

n s mṯkḥ(m,n) C343/3-4+; d mṯkḥnhn C26/7

INSCRIPTION, INSCRIPTIONAL TABLET

[Sense from contexts, which parallel those of msnd.]
C343/3-4: hqnyw twrn ddhbn wmtkhn "they dedicated this gold bull and this inscription"; C26/7: they dedicated mqtrm wtwrm wmsw[dnhn w]mtkhnhn "an incense burner, a bull, 2 altars and 2 inscriptional tablets"

TKM

n^{1} p tkmthmw C562/3*

SUBJECTS

[Ug tkm, Heb šékem "shoulder" > sense of "under the yoke"? (RycER3/284n4).]
C562/3: lk]brhmw w^{c}mthmw wtkmthmw "for their kabir, their people and their subjects"

n^{2} s tkmtn lr9/2+; var? 'tkmthmw Gl762/3

FIRST YEAR OF EPONYMOUS OFFICE

[From sense "shoulder" > "shouldering (the burden of) office" (RycER3/284). Or, cfing Ar takama "follow s.o.'s tracks" > year of "succession" to the office.]
Gl762/3: when he served the god ^{c}TTR as priest b'tkmthw "in his first year of eponymous office"; lr9/2: bxrf M bn N bn F tkmtn "in the year (named for) M..., (his) first year of eponymous office"

TLL

v pf/inf tll R3943/2+

PLUNDER, TAKE AS BOOTY

[Heb šālal id, Ar talla "tear down, destroy."]
R3943/2: he captured their children wtll qnyhmw ''blm wbqrm whmrm "and took their property/livestock as booty, camels, cattle and asses"; R3945/13: tll wstmly kl b^{c}rhmw wqnyhmw "plundered and took as booty all their herds and livestock"; sim ib/18,19

TL^{c}

h inf htl^{c}n J578/6+

BREAK an enemy's power

[Ar tala^{c}a "break, smash (the head)."]
J578/6: the god helped him bsbt wtbr whtl^{c}n whshtn K "in beating, crushing, breaking and destroying K."

Note: Once spelled ht^{c}ln (lr13) by error or metathesis.

TLT

n^{1} cardinal number: f tlt R4196/4+; m tltt(n) J657/3+

THREE (middle and late Sab; cf ŠLT)

[Ar talāt, talātat id.]
J657/3: hqny...tlttn 'slmn "he dedicated these three statues"; C6/4: dltltt wsb^{c}y wxms m'tm "in (the year) five hundred seventy-three"; R4196/4:

dlstt^{c}šr wtlt m'tm xryftm "in the year three hundred sixteen"; J665/23: mt^{c}...'sm rkbm wtltt rglm "rescued one mounted man and three footsoldiers"

n^2 s tlt(m,n) R3968/2+

(1) ONE THIRD (fraction)

[Ar tult id.]

R3968/2: SM^{c}]Y tlt dHGRM "(the clan) S., one-third of (the tribe) H."; R4187/3: s^{c}bn SM^{c}Y tltn dHŠDM "the tribe S., one-third of (the tribe) Ḥ."

(2) THIRD (ordinal) (?)

[Ar tālit id.]

J577/12: btltm ywmm ffxrw "on the third day, they gathered together"; also J631/28+; ltltm ywmm "on the third day" (var of normal "day three"?)

n^3 cardinal number: tltnhn C308/3; tlty J665/17+

THIRTY

[Ar talātūn id.]

C308/3: hqnyw...tltnhn 'ṣlmn "they dedicated these thirty statues"; J665/17,38: tlty rkbm...tlty 'frsm "thirty cameleers, thirty horses"

TMM

av tmt R4176/7*

THERE, THAT PLACE

[Ar tamma, tamma^{ta} "there."]

R4176/7: ltfr qsd T'LB ^{c}dy tmt w^{c}dy 'TMN "(the god) T.'s yeomen's journeying to there and to I."

TMN I

n cardinal number: f tmn R4988/1+; tmnym R2726/18; m? tmny R3112/2+; tmnyt(n) C546/1+; tmnt(n) C407/10+

EIGHT

[Ar tamān^{i}, tamāniya^{t} id.]

J665/34: xmsy wtmn m'tm "eight hundred fifty"; R2726/18: ywm tmnym dF "the eighth day (lit., day eight) of (the month) dF."; R3112/2: 'ṣb^{c}m bn tmny 'ṣb^{c} "one finger out of eight (i.e., one-eighth)"; J558/2: tmntn 'mtln "eight images"; R3945/3: sbyhmw tmnyt 'lfm "captured them (to the number of) eight thousand"

Note: tmnytn C546/1 prob n.pr.f.

n^1 s tmn C73/8*

ONE EIGHTH (but see Note)

[Ar tumn id.]

C73/8: ṣrb...dbhw kwn myrn tmn brm bdhbn "an autumn harvest in which (the price of) grain was one-eighth of a br-measure in gold"

Note: If br is f, tr phps "eight br-units"

n^2 cardinal number: tmnyy C537/9+

EIGHTY

[Ar ṯamānūn id. BeDGESA/35:14 characterizes the second y as the dual suffix, while the first "may perhaps represent a consonantization of a final i vowel characteristic of the unit numeral"--*ṯamani "eight": *ṯamanyê "eighty."]
C537/9: [bx]rf ḏlṯny wṯmnyy wxms m'tm "in the year five hundred hundred eighty-two"; Ir13/9: xmst wṯmnyy 'sdm "eighty-five soldiers"

ṮMN II

n s? mṯmn VanLessen 7/4*
VALUE (?)
[Cf Ar ṯaman "price" (BeNL10/421).]
VanLessen 7/4: mṯmn wmfẓr "in value (?) and extent (?)"

ṮMR

v ipf yṯm[rn] C615/6; tṯmrn C611/5
CAUSE TO BEAR FRUIT (said of a god and a canal)
[Ar ṯamara "bear fruit."]
C615/6: wb^{c}l BRD yṯm[rn... "may the lord of B. (a god?) cause (the land) to bear crops (?)" (context fragmentary); C611/5: kl 'ṯmr tṯmrn h' fnwtm "all crops (which) this canal causes (the land) to bear (?)"

h pf hṯmr R2865/3*
YIELD CROPS (said of land)
R2865/3: let no one cultivate (?) there 'l hṯmr kl ṯmrm 'l sqy "(lands) which yield any crop without irrigation"

n s ṯmr(m,n) C567/4+; p ṯmrtm R2726/15; 'ṯmr(m) C611/5+; 'ṯmrhmw R4141/2
CROP(S)
[Ar ṯamar "fruit; yield," ModYem aṯmār "cereal crops" (MüHāz/79).]
Gl537/7: ṯmr sqym w'klm wbql[m] "irrigated crops, cereals and vegetables"; C567/4: ^{c}šr...bn ṯmr 'rḍhmw "tithes from the crops of their land"; R2726/15: š'mtm...ṯmrtm "purchases (regarding?) crops"; R4938/18: may the god grant them 'ṯmr w'fql ṣdqm "satisfying crops and harvests" AND OFTEN SIM

ṮND

n s mṯnd P139b*
INSCRIPTION (cf msnd, mśnd)
[See etym under SND n and cf Ḥaḍ mṯnd id CT9/3.]
P139b: mṯnd ṮR "inscription of Ṯ. (n.pr)"

ṮNY

h pf hṯny R3945/3*
DOUBLE
[Ar ṯny D id.]
R3945/3: hṯny śl'hmw wbḍ^c b^{c}lhmw b^{c}m śl'hmw bqrm "he doubled their tribute

and imposed on them (payment of) cattle in addition to their tribute"

n^1 cardinal number: f ṯny(m) R4197/4+; m ṯty C369/2+; var ṯnty C460/5

TWO

[Ar iṯnān^i, iṯnatān^i, Heb šənāyim, štāyim id.]

R4197b/4: bxrfn ṯny wsb^{c}hy wm't xryftm "in the year one hundred seventy-two"; R4176/8: ṯny bxrf "two (banquets) a year"; C369/2: 'ḥt 'ṣb^{c}m bn ṯty yd "one finger from two hands (i.e., one tenth)"; J651/19: ywm šhrm wywm ṯnym "the day of the new moon and the second day (lit., day two) (of the month)"

used with dual: C343/15: ṯny 'sn "two men"; C398/3: ṯny ṣlmnhn "two statues"; J635/26: ṯty ḍb'tn "two battles"

Note esp C516/23: dbḥ ḏQ wW ṯnym "he sacrificed to (the gods) ḏQ. and W. two (victims?)" C cfs Ar ṯiny "two-year-old animal (sheep, camel, or the like)."

n^2 as adj: m ṯny(m,n) C461/5; f ṯntm Ry547/1; phps ṯnyt R4763/1

SECOND

[Ar ṯān^i, ṯāniya^t id.]

C461/5: ṯny šmlm "a second bad omen"; Ry547/1: snt ṯntm "a second year"; J631/34-5: b^{c}d ṯnym ywmm "after the second day" (var from normal "day two"); R3945/14: nš' ṯnym mnš'm "he made a second expedition"; C461/5: ṯnym t'twm "a second offering"; R4133/5: xrf N...ṯnyn "the year (named for) N., the second (of his eponymous years)"; R4763/1 (in obscure context): ṯnyt [sn]t "a second [yea]r (?)"

Note also ṯntn R3605b/1 in obscure context (prob not authentic).

n^3 p ṯnhw J702/12-3; var ṯnyhw ib/14

INCISOR TEETH

[Ar ṯanīya^t, p ṯanāyā id.]

J702/12-3: mr(ḍ) '(d)rshw wṯnhw "disease of his molars and incisors"; ib/14: t'hrn 'ḏrshw wṯnyhw "inflammation of his molars and incisors"

n^4 s ṯnytm R2861/16,21*

DOUBLE (?)

[Cf Ar ṯanya^t "fold, crease (in cloth)."]

R2861/16: whoever exports fodder shall be held responsible; ṯnytm (')ṯmr y'tw bn 'ṯwbthw "double (?) the crops shall come from his payments (i.e., he shall pay back double what he took illegally?)"; ib/21: [y]hšfqhw ṯmrn ṯnyt[m] "(the god?) granted him an abundant crop, (as the required?) double (?)"

Cf also ṯnyt R4763/1, cited under ṮNY n^2.

n^5 s mṯny Ry544/6* (D prt?)

DOUBLED > TWICE, TWO

[Cf Ar maṯnī "doubled."]

Ry544/6: he killed mṯny 'lfn 'w^{c}lm "a doubled thousand/twice a thousand ibexes"

T̲NN--For w-t̲nn R3156/3, read wt̲nn, see under WT̲N n^1

T̲^{c}D

tp ipf ytt̲^{c}d R3947/4*

IRRIGATE

[Ar t̲arâ^n t̲^{c}d^{un} "moist earth," cf t̲a'ida "moisten"; Irv/69 cfs Ar t̲a'ad "unripe dates, becoming soft" and t̲a^{c}d "ripe, soft dates."]

R3947/4: wl ytt̲^{c}d bd̲t ḥrtn wfnwtn "may he irrigate with this aqueduct and canal"; note also R4194/3-4: bql wšw^c wt̲[^{c}d?... "planted, watered and ir[rigated?]"--simple v?

n^1 s t̲^{c}d(m) R3945/15+; t̲^{c}dhw C518/3; var t̲^{c}dtm C318/4

IRRIGATED/CULTIVATED LAND (cf T̲^{c}D n^2)

R3945/15: fqḥ t̲^{c}d mlk...bn mwy M "he flooded (?) the irrigated land of the king (using) the waters of M."; C518/3: mḥfdn wt̲^{c}dhw "the tower and its irrigated land"

Note also C318/4: 'l s'l xdrn t̲^{c}dtm (sim C656/2): "let not this tomb be claimed as cultivated land"--i.e., "let no one incorporate it into a (neighboring?) cultivated area"?

n^2 s mt̲^{c}d R4815/8+

IRRIGATED/CULTIVATED LAND (cf T̲^{c}D n^1)

R4815/8: lsqy mt̲^{c}d bny R "for the irrigation (system) of the irrigated land of the b.R."

T̲^{c}Y

n^1 s tt̲^{c}t C411/8+; var tt̲^{c}yt NNAG5/20+

ABUSE, SLANDER

[Ar t̲ā^{ci} (root T̲^{c}Y) "one who insults, slanders" (RhSLG2/66); phps related to Mh t̲ây "odor" (cf Eng "bring into bad odor").]

C411/8: may the god protect him bn nḍ^c wšṣyt wšmt wtt̲^{c}t šn'm "from magic and evil eye, malice and abuse of (any) enemy" AND OFTEN SIM

n^2 s? mt̲[^{c}yt] C428/2; p mt̲^{c}y R3890#5/2

OFFERING OF INCENSE

[Ug t̲^{c}y "give, offer," Mh t̲ôye "smell (s.th.)" (MüW/34); Min mt̲^{c}(y)t "incense offering."]

R3890#5/2: rḥ]ś w^{c}rb mt̲^{c}y WD "(sprinkled?) and offered incense-offerings to (the god) W."; sim context C428/2

T̲^{c}L--For ht̲^{c}ln Irl3 read ht̲l^{c}n, see under T̲L^c h

T̲^{c}R

n p t̲^{c}rtm R3945/2*

SLUICES

[Cf Ar ṯaǵr, Heb š́a^{c}ar "opening," Heb ša^{c}ărê hannəhārôt "gates of the rivers (leading to canals)." Irv/75 remarks of R3945 "each section of land would have little walls with outflow openings."]
R3945/2: ^{c}sy ḥṣṣm wṯ^{c}rtm ḏnb M "he constructed sections (of land) and sluices for the area M."
Note: R prints ḍ^{c}rtm, erroneously (v6/396).

Ṯ^{c}, Ṯ^{c}T--For n ṯṯ^{c}t, see under Ṯ^{c}Y

ṮF'
n s? mhṯf'm Gl443*
sense doubtful; n.pr?
Gl443: ...] xdrn wmhdrn wmhṯf'm [... "the tomb and grave chamber; and..."
Note: SoSoSEG4/15 tr mhdrn wmhṯf'm as synonyms, "neighborhood and vicinity" (cf Ar ṯafā "follow, be near"), but the disagreement of nunation and mimation suggests the words are not alike syntactically.

ṮFṬ
n s ṯfṭ A452/6*
JUDGMENT, DECISION
[Cf Heb šāpaṭ "judge."]
A452/6: wkwn ḏ]n ṯfṭ bwrx... "and this judgment was (enacted) in the month..."

ṮQF
h pf hṯqf C350/13*
MAKE KNOWN
[Causative, cf Ar ṯaqifa "be smart, clever"?]
C350/13: ḏn m[t]kḥn ḏbhw hṯqf 'A...ḍr^{c}[n] ḏX "this inscriptional tablet on which A. has made known the defeat of (the tribe) ḏX."
st pf sṯṯqf J643/20+
sense doubtful; FIND ONE'S SELF in a place, HAPPEN TO BE (?)
[Cf Ar ṯaqifa "find, meet."]
J643/20: the army reached the city wftḥhmw 'ns sṯṯqf bhyt hgrn "and a man who happened to be (?) in that city opened to them"; J577/7: the god allowed the officer to return from campaign in safety w'sd sṯṯqf b^{c}mhw "along with the men who happened to be (?) with him"; sim ib/l

ṮQT--For n ṯqt, see under WṮQ

ṮRY
n p 'ṯry R2726/8*
KIND OF LEGAL DOCUMENT, phps (STATEMENT OF) SURPLUS
[MüW/34 cfs Akk šerū "grow abundant," Ar ṯariya "be moist, well-watered,

many."]

R2726/8: kl s'wlt w'sm^{c} w'zhd w'try "all claims (to the harvest), attestations, and (statements of) lack and surplus (?)"

TRT--For trt see under WTR n^{1}

TTY--For tty see under TNY n^{1}

Selective Bibliography

A — indicates inscriptions collected by Glaser but not included in the main sequence of the Glaser collection, published in various sources (but cf esp BoOr19)

AfO — *Archiv für Orientforschung*

AION — *Annali* of the Istituto Orientale di Napoli

ADSA — Bowen, R. LeBaron, Jr., and F.P. Albright, eds, *Archaeological discoveries in South Arabia.* Baltimore: Johns Hopkins Press, 1958.

BDB — Brown, Francis, S.R. Driver, and C.A. Briggs. *A Hebrew and English lexicon of the Old Testament...* Oxford: Clarendon Press, 1968.

BSOAS — *Bulletin* of the (London) School of Oriental and African Studies

BafIns — Bâfaqih, M. and Ch. Robin. "Inscriptions inédites de Yanbuq ..." *Raydān* 2 (1979) 15-76.

BeAIP — Beeston, A.F.L. "Appendix on the inscriptions published by Mr. Philby," in H.St.J. Philby, *Sheba's Daughters* (London: Methuen, 1939), pp.441-54.

BeAdd — __________. "Addenda" to IrvBSOAS30, q.v.

BeBSOAS17 — __________. "The 'Ta'lab Lord of Pastures' texts." *BSOAS* 17 (1955) 154-6.

BeDGESA — __________. *A descriptive grammar of epigraphic South Arabian.* London: Luzac, 1962

BeESACD — __________. *Epigraphic South Arabian calendars and dating.* London, 1956.

BeFSTI — __________. "Four Sabaean texts in the Istanbul Archeological Museum." *Museon* 65 (1953) 271-83.

BeGlean — __________. "Epigraphical and archaeological gleanings from South Arabia." *Oriens Antiquus* 1 (1962) 41-52.

BeJESHO15 — __________. "Kingship in ancient South Arabia." *JESHO* 15 (1972) 256-68.

BeJRAS'48 Beeston, A.F.L. "East and west in Sabaean inscriptions." *JRAS*, 1948, pp.177-80.

BeJSS14 ______. "A Sabaean trader's misfortunes." *JSS* 14 (1969) 227-30.

BeJSS20 ______. "Epigraphic South Arabian auxiliaries." *JSS* 20 (1975) 191-2.

BeJTS2 ______. "Angels in Deuteronomy 33^2." *JTS* 2 (1951) 30-31.

BeMus64 ______. "A Sabaean penal law." *Mus* 64 (1951) 304-315.

BeNL1 ______. "Notes on Old South Arabian lexicography, I." *Mus* 63 (1950) 53-7.

BeNL2 ______. "Notes on Old South Arabian lexicography, II." *Mus* 63 (1950) 261-8.

BeNL3 ______. "Notes on Old South Arabian lexicography, III." *Mus* 64 (1951) 137-42.

BeNL4 ______. "Notes on Old South Arabian lexicography, IV." *Mus* 65 (1952) 138-47.

BeNL5 ______. "Notes on Old South Arabian lexicography, V." *Mus* 66 (1953) 109-22.

BeNL6 ______. "Notes on Old South Arabian lexicography, VI." *Mus* 67 (1954) 311-22.

BeNL7 ______. "Notes on Old South Arabian lexicography, VII." *Mus* 85 (1972) 535-44.

BeNL8 ______. "Notes on Old South Arabian lexicography, VIII." *Mus* 86 (1973) 443-53.

BeNL9 ______. "Notes on Old South Arabian lexicography, IX." *Mus* 88 (1975) 187-98.

BeNL10 ______. "Notes on Old South Arabian lexicography, X." *Mus* 89 (1976) 407-23.

BeNewL ______. "New light on the himyaritic calendar," in *Arabian Studies*, ed R.B. Serjeant and R.L. Bidwell (London: Hurst, 1974), v.1, pp.1-6.

BeOr25 ______. Review of W. Caskel's *Entdeckungen in Arabien*. Or 25 (1956) 292-302.

BeOracle ______. "The oracle sanctuary of Jāral-Labbā." *Mus* 62 (1949) 207-28.

BePESA Beeston, A.F.L. "Phonology of the epigraphic South Arabian unvoiced sibilants." *Transactions* of the Philological Society, 1951, pp.1-26.

BeRev ______. Review of A. Jamme, *Sabaean inscriptions from Maḥram Bilqīs*. BSOAS 35 (1972) 349-53.

BeRitH	______________. "The ritual hunt. A study in Old South Arabian religious practice." *Mus* 61 (1948) 183-96.
BeSI	______________. *Sabaean inscriptions.* Oxford, 1937.
BeSM	______________. "Sabaean marginalia." *AION* 32 (1972) 394-400.
BeSabPL	= BeMus64
BeStI	______________. "Studies in Sabaic lexicography, I." *Raydān* 2 (1979) 89-100.
Be2SAIn	______________. "Two South Arabian inscriptions: some suggestions." *JRAS*, 1937, pp.59-78.
BiKa	Biberstein-Kazimirski, Albert de. *Dictionnaire arabe-francais* ... New ed. Paris: Maisonneuve, 1960.
BiOr	*Bibliotheca Orientalis*
BoOr19	Botterweck, G.J. "Altsüdarabische Glaser-Inschriften." *Or* 19 (1950) 435-44.
Bon2T	Boneschi, Paulo. "Duo tituli sabaei iterum interpretati." *RSO* 34 (1959) 137-40.
Bon3T	______________. "Tres tituli sabaei iterum interpretati." *RSO* 34 (1959) 27-32.
BonVar	______________. "Variazioni etimologiche sul tema 'lmqh." *Atti* dell'Accademia Nazionale dei Lincei, *Rendiconti*, series 8, vol.13, fasc.7-12 (1958), pp.327-55.
BronSem23	______________. "Notes de lexicographie sud-arabique." *Sem* 23 (1973) 135-7.
C	*Corpus inscriptionum semiticarum.* Pars quarta: Inscriptiones himyariticas et sabaeas continens. 3v, Paris, 1889-1930.
CoRoC	Conti-Rossini, C. *Chrestomathia arabica meridionalis epigraphica.* Rome: Istituto per l'Oriente, 1931.
CoRoSab	______________. "Sabaica." *RSO* 9 (1921-3) 27-31.
D	indicates inscriptions edited in A.J. Drewes, *Inscriptions de l'Éthiopie antique* (Leiden: Brill, 1962).
DJE	indicates inscriptions collected by the Deutsche Jemenische Expedition (cf esp MuBilinguis, Hāz, In566, Poly, Taᶜizz)
DiLLA	Dillmann, August. *Lexicon linguae aethiopicae.* Lipsiae, 1865.
DoJRAS'68	Doe, D.B., and A. Jamme. "New Sabaean inscriptions from South Arabia." *JRAS* 1968, 2-28.
Doughty	Doughty, Charles. *Travels in Arabia Deserta.* New York: Random House, 1936. 2v in 1.
Dozy	Dozy, R. *Supplément aux dictionnaires arabes.* Leyde: Brill, 1927. 2.ed, 2v.
DrNote	Drewes, A.J. "A note on ESA 'sy." *Raydān* 2 (1979) 101-103.

F — indicates inscriptions collected by A. Fakhry, edited in RyET

Freytag — Freytag, G.W. *Lexicon arabico-latinum praesertim ex Djeuharii Firuzabadiique et aliorum arabum...* Halle: Schwetschke, 1937. 4v.

G — indicates inscriptions collected by Eduard Glaser (cf esp SoSoSEG4, TsSEG6, SchSEG7, HöSEG8, TsSEG11)

GReise — Glaser, Eduard. *Eduard Glasers Reise nach Mārib,* ed D.H. Müller and N. Rhodokanakis. Wien, 1913.

GaAION31 — Garbini, G. "Frammenti epigrafici Sabei. I.--Un nuovo frammento di RES3968 + RES3979." *AION* 31 (1971) 538-40.

GaAION33 — ______________. "Nuove iscrizione sabee." *AION* 33 (1973) 31-46.

GaAntYem1 — ______________. "Antichità yemenite, I." *AION* 30 (1970) 400-404.

GaAntYem2 — ______________. "Antichità yemenite, II." *AION* 30 (1970) 537-48.

GaMosna^{c} — ______________, and Muṭahhar al-Iryani. "A Sabaean rock-engraved inscription at Mosna^{c}." *AION* 30 (1970) 405-8.

GaSY — ______________. "Una nuova iscrizione di Šaraḥbi'il Ya^{c}fur." *AION* 29 (1969) 559-66.

GoJ — Goitein, S.D.F. *Jemenica; Sprichwörter und Redensarten aus zentral-Jemen...* Leipzig: Harrassowitz, 1934.

GoTY — ______________. *Travels in Yemen, an account of Joseph Halevy's journey to Najran...* Jerusalem: Hebrew University Press, 1941.

GrOLZ9 — Grimme, H. "Südarabische Tempelstrafgesetze." *OLZ* 9 (1906) cols 256, 324, 395.

GressAOT — Gressman, H. *Altorientalische Texte zum alten Testament.* 2.ed. Berlin, 1926. The editions of OSA texts here are by Rhodokanakis.

GrohSudar — Grohmann, A.. *Südarabien als Wirtschaftsgebiet.* Wien, 1922.

HaAED — Hava, J.G. *An Arabic-English dictionary.* Beyrut: Catholic Press, 1899.

Ham — indicates inscriptions published esp in Brown, W.L., and A.F.L. Beeston, "Sculptures and inscriptions from Shabwa," *JRAS*, 1954, pp.51-62.

HoAA2 — Hommel, F. *Aufsätze und Abhandlungen, II: Die südarabischen Altertümer des Wiener Hofmuseums.* Munich, 1900.

HöASASühne — Hofner, Maria. "Eine altsüdarabische Sühne-Inschrift," in *Hebräische Wortforschung; Festschrift...Walter Baumgartner* (Leiden, 1967), pp.106-13.

HöASG — ______________. *Altsüdarabische Grammatik.* Leipzig: Otto Harrassowitz, 1943.

HöPW ________. "Drei sabäische Personen-widmungen." *WZ* 51 (1948) 38-42.

HöRel ________. "Die vorislamischen Religionen Arabiens; A. Südarabien," in Gese, H., M. Höfner, and K. Rudolph, *Religionen Altsyriens, Altarabiens und der Mandäer* (Religionen der Menschheit 10,2) (Stuttgart: Kohlhammer, 1970), pp.237-353.

HöRev ________. Review of A. Jamme, *Sabaean inscriptions from Maḥram Bilqīs*. ZDMG 114 (1964) 423-5.

HöSEG8 ________. *Inschriften aus Ṣirwāḥ, Ḫawlān, I. Teil.* (Sammlung Eduard Glaser, VIII) SBAW 291:1 (1973).

HöTPK ________. "Ta'lab als Patron der Kleinviehhirten," in *Serta Cantabrigiensia* (Wiesbaden, 1954), pp.29-36.

HöWdM ________. "Südarabien," in *Wörterbuch der Mythologie* (ed H.W. Haussig, 1962), pp.483-552.

HöWZ40 ________. "Die sabäische Inscriften der Südarabischen Expedition im Kunsthistorischen Museum in Wien (I)." *WZ* 40 (1933) 1-36.

HöWZ41 ________, K. Mlaker, and N. Rhodokanakis. "Zur altsüdarabischen Epigraphik und Archäologie II." *WZ* 41 (1934) 69-106.

HöWZ42 ________. "Die katabanischen und sabäischen Inschriften der südarabischen Expedition im kunsthistorischen Museum in Wien, II." *WZ* 42 (1936) 31-66.

HöWZ43 ________. "Zur interpretation altsüdarabischer Inschriften (II)." *WZ* 43 (1936) 77-108.

HöWar? ________. "War der sabäische Mukarrib ein 'Priesterfürst'?" *WZ* 54 (1957) 77-85.

HuZfA26 Snouck-Hurgronje, C. "Sa^{c}d ès Suwênî, ein seltsamer Walî aus Hadhramôt." *ZfA* 26 (1912) 223-4.

Ir indicates inscriptions published in al-Iryani, Muṭahhar ^{c}Ali, *Fī ta'rīx al-Yaman (In Yemen History)*, ed by the Center for Yemenite Studies at San^{c}a' (Cairo, 1973) (cf RycMus88)

Irv Irvine, A.K. *A survey of Old South Arabian lexical materials connected with irrigation techniques* (unpublished doctoral thesis). Oxford, 1962.

IrvBSOAS30 ________. "Homicide in pre-Islamic South Arabia." *BSOAS* 30 (1967) 277-92.

IrvJRAS'64 ________. "Some notes on Old South Arabian monetary terminology." *JRAS*, 1964, pp.18-36.

IrvRev ________. Review of A. Jamme, *Sabaean inscriptions from Maḥram Bilqīs*. JSS 10 (1965) 128-32.

J indicates inscriptions collected and/or edited by A. Jamme (cf esp JSIMB)

JDN	Jamme, A. "Un désastre nabatéen devant Nagrān." *Cahiers de Byrsa* 6 (1956) 165-71.
JESHO	*Journal of the Economic and Social History of the Orient*
JITDL	Jamme, A. "L'identification de Ta'lab au dieu lunaire et les textes sabéens GI 1142 et 1143." *BiOr* 13 (1956) 182-186.
JOrAnt9	______________. "The pre-Islamic inscriptions of the Riyādh Museum." *Oriens Antiquus* 9 (1970) 115-36.
JP	______________. "Le panthéon sud-arabe préislamique d'après les sources épigraphiques." *Mus* 60 (1947) 58-147.
JPDSM	______________. "Le pronom démonstratif sabéen *mhn* et les conjonctions composites *lqbl(y)/d(t)*, *kmhnmw* et *km*ᶜ*nmw*." *Cahiers de Byrsa* 6 (1956) 173-80.
JRAS	*Journal* of the Royal Asiatic Society
JSIMB	Jamme, A. *Sabaean inscriptions from Maḥram Bilqīs (Mārib).* Baltimore: Johns Hopkins Press, 1962.
JSS	*Journal of Semitic Studies*
JTS	*Journal of Theological Studies*
LA	*Lisān al-*ᶜ*Arab*, classical Arabic dictionary (only as cited by modern scholars)
LaGD	Landberg, Carl de. *Glossaire daṯînois.* Leiden, 1920-40.
LaH	______________. *Études sur les dialectes de l'Arabie méridionale. Vol I: Ḥaḍramoût.* Leyden: Brill, 1901.
Lane	Lane, Edward William. *Arabic-English lexicon..., Book I.* London: Williams and Norgate, 1863-93. 8 parts.
LeLS	Leslau, Wolf. *Lexique Soqotri (sudarabique moderne).* Paris, 1938.
LuDopol	Lundin, A.G. "Dopolnenija k spisku sabejskih eponimov." *Vestnik Drevnej Istorii* 97 (1966) 3, pp.82-91. "Compléments à la liste des éponymes sabéens."
LuMus76	______________. "'Il Très-Haut' dans les inscriptions sud-arabes." *Mus* 76 (1963) 207-209.
LuMus86	______________. "Deux inscriptions sabéennes de Mārib." *Mus* 86 (1973) 179-92.
LuSemAS5	______________. "Inscriptions from Jār al-Labbā." *Seminar for Arabian Studies (5th)*, London, 1972, p.65.
MoMiSI	Mordtmann, J.H., and Eugen Mittwoch. *Sabäische Inschriften.* Hamburg: Friedrichsen, De Gruyter, 1931 = Hamburgische Universität, Abhandlungen aus dem Gebiet der Auslandskunde, Band 36. Reihe B. Volkerkunde, Kulturgeschichte und Sprachen Band 17; Rathjens-v. Wissmannsche Südarabien-Reise Band I.
MüAfO24	Müller, W.W. "Ergebnisse der Deutschen Jemen-Expedition 1970." *AfO* 24 (1972) 15-61.

MüBeitrage ______. "Altsüdarabische Beiträge zum hebräischen Lexikon." *ZAW* 75 (1963) 304-316.

MüBilinguis ______, and Rainer Degen. "Eine hebräisch-sabäische Bilinguis aus Bait al-Aśwal." *NESE* 2 (1974) 117-23.

MüHāz Muller, W.W. "Epigraphische Nachlese aus Hāz." *NESE* 1 (1972) 75-85.

MüIn566 ______. "Eine sabäische Inschrift aus dem Jahre 566 der himjarischen Ära." *NESE* 2 (1974) 139-44.

MüOriens20 ______. Review of A.G. Lundin, *Die Eponymenliste von Saba.* Oriens 20 (1967) 266-8.

MüPoly ______. "Sabäische Texte zur Polyandrie." *NESE* 2 (1974) 125-38.

MüRev ______. Review of A. Jamme, *Sabaean inscriptions from Mahram Bilqis.* AfO 21 (1966) 104-9.

MüTa^{c}izz ______. "Sabäische Inschriften aus dem Museum in Ta^{c}izz." *NESE* 1 (1972) 87-101.

MüW ______. *Die Wurzeln mediae und tertiae Y/W im Altsüdarabischen* (doctoral thesis, University of Tübingen). Tübingen, 1962.

Mus *Le Muséon*

N indicates inscriptions published in H.Y. Nāmī, *Našr nuqūš šāmīya^{t} qadīma^{t} min janub bilād al-^{c}arab wašarḥuha* (Cairo, 1943).

NESE Degen, Rainer, Walter W. Müller, and Wolfgang Röllig. *Neue Ephemeris für Semitische Epigraphik.* Wiesbaden: O. Harrassowitz, 1972-

NNAG indicates inscriptions published in H.Y. Nāmī "Nuqūš ^{c}arabiya^{t} junubiya^{t}." Pt I, *Majalla^{t} Kullīya^{t} al-'Ādāb* 9 (1947) 15-27; Pt II, ib 16 (1954) 21-43; Pt III, ib 20 (1957) 55-63.

OLZ *Orientalistische Literaturzeitung*

Or *Orientalia*

OrAnt *Oriens Antiquus*

P indicates inscriptions collected by H. St.J. Philby (cf esp RyNE4, BeAIP, JDN)

PMidian Philby, H.ST.J. *The land of Midian.* London: Benn, 1957.

PalSb *Palestinskii sbornik*

PiMus69 Pirenne, J. "L'inscription 'Ryckmans 535' et la chronologie sud-arabe." *Mus* 69 (1956) 165-81.

PirenneGloss Pirenne, Jacqueline, ed. *Répertoire d'épigraphie sémitique,* v.VIII (Tables et Index des tomes V, VI, VII). Paris: Imprimerie Nationale, 1968. Glossary, pp.121-253.

Q *Qāmūs*, classical Arabic dictionary (only as cited by modern scholars)

R indicates inscriptions published in the *Répertoire d'épigraphie sémitique*, vols V-VII (Paris: Imprimerie Nationale, 1928-50)

RB *Revue Biblique*

RSO *Rivista degli Studi Orientali*

RabAncWAr Rabin, C. *Ancient West-Arabian*. London, 1951.

RhASI Rhodokanakis, N. "Altsüdarabische Inschriften," in GressAOT, pp.463-71.

RhAST ______________. *Altsabäische Texte*. Pt. I: SBAW 206:2 (1927); Pt. II: WZ 39 (1933) 173-226.

RhBod ______________. "Die Bodenwirtschaft im alten Südarabien." *Anzeiger* der Akademie der Wissenschaften (Wien), Jg 1916, pp. 173-98.

RhGr ______________. *Der Grundsatz der Öffentlichkeit in den südarabischen Urkunden*. SBAW 177:2 (1915).

RhKat ______________. *Katabanische Texte zur Bodenwirtschaft*. Pt. I: SBAW 194:2 (1919); Pt. II: SBAW 198:2 (1922).

RhSLG ______________. *Studien zur Lexikographie und Grammatik des Altsüdarabischen*. Pt. I: SBAW 178:4 (1915); Pt. II: SBAW 185:3 (1917); Pt. III: SBAW 213:3 (1931).

RhWZ37 ______________. "Dingliche Rechte im alten Südarabien." *WZ* 37 (1930) 121-73.

RoVoc Rossi, E. "Vocaboli sud-arabici nella odierne parlate arabe del Yemen." *RSO* 18 (1940) 299-314.

RobAtt Robin, Ch. and J. Ryckmans. "L'attribution d'un bassin à un divinité." *Raydān* I (1978) 39-64.

RodBiOr26 Rodinson, M. "Sur une nouvelle inscription du règne de Dhoû Nowâs." *BiOr* 26 (1969) 26-34.

RodConf'65-6 ______________. "Conferences," École Pratique des Hautes Études. IVème section, Sciences historiques et philologiques. *Annuaire* 1965/66, pp.125-40.

RodConf'66-7 ______________. As above; *Annuaire* 1966/67, pp.121-39.

RodConf'68-9 ______________. As above; *Annuaire* 1968/69, pp.97-118.

RodConf'69-70 ______________. As above; *Annuaire* 1969/70, pp.161-82.

Ry indicates inscriptions published by G. Ryckmans in *Le Muséon* (cf esp RyMus66, RyMus69)

RyCS Ryckmans, G. "Chronologie sabéenne." *Comptes-rendus de l'Academie des Inscriptions*, 1943, pp.236-46.

RyET ______________. "Epigraphical texts," in A. Fakhry, *An archaeological journey to Yemen* (Cairo, 1952), v.2.

RyGraf ________. "Graffites sabeens releves en Arabie sa^{c}udite." *RSO* 32 (1957) (*Scritti in onore di G. Furlani*) 557-63.

RýMus58 ________. "La confession publique des péchés en Arabie méridionale préislamique." *Mus* 58 (1945) 1-14.

RyMus66 ________. "Inscriptions sud-arabes, X." *Mus* 66 (1953) 267-317.

RyMus69 ________. "Inscriptions sud-arabes, XIII." *Mus* 69 (1956) 139-63; 369-89.

RyNEI-6 ________. "Notes épigraphiques." Pt I: *Mus* 43 (1930) 389-407; Pt II: *Mus* 50 (1937) 323-44; Pt III: *Mus* 54 (1941) 139-59; Pt IV: *Mus* 60 (1947) 149-70; Pt V: 71 (1958) 125-39; Pt VI: *Mus* 75 (1962) 459-68.

RyQayl ________. "Le *qayl* en Arabie méridionale préislamique," in *Hebrew and Semitic studies presented to G.R. Driver* (Oxford, 1963), pp.144-55.

RyRB58 ________. "De l'or (?), de l'encens, et de la myrrhe." *RB* 58 (1951) 372-6.

RycBiOr17 Ryckmans, J. Review of R.L. Bowen, *Archaeological discoveries in South Arabia*. *BiOr* 17 (1970) 204A-207B.

RycBiOr22 ________. Review of J.M. Solá Solé, *SEG4*. *BiOr* 22 (1965) 326A-327A.

RycBiOr25 ________. "Nouvelle interpretation d'un texte sabéen." *BiOr* 25 (1968) 5A-9A.

RycBiOr26 ________. Review of A. Jamme, *Sabaean and Ḥasaean inscriptions from Saudi Arabia*. *BiOr* 26 (1969) 246-9.

RycConf ________. "Les confessions publiques sabéennes: le code sud-arabe de pureté rituelle." *AION* 32 (1972) 1-15.

RycERI-8 ________. "Etudes d'épigraphie sud-arabe en russe." Pt I: *BiOr* 24 (1967) 271-3; Pt II: *BiOr* 25 (1968) 153-6; Pt III: *BiOr* 25 (1968) 283-6; Pt IV: *BiOr* 27 (1970) 3-4; Pt V: *BiOr* 27 (1970) 179; Pt VI: *BiOr* 27 (1970) 179; Pt VII: *BiOr* 29 (1972) 281-3; Pt VIII: *BiOr* 29 (1972) 283-4.

RycExpAst ________. "Une expression astrologique méconnue dans des inscriptions sabéennes." *Orientalia Lovanensia Periodica* 6/7 (1975/76) 521-29.

RycHimI-2 ________. "Himyaritica." Pt I: *Mus* 69 (1956) 91-98; Pt II: *Mus* 79 (1966) 475-500. Cf also RycMus87, RycMus88.

RycIMAM ________. *L'institution monarchique en Arabie Méridionale avant l'Islam (Ma^{c}in et Saba)*. Louvain, 1951.

RycIHS ________. "Inscriptions historiques sabéennes de l'Arabie centrale." *Mus* 66 (1953) 319-42.

RycInsAnc ________. *Les inscriptions anciennes de l'Arabie du sud: points de vue et problèmes actuels*. (Oosters Genootschap in Nederland, 4) Leiden: Brill, 1973.

RycMancie ______________. "La mancie par *ḥrb* en Arabie du sud ancienne: l'inscription Nami NAG 12," in *Festschrift W. Caskel...* (Leiden: Brill, 1968), pp.261-73.

RycMus66 ______________. "À propos du *m^cmr* en sud-arabe." *Mus* 66 (1953) 343-69.

RycMus67 ______________. "Le sens de *ḏ'l* en sud-arabe." *Mus* 67 (1954) 339-48.

RycMus87 ______________. "Himyaritica, III." *Mus* 87 (1974) 237-63; "Himyaritica, IV," ib, pp.493-521.

RycMus88 ______________. "Himyaritica, V." *Mus* 88 (1975) 199-219.

RycPCH ______________. *La persécution des chrétiens himyarites au sixième siècle.* Istanbul: Nederlands historisch-archaeologisch Instituut in het Nabije Osten, 1956.

RycVase ______________. "Un vase en bronze avec inscription sud-arabe." *Raydān* 2 (1979) 133-149.

RycRepas ______________. "Le repas rituel dans la religion sud-arabe," in *Symbolae biblicae et mesopotamicae F.M.Th. de Liagre dedicatae* (Leiden, 1973), pp.327-34.

RycRite Ryckmans, J. "Un rite d'istisqā' au temple sabéen de Mārib." *Annuaire* de l'Institut de Philologie et d'Histoire Orientales et Slaves 20 (1968-72) 379-88.

Rwala Musil, Alois. *The manners and customs of the Rwala bedouins.* New York, 1928.

SBAW *Sitzungsberichte* of the Akademie der Wissenschaften (Wien), philosophisch-historische Klasse.

SEG *Sammlung Eduard Glaser*

SchSEG7 Schaffer, B. *Sabäische Inschriften aus verschiedenen Fundorten* (Sammlung Eduard Glaser 7). SBAW 282:1 (1972).

Sem *Semitica*

SemAS *Seminar for Arabian Studies* (Cambridge University)

SerjMihr Serjeant, R.B. "Miḥrāb." *BSOAS* 22 (1959) 439-53.

Sh indicates inscriptions published in A. Sharafaddin, *Ta'rīx al-Yaman al-Ṯaqāfī* (1967).

SoSoDGI Solá Solé, J.M. *Las dos grandes inscripciones sudarábigas del dique de Mārib (edición crítica de sus textos)...* Barcelona-Tübingen, 1960.

SoSoSEG4 ______________. *Inschriften aus Riyām* (Sammlung Eduard Glaser 4). SBAW 243:4 (1964).

StSESA Stehle, Dorothy. "Sibilants and emphatics in South Arabic." *Journal* of the American Oriental Society 60 (1940) 507-43.

TA *Tāj al-^cArūs*, classical Arabic dictionary (only as cited by modern scholars)

TsSEG6 — Tschinkowitz, H. *Kleine Fragmente (I. Teil)* (Sammlung Eduard Glaser 6). SBAW 261:4

TsSEGII — ________. *Kleine Fragmente (II. Teil)* (Sammlung Eduard Glaser II). SBAW 301:3 (1975)

vSoden AHw — Von Soden, Wolfram. *Akkadische Handwörterbuch,* Lieferunge I- Wiesbaden, 1959-

WZ — *Wiener Zeitschrift für die Kunde des Morgenlandes*

Wehr — Wehr, Hans. *A dictionary of modern written Arabic,* ed J. Milton Cowan. Ithaca, N.Y.: Cornell University Press, 1961.

ZAW — *Zeitschrift für die alttestamentliche Wissenschaft*

ZfA — *Zeitschrift für Assyriologie und verwandte Gebiete*

ZDMG — *Zeitschrift* der Deutschen Morgenländischen Gesellschaft